Philosophy and Women

The Wadsworth Series in Social Philosophy
Richard Wasserstrom, Editor

Intervention and Reflection: Basic Issues in Medical Ethics, by Ronald Munson

Rights, by David Lyons

Philosophy and Women

edited by

Sharon Bishop and Marjorie Weinzweig

Wadsworth Publishing Company, Inc., Belmont, California

Philosophy Editor: Kenneth King
Production Editor: Connie Martin
Designer: Cynthia Bassett

Printed in the United States of America
1 2 3 4 5 6 7 8 9 10—83 82 81 80 79

**Library of Congress Cataloging in
Publication Data**

Main entry under title:

Philosophy and women.

   (The Wadsworth series in social philosophy)
   Bibliography: p.
1.1 Feminism—Addresses, essays, lectures.   2.
Sexism—Addresses, essays, lectures.   3.   Sex
role—Addresses, essays, lectures.   4.   Sexual
ethics—Addresses, essays,
lectures.   5.
Marriage—Addresses, essays, lectures.
I. Bishop, Sharon.   II. Weinzweig, Marjorie.
HQ1154.P52   301.41′2   78-11315
ISBN 0-534-00609-4

Contents

Introduction

Philosophy is sometimes said to consist of all those problems that no one knows how to solve. Sometimes its subject matter is said to consist of whatever remains unclaimed by another discipline. The serious point of these characterizations is that we do not always know how to proceed in thinking about an issue or topic because current methods or theories, for one reason or another, let us down. When this happens, we are ready for some sort of revolution —intellectual, moral, or both.

Social and political activists on behalf of women have been calling for moral revolution, asking that females be treated on an equal footing with males. Some of the reforms that they demand are required by straightforward applications of familiar moral principles (e.g., that a woman and a man should get the same pay for the same work). Within traditional moral outlooks, however, it is not easy to make sense of some of their demands, and many people find the moral fervor and depth of feeling with which these issues are discussed difficult to understand. For example, some persons profess to be genuinely puzzled about why the use of the term "man" as used to mean "human being" is offensive to many women. The innumerable jokes about "personhole" covers also attest to the fact that many do not understand the demand for change in our ways of speaking about men and women. Perhaps we only need to be more sensitive to the implications of commonly acceptable moral principles, but very probably the problems are deeper than that.

This selection of essays, focusing on women, has been collected and organized in the conviction that the problems *are* deeper and that we do not know how to resolve them. In order to understand the ways in which women are oppressed, we need new moral categories: new ways of thinking about human beings. With the moral revolution goes an intellectual revolution. What makes people angry,

resentful, and threatened about sex roles is now clearer than it once was. What is missing is an analysis of what it is for a role or comment to be sexist, what it is to be treated as a sex object, what it is to be exploited or oppressed. And no perspective seems sufficient for adequate discussion of what differing sex roles should be like. Or perhaps there should not be any differential treatment of the sexes; perhaps sexual differences ought to be no more interesting than differences in height or eye color.

This book is intended for the general reader and especially for students in philosophy and women's studies who undertake systematic rethinking of sex roles. Such a rethinking requires an effort to understand what is meant by notions like "sexual equality," "sexism," "liberation," and "oppression." In addition, because our family and personal lives are central areas for playing out sex roles, analyses of "sex," "love," and "marriage" are needed. Once these important ideas become clearer, one should be able to define more precisely what is wrong and unjust about current sex-role arrangements as well as to formulate in greater detail appropriate goals for liberated lives.

Raising and answering such questions is a distinctively philosophical enterprise, one that should be distinguished from others. For example, philosophical questions about sex roles should be distinguished from empirical questions about sex roles that are raised in recent work in the social sciences. Attempts in those disciplines aim at gathering new information about sex roles and explaining sex roles and their effects. Results include, for example, the surprising discovery that a piece of work believed to have been done by a woman is typically and systematically evaluated as lower in quality than the same piece of work believed to have been done by a man. The philosophical task is not to extend knowledge by collecting new data, but to analyze the assumptions of the empirical inquiry and to question them critically. In this way, one can achieve a better understanding of what the facts mean and of what follows from them. Empirical data are, of course, often relevant to philosophical investigations—and vice versa. Thus a philosophical analysis of what something is may point to certain empirical questions that are fit objects of scientific inquiry; and the answers to these may, in turn, help us decide what we want in our lives. For example, in raising questions about the nature of women, we must distinguish various senses of the word "nature" before we can begin the empirical studies to see which, if any, features are part of the nature of women in any of these senses. It is also a philosophical task to investigate the relevance of such results to questions about how our living arrangements should be designed. Finally, philosophers characteristically support their conclusions with rational argument. In this respect they differ from religious thinkers, who appeal to authority or faith, and from creative writers, whose work increases one's understanding by imaginative storytelling.

This anthology is divided into four parts. Part I, Chapter 1 contains five essays concerning sexism and sexual equality, what these concepts are, and how they are to be distinguished from other notions. Although John Stuart Mill does not use the modern term "sexism," he does argue that only perfect equality between the sexes would put their relations on a morally sound basis. Richard A. Wasserstrom explores some of the similarities and differences between racism and sexism, and Robert Baker points out some sexist features of our language and offers an explanation of them. Marilyn Frye analyzes the concept of "male chauvinism" as "phallism": the refusal to treat women as fully actualized, normal persons in the moral sense. Sandra Bartky claims that American women are subject to psychic alienation. Stereotyping, cultural domination, and sexual objectification are three forms of this alienation. Each of these involves "fragmentation", that is, the splitting of the whole person into parts—and "mystification"—the systematic obscuring of the fact of psychic oppression and the agencies by which it arises. The core notion for Bartky is the separation of the person from essential attributes of personhood. All five authors focus on the failure to recognize women as persons as central to the analysis of sexism.

There are rather widespread views that the nature of men and women make their assigned sex roles understandable and legitimate. Thus it is sometimes said that women's "natural passivity" makes them born followers, whereas men are "natural authorities." Chapter 2 considers questions about the nature of women and what connections there might be between that nature and sex roles. Several of the selections focus mainly on whether there is any such thing as woman's nature; and, if so, what it is and why it is difficult to have reasonable beliefs about it. Mill argues that no evidence is available on which to base judgments about the nature of women since women have been subjected to a variety of influences that induce the traits they exhibit. Margaret Mead draws from the results of her studies of three different communities to argue that males and females seem to function equally well with very disparate sex-role expectations. The passage from Sigmund Freud's essay "Femininity" gives some of the main elements of his views about feminine personality. To be mature and feminine, according to Freud, one must have a passive wish for a baby.

Some of the other selections discuss the connection between the nature of women and legitimate sex-role expectations. For example, Plato argues that men and women ought to receive equal and identical education because we do not and cannot have enough information about the nature of men and women to conclude that they ought to be filling certain roles. But Aristotle's "Reply to Plato" counters by claiming that men are by nature masters and that women are submissive followers (though not quite slaves). Sharon Bishop Hill suggests that to decide appropriate sex roles on the basis of the nature of males and females is incorrect. Instead we should set about developing conditions under which people can exercise their right to self-determination in a meaningful way. In arguing that sexual equality requires "full integration" of the sexes, Alison Jaggar also denies that beliefs about the nature of men and women are appropriately used for determining how sex roles should be assigned. In her view, a sexually integrated society would lack sex roles. Kathryn Morgan maintains that human beings are essentially sexual, but that fact does not determine what *gender* roles they should play.

There is a poem in which Byron says that love is to a man a thing apart, but to a woman her whole existence. This brings out poignantly the importance to women of their relations of intimacy. These relations involve women in sex, love, marriage, and family life. Part II is devoted to discussions of these topics. Chapter 3 attempts to analyze sexuality by considering alternative views of the nature of sex and its proper function. It has been said variously that the purpose of sex is reproduction, pleasure, communication and expression, and the development of intimacy between the partners. These models have been associated with opinions about the morality of sex, and these, in turn, have affected views on such issues as birth control, extramarital sex, open marriage, and the desirability of different sexual practices.

According to St. Thomas Aquinas, for instance, the essence of sex is seminal discharge, and procreation is its proper function. In his view, therefore, only married persons should have sex. He also believed that those who engage in intercourse ought to provide for the children they procreate in a nonadulterous, nondissolvable, monogamous marriage. In this family relationship, the male acts as governor both to the female and to the children because of his superior strength and reason.

Most subsequent articles in this section involve challenges to one or more of the principles of this classical, religious view. Robert Baker and Janice Moulton criticize the traditional notion of sexual intercourse. According to Baker, an examination of the words we use for sexual intercourse shows that our concept of it is incompatible with the concept of women as full human beings, and instead, the act involves harm done to the woman. According to Moulton, the polite expressions used for sexual intercourse suggest that intercourse is a reciprocal activity, but the vulgar expressions used imply that intercourse is solely a matter of male stimulation and orgasm. The resulting conceptual confusion leads to the demand for the occurrence of a simultaneous vaginal orgasm in the female in order to establish that sex really is a mutual activity. Moulton argues that this demand is unreasonable.

Sara Ruddick, developing a different view, argues for the moral desirability of "complete" sex acts—those in which each partner is "taken over" by a desire for the other's desire and responds to the other's desire. According to Ruddick, such acts involve respect for persons and are conducive to affection, tenderness, appreciation, and dependency. They dissolve the tension between the personal and the moral, for in them we are moral without cost. Richard A. Wasserstrom defends several forms of adultery against the charge of immorality. He raises the possibility of "demystifying" sexual behavior

from its implications of love for only one person, either by breaking the connection between sex and love or by dropping the implication that love requires sexual exclusivity.

Ann Garry uses Baker's results to suggest that the connotation of sex as involving harm done to the woman is responsible for the fact that pornography is more degrading to women than to men. It will be necessary to break this connection between sex and harm, she argues, in order to have nonsexist, nondegrading pornography.

The subject of rape has attracted the special interest of feminists, partly because the law treats women as collaborators in the crime until proven otherwise. Various attempts have been made to explain why the crime of rape is different from other crimes, such as assault. Pamela Foa discusses the special wrongness of rape and ties it to the Victorian conception of sex as something that must be enjoyed by men but ought not to be enjoyed by women. Rape becomes an activity that men understandably and naturally engage in, while women who have been raped are tainted with the suspicion of having enjoyed something not allowed to them.

"Love" is the subject of Chapter 4. Many people believe that sexual relations are only desirable or morally justifiable when shared with a person with whom one has a "love relationship." Some feminists, however, argue that there is a conflict between heterosexual love and women's liberation. To assess these views it is helpful to have a clear understanding of the concept of love. Analyzing this concept places one in a better position to see in some detail what kinds of love relations are possible and appropriate for persons committed to the values of mutual respect, independence, and self-development.

Sharon Bishop develops an analysis of love in terms of liking, natural commitment, and reciprocity, and discusses the creation of lover-dependent interests in a love relationship. She thinks that loving someone involves interests and desires, the satisfaction of which depends on one's lover, but that lovers also have an interest in maintaining each other's independent interests. Thus there will be tensions between dependent and independent interests, even when social conditions do not foster economic and psychological dependency.

The conflict between love and women's liberation under present conditions is dealt with by Shulamith Firestone. According to her, love in our society is the "pivot of women's oppression." The myth of romantic love serves to keep women in their traditional places even though technology has now freed them from the biological conditions of their oppression. Women are thus prevented from creating culture by a misguided pouring of their energy into love instead. The unequal power balance between men and women makes impossible the mutual exchange of selves that love requires.

Looking to the future, Virginia Held elaborates on Marx's suggestion that the relation of mutual concern and respect between a man and woman in a relation of sexual love constitutes a model for a cooperative society. In such a society individual self-interest would no longer be primary, and mutual exploitation and competition would be replaced by cooperation: that is, by a mutual pursuit of mutual values. Love is thus not a luxury that women in our society cannot afford, but is "the basic research . . . of this revolution."

Sara Ann Ketchum and Christine Pierce sketch a separatist position: the view that relationships between members of the oppressed group are particularly significant. These authors criticize Held's view that the present inequality in power between men and women can be eliminated and that relationships between men and women might serve as models of what relationships of mutual concern and respect could be like.

Many people think that love leads appropriately to marriage. Chapter 5 discusses the relation between marriage and oppression, the possibility of nonoppressive forms of marriage and of alternative social arrangements that would provide for child-rearing and intimate relations between persons. Friedrich Engels claims that the purpose of monogamous marriage is to produce children of undisputed paternity for the transmission of property. The "double standard" in sexual morality results from this. True sexual love, according to Engels, will not be possible until the economic basis of the family is abolished. Juliet Mitchell gives a contemporary Marxist analysis of the nuclear family, according to which the family is the focal point of the *idea* of private property in a system wherein the individual worker *has* no private property. The hope of accumulating private property for themselves and their families is what keeps the workers laboring in the social system to produce private property for the capitalists.

Sara Ann Ketchum argues for the application to marriage law of the liberal principles that govern other contracts: freedom of choice, equality of op-

portunity, and equal treatment under the law. Larry Blum, Marcia Homiak, Judy Hausman, and Naomi Scheman argue that a woman's ability to care for her husband and children is distorted by the structural features of marriage. The kind of altruism possible in marriage is thus of a negative nature, contrasting with the positive "caring with autonomy" that is possible, for example in consciousness-raising groups. And Shulamith Firestone sketches some alternatives to the nuclear family, including a communal form of child-rearing entered into on a voluntary basis by both adults and children.

Part III contains discussions of two controversial moral topics: abortion and preferential treatment. How we resolve each problem will have a serious impact on the life expectations of women. A society that does not allow a woman to decide whether to terminate a particular pregnancy seriously restricts her ability to arrange her life. Many women are convinced that because they have a right to plan their lives and decide whether and when to become parents, a prohibition on abortion would be unjust. On the other hand, many people believe that an abortion is an unjustified killing. In Chapter 6, Judith Jarvis Thomson discusses this conflict, arguing that a person's right to life does not create an obligation for other people to provide means of support and maintenance. Mary Anne Warren contributes to the debate on the morality of abortion by discussing the conditions for being a person, indicating that a fetus clearly does not meet them. There are other important and controversial issues surrounding abortion and the right to plan one's future. The Supreme Court decision in *Roe* v. *Wade*, guarantees women the right to terminate a pregnancy within the first trimester, but this means only that it cannot be illegal for a woman to seek and have an abortion during that period. If she does not have funds for the procedure, should financial help be made available through some public agency? Does recent federal and state legislation severely restricting the use of government funds for abortions discriminate against poor women?

Chapter 7 takes up some issues of preferential treatment. It is obvious that women and minorities are underrepresented in desirable vocations (i.e., in those that provide a good income, interesting work, or both). This situation results from a variety of practices involving outright discrimination or exclusionary quotas as well as from more subtle influences on the performance and motivation of minorities and women. Remedy for this underrepresentation is sought through programs of affirmative action and preferential treatment. The difficulty with preferential treatment is that it seems to pick a trait—race or sex—that appears to be irrelevant to performance, for example, as a medical student, and count it as relevant. The result is that people, in fact white males, who are more meritorious on standard criteria are excluded. Several different counters are offered to this objection.

Some say that preferential treatment is the best way to bring about a more nearly just distribution of desirable positions and to provide role models for the next generation. In this vein, Mary Anne Warren argues that "weak" quotas—those that would bring the percentage of women working in an institution or company in line with the percentage of qualified candidates—are justified in order to eliminate "secondary sexism." Under the latter heading Warren includes those practices whose *aim* is not sexist but whose *effects* are. Such a practice, according to Warren, would not be unfair to individual white males because it would do no more than create a situation in which men and women are hired according to merit.

Others, such as Judith Jarvis Thomson, suggest that preferential treatment of women and minorities should be seen as reparation for past harms and that the cost of righting those wrongs is appropriately borne by those who benefited from past unjust arrangements. Richard A. Wasserstrom argues that, at least with respect to university positions, minorities and women have special qualifications. The university is devoted to the pursuit of truth, and women and minorities, far from being short on "merit," have important experience to contribute to the university's task of advancing understanding.

In Part IV, Theoretical Frameworks for Women's Liberation, Sandra Lee Bartky describes the effects of living in an oppressive society on the consciousness of particular individuals. In her account of changes in consciousness that occur when one becomes a feminist, she claims that the resulting "raised" consciousness, which is experienced as liberating, is both a goal and a cause of the feminist movement. Alison Jaggar considers four different theories of what women's liberation would consist in, and how to bring it about. The differing

views held by feminists on these questions result from their differences on some of the fundamental questions of political and social philosophy (e.g., on what a good society is like and what the proper relationship is between an individual and his or her society and government). Differences on these questions reflect deeper disagreements about the nature of individuals. Classical liberal thinkers regard the individual as an independent unit, whereas socialist theorists think of individuals as dependent on society for their identity and powers. Thus, according to some feminist thinkers, liberation for women consists in the attainment of equality under the law, of legal access for all citizens to all institutions of society. On this theory legal reform within the framework of the present society would be sufficient for the liberation of women. According to other theorists, however, such "formal" equality of opportunity is not sufficient to bring about liberation; it is also necessary to change the economic balance of power and the correlative social class structure. Finally, radical feminist theorists hold that women's liberation requires a more radical change than the attainment of either legal or economic equality.

It is feminists who have been making the demands for radical shifts in behavior, policy, and attitude toward women. These demands have been made on behalf of women, though it has long been recognized that the results will involve gains and losses for both men and women. There is some controversy over who will lose and gain the most. Men are apt to lose powers they held in economic and family life, and women will probably lose privileges of support and security. Women stand to gain equal access to meaningful and rewarding careers, and men will win richer and healthier emotional lives. However the gains and losses balance out, such changes are regarded as required by justice. It is hard to see how the deep and pervasive changes that seem appropriate to feminists can be effected without widespread understanding and discussion of the issues raised in this volume. The editors hope that these essays will contribute to sensitive and constructive thinking about sex roles.

Sharon Bishop
Marjorie Weinzweig

Part One
Sexism and Sex Roles

1
Sexism

1/Sexism as Inequality
John Stuart Mill

The object of this Essay is to explain as clearly as I am able, the grounds of an opinion which I have held from the very earliest period when I had formed any opinions at all on social or political matters . . . : That the principle which regulates the existing social relations between the two sexes—the legal subordination of one sex to the other—is wrong in itself, and now one of the chief hindrances to human improvement; and that it ought to be replaced by a principle of perfect equality, admitting no power or privilege on the one side, nor disability on the other. . . .

The generality of a practice is in some cases a strong presumption that it is, or at all events once was, conducive to laudable ends. This is the case, when the practice was first adopted, or afterwards kept up, as a means to such ends, and was grounded on experience of the mode in which they could be most effectually attained. If the authority of men over women, when first established, had been the result of a conscientious comparison between different modes of constituting the government of society; if, after trying various other modes of social organization—the government of women over men, equality between the two, and such mixed and divided modes of government as might be invented —it had been decided, on the testimony of experience, that the mode in which women are wholly under the rule of men, having no share at all in public concerns, and each in private being under the legal obligation of obedience to the man with whom she has associated her destiny, was the arrangement most conducive to the happiness and well being of both; its general adoption might then be fairly thought to be some evidence that, at the time when it was adopted, it was the best. . . . But the state of the case is in every respect the reverse of this. In the first place, the opinion in favour of the present system, which entirely subordinates the weaker sex to the stronger, rests upon theory only; for there never has been trial made of any other: so that experience, in the sense in which it is vulgarly opposed to theory, cannot be pretended to have pronounced any verdict. And in the second place, the adoption of this system of inequality never was the result of deliberation, or forethought, or any social ideas, or any notion whatever of what conduced to the benefit of humanity or the good order of society. It arose simply from the fact that from the very earliest twilight of human society, every woman (owing to the value attached to her by men, combined with her inferiority in muscular strength) was found in a state of bondage to some man. Laws and systems of polity always begin by recognizing the relations they find already existing between individuals. They convert what was a mere physical fact into a legal right, give it the sanction of society, and principally aim at the substitution of public and organized means of asserting and protecting these rights, instead of the irregular and lawless conflict of physical strength. Those who had already been compelled to obedience became in this manner legally bound to it. Slavery, from being a mere affair of force between the master and the slave, became regularized and a matter of compact among the masters, who, binding themselves to one another for common protection, guaranteed by their collective strength the private possessions of each, including his slaves. In early times, the great majority of the male sex were slaves, as well as the whole of the female. And many ages elapsed, some of them ages of high cultivation, before any thinker was bold enough to question the rightfulness, and the absolute social necessity, either of the one slavery or of the other. By degrees such thinkers did arise: and (the general progress of society assisting) the slavery of the male sex has, in all the countries of Chris-

Adapted from *The Subjection of Women* (London, 1869).

tian Europe at least (though, in one of them, only within the last few years) been at length abolished, and that of the female sex has been gradually changed into a milder form of dependence. But this dependence, as it exists at present, is not an original institution, taking a fresh start from considerations of justice and social expediency—it is the primitive state of slavery lasting on, through successive mitigations and modifications occasioned by the same causes which have softened the general manners, and brought all human relations more under the control of justice and the influence of humanity. It has not lost the taint of its brutal origin. No presumption in its favour, therefore, can be drawn from the fact of its existence. . . .

Some will object, that a comparison cannot fairly be made between the government of the male sex and the forms of unjust power which I have adduced in illustration of it, since these are arbitrary, and the effect of mere usurpation, while it on the contrary is natural. But was there ever any domination which did not appear natural to those who possessed it? There was a time when the division of mankind into two classes, a small one of masters and a numerous one of slaves, appeared, even to the most cultivated minds, to be a natural, and the only natural, condition of the human race. No less an intellect, and one which contributed no less to the progress of human thought, than Aristotle, held this opinion without doubt or misgiving; and rested it on the same premises on which the same assertion in regard to the dominion of men over women is usually based, namely that there are different natures among mankind, free natures, and slave natures; that the Greeks were of a free nature, the barbarian races of Thracians and Asiatics of a slave nature. But why need I go back to Aristotle? Did not the slaveowners of the Southern United States maintain the same doctrine, with all the fanaticism with which men cling to the theories that justify their passions and legitimate their personal interests? Did they not call heaven and earth to witness that the dominion of the white man over the black is natural, that the black race is by nature incapable of freedom, and marked out for slavery? some even going so far as to say that the freedom of manual labourers is an unnatural order of things anywhere. . . . So true is it that unnatural generally means only uncustomary, and that everything which is usual appears natural. The subjection of women to men being a universal custom, any departure from it quite naturally appears unnatural. But how entirely, even in this case,

the feeling is dependent on custom, appears by ample experience. Nothing so much astonishes the people of distant parts of the world, when they first learn anything about England, as to be told that it is under a queen: the thing seems to them so unnatural as to be almost incredible. To Englishmen this does not seem in the least degree unnatural, because they are used to it; but they do feel it unnatural that women should be soldiers or members of parliament. In the feudal ages, on the contrary, war and politics were not thought unnatural to women, because not unusual; it seemed natural that women of the privileged classes should be of manly character, inferior in nothing but bodily strength to their husbands and fathers. The independence of women seemed rather less unnatural to the Greeks than to other ancients, on account of the fabulous Amazons (whom they believed to be historical), and the partial example afforded by the Spartan women; who, though no less subordinate by law than in other Greek states, were more free in fact, and being trained to bodily exercises in the same manner with men, gave ample proof that they were not naturally disqualified for them. There can be little doubt that Spartan experience suggested to Plato, among many other of his doctrines, that of the social and political equality of the two sexes.

But, it will be said, the rule of men over women differs from all these others in not being a rule of force: it is accepted voluntarily; women make no complaint, and are consenting parties to it. In the first place, a great number of women do not accept it. Ever since there have been women able to make their sentiments known by their writings (the only mode of publicity which society permits to them), an increasing number of them have recorded protests against their present social condition: and recently many thousands of them, headed by the most eminent women known to the public, have petitioned Parliament for their admission to the Parliamentary Suffrage. The claim of women to be educated as solidly, and in the same branches of knowledge, as men, is urged with growing intensity, and with a great prospect of success; while the demand for their admission into professions and occupations hitherto closed against them, becomes every year more urgent. . . . it [is not] only in our own country and in America that women are beginning to protest, more or less collectively, against the disabilities under which they labour. France, and Italy, and Switzerland, and Russia now afford examples of the same thing. How many more women there are who silently cherish similar aspirations, no one can possibly know; but there are abundant tokens how many *would* cherish them, were they not so strenuously taught to repress them as contrary to the proprieties of their sex. It must be remembered, also, that no enslaved class ever asked for complete liberty at once. When Simon de Montfort called the deputies of the commons to sit for the first time in Parliament, did any of them dream of demanding that an assembly, elected by their constituents, should make and destroy ministries, and dictate to the king in affairs of state? No such thought entered into the imagination of the most ambitious of them. The nobility had already these pretensions; the commons pretended to nothing but to be exempt from arbitrary taxation, and from the gross individual oppression of the king's officers. It is a political law of nature that those who are under any power of ancient origin, never begin by complaining of the power itself, but only of its oppressive exercise. There is never any want of women who complain of ill usage by their husbands. There would be infinitely more, if complaint were not the greatest of all provocatives to a repetition and increase of the ill usage. It is this which frustrates all attempts to maintain the power but protect the woman against its abuses. In no other case (except that of a child) is the person who has been proved judicially to have suffered an injury, replaced under the physical power of the culprit who inflicted it. Accordingly wives, even in the most extreme and protracted cases of bodily ill usage, hardly ever dare avail themselves of the laws made for their protection: and if, in a moment of irrepressible indignation, or by the interference of neighbours, they are induced to do so, their whole effort afterwards is to disclose as little as they can, and to beg off their tyrant from his merited chastisement.

All causes, social and natural, combine to make it unlikely that women should be collectively rebellious to the power of men. They are so far in a position different from all other subject classes, that their masters require something more from them than actual service. Men do not want solely the obedience of women, they want their sentiments. All men, except the most brutish, desire to have, in the woman most nearly connected with them, not a forced slave but a willing one, not a slave merely, but a favourite. They have therefore put everything in practice to enslave their minds. The masters of all other slaves rely, for maintaining obedience, on fear; either fear of themselves, or religious fears.

The masters of women wanted more than simple obedience, and they turned the whole force of education to effect their purpose. All women are brought up from the very earliest years in the belief that their ideal of character is the very opposite to that of men; not self-will, and government by self-control, but submission, and yielding to the control of others. All the moralities tell them that it is the duty of women, and all the current sentimentalities that it is their nature, to live for others; to make complete abnegation of themselves, and to have no life but in their affections. And by their affections are meant the only ones they are allowed to have—those to the men with whom they are connected, or to the children who constitute an additional and indefeasible tie between them and a man. When we put together three things—first, the natural attraction between opposite sexes; secondly, the wife's entire dependence on the husband, every privilege or pleasure she has being either his gift, or depending entirely on his will; and lastly, that the principal object of human pursuit, consideration, and all objects of social ambition, can in general be sought or obtained by her only through him, it would be a miracle if the object of being attractive to men had not become the polar star of feminine education and formation of character. And, this great means of influence over the minds of women having been acquired, an instinct of selfishness made men avail themselves of it to the utmost as a means of holding women in subjection, by representing to them meekness, submissiveness, and resignation of all individual will into the hands of a man, as an essential part of sexual attractiveness. Can it be doubted that any of the other yokes which mankind have succeeded in breaking, would have subsisted till now if the same means had existed, and had been as sedulously used, to bow down their minds to it? If it had been made the object of the life of every young plebeian to find personal favour in the eyes of some patrician, of every young serf with some seigneur; if domestication with him, and a share of his personal affections, had been held out as the prize which they all should look out for, the most gifted and aspiring being able to reckon on the most desirable prizes; and if, when this prize had been obtained, they had been shut out by a wall of brass from all interests not centering in him, all feelings and desires but those which he shared or inculcated; would not serfs and seigneurs, plebeians and patricians, have been as broadly distinguished at this day as men and women are? and would not all but a thinker here and there, have believed the distinction to be a fundamental and unalterable fact in human nature?

The preceding considerations are amply sufficient to show that custom, however universal it may be, affords in this case no presumption, and ought not to create any prejudice, in favour of the arrangements which place women in social and political subjection to men. But I may go farther, and maintain that the course of history, and the tendencies of progressive human society, afford not only no presumption in favour of this system of inequality of rights, but a strong one against it; and that, so far as the whole course of human improvement up to this time, the whole stream of modern tendencies, warrants any inference on the subject, it is, that this relic of the past is discordant with the future, and must necessarily disappear.

2/Racism and Sexism

Richard A. Wasserstrom

Introduction

Racism and sexism are two central issues that engage the attention of many persons living within the United States today. But while there is relatively little disagreement about their importance as topics, there is substantial, vehement, and apparently intractable disagreement about what individuals, practices, ideas, and institutions are either racist or sexist—and for what reasons. In dispute are a number of related questions concerning how individuals and institutions ought to regard and respond to matters relating to race or sex.

One particularly contemporary example concerns those programs variously called programs of "affirmative action," "preferential treatment," or "reverse discrimination" that are a feature of much of our institutional life. Attitudes and beliefs about these programs are diverse. Some persons are convinced that all such programs in virtually all of their forms are themselves racist and sexist and are for these among other reasons indefensible. The programs are causally explicable, perhaps, but morally reprehensible. Other persons—a majority, I suspect—are sorely troubled by these programs. They are convinced that some features of some programs, e.g., quotas, are indefensible and wrong. Other features and programs are tolerated, but not with fervor or enthusiasm. They are seen as a kind of moral compromise, as, perhaps, a lesser evil among a set of unappealing options. They are reluctantly perceived and implemented as a covert, euphemistic way to do what would clearly be wrong—even racist or sexist—to do overtly and with candor. And still a third group has a very different view. They think these programs are important and appropriate. They do not see these programs, quotas included, as racist or sexist, and they see much about the dominant societal institutions that is. They regard the racism and sexism of the society as accounting in substantial measure for the failure or refusal to adopt such programs willingly and to press vigorously for their full implementation.

I think that much of the confusion in thinking and arguing about racism, sexism and affirmative action results from a failure to see that there are three different perspectives within which the topics of racism, sexism and affirmative action can most usefully be examined. The first of these perspectives concentrates on what in fact is true of the culture, on what can be called the social realities. Here the fundamental question concerns the way the culture is: What are its institutions, attitudes and ideologies in respect to matters of race and sex?

The second perspective is concerned with the way things ought to be. From this perspective, analysis focuses very largely on possible, desirable states of affairs. Here the fundamental question

From "Racism, Sexism, and Preferential Treatment: An Approach to the Topics," *UCLA Law Review* (February 1977), pp. 581–615.

concerns ideals: What would the good society—in terms of its institutions, its attitudes, and its values—look like in respect to matters involving race and sex?

The third perspective looks forward to the means by which the ideal may be achieved. Its focus is on the question: What is the best or most appropriate way to move from the existing social realities, whatever they happen to be, to a closer approximation of the ideal society? This perspective is concerned with instrumentalities.[1]

Many of the debates over affirmative action and over what things are racist and sexist are un-illuminating because they neglect to take into account these three perspectives, which are important and must be considered separately. While I do not claim that all the significant normative and conceptual questions concerning race, sex, or affirmative action can be made to disappear, I do believe that an awareness and use of these perspectives can produce valuable insights that contribute to their resolution. In particular, it can almost immediately be seen that the question of whether something is racist or sexist is not as straightforward or unambiguous as may appear at first. The question may be about social realities, about how the categories of race or sex in fact function in the culture and to what effect. Or the question may be about ideals, about what the good society would make of race or sex. Or the question may be about instrumentalities, about how, given the social realities as to race and sex, to achieve a closer approximation of the ideal. It can also be seen, therefore, that what might be an impermissible way to take race or sex into account in the ideal society, may also be a desirable and appropriate way to take race or sex into account, given the social realities.

It is these three different perspectives and these underlying issues that I am interested in exploring. This framework is used to clarify a number of the central matters that are involved in thinking clearly about the topics of racism, sexism and affirmative action. Within this framework, some of the analogies and disanalogies between racism and sexism are explored—the ways they are and are not analytically interchangeable phenomena. I also provide an analytic scheme for distinguishing different respects in which a complex institution such as the legal system might plausibly be seen to be racist

or sexist. And I examine some of the key arguments that most often arise whenever these topics are considered. In respect to programs of affirmative action, or preferential treatment, I argue specifically that much of the opposition to such programs is not justifiable. It rests upon confusion in thinking about the relevant issues and upon a failure to perceive and appreciate some of the ways in which our society is racist and sexist. I argue that there is much to be said for the view that such programs, even when they include quotas, are defensible and right. My central focus is not, however, on affirmative action per se, but rather on how a consideration of affirmative action is linked to a deepened understanding of these larger, related issues.

I. Social Realities

One way to think and talk about racism and sexism is to concentrate upon the perspective of the social realities. Here one must begin by insisting that to talk about either is to talk about a particular social and cultural context. In this section I concentrate upon two questions that can be asked about the social realities of our culture. First, I consider the position of blacks and females in the culture vis-à-vis the position of those who are white, and those who are male. And second, I provide an analysis of the different ways in which a complex institution, such as our legal system, can be seen to be racist or sexist. The analysis is offered as a schematic account of the possible types of racism or sexism.

A. The Position of Blacks and Women

In our own culture the first thing to observe is that race and sex are socially important categories. They are so in virtue of the fact that we live in a culture which has, throughout its existence, made race and sex extremely important characteristics of and for all the people living in the culture.

It is surely possible to imagine a culture in which race would be an unimportant, insignificant characteristic of individuals. In such a culture race would be largely if not exclusively a matter of superficial physiology; a matter, we might say, simply of the way one looked. And if it were, then any analysis of race and racism would necessarily assume very different dimensions from what they do in our soci-

[1][See below, pp. 247–250 for Professor Wasserstrom's discussion of this perspective—eds.]

ety. In such a culture, the meaning of the term "race" would itself have to change substantially. This can be seen by the fact that in such a culture it would literally make no sense to say of a person that he or she was "passing." This is something that can be said and understood in our own culture and it shows at least that to talk of race is to talk of more than the way one looks.

Sometimes when people talk about what is wrong with affirmative action programs, or programs of preferential hiring, they say that what is wrong with such programs is that they take a thing as superficial as an individual's race and turn it into something important. They say that a person's race doesn't matter; other things do, such as qualifications. Whatever else may be said of statements such as these, as descriptions of the social realities they seem to be simply false. One complex but true empirical fact about our society is that the race of an individual is much more than a fact of superficial physiology. It is, instead, one of the dominant characteristics that affects both the way the individual looks at the world and the way the world looks at the individual. As I have said, that need not be the case. It may in fact be very important that we work toward a society in which that would not be the case, but it is the case now and it must be understood in any adequate and complete discussion of racism. That is why, too, it does not make much sense when people sometimes say, in talking about the fact that they are not racists, that they would not care if an individual were green and came from Mars, they would treat that individual the same way they treat people exactly like themselves. For part of *our* social and cultural history is to treat people of certain races in a certain way, and we do not have a social or cultural history of treating green people from Mars in any particular way. To put it simply, it is to misunderstand the social realities of race and racism to think of them simply as questions of how some people respond to other people whose skins are of different hues, irrespective of the social context.

I can put the point another way: Race does not function in our culture as does eye color. Eye color is an irrelevant category; nobody cares what color people's eyes are; it is not an important cultural fact; nothing turns on what eye color you have. It is important to see that race is not like that at all. And this truth affects what will and will not count as cases of racism. In our culture to be nonwhite—and especially to be black—is to be treated and seen to be a member of a group that is different from and infe-

rior to the group of standard, fully developed persons, the adult white males. To be black is to be a member of what was a despised minority and what is still a disliked and oppressed one. That is simply part of the awful truth of our cultural and social history, and a significant feature of the social reality of our culture today.

We can see fairly easily that the two sexual categories, like the racial ones, are themselves in important respects products of the society. Like one's race, one's sex is not merely or even primarily a matter of physiology. To see this we need only realize that we can understand the idea of a transsexual. A transsexual is someone who would describe himself or herself either as a person who is essentially a female but through some accident of nature is trapped in a male body, or a person who is essentially a male but through some accident of nature is trapped in the body of a female. His (or her) description is some kind of a shorthand way of saying that he (or she) is more comfortable with the role allocated by the culture to people who are physiologically of the opposite sex. The fact that we regard this assertion of the transsexual as intelligible seems to me to show how deep the notion of sexual identity is in our culture and how little it has to do with physiological differences between males and females. Because people do pass in the context of race and because we can understand what passing means; because people are transsexuals and because we can understand what transsexuality means, we can see that the existing social categories of both race and sex are in this sense creations of the culture.

It is even clearer in the case of sex than in the case of race that one's sexual identity is a centrally important, crucially relevant category within our culture. I think, in fact, that it is more important and more fundamental than one's race. It is evident that there are substantially different role expectations and role assignments to persons in accordance with their sexual physiology, and that the positions of the two sexes in the culture are distinct. We do have a patriarchal society in which it matters enormously whether one is a male or a female.[2] By almost all important measures it is more advantageous to be a male rather than a female.

[2]The best general account I have read of the structure of patriarchy and of its major dimensions and attributes is that found in SEXUAL POLITICS in the chapter, "Theory of Sexual Politics." K. MILLETT, SEXUAL POLITICS 23–58 (1970). The essay seems to me to be truly a major contribution to an understanding of

Women and men are socialized differently. We learn very early and forcefully that we are either males or females and that much turns upon which sex we are. The evidence seems to be overwhelming and well-documented that sex roles play a fundamental role in the way persons think of themselves and the world—to say nothing of the way the world thinks of them. Men and women are taught to see men as independent, capable, and powerful; men and women are taught to see women as dependent, limited in abilities, and passive. A woman's success or failure in life is defined largely in terms of her activities within the family. It is important for her that she marry, and when she does she is expected to take responsibility for the wifely tasks: the housework, the child care, and the general emotional welfare of the husband and children.[3] Her status in society is determined in substantial measure by the vocation and success of her husband.[4] Economically, women are substantially worse off than men. They do not receive any pay for the work that is done in the home. As members of the labor force their wages are significantly lower than those paid to men, even when they are engaged in similar work and have similar educational backgrounds.[5] The higher the prestige or the salary of the job, the less present women are in the labor force. And, of course, women are conspicuously absent from most positions of authority and power in the major economic and political institutions of our society.

As is true for race, it is also a significant social fact that to be a female is to be an entity or creature viewed as different from the standard, fully developed person who is male as well as white. But to be female, as opposed to being black, is not to be conceived of as simply a creature of less worth. That is one important thing that differentiates sexism from racism: The ideology of sex, as opposed to the ideology of race, is a good deal more complex and confusing. Women are both put on a pedestal and deemed not fully developed persons. They are idealized; their approval and admiration is sought; and they are at the same time regarded as less competent than men and less able to live fully de-

---

the subject. Something of the essence of the thesis is contained in the following:

[A] disinterested examination of our system of sexual relationship must point out that the situation between the sexes now, and throughout history, is a case of that phenomenon Max Weber defined as herrschaft, a relationship of dominance and subordinance. What goes largely unexamined, often even unacknowledged (yet is institutionalized nonetheless) in our social order, is the birthright priority whereby males rule females. Through this system a most ingenious form of "interior colonization" has been achieved. It is one which tends moreover to be sturdier than any form of segregation and more rigorous than class stratification, more uniform, certainly more enduring. However muted its present appearance may be, sexual dominion obtains nevertheless as perhaps the most pervasive ideology of our culture and provides its most fundamental concept of power.

This is so because our society, like all other historical civilizations, is a patriarchy. The fact is evident at once if one recalls that the military, industry, technology, universities, science, political office, and finance—in short, every avenue of power within the society, including the coercive force of the police, is entirely in male hands. . . .

Sexual politics obtains consent through the "socialization" of both sexes to basic patriarchal politics with regard to temperament, role, and status. As to status, a pervasive assent to the prejudice of male superiority guarantees superior status in the male, inferior in the female. The first item, temperament, involves the formation of human personality along stereotyped lines of sex category ("masculine" and "feminine"), based on the needs and values of the dominant group and dictated by what its members cherish in themselves and find convenient in subordinates: aggression, intelligence, force and efficacy in the male; passivity, ignorance, docility, "virtue," and ineffectuality in the female. This is complemented by a second factor, sex role, which decrees a consonant and highly elaborate code of conduct, gesture and attitude for each sex. In terms of activity, sex role assigns domestic service and attendance upon infants to the female, the rest of human achievement, interest and ambition to the male. . . . Were one to analyze the three categories one might designate status as the political component, role as the sociological, and

temperament as the psychological—yet their interdependence is unquestionable and they form a chain. Id. at 24–26 (footnotes omitted).

[3] For the married woman, her husband and children must always come first; her own needs and desires, last. When the children reach school age, they no longer require constant attention. The emotional-expressive function assigned to the woman is still required of her. Called the "stroking function" by sociologist Jessie Bernard, it consists of showing solidarity, raising the status of others, giving help, rewarding, agreeing, concurring, complying, understanding, and passively accepting. The woman is expected to give emotional support and comfort to other family members, to make them feel like good and worthwhile human beings. B. DECKARD, THE WOMEN'S MOVEMENT 59 (1975), citing J. BERNARD, WOMEN AND THE PUBLIC INTEREST 88 (1971).

Patriarchy's chief institution is the family. It is both a mirror of and a connection with the larger society; a patriarchal unit within a patriarchal whole. Mediating between the individual and the social structure, the family effects control and conformity where political and other authorities are insufficient. K. MILLETT, supra note [2] at 33.

[4] Even if the couple consciously try to attain an egalitarian marriage, so long as the traditional division of labor is maintained, the husband will be "more equal." He is the provider not only of money but of status. Especially if he is successful, society values what he does; she is just a housewife. Their friends are likely to be his friends and co-workers; in their company, she is just his wife. Because his provider function is essential for the family's survival, major family decisions are made in terms of how they affect his career. He need not and usually does not act like the authoritarian paterfamilias [sic] of the Victorian age. His power and status are derived from his function in the family and are secure so long as the traditional division of labor is maintained. B. DECKARD, supra note [3] at 62.

[5] In 1970, women workers were, on the average, paid only 59 percent of men's wages. And when wages of persons with similar educational levels are compared, women still were paid over 40 percent less than men. Id. at 79–81.

veloped, fully human lives—for that is what men do.[6] At best, they are viewed and treated as having properties and attributes that are valuable and admirable for humans of this type. For example, they may be viewed as especially empathetic, intuitive, loving, and nurturing. At best, these qualities are viewed as good properties for women to have, and, provided they are properly muted, are sometimes valued within the more well-rounded male. Because the sexual ideology is complex, confusing, and variable, it does not unambiguously proclaim the lesser value attached to being female rather than being male, nor does it unambiguously correspond to the existing social realities. For these, among other reasons, sexism could plausibly be regarded as a deeper phenomenon than racism. It is more deeply embedded in the culture, and thus less visible. Being harder to detect, it is harder to eradicate. Moreover, it is less unequivocally regarded as unjust and unjustifiable. That is to say, there is less agreement within the dominant ideology that sexism even implies an unjustifiable practice or attitude. Hence, many persons announce, without regret or embarrassment, that they are sexists or male chauvinists; very few announce openly that they are racists.[7] For all of these reasons sexism may be a more insidious

evil than racism, but there is little merit in trying to decide between two seriously objectionable practices which one is worse.

While I do not think that I have made very controversial claims about either our cultural history or our present-day culture, I am aware of the fact that they have been stated very imprecisely and that I have offered little evidence to substantiate them. In a crude way we ought to be able both to understand the claims and to see that they are correct if we reflect seriously and critically upon our own cultural institutions, attitudes, and practices. But in a more refined, theoretical way, I am imagining that a more precise and correct description of the social reality in respect to race and sex would be derivable from a composite, descriptive account of our society which utilized the relevant social sciences to examine such things as the society's institutions, practices, attitudes and ideology[8]—if the social sciences could be value-free and unaffected in outlook or approach by the fact that they, themselves, are largely composed of persons who are white and male.[9]

Viewed from the perspective of social reality it should be clear, too, that racism and sexism should not be thought of as phenomena that consist simply in taking a person's race or sex into account, or even

[6]*It is generally accepted that Western patriarchy has been much softened by the concepts of courtly and romantic love. While this is certainly true, such influence has also been vastly overestimated. In comparison with the candor of "machismo" or oriental behavior, one realizes how much of a concession traditional chivalrous behavior represents—a sporting kind of reparation to allow the subordinate female certain means of saving face. While a palliative to the injustice of woman's social position, chivalry is also a technique for disguising it. One must acknowledge that the chivalrous stance is a game the master group plays in elevating its subject to pedestal level. Historians of courtly love stress the fact that the raptures of the poets had no effect upon the legal or economic standing of women, and very little upon their social status. As the sociologist Hugo Beigel has observed, both the courtly and the romantic versions of love are "grants" which the male concedes out of his total powers. Both have the effect of obscuring the patriarchal character of Western culture and in their general tendency to attribute impossible virtues to women, have ended by confining them in a narrow and often remarkably conscribing sphere of behavior. It was a Victorian habit, for example, to insist the female assume the function of serving as the male's conscience and living the life of goodness he found tedious but felt someone ought to do anyway.*
K. MILLETT, *supra* note [2] at 36–37.

[7]Thus, even after his "joke" about black persons became known to the public, the former Secretary of Agriculture, Earl Butz, took great pains to insist that this in no way showed that he was a racist. This is understandable, given the strongly condemnatory feature of being described as a racist.
   Equally illuminating was the behavior of Butz's associates and superiors. Then-President Ford, for example, criticized Butz for the joke, but did not demand Butz's removal until there was a strong public outcry. It was as though Butz's problem was that he had been indiscreet; he had done something rude like belching in public. What Ford, Butz, and others apparently failed to grasp is

that it is just as wrong to tell these jokes in private because to tell a joke of this sort is to have a view about what black people are like: that they can appropriately be ridiculed as being creatures who care only about intercourse, shoes, and defecation. What these persons also failed to grasp is how implausible it is to believe that one can hold these views about black people and at the same time deal with them in a nonracist fashion.

[8]At a minimum, this account would include: (1) a description of the economic, political, and social positions of blacks and whites, males and females in the culture; (2) a description of the sexual and racial roles, *i.e.*, the rules, conventions and expectations concerning how males and females, blacks and whites, should behave, and the attitudes and responses produced by these roles; and (3) a description of the de facto ideology of racial and sexual differences. This would include popular beliefs about how males and females, blacks and whites, differ, as well as the beliefs as to what accounts for these differences, roles, and economic, political and social realities.

[9]The problem of empirical objectivity is compounded by the fact that part of the dominant, white male ideology is that white males are the one group in society whose members are able to be genuinely detached and objective when it comes to things like an understanding of the place of race and sex in the culture. Thus, for example, when a sex-discrimination suit was brought against a law firm and the case was assigned to Judge Constance Motley, the defendant filed a motion that she be disqualified partly because, as a woman judge, she would be biased in favor of the plaintiff. Judge Motley denied the motion. Blank v. Sullivan & Cromwell, 418 F. Supp. 1 (S.D.N.Y. 1975), *writ of mandamus denied sub nom.* Sullivan & Cromwell v. Motley, No. 75-3045 (2d Cir. Aug. 26, 1975). Explaining her decision, Judge Motley stated: "[I]f background or sex or race of each judge were, *by definition,* sufficient grounds for removal, no judge on this court could hear this case, or many others, by virtue of the fact that all of them were attorneys, of a sex, often with distinguished law firm or public service backgrounds." 418 F. Supp. at 4 (emphasis added).

simply in taking a person's race or sex into account in an arbitrary way. Instead, racism and sexism consist in taking race and sex into account in a certain way, in the context of a specific set of institutional arrangements and a specific ideology which together create and maintain a *system* of unjust institutions and unwarranted beliefs and attitudes. That system is and has been one in which political, economic, and social power and advantage are concentrated in the hands of those who are white and male.

One way to bring this out, as well as to show another respect in which racism and sexism are different, concerns segregated bathrooms—a topic that may seem silly and trivial but which is certainly illuminating and probably important. We know, for instance, that it is wrong, clearly racist, to have racially segregated bathrooms. There is, however, no common conception that it is wrong, clearly sexist, to have sexually segregated ones. How is this to be accounted for? The answer to the question of why it was and is racist to have racially segregated bathrooms can be discovered through a consideration of the role that this practice played in that system of racial segregation we had in the United States—from, in other words, an examination of the social realities. For racially segregated bathrooms were an important part of that system. And that system had an ideology; it was complex and perhaps not even wholly internally consistent. A significant feature of the ideology was that blacks were not only less than fully developed humans, but that they were also dirty and impure. They were the sorts of creatures who could and would contaminate white persons if they came into certain kinds of contact with them—in the bathroom, at the dinner table, or in bed, although it was appropriate for blacks to prepare and handle food, and even to nurse white infants. This ideology was intimately related to a set of institutional arrangements and power relationships in which whites were politically, economically, and socially dominant. The ideology supported the institutional arrangements, and the institutional arrangements reinforced the ideology. The net effect was that racially segregated bathrooms were both a part of the institutional mechanism of oppression and an instantiation of this ideology of racial taint. The point of maintaining racially segregated bathrooms was not in any simple or direct sense to keep both whites and blacks from using each other's bathrooms; it was to make sure that blacks would not contaminate bathrooms used

by whites. The practice also taught both whites and blacks that certain kinds of contacts were forbidden because whites would be degraded by the contact with the blacks.

The failure to understand the character of these institutions of racial oppression is what makes some of the judicial reasoning about racial discrimination against blacks so confusing and unsatisfactory. At times when the courts have tried to explain what is constitutionally wrong with racial segregation, they have said that the problem is that race is an inherently suspect category. What they have meant by this, or have been thought to mean, is that any differentiation among human beings on the basis of racial identity is inherently unjust, because arbitrary, and therefore any particular case of racial differentiation must be shown to be fully rational and justifiable. But the primary evil of the various schemes of racial segregation against blacks that the courts were being called upon to assess was not that such schemes were a capricious and irrational way of allocating public benefits and burdens. That might well be the primary wrong with racial segregation if we lived in a society very different from the one we have. The primary evil of these schemes was instead that they designedly and effectively marked off all black persons as degraded, dirty, less than fully developed persons who were unfit for full membership in the political, social, and moral community.

It is worth observing that the social reality of sexually segregated bathrooms appears to be different. The idea behind such sexual segregation seems to have more to do with the mutual undesirability of the use by both sexes of the same bathroom at the same time. There is no notion of the possibility of contamination; or even directly of inferiority and superiority. What seems to be involved —at least in part—is the importance of inculcating and preserving a sense of secrecy concerning the genitalia of the opposite sex. What seems to be at stake is the maintenance of that same sense of mystery or forbiddenness about the other sex's sexuality which is fostered by the general prohibition upon public nudity and the unashamed viewing of genitalia.

Sexually segregated bathrooms simply play a different role in our culture than did racially segregated ones. But that is not to say that the role they play is either benign or unobjectionable—only that it is different. Sexually segregated bathrooms may well be objectionable, but here too, the objection is not on the ground that they are prima facie capricious or arbitrary. Rather, the case against them now would rest on the ground that they are, perhaps, one small part of that scheme of sex-role differentiation which uses the mystery of sexual anatomy, among other things, to maintain the primacy of heterosexual sexual attraction central to that version of the patriarchal system of power relationships we have today.[10] Whether sexually segregated bathrooms would be objectionable, because irrational, in the good society depends once again upon what the good society would look like in respect to sexual differentiation.

B. Types of Racism or Sexism

Another recurring question that can profitably be examined within the perspective of social realities is whether the legal system is racist or sexist. Indeed, it seems to me essential that the social realities of the relationships and ideologies concerning race and sex be kept in mind whenever one is trying to assess claims that are made about the racism or sexism of important institutions such as the legal system. It is also of considerable importance in assessing such claims to understand that even within the perspective of social reality, racism or sexism can manifest itself, or be understood, in different ways. That these are both important points can be seen through a brief examination of the different, distinctive ways in which our own legal system might plausibly be understood to be racist. The mode of analysis I propose serves as well, I believe, for an analogous analysis of the sexism of the legal system, although I do not undertake the latter analysis in this paper.

The first type of racism is the simplest and the least controversial. It is the case of overt racism, in which a law or a legal institution expressly takes into account the race of individuals in order to assign benefits and burdens in such a way as to bestow an unjustified benefit upon a member or members of the racially dominant group or an unjustified burden upon members of the racial groups that are oppressed. We no longer have many, if any, cases of overt racism in our legal system today, although we certainly had a number in the past. Indeed, the historical system of formal, racial segregation

was both buttressed by, and constituted of, a number of overtly racist laws and practices. At different times in our history, racism included laws and practices which dealt with such things as the exclusion of nonwhites from the franchise, from decent primary and secondary schools and most professional schools, and the prohibition against interracial marriages.

The second type of racism is very similar to overt racism. It is covert, but intentional, racism, in which a law or a legal institution has as its purpose the allocation of benefits and burdens in order to support the power of the dominant race, but does not use race specifically as a basis for allocating these benefits and burdens. One particularly good historical example involves the use of grandfather clauses which were inserted in statutes governing voter registration in a number of states after passage of the fifteenth amendment.

Covert racism within the law is not entirely a thing of the past. Many instances of de facto school segregation in the North and West are cases of covert racism. At times certain school boards —virtually all of which are overwhelmingly white in composition—quite consciously try to maintain exclusively or predominantly white schools within a school district. The classifications such school boards use are not ostensibly racial, but are based upon the places of residence of the affected students. These categories provide the opportunity for covert racism in engineering the racial composition of individual schools within the board's jurisdiction.

What has been said so far is surely neither novel nor controversial. What is interesting, however, is that a number of persons appear to believe that as long as the legal system is not overtly or covertly racist, there is nothing to the charge that it is racist. So, for example, Mr. Justice Powell said in a speech a few years ago:

It is of course true that we have witnessed racial injustice in the past, as has every other country with significant racial diversity. But no one can fairly question the present national commitment to full equality and justice. Racial discrimination, by state action, is now proscribed by laws and court decisions which protect civil liberties more broadly than in any other country. But laws alone are not enough. Racial prejudice in the hearts of men cannot be legislated out of existence; it will pass only in time, and as human beings of all races learn in humility to respect each other—a process not

---

[10]This conjecture about the role of sexually segregated bathrooms may well be inaccurate or incomplete. The sexual segregation of bathrooms may have more to do with privacy than with patriarchy. However, if so, it is at least odd that what the institution makes relevant is sex rather than merely the ability to perform the eliminatory acts in private.

furthered by recrimination or undue self-accusation.[11]

I believe it is a mistake to think about the problem of racism in terms of overt or covert racial discrimination by state action, which is now banished, and racial prejudice, which still lingers, but only in the hearts of persons. For there is another, more subtle kind of racism—unintentional, perhaps, but effective—which is as much a part of the legal system as are overt and covert racist laws and practices. It is what some critics of the legal system probably mean when they talk about the "institutional racism" of the legal system.

There are at least two kinds of institutional racism. The first is the racism of sub-institutions within the legal system such as the jury, or the racism of practices built upon or countenanced by the law. These institutions and practices very often, if not always, reflect in important and serious ways a variety of dominant values in the operation of what is apparently a neutral legal mechanism. The result is the maintenance and reenforcement of a system in which whites dominate over nonwhites. One relatively uninteresting (because familiar) example is the case of de facto school segregation. As observed above, some cases of de facto segregation are examples of covert racism. But even in school districts where there is no intention to divide pupils on grounds of race so as to maintain existing power relationships along racial lines, school attendance zones are utilized which are based on the geographical location of the pupil. Because it is a fact in our culture that there is racial discrimination against black people in respect to housing, it is also a fact that any geographical allocation of pupils—unless one pays a lot of attention to housing patterns—will have the effect of continuing to segregate minority pupils very largely on grounds of race. It is perfectly appropriate to regard this effect as a case of racism in public education.

A less familiar, and hence perhaps more instructive, example concerns the question of the importance of having blacks on juries, especially in cases in which blacks are criminal defendants. The orthodox view within the law is that it is unfair to try a black defendant before an all-white jury if blacks were overtly or covertly excluded from the jury rolls used to provide the jury panel, but not otherwise. One reason that is often given is that the systematic

exclusion of blacks increases too greatly the chance of racial prejudice operating against the black defendant. The problem with this way of thinking about things is that it does not make much sense. If whites are apt to be prejudiced against blacks, then an all-white jury is just as apt to be prejudiced against a black defendant, irrespective of whether blacks were systematically excluded from the jury rolls. I suspect that the rule has developed in the way it has because the courts think that many, if not most, whites are not prejudiced against blacks, unless, perhaps, they happen to live in an area where there is systematic exclusion of blacks from the jury rolls. Hence prejudice is the chief worry, and a sectional, if not historical, one at that.

White prejudice against blacks is, I think, a problem, and not just a sectional one. However, the existence or nonexistence of prejudice against blacks does not go to the heart of the matter. It is a worry, but it is not the chief worry. A black person may not be able to get a fair trial from an all-white jury even though the jurors are disposed to be fair and impartial, because the whites may unknowingly bring into the jury box a view about a variety of matters which affects in very fundamental respects the way they will look at and assess the facts. Thus, for example, it is not, I suspect, part of the experience of most white persons who serve on juries that police often lie in their dealings with people and the courts. Indeed, it is probably not part of their experience that persons lie about serious matters except on rare occasions. And they themselves tend to take truth telling very seriously. As a result, white persons for whom these facts about police and lying are a part of their social reality will have very great difficulty taking seriously the possibility that the inculpatory testimony of a police witness is a deliberate untruth. However, it may also be a part of the social reality that many black persons, just because they are black, have had encounters with the police in which the police were at best indifferent to whether they, the police, were speaking the truth. And even more black persons may have known a friend or a relative who has had such an experience. As a result, a black juror would be more likely than his or her white counterpart to approach skeptically the testimony of ostensibly neutral, reliable witnesses such as police officers. The point is not that all police officers lie; nor is the point that all whites always believe everything police say, and blacks never do. The point is that because the world we live in is the way it is, it is likely that whites and blacks will on the

[11]N.Y. Times, Aug. 31, 1972, § 1, at 33, col. 3.

whole be disposed to view the credibility of police officers very differently. If so, the legal system's election to ignore this reality, and to regard as fair and above reproach the common occurrence of all-white juries (and white judges) passing on the guilt or innocence of black defendants is a decision in fact to permit and to perpetuate a kind of institutional racism within the law.

The second type of institutional racism is what I will call "conceptual" institutional racism. We have a variety of ways of thinking about the legal system, and we have a variety of ways of thinking within the legal system about certain problems. We use concepts. Quite often without realizing it, the concepts used take for granted certain objectionable aspects of racist ideology without our being aware of it. The second *Brown* case (*Brown II*) provides an example.[12] There was a second *Brown* case because, having decided that the existing system of racially segregated public education was unconstitutional (*Brown I*),[13] the Supreme Court gave legitimacy to a second issue—the nature of the relief to be granted—by treating it as a distinct question to be considered and decided separately. That in itself was striking because in most cases, once the Supreme Court has found unconstitutionality, there has been no problem about relief (apart from questions of retroactivity): The unconstitutional practices and acts are to cease. As is well known, the Court in *Brown II* concluded that the desegregation of public education had to proceed "with all deliberate speed."[14] The Court said that there were "complexities arising from the transition to a system of public education freed from racial discrimination."[15] More specifically, time might be necessary to carry out the ruling because of

problems related to administration, arising from the physical condition of the school plant, the school transportation system personnel, revision of school districts and attendance areas into compact units to achieve a system of determining admission to the public school on a non-racial basis, and revision of local laws and regulations which may be necessary in solving the foregoing problems.[16]

Now, I do not know whether the Court be-

[12]Brown v. Board of Educ., 349 U.S. 294 (1955).
[13]Brown v. Board of Educ., 347 U.S. 483 (1954).
[14]349 U.S. at 301.
[15]*Id.* at 299.
[16]*Id.* at 300–01.

lieved what it said in this passage, but it is a fantastic bit of nonsense that is, for my purposes, most instructive. Why? Because there was nothing complicated about most of the dual school systems of the southern states. Many counties, especially the rural ones, had one high school, typically called either "Booker T. Washington High School" or "George Washington Carver High School," where all the black children in the county went; another school, often called "Sidney Lanier High School" or "Robert E. Lee High School," was attended by all the white children in the county. There was nothing difficult about deciding that—as of the day after the decision—half of the children in the county, say all those who lived in the southern part of the county, would go to Robert E. Lee High School, and all those who lived in the northern half would go to Booker T. Washington High School. *Brown I* could have been implemented the day after the Court reached its decision. But it was also true that the black schools throughout the South were utterly wretched when compared to the white schools. There never had been any system of separate but equal education. In almost every measurable respect, the black schools were inferior. One possibility is that, without being explicitly aware of it, the members of the Supreme Court made use of some assumptions that were a significant feature of the dominant racist ideology. If the assumptions had been made explicit, the reasoning would have gone something like this: Those black schools are wretched. We cannot order white children to go to those schools, especially when they have gone to better schools in the past. So while it is unfair to deprive blacks, to make them go to these awful, segregated schools, they will have to wait until the black schools either are eliminated or are sufficiently improved so that there are good schools for everybody to attend.

What seems to me to be most objectionable, and racist, about *Brown II* is the uncritical acceptance of the idea that during this process of change, black schoolchildren would have to suffer by continuing to attend inadequate schools. The Supreme Court's solution assumed that the correct way to deal with this problem was to continue to have the black children go to their schools until the black schools were brought up to par or eliminated. That is a kind of conceptual racism in which the legal system accepts the dominant racist ideology, which holds that the claims of black children are worth less than the claims of white children in those cases in which conflict is inevitable. It seems to me that any minimally fair solution would have required that during the interim process, if anybody had to go to an inadequate school, it would have been the white children, since they were the ones who had previously had the benefit of the good schools. But this is simply not the way racial matters are thought about within the dominant ideology.

A study of *Brown II* is instructive because it is a good illustration of conceptual racism within the legal system. It also reflects another kind of conceptual racism—conceptual racism about the system. *Brown I* and *II* typically are thought of by our culture, and especially by our educational institutions, as representing one of the high points in the legal system's fight against racism. The dominant way of thinking about the desegregation cases is that the legal system was functioning at its very best. Yet, as I have indicated, there are important respects in which the legal system's response to the then existing system of racially segregated education was defective and hence should hardly be taken as a model of the just, institutional way of dealing with this problem of racial oppression. But the fact that we have, as well as inculcate, these attitudes of effusive praise toward *Brown I* and *II* and its progeny reveals a kind of persistent conceptual racism in talk about the character of the legal system, and what constitutes the right way to have dealt with the social reality of American racial oppression of black people.

In theory, the foregoing analytic scheme can be applied as readily to the social realities of sexual oppression as to racism. Given an understanding of the social realities in respect to sex—the ways in which the system of patriarchy inequitably distributes important benefits and burdens for the benefit of males, and the ideology which is a part of that patriarchal system and supportive of it—one can examine the different types of sexism that exist within the legal system. In practice the task is more difficult because we are inclined to take as appropriate even overt instances of sexist laws, *e.g.,* that it is appropriately a part of the definition of rape that a man cannot rape his wife. The task is also more difficult because sexism is, as I have suggested, a "deeper" phenomenon than racism.[17] As a result, there is less awareness of the significance of much of the social reality, *e.g.,* that the language we use to

talk about the world and ourselves has embedded within it ideological assumptions and preferences that support the existing patriarchal system. Cases of institutional sexism will therefore be systematically harder to detect. But these difficulties to one side, the mode of analysis seems to me to be in principle equally applicable to sexism, although, as I indicate in the next section on ideals, a complete account of the sexism of the legal system necessarily awaits a determination of what is the correct picture of the good society in respect to sexual differences.

II. Ideals

A second perspective is also important for an understanding and analysis of racism and sexism. It is the perspective of the ideal. Just as we can and must ask what is involved today in our culture in being of one race or of one sex rather than the other, and how individuals are in fact viewed and treated, we can also ask different questions: What would the good or just society make of race and sex, and to what degree, if at all, would racial and sexual distinctions ever be taken into account? Indeed, it could plausibly be argued that we could not have an adequate idea of whether a society was racist or sexist unless we had some conception of what a thoroughly nonracist or nonsexist society would look like. This perspective is an extremely instructive as well as an often neglected one. Comparatively little theoretical literature dealing with either racism or sexism has concerned itself in a systematic way with this perspective. Moreover, as I shall try to demonstrate, it is on occasion introduced in an inappropriate context, *e.g.,* in discussions of the relevance of the biological differences between males and females.

To understand more precisely what some of the possible ideals are in respect to racial or sexual differentiation, it is necessary to distinguish in a crude way among three levels or areas of social and political arrangements and activities. First, there is the area of basic political rights and obligations, including the right to vote and to travel and the obligation to pay taxes. Second, there is the area of important, nongovernmental institutional benefits

---

[17]For an example of a kind of analysis that is beginning to show some of the ways in which the law builds upon and supports the patriarchal system of marriage, see Johnston, *Sex and Property: The Common Law Tradition, The Law School Curriculum, and Developments Toward Equality,* 47 N.Y.U. L. Rev. 1033, 1071–89 (1972). Another very rich source is the recent casebook on sex discrimination by B. BABCOCK, A. FREEDMAN, E. NORTON & S. ROSS, SEX DISCRIMINATION AND THE LAW—CAUSES AND REMEDIES (1975).

and burdens. Examples are access to and employment in the significant economic markets, the opportunity to acquire and enjoy housing in the setting of one's choice, the right of persons who want to marry each other to do so, and the duties (nonlegal as well as legal) that persons acquire in getting married. Third, there is the area of individual, social interaction, including such matters as whom one will have as friends, and what aesthetic preferences one will cultivate and enjoy.

As to each of these three areas we can ask whether in a nonracist society it would be thought appropriate ever to take the race of the individuals into account. Thus, one picture of a nonracist society is that which is captured by what I call the assimilationist ideal: A nonracist society would be one in which the race of an individual would be the functional equivalent of the eye color of individuals in our society today.[18] In our society no basic political rights and obligations are determined on the basis of eye color. No important institutional benefits and burdens are connected with eye color. Indeed, except for the mildest sort of aesthetic preferences, a person would be thought odd who even made private, social decisions by taking eye color into account. And for reasons that we could fairly readily state, we could explain why it would be wrong to permit anything but the mildest, most trivial aesthetic preference to turn on eye color. The reasons would concern the irrelevance of eye color for any political or social institution, practice, or arrangement. It would, of course, be equally odd for a person to say that while he or she looked blue-eyed, he or she regarded himself or herself as really a brown-eyed person. That is, because eye color functions differently in our culture than does race or sex, there is no analogue in respect to eye color to passing or transsexuality. According to the assimilationist ideal, a nonracist society would be one in which an individual's race was of no more significance in any of these three areas than is eye color today.

The assimilationist ideal is not, however, the only possible, plausible ideal. There are two others that are closely related, but distinguishable. One is the ideal of diversity; the other, the ideal of tolerance. Both can be understood by considering how religion, rather than eye color, tends to be thought

about in our culture. According to the ideal of diversity, heterodoxy in respect to religious belief and practice is regarded as a positive good. In this view there would be a loss—it would be a worse society—were everyone to be a member of the same religion. According to the other view, the ideal of tolerance, heterodoxy in respect to religious belief and practice would be seen more as a necessary, lesser evil. In this view there is nothing intrinsically better about diversity in respect to religion, but the evils of achieving anything like homogeneity far outweigh the possible benefits.

Now, whatever differences there might be between the ideals of diversity and tolerance, the similarities are more striking. Under neither ideal would it be thought that the allocation of basic political rights and duties should take an individual's religion into account. We would want equalitarianism or nondiscrimination even in respect to most important institutional benefits and burdens—for example, access to employment in the desirable vocations. Nonetheless, on both views it would be deemed appropriate to have some institutions (typically those which are connected in an intimate way with these religions) which do in a variety of ways take the religion of members of the society into account. For example, it might be thought permissible and appropriate for members of a religious group to join together in collective associations which have religious, educational and social dimensions. And on the individual, interpersonal level, it might be thought unobjectionable, or on the diversity view, even admirable, were persons to select their associates, friends, and mates on the basis of their religious orientation. So there are two possible and plausible ideals of what the good society would look like in respect to religion in which religious differences would be to some degree maintained because the variety of religions was seen either as a valuable feature of the society, or as one to be tolerated. The picture is a more complex, less easily describable one than that of the assimilationist ideal.

The point of all this is its relevance to the case of sexism. One central and difficult question is what the ideal society would look like in respect to sex. The assimilationist ideal does not seem to be as readily plausible and obviously attractive here as it is in the case of race. Many persons invoke the possible realization of the assimilationist ideal as a reason for rejecting the equal rights amendment and indeed the idea of women's liberation itself. My view is that the assimilationist ideal may be just as good

---

[18]There is a danger in calling this ideal the "assimilationist" ideal. That term suggests the idea of incorporating oneself, one's values, and the like into the dominant group and its practices and values. I want to make it clear that no part of that idea is meant to be captured by my use of this term. Mine is a stipulative definition.

and just as important an ideal in respect to sex as it is in respect to race. But many persons think there are good reasons why an assimilationist society in respect to sex would not be desirable. One reason for their view might be that to make the assimilationist ideal a reality in respect to sex would involve more profound and fundamental revisions of our institutions and our attitudes than would be the case in respect to race. It is certainly true that on the institutional level we would have to alter radically our practices concerning the family and marriage. If a nonsexist society is a society in which one's sex is no more significant than eye color in our society today, then laws which require the persons who are being married to be of different sexes would clearly be sexist laws. Insofar as they are based upon the desirability of unifying the distinctive features of one male and one female, laws and institutions which conceive of the nuclear family as ideally composed of two and only two adults should also be thought of as anachronistic as well as sexist laws and institutions.

On the attitudinal and conceptual level, the assimilationist ideal would require the eradication of all sex-role differentiation. It would never teach about the inevitable or essential attributes of masculinity or femininity; it would never encourage or discourage the ideas of sisterhood or brotherhood; and it would be unintelligible to talk about the virtues as well as disabilities of being a woman or a man. Were sex like eye color, these things would make no sense. A nonsexist world might conceivably tolerate both homosexuality and heterosexuality (as peculiar kinds of personal erotic preference), but any kind of sexually *exclusive* preference would be either as anomalous or as statistically fortuitous as is a sexual preference connected with eye color in our society today. Just as the normal, typical adult is virtually oblivious to the eye color of other persons for all major interpersonal relationships, so the normal, typical adult in this kind of nonsexist society would be indifferent to the sexual, physiological differences of other persons for all interpersonal relationships. Bisexuality, not heterosexuality or homosexuality, would be the norm for intimate, sexual relationships in the ideal society that was assimilationist in respect to sex.

All of this seems to me to be worth talking about because unless and until we are clear about issues such as these we cannot be wholly certain about whether, from the perspective of the ideal, some of the institutions in our own culture are or are not sexist. We know that racially segregated bathrooms are racist. We know that laws that prohibit persons of different races from marrying are racist. But throughout our society we have sexually segregated bathrooms, and we have laws which prohibit individuals of the same sex from marrying. As I have argued above, from the perspective of the existing social reality there are important ways to distinguish the racial from the sexual cases and to criticize both practices. But that still leaves open the question of whether in the good society these sexual distinctions, or others, would be thought worth preserving either because they were meritorious, or at least to be tolerated because they were necessary.

As I have indicated, it may be that the problem is with the assimilationist ideal. It may be that in respect to sex (and conceivably, even in respect to race) something more like either of the ideals in respect to religion—pluralistic ideals founded on diversity or tolerance—is the right one. But the problem then—and it is a very substantial one—is to specify with a good deal of precision and care what the ideal really comes to. Which legal, institutional and personal differentiations are permissible and which are not? Which attitudes and beliefs concerning sexual identification and difference are properly introduced and maintained and which are not? Part, but by no means all, of the attractiveness of the assimilationist ideal is its clarity and simplicity. In the good society of the assimilationist sort we would be able to tell easily and unequivocally whether any law, practice or attitude was in any respect either racist or sexist. Part, but by no means all, of the unattractiveness of any pluralistic ideal is that it makes the question of what is racist or sexist a much more difficult and complicated one to answer. But although simplicity and lack of ambiguity may be virtues, they are not the only virtues to be taken into account in deciding among competing ideals. We quite appropriately take other considerations to be relevant to an assessment of the value and worth of alternative nonracist and nonsexist societies.

Nor do I even mean to suggest that all persons who reject the assimilationist ideal in respect to sex would necessarily embrace either something like the ideal of tolerance or the ideal of diversity. Some persons might think the right ideal was one in which substantially greater sexual differentiation and sex-role identification was retained than would be the case under either of these conceptions. Thus, someone might believe that the good society was, perhaps, essentially like the one they think we now have in respect to sex: equality of political rights, such as the right to vote, but all of the sexual differentiation in both legal and nonlegal institutions that is characteristic of the way in which our society has been and still is ordered. And someone might also believe that the usual ideological justifications for these arrangements are the correct and appropriate ones.[19] This could, of course, be regarded as a version of the ideal of diversity, with the emphasis upon the extensive character of the institutional and personal difference connected with sexual identity. Whether it is a kind of ideal of diversity or a different ideal altogether turns, I think, upon two things: first, how pervasive the sexual differentiation is; second, whether the ideal contains a conception of the appropriateness of significant institutional and interpersonal inequality, *e.g.,* that the woman's job is in large measure to serve and be dominated by the male. The more this latter feature is present, the clearer the case for regarding this as a distinctively different ideal.

The question of whether something is a plausible and attractive ideal turns in part on the nature of the empirical world. If it is true, for example, that race is not only a socially significant category in our culture but also largely a socially created one, then many ostensible objections to the assimilationist ideal appear to disappear immediately. What I mean is this: It is obvious that we could formulate and use some sort of a crude, incredibly imprecise physiological concept of race. In this sense we could even say that race is a naturally occurring rather than a socially created feature of the world. There are diverse skin colors and related physiological characteristics distributed among human beings. But the fact is that

except for skin hue and the related physiological characteristics, race is a socially created category. And skin hue, as I have shown, is neither a necessary nor a sufficient condition for being classified as black in our culture. Race as a naturally occurring characteristic is also a socially irrelevant category. There do not in fact appear to be any characteristics that are part of this natural concept of race and that are in any plausible way even relevant to the appropriate distribution of any political, institutional, or interpersonal concerns in the good society. Because in this sense race is like eye color, there is no plausible case to be made on this ground against the assimilationist ideal.[20]

There is, of course, the social reality of race. In creating and tolerating a society in which race matters, we must recognize that we have created a vastly more complex concept of race which includes what might be called the idea of ethnicity as well—a set of attitudes, traditions, beliefs, etc., which the society has made part of what it means to be of a race. It may be, therefore, that one could argue that a form of the pluralist ideal ought to be preserved in respect to race, in the socially created sense, for reasons similar to those that might be offered in support of the desirability of some version of the pluralist ideal in respect to religion. As I have indicated, I am skeptical, but for the purposes of this essay it can well be left an open question.

Despite appearances, the case of sex is more like that of race than is often thought. What opponents of assimilationism seize upon is that sexual difference appears to be a naturally occurring category of obvious and inevitable social relevance in a way, or to a degree, which race is not. The

---

[19]Thus, for example, a column appeared a few years ago in the *Washington Star* concerning the decision of the Cosmos Club to continue to refuse to permit women to be members. The author of the column (and a member of the club) defended the decision on the ground that women appropriately had a different status in the society. Their true distinction was to be achieved by being faithful spouses and devoted mothers. The column closed with this paragraph:

In these days of broken homes, derision of marriage, reluctance to bear children, contempt for the institution of the family—a phase in our national life when it seems more honorable to be a policewoman, or a model, or an accountant than to be a wife or mother—there is a need to reassert a traditional scale of values in which the vocation of homemaker is as honorable and distinguished as any in political or professional life. Such women, as wives and widows of members, now enjoy in the club the privileges of their status, which includes [sic] *their own drawing rooms, and it is of interest that they have been among the most outspoken opponents of the proposed changes in club structure.*

Groseclose, *Now—Shall We Join the Ladies?*, Washington Star, Mar. 13, 1975.

The same view may be held by Senator Daniel Moynihan. It is his view, apparently, that the United States government ought to

work primarily to strengthen the institution of the family. Moynihan is quoted as saying:

If the family is strong, the economy will be productive. If the family is strong, law will be respected and crime will decrease. If the family is strong, the welfare rolls will shrink. . . . All this is true, and its truth has been confirmed and reconfirmed by the evidence of history, of social science, of direct observation, and of simple common sense.

Buckley, *The Main Event East*, N.Y. Times, Oct. 31, 1976, § 6 (Magazine), at 16, 57.

For the reasons that I give below, I think any version of this ideal is seriously flawed. But it is one that is certainly much more widely held in respect to sex than is a comparable one held today in respect to race.

[20]This is not to deny that certain people believe that race is linked with characteristics that prima facie are relevant. Such beliefs persist. They are, however, unjustified by the evidence. *See,* *e.g.,* Block & Dworkin, *IQ, Heritability and Inequality* (pts. 1–2), 3 PHIL. & PUB. AFF. 331, 4 *id.* 40 (1974). More to the point, even if it were true that such a linkage existed, none of the characteristics suggested would require that political or social institutions, or interpersonal relationships, would have to be structured in a certain way.

problems with this way of thinking are twofold. To begin with, an analysis of the social realities reveals that it is the socially created sexual differences which tend in fact to matter the most. It is sex-role differentiation, not gender per se,[21] that makes men and women as different as they are from each other, and it is sex-role differences which are invoked to justify most sexual differentiation at any of the levels of society.[22]

More importantly, even if naturally occurring sexual differences were of such a nature that they were of obvious prima facie social relevance, this would by no means settle the question of whether in the good society sex should or should not be as minimally significant as eye color. Even though there are biological differences between men and women in nature, this fact does not determine the question of what the good society can and should make of these differences. I have difficulty understanding why so many persons seem to think that it does settle the question adversely to anything like the assimilationist ideal. They might think it does settle the question for two different reasons. In the first place, they might think the differences are of such a character that they substantially affect what would be possible within a good society of human persons. Just as the fact that humans are mortal

necessarily limits the features of any possible good society, so, they might argue, the fact that males and females are physiologically different limits the features of any possible good society.

In the second place, they might think the differences are of such a character that they are relevant to the question of what would be desirable in the good society. That is to say, they might not think that the differences *determine* to a substantial degree what is possible, but that the differences ought to be taken into account in any rational construction of an ideal social existence.

The second reason seems to me to be a good deal more plausible than the first. For there appear to be very few, if any, respects in which the ineradicable, naturally occurring differences between males and females *must* be taken into account. The industrial revolution has certainly made any of the general differences in strength between the sexes capable of being ignored by the good society in virtually all activities.[23] And it is sex-role acculturation, not biology, that mistakenly leads many persons to the view that women are both naturally and necessarily better suited than men to be assigned the primary responsibilities of child rearing. Indeed, the only fact that seems required to be taken into account is the fact that reproduction of the human species re-

---

[21] The term "gender" may be used in a number of different senses. I use it to refer to those anatomical, physiological, and other differences (if any) that are naturally occurring in the sense described above. Some persons refer to these differences as "sex differences," but that seems to me confusing. In any event, I am giving a stipulative definition to "gender."

[22] M. MEAD, SEX AND TEMPERAMENT IN THREE PRIMITIVE SOCIETIES (1935):

These three situations [the cultures of the Anapesh, the Mundugumor, and the Tchambuli] suggest, then, a very definite conclusion. If those temperamental attitudes which we have traditionally regarded as feminine—such as passivity, responsiveness, and a willingness to cherish children —can so easily be set up as the masculine pattern in one tribe, and in another to be outlawed for the majority of women as well as for the majority of men, we no longer have any basis for regarding such aspects of behaviour as sex-linked.... We are forced to conclude that human nature is almost unbelievably malleable, responding accurately and contrastingly to contrasting cultural conditions.... Standardized personality differences between the sexes are of this order, cultural creations to which each generation, male and female is trained to conform.

Id. at 190–91. [See pp. 59–67, this volume, eds.]

A somewhat different view is expressed in J. SHERMAN, ON THE PSYCHOLOGY OF WOMEN (1971). There, the author suggests that there are "natural" differences of a psychological sort between men and women, the chief ones being aggressiveness and strength of sex drive. See id. at 238. However, even if she is correct as to these biologically based differences, this does little to establish what the good society should look like.

Almost certainly the most complete discussion of this topic is E. MACOBY & C. JACKLIN, THE PSYCHOLOGY OF SEX DIFFERENCES (1974). The authors conclude that the sex differences which are, in their words, "fairly well established," are: (1) that girls have greater verbal ability than boys; (2) that boys excel in visual-spacial ability; (3) that boys excel in mathematical ability;

and (4) that males are aggressive. Id. at 351–52. They conclude, in respect to the etiology of these psychological sex differences, that there appears to be a biological component to the greater visual-spacial ability of males and to their greater aggressiveness. Id. at 360.

[23] As Sherman observes,

Each sex has its own special physical assets and liabilities. The principal female liability of less muscular strength is not ordinarily a handicap in a civilized, mechanized, society.... There is nothing in the biological evidence to prevent women from taking a role of equality in a civilized society.

J. SHERMAN, supra note [22] at 11.

There are, of course, some activities that would be sexually differentiated in the assimilationist society; namely, those that were specifically directed toward, say, measuring unaided physical strength. Thus, I think it likely that even in this ideal society, weight lifting contests and boxing matches would in fact be dominated, perhaps exclusively so, by men. But it is hard to find any significant activities or institutions that are analogous. And it is not clear that such insignificant activities would be thought worth continuing, especially since sports function in existing patriarchal societies to help maintain the dominance of males.

See K. MILLETT, supra note [2] at 48–49.

It is possible that there are some nontrivial activities or occupations that depend sufficiently directly upon unaided physical strength that most if not all women would be excluded. Perhaps being a lifeguard at the ocean is an example. Even here, though, it would be important to see whether the way lifeguarding had traditionally been done could be changed to render such physical strength unimportant. If it could be changed, then the question would simply be one of whether the increased cost (or loss of efficiency) was worth the gain in terms of equality and the avoidance of sex-role differentiation. In a nonpatriarchal society very different from ours, where sex was not a dominant social category, the argument from efficiency might well prevail. What is important, once again, is to see how infrequent and peripheral such occupational cases are.

quires that the fetus develop *in utero* for a period of months. Sexual intercourse is not necessary, for artificial insemination is available. Neither marriage nor the family is required for conception or child rearing. Given the present state of medical knowledge and the natural realities of female pregnancy, it is difficult to see why any important institutional or interpersonal arrangements *must* take the existing gender difference of *in utero* pregnancy into account.

But, as I have said, this is still to leave it a wholly open question to what degree the good society *ought* to build upon any ineradicable gender differences to construct institutions which would maintain a substantial degree of sexual differentiation. The arguments are typically far less persuasive for doing so than appears upon the initial statement of this possibility. Someone might argue that the fact of menstruation, for instance, could be used as a premise upon which to predicate different social roles for females than for males. But this could only plausibly be proposed if two things were true: first, that menstruation would be debilitating to women and hence relevant to social role even in a culture which did not teach women to view menstruation as a sign of uncleanliness or as a curse;[24] and second, that the way in which menstruation necessarily affected some or all women was in fact related in an important way to the role in question. But even if both of these were true, it would still be an open question whether any sexual differentiation ought to

be built upon these facts. The society could still elect to develop institutions that would nullify the effect of the natural differences. And suppose, for example, what seems implausible—that some or all women will not be able to perform a particular task while menstruating, *e.g.*, guard a border. It would be easy enough, if the society wanted to, to arrange for substitute guards for the women who were incapacitated. We know that persons are not good guards when they are sleepy, and we make arrangements so that persons alternate guard duty to avoid fatigue. The same could be done for menstruating women, even given these implausibly strong assumptions about menstruation. At the risk of belaboring the obvious, what I think it important to see is that the case against the assimilationist ideal—if it is to be a good one—must rest on arguments concerned to show why some other ideal would be preferable; it cannot plausibly rest on the claim that it is either necessary or inevitable.

There is, however, at least one more argument based upon nature, or at least the "natural," that is worth mentioning. Someone might argue that significant sex-role differentiation is natural not in the sense that it is biologically determined but only in the sense that it is a virtually universal phenomenon in human culture. By itself, this claim of virtual universality, even if accurate, does not directly establish anything about the desirability or undesirability of any particular ideal. But it can be made into an argument by the addition of the proposition that where there is a virtually universal social practice, there is probably some good or important purpose served by the practice. Hence, given the fact of sex-role differentiation in all, or almost all, cultures, we have some reason to think that substantial sex-role differentiation serves some important purpose for and in human society.

This is an argument, but I see no reason to be impressed by it. The premise which turns the fact of sex-role differentiation into any kind of a strong reason for sex-role differentiation is the premise of conservatism. And it is no more convincing here than elsewhere. There are any number of practices that are typical and yet upon reflection seem without significant social purpose. Slavery was once such a practice; war perhaps still is.

More to the point, perhaps, the concept of "purpose" is ambiguous. It can mean in a descriptive sense "plays some role" or "is causally relevant." Or it can mean in a prescriptive sense "does something desirable" or "has some useful function."

---

[24]*See, e.g.,* Paige, *Women Learn to Sing the Menstrual Blues,* in THE FEMALE EXPERIENCE 17 (C. Tavis ed. 1973).
    I have come to believe that the "raging hormones" theory of menstrual distress simply isn't adequate. All women have the raging hormones, but not all women have menstrual symptoms, nor do they have the same symptoms for the same reasons. Nor do I agree with the "raging neurosis" theory, which argues that women who have menstrual symptoms are merely whining neurotics, who need only a kind pat on the head to cure their problems.
    We must instead consider the problem from the perspective of women's subordinate social position, and of the cultural ideology that so narrowly defines the behaviors and emotions that are appropriately "feminine." Women have perfectly good reasons to react emotionally to reproductive events. Menstruation, pregnancy and childbirth—so sacred, yet so unclean—are the woman's primary avenues of achievement and self-expression. Her reproductive abilities define her femininity; other routes to success are only second-best in this society. . . . My current research on a sample of 114 societies around the world indicates that ritual observances and taboos about menstruation are a method of controlling women and their fertility. Men apparently use such rituals, along with those surrounding pregnancy and childbirth, to assert their claims to women and their children. . . . The hormone theory isn't giving us much mileage, and it's time to turn it in for a better model, one that looks to our beliefs about menstruation and women. It is no mere coincidence that women get the blue meanies along with an event they consider embarrassing, unclean—and a curse.
Id. at 21.

If "purpose" is used prescriptively in the conservative premise, then there is no reason to think that premise is true.

To put it another way, the question is whether it is desirable to have a society in which sex-role differences are to be retained at all. The straightforward way to think about that question is to ask what would be good and what would be bad about a society in which sex functioned like eye color does in our society. We can imagine what such a society would look like and how it would work. It is hard to see how our thinking is substantially advanced by reference to what has typically or always been the case. If it is true, as I think it is, that the sex-role differentiated societies we have had so far have tended to concentrate power in the hands of males, have developed institutions and ideologies that have perpetuated that concentration and have restricted and prevented women from living the kinds of lives that persons ought to be able to live for themselves, then this says far more about what may be wrong with any nonassimilationist ideal than does the conservative premise say what may be right about any nonassimilationist ideal.

Nor is this all that can be said in favor of the assimilationist ideal. For it seems to me that the strongest affirmative moral argument on its behalf is that it provides for a kind of individual autonomy that a nonassimilationist society cannot attain. Any nonassimilationist society will have sex roles. Any nonassimilationist society will have some institutions that distinguish between individuals by virtue of their gender, and any such society will necessarily teach the desirability of doing so. Any substantially nonassimilationist society will make one's sexual identity an important characteristic, so that there are substantial psychological, role, and status differences between persons who are males and those who are females. Even if these could be attained without systemic dominance of one sex over the other, they would, I think, be objectionable on the ground that they necessarily impaired an individual's ability to develop his or her own characteristics, talents and capacities to the fullest extent to which he or she might desire. Sex roles, and all that accompany them, necessarily impose limits —restrictions on what one can do, be or become. As such, they are, I think, at least prima facie wrong.

To some degree, all role-differentiated living is restrictive in this sense. Perhaps, therefore, all role-differentiation in society is to some degree troublesome, and perhaps all strongly role-differentiated societies are objectionable. But the case against sexual differentiation need not rest upon this more controversial point. For one thing that distinguishes sex roles from many other roles is that they are wholly involuntarily assumed. One has no choice whatsoever about whether one shall be born a male or female. And if it is a consequence of one's being born a male or a female that one's subsequent emotional, intellectual, and material development will be substantially controlled by this fact, then substantial, permanent, and involuntarily assumed restraints have been imposed on the most central factors concerning the way one will shape and live one's life. The point to be emphasized is that this would necessarily be the case, even in the unlikely event that substantial sexual differentiation could be maintained without one sex or the other becoming dominant and developing institutions and an ideology to support that dominance.

I do not believe that all I have said in this section shows in any conclusive fashion the desirability of the assimilationist ideal in respect to sex. I have tried to show why some typical arguments against the assimilationist ideal are not persuasive; and why some of the central ones in support of that ideal are persuasive. But I have not provided a complete account, or a complete analysis. At a minimum, what I have shown is how thinking about this topic ought to proceed, and what kinds of arguments need to be marshalled and considered before a serious and informed discussion of alternative conceptions of a nonsexist society can even take place. Once assembled, these arguments need to be individually and carefully assessed before any final, reflective choice among the competing ideals can be made. There does, however, seem to me to be a strong presumptive case for something very close to, if not identical with, the assimilationist ideal.

[25][The conclusion of this article, entitled "Preferential Treatment" is included in chapter 7 of this volume, pp. 247–250—eds.]

3/"Pricks" and "Chicks": A Plea for "Persons"

Robert Baker

There is a school of philosophers who believe that one starts philosophizing not by examining whatever it is one is philosophizing about but by examining the words we use to designate the subject to be examined. I must confess my allegiance to this school. The import of my confession is that this is an essay on women's liberation.

There seems to be a curious malady that affects those philosophers who in order to analyze anything must examine the way we talk about it; they seem incapable of talking about anything without talking about their talk about it—and, once again, I must confess to being typical. Thus I shall argue, first, that the way in which we identify something reflects our conception of it; second, that the conception of women embedded in our language is male chauvinistic; third, that the conceptual revisions proposed by the feminist movement are confused; and finally, that at the root of the problem are both our conception of sex and the very structure of sexual identification.

Identification and Conception

I am not going to defend the position that the terms we utilize to identify something reflect our conception of it; I shall simply explain and illustrate a simplified version of this thesis. Let us assume that any term that can be (meaningfully) substituted for x in the following statements is a term used to identify something: "Where is the x?" "Who is the x?" Some of the terms that can be substituted for x in the above expressions are metaphors; I shall refer to such metaphors as metaphorical identifications. For example, southerners frequently say such things as "Where did that girl get to?" and "Who is the new boy that Lou hired to help out at the filling station?" If the persons the terms apply to are adult Afro-Americans, then "girl" and "boy" are metaphorical

identifications. The fact that the metaphorical identifications in question are standard in the language reflects the fact that certain characteristics of the objects properly classified as boys and girls (for example, immaturity, inability to take care of themselves, need for guidance) are generally held by those who use identifications to be properly attributable to Afro-Americans. One might say that the whole theory of southern white paternalism is implicit in the metaphorical identification "boy" (just as the rejection of paternalism is implicit in the standardized Afro-American forms of address, "man" and "woman," as in, for example, "Hey, man, how are you?").

Most of what I am going to say in this essay is significant only if the way we metaphorically identify something is not a superficial bit of conceptually irrelevant happenstance but rather a reflection of our conceptual structure. Thus if one is to accept my analysis he must understand the significance of metaphorical identifications. He must see that, even though the southerner who identifies adult Afro-American males as "boys" feels that this identification is "just the way people talk"; but for a group to talk that way it must think that way. In the next few paragraphs I shall adduce what I hope is a persuasive example of how, in one clear case, the change in the way we identified something reflected a change in the way we thought about it.

Until the 1960s, Afro-Americans were identified by such terms as "Negro" and "colored" (the respectable terms) and by the more disreputable "nigger," "spook," "kink," and so on. Recently there has been an unsuccessful attempt to replace the respectable identifications with such terms as "African," and "Afro-American," and a more successful attempt to replace them with "black." The most outspoken champions of this linguistic reform were those who argued that nonviolence must be abandoned for Black Power (Stokely Carmichael, H. Rap

Brown), that integration must be abandoned in favor of separation (the Black Muslims: Malcolm X, Muhammad Ali), and that Afro-Americans were an internal colony in the alien world of Babylon who must arm themselves against the possibility of extermination (the Black Panthers: Eldridge Cleaver, Huey Newton). All of these movements and their partisans wished to stress that Afro-Americans were different from other Americans and could not be merged with them because the differences between the two was as great as that between black and white. Linguistically, of course, "black" and "white" are antonyms; and it is precisely this sense of oppositeness that those who see the Afro-American as alienated, separated, and nonintegratable wish to capture with the term "black." Moreover, as any good dictionary makes clear, in some contexts "black" is synonymous with "deadly," "sinister," "wicked," "evil," and so forth. The new militants were trying to create just this picture of the black man—civil rights and Uncle Tomism are dead, the ghost of Nat Turner is to be resurrected, Freedom Now or pay the price, the ballot or the bullet, "Violence is as American as cherry pie." The new strategy was that the white man would either give the black man his due or pay the price in violence. Since conceptually a "black man" was an object to be feared ("black" can be synonymous with "deadly," and so on), while a "colored man" or a "Negro" was not, the new strategy required that the "Negro" be supplanted by the "black man." White America resisted the proposed linguistic reform quite vehemently, until hundreds of riots forced the admission that the Afro-American was indeed black.

Now to the point: I have suggested that the word "black" replaced the word "Negro" because there was a change in our conceptual structure. One is likely to reply that while all that I have said above is well and good, one had, after all, no choice about the matter. White people are identified in terms of their skin color as whites; clearly, if we are to recognize what is in reality nothing but the truth, that in this society people are conscious of skin color, to treat blacks as equals is merely to identify them by their skin color, which is black. That is, one might argue that while there was a change in words, we have no reason to think that there was a parallel conceptual change. If the term "black" has all the associations mentioned above, that is unfortunate; but in the context the use of the term "black" to identify the people formerly identified as "Negroes" is natural,

inevitable, and, in and of itself, neutral; black is, after all, the skin color of the people in question. (Notice that this defense of the natural-inevitable-and-neutral conception of identification quite nicely circumvents the possible use of such seemingly innocuous terms as "Afro-American" and "African" by suggesting that in this society it is skin color that is the relevant variable.)

The great flaw in this analysis is that the actual skin color of virtually all of the people whom we call "black" is not black at all. The color tones range from light yellow to a deep umber that occasionally is literally black. The skin color of most Afro-Americans is best designated by the word "brown." Yet "brown" is not a term that is standard for identifying Afro-Americans. For example, if someone asked, "Who was the brown who was the architect for Washington, D.C.?" we would not know how to construe the question. We might attempt to read "brown" as a proper name ("Do you mean Arthur Brown, the designer?"). We would have no trouble understanding the sentence "Who was the black (Negro, colored guy, and so forth) who designed Washington, D.C.?" ("Oh, you mean Benjamin Banneker"). Clearly, "brown" is not a standard form of identification for Afro-Americans. I hope that it is equally clear that "black" has become the standard way of identifying Afro-Americans not because the term was natural, inevitable, and, in the context, neutral, but because of its occasional synonymy with "sinister" and because as an antonym to "white" it best fitted the conceptual needs of those who saw race relations in terms of intensifying and insurmountable antonymies. If one accepts this point, then one must admit that there is a close connection between the way in which we identify things and the way in which we conceive them—and thus it should be also clear why I wish to talk about the way in which women are identified in English.[1] (Thus, for example, one would expect Black Muslims, who continually use the term "black *man*"— as in "the black *man's* rights"—to be more male

---

[1] The underlying techniques used in this essay were all developed (primarily by Austin and Strawson) to deal with the problems of metaphysics and epistemology. All I have done is to attempt to apply them to other areas; I should note, however, that I rely rather heavily on metaphorical identifications, and that first philosophy tends not to require the analysis of such superficial aspects of language. Note also that it is an empirical matter whether or not people do use words in a certain way. In this essay I am just going to assume that the reader uses words more or less as my students do; for I gathered the data on which words we use to identify women, and so on, simply by asking students. If the reader does not use terms as my students do, then what I say may be totally inapplicable to him.

chauvinistic than Afro-Americans who use the term "black *people*" or "black *folk*.")

Ways of Identifying Women

It may at first seem trivial to note that women (and men) are identified sexually; but conceptually this is extremely significant. To appreciate the significance of this fact it is helpful to imagine a language in which proper names and personal pronouns do not reflect the sex of the person designated by them (as they do in our language). I have been told that in some oriental languages pronouns and proper names reflect social status rather than sex, but whether or not there actually exists such a language is irrelevant, for it is easy enough to imagine what one would be like. Let us then imagine a language where the proper names are sexually neutral (for example, "Xanthe"), so that one cannot tell from hearing a name whether the person so named is male or female, and where the personal pronouns in the language are "under" and "over." "Under" is the personal pronoun appropriate for all those who are younger than thirty, while "over" is appropriate to persons older than thirty. In such a language, instead of saying such things as "Where do you think *he* is living now?" one would say such things as "Where do you think *under* is living now?"

What would one say about a cultural community that employed such a language? Clearly, one would say that they thought that for purposes of intelligible communication it was more important to know a person's age grouping than the person's height, sex, race, hair color, or parentage. (There are many actual cultures, of course, in which people are identified by names that reflect their parentage; for example, Abu ben Adam means Abu son of Adam.) I think that one would also claim that this people would not have reflected these differences in the pronominal structure of their language if they did not believe that the differences between unders and overs was such that a statement would frequently have one meaning if it were about an under and a different meaning if it were about an over. For example, in feudal times if a serf said, "My lord said to do this," that assertion was radically different from "Freeman John said to do this," since (presumably) the former had the status of a command while the latter did not. Hence the conventions of Middle English required that one refer to people in such a way as to indicate their social status.

Analogously, one would not distinguish between pronominal references according to the age differences in the persons referred to were there no shift in meaning involved.

If we apply the lesson illustrated by this imaginary language to our own, I think that it should be clear that since in our language proper nouns and pronouns reflect sex rather than age, race, parentage, social status, or religion, we believe one of the most important things one can know about a person is that person's sex. (And, indeed, this is the first thing one seeks to determine about a newborn babe—our first question is almost invariably "Is it a boy or a girl?") Moreover, we would not reflect this important difference pronominally did we not also believe that statements frequently mean one thing when applied to males and something else when applied to females. Perhaps the most striking aspect of the conceptual discrimination reflected in our language is that man is, as it were, essentially human, while woman is only accidentally so.

This charge may seem rather extreme, but consider the following synonyms (which are readily confirmed by any dictionary). "Humanity" is synonymous with "mankind" but not with "womankind." "Man" can be substituted for "humanity" or "mankind" in any sentence in which the terms "mankind" or "humanity" occur without changing the meaning of the sentence, but significantly, "woman" cannot. Thus, the following expressions are all synonymous with each other: "humanity's great achievements," "mankind's great achievements," and "man's great achievements." "Woman's great achievements" is not synonymous with any of these. To highlight the degree to which women are excluded from humanity, let me point out that it is something of a truism to say that "man is a rational animal," while "woman is a rational animal" is quite debatable. Clearly, if "man" in the first assertion embraced both men and women, the second assertion would be just as much a truism as the first.[2] Humanity, it would seem, is a male prerogative. (And hence, one of the goals of women's liberation is to alter our conceptual structure so that someday "mankind" will be re-

---

[2]It is also interesting to talk about the technical terms that philosophers use. One fairly standard bit of technical terminology is "trouser word." J. L. Austin invented this bit of jargon to indicate which term in a pair of antonyms is important. Austin called the important term a "trouser word" because "it is the use which wears the trousers." Even in the language of philosophy, to be important is to play the male role. Of course, the antifeminism implicit in the language of technical philosophy is hardly comparable to the male chauvinism embedded in commonplaces of ordinary discourse.

garded as an improper and vestigial ellipsis for "humankind," and "man" will have no special privileges in relation to "human being" that "woman" does not have.[3])

The major question before us is, How are women conceived of in our culture? I have been trying to answer this question by talking about how they are identified. I first considered pronominal identification; now I wish to turn to identification through other types of noun phrases. Methods of nonpronominal identification can be discovered by determining which terms can be substituted for "woman" in such sentences as "Who is that woman over there?" without changing the meaning of the sentence. Virtually no term is interchangeable with "woman" in that sentence for all speakers on all occasions. Even "lady," which most speakers would accept as synonymous with "woman" in that sentence, will not do for a speaker who applies the term "lady" only to those women who display manners, poise, and sensitivity. In most contexts, a large number of students in one or more of my classes will accept the following types of terms as more or less interchangeable with "woman." (An asterisk indicates interchanges acceptable to both males and females; a plus sign indicates terms restricted to black students only. Terms with neither an asterisk nor a plus sign are accepted by all males but are not normally used by females.)

A. NEUTRAL TERMS: *lady, *gal, *girl (especially with regard to a coworker in an office or factory), *+sister, *broad (originally in the animal category, but most people do not think of the term as now meaning pregnant cow)

B. ANIMAL: *chick, bird, fox, vixen, filly, bitch (Many

[3]Although I thought it inappropriate to dwell on these matters in the text, it is quite clear that we do not associate many positions with females—as the following story brings out. I related this conundrum both to students in my regular courses and to students I teach in some experimental courses at a nearby community college. Among those students who had not previously heard the story, only native Swedes invariably resolved the problem; less than half of the students from an upper-class background would get it (eventually), while lower-class and black students virtually never figured it out. Radical students, women, even members of women's liberation groups fared no better than anyone else with their same class background. The story goes as follows: A little boy is wheeled into the emergency room of a hospital. The surgeon on emergency call looks at the boy and says, "I'm sorry I cannot operate on this child; he is my son." The surgeon was not the boy's father. In what relation did the surgeon stand to the child? Most students did not give any answer. The most frequent answer given was that the surgeon had fathered the boy illegitimately. (Others suggested that the surgeon had divorced the boy's mother and remarried and hence was not legally the boy's father.) Even though the story was related as a part of a lecture on women's liberation, at best only 20 percent of the written answers gave the correct and obvious answer—the surgeon was the boy's mother.

do not know the literal meaning of the term. Some men and most women construe this use as pejorative; they think of "bitch" in the context of "bitchy," that is, snappy, nasty, and so forth. But a large group of men claim that it is a standard nonpejorative term of identification—which may perhaps indicate that women have come to be thought of as shrews by a large subclass of men.)

C. PLAYTHING: babe, doll, cuddly

D. GENDER (association with articles of clothing typically worn by those in the female gender role): skirt, hem

E. SEXUAL: snatch, cunt, ass, twat, piece (of ass, and so forth), lay, pussy (could be put in the animal category, but most users associated it with slang expression indicating the female pubic region), +hammer (related to anatomical analogy between a hammer and breasts). There are many other usages, for example, "bunny," "sweat hog," but these were not recognized as standard by as many as 10 percent of any given class.

The students in my classes reported that the most frequently used terms of identification are in the neutral and animal classifications (although men in their forties claim to use the gender classifications quite a bit) and that the least frequently used terms of identification are sexual. Fortunately, however, I am not interested in the frequency of usage but only in whether the use is standard enough to be recognized as an identification among some group or other. (Recall that "brown" was not a standardized term of identification and hence we could not make sense out of "Who was the brown who planned Washington, D.C.?" Similarly, one has trouble with "Who was the breasts who planned Washington, D.C.?" but not with "Who was the babe (doll, chick, skirt, and so forth) who planned Washington, D.C.?")

Except for two of the animal terms, "chick" and "broad"—but note that "broad" is probably neutral today—women do not typically identify themselves in sexual terms, in gender terms, as playthings, or as animals; only males use nonneutral terms to identify women. Hence, it would seem that there is a male conception of women and a female conception. Only males identify women as "foxes," "babes," "skirts," or "cunts" (and since all the other nonneutral identifications are male, it is reasonable to assume that the identification of a woman as a "chick" is primarily a male conception that some women have adopted).

What kind of conception do men have of women? Clearly they think that women share certain properties with certain types of animals, toys, and playthings; they conceive of them in terms of the clothes associated with the female gender role; and, last (and, if my classes are any indication, least frequently), they conceive of women in terms of those parts of their anatomy associated with sexual intercourse, that is, as the identification "lay" indicates quite clearly, as sexual partners.

The first two nonneutral male classifications, animal and plaything, are prima facie denigrating (and I mean this in the literal sense of making one like a "nigger"). Consider the animal classification. All of the terms listed, with the possible exception of "bird," refer to animals that are either domesticated for servitude (to *man*) or hunted for sport. First, let us consider the term "bird." When I asked my students what sort of birds might be indicated, they suggested chick, canary (one member, in his forties, had suggested "canary" as a term of identification), chicken, pigeon, dove, parakeet, and hummingbird (one member). With the exception of the hummingbird, which like all the birds suggested is generally thought to be diminutive and pretty, all of the birds are domesticated, usually as pets (which reminds one that "my pet" is an expression of endearment). None of the birds were predators or symbols of intelligence or nobility (as are the owl, eagle, hawk, and falcon); nor did large but beautiful birds seem appropriate (for example, pheasants, peacocks, and swans). If one construes the bird terms (and for that matter, "filly") as applicable to women because they are thought of as beautiful, or at least pretty, *then there is nothing denigrating about them*. If, on the other hand, the common properties that underlie the metaphorical identification are domesticity and servitude, then they are indeed denigrating (as for myself, I think that both domesticity and prettiness underlie the identification). "Broad," of course, is, or at least was, clearly denigrating, since nothing renders more service to a farmer than does a pregnant cow, and cows are not commonly thought of as paradigms of beauty.

With one exception all of the animal terms reflect a male conception of women either as domesticated servants or as pets, or as both. Indeed, some of the terms reflect a conception of women first as pets and then as servants. Thus,

when a pretty, cuddly little chick grows older, she becomes a very useful servant—the egg-laying hen.

"Vixen" and "fox," variants of the same term, are the one clear exception. None of the other animals with whom women are metaphorically identified are generally thought to be intelligent, aggressive, or independent—but the fox is. A chick is a soft, cuddly, entertaining, pretty, diminutive, domesticated, and dumb animal. A fox too is soft, cuddly, entertaining, pretty, and diminutive, but it is neither dependent nor dumb. It is aggressive, intelligent, and a minor predator—indeed, it preys on chicks —and frequently outsmarts ("outfoxes") men.

Thus the term "fox" or "vixen" is generally taken to be a compliment by both men and women, and compared to any of the animal or plaything terms it is indeed a compliment. Yet, considered in and of itself, the conception of a woman as a fox is not really complimentary at all, for the major connection between *man* and fox is that of predator and prey. The fox is an animal that men chase, and hunt, and kill for sport. If women are conceived of as foxes, then they are conceived of as prey that it is fun to hunt.

In considering plaything identifications, only one sentence is necessary. *All the plaything identifications are clearly denigrating since they assimilate women to the status of mindless or dependent objects.* "Doll" is to male paternalism what "boy" is to white paternalism.

Up to this point in our survey of male conceptions of women, every male identification, without exception, has been clearly antithetical to the conception of women as human beings (recall that "man" was synonymous with "human," while "woman" was not). Since the way we talk of things, and especially the way we identify them, is the way in which we conceive of them, any movement dedicated to breaking the bonds of female servitude must destroy these ways of identifying and hence of conceiving of women. Only when both sexes find the terms "babe," "doll," "chick," "broad," and so forth, as objectionable as "boy" and "nigger" will women come to be conceived of as independent *human beings*.

The two remaining unexamined male identifications are gender and sex. There seems to be nothing objectionable about gender identifications per se. That is, women are metaphorically identified as skirts because in this culture, skirts, like women, are peculiarly female. Indeed, if one accepts the view that the slogan "female and proud" should play the same role for the women's liberation movement that the slogan "Black is beautiful" plays for the black-liberation movement, then female clothes should be worn with the same pride as Afro clothes. (Of course, one can argue that the skirt, like the cropped-down Afro, is a sign of bondage, and hence both the item of clothing and the identification with it are to be rejected—that is, cropped-down Afros are to Uncle Tom what skirts are to Uncle Mom.)

The terms in the last category are obviously sexual, and frequently vulgar. . . . [The concluding part of this article, titled "Sex and Language," is included in chapter 3 of this volume, pp. 100–103—ed.]

4/Male Chauvinism: A Conceptual Analysis

Marilyn Frye

Some years ago the new feminist rhetoric brought into common use the term "male chauvinist." The term found ready acceptance among feminists, and it seems to wear its meaning on its sleeve. But many males to whom it has been applied have found it rather puzzling. This puzzlement cannot properly be dismissed as a mere expression of defensiveness. In the first place, the term is frequently used as though it were interchangeable with the term "sexist," with the consequence that it can be difficult to see clearly that there may be different kinds of sin here. In the second place, a bit of analysis of the phenomenon called male chauvinism shows that it is not likely to work in male psychology quite as a chauvinism should work, though it bear considerable resemblance to a chauvinism when viewed from the position of the female. As if this were not enough to cloud the picture, male chauvinism involves self-deception, and thus it is bound to escape notice on the first round of self-examination. So for this reason also it is difficult for a male chauvinist, even one eager to repent, clearly to discern the nature of his offense and the extent of his guilt.

One of my tasks here is to disentangle the notions of a male chauvinist and a sexist. The other is to provide the outlines of an analysis of male chauvinism itself. I shall to some extent be describing feminist usage and theory as I understand it and to some extent be developing and improving upon it. There is no sharp line here between description and improvisation.

Sexism

The term "sexist" in its core and perhaps most fundamental meaning is a term that characterizes anything whatever that creates, constitutes, promotes, or exploits any irrelevant or impertinent marking of the distinctions between the sexes. I borrow the term "mark" here from a use in linguistics. Different distinctions may be "marked" in different languages. For example, the distinction between continuous and instantaneous present action is marked in some languages and not in others, that is, some do and some do not have different syntactic or semantic forms corresponding to this distinction. Behavior patterns very frequently mark the distinction between the sexes. For instance, behavior required in polite introductions differs according to the sexes of the participants. This means, curiously enough, that one must know a person's genital configuration before one has made that person's acquaintance, in order to know how to make her or his acquaintance. In general, "correct" or "appropriate" behavior, both nonlinguistic and linguistic, so frequently varies with (that is, marks) the sexes of the persons involved that it is of the utmost importance that a person's sex be immediately obvious upon the

I am heavily indebted to Carolyn Shafer, with whom I thoroughly and profitably discussed all parts of this essay at all stages of its development; her contribution is substantial. I also profited from discussion with an audience of philosophers and others at Michigan State University, and an audience at a meeting of the Eastern Division of the Society of Women in Philosophy, in April 1974, at Wellesley College.

This article first appeared in the book *Philosophy and Sex*, published by Prometheus Books, Buffalo, N.Y., and is reprinted by permission. Footnotes have been renumbered.

briefest encounter, even in conditions relatively unfavorable to observation. Hence our general need for abundant redundancy in sex marking.

The term "sexist" can be, and sometimes is, used in such a way that It is neutral with respect to what, if any, advantage or favor is associated with the marking of the distinction between the sexes and whether such advantage is enjoyed by the female or the male. But it is not standardly used in this neutral sense. As it is standardly used, the unqualified term denotes only those impertinent markings of the sexes that are in some way or sense associated with advantage to the male. To refer to such markings when they are associated with advantage to the female, one standardly must qualify the noun, using some such phrase as "reverse sexism." There is a kind of irony here with which one is now depressingly familiar. The word "sexist" is itself male-centered—one may perhaps say sexist. Nonetheless, for present purposes, I shall use and refer to the term "sexist" in its male-centered sense.

Although the term "sexist" is commonly applied to specific acts or behavior or to certain institutional processes, laws, customs, and so forth when they irrelevantly mark the distinction between the sexes, these uses seem to me to be relatively unproblematic, and I shall not directly discuss them. I shall focus instead on the characterization of persons as sexists—the notion of *a sexist.*

Three Kinds of Sexists and an Imposter

One would standardly characterize a person as a sexist in virtue of his sexist beliefs, opinions, convictions, and principles.[1] A person might also be called a sexist in virtue of his acts and practices, but in general only if they are seen as associated with sexist beliefs. There may be people whose sexist behavior is nothing but an unthinking adoption of the habits of those around them, for instance, a door-opening habit whose genesis is like that of peculiarities of dishwashing or driving techniques picked up from one's parents. If a person's sexist behavior consisted solely of such habits, perhaps he would be found innocent of sexist belief. In that case I think that though his behavior might be labeled sexist (and he might reasonably be expected to

change it), one should probably refrain from labeling *him* sexist.[2] Actually, it is a bit difficult to imagine someone having many such habits and not developing sexist beliefs to link the habits to each other and to various aspects of social life. Perhaps much of our sexist training takes this route, from unthinking habit to conviction.

Speaking quite generally, sexists are those who hold certain sorts of general beliefs about sexual differences and their consequences. They hold beliefs that would, for instance, support the view that physical differences between the sexes must always make for significant social and economic differences between them in any human society, such that males and females will in general occupy roles at least roughly isomorphic to those they now occupy in most extant human societies. In many cases, of course, these general beliefs might more accurately be represented by the simple proposition: Males are innately superior to females.

It is central to most feminist views that these general beliefs (assuming they are beliefs and not mere sentiments) are to be viewed as theories subject to the test of evidence and in principle falsifiable. And one kind of sexist is one who shares this attitude with respect to the epistemological status of such beliefs and differs from the feminist primarily in taking one version or another of them to be true, while the feminist holds that all such theories are false.[3] I call this person a *doctrinaire sexist.* When the feminist and the doctrinaire sexist are both fairly sophisticated, their debates tend to focus on preferred modes of empirical testing and the weights of various kinds of evidence.

There is another kind of sexist who would cheerfully assent to the same sorts of sexist propositions as those accepted by the doctrinaire sexist but who does not view them as mere theories. Such people, whom I call *primitive sexists,* are committed to these propositions as a priori truths, or ultimate metaphysical principles. A value-laden male/female dualism is embedded in their conceptual schemes more or less as a value-laden mind/body dualism is embedded in the conceptual schemes of many people of our culture. Looking at things from the point of view of the primitive sexist,

---

[1] I will refer to beliefs, opinions, convictions, and principles all indifferently as "beliefs." Not that it does not make any difference; a fuller analysis of sexism would take these distinctions into account.

[2] This might be seen as an instance when we condemn the sin but not the sinner.

[3] It should be noted that such theories are sexist only if they are false; for if true, they would not count as marking the sexes irrelevantly or impertinently. Consequently my own use of the terms "sexist" and "sexism" in connection with such theories constitutes a certain commitment in this regard.

these beliefs or principles cannot simply be refuted by empirical evidence, for they are among the principles of interpretation involved in *taking in* evidence. Even so, there is a point in challenging and haranguing the primitive sexist, for the turmoil of attack and defense may generate a reorganization of his conceptual scheme, changing the role of his sexist beliefs. One may be able to convert the primitive sexist to doctrinaire sexism, which is vulnerable to evidence and argument. (I am inclined to think that much of what feminists think of as unconscious sexism may really be primitive sexism.)

Borrowing a Quinean analogy, we might say that the sexist beliefs of the doctrinaire sexist are relatively near the periphery of his conceptual net, and that those of the primitive sexist have a central position. Sexist beliefs may indeed be anywhere between the center and the periphery of a conceptual net, and accordingly, sexists come in all shades, from empirical to metaphysical.

The stances of the doctrinaire and primitive sexists mark ends of a spectrum. Another spectrum of cases differs from the doctrinaire position in the degree to which a person's sexist beliefs are internally coherent and distinct from sundry other beliefs. Certainly, many people would assent (unless the new social pressure inhibited them) to quite a variety of statements the doctrinaire sexist would make; yet they could not in conscience be said to be adherents of a theory. There are those in whom such beliefs are scattered helter-skelter among religious persuasions, racist notions, beliefs and uncertainties about their own excellences and flaws, and so on. These sexist beliefs, though perhaps empirical enough, are not sufficiently organized or distinct from other networks of beliefs to constitute something so dignified as a theory. Sexists such as these I call *operational sexists*. They live pretty much as though they were doctrinaire sexists, but they are not so academic about it. Like the primitive sexist, the operational sexist may be more receptive to persuasion if first educated to the doctrinaire position.

There are other sorts of sexists that would have to be mentioned if we were striving for a complete catalog of members of the species according to the status of their sexist beliefs, but enough has been said to indicate the gist of the list. One other creature, however, should not go unmentioned—the *Opportunist*. The Opportunist is an impostor: he either has no particular beliefs about sexual differences and their consequences or in one degree or another accepts feminist claims about them, but he pretends to sexist convictions in order to gain the privileges and advantages associated with their acceptance by others. Regularly carrying on as though it is one's natural destiny to have some woman tend to one's laundry has, in the context of our present lives, a tendency to bring about the regular appearance of clean and mended clothes without effort on one's own part. Such opportunities abound in our society and are not missed by many persons of normal intelligence and normal distaste for distasteful tasks. (Many of us should recall here that in our youth we took advantage of such opportunities with respect to the rich variety of services our mothers were expected to perform but which we could well have performed for ourselves.) The Opportunist, furthermore, can share not only the advantages but also the excuses of the genuine sexists. The privilege attendant upon the opportunistic pretense of sexism can often be protected by availing oneself of the excuses and sympathy available to the genuine sexist—sexism is, after all, deeply ingrained in our society and in our individual lives, and who can blame the poor soul if he cannot rid himself of it overnight? One may well wonder how many of the people we identify as sexists are really cynical impostors; and while one's speculation on this question may place one on an optimist-pessimist spectrum, it is unfortunately not obvious which end of the spectrum is which.[4]

To accuse a person of being a sexist is to accuse him of having certain false beliefs and, in some cases, of having tendencies to certain reprehensible behavior presumed to be related in one way or another to such beliefs. Those justly accused of being sexists may or may not be blameworthy in this matter; personal responsibility for holding false beliefs varies greatly with persons and circumstances.

Male Chauvinism

The accusation of male chauvinism is a deeper matter than the accusation of sexism. "Male chauvinism" is one of the strongest terms in feminist

[4]Women are warmly encouraged to view belief in the ubiquity of Opportunists as paranoia. In this connection I refer the reader to a speech by William Lloyd Garrison, included under the title "Intelligent Wickedness" in *Feminism: The Essential Historical Writings*, edited by Miriam Schneir (New York: Vintage Books, 1972). He points out that men "manifest their guilt to a demonstration, in the manner in which they receive this movement [feminism] . . . they who are only ignorant, will never rage, and rave, and threaten, and foam, when the light comes. . . ." One cannot but believe that there are also some who, well aware of the point Garrison makes, prudently refrain from foaming in public.

rhetoric; "male chauvinist pig," which to some ears sounds pleonastic, belongs to a vocabulary of stern personal criticism. In the more extreme instances, persons called male chauvinists are not seen as ignorant or stupid, nor as hapless victims of socialization, but as wicked—one might almost say, perverted. They are accused of something whose relation to belief and action is like that of a defect of character, or a moral defect—a defect that might partially account for an otherwise reasonable and reasonably virtuous and self-critical person holding beliefs that are quite obviously false and behaving in ways that are obviously reprehensible. I believe the defect in question is a particularly nasty product of closely related moral failure and conceptual perversity.

Prior to its new association with the term "male," the concept of chauvinism was connected primarily, perhaps exclusively, with excessive and blind patriotism and closely similar phenomena. Patriotism seems at a glance to be an identification of some kind with one's country. One is personally affronted if one's country is criticized, and one takes personal pride in the country's real or imagined strengths and virtues. A national chauvinism is an exaggerated version of this identification, in which the righteousness and intolerance are extreme. Other chauvinisms will presumably be similar identifications with other sorts of groups, such as religious sects. In any of these cases the chauvinist will be convinced of the goodness, strength, and virtue—in general, the superiority—of his nation, sect, or so on, and will have some sort of psychological mechanisms linking this virtue with his own goodness, strength, and virtue—his own superiority.

Given roughly this view of chauvinisms, it might seem that if we could analyze and understand the mechanisms linking the supposed virtue and superiority of the nation or sect to the supposed personal virtue and superiority of the chauvinist, we could then transfer that understanding to the case of the male chauvinist to see how he is accused of ticking.

But there is a serious obstacle to pursuing this course. An analogy between national and male chauvinisms will not hold up because the objects of the identifications are not relevantly similar. Whatever the mechanisms of national and religious chauvinism might turn out to be, they are mechanisms that associate a person with an entity that is pseudo-personal. Nations and sects act and are responsible for their actions; they are therefore

pseudo-persons. Identification with such an entity is identification with a pseudo-person, and its mechanisms therefore will presumably be similar in some fairly important and enlightening ways to those of identifications with persons. Now, if we take the label "male chauvinism" at face value, male chauvinism should be an identification with the group consisting of all male human beings from which the chauvinist derives heightened self-esteem. But the group of all male human beings is not a pseudo-person: it does not have an internal structure that would give it an appropriate sort of unity; it does not act as a unit; it does not relate pseudo-personally to any other pseudo-persons; it is not virtuous or vicious. There cannot be a self-elevating identification with the group of all males the mechanisms of which would be like those of a national or sectarian chauvinism. The group with which the person supposedly identifies is the wrong sort of entity; in fact, one might say it is not an entity at all.

These reflections point to the conclusion that the phenomenon called male chauvinism is not in fact a chauvinism—a conclusion that should not be surprising. There clearly is some kind of mental set in which a male's knowledge that he is male is closely connected with his self-esteem and with the perception and treatment of females as "other," or "alien." But to picture this as a chauvinism is odd. So diverse, varied, and amorphous a group as that consisting of all male members of the species *homo sapiens* is an implausible peg on which to hang a self-esteem. I do think, however, that this phenomenon, like a chauvinism, critically involves an identification through which one gains support of one's self-esteem. Drawing on a prevalent current in feminist thought, I suggest it is at bottom a version of a self-elevating identification with Humanity or Mankind—a twisted version in which mankind is confused with malekind. Superficially it looks somewhat like a chauvinism, and a female's experience in confronting it is all too much like that of an Algerian in France; but actually the feminist is accusing the so-called male chauvinist not of improperly identifying with some *group* but of acting as though what really is *only* a group of human beings were all there is to the human race. Since that is not a chauvinism and calling it such can only be misleading, I shall hereafter refer to it as *phallism*.

Phallism

Feminists have always been sensitive to the

tendency to conflate and confuse the concepts of Man and male. We tend (we are explicitly taught) to think of distinctively human characteristics as distinctively masculine and to credit distinctively human achievements like culture, technology, and science, to men, that is, to males. This is one element of phallism: a picture of humanity as consisting of males. Blended with this, there is a (distinctively human?) tendency to romanticize and aggrandize the human species and to derive from one's rosy picture of it a sense of one's individual specialness and superiority.

Identifying with the human race, with the species, seems to involve a certain consciousness of the traits or properties one has qua member of the species. In this, we generally focus on those specific differences that we can easily construe as marking our elevation above the rest of the animal kingdom, among which the powers of speech and reason and moral sentiment are prime. Being the highest animals, the crowning achievement of evolution, we feel it morally acceptable to treat members of other species with contempt, condescension, and patronage. We supervise their safety, we decide what is best for them, we cultivate and train them to serve our needs and please us, we arrange that they shall be fed and sheltered as we please and shall breed and have offspring at our convenience (and often our concern for their welfare is sincere and our affection genuine). Every single human being, simply qua human being and regardless of personal virtues, abilities, or accomplishments, has these rights and, in some cases, duties with respect to members of any other species. All human beings can be absolutely confident of their unquestionable superiority over every creature of other species, however clever, willful, intelligent, or independently capable of survival.

We are all familiar enough with this self-serving arrogance. It might suitably be called *humanism*. It is just this sort of arrogance and assumption of superiority that is characteristic of the phallist. It is an assumption of superiority, with accompanying rights and duties, that is not seen as needing to be justified by personal virtue or individual merit, and is seen as justifying a contemptuous or patronizing attitude toward certain others. What the phallist does, generally, is to behave toward women with humanist contempt and patronage. The confusion of "man" with lowercase "m" and "Man" with uppercase "m" is revealed when the attitudes with which Man meets lower animals are

engaged in the male man's encounter with the female man.

It will be noted by the alert liberal that women are not the only human creatures that are not, or not generally, treated with the respect apparently due members of so elevated a species as ours. This is, of course, quite true. An arrogation of rights and duties fully analogous to humanism is carried out also in relation to infants, the aged, the insane, the criminal, the retarded, and other sorts of outcasts. It turns out that only certain of the creatures that are human (as opposed to equine, canine, and so on) are taken to be blessed with the superiority natural to the species; others are defective or underdeveloped and are not to be counted among the superior "us." The point here is just that phallists place females of the species in just this latter category. The words "defective" and "underdeveloped" and similar terms actually are used, with deadly seriousness, in descriptions of female psychology and anatomy broadcast by some of those assumed to have professional competence in such things.

With this degree of acquaintance with the phallist, I think one can see quite clearly why women complain of not being treated as persons by those who have been called male chauvinists. Those human creatures that we approach and treat with not the slightest trace of humanistic contempt are those we recognize unqualifiedly as fully actualized, fully normal, morally evaluable *persons.* The phallist approaches females with a superiority and condescension that we all take to be more or less appropriate to encounters with members of other species and with defective or underdeveloped members of our own. In other words, phallists do not treat women as persons.

I speak here of "the slightest trace of humanist contempt" and "fully actualized, fully normal, morally evaluable persons." These heavy qualifications are appropriate because much of our behavior suggests that there are degrees of personhood. But for now I wish to avoid this matter of degrees. I propose to simplify things by concentrating on unqualified fully actualized personhood. When in the rest of this essay I speak of persons or of the treatment or recognition of someone as a person, it is "full" personhood that I have in mind. Anything less than that, in any dimension, is covered by phrases like "not a person" or "not as a person." I shall also confine my attention to females and males who are not very young nor generally recognized as criminal or insane.

The Phallist Fantasy—I

The phallist does not treat women as persons. The obvious question is, Does he withhold this treatment in full awareness that women are persons? Are we dealing with simple malice? I have no doubt that there are cases of this transparent wickedness, but it may be more common for a person to shrink from such blatant immorality, guarding his conscience with a protective membrane of self-deception. The phallist can arrange things so that he does not experience females as persons in the first place, and thus will not have to justify to himself his failure to treat them as persons. In this and the succeeding section, I shall sketch out the phallist's characteristic strategies.

What makes a human creature a person is its possession of a range of abilities and traits whose presence is manifest in certain behavior under certain circumstances. Sacrificing elegance to brevity, I shall refer to these traits and abilities as person-abilities and to the behavior in which they are manifest as person-behavior. As with abilities in general, and their manifestations in behavior, certain circumstances are, and others are not, suitable for the manifestation of person-abilities in person-behavior.

Given this general picture one can easily see that the possibilities for self-deceptive avoidances of attributing personhood are plentiful. (1) One can observe a creature that is in fact person-behaving and deceive oneself straight out about the facts before one; one can come away simply denying that the behavior took place. (2) One can observe certain behavior and self-deceptively take it as a manifestation of a lower degree or smaller range of abilities than it in fact manifests. (3) One may self-deceptively judge circumstances that are adverse to the manifestation of the abilities to have been optimal and then conclude from the fact that the abilities were not manifest that they are not present. I have no doubt that persons anxious to avoid perceiving females as persons use all of these devices, singly and in combination. But another, more vicious device is at hand. It is not a matter of simple misinterpretation of presented data but a matter of rigging the data and then self-deceptively taking them at face value.

Person-abilities are manifest only in certain suitable circumstances; so one can ensure that an individual will seem not to have these abilities by arranging for the false appearance that the individual has been in suitable circumstances for their manifestation. The individual will not in fact have been in suitable circumstances, which guarantees that the abilities will not be manifest; but it will seem that the individual was in suitable circumstances and the deceived observer will perceive the individual to lack the abilities in question. Then to wrap it up, one can deceive oneself about having manipulated the data, take the position of the naive observer, and conclude for oneself that the individual lacks the abilities. Parents are often in a position to do this. Presenting their daughters with unsuitable learning situations self-deceptively arranged to appear suitable, they convince themselves that they have discovered the children's inability to learn those things. A simple but illuminating example is frequently acted out in a father's attempt to teach his daughter to throw a baseball. He goes through various superficial maneuvers and declares failure—her failure—without having engaged anything like the perseverence and ingenuity that he would have engaged in the training of his son.

But even this does not exhaust the tricks available to the phallist. A critical central range of the traits and abilities that go into a creature's being a person are traits and abilities that can be manifest only in circumstances of interpersonal interaction wherein another person maintains a certain level of communicativeness and cooperativeness. One cannot, for instance, manifest certain kinds of intelligence in interactions with a person who has a prior conviction of one's stupidity, lack of insight, absence of wit; one cannot manifest sensitivity or loyalty in interactions with someone who is distrustful and will not share relevant information. It is this sort of thing that opens up the possibility for the most elegant of the self-deceptive moves of the phallist, one that very nicely combines simplicity and effectiveness. He can avoid seeing the critical central range of a woman's person-abilities simply by being uncooperative and uncommunicative and can, at the same time, do it without knowing he has done it by self-deceptively believing he has been cooperative and communicative. The ease with which one can be uncooperative and uncommunicative while believing oneself to be the opposite is apparent from the most casual acquaintance with common interpersonal problems. The manipulation of the circumstances is easy, the deception is easy, and the effects are broad and conclusive.

The power and rigidity of the phallist's refusal to experience women as persons is exposed in a curious perceptual flip he performs when he is forced or tricked into experiencing as a person someone who is in fact female. Those of her female characteristics that in another woman would irresistibly draw his attention go virtually unnoticed, and she becomes "one of the boys." Confronted with the dissonant appearance of a female person in a situation where he is unable to deny that she is a person, he denies that she is female.

The frustration of trying to function as a person in interaction with someone who is self-deceptively exercising this kind of control over others and over his own perceptions is one of the primary sources of feminist rage.

The Phallist Fantasy—II

It has been assumed in the preceding section that it is obvious that women are persons. Otherwise, failure to perceive women as persons would not have to involve self-deception. Some women, however, clearly think there is some point in asserting that they are persons, and some women's experience is such that they are inclined to say that they are denied personhood.

To some, there seems to be a certain silliness about the assertion that women are persons, which derives from the fact that almost everybody, female and male alike, seems to *agree* that women are people. But in many instances this constitutes no more than an acceptance of the fact that females are biologically human creatures with certain linguistic capacities and emotional needs; in accepting this, one is committed to no more than the belief that women should be treated humanely, as we are enjoined to treat the retarded and the elderly. But the personhood of which I am speaking here is "full" personhood. I am speaking of unqualified participation in the radical superiority of the species, without justification by individual virtue or achievement —unqualified membership of that group of beings that may approach all other creatures with humanist arrogance. Members of this group are to be treated not humanely but with respect. It is plain that not everybody, not even almost everybody, agrees that women belong to this group. The assertion that they do is hardly the assertion of something so generally deemed obvious as to be unworthy of assertion.

The other claim—that women are denied personhood—also seems strange to some people. But it by no means emerges parthenogenetically from feminine fantasy. To some, the concept of a

person seems somewhat like the concepts that are sometimes called "institutional," such as the concepts of a lawyer or a knight. To some it seems that "person" denotes a social or institutional role and that one may be allowed or forbidden to adopt that role. It seems that we (persons) have some sort of power to admit creatures to personhood. I do not find this view plausible, but it surely recommends itself to some, and it must be attractive to the phallist, who would fancy the power to create persons. His refusal to perceive women as persons could then be taken by him as an exercise of this power. Some phallists give every sign of accepting this or a similar view, and some women seem to be taken in by it too. Hence, some women are worked into the position of asking to be granted personhood. It is a peculiar position for a person to be in, but such are the almost inevitable effects of phallist magic on those not forewarned. Of course, one cannot make what is a person not a person by wishing it so. And yet some vague impression lingers that phallists do just that—and it is not without encouragement that it lingers.

Even apart from the cases of institutional concepts, there is in the employment of concepts, as in the employment of words, a certain collective subjectivity. Every concept has some standard use or uses in some community—the "conceptual community" whose usage fixes its correct application. While admitting that various hedges and qualifications should be made here, one may say that, generally, if everyone in the community where the concept *Y* is in general use declares *X*s to be *Y*s, then *X*s are *Y*s. For concepts employed only by specialists or, say, used only within certain neighborhoods, the relevant conceptual communities consist of those specialists or the residents of those neighborhoods. In general, the conceptual community whose use of a concept fixes its correct application simply consists of all the people who use it. To determine its correct application, one identifies the people who use it and then describes or characterizes their use of it.

The concept of a person is a special case here. To discover the range of application of the concept of a person, one might identify the conceptual community in which that concept is used. It consists, of course, of all the persons who use the concept. To identify that conceptual community, one must decide which human creatures are persons. The upshot is that the phallist who self-deceptively adjusts the range of application of the concept of a person is also manipulating appearances with respect to the constitution of the conceptual community. Males who live their lives under the impression that only males are persons (and in the belief that this impression is shared by other males) will see *themselves* (the persons) as completely constituting the conceptual community and thence take *their* agreement in the (overt) application of the concept of a person as fixing its correct application, much as we all take our agreement in the application of the concept of a tree as fixing its correct application. We do not have the power to make what is a tree not a tree, but the collective subjectivity of conceptual correctness can be mistaken to mean that we do. Nor could the phallists, if they did constitute the conceptual community, thereby have the power to make what is a person not a person. But it is here, I think, that one finds the deepest source of the impression that women are *denied* personhood.

The self-deceptive denial that women are (full) persons adds up to an attempt to usurp the community's control over concepts in general by denying females membership in the conceptual community, or rather, by failing to see that they are members of the conceptual community. The effect is not simply the exclusion of females from the rights and duties of full persons but is a conceptual banishment that ensures that their complaints about this exclusion simply do not fit into the resulting conceptual scheme. Hence the phallist's almost incredible capacity for failure to understand what on earth feminists are talking about. His self-deception is locked into his conceptual framework, not simply as his analytic or a priori principles are, but in the underlying determinants of its entire structure and content. The self-deception fixes his conception of the constitution of the conceptual community whose existence makes conceptualization possible and whose collective perceptions determine in outline its progress.

The rejection of females by phallists is both morally and conceptually profound. The refusal to perceive females as persons is conceptually profound because it excludes females from that community whose conceptions of things one allows to influence one's own concepts—it serves as a police-lock on a closed mind. Furthermore, the refusal to treat women with the respect due to persons is in itself a violation of a moral principle that seems to many to be *the* founding principle of all morality. This violation of moral principle is sustained by an active manipulation of circumstances that is systematic and habitual and self-deceptively unacknowledged. The exclusion of women from the conceptual community simultaneously excludes them from the moral community. So the self-deception here is designed not just to dodge particular applications of moral principles but to narrow the moral community itself, and is therefore particularly insidious. It is the sort of thing that leavens the moral schizophrenia of the gentle, honest, god-fearing racist monster, the self-anointed *übermensch,* and other moral deviates. The phallist is confined with the worst of moral company in a self-designed conceptual closet—and he has taken great pains to ensure that this escape will not be abetted by any woman.

Postscript

It may seem that I have assumed here that all sexists and phallists are male. I do assume that in the paradigm cases phallists are male, but the suggestion that all sexists and all phallists are male arises innocently from the standard English usage of personal pronouns.

5/On Psychological Oppression

Sandra Lee Bartky

In *Black Skin, White Masks,* Frantz Fanon offers an anguished and eloquent description of the psychological effects of colonialism on the colonized, a "clinical study" of what he calls the "psychic alienation of the black man." "Those who recognize themselves in it," he says, "will have made a step forward."[1] Fanon's black American readers saw at once that he had captured the corrosive effects not only of classic colonial oppression but of domestic racism too, and that his study fitted well the picture of black America as an internal colony. Without wanting in any way to diminish the oppressive and stifling realities of black experience which Fanon has revealed, let me say that I, a white woman, recognize myself in this book too, not only in my "shameful livery of white incomprehension,"[2] but as myself the victim of a psychological oppression similar to what Fanon has described. In this paper I shall try to explore that moment of recognition, to reveal the ways in which the psychological effects of sexist oppression resemble those of racism and colonialism.

"To oppress," says Webster, is "to lie heavy on, to weigh down, to exercise harsh dominion over." When we describe a people as oppressed, what we have in mind most often is an oppression that is economic and political in character. But recent liberation movements, the black liberation movement and the women's movement in particular, have brought to light forms of oppression that are not immediately economic or political. Blacks and women can be oppressed in ways that need involve neither physical deprivation, legal inequality, nor economic exploitation;[3] both blacks and women can be victims of "psychic alienation" or psychological oppression. To be psychologically oppressed is to be weighed down in your mind; it is to have a harsh dominion exercised over your self-esteem. The psychologically oppressed become to themselves their own oppressors; they come to exercise harsh dominion over their *own* self-esteem. Differently put, psychological oppression can be regarded as the "internalization of intimations of inferiority."[4]

Like economic oppression, psychological oppression is institutionalized and systematic; it serves to make the work of domination easier by breaking the spirit of the dominated and by rendering them incapable of understanding the nature of those agencies responsible for their subjugation. This allows those who benefit from the established order of things to maintain their ascendancy with more appearance of legitimacy and with less recourse to overt acts of violence than they might otherwise require. Now poverty and powerlessness can destroy a person's self-esteem, and the fact that one occupies an inferior position in society is all too often racked up to one's being an inferior sort of person. Clearly, then, economic and political oppression are themselves psychologically oppressive. But there are *unique* modes of psychological oppression that can be distinguished from the usual forms of economic and political domination to which women and oppressed minorities are subject. Fanon offers a series of what are essentially phenomenological descriptions of psychic alienation.[5] In spite of considerable overlapping, the experiences of oppression he describes fall into three categories: experiences of stereotyping, of cultural domination, and of sexual objectification. These, I shall contend, are some of the ways in which the terrible messages of inferiority can be delivered even to those who may enjoy certain material benefits; they are special modes of psychic alienation. In what follows, I shall examine some of the ways in which American women are stereotyped, culturally dominated, and sexually objectified. In the course of the discussion, I shall argue that our ordinary concept of oppression needs to be altered and expanded, for it is too restricted to encompass what an analysis of psychological oppression reveals about the nature of oppression in general. Finally, I shall be concerned throughout to show how both fragmentation and mystification are present in each mode of psychological oppression, although in varying degrees: fragmentation, the splitting of the whole person into parts of a person which, in stereotyping, may take the form of a war between a "true" and "false" self—or, in sexual objectification, the form of an often-coerced and degrading identification of a person with her body;

---

[1] Frantz Fanon, *Black Skin, White Masks* (New York: Grove Press, 1967), p. 12.

[2] Ibid.

[3] For an excellent comparison of the concepts of exploitation and oppression, see Judith Farr Tormey, "Exploitation, Oppression and Self-Sacrifice," in *Women and Philosophy*, ed. Carol C. Gould and Marx W. Wartofsky (New York: G. P. Putnam's Sons, 1976), pp. 206–21.

[4] Joyce Mitchell Cook (Paper delivered at *Philosophy and the Black Liberation Struggle* Conference, University of Illinois, Chicago Circle, November 19–20, 1970).

[5] Fanon's phenomenology of oppression, however, is almost entirely a phenomenology of the oppression of colonized *men*. He seems unaware of the ways in which the oppression of women by their men in the societies he examines is itself similar to the colonization of natives by Europeans. Sometimes, as in *A Dying Colonialism* (New York: Grove Press, 1968), he goes so far as to defend the clinging to oppressive practices, such as the sequestration of women in Moslem countries, as an authentic resistance by indigenous people to Western cultural intrusion. For a penetrating critique of Fanon's attitude toward women, see Barbara Burris, "Fourth World Manifesto," in *Radical Feminism*, ed. A. Koedt, E. Levine, and A. Rapone (New York: Quadrangle, 1973), pp. 322–57.

mystification, the systematic obscuring of both the reality and agencies of psychological oppression so that its intended effect, the depreciated self, is lived out as destiny, guilt, or neurosis.

Few people will deny that women, like blacks, have been subject to stereotyping. What is perhaps not so immediately evident is that in our society the two groups have been stereotyped in remarkably similar ways. Both have been regarded as childlike, happiest when they are occupying their "place"; more intuitive than rational, more spontaneous than deliberate, closer to nature and less assimilable into the higher culture. Stereotyping is morally reprehensible as well as psychologically oppressive on two counts, at least. First, it can hardly be expected that those who hold a set of stereotyped beliefs about the sort of person I am will understand my needs or even respect my rights. Second, suppose that I, the victim of some stereotype, believe in it myself—for why should I not believe what everyone else believes? I may then find it difficult to achieve what existentialists call an "authentic choice of self," or what some psychologists have called a "state of self-actualization." Moral philosophers have quite correctly placed a high value, sometimes the highest value, on the development of autonomy and moral agency. Clearly, the economic and political domination of women—our concrete powerlessness—is what threatens our autonomy most. But stereotyping, in its own way, threatens our self-determination too. Even when economic and political obstacles on the path to autonomy are removed, a depreciated alterego still blocks the way. It is hard enough for me to determine what sort of person I am or ought to try to become without being shadowed by an alternate self, a truncated and inferior self that I have, in some sense, been doomed to be all the time. For many, the prefabricated self triumphs over a more authentic self which, with work and encouragement, might sometime have emerged. For the talented few, retreat into the

imago is raised to the status of art or comedy. Muhammad Ali has made himself what he could scarcely escape being made into—a personification of Primitive Man; while Zsa Zsa Gabor is not so much a woman as the parody of a woman.

The female stereotype threatens the autonomy of women not only by virtue of its existence but also by its nature.[6] In the conventional portrait, women deny their femininity when they undertake action that is too self-regarding or independent. The right to choose a husband was hard-won and long in coming; for many women still, this is virtually the only major decision we are thought capable of making without putting our womanly nature in danger; what follows ever after is or ought to be a properly feminine submission to the decisions of men. We cannot be autonomous, as men are thought to be autonomous, without in some sense ceasing to be women. When one considers how interwoven are traditional female stereotypes with traditional female roles—and these, in turn, with the ways in which we are socialized—all this is seen in an even more sinister light: women are psychologically *conditioned* not to develop into autonomous individuals.

The truncated self I am to be is not something manufactured out there by an anonymous Other which I encounter only in the pages of *Playboy* or the *Ladies Home Journal;* it is inside of me, a part of myself. I may become infatuated with my feminine persona and waste my powers in the more or less hopeless pursuit of a *Vogue* figure or a home that "expresses my personality." Or I may find the parts of myself fragmented and the fragments at war with one another. Women are only now learning to identify and struggle against the forces that have laid these psychic burdens upon us. More often than not, we live out this struggle, which is really a struggle against oppression, in a mystified way: What we are enduring we believe to be entirely intrapsychic in character, the result of immaturity, maladjustment, or even neurosis.

---

[6] I have in mind Abraham Maslow's concept of autonomy, a notion which has the advantage of being neutral as regards the controversy between free-will and determinism. For Maslow, the sources of behavior of autonomous or "psychologically free" individuals are more internal than reactive:

Such people become far more self-sufficient and self-contained. The determinants which govern them are now primarily inner ones . . . They are the laws of their own inner nature, their potentialities and capacities, their talents, their latent resources, their creative impulses, their needs to know themselves and to become more and more integrated and unified, more and more aware of what they really are, of what they really want, of what their call or vocation or fate is to be.

Toward a Psychology of Being, 2d ed. (New York: D. Van Nostrand Co., 1968), p. 35.

It would be absurd to suggest that most men are autonomous in this sense of the term. Nevertheless, insofar as there are individuals who resemble this portrait, I think it likelier that they will be men than women. Furthermore, more men than women *believe* themselves to be autonomous; this belief, even if false, is widely held, and this in itself has implications that are important to consider. Whatever the facts may be in regard to men's lives, the point to remember is this: Women have been thought to have neither the capacity nor the right to aspire to an ideal of autonomy, an ideal to which there accrues, whatever its relation to mental health, an enormous social prestige.

Tylor, the great classical anthropologist, defined culture as all the items in the general life of a people. To claim that we women are victims of cultural domination is to claim that all the items in the general life of our people—our language, our institutions, our art and literature, our popular culture—are sexist; that all, to a greater or lesser degree, manifest male supremacy. There is some exaggeration in this claim, but not much. Unlike the black colonial whom Fanon describes with such pathos, women are not now in possession of an alternate culture, a "native" culture which, even if regarded by everyone including ourselves as decidedly inferior to the dominant culture, we could at least recognize as our own. However degraded or distorted an image of ourselves we see reflected in the patriarchal culture, the culture of our men is still our culture. Certainly in some respects, the condition of women is like the condition of a colonized people, but we are not a colonized people; we have never been more than half a people.[7]

This lack of cultural autonomy has several important consequences for an understanding of the condition of women. A culture has a global character; the limits of my culture are the limits of my world. The subordination of women, then, because it is so pervasive a feature of my culture, will (if uncontested) appear to be natural—and because it is natural, unalterable. Unlike a colonized people, women have no memory of a "time before": a time before the masters came, a time before we were subjugated and ruled. Further, since one function of cultural identity is to allow me to distinguish those who are like me from those who are not, I may feel more kinship with those who share my culture, even though they oppress me, than with the women of another culture, whose whole experience of life may well be closer to my own than to any man's.

Our true situation in regard to male supremacist culture is one of domination and exclusion. But this manifests itself in an extremely deceptive way; mystification once more holds sway. Our relative absence from the "higher" culture is taken as proof that we are unable to participate in it ("Why are there no great women artists?"). Theories of the female nature must then be brought forward to try to account for this.[8] The splitting or fragmenting of women's consciousness which takes place in the cultural sphere is also apparent. While remaining myself, I must at the same time transform myself into that abstract and "universal" subject for whom cultural artifacts are made and whose values and experience they express. This subject is not universal at all, however, but *male*. Thus I must approve the taming of the shrew, laugh at the mother-in-law or the dumb blonde, and somehow identify with all those heroes of fiction from Faust to the personae of Norman Mailer and Henry Miller, whose *Bildungsgeschichten* involve the sexual exploitation of women.

Women and blacks are subject not only to cultural depreciation and to stereotyping but to sexual objectification as well. Even though much has been written about sexual objectification in the literature of both liberation movements, the notion itself is complex, obscure, and much in need of philosophical clarification. I offer the following preliminary characterization of sexual objectification: A person is sexually objectified when her sexual parts or sexual functions are separated out from the rest of her personality and reduced to the status of mere instruments or else regarded as if they were capable of representing her. On this definition, then, the prostitute would be a victim of sexual objectification, as would the *Playboy* bunny, the female breeder, and the bathing beauty.

To say that the sexual part of a person is regarded as if it could represent her is to imply that it cannot, that the part and the whole are incommensurable. But surely there are times, in the sexual embrace perhaps, when a woman might want to be regarded as nothing but a sexually intoxicating body and when attention paid to some other aspect of her person—say to her mathematical ability—would be absurdly out of place. If sexual relations involve some sexual objectification, then it becomes necessary to distinguish situations in which sexual objectification is oppressive from the sorts of situations in

[7]Many feminists would object vigorously to my claim that there has been no female culture (see, e.g., Burris, "Fourth World Manifesto"). I am not claiming that women have had no enclaves within the dominant culture, that we have never made valuable contributions to the larger culture, or even that we have never dominated *any* avenue of cultural expression—one would have to think only of the way in which women have dominated certain forms of folk art (e.g., quilting). What I am claiming is that none of this adds up to a "culture," in the sense in which we speak of Jewish culture, Arapesh culture, or Afro-American culture. Further, the fact that many women are today engaged in the self-conscious attempt to create a female culture testifies, I think, to the situation regarding culture being essentially as I describe it.

[8]The best-known modern theory of this type is, of course, Freud's. He maintains that the relative absence of women from the higher culture is the consequence of a lesser ability to sublimate libidinal drives. See "Femininity" in *New Introductory Lectures in Psychoanalysis* (New York: W. W. Norton, 1933). [See selection 8, pp. 47–52, this volume—eds.]

which it is not.[9] The identification of a person with her sexuality becomes oppressive, one might venture, when such an identification becomes habitually extended into every area of her experience. To be routinely perceived by others in a sexual light on occasions when such a perception is inappropriate is to have one's very being subjected to that compulsive sexualization that has been the traditional lot of women and blacks. "For the majority of white men," says Fanon, "the Negro is the incarnation of a genital potency beyond all moralities and prohibitions."[10] And later, again from *Black Skin, White Masks,* "the Negro is the genital."[11]

One way to be sexually objectified, then, is to be the object of a kind of perception, unwelcome and inappropriate, that takes the part for the whole. An example may make this clearer. A young woman was recently interviewed for a teaching job in philosophy by the academic chairman of a large department. During most of the interview, so she reported, the man stared fixedly at her breasts. In this situation, the woman is a bosom, not a job candidate. Was this department chairman guilty only of a confusion between business and pleasure? Scarcely. He stares at her breasts for his sake, not hers. Her wants and needs not only play no role in the encounter but, because of the direction of his attention, she is discomfited, feels humiliated, and performs badly. Not surprisingly, she fails to get the job. Much of the time, sexual objectification occurs independently of what women want; it is something done to us against our will. It is clear from this example that the objectifying perception that splits a person into parts serves to elevate one interest above another. Now it stands revealed not only as a way of perceiving, but as a way of maintaining dominance as well. It is not clear to me that the sexual and nonsexual spheres of experience can or ought to be kept separate forever (Marcuse, for one, has envisioned the eroticization of all areas of human life); but as

things stand now, sexualization is one way of fixing disadvantaged persons in their disadvantage, to their clear detriment and within a narrow and repressive eros.

Consider now a second example of the way in which that fragmenting perception, which is so large an ingredient in the sexual objectification of women, serves to maintain the dominance of men. It is a fine, spring day, and with an utter lack of self-consciousness I am bouncing down the street. Suddenly I hear men's voices. Catcalls and whistles fill the air. These noises are clearly sexual in intent and they are meant for me; they come from a group of men hanging about a corner across the street. I freeze. As Sartre would say, I have been petrified by the gaze of the Other. My face flushes and my motions become stiff and self-conscious. The body which, only a moment before, I inhabited with such ease now floods my consciousness. I have been made into an object. While it is true that for these men I am nothing but, let us say, a "nice piece of ass," there is more involved in this encounter than their mere fragmented perception of me. They could, after all, have enjoyed me in *silence*. Blissfully unaware, breasts bouncing, eyes on the birds in the trees, I could have passed by without having been turned to stone. But I must be *made* to know that I am a "nice piece of ass"; I must be made to see myself as they see me. There is an element of compulsion in this encounter, in this being-made-to-be-aware of one's own flesh; like being made to apologize, it is humiliating. It is unclear what role is played by sexual arousal or even sexual connoisseurship in encounters like these. The encounter described seems less the spontaneous expression of a healthy eroticism than a ritual of subjugation.

The paradigm case of sexual objectification as I have characterized it involves two persons: the one who objectifies and the one who is objectified. But the observer and the one observed can be the same person. I can, of course, take pleasure in my

[9]There might be some objection to regarding ordinary sexual relations as involving sexual objectification, since this use of the term seems not to jibe with its use in more ordinary contexts. For Hegel, Marx, and Sartre, "objectification" is an important moment in the dialectic of consciousness. My decision to treat ordinary sexual relations or even sexual desire alone as involving some objectification is based on a desire to remain within this tradition. Further, Sartre's phenomenology of sexual desire in *Being and Nothingness* (New York: Philosophical Library, 1968) draws heavily on a concept of objectification in an unusually compelling description of the experienced character of the state:
The caress by realizing the Other's incarnation reveals to me my own incarnation; that is, I make myself flesh in order to impel the Other to realize for-herself and for-me her own flesh, and my caresses cause my flesh to be born for me in so far as it

is for the Other flesh causing her to be born as flesh. I make her enjoy my flesh through her flesh in order to compel her to feel herself flesh. And so possession truly appears as a double reciprocal incarnation. [*P. 508*]
What I call "objectification," Sartre here calls "incarnation," a refinement not necessary for my purposes. What he calls "sadism" is incarnation without reciprocity. Most of my examples of sexual objectification would fall into the latter category.

[10]Fanon, *Black Skin, White Masks,* p. 177. Eldridge Cleaver sounds a similar theme in *Soul on Ice* (New York: Dell Publishing Co., 1968). The archetypal white man in American society, he claims, is the "Omnipotent Administrator"; the archetypal black man is the "Super-Masculine Menial."

[11]Fanon, *Black Skin, White Masks,* p. 180.

own body as another might take pleasure in it; and it would be naive not to notice that there are delights of a narcissistic kind that go along with the status "sex object." But the extent to which the identification of women with their bodies feeds an essentially infantile narcissism—an attitude of mind in keeping with our forced infantilization in other areas of life—is, at least for me, an open question. Subject to the evaluating eye of the male connoisseur, women learn to evaluate themselves first and best. Our identities can no more be kept separate from how our bodies look than they can be kept separate from the shadow selves of the female stereotype. "Much of a young woman's identity is already defined in her kind of attractiveness and in the selectivity of her search for the man (or men) by whom she wishes to be sought."[12] There is something obsessional in the preoccupation of many women with their bodies, although the magnitude of the obsession will vary somewhat with the presence or absence in a woman's life of other sources of self-esteem and with her capacity to gain a living independent of her looks. Surrounded on all sides by images of perfect female beauty—for, in modern advertising, the needs of capitalism and the traditional values of patriarchy are happily married—of course we fall short. The narcissism encouraged by our identification with the body is shattered by these images. Whose nose is not the wrong shape, whose hips are not too wide or too narrow? Anyone who believes that such concerns are too trivial to weigh very heavily with most women has failed to grasp the realities of the feminine condition.

The idea that women ought always to make themselves as pleasing to the eye as possible is very widespread indeed. It was dismaying to come across this passage in a paper written by an eminent Marxist humanist in defense of the contemporary women's movement:

There is no reason why a women's liberation activist should not try to look pretty and attractive. One of the universal human aspirations of all times was to raise reality to the level of art, to make the world more beautiful, to be more beautiful within given limits. Beauty is a value in itself; it will always be respected and will attract—to be sure various forms of beauty but not to the exclusion of physical *beauty. A woman does not become a sex object in herself, or only because of her pretty appearance. She becomes a sexual object in a relationship, when she allows man to treat her in a certain depersonalizing, degrading way; and vice versa, a woman does not become a sexual subject by neglecting her appearance.*[13]

Here, it is not for the sake of mere men that we women—not just we women, but we women's liberation activists—ought to look "pretty and attractive," but for the sake of something much more exalted—the sake of beauty. This preoccupation with the way we look and the fear that women might stop trying to make themselves pretty and attractive (so as to "raise reality to the level of art") would be a species of objectification anywhere; but it is absurdly out of place in a paper on women's emancipation. It is as if an essay on the black liberation movement were to end by admonishing blacks not to forget their natural rhythm, or as if Marx had warned the workers of the world not to neglect their appearance while throwing off their chains.

Marković's concern with women's appearance merely reflects a larger cultural preoccupation. It is a fact that women in our society are regarded as having a virtual duty "to make the most of what we have." But the imperative not to neglect our appearance suggests that we *can* neglect it, that it is within our power to make ourselves look better—not just neater and cleaner, but prettier and more attractive. What is presupposed by this is that we don't look good enough already, that attention to the ordinary standards of hygiene would be insufficient, *that there is something wrong with us as we are.* Here, the intimations of inferiority are clear: Not only must we continue to produce ourselves as beautiful bodies, but the bodies we have to work with are deficient to begin with. Even within an already inferiorized identity (i.e., the identity of one who is principally and most importantly a body), I turn out once more to be inferior, for the body I am to be, never sufficient unto itself, stands forever in need of plucking or painting, of slimming down or fattening up, of firming or flattening.

The foregoing examination of three modes of psychological oppression, so it appears, points up

[12]Erik Erikson, "Inner and Outer Space: Reflections on Womanhood," *Daedalus* 93 (1961); 582–606; quoted by Naomi Weisstein, "Psychology Constructs the Female," in *Radical Feminism*, p. 179.

[13]Mihailo Marković, "Women's Liberation and Human Emancipation," in *Women and Philosophy*, p. 165–66. In spite of this lapse and some questionable opinions concerning the nature of female sexuality, Marković's paper is a most compelling defense of the claim that the emancipation of women cannot come about under capitalism.

the need for an alteration in our ordinary concept of oppression. Oppression, I believe, is ordinarily conceived in too limited a fashion. This has placed undue restrictions both on our understanding of what oppression itself *is* and on the categories of persons we might want to classify as oppressed. Consider, for example, the following paradigmatic case of oppression:

And the Egyptians made the children of Israel to serve with rigor; and they made their lives bitter with hard bondage, in mortar and in brick, and in all manner of service in the field; all their service, wherein they made them serve, was with rigor.[14]

Here the Egyptians, one group of persons, exercise harsh dominion over the Israelites, another group of persons. It is not suggested that the Israelites, however great their sufferings, have lost their integrity and wholeness qua persons. But psychological oppression is dehumanizing and depersonalizing; it attacks the person in her personhood. I mean by this that the nature of psychological oppression is such that oppressor and oppressed alike come to doubt that the oppressed have the capacity to do the sorts of things that only persons can do, to be what persons, in the fullest sense of the term, can be. The possession of autonomy, for example, is widely thought to distinguish persons from nonpersons; but stereotyping, as we have seen, threatens the autonomy of women. Oppressed people might or might not be in a position to exercise their autonomy, but the psychologically oppressed come to believe that they lack the capacity to be autonomous whatever their position.

Similarly, the creation of culture is a distinctly human function, perhaps the most human function. In its cultural life, a group is able to affirm its values and to grasp its identity in acts of self-reflection. Frequently women and blacks, cut off from the cultural apparatus, are denied the exercise of this function entirely. To the extent that we are able to catch sight of ourselves in the dominant culture at all, the images we see are distorted or demeaning. Finally, sexual objectification leads to the identification of those who undergo it with what is both human and not-quite-human—the body. Thus psychological oppression is just what Fanon said it

was—"psychic alienation"—the estrangement or separating of a person from some of the essential attributes of personhood.

Some final thoughts on mystification: The special modes of psychological oppression can be regarded as some of the many ways in which messages of inferiority are delivered to those who are to occupy an inferior position in society. But it is important to remember that messages of this sort are neither sent nor received in an unambiguous way. We are taught that we are deficient in those capacities that distinguish persons from nonpersons, but at the same time we are assured that we are persons after all. *Of course* women are persons; *of course* blacks are human beings. Who but the lunatic fringe would deny it? The Antillean Negro, Fanon is fond of repeating, is a *Frenchman.* The official ideology announces with conviction that "all men are created equal"; and in spite of the suspect way in which this otherwise noble assertion is phrased, we women learn that they mean to include us after all.

But it is psychologically oppressive to believe and at the same time *not* to believe that one is inferior—in other words, to believe a contradiction. Lacking an analysis of the larger system of social relations which produced it, one can only "make sense" of this contradiction in two ways. First, while accepting in some quite formal sense the proposition that "all men are created equal," I can believe, inconsistently, what my oppressors have always believed: that some types of persons are less equal than others. I may then live out my membership in my sex or race in *shame;* I am "only a woman" or "just a nigger." Or, somewhat more consistently, I may reject entirely the belief that my disadvantage is generic; but having still to account for it somehow, I may locate the cause squarely within myself, a bad destiny of an entirely private sort—a character flaw, an "inferiority complex," or a neurosis.

Many blacks and women regard themselves as uniquely unable to satisfy normal criteria of psychological health or moral adequacy. Indeed, if victims of oppression *could* somehow believe themselves to be innately inferior *merely* by virtue of being black or female, for some at least, their anguish might be diminished. A lack I share with many others just because of an accident of birth would be unfortunate indeed, but at least I would not have to regard myself as having failed to measure up to standards that people like myself are expected to meet. It should be pointed out

[14]Exod. 1:13–14.

that both of these "resolutions" produce a "poor self-image"—a bloodless term of the behavioral sciences that refers to a very wide variety of possible ways to suffer.[15]

To take one's oppression to be an inherent flaw of birth, or of psychology, is to have what Marxists call a "false consciousness." Systematically deceived about the nature and origin of our unhappiness, our struggles are directed inward upon the self, not outward upon those social forces responsible for our predicament. Like the psychologically disturbed, the psychologically oppressed often lack a viable indentity. Frequently we are unable to make sense of our own impulses or feelings, not only because our drama of fragmentation gets played out on an inner psychic stage, but because we are forced to find our way about in a world which presents itself to us in a masked and deceptive fashion. Regarded as persons, yet depersonalized, we are treated by our society the way the parents of some schizophrenics are said by R. D. Laing to treat their children—professing to love them at the very moment they shrink from their touch.

In sum, then, to be psychologically oppressed is to be caught in the double bind of a society which both affirms my human status and at the same time bars me from the exercise of many of those typically human functions that bestow this status. To be denied autonomy, forbidden cultural expression, and condemned to the immanence of mere bodily being is to be cut off from the sorts of activities that define what it is to be human. A person whose being has been subjected to these cleavages may be described as "alienated." Alienation in any form causes a rupture within the human person, an estrangement from self, a "splintering of human nature into a number of misbegotten parts."[16] Any adequate theory of the nature and varieties of human alienation, then, must encompass psychological oppression—or, to use Fanon's term once more, "psychic alienation."

Much has been written about alienation, but it is Marx's theory of alienation that speaks most compellingly to the concerns of feminist political theory.

Alienation for Marx is primarily the alienation of labor. What distinguishes human beings from animals is "labor," for Marx the free, conscious, and creative transformation of nature in accordance with human needs. But under capitalism, workers are alienated in production, estranged from the products of their labor, from their own productive activity, and from their fellow creatures. Since labor is the most characteristic human life activity, to be alienated from one's own labor is to be alienated from oneself.

Human productive activity, according to Marx, is "objectified" in its products. What this means is that we are able to grasp ourselves reflectively primarily in the things we have produced; human needs and powers become concrete "in their products as the amount and type of change which their exercise has brought about."[17] But in capitalist production, the capitalist has a right to appropriate what workers have produced. Thus the product goes to augment capital, where it becomes part of an alien force exercising power over those who produced it. An "objectification" or extension of the worker's self, the product is split off from this self and turned against it. Workers are alienated not only from the products they produce but from their own laboring activity as well. The activity of production, as Marx views it, offers the worker an opportunity to exercise his specifically human powers and capacities; it is the ideal expression and realization of the human essence. But labor under capitalism does not become an occasion for human self-realization. It is mere drudgery, which mortifies the body and ruins the mind. The worker's labor "is therefore not voluntary, but coerced; it is forced labor. It is therefore not the satisfaction of a need; it is merely a means to satisfy needs external to it."[18] When the free and creative productive activity that should define human functioning is reduced to a mere means to sustain life, to "forced labor," workers suffer fragmentation and loss of self. Workers are set against owners of the means of production—and, in the competitive relations of the marketplace, against one another too. Since Marx regards sociality as something intrinsic to the self, this species of alienation (i.e., estrangement from the Other), like the other forms of estranged labor, is also an estrangement from the self.

[15]The available clinical literature on the psychological effects of social inferiority supports this claim. See William H. Grier and Price M. Cobbs, *Black Rage* (New York: Grosset & Dunlap, (1969); Pauline Bart, "Depression in Middle-Aged Women," in *Women in Sexist Society,* ed. Vivian Gornick and Barbara Moran (New York: New American Library, 1971), pp. 163–86; also Phyllis Chesler, *Women and Madness* (New York: Doubleday, 1972).

[16]Bertell Ollman, *Alienation: Marx's Conception of Man in Capitalist Society* (London: Cambridge University Press, 1971), p. 135.

[17]Ibid., p. 143.

[18]Karl Marx, *Economic and Philosophic Manuscripts of 1844,* ed. with an Introduction by Dirk J. Struik, trans. Martin Milligan (New York: International Publishers, 1964), p. 70.

In many ways, psychic alienation and the alienation of labor are profoundly alike. Both involve a splitting off of human functions from the human person, a forbidding of activities thought to be essential to a fully human existence. Both subject the individual to fragmentation and impoverishment. Alienation is not a condition into which someone might stumble by accident; it has come both to the victim of psychological oppression and to the alienated worker from without as a usurpation by someone else of what is, by rights, mine. Alienation occurs in each case when activities, which not only belong to the domain of the self but define, in large measure, the proper functioning of this self, fall under the control of others. To be a victim of alienation is to have a part of one's being stolen by another.[19] Both psychic alienation and the alienation of labor might be regarded as varieties of alienated productivity. From this perspective, cultural domination would be the estrangement or alienation of production in the cultural sphere; while stereotyping and sexual objectification could be seen as the alienated production of *one's own person.*

All the modes of oppression—psychological, political, and economic—and the kinds of alienation which accompany them serve to maintain a vast system of privilege—privilege of race, of sex, and of class. Every mode of oppression within the system has its own part to play, but each serves to support and to maintain the others. Thus, for example, the assault on the self-esteem of women and blacks prepares us for the historic role that a disproportionate number of us are destined to play within the process of capitalist production: that of a cheap or reserve labor supply. Class oppression, in turn, encourages those who are somewhat higher in the social hierarchy to cling to a false sense of racial or sexual superiority. Because of the interlocking character of the modes of oppression, I think it highly unlikely that any form of oppression will disappear entirely until the system of oppression as a whole is overthrown.

---

[19]The *agents* of alienation differ for each type; and for this reason, psychic alienation and the alienation of labor do not fit entirely comfortably under the same theoretical framework. A discussion of the ways in which Marx's theory of alienated labor would have to be altered in order to include other forms of alienation would go far beyond the scope of this paper.

2
Female Nature and Sex Roles

6/The Equality of Women

Plato

Editor's Note: [In this section of the *Republic,* Socrates discusses with Glaucon the position of women in his ideal society.]

Well, I replied, I suppose that I must retrace my steps and say what I perhaps ought to have said before in the proper place. The part of the men has been played out, and now properly enough comes the turn of the women. Of them I will proceed to speak, and the more readily since I am invited by you.

For men born and educated like our citizens, the only way, in my opinion, of arriving at a right conclusion about the possession and use of women and children is to follow the path on which we originally started, when we said that the men were to be the guardians and watchdogs of the herd.

True.

Let us further suppose the birth and education of our women to be subject to similar or nearly similar regulations; then we shall see whether the result accords with our design.

What do you mean?

What I mean may be put into the form of a question, I said: Are dogs divided into hes and shes, or do they both share equally in hunting and in keeping watch and in the other duties of dogs? or do we entrust to the males the entire and exclusive care of the flocks, while we leave the females at home, under the idea that the bearing and suckling their puppies is labour enough for them?

No, he said, they share alike; the only difference between them is that the males are stronger and the females weaker.

But can you use different animals for the same purpose, unless they are bred and fed in the same way?

You cannot.

Then, if women are to have the same duties as men, they must have the same nurture and education?

Yes.

The education which was assigned to the men was music and gymnastic.

Yes.

Then women must be taught music and gymnastic and also the art of war, which they must practice like the men?

That is the inference, I suppose.

I should rather expect, I said, that several of our proposals, if they are carried out, being unusual, may appear ridiculous.

No doubt of it.

Yes, and the most ridiculous thing of all will be the sight of women naked in the palaestra, exercising with the men, especially when they are no longer young; they certainly will not be a vision of beauty, any more than the enthusiastic old men who in spite of wrinkles and ugliness continue to frequent the gymnasia.

Yes, indeed, he said: according to present notions the proposal would be thought ridiculous.

But then, I said, as we have determined to speak our minds, we must not fear the jests of the wits which will be directed against this sort of innovation; how they will talk of women's attainments both in music and gymnastic, and above all about their wearing armour and riding upon horseback!

Very true, he replied.

Yet having begun we must go forward to the rough places of the law; at the same time begging of these gentlemen for once in their life to be serious. Not long ago, as we shall remind them, the Hellenes were of the opinion, which is still generally received

---

From *Republic,* trans. B. Jowett, 3d ed. (Oxford University Press, 1892). Notes have been deleted.

among the barbarians, that the sight of a naked man was ridiculous and improper; and when first the Cretans and then the Lacedaemonians introduced the custom, the wits of that day might equally have ridiculed the innovation.

No doubt.

But when experience showed that to let all things be uncovered was far better than to cover them up, and the ludicrous effect to the outward eye vanished before the better principle which reason asserted, then the man was perceived to be a fool who directs the shafts of his ridicule at any other sight but that of folly and vice, or seriously inclines to weigh the beautiful by any other standard but that of the good.

Very true, he replied.

First, then, whether the question is to be put in jest or in earnest, let us come to an understanding about the nature of woman: Is she capable of sharing either wholly or partially in the actions of men, or not at all? And is the art of war one of those arts in which she can or cannot share? That will be the best way of commencing the enquiry, and will probably lead to the fairest conclusion.

That will be much the best way.

Shall we take the other side first and begin by arguing against ourselves; in this manner the adversary's position will not be undefended.

Why not? he said.

Then let us put a speech into the mouths of our opponents. They will say: 'Socrates and Glaucon, no adversary need convict you, for you yourselves, at the first foundation of the State, admitted the principle that everybody was to do the one work suited to his own nature.' And certainly, if I am not mistaken, such an admission was made by us. 'And do not the natures of men and women differ very much indeed?' And we shall reply: Of course they do. Then we shall be asked, 'Whether the tasks assigned to men and to women should not be different, and such as are agreeable to their different natures?' Certainly they should. 'But if so, have you not fallen into a serious inconsistency in saying that men and women, whose natures are so entirely different, ought to perform the same actions?'— What defense will you make for us, my good Sir, against any one who offers these objections?

That is not an easy question to answer when asked suddenly; and I shall and I do beg of you to draw out the case on our side.

These are the objections, Glaucon, and there are many others of a like kind, which I foresaw long ago; they made me afraid and reluctant to take in hand any law about the possession and nurture of women and children.

By Zeus, he said, the problem to be solved is anything but easy.

Why yes, I said, but the fact is that when a man is out of his depth, whether he has fallen into a little swimming bath or into mid ocean, he has to swim all the same.

Very true.

And must not we swim and try to reach the shore: we will hope that Arion's dolphin or some other miraculous help may save us?

I suppose so, he said.

Well then, let us see if any way of escape can be found. We acknowledged—did we not? that different natures ought to have different pursuits, and that men's and women's natures are different. And now what are we saying?—that different natures ought to have the same pursuits,—this is the inconsistency which is charged upon us.

Precisely.

Verily, Glaucon, I said, glorious is the power of the art of contradiction!

Why do you say so?

Because I think that many a man falls into the practice against his will. When he thinks that he is reasoning he is really disputing, just because he cannot define and divide, and so know that of which he is speaking; and he will pursue a merely verbal opposition in the spirit of contention and not of fair discussion.

Yes, he replied, such is very often the case; but what has that to do with us and our argument?

A great deal; for there is certainly a danger of our getting unintentionally into a verbal opposition.

In what way?

Why we valiantly and pugnaciously insist upon the verbal truth, that different natures ought to have different pursuits, but we never considered at all what was the meaning of sameness or difference of nature, or why we distinguished them when we assigned different pursuits to different natures and the same to the same natures.

Why, no, he said, that was never considered by us.

I said: Suppose that by way of illustration we were to ask the question whether there is not an opposition in nature between bald men and hairy men; and if this is admitted by us, then, if bald men are cobblers, we should forbid the hairy men to be cobblers, and conversely?

That would be a jest, he said.

Yes, I said, a jest; and why? because we never meant when we constructed the State, that the opposition of natures should extend to every difference, but only to those differences which affected the pursuit in which the individual is engaged; we should have argued, for example, that a physician and one who is in mind a physician may be said to have the same nature.

True.

Whereas the physician and the carpenter have different natures?

Certainly.

And if, I said, the male and female sex appear to differ in their fitness for any art or pursuit, we should say that such pursuit or art ought to be assigned to one or the other of them; but if the difference consists only in women bearing and men begetting children, this does not amount to a proof that a woman differs from a man in respect of the sort of education she should receive; and we shall therefore continue to maintain that our guardians and their wives ought to have the same pursuits.

Very true, he said.

Next, we shall ask our opponent how, in reference to any of the pursuits or arts of civic life, the nature of a woman differs from that of a man?

That will be quite fair.

And perhaps he, like yourself, will reply that to give a sufficient answer on the instant is not easy; but after a little reflection there is no difficulty.

Yes, perhaps.

Suppose then that we invite him to accompany us in the argument, and then we may hope to show him that there is nothing peculiar in the constitution of women which would affect them in the administration of the State.

By all means.

Let us say to him: Come now, and we will ask you a question:—when you spoke of a nature gifted or not gifted in any respect, did you mean to say that one man will acquire a thing easily, another with difficulty; a little learning will lead the one to discover a great deal; whereas the other, after much study and application, no sooner learns than he forgets; or again, did you mean, that the one has a body which is a good servant to his mind, while the body of the other is a hindrance to him?—would not these be the sort of differences which distinguish the man gifted by nature from the one who is ungifted?

No one will deny that.

And can you mention any pursuit of mankind in which the male sex has not all these gifts and qualities in a higher degree than the female? Need I waste time in speaking of the art of weaving, and the management of pancakes and preserves, in which womankind does really appear to be great, and in which for her to be beaten by a man is of all things the most absurd?

You are quite right, he replied, in maintaining the general inferiority of the female sex: although many women are in many things superior to many men, yet on the whole what you say is true.

And if so, my friend, I said, there is no special faculty of administration in a State which a woman has because she is a woman, or which a man has by virtue of his sex, but the gifts of nature are alike diffused in both; all the pursuits of men are the pursuits of women also, but in all of them a woman is inferior to a man.

Very true.

Then are we to impose all our enactments on men and none of them on women?

That will never do.

One woman has a gift of healing, another not; one is a musician, and another has no music in her nature?

Very true.

And one woman has a turn for gymnastic and military exercises, and another is unwarlike and hates gymnastics?

Certainly.

And one woman is a philosopher, and another is an enemy of philosophy; one has spirit, and another is without spirit?

That is also true.

Then one woman will have the temper of a guardian, and another not. Was not the selection of the male guardians determined by differences of this sort?

Yes.

Men and women alike possess the qualities which make a guardian; they differ only in their comparative strength or weakness.

Obviously.

And those women who have such qualities are to be selected as the companions and colleagues of men who have similar qualities and whom they resemble in capacity and in character?

Very true.

And ought not the same natures to have the same pursuits?

They ought.

Then, as we were saying before, there is

nothing unnatural in assigning music and gymnastic to the wives of the guardians—to that point we come round again.

Certainly not.

The law which we then enacted was agreeable to nature, and therefore not an impossibility or mere aspiration; and the contrary practice, which prevails at present, is in reality a violation of nature.

That appears to be true.

We had to consider, first, whether our proposals were possible, and secondly whether they were the most beneficial?

Yes.

And the possibility has been acknowledged?

Yes.

The very great benefit has next to be established?

Quite so.

You will admit that the same education which makes a man a good guardian will make a woman a good guardian; for their original nature is the same?

Yes.

I should like to ask you a question.

What is it?

Would you say that all men are equal in excellence, or is one man better than another?

The latter.

And in the commonwealth which we were founding do you conceive the guardians who have been brought up on our model system to be more perfect men, or the cobblers whose education has been cobbling?

What a ridiculous question!

You have answered me, I replied: Well, and

may we not further say that our guardians are the best of our citizens?

By far the best.

And will not their wives be the best women?

Yes, by far the best.

And can there be anything better for the interests of the State than that the men and women of a State should be as good as possible?

There can be nothing better.

And this is what the arts of music and gymnastic, when present in such manner as we have described, will accomplish?

Certainly.

Then we have made an enactment not only possible but in the highest degree beneficial to the State?

True.

Then let the wives of our guardians strip, for their virtue will be their robe, and let them share in the toils of war and the defence of their country; only in the distribution of labours the lighter are to be assigned to the women, who are the weaker natures, but in other respects their duties are to be the same. And as for the man who laughs at naked women exercising their bodies from the best of motives, in his laughter he is plucking

A fruit of unripe wisdom,

and he himself is ignorant of what he is laughing at, or what he is about;—for that is, and ever will be, the best of sayings, *That the useful is the noble and the hurtful is the base.*

Very true.

7/Reply to Plato
Aristotle

Of household management we have seen that there are three parts—one is the rule of a master over slaves, . . . another of a father, and the third of a husband. A husband and father . . . rules over wife and children, both free, but the rule differs, the rule over his children being a royal, over his wife a constitutional rule. For although there may be exceptions to the order of nature, the male is by nature fitter for command than the female, just as the elder

and full-grown is superior to the younger and more immature. But in most constitutional states the citizens rule and are ruled by turns, for the idea of a constitutional state implies that the natures of the citizens are equal, and do not differ at all. Nevertheless, when one rules and the other is ruled we endeavour to create a difference of outward forms and names and titles of respect, . . . The relation of the male to the female is of this kind, but there the

From *The Works of Aristotle,* ed. W. David Ross, trans. J. I. Beare *et al.,* vol. 10 (Oxford University Press, 1921). Footnotes have been deleted.

inequality is permanent. A question may indeed be raised, whether there is any excellence at all in a slave beyond and higher than merely instrumental and ministerial qualities—whether he can have the virtues of temperance, courage, justice, and the like; or whether slaves possess only bodily and ministerial qualities. And, whichever way we answer the question, a difficulty arises; for, if they have virtue, in what will they differ from freemen? On the other hand, since they are men and share in rational principle, it seems absurd to say that they have no virtue. A similar question may be raised about women and children, whether they too have virtues: ought a woman to be temperate and brave and just, and is a child to be called temperate, and intemperate, or not? So in general we may ask about the natural ruler, and the natural subject, whether they have the same or different virtues. For if a noble nature is equally required in both, why should one of them always rule, and the other always be ruled? Nor can we say that this is a question of degree, for the difference between ruler and subject is a difference of kind, which the difference of more and less never is. Yet how strange is the supposition that the one ought, and that the other ought not, to have virtue! For if the ruler is intemperate and unjust, how can he rule well? if the subject, how can he obey well? If he be licentious and cowardly, he will certainly not do his duty. It is evident, therefore, that both of them must have a share of virtue, but varying as natural subjects also vary among themselves. Here the very constitution of the soul has shown us the way; in it one part naturally rules, and the other is subject, and the virtue of the ruler we maintain to be different from that of the subject;—the one being the virtue of the rational, and the other of the irrational part. Now, it is obvious that the same principle applies generally, and therefore almost all things rule and are ruled according to nature. But the kind of rule differs;—the freeman rules over the slave after another manner from that in which the male rules over the female, or the man over the child; although the parts of the soul are present in all of them, they are present in different degrees. For the slave has no deliberative faculty at all; the woman has, but it is without authority, and the child has, but it is immature. So it must necessarily be supposed to be with the moral virtues also; all should partake of them, but only in such manner and degree as is required by each for the fulfilment of his duty. Hence the ruler ought to have moral virtue in perfection, for his function, taken absolutely, demands a master artificer,

and rational principle is such an artificer; the subjects, on the other hand, require only that measure of virtue which is proper to each of them. Clearly, then, moral virtue belongs to all of them; but the temperance of a man and of a woman, or the courage and justice of a man and of a woman, are not, as Socrates maintained, the same; the courage of a man is shown in commanding, of a woman in obeying. And this holds of all other virtues, as will be more clearly seen if we look at them in detail. . . . All classes must be deemed to have their special attributes; as the poet says of women,

Silence is a woman's glory,

but this is not equally the glory of man. The child is imperfect, and therefore obviously his virtue is not relative to himself alone, but to the perfect man and to his teacher, and in like manner the virtue of the slave is relative to a master. Now we determined that a slave is useful for the wants of life, and therefore he will obviously require only so much virtue as will prevent him from failing in his duty through cowardice or lack of self-control. . . . the slave shares in his master's life; the artisan is less closely connected with him, and only attains excellence in proportion as he becomes a slave. The meaner sort of mechanic has a special and separate slavery; and whereas the slave exists by nature, not so the shoemaker or other artisan. It is manifest, then, that the master ought to be the source of such excellence in the slave, and not a mere possessor of the art of mastership which trains the slave in his duties. Wherefore they are mistaken who forbid us to converse with slaves and say that we should employ command only, for slaves stand even more in need of admonition than children.

So much for this subject; the relations of husband and wife, parent and child, their several virtues, what in their intercourse with one another is good, and what is evil, will have to be discussed when we speak of the different forms of government. For, inasmuch as every family is a part of a state, and these relationships are the parts of a family, and the virtue of the part must have regard to the virtue of the whole, women and children must be trained by education with an eye to the constitution, if the virtues of either of them are supposed to make any difference in the virtues of the state. And they must make a difference: for the children grow up to be citizens, and half the free persons in a state are women.

8/Femininity

Sigmund Freud

It might be thought indeed that this first love-relation of the child's is doomed to dissolution for the very reason that it is the first, for these early object-cathexes are regularly ambivalent to a high degree. A powerful tendency to aggressiveness is always present beside a powerful love, and the more passionately a child loves its object the more sensitive does it become to disappointments and frustrations from that object; and in the end the love must succumb to the accumulated hostility. Or the idea that there is an original ambivalence such as this in erotic cathexes may be rejected, and it may be pointed out that it is the special nature of the mother-child relation that leads, with equal inevitability, to the destruction of the child's love; for even the mildest upbringing cannot avoid using compulsion and introducing restrictions, and any such intervention in the child's liberty must provoke as a reaction an inclination to rebelliousness and aggressiveness. A discussion of these possibilities might, I think, be most interesting; but an objection suddenly emerges which forces our interest in another direction. All these factors—the slights, the disappointments in love, the jealousy, the seduction followed by prohibition—are, after all, also in operation in the relation of a *boy* to his mother and are yet unable to alienate him from the maternal object. Unless we can find something that is specific for girls and is not present or not in the same way present in boys, we shall not have explained the termination of the attachment of girls to their mother.

I believe we have found this specific factor, and indeed where we expected to find it, even though in a surprising form. Where we expected to find it, I say, for it lies in the castration complex. After all, the anatomical distinction [between the sexes] must express itself in physical consequences. It was, however, a surprise to learn from analyses that girls hold their mother responsible for their lack of a penis and do not forgive her for their being thus put at a disadvantage.

As you hear, then, we ascribe a castration complex to women as well. And for good reasons, though its content cannot be the same as with boys. In the latter the castration complex arises after they have learnt from the sight of the female genitals that the organ which they value so highly need not necessarily accompany the body. At this the boy recalls to mind the threats he brought on himself by his doings with that organ, he begins to give credence to them and falls under the influence of fear of castration, which will be the most powerful motive force in his subsequent development. The castration complex of girls is also started by the sight of the genitals of the other sex. They at once notice the difference and, it must be admitted, its significance too. They feel seriously wronged, often declare that they want to 'have something like it too', and fall a victim to 'envy for the penis', which will leave ineradicable traces on their development and the formation of their character and which will not be surmounted in even the most favourable cases without a severe expenditure of psychical energy. The girl's recognition of the fact of her being without a penis does not by any means imply that she submits to the fact easily. On the contrary, she continues to hold on for a long time to the wish to get something like it herself and she believes in that possibility for improbably long years; and analysis can show that, at a period when knowledge of reality has long since rejected the fulfilment of the wish as unattainable, it persists in the unconscious and retains a considerable cathexis of energy. The wish to get the longed-for penis eventually in spite of everything may contribute to the motives that drive a mature woman to analysis, and what she may reasonably expect from analysis—a capacity, for instance, to carry on an intellectual profession—may often be recognized as a sublimated modification of this repressed wish.

One cannot very well doubt the importance of envy for the penis. You may take it as an instance of

From *New Introductory Lectures on Psychoanalysis* by Sigmund Freud. Translated and edited by James Strachey. Copyright © 1965, 1964 by James Strachey. Reprinted by permission of W. W. Norton & Company, Inc. Bracketed footnotes are by the translator.

male injustice if I assert that envy and jealousy play an even greater part in the mental life of women than of men. It is not that I think these characteristics are absent in men or that I think they have no other roots in women than envy for the penis; but I am inclined to attribute their greater amount in women to this latter influence. Some analysts, however, have shown an inclination to depreciate the importance of this first instalment of penis-envy in the phallic phase. They are of opinion that what we find of this attitude in women is in the main a secondary structure which has come about on the occasion of later conflicts by regression to this early infantile impulse. This, however, is a general problem of depth psychology. In many pathological—or even unusual—instinctual attitudes (for instance, in all sexual perversions) the question arises of how much of their strength is to be attributed to early infantile fixations and how much to the influence of later experiences and developments. In such cases it is almost always a matter of complemental series such as we put forward in our discussion of the aetiology of the neuroses.[1] Both factors play a part in varying amounts in the causation; a less on the one side is balanced by a more on the other. The infantile factor sets the pattern in all cases but does not always determine the issue, though it often does. Precisely in the case of penis-envy I should argue decidedly in favour of the preponderance of the infantile factor.

The discovery that she is castrated is a turning-point in a girl's growth. Three possible lines of development start from it: one leads to sexual inhibition or to neurosis, the second to change of character in the sense of a masculinity complex, the third, finally, to normal femininity. We have learnt a fair amount, though not everything, about all three.

The essential content of the first is as follows: the little girl has hitherto lived in a masculine way, has been able to get pleasure by the excitation of her clitoris and has brought this activity into relation with her sexual wishes directed towards her mother, which are often active ones; now, owing to the influence of her penis-envy, she loses her enjoyment in her phallic sexuality. Her self-love is mortified by the comparison with the boy's far superior equipment and in consequence she renounces her masturbatory satisfaction from her clitoris, repudiates her love for her mother and at the same time not infrequently represses a good part of her sexual trends in general. No doubt her turning away from her mother

does not occur all at once, for to begin with the girl regards her castration as an individual misfortune, and only gradually extends it to other females and finally to her mother as well. Her love was directed to her *phallic* mother; with the discovery that her mother is castrated it becomes possible to drop her as an object, so that the motives for hostility, which have long been accumulating, gain the upper hand. This means, therefore, that as a result of the discovery of women's lack of a penis they are debased in value for girls just as they are for boys and later perhaps for men.

You all know the immense aetiological importance attributed by our neurotic patients to their masturbation. They make it responsible for all their troubles and we have the greatest difficulty in persuading them that they are mistaken. In fact, however, we ought to admit to them that they are right, for masturbation is the executive agent of infantile sexuality, from the faulty development of which they are indeed suffering. But what neurotics mostly blame is the masturbation of the period of puberty; they have mostly forgotten that of early infancy, which is what is really in question. I wish I might have an opportunity some time of explaining to you at length how important all the factual details of early masturbation become for the individual's subsequent neurosis or character: whether or not it was discovered, how the parents struggled against it or permitted it, or whether he succeeded in suppressing it himself. All of this leaves permanent traces on his development. But I am on the whole glad that I need not do this. It would be a hard and tedious task and at the end of it you would put me in an embarrassing situation by quite certainly asking me to give you some practical advice as to how a parent or educator should deal with the masturbation of small children.[2] From the development of girls, which is what my present lecture is concerned with, I can give you the example of a child herself trying to get free from masturbating. She does not always succeed in this. If envy for the penis has provoked a powerful impulse against clitoridal masturbation but this nevertheless refuses to give way, a violent struggle for liberation ensues in which the girl, as it were, herself takes over the role of her deposed mother and gives expression to her entire dissatisfaction with her inferior clitoris in her efforts against obtaining satisfaction from it. Many years later,

---

[1] [See *Introductory Lectures*, XXII and XXIII.]

[2] [Freud's fullest discussion of masturbation was in his contributions to a symposium on the subject in the Vienna Psycho-Analytical Society (1912).]

when her masturbatory activity has long since been suppressed, an interest still persists which we must interpret as a defence against a temptation that is still dreaded. It manifests itself in the emergence of sympathy for those to whom similar difficulties are attributed, it plays a part as a motive in contracting a marriage and, indeed, it may determine the choice of a husband or lover. Disposing of early infantile masturbation is truly no easy or indifferent business.

Along with the abandonment of clitoridal masturbation a certain amount of activity is renounced. Passivity now has the upper hand, and the girl's turning to her father is accomplished principally with the help of passive instinctual impulses. You can see that a wave of development like this, which clears the phallic activity out of the way, smooths the ground for femininity. If too much is not lost in the course of it through repression, this femininity may turn out to be normal. The wish with which the girl turns to her father is no doubt originally the wish for the penis which her mother has refused her and which she now expects from her father. The feminine situation is only established, however, if the wish for a penis is replaced by one for a baby, if, that is, a baby takes the place of a penis in accordance with an ancient symbolic equivalence. . . . It has not escaped us that the girl has wished for a baby earlier, in the undisturbed phallic phase: that, of course, was the meaning of her playing with dolls. But that play was not in fact an expression of her femininity; it served as an identification with her mother with the intention of substituting activity for passivity. *She* was playing the part of her mother and the doll was herself: now she could do with the baby everything that her mother used to do with her. Not until the emergence of the wish for a penis does the doll-baby become a baby from the girl's father, and thereafter the aim of the most powerful feminine wish. Her happiness is great if later on this wish for a baby finds fulfilment in reality, and quite especially so if the baby is a little boy who brings the longed-for penis with him.[3] Often enough in her combined picture of 'a baby from her father' the emphasis is laid on the baby and her father left unstressed. In this way the ancient masculine wish for the possession of a penis is still faintly visible through the femininity now achieved. But perhaps we ought rather to recognize this wish for a penis as being *par excellence* a feminine one.

With the transference of the wish for a penis-

[3][See p. 51 below.]

baby on to her father, the girl has entered the situation of the Oedipus complex. Her hostility to her mother, which did not need to be freshly created, is now greatly intensified, for she becomes the girl's rival, who receives from her father everything that she desires from him. For a long time the girl's Oedipus complex concealed her pre-Oedipus attachment to her mother from our view, though it is nevertheless so important and leaves such lasting fixations behind it. For girls the Oedipus situation is the outcome of a long and difficult development; it is a kind of preliminary solution, a position of rest which is not soon abandoned, especially as the beginning of the latency period is not far distant. And we are now struck by a difference between the two sexes, which is probably momentous, in regard to the relation of the Oedipus complex to the castration complex. In a boy the Oedipus complex, in which he desires his mother and would like to get rid of his father as being a rival, develops naturally from the phase of his phallic sexuality. The threat of castration compels him, however, to give up that attitude. Under the impression of the danger of losing his penis, the Oedipus complex is abandoned, repressed and, in the most normal cases, entirely destroyed . . . and a severe super-ego is set up as its heir. What happens with a girl is almost the opposite. The castration complex prepares for the Oedipus complex instead of destroying it; the girl is driven out of her attachment to her mother through the influence of her envy for the penis and she enters the Oedipus situation as though into a haven of refuge. In the absence of fear of castration the chief motive is lacking which leads boys to surmount the Oedipus complex. Girls remain in it for an indeterminate length of time; they demolish it late and, even so, incompletely. In these circumstances the formation of the super-ego must suffer; it cannot attain the strength and independence which give it its cultural significance, and feminists are not pleased when we point out to them the effects of this factor upon the average feminine character.

To go back a little. We mentioned [p. 48] as the second possible reaction to the discovery of female castration the development of a powerful masculinity complex. By this we mean that the girl refuses, as it were, to recognize the unwelcome fact and, defiantly rebellious, even exaggerates her previous masculinity, clings to her clitoridal activity and takes refuge in an identification with her phallic mother or her father. What can it be that decides in favour of this outcome? We can only suppose that it is a constitutional factor, a greater amount of activity, such as is ordinarily characteristic of a male. However that may be, the essence of this process is that at this point in development the wave of passivity is avoided which opens the way to the turn towards femininity. The extreme achievement of such a masculinity complex would appear to be the influencing of the choice of an object in the sense of manifest homosexuality. Analytic experience teaches us, to be sure, that female homosexuality is seldom or never a direct continuation of infantile masculinity. Even for a girl of this kind it seems necessary that she should take her father as an object for some time and enter the Oedipus situation. But afterwards, as a result of her inevitable disappointments from her father, she is driven to regress into her early masculinity complex. The significance of these disappointments must not be exaggerated; a girl who is destined to become feminine is not spared them, though they do not have the same effect. The predominance of the constitutional factor seems indisputable; but the two phases in the development of female homosexuality are well mirrored in the practices of homosexuals, who play the parts of mother and baby with each other as often and as clearly as those of husband and wife. . . .

It is not my intention to pursue the further behaviour of femininity through puberty to the period of maturity. Our knowledge, moreover, would be insufficient for the purpose. But I will bring a few features together in what follows. Taking its prehistory as a starting-point, I will only emphasize here that the development of femininity remains exposed to disturbance by the residual phenomena of the early masculine period. Regressions to the fixations of the pre-Oedipus phases very frequently occur; in the course of some women's lives there is a repeated alternation between periods in which masculinity or femininity gains the upper hand. Some portion of what we men call 'the enigma of women' may perhaps be derived from this expression of bisexuality in women's lives. But another question seems to have become ripe for judgement in the course of these researches. We have called the motive force of sexual life 'the libido'. Sexual life is dominated by the polarity of masculine–feminine; thus the notion suggests itself of considering the relation of the libido to this antithesis. It would not be surprising if it were to turn out that each sexuality had its own special libido appropriated to it, so that one sort of libido would pursue the aims of a masculine sexual

life and another sort those of a feminine one. But nothing of the kind is true. There is only one libido, which serves both the masculine and the feminine sexual functions. To it itself we cannot assign any sex; if, following the conventional equation of activity and masculinity, we are inclined to describe it as masculine, we must not forget that it also covers trends with a passive aim. Nevertheless the juxtaposition 'feminine libido' is without any justification. Furthermore, it is our impression that more constraint has been applied to the libido when it is pressed into the service of the feminine function, and that—to speak teleologically—Nature takes less careful account of its [that function's] demands than in the case of masculinity. And the reason for this may lie—thinking once again teleologically—in the fact that the accomplishment of the aim of biology has been entrusted to the aggressiveness of men and has been made to some extent independent of women's consent.

The sexual frigidity of women, the frequency of which appears to confirm this disregard, is a phenomenon that is still insufficiently understood. Sometimes it is psychogenic and in that case accessible to influence; but in other cases it suggests the hypothesis of its being constitutionally determined and even of there being a contributory anatomical factor.

I have promised to tell you of a few more psychical peculiarities of mature femininity, as we come across them in analytic observation. We do not lay claim to more than an average validity for these assertions; nor is it always easy to distinguish what should be ascribed to the influence of the sexual function and what to social breeding. Thus, we attribute a larger amount of narcissism to femininity, which also affects women's choice of object, so that to be loved is a stronger need for them than to love. The effect of penis-envy has a share, further, in the physical vanity of women, since they are bound to value their charms more highly as a late compensation for their original sexual inferiority.[4] Shame, which is considered to be a feminine characteristic *par excellence* but is far more a matter of convention than might be supposed, has as its purpose, we believe, concealment of genital deficiency. We are not forgetting that at a later time shame takes on other functions. It seems that women have made few contributions to the discoveries and inventions in the history of civilization; there is, however, one

[4][Cf. Section II of 'On Narcissism' (1914).]

technique which they may have invented—that of plaiting and weaving. If that is so, we should be tempted to guess the unconscious motive for the achievement. Nature herself would seem to have given the model which this achievement imitates by causing the growth at maturity of the pubic hair that conceals the genitals. The step that remained to be taken lay in making the threads adhere to one another, while on the body they stick into the skin and are only matted together. If you reject this idea as fantastic and regard my belief in the influence of lack of a penis on the configuration of femininity as an *idée fixe*, I am of course defenceless.

The determinants of women's choice of an object are often made unrecognizable by social conditions. Where the choice is able to show itself freely, it is often made in accordance with the narcissistic ideal of the man whom the girl had wished to become. If the girl has remained in her attachment to her father—that is, in the Oedipus complex— her choice is made according to the paternal type. Since, when she turned from her mother to her father, the hostility of her ambivalent relation remained with her mother, a choice of this kind should guarantee a happy marriage. But very often the outcome is of a kind that presents a general threat to such a settlement of the conflict due to ambivalence. The hostility that has been left behind follows in the train of the positive attachment and spreads over on to the new object. The woman's husband, who to begin with inherited from her father, becomes after a time her mother's heir as well. So it may easily happen that the second half of a woman's life may be filled by the struggle against her husband, just as the shorter first half was filled by her rebellion against her mother. When this reaction has been lived through, a second marriage may easily turn out very much more satisfying.[5] Another alteration in a woman's nature, for which lovers are unprepared, may occur in a marriage after the first child is born. Under the influence of a woman's becoming a mother herself, an identification with her own mother may be revived, against which she had striven up till the time of her marriage, and this may attract all the available libido to itself, so that the compulsion to repeat reproduces an unhappy marriage between her parents. The difference in a mother's reaction to the birth of a son or a daughter shows that the old factor of lack of a penis has even now not lost its

strength. A mother is only brought unlimited satisfaction by her relation to a son; this is altogether the most perfect, the most free from ambivalence of all human relationships.[6] A mother can transfer to her son the ambition which she has been obliged to suppress in herself, and she can expect from him the satisfaction of all that has been left over in her of her masculinity complex. Even a marriage is not made secure until the wife has succeeded in making her husband her child as well and in acting as a mother to him.

A woman's identification with her mother allows us to distinguish two strata: the pre-Oedipus one which rests on her affectionate attachment to her mother and takes her as a model, and the later one from the Oedipus complex which seeks to get rid of her mother and take her place with her father. We are no doubt justified in saying that much of both of them is left over for the future and that neither of them is adequately surmounted in the course of development. But the phase of the affectionate pre-Oedipus attachment is the decisive one for a woman's future: during it preparations are made for the acquisition of the characteristics with which she will later fulfil her role in the sexual function and perform her invaluable social tasks. It is in this identification too that she acquires her attractiveness to a man, whose Oedipus attachment to his mother it kindles into passion. How often it happens, however, that it is only his son who obtains what he himself aspired to! One gets an impression that a man's love and a woman's are a phase apart psychologically.

The fact that women must be regarded as having little sense of justice is no doubt related to the predominance of envy in their mental life; for the demand for justice is a modification of envy and lays down the condition subject to which one can put envy aside. We also regard women as weaker in their social interests and as having less capacity for sublimating their instincts than men. The former is no doubt derived from the dissocial quality which unquestionably characterizes all sexual relations. Lovers find sufficiency in each other, and families too resist inclusion in more comprehensive associations.[7] The aptitude for sublimation is subject to the greatest individual variations. On the

---

[5][This had already been remarked upon earlier, in 'The Taboo of Virginity' (1918).]

[6][This point seems to have been made by Freud first in a footnote to Chapter VI of *Group Psychology* (1921). He repeated it in the *Introductory Lectures*, XIII, and in Chapter V of *Civilization and its Discontents* (1930). . . .]

[7][Cf. some remarks on this in Chapter XII (D) of *Group Psychology* (1921).]

other hand I cannot help mentioning an impression that we are constantly receiving during analytic practice. A man of about thirty strikes us as a youthful, somewhat unformed individual, whom we expect to make powerful use of the possibilities for development opened up to him by analysis. A woman of the same age, however, often frightens us by her psychical rigidity and unchangeability. Her libido has taken up final positions and seems incapable of exchanging them for others. There are no paths open to further development; it is as though the whole process had already run its course and remains thenceforward insusceptible to influence —as though, indeed, the difficult development to femininity had exhausted the possibilities of the person concerned. As therapists we lament this state of things, even if we succeed in putting an end to our patient's ailment by doing away with her neurotic conflict.

That is all I had to say to you about femininity. It is certainly incomplete and fragmentary and does not always sound friendly. But do not forget that I have only been describing women in so far as their nature is determined by their sexual function. It is true that that influence extends very far; but we do not overlook the fact that an individual woman may be a human being in other respects as well. If you want to know more about femininity, enquire from your own experiences of life, or turn to the poets, or wait until science can give you deeper and more coherent information.

9/The Nature of Women

John Stuart Mill

Neither does it avail anything to say that the *nature* of the two sexes adapts them to their present functions and position, and renders these appropriate to them. Standing on the ground of common sense and the constitution of the human mind, I deny that anyone knows, or can know, the nature of the two sexes, as long as they have only been seen in their present relation to one another. If men had ever been found in society without women, or women without men, or if there had been a society of men and women in which the women were not under the control of the men, something might have been positively known about the mental and moral differences which may be inherent in the nature of each. What is now called the nature of women is an eminently artificial thing—the result of forced repression in some directions, unnatural stimulation in others. It may be asserted without scruple, that no other class of dependents have had their character so entirely distorted from its natural proportions by their relation with their masters; for, if conquered and slave races have been, in some respects, more forcibly repressed, whatever in them has not been crushed down by an iron heel has generally been let alone, and if left with any liberty of development, it has developed itself according to its own laws; but in the case of women, a hothouse and stove cultivation has always been carried on of some of the capabilities of their nature, for the benefit and pleasure of their masters. Then, because certain products of the general vital force sprout luxuriantly and reach a great development in this heated atmosphere and under this active nurture and watering, while other shoots from the same root, which are left outside in the wintry air, with ice purposely heaped all round them, have a stunted growth, and some are burnt off with fire and disappear; men, with that inability to recognise their own work which distinguishes the unanalytic mind, indolently believe that the tree grows of itself in the way they have made it grow, and that it would die if one half of it were not kept in a vapour bath and the other half in the snow.

Of all difficulties which impede the progress of thought, and the formation of well-grounded opinions on life and social arrangements, the greatest is now the unspeakable ignorance and inattention of mankind in respect to the influences which form human character. Whatever any portion of

From *The Subjection of Women* (London, 1869).

the human species now are, or seem to be, such, it is supposed, they have a natural tendency to be: even when the most elementary knowledge of the circumstances in which they have been placed, clearly points out the causes that made them what they are. . . .

Hence, in regard to that most difficult question, what are the natural differences between the two sexes—a subject on which it is impossible in the present state of society to obtain complete and correct knowledge—while almost everybody dogmatizes upon it, almost all neglect and make light of the only means by which any partial insight can be obtained into it. This is, an analytic study of the most important department of psychology, the laws of the influence of circumstances on character. For, however great and apparently ineradicable the moral and intellectual differences between men and women might be, the evidence of their being natural differences could only be negative. Those only could be inferred to be natural which could not possibly be artificial—the residuum, after deducting every characteristic of either sex which can admit of being explained from education or external circumstances. The profoundest knowledge of the laws of the formation of character is indispensable to entitle anyone to affirm even that there is any difference, much more what the difference is, between the two sexes considered as moral and rational beings; and since no one, as yet, has that knowledge, (for there is hardly any subject which, in proportion to its importance, has been so little studied), no one is thus far entitled to any positive opinion on the subject. Conjectures are all that can at present be made; conjectures more or less probable, according as more or less authorized by such knowledge as we yet have of the laws of psychology, as applied to the formation of character.

Even the preliminary knowledge, what the differences between the sexes now are, apart from all questions as to how they are made what they are, is still in the crudest and most incomplete state. Medical practitioners and physiologists have ascertained, to some extent, the differences in bodily constitution; and this is an important element to the psychologist: but hardly any medical practitioner is a psychologist. Respecting the mental characteristics of women; their observations are of no more worth than those of common men. It is a subject on which nothing final can be known, so long as those who alone can really know it, women themselves, have given but little testimony, and that little, mostly sub-

orned. It is easy to know stupid women. Stupidity is much the same all the world over. A stupid person's notions and feelings may confidently be inferred from those which prevail in the circle by which the person is surrounded. Not so with those whose opinions and feelings are an emanation from their own nature and faculties. It is only a man here and there who has any tolerable knowledge of the character even of the women of his own family. I do not mean, of their capabilities; these nobody knows, not even themselves, because most of them have never been called out. I mean their actually existing thoughts and feelings. Many a man thinks he perfectly understands women, because he has had amatory relations with several, perhaps with many of them. If he is a good observer, and his experience extends to quality as well as quantity, he may have learnt something of one narrow department of their nature—an important department, no doubt. But of all the rest of it, few persons are generally more ignorant, because there are few from whom it is so carefully hidden. The most favourable case which a man can generally have for studying the character of a woman, is that of his own wife: for the opportunities are greater, and the cases of complete sympathy not so unspeakably rare. And in fact, this is the source from which any knowledge worth having on the subject has, I believe, generally come. But most men have not had the opportunity of studying in this way more than a single case: accordingly one can, to an almost laughable degree, infer what a man's wife is like, from his opinions about women in general. To make even this one case yield any result, the woman must be worth knowing, and the man not only a competent judge, but of a character so sympathetic in itself, and so well adapted to hers, that he can either read her mind by sympathetic intuition, or has nothing in himself which makes her shy of disclosing it. Hardly anything, I believe, can be more rare than this conjunction. It often happens that there is the most complete unity of feeling and community of interests as to all external things, yet the one has as little admission into the internal life of the other as if they were common acquaintance. Even with true affection, authority on the one side and subordination on the other prevent perfect confidence. Though nothing may be intentionally withheld, much is not shown. In the analogous relation of parent and child, the corresponding phenomenon must have been in the observation of everyone. As between father and son, how many are the cases in which the father, in spite of real affection on both sides, obviously to all the world does not know, nor suspect, parts of the son's character familiar to his companions and equals. The truth is, that the position of looking up to another is extremely unpropitious to complete sincerity and openness with him. The fear of losing ground in his opinion or in his feelings is so strong, that even in an upright character, there is an unconscious tendency to show only the best side, or the side which, though not the best, is that which he most likes to see: and it may be confidently said that thorough knowledge of one another hardly ever exists, but between persons who, besides being intimates, are equals. How much more true, then, must all this be, when the one is not only under the authority of the other, but has it inculcated on her as a duty to reckon everything else subordinate to his comfort and pleasure, and to let him neither see nor feel anything coming from her, except what is agreeable to him. All these difficulties stand in the way of a man's obtaining any thorough knowledge even of the one woman whom alone, in general, he has sufficient opportunity of studying. When we further consider that to understand one woman is not necessarily to understand any other woman; that even if he could study many women of one rank, or of one country, he would not thereby understand women of other ranks or countries; and even if he did, they are still only the women of a single period of history; we may safely assert that the knowledge which men can acquire of women, even as they have been and are, without reference to what they might be, is wretchedly imperfect and superficial, and always will be so, until women themselves have told all that they have to tell.

And this time has not come; nor will it come otherwise than gradually. It is but of yesterday that women have either been qualified by literary accomplishments, or permitted by society, to tell anything to the general public. As yet very few of them dare tell anything, which men, on whom their literary success depends, are unwilling to hear. Let us remember in what manner, up to a very recent time, the expression, even by a male author, of uncustomary opinions, or what are deemed eccentric feelings, usually was, and in some degree still is, received; and we may form some faint conception under what impediments a woman, who is brought up to think custom and opinion her sovereign rule, attempts to express in books anything drawn from the depths of her own nature. The greatest woman who has left writings behind her sufficient to give her an eminent rank in the literature of her country,

thought it necessary to prefix as a motto to her boldest work, "Un homme peut braver l'opinion; une femme doit s'y soumettre."[1] The greater part of what women write about women is mere sycophancy to men. In the case of unmarried women, much of it seems only intended to increase their chance of a husband. Many, both married and unmarried, overstep the mark, and inculcate a servility beyond what is desired or relished by any man, except the very vulgarest. But this is not so often the case as, even at a quite late period, it still was. Literary women are becoming more freespoken, and more willing to express their real sentiments. Unfortunately, in this country especially, they are themselves such artificial products, that their sentiments are compounded of a small element of individual observation and consciousness, and a very large one of acquired associations. This will be less and less the case, but it will remain true to a great extent, as long as social institutions do not admit the same free development of originality in women which is possible to men. When that time comes, and not before, we shall see, and not merely hear, as much as it is necessary to know of the nature of women, and the adaptation of other things to it.

I have dwelt so much on the difficulties which at present obstruct any real knowledge by men of the true nature of women, because in this as in so many other things "opinio copiae inter maximas causas inopiae est"; and there is little chance of reasonable thinking on the matter, while people flatter themselves that they perfectly understand a subject of which most men know absolutely nothing, and of which it is at present impossible that any man, or all men taken together, should have knowledge which can qualify them to lay down the law to women as to what is, or is not, their vocation. Happily, no such knowledge is necessary for any practical purpose connected with the position of women in relation to society and life. For, according to all the principles involved in modern society, the question rests with women themselves—to be decided by their own experience, and by the use of their own faculties. There are no means of finding what either one person or many can do, but by trying—and no means by which anyone else can discover for them what it is for their happiness to do or leave undone.

One thing we may be certain of—that what is contrary to women's nature to do, they never will be made to do by simply giving their nature free play.

---

[1]Title page of Mme. de Stael's "Delphine."

The anxiety of mankind to interfere in behalf of nature, for fear lest nature should not succeed in effecting its purpose, is an altogether unnecessary solicitude. What women by nature cannot do, it is quite superfluous to forbid them from doing. What they can do, but not so well as the men who are their competitors, competition suffices to exclude them from; since nobody asks for protective duties and bounties in favour of women; it is only asked that the present bounties and protective duties in favour of men should be recalled. If women have a greater natural inclination for some things than for others, there is no need of laws or social inculcation to make the majority of them do the former in preference to the latter. Whatever women's services are most wanted for, the free play of competition will hold out the strongest inducements to them to undertake. And, as the words imply, they are most wanted for the things for which they are most fit; by the apportionment of which to them, the collective faculties of the two sexes can be applied on the whole with the greatest sum of valuable result.

The general opinion of men is supposed to be, that the natural vocation of a woman is that of a wife and mother. I say, is supposed to be, because, judging from acts—from the whole of the present constitution of society—one might infer that their opinion was the direct contrary. They might be supposed to think that the alleged natural vocation of women was of all things the most repugnant to their nature; insomuch that if they are free to do anything else—if any other means of living, or occupation of their time and faculties, is open, which has any chance of appearing desirable to them—there will not be enough of them who will be willing to accept the condition said to be natural to them. If this is the real opinion of men in general, it would be well that it should be spoken out. I should like to hear somebody openly enunciating the doctrine (it is already implied in much that is written on the subject)—"It is necessary to society that women should marry and produce children. They will not do so unless they are compelled. Therefore it is necessary to compel them." The merits of the case would then be clearly defined. It would be exactly that of the slaveholders of South Carolina and Louisiana. "It is necessary that cotton and sugar should be grown. White men cannot produce them. Negroes will not, for any wages which we choose to give. *Ergo* they must be compelled." An illustration still closer to the point is that of impressment. Sailors must absolutely be had to defend the country. It

often happens that they will not voluntarily enlist. Therefore there must be the power of forcing them. How often has this logic been used! and, but for one flaw in it, without doubt it would have been successful up to this day. But it is open to the retort—First pay the sailors the honest value of their labour. When you have made it as well worth their while to serve you, as to work for other employers, you will have no more difficulty than others have in obtaining their services. To this there is no logical answer except "I will not": and as people are now not only ashamed, but are not desirous, to rob the labourer of his hire, impressment is no longer advocated. Those who attempt to force women into marriage by closing all other doors against them, lay themselves open to a similar retort. If they mean what they say, their opinion must evidently be, that men do not render the married condition so desirable to women, as to induce them to accept it for its own recommendations. It is not a sign of one's thinking the boon one offers very attractive, when one allows only Hobson's choice, "that or none." And here, I believe, is the clue to the feelings of those men, who have a real antipathy to the equal freedom of women. I believe they are afraid, not lest women should be unwilling to marry, for I do not think that anyone in reality has that apprehension; but lest they should insist that marriage should be on equal conditions; lest all women of spirit and capacity should prefer doing almost anything else, not in their own eyes degrading, rather than marry, when marrying is giving themselves a master, and a master too of all their earthly possessions. And truly, if this consequence were necessarily incident to marriage, I think that the apprehension would be very well founded. I agree in thinking it probable that few women, capable of anything else, would, unless under an irresistible *entrainement*, rendering them for the time insensible to anything but itself, choose such a lot, when any other means were open to them of filling a conventionally honourable place in life: and if men are determined that the law of marriage shall be a law of despotism, they are quite right, in point of mere policy, in leaving to women only Hobson's choice. But in that case, all that has been done in the modern world to relax the chain on the minds of women, has been a mistake. They never should have been allowed to receive a literary education. . . .

With regard to the fitness of women, not only to participate in elections, but themselves to hold offices or practice professions involving important public responsibilities; I have already observed that this consideration is not essential to the practical question in dispute: since any woman, who succeeds in an open profession, proves by that very fact that she is qualified for it. And in the case of public offices, if the political system of the country is such as to exclude unfit men, it will equally exclude unfit women: while if it is not, there is no additional evil in the fact that the unfit persons whom it admits may be either women or men. As long therefore as it is acknowledged that even a few women may be fit for these duties, the laws which shut the door on those exceptions cannot be justified by any opinion which can be held respecting the capacities of women in general. But, though this last consideration is not essential, it is far from being irrelevant. An unprejudiced view of it gives additional strength to the arguments against the disabilities of women, and reinforces them by high considerations of practical utility.

Let us at first make entire abstraction of all psychological considerations tending to show, that any of the mental differences supposed to exist between women and men are but the natural effect of the differences in their education and circumstances, and indicate no radical difference, far less radical inferiority, of nature. Let us consider women only as they already are, or as they are known to have been; and the capacities which they have already practically shown. What they have done, that at least, if nothing else, it is proved that they can do. When we consider how sedulously they are all trained away from, instead of being trained towards, any of the occupations or objects reserved for men, it is evident that I am taking a very humble ground for them, when I rest their case on what they have actually achieved. For, in this case, negative evidence is worth little, while any positive evidence is conclusive. It cannot be inferred to be impossible that a woman should be a Homer, or an Aristotle, or a Michael Angelo, or a Beethoven, because no woman has yet actually produced works comparable to theirs in any of those lines of excellence. This negative fact at most leaves the question uncertain, and open to psychological discussion. But it is quite certain that a woman can be a Queen Elizabeth, or a Deborah, or a Joan of Arc, since this is not inference, but fact. Now it is a curious consideration, that the only things which the existing law excludes women from doing, are the things which they have proved

that they are able to do. There is no law to prevent a woman from having written all the plays of Shakspeare, or composed all the operas of Mozart. But Queen Elizabeth or Queen Victoria, had they not inherited the throne, could not have been intrusted with the smallest of the political duties, of which the former showed herself equal to the greatest. . . .

Is it reasonable to think that those who are fit for the greater functions of politics, are incapable of qualifying themselves for the less? Is there any reason in the nature of things, that the wives and sisters of princes should, whenever called on, be found as competent as the princes themselves to *their* business, but that the wives and sisters of statesmen, and administrators, and directors of companies, and managers of public institutions, should be unable to do what is done by their brothers and husbands? The real reason is plain enough; it is that princesses, being more raised above the generality of men by their rank than placed below them by their sex, have never been taught that it was improper for them to concern themselves with politics; but have been allowed to feel the liberal interest natural to any cultivated human being, in the great transactions which took place around them, and in which they might be called on to take a part. The ladies of reigning families are the only women who are allowed the same range of interests and freedom of development as men; and it is precisely in their case that there is not found to be any inferiority. Exactly where and in proportion as women's capacities for government have been tried, in that proportion have they been found adequate.

This fact is in accordance with the best general conclusions which the world's imperfect experience seems as yet to suggest, concerning the peculiar tendencies and aptitudes characteristic of women, as women have hitherto been. I do not say, as they will continue to be; for, as I have already said more than once, I consider it presumption in any one to pretend to decide what women are or are not, can or cannot be, by natural constitution. They have always hitherto been kept, as far as regards spontaneous development, in so unnatural a state, that their nature cannot but have been greatly distorted and disguised; and no one can safely pronounce that if women's nature were left to choose its direction as freely as men's, and if no artificial bent were attempted to be given to it except that required by the conditions of human society, and given to both sexes alike, there would be any material difference, or perhaps any difference at all, in the character and capacities which would unfold themselves. I shall presently show, that even the least contestable of the differences which now exist, are such as may very well have been produced merely by circumstances, without any difference of natural capacity. But, looking at women as they are known in experience, it may be said of them, with more truth than belongs to most other generalizations on the subject, that the general bent of their talents is towards the practical. This statement is conformable to all the public history of women, in the present and the past. It is no less borne out by common and daily experience. Let us consider the special nature of the mental capacities most characteristic of a woman of talent. They are all of a kind which fits them for practice, and makes them tend towards it. What is meant by a woman's capacity of intuitive perception? It means, a rapid and correct insight into present fact. It has nothing to do with general principles. Nobody ever perceived a scientific law of nature by intuition, nor arrived at a general rule of duty or prudence by it. These are results of slow and careful collection and comparison of experience; and neither the men nor the women of intuition usually shine in this department, unless, indeed, the experience necessary is such as they can acquire by themselves. For what is called their intuitive sagacity makes them peculiarly apt in gathering such general truths as can be collected from their individual means of observation. When, consequently, they chance to be as well provided as men are with the results of other people's experience, by reading and education, (I use the word chance advisedly, for, in respect to the knowledge that tends to fit them for the greater concerns of life, the only educated women are the self-educated) they are better furnished than men in general with the essential requisites of skillful and successful practice. Men who have been much taught, are apt to be deficient in the sense of present fact; they do not see, in the facts which they are called upon to deal with, what is really there, but what they have been taught to expect. This is seldom the case with women of any ability. Their capacity of "intuition" preserves them from it. With equality of experience and of general faculties, a woman usually sees much more than a man of what is immediately before her. Now this sensibility to the present, is the main quality on which the capacity for practice, as distinguished from theory, depends. To discover general principles, belongs to the speculative faculty: to discern and discriminate the particular cases in which they are and are not applicable, constitutes practical talent: and for this, women as they now are have a peculiar aptitude. I admit that there can be no good practice without principles, and that the predominant place which quickness of observation holds among a woman's faculties, makes her particularly apt to build over-hasty generalizations upon her own observation; though at the same time no less ready in rectifying those generalizations, as her observation takes a wider range. But the corrective to this defect, is access to the experience of the human race; general knowledge—exactly the thing which education can best supply. A woman's mistakes are specifically those of a clever self-educated man, who often sees what men trained in routine do not see, but falls into errors for want of knowing things which have long been known. Of course he has acquired much of the pre-existing knowledge, or he could not have got on at all; but what he knows of it he has picked up in fragments and at random, as women do.

But this gravitation of women's minds to the present, to the real, to actual fact, while in its exclusiveness it is a source of errors, is also a most useful counteractive of the contrary error. The principal and most characteristic aberration of speculative minds as such, consists precisely in the deficiency of this lively perception and ever-present sense of objective fact. For want of this, they often not only overlook the contradiction which outward facts oppose to their theories, but lose sight of the legitimate purpose of speculation altogether, and let their speculative faculties go astray into regions not peopled with real beings, animate or inanimate, even idealized, but with personified shadows created by the illusions of metaphysics or by the mere entanglement of words, and think these shadows the proper objects of the highest, the most transcendent, philosophy. Hardly anything can be of greater value to a man of theory and speculation who employs himself not in collecting materials of knowledge by observation, but in working them up by processes of thought into comprehensive truths of science and laws of conduct, than to carry on his speculations in the companionship, and under the criticism, of a really superior woman. There is nothing comparable to it for keeping his thoughts within the limits of real things, and the actual facts of nature. A woman seldom runs wild after an abstraction. The habitual direction of her mind to dealing with things as individuals rather than in groups, and (what is closely connected with it) her more lively interest in the present feelings of persons, which makes her consider first of all, in anything which claims to be applied to practice, in what manner persons will be affected by it—these two things make her extremely unlikely to put faith in any speculation which loses sight of individuals, and deals with things as if they existed for the benefit of some imaginary entity, some mere creation of the mind, not resolvable into the feelings of living beings. Women's thoughts are thus as useful in giving reality to those of thinking men, as men's thoughts in giving width and largeness to those of women. In depth, as distinguished from breadth, I greatly doubt if even now, women, compared with men, are at any disadvantage.

If the existing mental characteristics of women are thus valuable even in aid of speculation, they are still more important, when speculation has done its work, for carrying out the results of speculation into practice. For the reasons already given, women are comparatively unlikely to fall into the common error of men, that of sticking to their rules in a case whose specialties either take it out of the class to which the rules are applicable, or require a special adaptation of them. Let us now consider another of the admitted superiorities of clever women, greater quickness of apprehension. Is not this pre-eminently a quality which fits a person for practice? In action, everything continually depends upon deciding promptly. In speculation, nothing does. A mere thinker can wait, can take time to consider, can collect additional evidence; he is not obliged to complete his philosophy at once, lest the opportunity should go by. The power of drawing the best conclusion possible from insufficient data is not indeed useless in philosophy; the construction of a provisional hypothesis consistent with all known facts is often the needful basis for further inquiry. But this faculty is rather serviceable in philosophy, than the main qualification for it: and, for the auxiliary as well as for the main operation, the philosopher can allow himself any time he pleases. He is in no need of the capacity of doing rapidly what he does; what he rather needs is patience, to work on slowly until imperfect lights have become perfect, and a conjecture has ripened into a theorem. For those, on the contrary, whose business is with the fugitive and perishable—with individual facts, not kinds of facts—rapidity of thought is a qualification next only in importance to the power of thought itself. He who has not his faculties under immediate command, in the contingencies of action, might as well not have them at all. He may be fit to criticize, but he is not fit to

act. Now it is in this that women, and the men who are most like women, confessedly excel. The other sort of man, however pre-eminent may be his faculties, arrives slowly at complete command of them: rapidity of judgment and promptitude of judicious action, even in the things he knows best, are the gradual and late result of strenuous effort grown into habit.

It will be said, perhaps, that the greater nervous susceptibility of women is a disqualification for practice, in anything but domestic life, by rendering them mobile, changeable, too vehemently under the influence of the moment, incapable of dogged perseverance, unequal and uncertain in the power of using their faculties. I think that these phrases sum up the greater part of the objections commonly made to the fitness of women for the higher class of serious business. Much of all this is the mere overflow of nervous energy run to waste, and would cease when the energy was directed to a definite end. Much is also the result of conscious or unconscious cultivation; as we see by the almost total disappearance of "hysterics" and fainting fits, since they have gone out of fashion. Moreover, when people are brought up, like many women of the higher classes (though less so in our own country than in any other) a kind of hothouse plants, shielded from the wholesome vicissitudes of air and temperature, and untrained in any of the occupations and exercises which give stimulus and development to the circulatory and muscular system, while their nervous system, especially in its emotional department, is kept in unnaturally active play; it is no wonder if those of them who do not die of consumption, grow up with constitutions liable to derangement from slight causes, both internal and external, and without stamina to support any task, physical or mental, requiring continuity of effort. But women brought up to work for their livelihood show none of these morbid characteristics, unless indeed they are chained to an excess of sedentary work in confined and unhealthy rooms. Women who in their early years have shared in the healthful physical education and bodily freedom of their brothers, and who obtain a sufficiency of pure air and exercise in after-life, very rarely have any excessive susceptibility of nerves which can disqualify them for active pursuits. . . .

Supposing it, however, to be true that women's minds are by nature more mobile than those of men, less capable of persisting long in the same continuous effort, more fitted for dividing their faculties among many things than for travelling in any one path to the highest point which can be reached by it: this may be true of women as they now are (though not without great and numerous exceptions), and may account for their having remained behind the highest order of men in precisely the things in which this absorption of the whole mind in one set of ideas and occupations may seem to be most requisite. Still, this difference is one which can only affect the kind of excellence, not the excellence itself, or its practical worth: and it remains to be shown whether this exclusive working of a part of the mind, this absorption of the whole thinking faculty in a single subject, and concentration of it on a single work, is the normal and healthful condition of the human faculties, even for speculative uses. I believe that what is gained in special development by this concentration, is lost in the capacity of the mind for the other purposes of life; and even in abstract thought, it is my decided opinion that the mind does more by frequently returning to a difficult problem, than by sticking to it without interruption. For the purposes, at all events, of practice, from its highest to its humblest departments, the capacity of pass-

ing promptly from one subject of consideration to another, without letting the active spring of the intellect run down between the two, is a power far more valuable; and this power women pre-eminently possess, by virtue of the very mobility of which they are accused. They perhaps have it from nature, but they certainly have it by training and education; for nearly the whole of the occupations of women consist in the management of small but multitudinous details, on each of which the mind cannot dwell even for a minute, but must pass on to other things, and if anything requires longer thought, must steal time at odd moments for thinking of it. The capacity indeed which women show for doing their thinking in circumstances and at times which almost any man would make an excuse to himself for not attempting it, has often been noticed: and a woman's mind, though it may be occupied only with small things, can hardly ever permit itself to be vacant, as a man's so often is when not engaged in what he chooses to consider the business of his life. The business of a woman's ordinary life is things in general, and can as little cease to go on as the world to go round. . . .

10/Sex and Temperament in Three Primitive Societies

Margaret Mead

We have now considered in detail the approved personalities of each sex among three primitive peoples. We found the Arapesh—both men and women—displaying a personality that, out of our historically limited preoccupations, we would call maternal in its parental aspects, and feminine in its sexual aspects. We found men, as well as women, trained to be co-operative, unaggressive, responsive to the needs and demands of others. We found no idea that sex was a powerful driving force either for men or for women. In marked contrast to these attitudes, we found among the Mundugumor that both men and women developed as ruthless, aggressive, positively sexed individuals, with the

maternal cherishing aspects of personality at a minimum. Both men and women approximated to a personality type that we in our culture would find only in an undisciplined and very violent male. Neither the Arapesh nor the Mundugumor profit by a contrast between the sexes; the Arapesh ideal is the mild, responsive man married to the mild, responsive woman; the Mundugumor ideal is the violent aggressive man married to the violent aggressive woman. In the third tribe, the Tchambuli, we found a genuine reversal of the sex-attitudes of our own culture, with the woman the dominant, impersonal, managing partner, the man the less responsible and the emotionally dependent person. These three situations suggest, then, a very definite conclusion. If those temperamental attitudes which we have traditionally regarded as feminine—such as passivity, responsiveness, and a willingness to cherish children—can so easily be set up as the masculine pattern in one tribe, and in another be outlawed for the majority of women as well as for the majority of men, we no longer have any basis for regarding such aspects of behaviour as sex-linked. And this conclusion becomes even stronger when we consider the actual reversal in Tchambuli of the position of dominance of the two sexes, in spite of the existence of formal patrilineal institutions.

The material suggests that we may say that many, if not all, of the personality traits which we have called masculine or feminine are as lightly linked to sex as are the clothing, the manners, and the form of head-dress that a society at a given period assigns to either sex. When we consider the behaviour of the typical Arapesh man or woman as contrasted with the behaviour of the typical Mundugumor man or woman, the evidence is overwhelmingly in favor of the strength of social conditioning. In no other way can we account for the almost complete uniformity with which Arapesh children develop into contented, passive, secure persons, while Mundugumor children develop as characteristically into violent, aggressive, insecure persons. Only to the impact of the whole of the integrated culture upon the growing child can we lay the formation of the contrasting types. There is no other explanation of race, or diet, or selection that can be adduced to explain them. We are forced to conclude that human nature is almost unbelievably malleable, responding accurately and contrastingly to contrasting cultural conditions. The differences between individuals who are members of different cultures, like the differences between individuals within a culture, are almost entirely to be laid to differences in conditioning, especially during early childhood, and the form of this conditioning is culturally determined. Standardized personality differences between the sexes are of this order, cultural creations to which each generation, male and female, is trained to conform. There remains, however, the problem of the origin of these socially standardized differences.

While the basic importance of social conditioning is still imperfectly recognized—not only in lay thought, but even by the scientist specifically concerned with such matters—to go beyond it and consider the possible influence of variations in hereditary equipment is a hazardous matter. The following pages will read very differently to one who has made a part of his thinking a recognition of the whole amazing mechanism of cultural conditioning—who has really accepted the fact that the same infant could be developed into a full participant in any one of these three cultures—than they will read to one who still believes that the minutiae of cultural behaviour are carried in the individual germ-plasm. If it is said, therefore, that when we have grasped the full significance of the malleability of the human organism and the preponderant importance of cultural conditioning, there are still further problems to solve, it must be remembered that these problems come *after* such a comprehension of the force of conditioning; they cannot precede it. The forces that make children born among the Arapesh grow up into typical Arapesh personalities are entirely social, and any discussion of the variations which do occur must be looked at against this social background.

With this warning firmly in mind, we can ask a further question. Granting the malleability of human nature, whence arise the differences between the standardized personalities that different cultures decree for all of their members, or which one culture decrees for the members of one sex as contrasted with the members of the opposite sex? If such differences are culturally created, as this material would most strongly suggest that they are, if the new-born child can be shaped with equal ease into an unaggressive Arapesh or an aggressive Mundugumor, why do these striking contrasts occur at all? If the clues to the different personalities decreed for men and women in Tchambuli do not lie in the physical constitution of the two sexes—an assumption that we must reject both for the Tchambuli and for our own society—where can we find the clues upon which the Tchambuli, the Arapesh, the Mundugumor, have built? Cultures are man-made, they are built of human materials; they are diverse but comparable structures within which human beings can attain full human stature. Upon what have they built their diversities?

We recognize that a homogeneous culture committed in all of its gravest institutions and slightest usages to a co-operative, unaggressive course can bend every child to that emphasis, some to a perfect accord with it, the majority to an easy acceptance, while only a few deviants fail to receive the cultural imprint. To consider such traits as aggressiveness or passivity to be sex-linked is not possible in the light of the facts. Have such traits, then, as aggressiveness or passivity, pride or humility, objectivity or a preoccupation with person relationships, an easy response to the needs of the young and the weak or a hostility to the young and the weak, a tendency to initiate sex-relations or merely to respond to the dictates of a situation or another person's advances—have these traits any basis in temperament at all? Are they potentialities of all human temperaments that can be developed by different kinds of social conditioning and which will not appear if the necessary conditioning is absent?

When we ask this question we shift our emphasis. If we ask why an Arapesh man or an Arapesh woman shows the kind of personality that we have considered . . . the answer is: Because of the Arapesh culture, because of the intricate, elaborate, and unfailing fashion in which a culture is able to shape each new-born child to the cultural image. And if we ask the same question about a Mundugumor man or woman, or about a Tchambuli man as compared with a Tchambuli woman, the answer is of the same kind. They display the personalities that are peculiar to the cultures in which they were born and educated. Our attention has been on the differences between Arapesh men and women as a group and Mundugumor men and women as a group. It is as if we had represented the Arapesh personality by a soft yellow, the Mundugumor by a deep red, while the Tchambuli female personality was deep orange, and that of the Tchambuli male, pale green. But if we now ask whence came the original direction in each culture, so that one now shows yellow, another red, the third orange and green by sex, then we must peer more closely. And leaning closer to the picture, it is as if behind the bright consistent yellow of the Arapesh, and the deep equally consistent red of the Mundugumor, behind the orange and green that are Tchambuli, we found in each case the delicate, just discernible outlines of the whole spectrum, differently overlaid in each case by the monotone which covers it. This spectrum is the range of individual differences which lie back of the so much more conspicuous cultural emphases, and it is to this that we must turn to find the explanation of cultural inspiration, of the source from which each culture has drawn.

There appears to be about the same range of basic temperamental variation among the Arapesh and among the Mundugumor, although the violent man is a misfit in the first society and a leader in the second. If human nature were completely homogeneous raw material, lacking specific drives

and characterized by no important constitutional differences between individuals, then individuals who display personality traits so antithetical to the social pressure should not reappear in societies of such differing emphases. If the variations between individuals were to be set down to accidents in the genetic process, the same accidents should not be repeated with similar frequency in strikingly different cultures, with strongly contrasting methods of education.

But because this same relative distribution of individual differences does appear in culture after culture, in spite of the divergence between the cultures, it seems pertinent to offer a hypothesis to explain upon what basis the personalities of men and women have been differently standardized so often in the history of the human race. This hypothesis is an extension of that advanced by Ruth Benedict in her *Patterns of Culture.* Let us assume that there are definite temperamental differences between human beings which if not entirely hereditary at least are established on a hereditary base very soon after birth. (Further than this we cannot at present narrow the matter.) These differences finally embodied in the character structure of adults, then, are the clues from which culture works, selecting one temperament, or a combination of related and congruent types, as desirable, and embodying this choice in every thread of the social fabric—in the care of the young child, the games the children play, the songs the people sing, the structure of political organization, the religious observance, the art and the philosophy.

Some primitive societies have had the time and the robustness to revamp all of their institutions to fit one extreme type, and to develop educational techniques which will ensure that the majority of each generation will show a personality congruent with this extreme emphasis. Other societies have pursued a less definitive course, selecting their models not from the most extreme, most highly differentiated individuals, but from the less marked types. In such societies the approved personality is less pronounced, and the culture often contains the types of inconsistencies that many human beings display also; one institution may be adjusted to the uses of pride, another to a casual humility that is congruent neither with pride nor with inverted pride. Such societies, which have taken the more usual and less sharply defined types as models, often show also a less definitely patterned social structure. The culture of such societies may be likened to a house the decoration of which has been informed by no definite and precise taste, no exclusive emphasis upon dignity or comfort or pretentiousness or beauty, but in which a little of each effect has been included.

Alternatively, a culture may take its clues not from one temperament, but from several temperaments. But instead of mixing together into an inconsistent hotchpotch the choices and emphases of different temperaments, or blending them together into a smooth but not particularly distinguished whole, it may isolate each type by making it the basis for the approved social personality for an age-group, a sex-group, a caste-group, or an occupational group. In this way society becomes not a monotone with a few discrepant patches of an intrusive colour, but a mosaic, with different groups displaying different personality traits. Such specializations as these may be based upon any facet of human endowment—different intellectual abilities, different artistic abilities, different emotional traits. So the Samoans decree that all young people must show the personality trait of unaggressiveness and punish with opprobrium the aggressive child who displays traits regarded as appropriate only in titled middle-aged men. In societies based upon elaborate ideas of rank, members of the aristocracy will be permitted, even compelled, to display a pride, a sensitivity to insult, that would be deprecated as inappropriate in members of the plebeian class. So also in professional groups or in religious sects some temperamental traits are selected and institutionalized, and taught to each new member who enters the profession or sect. Thus the physician learns the bedside manner, which is the natural behaviour of some temperaments and the standard behaviour of the general practitioner in the medical profession; the Quaker learns at least the outward behaviour and the rudiments of meditation, the capacity for which is not necessarily an innate characteristic of many of the members of the Society of Friends.

So it is with the social personalities of the two sexes. The traits that occur in some members of each sex are specially assigned to one sex, and disallowed in the other. The history of the social definition of sex-differences is filled with such arbitrary arrangements in the intellectual and artistic field, but because of the assumed congruence between physiological sex and emotional endowment we have been less able to recognize that a similar arbitrary selection is being made among emotional traits also. We have assumed that because it is

convenient for a mother to wish to care for her child, this is a trait with which women have been more generously endowed by a carefully teleological process of evolution. We have assumed that because men have hunted, an activity requiring enterprise, bravery, and initiative, they have been endowed with these useful attitudes as part of their sex-temperament.

Societies have made these assumptions both overtly and implicitly. If a society insists that warfare is the major occupation for the male sex, it is therefore insisting that all male children display bravery and pugnacity. Even if the insistence upon the differential bravery of men and women is not made articulate, the difference in occupation makes this point implicitly. When, however, a society goes further and defines men as brave and women as timorous, when men are forbidden to show fear and women are indulged in the most flagrant display of fear, a more explicit element enters in. Bravery, hatred of any weakness, of flinching before pain or danger—this attitude which is so strong a component of *some human* temperaments has been selected as the key to masculine behaviour. The easy unashamed display of fear or suffering that is congenial to a different temperament has been made the key to feminine behaviour.

Originally two variations of human temperament, a hatred of fear or willingness to display fear, they have been socially translated into inalienable aspects of the personalities of the two sexes. And to that defined sex-personality every child will be educated, if a boy, to suppress fear, if a girl, to show it. If there has been no social selection in regard to this trait, the proud temperament that is repelled by any betrayal of feeling will display itself, regardless of sex, by keeping a stiff upper lip. Without an express prohibition of such behaviour the expressive unashamed man or woman will weep, or comment upon fear or suffering. Such attitudes, strongly marked in certain temperaments, may by social selection be standardized for everyone, or outlawed for everyone, or ignored by society, or made the exclusive and approved behaviour of one sex only.

Neither the Arapesh nor the Mundugumor have made any attitude specific for one sex. All of the energies of the culture have gone towards the creation of a single human type, regardless of class, age, or sex. There is no division into age-classes for which different motives or different moral attitudes are regarded as suitable. There is no class of seers or mediums who stand apart drawing inspiration from psychological sources not available to the majority of the people. The Mundugumor have, it is true, made one arbitrary selection, in that they recognize artistic ability only among individuals born with the cord about their necks, and firmly deny the happy exercise of artistic ability to those less unusually born. The Arapesh boy with a tinea infection has been socially selected to be a disgruntled, antisocial individual, and the society forces upon sunny co-operative children cursed with this affliction a final approximation to the behaviour appropriate to a pariah. With these two exceptions no emotional role is forced upon an individual because of birth or accident. As there is no idea of rank which declares that some are of high estate and some of low, so there is no idea of sex-difference which declares that one sex must feel differently from the other. One possible imaginative social construct, the attribution of different personalities to different members of the community classified into sex-, age-, or caste-groups, is lacking.

When we turn however to the Tchambuli, we find a situation that while bizarre in one respect, seems nevertheless more intelligible in another. The Tchambuli have at least made the point of sex-difference; they have used the obvious fact of sex as an organizing point for the formation of social personality, even though they seem to us to have reversed the normal picture. While there is reason to believe that not every Tchambuli woman is born with a dominating, organizing, administrative temperament, actively sexed and willing to initiate sex-relations, possessive, definite, robust, practical and impersonal in outlook, still most Tchambuli girls grow up to display these traits. And while there is definite evidence to show that all Tchambuli men are not, by native endowment, the delicate responsive actors of a play staged for the women's benefit, still most Tchambuli boys manifest this coquettish play-acting personality most of the time. Because the Tchambuli formulation of sex-attitudes contradicts our usual premises, we can see clearly that Tchambuli culture has arbitrarily permitted certain human traits to women, and allotted others, equally arbitrarily, to men.

If we then accept this evidence drawn from these simple societies which through centuries of isolation from the main stream of human history have been able to develop more extreme, more striking cultures than is possible under historical conditions of great intercommunication between peoples and the resulting heterogeneity, what are the implications of these results? What conclusions can we draw from a study of the way in which a culture can select a few traits from the wide gamut of human endowment and specialize these traits, either for one sex or for the entire community? What relevance have these results to social thinking? . . .

Conclusion

The knowledge that the personalities of the two sexes are socially produced is congenial to every program that looks forward towards a planned order of society. It is a two-edged sword that can be used to hew a more flexible, more varied society than the human race has ever built, or merely to cut a narrow path down which one sex or both sexes will be forced to march, regimented, looking neither to the right nor to the left. . . .

There are at least three courses open to a society that has realized the extent to which male and female personality are socially produced. Two of these courses have been tried before, over and over again, at different times in the long, irregular, repetitious history of the race. The first is to standardize the personality of men and women as clearly contrasting, complementary, and antithetical, and to make every institution in the society congruent with this standardization. If the society declared that woman's sole function was motherhood and the teaching and care of young children, it could so arrange matters that every woman who was not physiologically debarred should become a mother and be supported in the exercise of this function. It could abolish the discrepancy between the doctrine that women's place is the home and the number of homes that were offered to them. It could abolish the discrepancy between training women for marriage and then forcing them to become the spinster supports of their parents.

Such a system would be wasteful of the gifts of many women who could exercise other functions far better than their ability to bear children in an already overpopulated world. It would be wasteful of the gifts of many men who could exercise their special personality gifts far better in the home than in the marketplace. It would be wasteful, but it would be clear. It could attempt to guarantee to each individual the role for which society insisted upon training him or her, and such a system would penalize only those individuals who, in spite of all the training, did not display the approved personalities. There are millions of persons who would gladly return to such a standardized method of treating the relationship between the sexes, and we must bear in mind the possibility that the greater opportunities open in the twentieth century to women may be quite withdrawn, and that we may return to a strict regimentation of women.

The waste, if this occurs, will be not only of many women, but also of as many men, because regimentation of one sex carries with it, to greater or less degree, the regimentation of the other also. Every parental behest that defines a way of sitting, a response to a rebuke or a threat, a game, or an attempt to draw or sing or dance or paint, as feminine, is moulding the personality of each little girl's brother as well as moulding the personality of the sister. There can be no society which insists that women follow one special personality-pattern, defined as feminine, which does not do violence also to the individuality of many men.

Alternatively, society can take the course that has become especially associated with the plans of most radical groups: admit that men and women are capable of being moulded to a single pattern as easily as to a diverse one, and cease to make any distinction in the approved personality of both sexes. Girls can be trained exactly as boys are trained, taught the same code, the same forms of expression, the same occupations. This course might seem to be the logic which follows from the conviction that the potentialities which different societies label as either masculine or feminine are really potentialities of some members of each sex, and not sex-linked at all. If this is accepted, is it not reasonable to abandon the kind of artificial standardizations of sex differences that have been so long characteristic of European society, and admit that they are social fictions for which we have no longer any use? In the world today, contraceptives make it possible for women not to bear children against their will. The most conspicuous actual difference between the sexes, the difference in strength, is progressively less significant. Just as the difference in height between males is no longer a realistic issue, now that lawsuits have been substituted for hand-to-hand encounters, so the difference in strength between men and women is no longer worth elaboration in cultural institutions.

In evaluating such a program as this, however, it is necessary to keep in mind the nature of the gains that society has achieved in its most complex forms. A sacrifice of distinctions in sex-personality may mean a sacrifice in complexity. The Arapesh

recognize a minimum of distinction in personality between old and young, between men and women, and they lack categories of rank or status. We have seen that such a society at the best condemns to personal frustration, and at the worst to maladjustment, all of those men and women who do not conform to its simple emphases. The violent person among the Arapesh cannot find, either in the literature, or in the art, or in the ceremonial, or in the history of his people, any expression of the internal drives that are shattering his peace of mind. Nor is the loser only the individual whose own type of personality is nowhere recognized in his society. The imaginative, highly intelligent person who is essentially in tune with the values of his society may also suffer by the lack of range and depth characteristic of too great simplicity. The active mind and intensity of one Arapesh boy whom I knew well was unsatisfied by the laissez-faire solutions, the lack of drama in his culture. Searching for some material upon which to exercise his imagination, his longing for a life in which stronger emotions would be possible, he could find nothing with which to feel his imagination but tales of the passionate outbursts of the maladjusted, outbursts characterized by a violent hostility to others that he himself lacked.

Nor is it the individual alone who suffers. Society is equally the loser, and we have seen such an attenuation in the dramatic representations of the Mundugumor. By phrasing the exclusion of women as a protective measure congenial to both sexes, the Arapesh kept their *tamberan* cult, with the necessary audiences of women. But the Mundugumor developed a kind of personality for both men and women to which exclusion from any part of life was interpreted as a deadly insult. And as more and more Mundugumor women have demanded and been given the right of initiation, it is not surprising that the Mundugumor ceremonial life has dwindled, the actors have lost their audience, and one vivid artistic element in the life of the Mundugumor community is vanishing. The sacrifice of sex-differences has meant a loss in complexity to the society.

So in our own society. To insist that there are no sex-differences in a society that has always believed in them and depended upon them may be as subtle a form of standardizing personality as to insist that there are many sex-differences. This is particularly so in a changing tradition, when a group in control is attempting to develop a new social personality, as is the case today in many European countries. Take, for instance, the current assumption that women are more opposed to war than men, that any outspoken approval of war is more horrible, more revolting, in women than in men. Behind this assumption women can work for peace without encountering social criticism in communities that would immediately criticize their brothers or husbands if they took a similarly active part in peace propaganda. This belief that women are naturally more interested in peace is undoubtedly artificial, part of the whole mythology that considers women to be gentler than men. But in contrast let us consider the possibility of a powerful minority that wished to turn a whole society wholeheartedly towards war. One way of doing this would be to insist that women's motives, women's interests, were identical with men's, that women should take as bloodthirsty a delight in preparing for war as ever men do. The insistence upon the opposite point of view, that the woman as a mother prevails over the woman as a citizen at least puts a slight drag upon agitation for war, prevents a blanket enthusiasm for war from being thrust upon the entire younger generation. The same kind of result follows if the clergy are professionally committed to a belief in peace. The relative bellicosity of different individual clerics may be either offended or gratified by the prescribed pacific role, but a certain protest, a certain dissenting note, will be sounded in society. The dangerous standardization of attitudes that disallows every type of deviation is greatly reinforced if neither age nor sex nor religious belief is regarded as automatically predisposing certain individuals to hold minority attitudes. The removal of all legal and economic barriers against women's participating in the world on an equal footing with men may be in itself a standardizing move towards the wholesale stamping-out of the diversity of attitudes that is such a dearly bought product of civilization.

Such a standardized society, in which men, women, children, priests, and soldiers were all trained to an undifferentiated and coherent set of values, must of necessity create the kind of deviant that we found among the Arapesh and the Mundugumor, the individual who, regardless of sex or occupation, rebels because he is temperamentally unable to accept the one-sided emphasis of his culture. The individuals who were specifically unadjusted in terms of their psycho-sexual role would, it is true, vanish, but with them would vanish the knowledge that there is more than one set of possible values.

To the extent that abolishing the differences in the approved personalities of men and women

means abolishing any expression of the type of personality once called exclusively feminine, or once called exclusively masculine, such a course involves a social loss. Just as a festive occasion is the gayer and more charming if the two sexes are dressed differently, so it is in less material matters. If the clothing is in itself a symbol, and a woman's shawl corresponds to a recognized softness in her character, the whole plot of personal relations is made more elaborate, and in many ways more rewarding. The poet of such a society will praise virtues, albeit feminine virtues, which might never have any part in a social Utopia that allowed no differences between the personalities of men and women.

To the extent that a society insists upon different kinds of personality so that one age-group or class or sex-group may follow purposes disallowed or neglected in another, each individual participant in that society is the richer. The arbitrary assignment of set clothing, set manners, set social responses, to individuals born in a certain class, of a certain sex, or of a certain colour, to those born on a certain day of the week, to those born with a certain complexion, does violence to the individual endowment of individuals, but permits the building of a rich culture. The most extreme development of a society that has attained great complexity at the expense of the individual is historical India, based, as it was, upon the uncompromising association of a thousand attributes of behaviour, attitude, and occupation with an accident of birth. To each individual there was given the security, although it might be the security of despair, of a set role, and the reward of being born into a highly complex society.

Furthermore, when we consider the position of the deviant individual in historical cultures, those who are born into a complex society in the wrong sex or class for their personalities to have full sway are in a better position than those who are born into a simple society which does not use in any way their special temperamental gifts. The violent woman in a society that permits violence to men only, the strongly emotional member of an aristocracy in a culture that permits downright emotional expression only in the peasantry, the ritualistically inclined individual who is bred a Protestant in a country which has also Catholic institutions—each one of these can find expressed in some other group in the society the emotions that he or she is forbidden to manifest. He is given a certain kind of support by the mere existence of these values, values so congenial to him and so inaccessible because of an accident of birth. For those who are content with a vicarious spectator-role, or with materials upon which to feast the creative imagination, this may be almost enough. They may be content to experience from the sidewalks during a parade, from the audience of a theatre or from the nave of a church, those emotions the direct expression of which is denied to them. The crude compensations offered by the moving pictures to those whose lives are emotionally starved are offered in subtler forms by the art and literature of a complex society to the individual who is out of place in his sex or his class or his occupational group.

Sex-adjustments, however, are not a matter of spectatorship, but a situation in which the most passive individual must play some part if he or she is to participate fully in life. And while we may recognize the virtues of complexity, the interesting and charming plots that cultures can evolve upon the basis of accidents of birth, we may well ask: Is not the price too high? Could not the beauty that lies in contrast and complexity be obtained in some other way? If the social insistence upon different personalities for the two sexes results in so much confusion, so many unhappy deviants, so much disorientation, can we imagine a society that abandons these distinctions without abandoning the values that are at present dependent upon them?

Let us suppose that, instead of the classification laid down on the "natural" bases of sex and race, a society had classified personality on the basis of eye-colour. It had decreed that all blue-eyed people were gentle, submissive, and responsive to the needs of others, and all brown-eyed people were arrogant, dominating, self-centered, and purposive. In this case two complementary social themes would be woven together—the culture, in its art, its religion, its formal personal relations, would have two threads instead of one. There would be blue-eyed men and blue-eyed women, which would mean that there were gentle, "maternal" women, and gentle, "maternal" men. A blue-eyed man might marry a woman who had been bred to the same personality as himself, or a brown-eyed woman who had been bred to the contrasting personality. One of the strong tendencies that makes for homosexuality, the tendency to love the similar rather than the antithetical person, would be eliminated. Hostility between the two sexes as groups would be minimized, since the individual interests of members of each sex could be woven together in different ways, and marriages of similarity and friendships of contrast

need carry no necessary handicap of possible psycho-sexual maladjustment. The individual would still suffer a mutilation of his temperamental preferences, for it would be the unrelated fact of eye-colour that would determine the attitudes which he was educated to show. Every blue-eyed person would be forced into submissiveness and declared maladjusted if he or she showed any traits that it had been decided were only appropriate to the brown-eyed. The greatest social loss, however, in the classification of personality on the basis of sex would not be present in this society which based its classification on eye-colour. Human relations, and especially those which involve sex, would not be artificially distorted.

But such a course, the substitution of eye-colour for sex as a basis upon which to educate children into groups showing contrasting personalities, while it would be a definite advance upon a classification by sex, remains a parody of all the attempts that society has made through history to define an individual's role in terms of sex, or colour, or date of birth, or shape of head.

However, the only solution of the problem does not lie between an acceptance of standardization of sex-differences with the resulting cost in individual happiness and adjustment, and the abolition of these differences with the consequent loss in social values. A civilization might take its cues not from such categories as age or sex, race or hereditary position in a family line, but instead of specializing personality along such simple lines recognize, train, and make a place for many and divergent temperamental endowments. It might build upon the different potentialities that it now attempts to extirpate artificially in some children and create artificially in others.

Historically the lessening of rigidity in the classification of the sexes has come about at different times, either by the creation of a new artificial category, or by the recognition of real individual differences. Sometimes the idea of social position has transcended sex-categories. In a society that recognizes gradations in wealth or rank, women of rank or women of wealth have been permitted an arrogance which was denied to both sexes among the lowly or the poor. Such a shift as this has been, it is true, a step towards the emancipation of women, but it has never been a step towards the greater freedom of the individual. A few women have shared the upper-class personality, but to balance this a great many men as well as women have been condemned to a personality characterized by subservience and fear. Such shifts as these mean only the substitution of one arbitrary standard for another. A society is equally unrealistic whether it insists that only men can be brave, or that only individuals of rank can be brave.

To break down one line of division, that between the sexes, and substitute another, that between classes, is no real advance. It merely shifts the irrelevancy to a different point. And meanwhile, individuals born in the upper classes are shaped inexorably to one type of personality, to an arrogance that is again uncongenial to at least some of them, while the arrogant among the poor fret and fume beneath their training for submissiveness. At one end of the scale is the mild, unaggressive young son of wealthy parents who is forced to lead, at the other the aggressive, enterprising child of the slums who is condemned to a place in the ranks. If our aim is greater expression for each individual temperament, rather than any partisan interest in one sex or its fate, we must see these historical developments which have aided in freeing some women as nevertheless a kind of development that also involved major social losses.

The second way in which categories of sex-differences have become less rigid is through a recognition of genuine individual gifts as they occurred in either sex. Here a real distinction has been substituted for an artificial one, and the gains are tremendous for society and for the individual. Where writing is accepted as a profession that may be pursued by either sex with perfect suitability, individuals who have the ability to write need not be debarred from it by their sex, nor need they, if they do write, doubt their essential masculinity or femininity. An occupation that has no basis in sex-determined gifts can now recruit its ranks from twice as many potential artists. And it is here that we can find a ground-plan for building a society that would substitute real differences for arbitrary ones. We must recognize that beneath the superficial classifications of sex and race the same potentialities exist, recurring generation after generation, only to perish because society has no place for them. Just as society now permits the practice of an art to members of either sex, so it might also permit the development of many contrasting temperamental gifts in each sex. It might abandon its various attempts to make boys fight and to make girls remain passive, or to make all children fight, and instead shape our educational institutions to develop to the full the boy who shows a capacity for maternal behaviour, the girl who shows an opposite capacity that is stimulated by fighting against obstacles. No skill, no special aptitude, no vividness of imagination or precision of thinking would go unrecognized because the child who possessed it was of one sex rather than the other. No child would be relentlessly shaped to one pattern of behaviour, but instead there should be many patterns, in a world that had learned to allow to each individual the pattern which was most congenial to his gifts.

Such a civilization would not sacrifice the gains of thousands of years during which society has built up standards of diversity. The social gains would be conserved, and each child would be encouraged on the basis of his actual temperament. Where we now have patterns of behaviour for women and patterns of behaviour for men, we would then have patterns of behaviour that expressed the interests of individuals with many kinds of endowment. There would be ethical codes and social symbolisms, an art and a way of life, congenial to each endowment.

Historically our own culture has relied for the creation of rich and contrasting values upon many artificial distinctions, the most striking of which is sex. It will not be by the mere abolition of these distinctions that society will develop patterns in which individual gifts are given place instead of being forced into an ill-fitting mould. If we are to achieve a richer culture, rich in contrasting values, we must recognize the whole gamut of human potentialities, and so weave a less arbitrary social fabric, one in which each diverse human gift will find a fitting place.

11/Self-Determination and Autonomy

Sharon Bishop Hill

Some have spoken as if the sexual revolution amounts to greatly increased liberality about sex. Recently there is talk that it will not be accomplished until there is an end to sexual discrimination and women as well as men are liberated. Not a few are certain that they know what changes are required to liberate women. Many are content with things as they are, and some are merely complacent about this revolution. Others are perplexed though not unwilling to change, for those they love seem unhappy. In winding a way through an unreal but not unlikely dispute, I suggest a way of allaying these perplexities and justifying some of these demands. If what I say about how to set aside certain doubts about women's liberation is plausible, then I imagine radical changes are in order, not just about how we view and treat women, but also about how we view and treat men and children. What these changes are is difficult to say. In any case, my interest here is primarily in principles and arguments which might be used to explain and justify some of the demands now being made in the name of women's liberation. But to begin with, the dispute.

I. The Dispute

Over the years, John and Harriet have had long arguments about women's liberation. Both have come a long way. When Harriet first decided that she could not find self-fulfillment without a paying job, John felt threatened and protested that it would not be proper. But now he is reconciled and even insists that women get equal pay for equal work. He supports the Equal Rights Amendment and urges his company to give talented and well-trained women an equal chance at job opportunities. He has given up as muddled his old belief that women are naturally inferior to men in intelligence, objectivity, emotional stability and the like. He acknowledges that women have often been treated

in degrading ways, and like many liberals, he has tried hard to purge his vocabulary of such words as "chick," "broad," and "piece." He even tries, not always successfully, to avoid references like "the girls in the office." Women, he says, have as much right to happiness as men, and so he is ready to oppose any social scheme which makes them, relative to men, systematically discontent or unhappy. But this is as far as he will go.

Harriet says that this is not far enough. And the dispute came to a head when she protested to the school principal and finally to the school board about their daughter's education. Harriet was distressed that girls were encouraged in numerous ways to accept the traditional feminine role. For example, the practice at most school dances was for girls to wait to be asked by boys. The school had well-developed and financed athletic programs for boys, but few for girls, and very little staff to help girls to develop their skills. The counselors were comparatively uninterested in advising girls about their futures. When they did, they assumed that, for the most part, appropriate careers for girls were as secretaries, decorators, teachers, nurses or medical assistants. Students' programs were then tailored for these vocations. These, in turn, were viewed as stop-gap or carry-over measures to enable girls to get through any periods in which they were not married or supported by someone. If they did marry, it was assumed that there would be children and a home to which the woman should devote herself.

Harriet gradually came to see that her objections to these practices arose as she faced her own feelings of resentment and betrayal at the kinds of opportunities and counseling she had early in life. Though she acknowledged the occasion of her objections, she also became convinced that her com-

I wish to thank Thomas Hill, Jr., and Richard Wasserstrom, who read earlier versions of this paper and made many helpful comments and suggestions.

From *Today's Moral Problems* (New York: Macmillan Co., 1975). Reprinted by permission of the author. Sharon Bishop Hill is now publishing under the name Sharon Bishop.

plaints were well founded. She was less clear how to support them, but her way of life seemed unnecessarily restrictive and she believed that she had interests and capacities which should have been developed but were not. She was irked, too, that she had never had a genuine opportunity to choose the way of life in which she and other women were so deeply involved. Whatever she might have chosen and whether or not she liked having a family and the feminine virtues, she felt that she had never really had any choice. She realized that part of the problem was that she herself had not regarded these as proper objects of her own choice. The failure she thought was the result of a complicated and overlapping set of teachings which had it that women were almost inevitably unfulfilled without having children, that normally they were better at raising children than men and men better suited for earning a living. Consequently, as the story went, the current division of labor is really most efficient, better for almost everyone and thus best. Both men and women were said to have duties associated with these roles. She now resents these teachings, justifiably she believes. She became especially anxious as she saw her daughter falling into the patterns of behavior and belief to which she now objects and so she complained to the school board.

John found Harriet less than convincing on these matters. It is important to oppose sex roles, he argued, if the roles function in a way which humiliates or degrades women or deprives them of political or economic rights. If these abuses could be avoided, he thinks the current standard division of labor and roles would not only be legitimate but quite a good way to arrange things. Someone, after all, needs to care for children and most women seem quite content. These arrangements seem natural to him. He suspects that women are naturally more sensitive and so make better parents for the very young; moreover, those he knows who have either not married or not had children seem to be weak and stunted characters or else hostile and aggressive. These observations suggest to him that most people, including women, are well off under something like the current division of labor and role. He acknowledges some, at least, of the difficulties about his belief that women are naturally suited for the domestic role. He does not, for example, rely on personality inventories of women versus men, because the traits they test for are bound to be influenced by the culture in which people grow up including, of course, some of the practices Harriet finds obnoxious. He

does not appeal to the obvious physical differences between men and women, and he regards as irrelevant, at least in the modern world, appeals to differences in brute strength. Still he believes that some of the relevant differences are natural. He supports his suspicion by appeals to anthropological evidence about widely divergent groups in which women have almost invariably had the domestic role and quite often the traits which suit them for raising children and managing households. Were this not natural, he thinks it would not be so frequent. He has been known to remark that estrogen is associated with passive as opposed to aggressive personality traits, reminding Harriet that women maintain a higher level of this hormone than men. He suspects that the thwarted and hostile women he finds among the unmarried and childless result from frustration of the natural capacities of women for close emotional relations. There are, he admits, extraordinarily ambitious women who would be frustrated in following the traditional pattern; but a society which grants full political and economic rights to all adults can accommodate these exceptional people. Consequently, he resists the idea that there is something wrong with encouraging in young girls the feminine traits he so likes. He wants his daughter to be ladylike in figure and personality and hopes, for her sake, that she will never choose a career at the expense of having a family. He communicates this to her in innumerable, sometimes subtle, sometimes direct ways.

It is at this point that Harriet becomes most exasperated and even despairing. By all the conventional criteria, John seems liberal enough. He believes in equal pay for equal work and equal opportunities for those of equal achievement, motivation and talent. He acknowledges that women have been deprived of income, opportunities, power and their associated satisfactions by unfair social practices of various sorts. What he envisages is a world in which these injustices are eradicated but one in which women remain sensitive, understanding and charming, and in which most take up a domestic life while most men take up a paying vocation. Since he thinks it only efficient to prepare people for these likely different but quite natural futures, he thinks sound educational policy calls for certain subtle differences in the training of males and females. Harriet, on the other hand, believes that her resentment is justified, that she has been wronged in some way and would continue to be wronged if the world were magically transformed to match John's dreams. She becomes most desperate when she thinks of her daughter who is being similarly wronged.

The perplexed, like John, may say, "But where is the difficulty?" They understand complaints about violations of political and economic rights, like the right to vote, hold office and receive equal pay for equal work. They admit that a person would be wronged if gratuitously insulted or deliberately injured. But none of these seem to fit the case of Harriet or her daughter at least in the world John wants. There is no reason to believe they will be insulted, and it is difficult to pick out any political or economic right which we could confidently claim would be violated. Even if we think that Harriet and her daughter have been injured by the workings of the social system in this world, it is not clear that the harm was deliberate. No definite person designed the social system for the purpose of keeping women down, much less for the purpose of harming Harriet; it, like Topsy, just growed. If that is the case, whatever harm they may have suffered seems in important respects like a natural misfortune and not a deliberate wrong. If Harriet's objections to John's views can be defended, it must be on some other pattern of reasoning.

In the following, I shall try to isolate and explain some principles which could be used to justify Harriet's feelings about her own life and her protests of school practices. Roughly, I shall argue that if adults are viewed as having a right of self-determination, then Harriet and other adult women do nothing inappropriate in eschewing a traditional role nor do they have duties directly associated with such a role. Moreover, if as adults, we are to have a right of self-determination which is meaningful, we ought not to be treated in ways which distort or prevent the development of the capacity for autonomous choice. I do not attempt to justify the claim that adults have a right of self-determination nor the claim that viewing adults as having such a right is better than any of a variety of other ways of regarding them, for example, as potential contributors to the general welfare or to some social or economic ideal. I hope that some of what I say will make respect for a right of self-determination attractive, but here I only set out to explain something about the right.

I try this line of argument, first, because I think it is a promising one to explain the depth and kind of feeling generated in women who begin thinking seriously about their lives and their daughters' pros-

pects. In the end, it may help explain why such pervasive changes are required and why some of them must be changes in attitude. Secondly, it seems possible with this reasoning to avoid some philosophical and empirical difficulties involved in more familiar arguments. For example, a number of people argue for sweeping changes in the treatment of women on the grounds that the resulting system will be more efficient in turning out happy individuals or in using the available pool of natural abilities. One problem here, of course, is to determine what is to count as being happy and so what is to count as evidence that some new system will be more efficient producing it than the present one. Others suggest that there has been a deliberate male conspiracy to keep women in the kitchen and out of the most lucrative and satisfying jobs. There are innumerable problems about what could be meant by "deliberate conspiracy" in this case; there does not seem to have been a conspiratorial meeting attended by anyone much less by most men or by representative men. It does not even seem plausible that some rather large number of men have consciously intended to keep women out of the mainstream of social and economic life at least in recent history. Even if some clear sense can be given to the notion, successful completion of the argument would require complicated empirical inquiries. Although it is true that a deliberate conspiracy to do wrong makes things rather worse, what seems important here is rather the wrong that has been done. If questions about the deliberateness of the wrongs are important at all, they seem to belong rather with attempts to decide to whom the burdens of change may legitimately fall. Finally, the line of reasoning I propose directly undercuts two of the kinds of arguments John suggested against Harriet. In the end, he claimed that his views about women and educational policy could be supported by appeals to efficient ways of arranging for child rearing as well as the natural suitability of current sex roles and the division of labor. Once a right of self-determination is granted, however, it does not matter whether the complex facts John appeals to are true or not, that is, it does not matter whether current sex roles are efficient means of rearing children or whether women, on the average, are better at domestic affairs than men. There are other considerations having to do with self-determination and autonomy which make these alleged facts irrelevant and which do justice to Harriet's response. She does not need to await empirical evidence about what is suitable for women and what makes women and children happy in order to know that something is wrong.

II. The Right of Self-Determination

To say that persons or states have a right of self-determination is to say minimally that they and only they have the authority to determine certain sorts of things. This does not necessarily mean that they have the power or capacity to determine these things, but rather that they have the title to. Sovereign states, for example, are widely regarded as having rather extensive authority to choose for themselves; they are said to have a right to determine how and who shall govern them, to have rights to determine for themselves what their ideals shall be, how they will allocate funds, what forms of culture they will support and devote themselves to, and the like. Having title to make these choices means that they have a right to expect others not to interfere with the legitimate exercise of their authority and a right to protect themselves from interference. It means, too, that they have a right to expect to carry on the processes of their government without foreign interest groups bribing their officials, and without being flooded with propaganda designed to influence the outcome of elections and the like. All this seems rather uncontroversial. More controversially, a small dependent state might claim that its right of self-determination was violated by threats of loss of essential support just because it failed to adopt the policies its larger, more affluent neighbor wanted. Withdrawal of such support makes it impossible to exercise its right of self-determination, consequently, threatening such withdrawal may be counted as incompatible with respecting the small nation's right. This may seem especially plausible where the support is well established, and where the threat is given for failure, say, to give up some local ritual or some trading policy mildly contrary to the interests of the affluent. Mature adults are often said to have a similar right, for example, to determine for themselves what their vocations shall be, whether to use their money for steaks or tennis balls, their leisure time for concerts or back-packing, and so on. Again, what is meant is that only they have the authority to make such choices, that others ought to refrain from interfering with the legitimate exercise of the title, and that they have the right to protect

themselves from interference. Individuals may, if they wish, delegate parts of that authority. They give up some of it when they take a job, put themselves under the tutelage of an instructor or decide to let a friend choose the day's activities. Even in these cases, however, it is only they who may decide not to exercise the right.

Like other rights, this one is limited. Sovereign states do not have a right to make war on their neighbors for profit. Individuals do not have the right to harm or restrain one another simply for the fun of it however much they may want to. The limitations on this right will be roughly what is prohibited by other moral principles. Although these limitations cannot be spelled out here, we could get agreement about a number of cases like injuring another for one's own pleasure. While this does not give us a satisfactory criterion for what morality forbids, it is enough to permit us to focus on the right of self-determination confident that it need not commit us to silly views about the rights of sadists.

Obviously the right is not in fact granted or guaranteed to everyone by the state or culture in which they live. Like the rights to life, liberty and security, it is a natural right, that is, it is thought of as belonging to everyone simply by virtue of their being human and so it is a right which everyone has equally. Society can and should protect us in exercising it in some ways, for example, in choosing a vocation. A state should not, however, enforce all the behavior and attitudes which might be appropriate in someone who believes in the right of self-determination. For example, I suspect that some committed to honoring the right of self-determination would regard themselves as bound not to influence those close to them by exploiting any emotional dependence they might have. If this is a reasonable attitude, it does not seem that it would be wise for a society to protect us from the influence of those on whom we are dependent emotionally. The right of self-determination does not, in general, determine a particular outcome as the just or only acceptable one. It rather outlines a range of considerations which should come into play whenever we are trying to adjust our behavior or attitudes to persons making permissible choices. I call it a right because it is thought of as a title and because the considerations it picks out as relevant mark off an area in which we do not allow conclusions about either the general good or an individual's good to be decisive. The point of the right of self-determination is to enable people to work out their own way of life in response to their own assessments of current conditions and their own interests, capacities and needs, rather than to secure the minimal conditions for living or to maximize a person's expectations for satisfaction. In respecting an individual's right of self-determination, one expresses a certain view about that person which is not a belief that one is acting for the good of that person (at least in some narrow sense of the person's good having to do with his or her welfare or happiness). The rough idea is that persons are, among other things, creatures who have title to select what they will do from among the permitted options. This establishes a presumption that other people should refrain from interfering with our selections whatever their content. They should refrain even if they do not like the particular choice or if they correctly believe that it is not in the chooser's or society's long-term interests.

Applying the right of self-determination to questions about the treatment of women, John and Harriet readily agree on a number of conclusions. First, bending the will of a woman by force is wrong. Conquering nations violate the right of self-determination and so does the man who keeps a woman or harem in servitude however nice he may make their lives. The man who prevents his wife from attending her therapy session or sky-diving lessons by force also violates this right. He does not allow her to do what she has a right to do. He violates the right whether he prevents her because he fears the changes in her personality, or is jealous of her handsome teacher, or because he correctly and sincerely believes the group is harming her or that sky-diving is dangerous. So long as we are talking about a mature woman who is choosing nothing prohibited by morality, it does not matter whether he acts in her own interests or not, he will still have violated her right to determine on her own what she will do.

The husband who achieves similar results by threatening to divorce his wife who has no other means of support may also violate her right to self-determination. This would be like a powerful state that threatens to cut off aid whenever a dependent state acts contrary to its wishes. Some may feel more certain that the threatening husband makes a mistake than that the powerful state violates the right of self-determination of the smaller state. Someone may note that it is quite accepted that relations among nations proceed by threat and counter threat. Things do not go all that well when

carried on in this manner, but they go on. When husband, wife, parents or friends resort to such tactics, the relation of friendship or love is effectively off. Someone who is prepared to use such tactics displays special callousness toward the friendship. If they care about maintaining it at all, they will have made a grave blunder. They will also have indicated that they are indifferent to the feelings of the individual they threaten. They show a willingness to harm them, and this may be considered a moral fault for which there is no analogue in the threatening state. These observations can be accepted, I think, without weakening the original claim. We began by saying that states and persons have a right to make certain sorts of choices for themselves without interference by force or threat of force or withdrawal of essential support. This implies in both the case of states and individuals that there is a special wrong in threatening those who are making perfectly permissible policy, namely the violation of this right; that other wrongs and blunders may also be involved is beside the point.

Finally, if a group of men were to conspire together to discourage their wives from taking jobs or joining groups where women work through their problems together, they would violate the women's right of self-determination. These conclusions are not a problem for a liberal like John. He is not tempted to prevent his wife from going anywhere by force. Nor is he tempted to use the threat of loss of support in order to win a battle. He knows that would be to lose the war, and he wants her love and respect, not simply her presence and obedience. He knows, too, that his wife could find other means of support in this world. She is able, and this is not the nineteenth century where his support may well have been essential. Moreover, he has always been inclined to resist the temptation to adjust his relation to his wife in response to or in concert with others. So far the right of self-determination adds nothing startling to the list of legitimate complaints that women might have.

It does, however, add something to the reasons we may have for objecting to a variety of policies. For example, it means that some wrong is involved in the above cases apart from the objectionable techniques used to bring about the desired result. The wrong is not either simply that someone made a conscious attempt to interfere with someone's legitimate choice, but rather that someone's selections were blocked or interfered with. In addition, the right of self-determination takes us a good way toward directly undermining John's views about women. He seemed to think that it was perfectly all right to advise adult women to engage in and stick with traditional domestic life styles on the grounds that it was efficient and natural for women to have them. What appears to be the case now, is that, even if it is efficient and natural, enticing women to take this role for these reasons is likely to interfere with their right of self-determination. It is likely to do this because it encourages the false belief that these reasons are or should be decisive in determining an important lifetime commitment. Instead the right of self-determination establishes a presumption that within the range of permissible selections a person's uncoerced, unforced spontaneous responses to her own interests and circumstances are or should be decisive. It does not matter whether the interference is deliberate or non-deliberate or whether it is well-intended guidance. Once it is known that a practice, policy or teaching interferes, there is good reason to believe it should be revised. That is not to say that there is always sufficient reason, for this presumption like others can be rebutted. If the rebuttal is to work, however, it must give something like an equally important reason, for example, that revising the policy will cause perpetual or irremediable disaster, that it represents the only possible way for anyone to have a decent life, that some other natural right would be violated or that some particular person is not capable of exercising the right for some special reason. While this is not an adequate account of what will rebut the presumption established by the right of self-determination, it does suggest that John's arguments were simply beside the point if he was trying to justify policies which encourage a group of people to take up some lifetime role.

It is even difficult to see why the argument from efficiency should be effective in persuading a particular person like Harriet to exercise her right of self-determination by choosing a traditional domestic role. It seemed to be an argument that society in general will run more efficiently under the current role division, and it is not obvious that it is wise to make important lifetime commitments on the grounds that society in general is likely to run more efficiently. If the argument is rather that Harriet's life would work more smoothly and efficiently if she has a domestic role, then the right of self-determination says that it is up to her whether to take these facts (supposing them to be determinate) as decisive. If she does not want to struggle or if she does not

fancy some other definite way of life, she may prefer the so-called efficient way. At the same time, it should be noted that it is a little difficult to determine what is meant by saying that her life would be more efficient, for surely that will depend to some very great extent on what her ends are. If her ends are to develop some talents she has or even to remain a lively and developing person, this may not be an efficient route at all. Nor is the evidence clear that this is the most efficient way for her to raise healthy children; that will depend to some extent on whom she thinks of raising them with, how that is likely to work, and so on.

The argument that the current division of labor and role is in some deep and important sense natural is also beside the point. If these roles are "natural," then persons who are taught that they have a right of self-determination will tend to choose them. There is, then, no need to worry about what it might mean to say that the sex roles are natural, nor to await the empirical evidence about whether they are before we decide whether it is justifiable to encourage them or not. Moreover, taking the perspective of someone committed to the right of self-determination accords nicely with a reasonable suspicion that what is natural for persons is not determinate. Sometimes when people talk about a person being a natural in a role, they have in mind that given the person's background, achievement and current interests, he or she would do well at it and flourish in it. Sometimes, however, they attempt to tie success and satisfaction with a role more closely to a person's genetic heritage. In this sense, a role is natural for persons if because of their genetic endowment, they have certain special capacities which enable them to play the role well, the role does not frustrate some deep need and it provides opportunities for them to express their central interests. In the former sense, it is probably true that the domestic role is a natural for most women now, but it is the latter sense that plays a part in arguments that the current division of labor and role is natural and therefore justifiable. In a modern industrial community, however, there must be at the very least several life styles which could be natural in this sense for most any normal person. That is, there must be several ways of life in which their natural talents could be used and which would provide circumstances for the expression of a range of strong human interests without tending to frustrate deep needs. What the right of self-determination gives people is the title to let their own preferences put together a way of life. If these preferences are properly weighted by themselves and others, then the style they put together is very likely to be one which makes use of their special capacities, does not frustrate and provides opportunities for the expression of central interests.

Unfortunately, it is not clear that the right of self-determination will complete the job Harriet hoped it would; that is, adjudicate in her favor the dispute with John over their daughter's education. John, we may suppose, says that it will not do this because the right of self-determination is a right of adults and not of children. He says that it would be absurd if not impossible and immoral to treat young children as if they had the right to make major choices regarding their futures. Either we would give the children no guidance at all, in which case they may well feel lost and have too little discipline to gain what they will want as adults, or we would be required to use the techniques of rational persuasion that we use with adults. This, too, is likely to have disastrous consequences. At best it leads children to confuse the forms of reasoning with reasonable choosing and tends to make them overrate their capacities and status. Guidance must be given to children for their own sakes, and it will be guidance which inevitably will influence what they want later in life. The question is what kind of guidance to give. John wants to encourage in his daughter the feminine virtues. He wants her to be graceful in figure and movement, he is afraid that too much concentration on competitive athletic games will spoil her development. He thinks the modern dance and figure control programs the school has for girls are all that is important for them. He wants her to remain sweet and coy, affectionate and sensitive, and to develop feminine interests in cooking, sewing and children. Not only does he do what he can to encourage these traits in her, but he wants the school to. He thinks that Harriet and her friends have gone too far in complaining about the fact that only a few exceptionally talented or stubborn women are presented as professionals, and in demanding that the girls be taught the manual arts as well as home economics.

In the following section, I argue that even if the right of self-determination is reserved for adults, John's arguments about his daughter's education do not succeed. Even if the right of self-determination does not itself directly limit the kinds of guidance we may give our children, it does in an indirect way.

III. The Importance of Autonomy

Let us say that parents have the authority to make certain decisions affecting the welfare of their offspring. They have this authority because children lack the know-how and the physical and psychological resources to make it on their own. Typically parents are supposed to exercise this authority in the interests of their children though sometimes they may exercise it for their own peace of mind, especially after nine and on weekends. Even given this picture of legitimate parental authority, there is something wrong with John's educational policies. There are, I think, two objections to teaching girls the traditional feminine virtues and role. First (A), such teaching interferes subtly with their exercise of the right of self-determination as mature women. Second (B), anyone committed to the right of self-determination and its importance has reasons for attaching special significance to the development of the capacity to exercise it autonomously.

(A)   To begin with, when we say that mature persons have a right of self-determination, we mean that they are entitled to decide for themselves which career they will attempt, whether or whom to marry, whether to have children, how to spend their leisure time and the like. We all know that deciding for oneself is incompatible with being coerced at the time of choice, but there are subtle influences which may occur earlier and which interfere with the exercise of the right of self-determination.

Let us imagine that a school system has the following practices. First, the system leads girls to take up domestic activities and keeps them from others like competitive games and mechanics. Then, when women reach the age to choose how to spend their time, they have already developed the skills to enjoy cooking and sewing at a high level and discover, not surprisingly, that they like domestic tasks, and not car repair, carpentry or basketball. Surely the possibility that these latter might have been objects of their choice is virtually extinguished. By hypothesis, home economics training for the girls has been successful, that is, many of them really have learned to manage themselves in the kitchen or sewing room so that they are creative and effective, and they have not made similar progress in the workroom. People tend to prefer doing what they are good at, and so women will tend to prefer cooking.

It might be said that at the age of reason, women have the right of self-determination, to choose, for example, to learn carpentry or mechanics, but the right to choose these things will not be worth much if at that time they do not have the possibility of getting satisfaction from these activities at some fairly advanced level because whatever original interest they might have had was never exposed. Not, of course, that everyone should be forced to take home economics, mechanics, and so on, but adults would have a reason to complain if they were systematically deprived of the opportunity to develop some legitimate interest; whereas, if the opportunity had been there and they failed to take it, they would not.

Secondly, the schools do not provide girls with information about women's capacities except for domestic affairs like mothering and cooking. If this occurs, then when the girls become women, they will be unlikely to imagine alternatives and choose intelligently between them. If this were to happen, then women could not even freely choose a domestic life, since they would be likely to see it as the only possibility instead of one among several. Alternatively, suppose that girls are presented with a few examples of women professionals, but these are always presented as rare, extraordinary persons who had to pay a high price for their aspirations. They either gave up the possibility of developing a marriage or they withstood criticism and ostracism for their strange ambitions or both. This makes the cost of choosing another way of life seem so high that most would be unwilling to select it.

Imagine next that girls are rewarded for being patient, sensitive, responsive and obedient, but that displays of ambition and curiosity are met with frowns or silence. The result is that the girls learn to be passive, understanding and sensitive, and not at the same time confident, interested and active. What has happened is that the pattern of traits they develop suits them for domestic life, and when they come to choose between being a housewife and a doctor, they may judge quite correctly that given their current wants and temperament, housewifery is a better prospect for them. If, however, they had been rewarded for curiosity and ambition, the pattern of their personalities would have been different, and it might have been worthwhile for them to develop interests they have in, say, some science, and so to choose another style of life. The difficulty with the training they in fact had is that it has made such a choice unreasonable and done so without attending to the spontaneous and quite legitimate preferences of girls as they developed.

Finally, suppose that certain styles of dress and standards of etiquette are insisted upon for girls and that boys are encouraged to expect girls to meet these and admire those who meet them well. Anyone who deviates from the norm is made to feel uneasy or embarrassed. Imagine, too, that style of dress, while insignificant in itself, is associated with certain career roles and basic life styles. Dress in such a world serves to symbolize the career role and set up important expectations. When the time comes for a woman to choose what she will do, her expectations tend to be fixed not just with regard to the otherwise insignificant matter of dress, but also with regard to what role she will take up. When this happens, it is difficult for her to choose any unexpected role, for any deviation from expectations about her will produce stress and recall the uneasiness she felt upon breaking the dress code.

If the above practices in fact have the effects I envisage, they interfere with the right of self-determination of mature women. To believe that mature persons have a right of self-determination and that such practices are justifiable is rather like believing that Southern Blacks have a right to vote, but that Whites may legitimately ostracize those who exercise it. It would be like believing that Blacks have a right to eat where Whites do and that it would be merely impolite for Whites to stare as if they did not. In some important respects, it would be like a government maintaining that its citizens have a right to travel wherever they choose, but confiscating the passports of those who go to Cuba. If these analogies are acceptable, then even though the educational policies described above do not violate the right of self-determination, they should be changed. Or rather they should be revised unless it can be argued reasonably that each proposed revision would cause disaster or violate some equally important right.

(B)   So far Harriet's commitment to the right of self-determination inclines her to prevent and avoid violations and to minimize interferences like those described above. If, however, she is also committed to the importance of the right, she will want those she cares about to exercise it and to exercise it in a worthwhile way. It is not in general true that belief that one has a right means that one cares about having it or exercising it; for example, the right to travel or to marry do not seem to be rights that one need care about exercising or having. The right of self-determination, however, seems importantly different at least when it is accepted for the suggested rationale. The right was granted to persons to enable them to work out their own way of life in response to their own assessment of their situation, interests and capacities because it was thought appropriate and important that persons work out their own way of life believing that they have a right to. We may ask why this is important, but that is beyond the scope of the present inquiry. It would require explaining the advantages of regarding persons in part as creators of their own way of life rather than merely contributors to the general welfare or some other social ideal.

Assuming, then, that Harriet is also committed to the importance of the right of self-determination, she will want those she loves to exercise it and that its exercise be worthwhile for them. The right of self-determination tends to be worth less to mature persons the fewer opportunities and more interferences they are confronted with and the more they have been trained to have personality traits which make them suited for some definite life role. To say further what tends to make the right worth more, it helps to ask what one would want for persons one loves as they exercise the right of self-determination. Using this device, we are blocked from regarding ourselves as proper determiners of their life style. We do, however, want their good, but partly because we cannot properly determine it and partly because we do not know what will confront them, we do not know what in particular will be good or best for them. Still something can be said about what we want for them.

First, talking of our children and not knowing what they will face, we shall want them to develop the kind of personality which will enable them to respond well to their circumstances whatever they are. We shall want them to have what might be called broadly useful traits, that is, traits which will be helpful whatever their interests and circumstances, traits like confidence, intelligence and discipline. Self-confidence is, for example, a trait which it is good to have because it is useful in a wide variety of ways and inevitably satisfying. Broadly useful traits are the kinds which make a wider range of alternatives feasible for those who have them and so are important for exercising the right of self-determination. We should set about teaching these, then, rather than those associated with some culturally variable sex role.

Secondly, given that our children when mature will have a right of self-determination and given

our ignorance of what they will face, it is not in general reasonable for us to aim for a particular outcome of our children's choices, but rather to develop their capacity to make choices in a certain way, namely, autonomously. That is, at least we want them to make the selections free from certain kinds of pressure. We do not want their selections to be coerced, threatened or bribed, and we do not want them to succumb easily to seductive advice or the bare weight of tradition. Neither do we want their preferences to be neurotic or self-destructive even though there are admittedly circumstances in which neurotic responses pay. In short, we want them to have certain psychological strengths which will enable them to make sensible use of the right of self-determination.

To want our children's choices to be autonomous is also to want their selections to express genuine interests of theirs which arise spontaneously under certain conditions. These are the circumstances in which they have the above psychological strengths and as they are making rational assessments of their capacities and situation. The selections should be spontaneous under these conditions because those are the choices we think of as expressive of us as individuals, and those in turn are the selections we tend to find most deeply satisfying and with which we feel most comfortable. Although we do not usually know what in particular these interests will be, we do know that there are certain basic human interests which anyone might have regardless of their sex or other peculiarities about them. Basic human interests are those taken in the kinds of activities which typically individuals find satisfying and which are potentially healthy. For example, people are capable of gaining satisfaction directly in their work or indirectly because it provides them with income, they find successful friendships and love relations satisfying, they enjoy play and developing their talents. The capacities to enjoy each of these interests, unlike other human capacities—for example, for self-destruction, enmity, hostility, envy and so on—are potentially healthy. They are potentially healthy in that they can be coordinated in one person to produce a satisfying way of life, and styles of life in which these capacities are exploited (and the others minimized) are styles which can be coordinated together in a smooth way. What we can legitimately want and hope that our children have, then, are the satisfactions associated with each of these kinds of interests, and more rather than less. These are legitimate aspirations for us to have for our children because they are the kinds they would want to build their lives around if they were mature and reasonable and if the background conditions of life were decent. Given that these are legitimate aspirations, we should set about helping children understand these potential satisfactions vividly and not to suiting them for some particular lifetime role. Then when people are of an age to warrant saying they have a right of self-determination, ideally they will have psychological strengths and a vivid appreciation of the range of enjoyments possible for them so that they are able to work out a satisfying way of life which is an expression of their spontaneous preferences. This does not require that each be equally capable of fitting in anywhere, but only that there is for everyone some array of feasible options.

According to the preceding argument, young persons should be treated in whatever ways give them the strength and imagination to make use of their right of self-determination autonomously when they reach maturity. Treating them in ways which are believed to do this is a way of respecting the right

they will have when they reach maturity. In addition, if one is to respect someone's right of self-determination fully, one must be willing to allow its exercise even when one believes it is being done badly. This suggests that some importance should be attached to the choices of people simply because they are attempts to arrive at the available alternative most in line with their autonomous preferences. For the most part, this will probably amount to keeping out of others' business. In those we care about and love, however, it will mean valuing and appreciating what they choose simply because it is their choice. This is, perhaps, one way of expressing our love. If so, then Harriet may have taken John's reticence about some of her projects as signs that he did not love her. Equally, of course, he may have believed that Harriet was a bit wacky and irresponsible, or he may not be committed to the right of self-determination or its importance. None of these is likely to sit well with Harriet, who we might imagine really has reached a vision about the moral life which is incompatible with John's view and with which she feels quite comfortable.

12/On Sexual Equality

Alison Jaggar

Oh Ma, what is a feminist?
A feminist, my daughter,
Is any woman now who cares
To organize her own affairs
As men don't think she oughter.

I. Sexual Equality:
Integration or Separation?

A more conventional, though not more apt, definition of a feminist is one who believes that justice requires equality between women and men. Not that equality is a sufficient condition of human or of women's liberation, but it is at least a necessary one. For this reason, and since the concept of equality is already notoriously elusive, it seems worthwhile to

spend a little time reflecting on what it would mean for the sexes to be equal.

Equality, in the sense with which social philosophers are concerned, is a social ideal. Therefore, sexual equality does not mean that individuals of different sexes should be physically indistinguishable from each other (as misogynists sometimes pretend is the goal of women's liberation). It

Various versions of this paper, under different titles, have been read at Kenyon College, at Michigan State University, at the State University of New York at Buffalo, at the fall 1972 meeting of the Society for Women in Philosophy, and at the Western Division meetings of the American Philosophical Association in April 1973. As a result of discussion following my readings, I have made many revisions of the paper, and I am grateful to all those who have forced me to clarify or modify my views. I am especially grateful to Hilda Hein, Marcia Keller, Alice Koller, Caroline Korsmeyer, Maryellen McGuigan, Susan Nicholson, and Beatrice Stegeman, who were all kind enough to send me their written comments and thus made important contributions to this essay.

---

means rather that those of one sex, in virtue of their sex, should not be in a socially advantageous position vis-à-vis those of the other sex. A society in which this condition obtained would be a nonsexist society. Although all feminists, by definition, agree that sexism should be eliminated, disagreement arises among us over how this should be done and how our common goal of sexual equality should be achieved.

The traditional feminist answer to this question has been that a sexually egalitarian society is one in which virtually no public recognition is given to the fact that there is a physiological sex difference between persons. This is not to say that the different reproductive function of each sex should be unacknowledged in such a society nor that there should be no physicians specializing in female and male complaints, etc. But it is to say that, except in this sort of context, the question whether someone is female or male should have no significance.

It is easy to see why both traditional feminism and much of the contemporary women's liberation movement take this view of sexual equality. Since the distinction between the sexes is embedded in our most basic institutions (employment, marriage, the draft, even our language),[1] and since the societal disadvantages of being female are well known, it is natural to suppose that the one is the cause of the other and hence that equality requires the de-institutionalization of sexual differences. For this reason, feminists have always fought hard against the notion that an individual's sex should be an acceptable test for ter[2] fitness to do such things as fill a certain job, borrow money, etc. Much of their effort has been expended in trying to provide legal guarantees to protect women from differential treatment in so-called public life. Recently, and in accord with the contemporary rejection of the old public/private dichotomy on which classical liberalism laid so much stress, some radical feminists have extended the principle that equality requires the minimization of sexual differences even into what used to be called private life. Thus, Shulamith Firestone believes that a sexually

egalitarian society requires that an individual may freely express ter "natural" "polymorphous perversity" by sexual encounters with other people of any age and of either sex,[3] and Ti-Grace Atkinson advocates the total abolition of what she calls "the institution of sexual intercourse."[4]

In order to understand more clearly what is meant by this call for the de-institutionalization of sexual differences, let me pause for a moment to consider what it is for an activity to be institutionalized. Some of the radical feminists' proposals may be confusing if they are thought to suggest that every cooperative activity constitutes a social institution. One unfortunate consequence of taking this suggestion seriously would be to undermine the distinction between individual and institutional prejudice, a distinction which is very useful in the analysis of discriminatory behavior.[5] At least for present purposes, then, I shall take a social institution to be a relatively stable way of organizing a significant social activity. To institutionalize activity streamlines social intercourse by defining socially recognized roles and thus enables prediction of what those participating in the practice are likely to do. It also, and perhaps more importantly, provides a standard of correctness by reference to which the propriety of certain kinds of behavior may be judged. It is clear from this definiion why even such an apparently individual matter as sexual intercourse, to the extent that it is governed by community norms and even regulated by law, should be acknowledged as a social institution. This definition also makes it clear that some forms of activity may be institutionalized in one society and not in another; it depends on the extent of social regulation and control.

Institutional sexism is a social disadvantage which attaches to individuals of one sex or the other as the result of a certain way of institutionalizing activity. In this, it differs from individual sexism which occurs when a certain individual or group of individuals express hatred or contempt for an individual or group of (usually) the other sex by an act of hostility which may or may not be violent but which is

---

[1] The sexism implicit in our language is documented by Robert Baker of Wayne State University in a paper . . . entitled "'Pricks' and 'Chicks': A Plea for 'Persons.'" [See chapter 1, this volume—ed.] It is also shown by Kate Miller and Casey Swift in an article called "De-Sexing the English Language," *Ms.* (Spring 1972).

[2] In this paper I adopt the suggestions of Miller and Swift for a new form of the generic singular pronoun. Instead of using "he," "him," and "his," I employ their suggested common-gender form, derived from the plural, namely, "tey," "tem," and "ter(s)."

[3] Shulamith Firestone, *The Dialectic of Sex: The Case for Feminist Revolution* (New York: Bantam Books, 1971).

[4] Ti-Grace Atkinson, "The Institution of Sexual Intercourse" and "Radical Feminism," in *Notes from the Second Year*, ed. S. Firestone (New York, 1970).

[5] As far as I know, this distinction was first made with respect to racial prejudice by Stokely Carmichael and Charles V. Hamilton in their book *Black Power: The Politics of Liberation in America* (New York: Vintage Books, 1967).

not part of a socially stabilized pattern of discrimination. As social philosophers, we must obviously be concerned primarily with the former type of discrimination, for our first task is to articulate a social ideal.

Let us now return to what I see as my central question, namely, does equality between the sexes require that there should be no institutional recognition of sexual differences, that is, no institutions which differentiate systematically between women and men? I have already remarked that the mainstream of feminist thought has held almost continuously that the answer to this question is yes. In the mainstream tradition, the nonsexist society is one which is totally integrated sexually, one in which sexual differences have ceased to be a matter of public concern. That this should be the ultimate goal of the women's liberation movement follows logically from one very natural interpretation of such familiar slogans as "Women want to be treated as human beings" or "as persons" or "as individuals." On this interpretation, to treat someone as a person is to ignore ter sex.[6]

Recently, however, the traditional feminist goal of sexual integration has been challenged —and challenged by those who, on the criterion of their belief in sexual equality, are undeniably feminists. Just as there is a faction within the black liberation movement which rejects the ideals of "color blindness" and racial integration in favor of black pride and racial separatism, so there are now some feminists who argue that a person's sex is an inescapable and important fact about tem which ought to be socially recognized rather than ignored.

The issue between these two groups of feminists is not entirely clear. In some cases, it seems to be merely a matter of tactics or strategy: what is the best way of improving the position of women in this society? But the disagreement is also a philosophical one, philosophical in two senses. On the one hand, it involves certain more or less familiar conceptual problems: what constitutes justice or equality? what constitutes a person? even, what constitutes a sexual difference? And, on the other hand, it involves a normative disagreement over the kind of society for which we should aim.[7]

In this paper, I shall explore the philosophical differences between these two groups of feminists

and try to establish that sexual separation, or the institutionalization of sexual differences, is neither necessary nor desirable. I shall begin by attempting to refute various philosophical arguments to the conclusion that it is impossible, logically and practically, to ignore a person's sex. I shall then deal with other arguments which purport to present good reasons for the institutionalization of sexual differences. Thus, I shall move from the more clearly conceptual to the more explicitly normative claims. My overriding aim will be to defend the traditional feminist conception of sexual equality as the deinstitutionalization of sexual differences.

II. Are Persons Necessarily Sexual?

Those who deny that complete "sexual blindness" is an appropriate goal for the women's liberation movement may do so on the ground that such blindness is not even a logical possibility. They may argue that in recognizing someone as a person, one must simultaneously recognize ter sex, since sexuality is a category which necessarily applies to persons. In this case, it would be held to be logically true that a person could not exist devoid of sexuality; it would be self-contradictory to speak of a person who was neither male nor female. Such a claim may seem to be supported by the contemporary rejection of dualism and the widespread acceptance of the view that it is incoherent to regard persons simply as disembodied minds. If persons are necessarily embodied, then it might be thought to follow that we are necessarily either female or male. If this were so, one's awareness of another's sex would be built into one's recognition of tem as a person, so that to be "sexually blind" would disqualify one from recognizing others as persons—and hence, perhaps, from being a person oneself.

This argument does not work. There is no reason to believe that sexuality is a category which must be applied to persons so that it becomes necessarily true that we are all either female or male. Certainly this is not entailed by the claim that we are necessarily embodied. The conceptual truth that there must be a physical basis for the ascription of personal characteristics provides no grounds for the belief that this physical basis must also be sexual. The very neglect of the topic of sexuality in the innumerable recent (and, admittedly, mostly male) discussions of the criteria for being a person suggests that the concept of sex is in no way essen-

---

[6]This is suggested, for example, by the subtitle of Baker's paper (n. 1 above).

[7]I am aware that the distinction between a normative and a conceptual disagreement, like that between a factual and a conceptual disagreement, is far from clear.

tial to the concept of a person. In fact, it has even been argued that the retention of sexual identity is not essential to the maintenance of personal identity,[8] though this is a more dubious claim.[9]

That not all persons must be either female or male becomes clearer when one reflects that "person" is not a purely descriptive concept. To call someone a person is not only (if at all) to make an empirical claim about ter biological construction but, rather, to ascribe a moral status, with attendant rights and responsibilities. Some capacities are relevant to the ascription of this status. They include the ability to enjoy and to suffer, to reason, to engage in moral deliberation, and so on. So far, we believe that these capacities belong only to human beings, although the rapid advance of technology has rendered this belief notoriously open to question. But surely we would not want to *insist,* as a matter of principle, that the physical basis of a person must always resemble our familiar human body. After all, we don't want to say that all human beings, including idiots, are persons in the full-fledged moral sense. So why should we deny that it is possible in principle for machines or creatures from outer space (both of which we may assume to be asexual)[10] to qualify for the status of personhood?

The question whether persons are necessarily sexual is ultimately a moral rather than a conceptual question. It depends on one's decision whether the capacity to engage in sexual activity affects the fundamental rights and responsibilities of persons. For me, the answer is clearly no, although I would not deny that this ability raises its own moral issues. It may be that one's sexual capacity has a relevance to the question of personhood which I have failed to see. But if this is so, then the claim must be argued. The onus is on whoever would discriminate, whether it be the discrimination against certain people, against animals, even against machines or Martians, to justify ter discrimination.

For these reasons, I deny that it is either a conceptual or a moral truth that all persons are

either female or male. Of course, even if this argument were fallacious, and all persons did have a sex, it would not follow logically that the difference between the sexes was something that ought to be institutionally reinforced—but it might well seem somewhat unreasonable to refuse to recognize publicly one of the defining characteristics of a person. However, if having a sex is *not* one of the defining characteristics of a person, as I have argued, then we can draw no justification from the concept of a person for arguing that our ideal society requires a social distinction between persons of different sexes.

To argue that it is not self-contradictory to postulate a nonsexual person is not, however, a very strong claim. In response to it, many feminists would simply retort that they are not interested in the remote logical possibilities for science fiction creatures but, rather, in the real possibilities for those who now qualify as persons and who are, after all, indisputably female or male.[11] Given that the only persons we now encounter are women and men, it might plausibly be argued that, whatever the logical possibilities, practically speaking we cannot ignore the sexual distinction between persons. It is this claim that I shall consider next.

III. The Distinction Between the Sexes

The traditional feminist claim that sexual equality is to be achieved by ignoring sexual differences obviously presupposes a certain view of what a sexual difference is. As a matter of historical fact (though not conceptual necessity), sexual integrationists have regarded an individual's sex as being an entirely physiological characteristic.[12] It is assumed that the physiological differences are not accompanied by any significant differences between the sexes in such apparently nonphysical functions as sensitivity, reasoning, moral deliberation, etc. This makes it plausible to claim that sexual differences can be ignored in most social contexts except those directly concerned with reproduction.

The picture might change, however, if this view about what constitutes a sexual difference

---

[8]This claim is made by Roland Puccetti in an article entitled "Brain Transplantation and Personal Identity," *Analysis* 29, no. 3 (January 1969): 65–77.

[9]Puccetti's claim is challenged by Andrew Brennan in "Persons and Their Brains," *Analysis* 30, no. 1 (October 1969): 27–31. Puccetti's reply to Brennan was published in *Analysis* 31, no. 1 (October 1970): 30–32.

[10]Everyone, however, may not share this assumption. I understand that when the new word for "computers" was entering the German language, there was considerable dispute about whether it should be given the masculine or the neuter gender. That it should have the feminine gender apparently was not even considered.

[11]In our society a sex must be ascribed to each individual at birth, regardless of the uncertainty of ter physical characteristics.

[12]Although the difference in reproductive capacity is what makes the physiological differences between the sexes important to us, the physiological distinction is normally taken as the primary criterion for determining the sex of an individual, and one who is unable to reproduce is not thereby described as sexless. Therefore, I call the distinction physiological rather than functional.

were shown to be inadequate, if it could be argued successfully that the concept of sex should include not only a difference in reproductive organs but also certain nonphysical differences. Empirical research in this area is still inconclusive, to say the least, but if a philosophical argument could demonstrate that sexual differences necessarily stretch beyond the physical, this should force us to rethink the claim that such differences are socially irrelevant. And if sexual differences were shown to be much more far-reaching than we had hitherto supposed, we might come to believe that it was practically if not logically impossible to ignore a person's sex.

There are, of course, a number of arguments by misogynists purporting to show that women are intellectually and morally inferior to men. But I shall take these as already refuted by other writers and turn instead to the one author I have been able to discover who deals with the question in a manner which is both philosophical and feminist. This is Professor Christine Garside, who first takes up the issue in a paper entitled "Women and Persons":[13]

. . . Women will always be different from men as the result of self-determination, because we differ in physical structure, we differ in our present social experience, we differ in our inherited past and so on.

I suspect that it was in some part the fear of loss of polarity between the sexes which led to the traditional denial of self-determination for women. This fear, however, is groundless for a true polarity will emerge when women and men press forward in active self-determination.[14]

The concluding paragraph of her paper runs thus:

Finally, I would like to reiterate my belief that there is no need to fear loss of polarity when women do achieve liberation on the level of self-determination. . . . There is no way that women can ever become identical to men. Nor is there any reason why they should desire to do so. The heritage and experience of women is as rich as the heritage and experience as [of?] men; and once women recognize their right to self-determination

and release their creative energies into the world this will be obvious.[15]

Now, in its narrowest interpretation, the claim that women can never be identical to men is simply tautologous, trivially true, just like the claim that people with big feet can never be identical to people with small ones. But of course Garside is saying more than this, and her most recent paper, "True Sex-Polarity,"[16] gives a fuller exposition of her views. In this account, she utilizes Scriven's notion of "normical" properties, properties which do not belong analytically to an object but whose presence is not purely accidental or, as she says, "arbitrary." "A normical property is one which is needed in a thorough explanation of the thing which has the property."[17] An object may lack any one of its normical properties, but it could not lack them all and still be an object of that type.

Garside claims that there is only one property which belongs analytically to women, namely, that of being a person, but she believes that this one property is supplemented by a number of normical properties. "What it is to be a woman includes having a particular kind of body, having a recent history of being brought up in a patriarchal society, having an inherited history of female archetypes, having present experiences which occur because one is female, and having a future which calls for a revolution from being oppressed. There are other things as well, but these are most central."[18]

In elaborating this definition, Garside gives a rich and evocative account of what it is to be female. The alternative account, which I wish to espouse, is much starker. For me, to be a woman is no more and no less than to be a female human being. All and only female human beings are women. To be female and to be human are the necessary and sufficient conditions for being a woman.

I therefore deny Garside's claim that the property which she regards as belonging analytically to women, namely, that of being a person, is in fact an analytic property. Acceptance of my argument in the last section that the concept of a person is a moral category entails the possibility that not all human beings are persons in the full-fledged moral

[13]Christine Garside's "Women and Persons" was the winning entry in "The Problem of Women" prize essay competition. It is published in *Mother Was Not a Person,* an anthology compiled by Margret Andersen (Montreal: Content, 1972). My criticism of Garside's argument should in no way be taken, of course, as reflecting a lack of admiration for her work.

[14]Ibid., p. 196.

[15]Ibid., p. 202.

[16]Parts of this paper were read in response to mine at the Western Division meetings of the American Philosophical Association in April 1973.

[17]Christine Garside, "True Sex-Polarity."

[18]Ibid.

sense. For example, mental defectives are not persons in this sense. Therefore, not all women are persons.

I take issue further with Garside's explanation of womanhood in terms of normical properties. It may indeed be true that all women do in fact possess some or even all of the properties she lists (although we may well not be aware of all of them, for example, our inherited history of female archetypes). But it seems plainly false to assert that if we came across a female human being who lacked these characteristics, we should deny her the name of woman. So, contrary to Garside, I claim that we have no need to talk about normical properties in talking about what it is to be a woman. This would change only if we found reason to be uncertain of what it was to be human or what it was to have a female body, for example, if a case occurred where an individual's endocrine system was not in conformity with ter reproductive organs or something like that.

My account of the distinction between the sexes rests on an analysis of our present concepts of what it is to be a woman and what it is to be a man. On my account, which is faithful to the way in which the words are ordinarily used, these are very simple concepts. However, it might be replied that what is wanted here is more than analysis. Someone might argue that our concept of woman needs to be reformed or enriched, much as Garside has tried to do. This may indeed be so. But such reforms should be made only in response to a clear deficiency in our ordinary ways of thinking. And in pointing out these facts about women, I don't think Garside has shown this deficiency. All that she has done is to point out that there are certain characteristics which most women in fact share (except the having of a female body, which I see as a necessary rather than a normical property). But Garside's comments do not yet indicate a lack in our concept of woman. It may be that future scientific discoveries will do so, but a convincing philosophy cannot rest on such speculation.

So much for the conceptual side of our disagreement. Now to its implications. Neither Garside nor I dispute the empirical facts regarding women's history, socialization, etc. But we do differ, apparently, in the significance that we attach to those facts. Garside seems to believe that they are of great importance, that they result in distinct and permanent differences between male and female nature, if that is an acceptable gloss for her term

"sex-polarity." I'm less sure about this. I simply don't know how important these factors are. I suppose the importance of at least some of them might be investigated empirically—although I don't know how one could investigate empirically her claim that "it feels different to be a woman than to be a man."[19] At the moment, given the oppressive conditions of the present and the past, those factors may be very important. But one may hope that, as conditions improve, as women experience less discrimination, for example, those factors may weigh less heavily. So not only is it not conceptually true, it may not even be empirically true that, in a more than trivial philosophical sense, there will always be a sexual polarity.

Garside's presumption that there are certain necessary features of personal experience seems to be philosophically sound. I would accept that it is indeed a conceptual truth that persons must have physical experiences, social experiences, and some kind of cultural heritage. But what does not seem to be conceptually true is that these features have an inescapably sexual character. I am not, of course, asserting, a priori, that the differences between women and men have been shown conclusively to be limited to the purely reproductive and that, therefore, complete sexual integration is possible in all social contexts except those directly involving reproduction. What I am claiming, however, is that we have as yet no good reason, either a priori or empirical, for denying the possibility of sexual integration. So, since I believe that integration is a desirable ideal, I claim that we should work on the assumption that it is possible. Only if empirical research or new philosophical arguments demonstrate other differences between the sexes shall we need to question again the possibility of this ideal.

IV. The Rights of Women

Even in the absence of reason to believe in a sexual polarity which transcends the physiological distinction, it might be argued that the simple physiological differences between women and men

[19]For a discussion of some of the problems of investigating empirically whether there are innate psychological differences between the sexes, see my "On Female Nature," forthcoming in *The Problem of Women,* incorporating prize essays on "The Problem of ♀, a competition sponsored by SUNY at Fredonia. SUNY at Fredonia organized "The Problem of ♀" prize essay competition and planned to publish some of the entries. Apparently they are now having difficulty finding a publisher. I have not heard from them for months.

were alone sufficient to justify the institutionalization of sexual differences. The facts that women are, in general, smaller and (in some ways) weaker than men, that we give birth to children, and so on, may be thought to constitute in themselves inequalities which require social remedy. In the past, such arguments have been used by male supremacists as justification for forcing on women a kind of "protection" which guarantees to us an inferior social position, but the biological facts may also be used by feminists as grounds for arguing that women should receive special treatment in order to offset our biological inequality. Such a feminist is Shulamith Firestone, who believes that the goal of social equality between the sexes requires a technological advance which will allow for the extrauterine reproduction of children, thus freeing women from what Firestone calls "the fundamental inequality of the bearing and raising of children."[20]

This claim apparently takes for granted the conclusion of my argument in the last section that one's sex should be essentially determined by the shape of ter reproductive organs. Its novelty seems to lie in its view of equality. For it presupposes that equality is not merely equality of opportunity, that is not merely the absence of social impediments based on sex to any individual's attaining whatever position in society tey chooses to aim for. Instead, equality is viewed in a more positive sense, as a certain level of physical and economic security which society ought to provide for each of its members. In order that each individual should reach this level, it may be necessary to grant special social rights to certain disadvantaged groups, and it is claimed that women constitute a group which requires such rights in order to achieve social equality with men.

In order to qualify as a genuine female right, any proposal must be envisioned as a permanent feature of a nonsexist society. It cannot be viewed simply as a temporary measure, like alimony or the preferential hiring of women, which are usually advocated as necessary only to correct an unequal situation but which should be discontinued as soon as the imbalance is remedied. To be a genuine "female right," the alleged right must be seen as belonging permanently to all women simply in virtue of our sex and not, for example, in virtue of our social status or in virtue simply of our being human. When the sexual distinction is seen primarily as a differ-

ence in reproductive organs, it follows that the kind of special rights which women are said to need in a sexually egalitarian society should be connected with our reproductive function. They include the right to protection from assault and rape, the right to abortion, the right to maternity leave, and the right to guaranteed care and/or financial support for our children.

In my opinion, the trouble with this position lies not in its vision of social equality as a positive condition but, rather, in its view of the sexual distinction. Despite its apparent acceptance of the view that sex is merely physiological, I think that those who claim the need for special female rights are surreptitiously extending the sexual distinction to cover more than a physiological difference. For example, it may well be true that society in general should take on the responsibility of providing and caring for children, but this proposal should not be presented as a *female* right. To do so is to make the obviously false assumption that the sexual difference consists not only in women's capacity to give birth to children but also in our having an obligation to raise them. Even on the dubious presumption that the welfare of children is the total responsibility of whoever produced them, it is clear that this measure would provide relief to *both* parents of the children, the father as well as the mother. But perhaps a preferable way of seeing this proposal is not as a right of parents at all but rather as a right of children.

Similarly, to suggest that the right to freedom from assault and rape is a specifically female right is to presuppose that women alone are desirable sexual objects or that women alone are incapable of defending themselves. Such suggested female rights are far better viewed as applications of general human rights, so that adequate protection may be afforded to any individual, male or female, who needs it. Thus, the right to maternity leave should be covered by the statement that those who are temporarily incapable of contributing to material production should not be expected to do so. The stress on the special nature of maternity leave does indeed emphasize that pregnancy and childbirth are not sicknesses, but it also suggests that women need special privileges which men don't require. This suggestion is misleading. We do not, after all, elevate "prostate leave" into a special right of men.

The proposed female right to abortion is more complicated. It is certainly something which does not apply to men, but it is often defended either as a way of allowing women to enjoy the general human

[20]*The Dialectic of Sex* (n. 3 above).

right of "control over one's own body" or, perhaps more plausibly, as a way of allowing women the general human right of sexual freedom.[21] The former right, however, is extremely ill-determined and controversial; how much control over ter own body should a typhoid carrier have, for example? And the latter right, of sexual freedom, may well be thought to be limited by a consideration of the rights of the fetus. If this is so, however, then a feminist could argue that, in the absence of foolproof contraceptive methods, the right to sexual freedom should be limited for men as well as for women. The complexity of this special case makes it impossible to discuss adequately here, but it certainly does not seem to me to present a clear case of special female right which ought to be guaranteed by a sexually egalitarian society.

In general, I would argue that, so long as we view the difference between the sexes as a simple physiological difference—and we have no conclusive grounds for doing more—then there is no reason to draw up a special bill of rights for women in order to ensure our equality. The rights of women can be protected quite adequately in a society which recognizes basic human rights.

V. The Preservation of Female "Culture"

Another challenge to the belief that sexual equality requires complete sexual integration is rooted in the rejection of the classical liberal model of a society as composed of a multitude of isolated individuals, each intent on pursuing ter own private advantage to the best of ter ability. It is now frequently argued that this model is inadequate to account for the complexities of modern society and that it should be superseded by a different picture of society as composed of a series of groups organized on a variety of different bases. It is this latter model which underlies the arguments of some feminists who argue for a kind of sexual separation. These feminists claim that women, like it or not, form a series of special-interest groups and that in order to gain social equality we ought to seek power for our groups as a whole in order to rival the power of the groups presently formed by men. Such feminists often deny that integration on an individual level is a realistic goal. This pluralist model of equality contrasts sharply with that view which sees equality in

terms of assimilation and integration by individuals. It is generally associated with the type of conservatism and reaction which is perhaps most clearly typified by the South African system of apartheid, so it is interesting to see that the motto of "separate but equal" can also be adopted by genuine feminists.[22]

The pluralistic model of equality is supported by arguments which are sometimes strikingly similar to those used by the factions of the U.S. black liberation movement which advocate racial separatism. One such argument is that women have a distinctive culture which would be lost if complete sexual integration were to occur. It is also contended that individual women will not be recognized by men as genuine equals in any sphere so long as we belong to an inferior "caste." For this reason, it is claimed, the assimilation of individuals is impossible until the prestige of women as a group has been raised through the establishment of strong female institutions capable of challenging the power of the present male-dominated institutions. The institutions most generally regarded as crucial to feminism are education, health, and the media, but there are some advocates of separate female financial institutions and even a female military force. Persuaded by such arguments, a number of women even deny that a genuine heterosexual love relationship is possible in the present conditions of male/female inequality and they therefore recommend exclusively lesbian sexual arrangements. Finally, it is claimed that women need to have strong supportive female groups behind them before they can "get it together" as individuals sufficiently to face integration with men. For this reason, too, therefore, sexual separation is seen as a more appropriate goal for the women's liberation movement than complete sexual integration on an individual level.

The trouble with most of these arguments is that they rest on empirical premises about the psychology of oppressed groups whose truth is, to say the least, controversial. But in any case, they do not directly attack the notion of individual sexual integration as an ideal; they claim merely that sexual separation is a necessary step on the way to this ultimate goal. The only argument which challenges the *ultimate* desirability of complete sexual integration is the one which advocates the preservation of a distinctive female "culture" and sees separation as the only way of achieving this.

[21]The latter suggestion was made by Caroline Korsmeyer of the State University of New York at Buffalo.

[22]I am using here my original definition of a feminist, namely, someone who believes in sexual equality.

For the sake of evaluating this argument, let us assume that there does indeed exist a worldwide split between female and male "culture."[23] "Male culture" consists of the art, philosophy, and science which are identified with national culture and from which, it is claimed, women have been excluded almost totally. "Female culture," on the other hand, is less visible and less closely tied to national boundaries. In the past, it has included many invaluable contributions to civilization, such as folk medicine, the preparation and preservation of food, spinning, weaving, pottery, and so on. Nowadays, however, it has been reduced to a number of relatively simple domestic skills, mainly involving such tasks as cooking, cleaning, and child care, in a few unprestigious skills such as typing which are used in work outside the home, and in the subtle skills which women use to make themselves attractive to men. "Female culture" is said to embody values which are contrary, antipathetic, to those embodied in the institutions of "male culture" such as the government, army, religion, and economy. In particular, it is claimed that "female culture" demands and fosters such values as empathy, intuition, love, responsibility, endurance, practicality, and humanization.

It is certainly true that the above-mentioned characteristics are highly valued in few, if any, national or "male" cultures. Instead, these cultures often emphasize such qualities as discipline, self-control, efficiency, etc. But there are other aspects of "female culture," especially in its debased modern aspect, which are perhaps less admirable. They include lack of initiative, dependence, timidity, narcissism, cunning, manipulativeness, etc. Nor can the existence of these features be written off entirely as propagandist examples of sexual stereotyping. On the contrary, they are the necessary concomitants of the culture of an economically dependent group; they typify a slave culture. And this being so, it seems obvious that they represent aspects of "female culture" which liberated women will not want to preserve.

It is doubtful, indeed, whether those aspects even could be preserved in a society where women were organizing their own institutions in competition with those of men. The necessity of competition would entail that women would have to adopt the "male" values of discipline, efficiency, etc., simply in order to face the male challenge. This is, of course, the same problem that faces utopian socialist or anarchist groups who wish to institute values different from those which prevail at present but who have to survive in a world where their values are at a practical disadvantage, at least with respect to quantity of production.

Whatever may be the solution to this dilemma in other spheres, it seems clear that the problem as it arises for women cannot be solved by sexual separation. Not only is it extremely unlikely that female institutions could ever challenge successfully the dominant male ones, but they would be corrupted if they did so. They would have to abandon those values we have designated as characteristically female ones, and thus women would be forced to become imitations of men.

What we now call female culture could not survive if it were placed in competition with, instead of in subordination to, the male culture. Nor, I would argue, should we want it to. We should recognize that our culture is to a large extent the culture of an oppressed group, and while we may not wish to let it be forgotten entirely, at the same time we should distinguish those elements which we want to keep alive. Obviously we do not really want to perpetuate the supposedly feminine skills of hair curling or straightening, makeup, and the "arts" of seduction. What we must do instead is to create a new androgynous culture which incorporates the best elements of both the present male and the present female cultures, which values both personal relationships and efficiency, both emotion and rationality.

This result cannot be achieved through sexual separation. Our ideal of sexual equality must go beyond the achievement of a balance of economic and political power for contending female and male groups. Ultimately, I believe that we must seek total integration on a personal level, so that an individual's sex is viewed as a fact which is irrelevant to ter place in society.

VI. Sexual Differentiation as Intrinsically Valuable

I want to consider one more argument against sexual integration. The proponents of this argument

[23]It has become fashionable to use the term "culture" very loosely to describe the special practices of a certain group within a larger society. A more accurate term might be "subculture," but in this discussion I shall follow the usage of the writers whose views I am discussing. Much of the characterization of male and female "culture" which follows is taken from the *Fourth World Manifesto*, by Barbara Burris, reprinted in *Notes from the Third Year* (Women's Liberation), edited by Anne Koedt and Shulamith Firestone (New York, 1971), pp. 102–19.

may well accept the simple physiological view of the sexual distinction, but they still propose, on what seem to be semiaesthetic grounds, that it is desirable to preserve a social distinction between the sexes. Freud seems to be taking this position when he suggests that, if women leave "the calm uncompetitive activity of home" and join "the struggle for existence exactly as men," we should mourn "the passing away of the most delightful thing the world can offer us—our ideal of womanhood."[24]

I call arguments on these lines *vive la différence* arguments. They recur with predictable regularity whenever women's liberation is being discussed. They claim that the basic physiological differences between the sexes should be the grounds of social differentiation because in this way we can add a spice of pleasurable variety to life. They argue that sexual equality in the sense that one sex should not have more social advantages than the other does not entail that the sexes should have identical social roles. They ask, rhetorically, "Wouldn't it be unfortunate if we were all alike?" These arguments are persuasive because of their suggestion that those who do not recognize the pleasures of institutionalizing sexual differences are gloomy puritans. They suggest that their proponents are advocating not sexual inequality but merely a kind of healthy hedonism.

Simone de Beauvoir's response to Freud's argument is to point out what both women and men invariably lose as well as what we gain when a sexual role system is established. She agrees "that he would be a barbarian indeed who failed to appreciate exquisite flowers, rare lace, the crystal-clear voice of the eunuch, and feminine charm."[25] But then she asks, "Does a fugitive miracle—and one so rare—justify us in perpetuating a situation that is baneful for both sexes? One can appreciate the beauty of flowers, the charm of women, and appreciate them at their true value; if these treasures cost blood or misery, they must be sacrificed."[26]

De Beauvoir's point is well taken. The forcing of women into a socially shaped mold of femininity may indeed have its compensations; but, as contemporary women's liberation literature never tires

of reminding us, those advantages have been more than offset in practice by their corresponding disadvantages. Such disadvantages include not only female frustration, the wasting of female potential and talent, loss of female initiative, and so on, but also a corresponding denial of self-realization to men. Insofar as sexual discrimination exists in contexts other than the reproductive, and hence is based on a difference which is irrelevant in those contexts, it is bound to limit arbitrarily the options of both women and men.

There is, however, a more far-reaching argument against sexual separation. This is hinted at by some radical feminists, such as Ti-Grace Atkinson, when they claim that the sexual role system should be abolished not just because the goal of "separate but equal" seems to be unrealizable in fact but because it is one aspect of a role system which ideally should be abolished in its entirety. I take such talk about the desirability of a "role system" to be a way of talking about the desirability of institutionalizing human activity. This claim is sometimes thought to be involved in the political theory of anarchism, and since many of the radical feminist writings, especially those of Firestone and Atkinson, pay homage to some fundamental anarchist ideals, I shall draw on the anarchist tradition in an attempt to reconstruct the kind of considerations which may well have influenced Atkinson in rejecting a role system.[27]

One general objection to a role system is that it might tempt us to define a person by ter relation to a social institution. Thus, a person comes to be seen simply as a tinker, a tailor, a soldier, or a sailor. Not only is such stereotyping an obvious disfigurement of an individual's humanity, but it seems to conflict with the anarchist ideal of a person able to do many different kinds of work in a society where specialization of human function has been minimized if not eliminated.

The institutionalization of human activity might also be thought inimical to the anarchist ideal of social freedom. To the extent that social institutions embody norms of behavior and impose sanctions, even if only as mild as social disapproval, on individuals who depart from those norms, the freedom of the individual might be thought to be compromised. Indeed, it is a conceptual truth that, in

---

[24] This well-known passage from one of Freud's letters to his fiancée is quoted in *Masculine/Feminine: Readings in Sexual Mythology and the Liberation of Women,* ed. Betty Roszak and Theodore Roszak (New York: Harper & Row, 1969).

[25] Simone de Beauvoir, *The Second Sex* (New York: Bantam Books, 1961), p. 686.

[26] Ibid., p. 687.

[27] For some of the following ideas I am indebted to my former colleague, Peter M. Schuller of Miami University, Ohio, who explains them in an unpublished paper entitled "Antinomic Elements in Higher Education."

order to be playing a role at all, the behavior of the player must be circumscribed by the requirements of that role.

Finally, the existence of a role system might appear to be incompatible with the moral autonomy of the individual.[28] If the obligations of a person's role are taken as defining the whole of ter moral obligations, then it becomes impossible for that individual to rise above the conventional morality of professional ethics. Insofar as one conforms to ter role, one may be forced to do what is morally wrong or be unable to do what is morally right. A soldier may have to kill and a salaried employee may be unable to avoid contributing to the war effort. In order to act morally, therefore, it seems to be necessary to transcend one's role, to examine critically the obligations which define it. Thus, a morally autonomous person must, despite the functionalist theory of contemporary sociologists, be more than the sum of ter roles.

These arguments are very persuasive, and in my original draft of this paper I accepted them. However, I now believe that they can be answered, that human freedom and equality do not require the de-institutionalization of all human activity.[29] I doubt, in fact, whether the very concept of a society without some kind of "role system" is coherent. It seems to me now that a society necessarily includes social institutions which define social roles, in fact, that it is precisely the norms embodied in those institutions which provide the criteria for the identification of that society.

Not only are norms logically necessary to a society; by ensuring a certain degree of social predictability, they are also practically necessary. However, in order that social institutions should not be oppressive, certain conditions must be fulfilled. The norms which we endorse should be determined rationally by all concerned. Such norms should help rather than hinder justice and personal self-determination; to use a couple of obvious examples, such things as exploitation and rape should not be permissible. And the norms which define a social role should not be viewed as absolutely binding on the one who is performing that role: roles should be seen, rather, as imposing prima facie duties which may, in certain circumstances, be overridden. In this case, to adopt a role will not per se limit one's moral autonomy.[30] Finally, a person should not be assigned any role involuntarily; instead, tey should be able to choose from a variety of roles.

These requirements necessitate the abolition of a role system based on sex. Sex roles are not determined by those concerned. They are irrational whenever they regulate our behavior in contexts other than the reproductive, for in doing so they unwarrantably presuppose that the difference between the sexes is more than a simple physiological distinction. Sex roles are restrictive and oppressive, in fact if not in principle. And, necessarily, they are ascribed by others rather than assumed voluntarily. Hence, while I cannot agree that personal liberation and equality require the total de-institutionalization of all human activity, I do believe that women's and men's liberation and sexual equality require that the distinction between the sexes should ultimately be de-institutionalized. I am not, of course, advocating that a genuine feminist should refuse to recognize physiological sexual differences. To do this would suggest that feminism involves a reversion to the kind of Victorian hypocrisy which preferred to call a woman's legs her "limbs." But I do claim that a sexually egalitarian society must be integrated in the sense that sexual differences should not be institutionally recognized.

VII. Conclusion

This account of sexual equality is obviously not purely analytic, nor is it intended to be. It is designed to persuade. And if it is accepted, various practical conclusions follow from it. If sexual equality requires integration, then a feminist should seek to modify our language by the use of neuter proper names and the elimination of gender in order to undermine the sexist consciousness which presently permeates it.[31] Tey must, of course, continue the long and tedious struggle against institutionalized sexual discrimination. And when people complain that you can't tell the boys from the girls nowadays, the feminist response must be to point out that it should make no difference. As Florynce Kennedy demanded, "Why do they want to know anyway? So that they can discriminate?"

[28] This seems to be an implication of Robert Paul Wolff's thesis in his *In Defense of Anarchism* (New York: Harper & Bros, 1970).

[29] I was forced to this realization by argument with Marlene Freed.

[30] For a fuller discussion of this claim, see my "The Just State as a Round Square," *Dialogue* 11, no. 4 (December 1972): 580–83.

[31] These measures are among those suggested by Baker (n. 1, above).

13/Sexuality as a Metaphysical Dimension

Kathryn Morgan

Off the Great Barrier Reef lives a little scavenger fish which is able to reverse its sex.[1] Such fish travel in small groups. The biggest and strongest of each group is the leader. The leader is a male. All the rest are female. Should something happen to the male, one of the females takes its place at the head of the group. She adopts territorial behavior and, within a short period, starts producing sperm. Should another fish join the group and succeed in challenging the leader, the deposed leader drops back in the ranks and resumes her production of viable eggs. Unfortunately, human beings are not so flexible—or so we have been led to think.

In this paper, I distinguish two claims. The first is that human beings are necessarily sexual. I argue in favor of this claim. The second is that sexual dimorphism, the division of human beings into exclusive male and female classes, is also a necessary feature of human existence. I argue against this claim.

The General Claim:
That Sexuality, per se, is a
Metaphysical Dimension of Human Beings

In making this claim, I am not saying that every aspect of human existence has *sexual* significance nor that every aspect of human sexuality has *metaphysical* significance. Rather, I am claiming that sexuality is an essential constituent structure on a par with rationality and volition. These are logically independent of human sexuality although they may be highly integrated in a particular human being. In arguing for this thesis, a number of strategies might be used. I shall sketch just two arguments here.

The Argument from Ordinary Experience

It is generally agreed that sexuality is involved in an extremely broad range of human concerns. This is suggested by the variety of contexts in which we speak of it. At the biological level, we speak about sex organs, cells, hormones, health, excitement, stimuli, anatomy. At the individual psychological level, we speak about sexual pleasure, zones, deprivation, appeal, development, history, expression, perversion, identity, dreams, fantasies, and life. At the social level, we speak about sexual performance, partners, objects, communication, art, education, games, toys, symbols, rituals, roles, slavery, bargaining, play, mores, and ideology. At the level of reflective theory, we speak of sexual morality, sociology, politics, and philosophy. This is a fairly impressive array.

Reports given by human beings who have changed part of their sexual identity also bear witness to the pervasiveness of various aspects of sexuality throughout human experience. For example, Jan Morris says:

Having experienced life in both roles, there seems to me no aspect of existence, no moment of the day, no contact, no arrangement, no response, which is not different for men and for women. The very tone of voice in which I was now addressed, the very posture of the person next in the queue, the very feel in the air when I entered a room or sat at a restaurant table constantly emphasized my change of status.[2]

Beyond the phenomenal level of everyday experience, psychoanalysis has shown how an individual's sexuality plays a formal structuring role that is central to the multidimensional entity we

*I wish to express my gratitude for comments received from audiences of the Department of Philosophy, the University of Toronto; the Canadian Philosophical Association; and the Society for Women in Philosophy.

[1]The species referred to is *Labroides dimidiatus*. It is re-

ported by John Money and Patricia Tucker, *Sexual Signatures: On Being a Man or a Woman* (Boston: Little, Brown & Co., 1975), p. 64.

[2]Jan Morris, *Conundrum* (New York: Harcourt Brace Jovanovich, 1974); quoted by Money and Tucker, p. 123.

refer to as the self. It is not merely in the Freudian perspective that human sexual interrelations can symbolize human relationships. In the *1844 Manuscripts*, Marx says:

The direct, natural and necessary relation of person to person is the relation of man to woman. *In this natural relation of the sexes, man's relation to nature is immediately his relation to man, just as his relation to man is immediately his relation to nature—his own* natural *function.*

In this relationship, therefore, is sensuously manifested, *reduced to an observable* fact, *the extent to which the human essence has become nature to man, or to which nature has to him become the human essence of man. From this relationship one can therefore judge man's whole level of development.*[3]

In interpreting Marx, Avineri points out that sexual interaction has a systematic significance with reference to important social and political dimensions. In particular, the reciprocity and mutual interpersonal satisfaction, which are central to a fulfilling act of sexual intercourse, can be regarded as central to relationships in society based on genuine recognition and mutuality of concern among all the members.[4] Thus sexual interaction can serve both as an indicator of the present state of social relations and as a normative model for relations between persons in an ideal society.

Finally, the nature of the sexes, as conceived through various evolutionary stages, has prompted complementary world views. For example, one might argue in favour of a gynocentric view of the world.[5] Such a view would claim primacy for the female on the grounds of her greater importance for the preservation of the race.[6] At present, the competing androcentric world view dominates our collective consciousness. Such a view sees males as the chief protagonists in the development of culture and evolutionary advance in general. Here again, biological facts concerning sexuality have been cited as a springboard for the construction of a *Weltanschauung*.

I have argued that sexuality is a dimension whose significance ranges through the biological, psychological, social, aesthetic, political, and moral spheres of human existence. Such a dimension may plausibly be called essential.

The Argument from an Analysis of Sexual Identity

This argument is designed to show that, given that sexual identity is a complex structure which includes gender, sexuality is a necessary condition for being human.

Theoreticians are agreed that seven features together contribute to sexual identity.[7] These are: chromosomal sex, gonadal sex in the form of ovaries or testes, internal reproductive features, external reproductive features, hormonal sex, psychologic sex, and the sex of assignment and rearing (sometimes referred to as "gender" or socially ascribed sex). These features suggest a duality of dimension: the biological and the social.

Human beings display a high level of cortical development. Among its consequences are the variable behavior patterns and receptivity to behavioral modification that make for the complexity of human experience. The role of learning is important for an understanding of human sexuality. It is now known that the kinds of stimulation and the types of situation that can evoke sexual excitement are determined by learning. So is overt sexual behavior.[8] The variability of human sexual behavior is underscored by the fact that almost *any* visual feature of the human body, dependent upon a given cultural context, can serve as a sexual stimulus. In societies where complete nudity is the practice, specific motions and gestures are codified as sexually inviting.

Moreover, patterns of upbringing and social structure serve as powerful devices for defining legitimate sexual activities and attitudes. For example, we know that in every infrahuman species, the

---

[3]Karl Marx, "Economic and Philosophical Manuscripts of 1844," in *Marx-Engels Reader,* ed. Robert C. Tucker (New York: Norton, 1972), p. 69.

[4]Shlomo Avineri, *The Social and Political Thought of Karl Marx* (Cambridge: Cambridge University Press, 1971).

[5]See, for example, the work of Lester Ward, *Pure Sociology: A Treatise on the Origin and Spontaneous Development of Society* (New York: Macmillan, 1914).

[6]Ibid., p. 373.

[7]Cf. Leon Salzman, "Psychology of the Female," in *Psychoanalysis and Women,* ed. Jean Baker (Baltimore: Penguin, 1973), p. 211; J. L. Hampson and Joan Hampson, "The Ontogenesis of Sexual Behaviour in Man," in *Sex and Internal Secretions,* ed. William Young (Baltimore: Williams & Wilkins, 1961); M. Kay Martin and Barbara Voorhies, *Female of the Species* (New York: Columbia University Press, 1975), p. 27; John Money and Anke Erhardt, *Man and Woman, Boy and Girl: The Differentiation and Dimorphism of Gender Identity from Conception to Maturity* (Baltimore: Johns Hopkins University Press, 1972).

[8]The research of Ford and Beach is extremely important for determining cross-species common factors. Clellan S. Ford and Frank Beach, *Patterns of Sexual Behavior* (New York: Harper & Row, 1951), p. 262.

distribution of sexual initiative is bilateral.[9] This would lead us to expect the same distribution among humans. This is not so. Societies that severely restrict adolescent and preadolescent sex play and enjoin girls to be modest and retiring produce adult women who are either incapable of assuming or unwilling to assume sexual initiative.

Considerations such as these have led some philosophers and many contemporary radical feminists to claim that "Man is a historical idea and not a natural species."[10] I am unwilling to accept this exclusive disjunction. The evidence concerning human sexuality is too compelling to abandon either side. For example, the chemistry of the blood is extremely important in determining the glandular secretions that regulate one's susceptibility to sexual arousal and capacity for sexual performance. Similarly, the structural and functional capacities of one's central nervous system and musculature also determine the kinds of behavior that can occur and toward which certain individuals are or are not inclined.[11] Thus it is more reasonable to resist the temptation to reductionism in either direction. Man is both a social and a biological species.

I designate the social dimension by the term 'gender'. This includes the person's self-awareness of being genderized in a particular way, nongenital behaviors that are characteristic of most males or females in a particular culture, and a particular genital orientation.[12]

It is a universal practice among human beings that social gender categories are assigned on a one-to-one basis corresponding to externally visible biological sex. In most (but not all) societies, this implies that a newborn will be assigned either a masculine or a feminine gender. One of the most important findings of researchers in the field of human genderization is the psychosexual *neutrality* at birth of a newborn infant.[13] This means that prior to the ascription of gender and at the beginning of the complex process of gender typing, the infant is completely flexible and open to an indeterminate set of gender possibilities. Evidence for this comes from matched pairs of hermaphrodites. In each pair, the biological sex is identical, but one has been raised successfully as a male, one as a female. These individuals have adopted completely the gender identity ascribed to them regardless of whether they are biologically male, female, or ambiguous. Further evidence is provided by data on transsexuals. These show that although biologic sex has developed consistently, a particular family syndrome is responsible for producing a consciousness of gender that is completely at odds with the biologic sex. In short, gender is not determined by inborn factors, it results from social behavior and learning.[14]

Differential genderization begins, quite literally, from the moment that the infant emerges from the womb and is assigned a gender. It has been documented that males and females are handled differently as soon as they are born.[15] Many other differential forms of behavior could be cited.[16] The important point is that the infant is learning gender-related behavior as soon as it is capable of learning anything whatever. More specifically, it is now known that by the age of nine months the child can differentiate genders. By the age of two, the child recognizes its own gender, acts appropriately, and identifies the cultural and familial behavior that is appropriate for its own particular gender.[17] Further, by the age of two, the child's awareness of its own gender can be fixed to such an extent that any

[9]Ibid., p. 266.

[10]Maurice Merleau-Ponty, *The Phenomenology of Perception,* trans. Colin Smith (London: Routledge & Kegan Paul, 1962), p. 170.

[11]Cf. Ford and Beach, *Patterns of Sexual Behavior,* p. 251; Money and Tucker, *Sexual Signatures,* p. 163; Kenneth Moyer, "Sex Differences in Aggression," in *Sex Differences in Behavior,* ed. Richard Friedman, Ralph Richart, and Raymond Vande Wiele. (New York: Wiley, 1974), pp. 335–72.

[12]Money and Erhardt, *Man and Woman, Boy and Girl,* make the following distinction between gender identity and gender role:
gender identity: *the sameness, unity, and persistence of one's individuality as male, female, or ambivalent, in greater or lesser degree, especially as it is experienced in self-awareness and behavior.*
gender role: *everything that a person says and does, to indicate to others or to the self the degree that one is either male or female, or ambivalent; it includes but is not restricted to sexual arousal and response; gender role is the public expression of gender identity.*

I find the distinction between gender identity and gender role to be an important one. However, I think that the above definitions are lacking clarity in important areas. For purposes of this paper, I have collapsed the distinction, referring to the social dimension of sexuality as *gender.*

[13]Cf. John Hampson, "Determinants of Psycho-Sexual Orientations," in *Sex and Behavior,* ed., Frank Beach (New York: Wiley, 1965), p. 115; Paul Chodoff, "Feminine Psychology and Infantile Sexuality," in *Psychoanalysis and Woman,* pp. 184–200; Mary Jane Sherfey, *The Nature and Evolution of Female Sexuality* (New York: Random House, 1973), p. 36.

[14]Money and Erhardt, *Man and Woman, Boy and Girl;* quoted by Money and Tucker, *Sexual Signatures,* p. 9 n.

[15]See the research done by Kagan and Moss reported by Mabel Blake Cohen, "Personal Identity and Sexual Identity," in *Psychoanalysis and Women,* pp. 163–64.

[16]Ibid., p. 159; Money and Tucker, *Sexual Signatures,* p. 87.

[17]Michael Lewis and Marsha Weinraub, "Sex of Parent X Sex of Child: Socioemotional Development," in *Sex Differences in Behavior,* pp. 165–89.

attempt to alter it produces extreme psychological anguish. By the age of four, it can be fixed beyond the point of any significant alteration whatever. Evidence for this is that any attempts to reassign gender after this age have failed. Such attempts have included all known forms of therapy.[18] This stability of gender is the first relevant feature for my argument.

The second relevant feature of gender is its pervasiveness. Gender identity refers to broad, extremely pervasive aspects of personality and character. These complex, highly integrated patterns result partially from the identification of the child with various role models. Such identification consists not only in imitation of discrete bits of behavior but, more importantly, in the systematic emulation of ways of behaving, thinking, and feeling. In addition, the child responds to particular kinds of milieus. In a relaxed and permissive milieu, a child is rewarded for exploring and experimenting, seeking outgoing activity, and adopting a generally aggressive posture toward the world. In a restrictive milieu, a child is rewarded for obedience, passivity, and the inhibition of strong overt reactions.[19] Thus, pervasive world orientations, with profound consequences for cognitive development, result from the processes of identification and interaction in a particular type of milieu. Moreover, in most societies different gender assignments entail widely different milieus. Hence, as one psychologist has put it:

It is a banal truth that the individual's sex role is the most salient of his many social roles. No other social role directs more of his overt behavior, emotional reactions, cognitive functioning, covert attitudes and general psychological and social adjustment.[20]

So it is not surprising that gender provides an important means of specialization affecting all areas of social organization.

In sum, the argument is this: Sexual identity involves a complex of biological, psychological, and social features that constitute the most pervasive structuring dimension of an individual's personal identity. The various elements that constitute sexual identity are logically independent of each other.[21] Nevertheless they are all, in one form or other, present in a human being. In particular, an individual always has a sense of gender. Thus I conclude, first, that sexual identity is a necessary condition for the development of personal identity;[22] and, second, given its crucial role and pervasiveness in human experience, sexual identity may be said to be a metaphysical dimension of human existence.

The Specific Claim: That Sexual Dimorphism is a Metaphysical Dimension of the Human Species

I now turn to a more specific claim, which is not always kept separate from the first. This is the thesis that any individual member of the human species must be either a male or a female, cannot be neither nor both. I regard this claim as false.

The attempt to polarize the human species is a common one. Witnesses Martin Luther:

Men have broad and large chests, and small narrow hips and more understanding than the women, who have but small and narrow breasts, and broad hips, to the end they should remain at home, sit still, keep house, and bear and bring up children. . . . A woman is . . . a friendly, courteous, and merry companion in life, whence they are named, by the Holy Ghost, the honour and ornament of the house, and inclined to tenderness, for thereunto are they chiefly created, to bear children, and be the pleasure, joy, and solace of their husbands.[23]

[18]Cf. Money and Tucker, *Sexual Signatures,* p. 98: Hampson in *Sex and Behavior,* pp. 108–32; Paul H. Mussen, "Early Sex-Role Development," in *Handbook of Socialization Theory and Research,* ed. David Goslin (Chicago: Rand McNally, 1969), pp. 707–29; reprinted in Nancy Reeves, *Womankind: Beyond the Stereotypes* (Chicago: Aldine-Atherton, 1971), pp. 393–415.

[19]Cf. Mussen, *Womankind,* p. 402.; R. R. Sears "Development of Gender Role," in *Sex and Behavior,* p. 133; R. R. Sears, Lucy Rau, and P. Alpert, *Identification and Child Rearing* (Stanford, Calif.: Stanford University Press, 1965).

[20]Mussen, *Womankind,* p. 393. See also Martin and Voorhies, *Female of the Species,* pp. 7–8.

[21]That all the biological components are independent of each other is shown by research dealing with various abnor-

malities. This research is reported by Money and Erhardt, *Man and Woman, Boy and Girl,* and is reported in many other contexts. I have already cited sources documenting the independence of the psychological and social factors (see n. 13).

[22]These remarks have a direct bearing on the debate concerning the relevance of sexual identity in brain transplants. For an account of the debate between Roland Puccetti and Andrew Brennan, see Puccetti, "Brain Transplantation and Personal Identity," *Analysis* 29 (1969); Brennan, "Persons and their Brains," *Analysis* 30 (1970); Puccetti, "Mr. Brennan on Persons' Brains," *Analysis* 31 (1971).

[23]Martin Luther, *Table Talk* (first published 1566), ed. and trans. William Hazlitt (London: 1884); Quoted by Reeves, *Womankind,* p. 99.

In addition to assorted prejudices, theological or otherwise, various arguments have been brought forward to support the claim that the human species is necessarily dimorphically divided. I will consider five such arguments.

Arguments Drawn from Ethology

Arguments based on ethological findings have a prima facie plausibility. Similarity in the areas of anatomy, genetic structure, biochemical make-up and susceptibility to disease have been demonstrated. Moreover, various species share various forms of social behavior with human beings, including such dimensions as facial expression, greeting behavior, food sharing, and tool using.[24] Nevertheless, ethological findings must be used with a great deal of caution. A characteristic example of how such findings can be used to further androcentric purposes is the work of Lionel Tiger.[25] Tiger bases his inferences on observations of the social life of savanna baboons. Savanna baboons are sharply sexually differentiated in such a way that the females are essentially child oriented, while the males are capable of bonding behavior with other males, thereby providing group cohesion and defense. Tiger then reconstructs the early social life of the human species from these observations. Perceptive researchers have noticed how conveniently Tiger's selected group exemplifies Western gender stereotypes. They have also pointed out that had Tiger selected some other group for study—for example, chimpanzees (which are more closely related to humans)—he could not have arrived at the same conclusions regarding the primacy of male bonding behavior.[26]

More important are the significant differences between human and nonhuman primates. One of these differences is the relative emancipation of human sexuality from hormonal domination.[27] Another is the fact that, insofar as almost all human sexuality is mediated through socially derived conceptual structures and is controlled by the cerebral cortex, it differs significantly from most primate behavior, which is gonadally regulated. Thirdly,

cortical mediation is visible in human sexual practice, at both the individual and social level, when human beings regulate their sexuality according to moral rules or subordinate various aspects of it to higher, collective ends. Finally, the demonstrated fact of the psychosexual neutrality of the human infant must be kept clearly in mind. These facts constitute relevant differences that invalidate inferences about human sexuality drawn from information about other primates.

Arguments Based on the Effects of Prenatal Hormones on the Brain

In the second and third month, the central nervous system of the human embryo is highly susceptible to the influences of the specific hormones that dominate in gonadal males or females. Males and females differ in the proportion of particular hormones. Such hormones enter the brain and alter its character, particularly that of the hypothalamus. This alteration carries with it a preferred pattern of physiological responses.[28] Proponents of this argument point out that children who receive concentrations of estrogen during this period of gestation are prone to engage in play with dolls; while genetically male or female children whose brains are prenatally exposed to androgen do not demonstrate this form of play. Hence the proponents conclude that physiological, sex-typed patterns in the brain are directly related to various sex-typed behaviors. In particular, they claim that maternalism is, to some extent, neurally programed.[29] Generalizing from the above information, advocates of this view also claim that the observed polarity of human males and females is built into the brain itself at birth.

There are at least two objections to this argument. First, the conclusions go beyond what may be drawn from the present data. Present research indicates that the prenatal hormone mix does not create any new brain pathways or eliminate any such pathways that are already present. What the different hormone mixes do is lower the threshold to various sorts of stimuli.[30] For example, prenatal exposure to androgen lowers an individual's sensitivity to challenges of peers and to strenuous physical activity. Exposure to estrogen lowers the threshold

---

[24]Martin and Voorhies, *Female of the Species*, pp. 140–41.

[25]Lionel Tiger, *Men in Groups* (New York: Vintage, 1970); Lionel Tiger, "The Possible Biological Origins of Sexual Discrimination," *Impact of Science on Society* 20 (1970): 29–44.

[26]Martin and Voorhies, *Female of the Species*, pp. 135–40.

[27]The rhesus monkey is the one known exception to this rule. The sexual behavior of this monkey displays a certain amount of freedom from the estrus cycle. However, this freedom does not begin to approximate that of humans. See the research by Ford and Beach, *Patterns of Sexual Behavior*.

[28]Martin and Voorhies, *Female of the Species,* pp. 135–40.

[29]Richard Green, "The Behaviorally Feminine Male Child: Pretranssexual? Pretransvestic? Prehomosexual? Preheterosexual?" in *Sex Differences in Behavior,* pp. 301–14 (esp. p. 312).

[30]Money and Tucker, *Sexual Signatures,* pp. 78–81.

of one's response to helpless young. Prenatal hormone exposure does not, however, rule out any behavior patterns for either sex, regardless of which hormone is dominant. Thus the conclusion reached is too broad, given the available data. Serious social implications cannot be drawn from the present state of research.

Secondly, the argument trades on a spurious disjunction between the two sex hormones. It would appear from the way the argument is structured either that the brain is exposed to androgen or to estrogen. In fact, all embryos produce both hormones in varying proportions. Thus the brain is exposed to a particular mixture which could, in principle, vary with each individual. Rather than serving as an argument for sexual dimorphism, the data regarding prenatal hormone exposure would suggest the possibility of sexual polymorphism and an indeterminate multiplicity of corresponding gender styles.

Arguments Based on Biological Differences

One respected contemporary psychoanalyst puts the biological argument in the following way:

The anatomical differences between the sexes must inevitably be reflected in some personality differences, regardless of variations in cultural patterns . . . body image, menstruation at puberty, monthly cyclical variations of endocrine function, . . . experiences of sexual intercourse, pregnancy, child-birth and menopause are all aspects of bodily sensation and function that are uniquely different for the woman as compared to the man: and in the biological-environmental interaction that leads to personality formation, these must *result in significant personality variances between the sexes.*[31]

Unfortunately this argument does not hold up. Contemporary practices are designed to eliminate most of the elements which Marmor cities. For example, unisex clothing minimizes differences in body image, menstrual extraction eliminates periods for women, hormonal control allows a woman to eliminate her menstrual periods completely as well as regulate hormonal variation, sterilization is available, and women are no longer being primarily defined by proven fertility and childbearing. Should

these practices become widespread and incorporated into the normal psychosexual development of a woman, the important personality variances cited by Marmor would no longer occur. Hence such differences are relatively low on the scale of definitional importance to the nature of human beings.

Moreover, it is not clear that even granted the biological differences, the personality differences between sexes would be any sharper than intrasex personality differences. Because of different socially derived ways of responding to those biological universals, it is quite conceivable that personality differences would be greater cross-culturally than between males and females in a given culture. For example, two females might respond to the onset of menstruation in different ways—one regarding it as the "curse," with all of its medieval overtones, the other regarding it as an occasion for the public celebration of her fertility. Given the widely varying significance of the process, one would reasonably infer varying personality differences between such members of the same sex. Again, a plurality of genderized personality configurations, not a strict dimorphism, would seem to be the logical conclusion to draw.

A second type of argument concerning biological determinism of sexual dimorphism is based on the biological facts of sexual reproduction. Human sexual reproduction requires two members of the species in order to insure fertilization. But acceptance of this fact does not commit one to acceptance of full human sexual dimorphism. At most, it commits one to recognize the necessity of *at least* two recognizable physical sexes. It establishes a *minimum* number for ensuring reproduction (assuming that human reproduction continues to be sexual rather than asexual) but does not establish a maximum number. Survival of the species requires merely that *some* members reproduce; it does not require, on the individual level, that every member of the species be either male or female. Nor, on the social level, does it require *only* two recognized genders. Here again, arguments from biology fail to establish sexual dimorphism as a necessary property of the species.

Arguments Based on
Psychological Necessity

These refer to much of the same data on gender identity that I reported earlier. Appeal to this data is coupled with an assumption that a carefully delineated, rigidly maintained family complex is

---

[31]Judd Marmor, "Changing Patterns of Femininity," in *Psychoanalysis and Women*, pp. 228–29.

necessary to provide the individual child with the psychological security needed to allow the fullest development of his or her human potentialities. Sexual differentiation into men and women is necessary to such a family structure. Hence sexual dimorphism is necessary to human development.

I agree that the development of a stable gender identity is necessary for personal development. However, it does not follow that gender identity must be either a masculine or feminine gender. It is clear that the sort of family structure mentioned can provide the child with the required psychological security. But the argument treats families as natural entities rather than as social groupings. If the family is regarded as a social group, then no implications regarding gender follow. In this context, the existence of intersexes and supernumerary sexes is particularly relevant. Societies in which three or more sexes are recognized have survived over many generations and appear to consist of the usual number of psychologically stable individuals.[32] For example, the Navajo recognize a third sex, an intersex, whose status is quite different from that of either men or women in the culture. Members of this intersex have an extremely variable dress code, are entitled to perform all the Navajo tasks, have special rights over the personal property of other members of their households, function as mediators in disputes between a man and a woman, have unusual sexual license, and may marry a spouse of either biologic sex. Anthropological investigations have revealed multisexed societies in North America, India, Siberia, and East Africa. In each of these societies, varying sorts of family structures prevail and individuals grow up with a gender identity. These facts make it impossible to show that sexual dimorphism is necessary for human psychological development.

Arguments Based on Social Necessity

These are based on the observation that there are universal, cross-cultural, sex-role differences. Given that all societies emphasize nongenital, visible differences between the sexes, it is inferred that sex-roles have some adaptive advantage for society. Evidence for this argument is impressive, especially considering the wide cultural variation in the actual definition of the specific sex-roles, and I think the conclusion is a reasonable one. This is, how-

ever, where the reasonableness ends. Consider the following argument:

Gender stereotypes, with all their many more or less arbitrary sex distinctions, provide the framework for that cooperation. . . . Achieving even a minimum degree of cooperation depends on some kind of division of labor between the sexes, a sorting of behavior in sex, love, work and play.[33]

Here again, the data regarding intersexes are relevant. Insofar as there are societies which have three or more gender stereotypes and which satisfy the requirements for stability and cooperation, the requirement of just two gender stereotypes cannot be a necessary one for a successful society. Moreover, even though one might agree to a dichotomous split of gender stereotypes, it does not follow that all of the complex behavior involved in sex, love, work, and play must be gender-coded. One might argue, in contrast to the above argument, that if many of the behaviors involved in work and play are *nongenderized,* cooperation would be greatly facilitated rather than undercut. This is certainly true during times that call for high adaptability.

A different sort of argument is based on the necessary requirements for cultural development and social evolution. One version of this argument is stated by Mary Jane Sherfey, who says:

A potentially similar inordinately high level of sexual drive and orgasmic capacity existing in the primate females continues to exist in women. . . . the suppression by cultural forces of women's inordinately high sexual drive and orgasmic capacity must have been an important prerequisite for the evolution of modern human societies and has continued, of necessity, to be a major preoccupation of practically every civilization.[34]

Sherfey goes on to claim that the human mating system, with its permanent family and kinship ties based on two sexes, is necessary to sustain a civilized level of human development. Although she admits that hormonal controls could be imposed on women, she states that the division of men and women through inhibiting and dominant-

---

[32]For an extended account of these societies, see Martin and Voorhies, *Female of the Species,* pp. 84–107.

[33]Money and Tucker, *Sexual Signatures,* pp. 38–39. A similar argument is advanced by Mussen, who claims that sex-roles are the most fundamental roles in the maintenance and continuity of society (see Mussen, *Womankind,* p. 393).

[34]Sherfey, *Nature and Evolution of Female Sexuality,* p. 52.

gender stereotypes has been shown to serve this purpose well.

It is possible to grant Sherfey's premises without accepting her conclusion. She is concerned with the maintenance and stability of child-raising patterns in order to ensure the existence of a competent and stable younger generation. It is presently desirable, from a species perspective, to diminish our numbers; this should relieve many from the task and obligation of child raising. Multiple-gender stereotypes might, therefore, evolve, even while the childbearing members of society control their sexuality. Even should this not be possible, *alternative* methods of child raising are possible. Such an important practice might be allocated to the males of the species. In short, while Sherfey's premises raise important normative issues about the effects of women's sexuality, they do not lead to the conclusion of the social necessity of sexual dimorphism.

In this section, I have argued that the standard types of argument designed to show the necessity of human sexual polarization into masculine and feminine fail. While it *is* reasonable to maintain that human beings are essentially sexual, it is *not* reasonable to hold that this sexuality is necessarily either masculine or feminine.

Conclusion

Human beings have the potential to display the same high level of sexual adaptibility as the little scavenger fish described at the beginning of this paper. We have the technology and developmental theory at our disposal to control and change both our own and others' sexual identities. How we use this power will, to some extent, depend on our understanding of sexuality and the role it can play in individual and social existence. This paper has attempted to provide some of that understanding.

Part Two
Sex, Love, and Marriage

3
Sex and Sexual Morality

14/The Purpose of Sex
St. Thomas Aquinas

**The Reason Why Simple
Fornication Is a Sin According to
Divine Law, and that Matrimony is Natural**

(1) We can see the futility of the argument of certain people who say that simple fornication is not a sin. For they say: Suppose there is a woman who is not married, or under the control of any man, either her father or another man. Now, if a man performs the sexual act with her, and she is willing, he does not injure her, because she favors the action and she has control over her own body. Nor does he injure any other person, because she is understood to be under no other person's control. So, this does not seem to be a sin.

(2) Now, to say that he injures God would not seem to be an adequate answer. For we do not offend God except by doing something contrary to our own good, as has been said. But this does not appear contrary to man's good. Hence, on this basis, no injury seems to be done to God.

(3) Likewise, it also would seem an inadequate answer to say that some injury is done to one's neighbor by this action, inasmuch as he may be scandalized. Indeed, it is possible for him to be scandalized by something which is not in itself a sin. In this event, the act would be accidentally sinful. But our problem is not whether simple fornication is accidentally a sin, but whether it is so essentially.

(4) Hence, we must look for a solution in our earlier considerations. We have said that God exercises care over every person on the basis of what is good for him. Now, it is good for each person to attain his end, whereas it is bad for him to swerve away from his proper end. Now, this should be considered applicable to the parts, just as it is to the whole being; for instance, each and every part of man, and every one of his acts, should attain the proper end. Now, though the male semen is superfluous in regard to the preservation of the individual, it is nevertheless necessary in regard to the propagation of the species. Other superfluous things, such as excrement, urine, sweat, and such things, are not at all necessary; hence, their emission contributes to man's good. Now, this is not what is sought in the case of semen, but, rather, to emit it for the purpose of generation, to which purpose the sexual act is directed. But man's generative process would be frustrated unless it were followed by proper nutrition, because the offspring would not survive if proper nutrition were withheld. Therefore, the emission of semen ought to be so ordered that it will result in both the production of the proper offspring and in the upbringing of this offspring.

(5) It is evident from this that every emission of semen, in such a way that generation cannot follow, is contrary to the good for man. And if this be done deliberately, it must be a sin. Now, I am speaking of a way from which, *in itself,* generation could not result: such would be any emission of semen apart from the natural union of male and female. For which reason, sins of this type are called *contrary to nature.* But, if by accident generation cannot result from the emission of semen, then this is not a reason for it being against nature, or a sin; as for instance, if the woman happens to be sterile.

(6) Likewise, it must also be contrary to the good for man if the semen be emitted under conditions such that generation could result but the proper upbringing would be prevented. We should take into consideration the fact that, among some animals where the female is able to take care of the upbringing of offspring, male and female do not remain together for any time after the act of genera-

From St. Thomas Aquinas' *On the Truth of the Catholic Faith, Summa Contra Gentiles,* Book Three: Providence, Part II, translated and with an introduction by Vernon J. Bourke. Copyright © 1956 by Doubleday & Company, Inc. Reprinted by permission of Doubleday & Company, Inc. Footnotes have been deleted.

tion. This is obviously the case with dogs. But in the case of animals of which the female is not able to provide for the upbringing of offspring, the male and female do stay together after the act of generation as long as is necessary for the upbringing and instruction of the offspring. Examples are found among certain species of birds whose young are not able to seek out food for themselves immediately after hatching. In fact, since a bird does not nourish its young with milk, made available by nature as it were, as occurs in the case of quadrupeds, but the bird must look elsewhere for food for its young, and since besides this it must protect them by sitting on them, the female is not able to do this by herself. So, as a result of divine providence, there is naturally implanted in the male of these animals a tendency to remain with the female in order to bring up the young. Now, it is abundantly evident that the female in the human species is not at all able to take care of the upbringing of offspring by herself, since the needs of human life demand many things which cannot be provided by one person alone. Therefore, it is appropriate to human nature that a man remain together with a woman after the generative act, and not leave her immediately to have such relations with another woman, as is the practice with fornicators.

(7) Nor, indeed, is the fact that a woman may be able by means of her own wealth to care for the child by herself an obstacle to this argument. For natural rectitude in human acts is not dependent on things accidentally possible in the case of one individual, but, rather, on those conditions which accompany the entire species.

(8) Again, we must consider that in the human species offspring require not only nourishment for the body, as in the case of other animals, but also education for the soul. . . . children must be instructed by parents who are already experienced people. Nor are they able to receive such instruction as soon as they are born, but after a long time, and especially after they have reached the age of discretion. Moreover, a long time is needed for this instruction. Then, too, because of the impulsion of the passions, through which prudent judgment is vitiated, they require not merely instruction but correction. Now, a woman alone is not adequate to this task; rather, this demands the work of a husband, in whom reason is more developed for giving instruction and strength is more available for giving punishment. Therefore, in the human species, it is

not enough, as in the case of birds, to devote a small amount of time to bringing up offspring, for a long period of life is required. Hence, since among all animals it is necessary for male and female to remain together as long as the work of the father is needed by the offspring, it is natural to the human being for the man to establish a lasting association with a designated woman, over no short period of time. Now, we call this society *matrimony*. Therefore, matrimony is natural for man, and promiscuous performance of the sexual act, outside matrimony, is contrary to man's good. For this reason, it must be a sin.

(9) Nor, in fact, should it be deemed a slight sin for a man to arrange for the emission of semen apart from the proper purpose of generating and bringing up children, on the argument that it is either a slight sin, or none at all, for a person to use a part of the body for a different use than that to which it is directed by nature (say, for instance, one chose to walk on his hands, or to use his feet for something usually done with the hands) because man's good is not much opposed by such inordinate use. However, the inordinate emission of semen is incompatible with the natural good; namely, the preservation of the species. Hence, after the sin of homicide whereby a human nature already in existence is destroyed, this type of sin appears to take next place, for by it the generation of human nature is precluded.

(10) Moreover, these views which have just been given have a solid basis in divine authority. That the emission of semen under conditions in which offspring cannot follow is illicit is quite clear. There is the text of Leviticus (18:22–23): "thou shalt not lie with mankind as with womankind . . . and thou shalt not copulate with any beast." And in I Corinthians (6:10): "Nor the effeminate, nor liers with mankind . . . shall possess the kingdom of God."

(11) Also, that fornication and every performance of the act of reproduction with a person other than one's wife are illicit is evident. For it is said: "There shall be no whore among the daughters of Israel, nor whoremonger among the sons of Israel" (Deut. 23:17); and in Tobias (4:13): "Take heed to keep thyself from all fornication, and beside thy wife never endure to know a crime"; and in I Corinthians (6:18): "Fly fornication."

(12) By this conclusion we refute the error of those who say that there is no more sin in the emis-

sion of semen than in the emission of any other superfluous matter, and also of those who state that fornication is not a sin. . . .

That Matrimony Should Be Indivisible

(1) If one will make a proper consideration, the preceding reasoning will be seen to lead to the conclusion not only that the society of man and woman of the human species, which we call matrimony, should be long-lasting, but even that it should endure throughout an entire life.

(2) Indeed, possessions are ordered to the preservation of natural life, and since natural life, which cannot be preserved perpetually in the father, is by a sort of succession preserved in the son in its specific likeness, it is naturally fitting for the son to succeed also to the things which belong to the father. So, it is natural that the father's solicitude for his son should endure until the end of the father's life. Therefore, if even in the case of birds the solicitude of the father gives rise to the cohabitation of male and female, the natural order demands that father and mother in the human species remain together until the end of life.

(3) It also seems to be against equity if the aforesaid society be dissolved. For the female needs the male, not merely for the sake of generation, as in the case of other animals, but also for the sake of government, since the male is both more perfect in reasoning and stronger in his powers. In fact, a woman is taken into man's society for the needs of generation; then, with the disappearance of a woman's fecundity and beauty, she is prevented from association with another man. So, if any man took a woman in the time of her youth, when beauty and fecundity were hers, and then sent her away after she had reached an advanced age, he would damage that woman contrary to natural equity.

(4) Again, it seems obviously inappropriate for a woman to be able to put away her husband, because a wife is naturally subject to her husband as governor, and it is not within the power of a person subject to another to depart from his rule. So, it would be against the natural order if a wife were able to abandon her husband. Therefore, if a husband were permitted to abandon his wife, the society of husband and wife would not be an association of equals, but, instead, a sort of slavery on the part of the wife.

(5) Besides, there is in men a certain natural solicitude to know their offspring. This is necessary for this reason: the child requires the father's direction for a long time. So, whenever there are obstacles to the ascertaining of offspring they are opposed to the natural instinct of the human species. But, if a husband could put away his wife, or a wife her husband, and have sexual relations with another person, certitude as to offspring would be precluded, for the wife would be united first with one man and later with another. So, it is contrary to the natural instinct of the human species for a wife to be separated from her husband. And thus, the union of male and female in the human species must be not only lasting, but also unbroken.

(6) Furthermore, the greater that friendship is, the more solid and long-lasting will it be. Now, there seems to be the greatest friendship between husband and wife, for they are united not only in the act of fleshly union, which produces a certain gentle association even among beasts, but also in the partnership of the whole range of domestic activity. Consequently, as an indication of this, man must even "leave his father and mother" for the sake of his wife, as is said in Genesis (2:24). Therefore, it is fitting for matrimony to be completely indissoluble. . . .

15/Sex and Language

Robert Baker

Our Conception of Sexual Intercourse

There are two profound insights that underlie the slogan "men ought not conceive of women as sexual objects"; both have the generality of scope that justifies the universality with which the feminists apply the slogan; neither can be put as simply as the slogan. The first is that the conception of sexual intercourse that we have in this culture is antithetical to the conception of women as human beings—as persons rather than objects. (Recall that this is congruent with the fact . . . that "man" can be substituted for "humanity," while "woman" cannot.)

Many feminists have attempted to argue just this point. Perhaps the most famous defender of this view is Kate Millett,[1] who unfortunately faces the problem of trying to make a point about our conceptual structure without having adequate tools for analyzing conceptual structures.

The question Millett was dealing with was conceptual—Millett, in effect, asking about the nature of our conception of sexual roles. She tried to answer this question by analyzing novels; I shall attempt to answer this question by analyzing the terms we use to identify coitus, or more technically, in terms that function synonymously with "had sexual intercourse with" in a sentence of the form "**A** had sexual intercourse with **B**." The following is a list of some commonly used synonyms (numerous others that are not as widely used have been omitted, for example, "diddled," "laid pipe with"):

screwed
laid
fucked
had
did it with (to)
banged

balled
humped
slept with
made love to

Now, for a select group of these verbs, names for males are the subjects of sentences with active constructions (that is, where the subjects are said to be doing the activity); and names for females require passive constructions (that is, they are the recipients of the activity—whatever is done is done to them). Thus, we would not say "Jane did it to Dick," although we would say "Dick did it to Jane." Again, Dick bangs Jane, Jane does not bang Dick; Dick humps Jane, Jane does not hump Dick. In contrast, verbs like "did it with" do not require an active role for the male; thus, "Dick did it with Jane, and Jane with Dick." Again, Jane may make love to Dick, just as Dick makes love to Jane; and Jane sleeps with Dick as easily as Dick sleeps with Jane. (My students were undecided about "laid." Most thought that it would be unusual indeed for Jane to lay Dick, unless she played the masculine role of seducer-aggressor.)

The sentences thus form the following pairs. (Those nonconjoined singular noun phrases where a female subject requires a passive construction are marked with a cross. An asterisk indicates that the sentence in question is not a sentence of English if it is taken as synonymous with the italicized sentence heading the column.[2])

[1]*Sexual Politics* (New York: Doubleday, 1971); but see also *Sisterhood Is Powerful,* ed. Robin Morgan (New York: Vintage Books, 1970).

[2]For further analysis of verbs indicating copulation see "A Note on Conjoined Noun Phrases," *Journal of Philosophical Linguistics,* vol. 1, no. 2, Great Expectations, Evanston, Ill. Reprinted with "English Sentences Without Overt Grammatical Subject," in Zwicky, Salus, Binnick, and Vanek, eds., *Studies Out in Left Field: Defamatory Essays Presented to James D. McCawley* (Edmonton: Linguistic Research, Inc., 1971). The puritanism in our society is such that both of these articles are pseudoanonymously published under the name of Quang Phuc Dong; Mr. Dong, however, has a fondness for citing and criticizing the articles and theories of Professor James McCawley, Department of Linguistics, University of Chicago. Professor McCawley himself was kind enough to criticize an earlier draft of this essay. I should also like to thank G. E. M. Anscombe for some suggestions concerning this essay.

From "Pricks and Chicks: A Plea for Persons," in *Philosophy and Sex,* pp. 57–64, published by Prometheus Books, Buffalo, N.Y. Copyright 1971, 1973, 1975, 1977 by Robert Baker. Reprinted by permission. The first part of this article, titled "'Pricks' and 'Chicks': A Plea for 'Persons,'" is included in chapter 1 of this volume, pp. 21–26. Footnotes have been renumbered.

Dick had sexual intercourse with Jane
Dick screwed Jane†
Dick laid Jane†
Dick fucked Jane†
Dick had Jane†
Dick did it to Jane†
Dick banged Jane†
Dick humped Jane†
Dick balled Jane(?)
Dick did it with Jane
Dick slept with Jane
Dick made love to Jane

Jane had sexual intercourse with Dick
Jane was banged by Dick
Jane was humped by Dick
*Jane was done by Dick
Jane was screwed by Dick
Jane was laid by Dick
Jane was fucked by Dick
Jane was had by Dick
Jane balled Dick (?)
Jane did it with Dick
Jane slept with Dick
Jane made love to Dick
*Jane screwed Dick
*Jane laid Dick
*Jane fucked Dick
*Jane had Dick
*Jane did it to Dick
*Jane banged Dick
*Jane humped Dick

These lists make clear that within the standard view of sexual intercourse, males, or at least names for males, seem to play a different role than females, since male subjects play an active role in the language of screwing, fucking, having, doing it, and perhaps, laying, while female subjects play a passive role.

The asymmetrical nature of the relationship indicated by the sentences marked with an asterisk is confirmed by the fact that the form "—ed with each other" is acceptable for the sentences not marked with an asterisk, but not for those that require a male subject. Thus:

Dick and Jane had sexual intercourse with each other
Dick and Jane made love to each other

Dick and Jane slept with each other
Dick and Jane did it with each other
Dick and Jane balled with each other (*?)
*Dick and Jane banged with each other
*Dick and Jane did it to each other
*Dick and Jane had each other
*Dick and Jane fucked each other
*Dick and Jane humped each other
*(?) Dick and Jane laid each other
*Dick and Jane screwed each other

It should be clear, therefore, that our language reflects a difference between the male and female sexual roles, and hence that we conceive of the male and female roles in different ways. The question that now arises is, What difference in our conception of the male and female sexual roles requires active constructions for males and passive for females?

One explanation for the use of the active construction for males and the passive construction for females is that this grammatical asymmetry merely reflects the natural physiological asymmetry between men and women: the asymmetry of "to screw" and "to be screwed," "to insert into" and "to be inserted into." That is, it might be argued that the difference between masculine and feminine grammatical roles merely reflects a difference naturally required by the anatomy of males and females. This explanation is inadequate. Anatomical differences do not determine how we are to conceptualize the relation between penis and vagina during intercourse. Thus one can easily imagine a society in which the female normally played the active role during intercourse, where female subjects required active constructions with verbs indicating copulation, and where the standard metaphors were terms like "engulfing"—that is, instead of saying "he screwed her," one would say "she engulfed him." It follows that the use of passive constructions for female subjects of verbs indicating copulation does not reflect differences determined by human anatomy but rather reflects those generated by human customs.

What I am going to argue next is that the passive construction of verbs indicating coitus (that is, indicating the female position) can *also* be used to indicate that a person is being harmed. I am then going to argue that the metaphor involved would only make sense if we conceive of the female role in intercourse as that of a person being harmed (or being taken advantage of).

Passive constructions of "fucked," "screwed," and "had" indicate the female role. They also can be used to indicate being harmed. Thus, in all of the following sentences, Marion plays the female role: "Bobbie fucked Marion"; "Bobbie screwed Marion"; "Bobbie had Marion"; "Marion was fucked"; "Marion was screwed"; and "Marion was had." All of the statements are equivocal. They might literally mean that someone had sexual intercourse with Marion (who played the female role); or they might mean, metaphorically, that Marion was deceived, hurt, or taken advantage of. Thus, we say such things as "I've been screwed" ("fucked," "had," "taken," and so on) when we have been treated unfairly, been sold shoddy merchandise, or conned out of valuables. Throughout this essay[3] I have been arguing that metaphors are applied to things only if what the term *actually* applies to shares one or more properties with what the term *metaphorically* applies to. Thus, the female sexual role must have something in common with being conned or being sold shoddy merchandise. The only common property is that of being harmed, deceived, or taken advantage of. *Hence we conceive of a person who plays the female sexual role as someone who is being harmed* (that is, "screwed," "fucked," and so on).

It might be objected that this is clearly wrong, since the unsignated terms do not indicate someone's being harmed, and hence we do not conceive of having intercourse as being harmed. The point about the unsignated terms, however, is that they can take both females and males as subjects (in active constructions) and thus *do not pick out the female role*. This demonstrates that we conceive of sexual roles in such a way that only females are thought to be taken advantage of in intercourse.

The best part of solving a puzzle is when all the pieces fall into place. If the subjects of the passive construction are being harmed, presumably the subjects of the active constructions are doing harm, and, indeed, we do conceive of these subjects in precisely this way. Suppose one is angry at someone and wishes to express male violence as forcefully as possible without actually committing an act of physical violence. If one is inclined to be vulgar one can make the sign of the erect male cock by clenching one's fist while raising one's middle finger,

or by clenching one's fist and raising one's arm and shouting such things as "screw you," "up yours," or "fuck you." In other words, one of the strongest possible ways of telling someone that you wish to harm him is to tell him to assume the female sexual role relative to you. Again, to say to someone "go fuck yourself" is to order him to harm himself, while to call someone a "mother fucker" is not so much a play on his Oedipal fears as to accuse him of being so low that he would inflict the greatest imaginable harm (fucking) upon that person who is most dear to him (his mother).

Clearly, we conceive of the male sexual role as that of hurting the person in the female role—but lest the reader have any doubts, let me provide two further bits of confirming evidence: one linguistic, one nonlinguistic. One of the English terms for a person who hurts (and takes advantage of) others is the term "prick." This metaphorical identification would not make sense unless the bastard in question (that is, the person outside the bonds of legitimacy) was thought to share some characteristics attributed to things that are literally pricks. As a verb, "prick" literally means "to hurt," as in "I pricked myself with a needle"; but the usage in question is as a noun. As a noun, "prick" is a colloquial term for "penis." Thus, the question before us is what characteristic is shared by a penis and a person who harms others (or, alternatively, by a penis and by being stuck by a needle). Clearly, no physical characteristic is relevant (physical characteristics might underlie the Yiddish metaphorical attribution "schmuck," but one would have to analyze Yiddish usage to determine this); hence the shared characteristic is nonphysical; the only relevant shared nonphysical characteristic is that both a literal prick and a figurative prick are agents that harm people.

Now for the nonlinguistic evidence. Imagine two doors: in front of each door is a line of people; behind each door is a room; in each room is a bed; on each bed is a person. The line in front of one room consists of beautiful women, and on the bed in that room is a man having intercourse with each of these women in turn. One may think any number of things about this scene. One may say that the man is in heaven, or enjoying himself at a bordello; or perhaps one might only wonder at the oddness of it all. One does not think that the man is being hurt or violated or degraded—or at least the possibility does not immediately suggest itself, although one could conceive of situations where this was what was happening (especially, for example, if the man was

---

[3]["'Pricks' and 'Chicks': A Plea for "Persons'"—see pp. 21–26, chapter 1 of this book—eds.]

impotent). Now, consider the other line. Imagine that the figure on the bed is a woman and that the line consists of handsome, smiling men. The woman is having intercourse with each of these men in turn. It immediately strikes one that the woman is being degraded, violated, and so forth —"that poor woman."

When one man fucks many women he is a playboy and gains status; when a woman is fucked by many men she degrades herself and loses stature.

Our conceptual inventory is now complete enough for us to return to the task of analyzing the slogan that men ought not to think of women as sex objects.

I think that it is now plausible to argue that the appeal of the slogan "men ought not to think of women as sex objects," and the thrust of much of the literature produced by contemporary feminists, turns on something much deeper than a rejection of "scoring" (that is, the utilization of sexual "conquests" to gain esteem) and yet is a call neither for homosexuality nor for puritanism.

The slogan is best understood as a call for a new conception of the male and female sexual roles. If the analysis developed above is correct, our present conception of sexuality is such that to be a man is to be a person capable of brutalizing women (witness the slogans "The marines will make a man out of you!" and "The army builds *men*!" which are widely accepted and which simply state that learning how to kill people will make a person more manly). Such a conception of manhood not only bodes ill for a society led by such men, but also is clearly inimical to the best interests of women. It is only natural for women to reject such a sexual role, and it would seem to be the duty of any moral person

to support their efforts—to redefine our conceptions not only of fucking, but of the fucker (man) and the fucked (woman).

This brings me to my final point. We are a society preoccupied with sex. As I noted previously, the nature of proper nouns and pronouns in our language makes it difficult to talk about someone without indicating that person's sex. This convention would not be part of the grammar of our language if we did not believe that knowledge of a person's sex was crucial to understanding what is said about that person. Another way of putting this point is that sexual discrimination permeates our conceptual structure. Such discrimination is clearly inimical to any movement toward sexual egalitarianism and virtually defeats its purpose at the outset. (Imagine, for example, that black people were always referred to as "them" and whites as "us" and that proper names for blacks always had an "x" suffix at the end. Clearly any movement for integration as equals would require the removal of these discriminatory indicators. Thus at the height of the melting-pot era, immigrants Americanized their names: "Bellinsky" became "Bell," "Burnstein" became "Burns," and "Lubitch" became "Baker.")

I should therefore like to close this essay by proposing that contemporary feminists should advocate the utilization of neutral proper names and the elimination of gender from our language (as I have done in this essay); and they should vigorously protest any utilization of the third-person pronouns "he" and "she" as examples of sexist discrimination (perhaps "person" would be a good third-person pronoun)—for, as a parent of linguistic analysis once said, "The limits of our language are the limits of our world."

16/Sex and Reference

Janice Moulton

I

In this essay I shall discuss the infrequency of

female orgasms in sexual intercourse. I shall claim that concern about this infrequency embodies a confusion about the concept of sexual intercourse. The confusion is reflected in our language and in other

---

Reprinted by permission of Janice Moulton.

widespread, although factually unsubstantiated, beliefs about sexual intercourse.[1]

Hardly anyone today denies that women are capable of orgasms, even as capable as men when sufficiently stimulated. Kinsey says: "In general females and males appear to be equally responsive to the whole range of physical stimuli which may initiate erotic reactions . . . and the specific data show that the average female is no slower in response than the average male when she is sufficiently stimulated and when she is not inhibited in her activity."[2] The key words are "sufficiently stimulated." Although women have the same capacity for orgasm as men, they reach orgasm far less frequently during sexual intercourse.[3]

Invariably, suggestions for increasing the possibility of female orgasms focus on releasing inhibitions of the female, prolonging intercourse, or stimulating the female before intercourse. However, these methods often create new problems. Direct stimulation of the female before intercourse usually ceases when intercourse begins. If these procedures fail, the woman may be considered sexually inadequate, or the man sexually incompetent. Sexual activity, instead of being a source of pleasure and enjoyment, is treated as a complicated and difficult skill, something not to be enjoyed, but mastered. Often the female is advised to fake orgasm (men, the marriage manuals point out, obviously cannot fake it and so could never be under an obligation to try).[4] Faking relieves the obligations of the male but certainly does not solve the problems of the female. The old disparity between the frequency of male and female orgasms remains, to which the need for deception has been added.

In spite of this disparity, many people who are interested in orgasm for the female still rely on sexual intercourse as the main or only method of interpersonal sexual stimulation.[5] The continued belief, despite the facts, that intercourse is the appropriate sexual activity to bring about the orgasms of both male and female involves a conceptual confusion. Sexual intercourse is an activity in which male arousal is a necessary condition, and male satisfaction, if not also a necessary condition, is the primary aim. Despite this, sexual intercourse is thought by many to be an activity that involves (or ought to) both male and female equally. But female arousal and satisfaction, although they may be concomitant events occasionally, are not even constituents of sexual intercourse.

II

Our language mirrors this confusion. Grammatically, polite expressions for sexual intercourse tend to be symmetric, giving the impression that what A does to B, B likewise does to A. Yet their definitions give a different picture. Although both male and female genitals are mentioned, the activity is characterized solely in terms of the *male* responses that constitute it.

Most expressions for sexual intercourse have the symmetry of other relations, like "shaking hands with," "being a sibling of" and "dancing with."[6] If a woman has sexual intercourse with a man, then it follows from the meaning of the terms that he has had sexual intercourse with her. If he has gone all the way with her, then, logically, she has gone all the

[1]This essay does not question the sociological data of Kinsey or Masters and Johnson. Nor does it raise any epistemological questions concerning their data, since I assume that knowledge about the sexual pleasure of others is just as possible as knowledge about any other feelings. And I assume that women are just as able as men to know about their own feelings of sexual pleasure.

[2]Alfred Kinsey et al., *Sexual Behavior in the Human Female* (Philadelphia: W. R. Saunders, 1953), p. 163.

[3]According to Kinsey's research "something between 36 and 44 per cent of the females in the sample had responded to [experienced] orgasm in a part but not all of their coitus in marriage. About one-third of those females had responded only a small part of the time, and the other third had responded a major portion of the time, even though it was not a hundred per cent of the time . . ." (ibid., p. 375). That is, fewer than 14 percent managed to have orgasms a major portion of the time, while over 56 percent had never had an orgasm during coitus. Objections to Kinsey's statistics (cf. Abram Kardiner, *Sex and Morality* [London: Routledge & Kegan Paul, 1955], p. 73) claim that his percentages of female orgasms during intercourse are much too *high*, giving women expectations that could never be met. Yet men, with rare exceptions, experience orgasms in sexual intercourse every time, without special techniques or partner skill.

[4]Eustace Chesser, *An Outline of Human Relationships* (London: William Heinemann, Ltd., 1959), p. 66: ". . . the misfortune of premature [preceeding the female's orgasm] ejaculation is extremely common. It cannot be too strongly emphasized that intercourse is more beset with difficulties for a man than a woman. A woman may take no pleasure in it for a variety of reasons, but if she cares deeply for her husband, she can pretend."

[5]The popularity of David Reuben's book *Any Woman Can* [have an orgasm in intercourse] shows that (1) it is widely known that many women do not have orgasms, and (2) many people who are interested in orgasm for the female think of sexual intercourse as the appropriate sexual activity.

[6]A selection of verbs and verb phrases for sexual intercourse from the *Dictionary of American Slang* and from *Webster's Third New International Dictionary* includes the taboo: "screw," "lay," "fuck," and "ball"; the slang: "do it (with)," "make," "make it (with)," "go all the way," and "give it to"; more acceptable expressions: "mate," "copulate," "couple," "have sex," "engage in coitus," and "sleep with"; expressions for intercourse outside marriage: "fornicate," "commit adultery"; and expressions for intercourse on a regular basis: "have an affair," "shack up," "have a relationship."

way with him. Since so many of the expressions for intercourse exhibit this symmetry, one might be led to expect that he and she are equally involved in this activity. Thus, if a male orgasm is a primary aim and usual constituent of the activity, it would seem that a female orgasm should be an aim and constituent too.

The exceptions, the expressions for sexual intercourse that are not symmetric, are significant in that they are vulgar. If he fucked her, it does not follow that she has fucked him, but only that she has been fucked by him. The grammar of the word "fuck" does not imply that he and she are equally involved in the activity.[7]

Acceptable expressions for sexual intercourse are symmetric; unacceptable expressions usually are not. Thus the grammar reflects the expectation of many people that if sexual intercourse is considered a decent and nice thing to do, men and women are likely to find it equally satisfying; and if it is considered a vulgar, dirty experience, they will not. This contrast reinforces the idea that a man and a woman *should,* if they are decent and nice, find this activity equally pleasurable. The belief is further reinforced by the slang use of the vulgar expressions such as "fuck" and "screw" to mean take advantage of, deceive, and injure. Thus, the grammar of these expressions invites us to believe that sexual intercourse, if it does not involve deceit and injury, is an activity that pertains to both parties equally. Viewed as an activity in genetics, sexual intercourse does involve both parties equally. But as an activity for producing pleasure, it is not an equal-opportunity experience.

III

What purports to be a mutually pleasurable activity, what is politely expressed in terms of a symmetric relation, in fact results in far fewer orgasms for women than for men. The reasons for this become obvious when we consider the definitions of expressions for sexual intercourse.

For sexual subjects dictionaries are usually barren sources. However, *Webster's Third New In-ternational Dictionary of the English Language* gives a definition under "coitus," and refers one to this word for all synonymous expressions. Coitus is defined as "the act of conveying the male semen to the female reproductive tract involving insertion of the penis in the vaginal orifice followed by ejaculation."[8] If we look up "ejaculation" we find: "the sudden or spontaneous discharging of a fluid (as semen in orgasm) from a duct"; and for "orgasm": "the climax of sexual excitement typically occurring toward the end of coitus."

According to these definitions the male orgasm is a necessary condition for sexual intercourse (coitus). To many people the only necessary condition for sexual intercourse is penetration; *coitus interruptus* is still coitus. But male orgasm is such a regular and expected part of sexual intercourse that the *Webster's Third* definition is widely accepted. For example, the law, which defines rape in terms of penetration, requires the presence of semen in the vaginal tract as *evidence* of the penetration. (Of course, this is because the testimony of the victim is not considered sufficient. If the law thought victims of other crimes were as likely to be liars, it might require other evidence to substantiate the charge. Significantly, for this paper, although many people object to the way rape victims are treated by the law, to my knowledge no one has objected to the semen test on the grounds that male orgasm is not an invariable aspect of rape.)

Thus, although there are exceptions, sexual intercourse is widely accepted as a process that is brought to a conclusion by the male orgasm. Physiologically it is usually impossible to continue intercourse after male orgasm. Thus, any discussion of the female orgasm during sexual intercourse is actually a discussion of the female orgasm before or during the male orgasm. Once the male orgasm occurs, sexual intercourse ends. This puts an arbitrary restriction on the period during which the female orgasm may occur. In addition, sexual intercourse formally begins when the primary focus for sexual stimulation in the male (the penis) is inserted in a container particularly well suited to bring about the male orgasm (the vaginal orifice). Although the dictionary merely says that sexual intercourse "involves" this insertion, anything

---

[7]It has even been claimed that it is ungrammatical for "fuck" to have a female subject (cf. Robert Baker, "'Pricks' and 'Chicks': A Plea for 'Persons,'" [see chapter 1, pp. 21–26, and chapter 3 ("Sex and Language"), pp. 100–103, this volume—eds.]. However, the *Dictionary of American Slang* says about "lay": "As most taboo words, this is primarily used by, but not restricted to use by, males" (p. 313). My experience supports the latter source.

[8]Even this definition is incorrect. If the male semen is deliberately prevented by a condom from entering the female reproductive tract, it would still be an act of coitus. A more accurate definition might be: That act involving insertion of the penis in the vaginal orifice followed by ejaculation.

prior to this insertion is termed "foreplay" or "pre-liminaries"; the real thing does not begin until the insertion occurs.[9]

The important point to notice is that this activity, which is described by verbs that are logically symmetrical, is in fact *defined* exclusively in terms of *male* stimulation by contact with the female, leading to (or at least aiming at) *male* orgasm. Thus, discussions of the female orgasm during sexual intercourse amount to discussions of the female orgasm after the source of *male* stimulation is placed in its container and before or during the *male* orgasm. The female locus of stimulation and the female orgasm are not even part of the definition of sexual intercourse. From this view, one might wonder why anyone ever thought the female orgasm had anything to do with sexual intercourse, except as an occasional and accidental co-occurrence. Sometimes the telephone rings, too.

IV

Some claims about the nature of sexual behavior can be seen as attempts to explain the asymmetry between male and female orgasms. Ignoring the definition of sexual intercourse, they assume that sexual intercourse would ordinarily involve the mutual pleasure of both male and female, and blame the inadequacies of the participants when it does not.

The claim about vaginal orgasms says, in effect, that for sexual intercourse to be a mutually pleasurable activity, the anatomical source of female stimulation must be the container that stimulates the male, and if it is not, there is something wrong with the female. The claim does not deny that women have orgasms for which the clitoris is the anatomical source. But such orgasms, it is claimed, (1) are not very good and (2) indicate immaturity.[10] In childhood masturbation the anatomical source may be the clitoris, but in sexual intercourse it should become the vagina. Significantly, no analogous difference between the locus of stimulation in mastur-

bation and intercourse is claimed for the male. Nor is it claimed that a male must mature to experience an intense orgasm during intercourse.

The claim about vaginal orgasms contradicts physiological evidence. All female orgasms share the same physiological characteristics: all may result in contractions of the vagina, but direct stimulation of the clitoral area produces more intense and rapid orgasms.[11]

It might be argued against this evidence that orgasm is not mainly a physiological, but a psychological, state. However, psychological (introspective) data are not allowed as falsifications by this claim for the superiority of vaginal orgasms. If a woman denies having orgasms produced by vaginal stimulation, her report can be discredited by the claim that she is fixated in childhood and does not experience a real orgasm because of her lack of sexual maturity. If a woman reports that vaginal orgasms are less intense than clitorally oriented ones, according to the claim, she does not know what a vaginal orgasm is. If it is less intense than a clitoral orgasm, it could not be a vaginal orgasm, which by definition is the more intense.

Psychologically the above claim is untestable; physiologically it is groundless. What purpose does this myth serve? It gives an account that hails sexual intercourse as a mutually pleasurable activity despite the facts against it. It also gives an explanation for this discordance with the facts: the female may still be more interested in the childish, self-centered sexual pleasures of masturbation and not mature enough to enjoy intercourse. The supposed symmetry of sexual intercourse presupposes this maturity; the facts are sometimes otherwise.

Another such claim is that in the best sexual experiences the male and female orgasms occur simultaneously. There is little specific physiological evidence to support this. In fact there is a loss of perceptual awareness that accompanies orgasm.[12] Thus, with simultaneous orgasms, neither participant is very aware of what is happening to the other. Part of the reason for interpersonal sexual activity is to enjoy the pleasure given to the other person. But with simultaneous orgasms one is less able to appreciate the partner's experience because one is overwhelmed by one's own.

What rationale supports this widely believed

---

[9]In the standard coital position sexual stimulation of the penis actually prevents similar stimulation of the primary area of sexual stimulation of the female. (William Masters and Virginia Johnson, *Human Sexual Response* [Boston: Little, Brown, and Co.], 1966, p. 60.)

[10]Kardiner, p. 67; Noel Lamare, *Love and Fulfillment in Woman* (New York: Macmillan, 1957), p. 21; Sigmund Freud, "The Transformation of Puberty," in *The Basic Writings of Sigmund Freud,* trans. A. A. Brill (New York: Random House, 1938), pp. 613–14; and Freud, "Female Sexuality," in *Collected Papers,* vol. 5, ed. J. V. Strachey (London: Hogarth Press, 1953), p. 252.

[11]Masters and Johnson, *Human Sexual Response,* pp. 59, 66–67.

[12]Ibid., p. 135.

claim about simultaneous orgasms?[13] Sexual intercourse is an event that regularly and expectedly culminates in the male orgasm. So if the female orgasm happened at the same time, then intercourse would have culminated in a female orgasm too. Simultaneous orgasms would provide the female's orgasm with the same status as the male's and would guarantee that sexual intercourse really had been a mutual activity. If people only did it right, sexual intercourse would merit the symmetry of its polite expressions.

V

Once it is recognized that sexual intercourse is an activity characterized in terms of male arousal and orgasm, for which female arousal and orgasm is irrelevant, the disparity between male and female orgasms in sexual intercourse should not be a problem. The disparity would be reduced if the standard sexual activity were a process characterized by the arousal and satisfaction of both sexes, rather than, as it is now, the process of sexual intercourse.[14] When sexual intercourse occurs, the male must be sexually aroused and regularly is orgasmic. If this activity included the same responses for the female, everything would be fine. But, as we know, it does not. The whole problem arises from trying to produce a female orgasm as a useful by-product of a process aimed at producing the male orgasm. And this attempt arises from the belief that the process will be, or should be, a mutually pleasurable activity involving both partners equally.

VI

One might object to blaming a conceptual confusion for the infrequency of female orgasms in sexual intercourse. It may be agreed that for most people sexual intercourse begins with stimulation of the male and ends with the male orgasm. But the objection would claim that this is the result of a male-oriented society. The contrast between grammar and definition may exist, but that too is the result of a male-oriented culture.

If the discrepancy in orgasm attainment were simply the result of male orientation, sexual intercourse could be represented as something to be initiated and carried out solely by the male for his own pleasure, with or without the use of the female. No one would be concerned about female orgasms at all.

It might be diplomatic to misrepresent sexual intercourse as a mutually pleasurable activity, a pretense that would help keep women in their place. One would not expect such deception to fool anyone acquainted with the facts. Yet many people (both male and female) believe that sexual activity should provide maximum satisfaction for both parties, recognize that women reach orgasm in intercourse far less often than men, and yet, thinking that sexual intercourse is a symmetric activity, continue to believe that it should provide the same sort of satisfaction for both sexes. If there were no conceptual confusion, then those who were only concerned with male satisfaction in sexual activity between males and females could restrict that activity to intercourse, while those concerned with female satisfaction as well would not be so restricted.

VII

Perhaps the nature of the confusion can be best brought out by an analogy. Let us imagine a culture in which the women prepared all the food and spoon-fed it to the men, but fed none to themselves. And suppose this feeding activity was described as if it were a mutual activity, that is, by expressions that indicated symmetric relations. This custom would be described by expressions such as "have feeding behavior with." Logically it would follow that if he had feeding behavior with her, then she had feeding behavior with him. Despite this symmetry and the universal and frequent practice of feeding behavior, a great many women in this culture suffered from malnutrition. Instead of changing or expanding the custom, so that women got a chance to eat too, the society attributed the malnutrition to biological differences. It was argued that women's bodies were not as able to be nourished as

---

[13]After orgasm the genital areas of both sexes may become oversensitive, so that continued stimulation is painful. Simultaneous orgasms would avoid this problem, but at the cost of delicate and difficult timing that often diminishes the intensity of the orgasm. More important, I suspect, is that the loss of awareness actually encourages the support for simultaneity, as it provides an ideal time for the faking recommended by the marriage manuals. The male is excused from not knowing and can ask "Did you?" when at any other time the answer would be obvious to him.

[14]For some people this change might result in no variation of physical behavior. This is not a recommendation for any particular sort of physical behavior—let that be the province of physiologists—but a recommendation that the physical behavior engaged in, whatever it is, fit (or try to) this description: a process that involves the arousal and satisfaction of all participants equally.

were men's. Malnutrition was considered a consequence of a sex-linked congenital defect. Experts claimed that women, unlike men, could not be satisfied with mere hunger-satiation anyway. Instead, the satisfaction women derived from feeding behavior was in the warmth and closeness of a meaningful relationship.

Educated women introduced variations of feeding behavior that included spoon-licking while cooking. This was called "foretaste." Men often encouraged it, although it was rarely continued when feeding behavior began. Other women relied on self-feeding to survive, but this was frowned on by the whole community as perverted, antisocial behavior. The influence of custom was so strong that few believed that women in the kitchen together might feed each other. It was commonly thought that women who fed each other did so only because they could not get men to feed. No one ever thought they did it to get food.

Gourmet cookbooks claimed that in truly gourmet feeding both male and female got nourished together. However, since only one spoon was used in feeding behavior, simultaneous nourishment was very unusual. Even when it was managed most of the food spilled and neither party got very much.

Nutrition manuals argued that since feeding behavior *should* be a mutual activity, the female *should* receive nourishment through the spoon that feeds the male, and if she did not there was something inadequate about her. The books did not deny that a female could be nourished through her mouth. But such nourishment, they claimed, (1) is not very satisfying and (2) indicates immaturity. In childhood self-feeding, the focus of feeding satisfaction may be the mouth, but in mature feeding behavior, it should become the spoon. Of course, the locus of nourishment in the male was not thought to be different in mature feeding behavior from that of childhood self-feeding.

In this imaginary culture the problem of how to provide nourishment for the female during feeding behavior is beset with the same conceptual difficulties as the problem in our culture of how to provide orgasm for the female during sexual intercourse. Attributing either problem to basic anatomic differences between men and women is absurd. It is not anatomic differences that account for female malnutrition in the feeding-behavior culture. The female is just not getting enough food. Note that a larger female would not get enough food just by getting the same amount of food as a smaller male. What counts as "enough" varies with the individual.

Similarly, it is not anatomical differences that account for lack of female orgasms during sexual intercourse. The female is just not getting enough stimulation.

VIII

It is often said that for women the sympathy and understanding expressed in sexual relations is more satisfying than an orgasm.[15] Many critics of physiological research claim that it ignores these psychological aspects of sexual behavior. Now of course these psychological aspects are important. They are the whole reason for engaging in interpersonal sexual activity rather than masturbation. But if a woman spends the time and energy to produce someone else's orgasm, with the understanding that she is participating in a mutual activity, it is only fair that her partner do the same for her. If she has to be satisfied with sympathy and understanding alone, then so should her partner.

IX

Sexual activities, as with most social behaviors, are stylized, deriving much of their immutability from the language that describes them. For each new generation of humans, lacking the instinctual control of other species, the "rediscovery" of sexual activity is greatly influenced by information carried by spoken and written language. There is a big difference between pointing out a conceptual confusion and its remedy and actually changing the behavior that the confusion helps maintain. To do the latter it is necessary to change the concept of the standard sexual activity to one that involves the arousal and satisfaction of all participants. That involves changing the romantic looks and smiles that now convey "I'm interested in sexual intercourse with you" so that they convey "I'm interested in our both having a satisfying sexual experience together."

[15] Eustace Chesser, *Is Chastity Outmoded?* (London: William Heinemann, Ltd., 1960), p. 88.

17/Better Sex

Sara Ruddick

It might be argued that there is no specifically sexual morality. We have, of course, become accustomed to speaking of sexual morality, but the "morality" of which we speak has a good deal to do with property, the division of labor, and male power, and little to do with our sexual lives. Sexual experiences, like experiences in driving automobiles, render us liable to specific moral situations. As drivers we must guard against infantile desires for revenge and excitement. As lovers we must guard against cruelty and betrayal, for we know sexual experiences provide special opportunities for each. We drive soberly because, before we get into a car, we believe that it is wrong to be careless of life. We resist temptations to adultery because we believe it wrong to betray trust, whether it be a parent, a sexual partner, or a political colleague who is betrayed. As lovers and drivers we act on principles that are particular applications of general moral principles. Moreover, given the superstitions from which sexual experience has suffered, it is wise to free ourselves, as lovers, from any moral concerns, other than those we have as human beings. There is no specifically sexual morality, and none should be invented. Or so it might be argued.

When we examine our moral "intuitions," however, the analogy with driving fails us. Unburdened of *sexual* morality, we do not find it easy to apply general moral principles to our sexual lives. The "morally average" lover can be cruel, violate trust, and neglect social duties with less opprobrium precisely *because* he is a lover. Only political passions and psychological or physical deprivation serve as well as sexual desire to excuse what would otherwise be seriously and clearly immoral acts. (Occasionally, sexual desire is itself conceived of as a deprivation, an involuntary lust. And there is, of course, a tradition that sees sexual morality as a way of controlling those unable to be sexless: "It is better to marry than to burn.") Often, in our sexual lives, we neither flout nor simply apply general moral principles. Rather, the values of sexual experience themselves figure in the construction of moral dilemmas. The conflict between better sex (more complete, natural, and pleasurable sex acts) and, say, social duty is not seen as a conflict between the immoral and compulsive, on one hand, and the morally good, on the other, but as a conflict between alternative moral acts.

Our intuitions vary but at least they suggest we can use "good" sex as a positive weight on some moral balance. What is that weight? Why do we put it there? How do we, in the first place, evaluate sexual experiences? On reflection, should we endorse these evaluations? These are the questions whose answers should constitute a specifically sexual morality.

In answering them, I will first consider three characteristics that have been used to distinguish some sex acts as better than others—greater pleasure, completeness, and naturalness. Other characteristics may be relevant to evaluating sex acts, but these three are central. If they have *moral* significance, then the sex acts characterized by them will be better than others not so characterized.

After considering those characteristics in virtue of which some sex acts are allegedly better than others, I will ask whether the presence of those characteristics renders the acts *morally* superior. I will not consider here the unclear and overused distinction between the moral and the amoral, nor the illegitimate but familiar distinction between the moral and the prudent. I hope it is sufficient to set out dogmatically and schematically the moral notions I will use. I am confident that better sex is morally

An earlier version of this paper was published in *Moral Problems*, edited by James Rachels (New York: Harper & Row, 1971). I am grateful to many friends and students for their comments on the earlier version, especially to Bernard Gert, Evelyn Fox Keller, and James Rachels.

preferable to other sex, but I am not at all happy with my characterization of its moral significance. Ultimately, sexual morality cannot be considered apart from a "prudential" morality in which it is shown that what is good is good for us and what is good for us makes us good. In such a morality, not only sex, but art, fantasy, love, and a host of other intellectual and emotional enterprises will regain old moral significances and acquire new ones. My remarks here, then, are partial and provisional.

A characteristic renders a sex act morally preferable to one without that characteristic if it gives, increases, or is instrumental in increasing the "benefit" of the act for the person engaging in it. Benefits can be classified as peremptory or optional. Peremptory benefits are experiences, relations, or objects that anyone who is neither irrational nor anhedonic will want so long as s/he wants anything at all. Optional benefits are experiences, relations, or objects that anyone, neither irrational nor anhedonic, will want so long as s/he will not thereby lose a peremptory benefit. There is widespread disagreement about which benefits are peremptory. Self-respect, love, and health are common examples of peremptory benefits. Arms, legs, and hands are probably optional benefits. A person still wanting a great deal might give up limbs, just as s/he would give up life, when mutilation or death is required by self-respect. As adults we are largely responsible for procuring our own benefits and greatly dependent on good fortune for success in doing so. However, the moral significance of benefits is most clearly seen not from the standpoint of the person procuring and enjoying them but from the standpoint of another *caring* person, for example, a lover, parent, or political leader responsible for procuring benefits for specific others. A benefit may then be described as an experience, relation, or object that anyone who properly cares for another is obliged to attempt to secure for him/her. Criteria for the virtue of care and for benefit are reciprocally determined, the virtue consisting in part in recognizing and attempting to secure benefits for the person cared for, the identification of benefit depending on its recognition by those already seen to be properly caring.

In talking of benefits I shall be looking at our sexual lives from the vantage point of hope, not of fear. The principal interlocutor may be considered to be a child asking what s/he should rightly and reasonably hope for in living, rather than a potential criminal questioning conventional restraints. The specific question the child may be imagined to ask

can now be put: In what way is better sex beneficial or conducive to experiences or relations or objects that are beneficial?

A characteristic renders a sex act morally preferable to one without that characteristic if either the act is thereby more just or the act is thereby likely to make the person engaging in it more just. Justice includes giving others what is due them, taking no more than what is one's own, and giving and taking according to prevailing principles of fairness.

A characteristic renders a sex act morally preferable to one without that characteristic if because of the characteristic the act is more virtuous or more likely to lead to virtue. A virtue is a disposition to attempt, and an ability to succeed in, good acts —acts of justice, acts that express or produce excellence, and acts that yield benefits to oneself or others.

Sexual Pleasure

Sensual experiences give rise to sensations and experiences that are paradigms of what is pleasant. Hedonism, in both its psychological and ethical forms, has blinded us to the nature and to the benefits of sensual pleasure by overextending the word "pleasure" to cover anything enjoyable or even agreeable.[1] The paradigmatic type of pleasure is sensual. Pleasure is a temporally extended, more or less intense quality of particular experiences. Pleasure is enjoyable independent of any function pleasurable activity fulfills. The infant who continues to suck well after s/he is nourished, expressing evident pleasure in doing so, gives us a demonstration of the nature of pleasure.[2]

As we learn more about pleasant experiences we not only apply but also extend and attenuate the primary notion of "pleasure." But if pleasure is to have any nonsophistical psychological or moral interest, it must retain its connections with those paradigm instances of sensual pleasure that give rise to it. We may, for example, extend the notion of

[1] This may be a consequence of the tepidness of the English "pleasant." It would be better to speak of lust and its satisfaction if our suspicion of pleasure had not been written into that part of our language.

[2] The example is from Sigmund Freud, *Three Essays on Sexuality,* standard ed., vol. 7 (London: Hogarth, 1963), p. 182. The concept of pleasure I urge here is narrower but also, I think, more useful than the popular one. It is a concept that, to paraphrase Wittgenstein, we (could) learn when we learn the language. The idea of paradigmatic uses and subsequent more-or-less-divergent, more-or-less-"normal" uses also is derived from Wittgenstein.

pleasure so that particular episodes in the care of children give great pleasure; but the long-term caring for children, however intrinsically rewarding, is not an experience of pleasure or unpleasure.

Sexual pleasure is a species of sensual pleasure with its own conditions of arousal and satisfaction. Sexual acts vary considerably in pleasure, the limiting case being a sexual act where no one experiences pleasure even though someone may experience affection or "relief of tension" through orgasm. Sexual pleasure can be considered either in a context of deprivation and its relief or in a context of satisfaction. Psychological theories have tended to emphasize the frustrated state of sexual desire and to construe sexual pleasure as a relief from that state. There are, however, alternative accounts of sexual pleasure that correspond more closely with our experience. Sexual pleasure is "a primary distinctively poignant pleasure experience that manifests itself from early infancy on. . . . Once experienced it continues to be savored. . . ."[3] Sexual desire is not experienced as frustration but as part of sexual pleasure. Normally, sexual desire transforms itself gradually into the pleasure that appears, misleadingly, to be an aim extrinsic to it. The natural structure of desire, not an inherent quality of frustration, accounts for the pain of an aroused but unsatisfied desire.

Sexual pleasure, like addictive pleasure generally, does not, except very temporarily, result in satiety. Rather, it increases the demand for more of the same while sharply limiting the possibility of substitutes. The experience of sensual pleasures, and particularly of sexual pleasures, has a pervasive effect on our perceptions of the world. We find bodies inviting, social encounters alluring, and smells, tastes, and sights resonant because our perception of them includes their sexual significance. Merleau-Ponty has written of a patient for whom "perception had lost its erotic structure, both temporally and physically."[4] As the result of a brain injury the patient's capacity for sexual desire and pleasure (though not his capacity for performing sexual acts) was impaired. He no longer sought sexual intercourse of his own accord, was left indif-

ferent by the sights and smells of available bodies, and if in the midst of sexual intercourse his partner turned away, he showed no signs of displeasure. The capacity for sexual pleasure, upon which the erotic structure of perception depends, can be accidentally damaged. The question that this case raises is whether it would be desirable to interfere with this capacity in a more systematic way than we now do. With greater biochemical and psychiatric knowledge we shall presumably be able to manipulate it at will.[5] And if that becomes possible, toward what end should we interfere? I shall return to this question after describing the other two characteristics of better sex—completeness and naturalness.

Complete Sex Acts

The completeness of a sexual act depends upon the *relation* of the participants to their own and each other's *desire*. A sex act is complete if each partner allows him/herself to be "taken over" by an active desire, which is desire not merely for the other's body but also for her/his active desire. Completeness is hard to characterize, though complete sex acts are at least as natural as any others —especially, it seems, among those people who take them casually and for granted. The notion of "completeness" (as I shall call it) has figured under various guises in the work of Sartre, Merleau-Ponty, and more recently Thomas Nagel. "The being which desires is consciousness making itself body."[6] "What we try to possess, then, is not just a body, but a body brought to life by consciousness."[7] "It is important that the partner be aroused, and not merely aroused, but aroused by the awareness of one's desire."[8]

The precondition of complete sex acts is the "embodiment" of the participants. Each participant submits to sexual desires that take over consciousness and direct action. It is sexual desire and not a separable satisfaction of it (for example, orgasm) that is important here. Indeed, Sartre finds pleasure external to the essence of desire, and Nagel gives

[3]George Klein, "Freud's Two Theories of Sexuality," in L. Berger, ed., *Clinical-Cognitive Psychology: Models and Integrations* (Englewood Cliffs, N.J.: Prentice-Hall, 1969), pp. 131–81. This essay gives a clear idea of alternative psychological accounts of sexual pleasure.

[4]Maurice Merleau-Ponty, *Phenomenology of Perception*, trans. Colin Smith (London: Routledge & Kegan Paul, 1962), p. 156.

[5]See Kurt Vonnegut, Jr., "Welcome to the Monkey House," in *Welcome to the Monkey House* (New York: Dell, 1968), which concerns both the manipulation and the benefit of sexual pleasure.

[6]Jean-Paul Sartre, *Being and Nothingness*, trans. Hazel E. Barnes (New York: Philosophical Library, 1956), p. 389.

[7]Merleau-Ponty, *Phenomenology of Perception*, p. 167.

[8]Thomas Nagel, "Sexual Perversion," *The Journal of Philosophy* 66, no. 1 (January 16, 1969): 13. . . . My original discussion of completeness was both greatly indebted to and confused by Nagel's. I have tried here to dispel some of the confusion.

an example of embodiment in which the partners do not touch each other. Desire is pervasive and "overwhelming," but it does not make its subject its involuntary victim (as it did the Boston Strangler, we are told), nor does it, except at its climax, alter capacities for ordinary perceptions, memories, and inferences. Nagel's embodied partners can presumably get themselves from bar stools to bed while their consciousness is "clogged" with desire. With what, then, is embodiment contrasted?

Philosophers make statements that when intended literally are evidence of pathology: "Human beings are automata"; "I never really see physical objects"; "I can never know what another person is feeling." The clearest statement of disembodiment that I know of is W. T. Stace's claim: "I become aware of my body in the end chiefly because it insists on accompanying me wherever I go."[9] What "just accompanies me" can also stay away. "When my body leaves me/I'm lonesome for it./ ... body/goes away I don't know where/and it's lonesome to drift/above the space it/fills when it's here."[10] If "the body is felt more as one object among other objects in the world than as the core of the individual's own being,"[11] then what appears to be bodily can be dissociated from the "real self." Both a generalized separation of "self" from body and particular disembodied experiences have had their advocates. The attempt at disembodiment has also been seen as conceptually confused and psychologically disastrous.

We may often experience ourselves as relatively disembodied, observing or "using" our bodies to fulfill our intentions. On some occasions, however, such as in physical combat, sport, physical suffering, or danger, we "become" our bodies; our consciousness becomes bodily experience of bodily activity.[12] Sexual acts are occasions for such embodiment; they may, however, fail for a variety of reasons, for example, because of pretense or an excessive need for self-control. If someone is em-

bodied by sexual desire, s/he submits to its direction. Spontaneous impulses of desire become her/his movements—some involuntary, like gestures of "courting behavior" or physical expressions of intense pleasure, and some deliberate. Her/his consciousness, or "mind," is taken over by desire and the pursuit of its object, in the way that at other times it may be taken over by an intellectual problem or by obsessive fantasies. But unlike the latter takeovers, this one is bodily. A desiring consciousness is flooded with specifically sexual feelings that eroticize all perception and movement. Consciousness "becomes flesh."

Granted the precondition of embodiment, complete sex acts occur when each partner's embodying desire is active and actively responsive to the other's. This second aspect of complete sex constitutes a "reflexive mutual recognition" of desire by desire.[13]

The partner *actively* desires another person's desire. Active desiring includes more than embodiment, which might be achieved in objectless masturbation. It is more, also, than merely being aroused by and then taken over by desire, though it may come about as a result of deliberate arousal. It commits the actively desiring person to her/his desire and requires her/him to identify with it—that is, to recognize him/herself as a sexual agent as well as respondent. (Active desiring is less encouraged in women, and probably more women than men feel threatened by it.)

The other recognizes and responds to the partner's desire. Merely to recognize the desire as desire, not to reduce it to an itch or to depersonalize it as a "demand," may be threatening. Imperviousness to desire is the deepest defense against it. We have learned from research on families whose members tend to become schizophrenic that such imperviousness, the refusal to recognize a feeling for what it is, can force a vulnerable person to deny or to obscure the real nature of her/his feelings. Imperviousness tends to deprive even a relatively invulnerable person of her/his efficacy. The demand that our feelings elicit a response appropriate to them is part of a general demand that *we* be recognized, that our feelings be allowed to make a difference.

There are many ways in which sexual desire may be recognized, countless forms of submission and resistance. In complete sex, desire is recog-

[9]W. T. Stace, "Solipsism," from *The Theory of Knowledge and Existence;* reprinted in Tillman, Berofsky, and O'Connor, eds. *Introductory Philosophy* (New York: Harper & Row, 1967), p. 113.

[10]Denise Levertov, "Gone Away," in *O Taste and See* (New York: New Directions, 1962), p. 59. Copyright by Denise Levertov Goodman, New Directions Publishing Corporation, New York.

[11]R. D. Laing, *The Divided Self* (Baltimore: Pelican Books, 1965), p. 69.

[12]We need not become our bodies on such occasions. Pains, muscular feelings, and emotions can be reduced to mere "sensations" that may impinge on "me" but that I attempt to keep at a distance. Laing describes the case of a man who when beaten up felt that any damage to his body could not really hurt *him*. See *The Divided Self,* p. 68.

[13]Nagel, "Sexual Perversion," p. 254.

nized by a responding and active desire that commits the other, as it committed the partner. Given responding desire, both people identify themselves as sexually desiring the other. They are neither seducer nor seduced, neither suppliant nor benefactress, neither sadist nor victim, but sexual agents acting sexually out of their recognized desire. Indeed, in complete sex one not only welcomes and recognizes active desire, one desires it. Returned and endorsed desire becomes one of the features of an erotically structured perception. Desiring becomes desirable. (Men are less encouraged to desire the other's active and demanding desire, and such desiring is probably threatening to more men than women.)

In sum, in complete sex two persons embodied by sexual desire actively desire and respond to each other's active desire. Although it is difficult to write of complete sex without suggesting that one of the partners is the initiator, while the other responds, complete sex is reciprocal sex. The partners, whatever the circumstances of their coming together, are equal in activity and responsiveness of desire.

Sexual acts can be partly incomplete. A necrophiliac may be taken over by desire, and one may respond to a partner's desire without being embodied by one's own. Partners whose sexual activities are accompanied by private fantasies engage in an incomplete sex act. Consciousness is used by desire but remains apart from it, providing it with stimulants and controls. Neither partner responds to the other's desire, though each may appear to. Sartre's "dishonest masturbator," for whom masturbation is the sex act of choice, engages in a paradigmatically incomplete sex act: "He asks only to be slightly distanced from his own body, only for there to be a light coating of otherness over his flesh and over his thoughts. His personae are melting sweets. . . . The masturbator is enchanted at never being able to feel himself sufficiently another, and at producing for himself alone the diabolic appearance of a couple that fades away when one touches it. . . . Masturbation is the derealisation of the world and of the masturbator himself."[14]

Completeness is more difficult to describe than incompleteness, for it turns on precise but subtle ways of responding to a particular person's desire with specific expressions of impulse that are both spontaneous and responsive.

There are many possible sex acts that are pleasurable but not complete. Sartre, Nagel, and Merleau-Ponty each suggest that the desire for the responsive desire of one's partner is the "central impulse" of sexual desire.[15] The desire for a sleeping woman, for example, is possible only "in so far as this sleep appears on the ground of consciousness."[16] This seems much too strong. Some lovers desire that their partners resist, other like them coolly controlled, others prefer them asleep. We would not say that there was anything abnormal or less fully sexual about desire. Whether or not complete sex is preferable to incomplete sex (the question to which I shall turn shortly), incompleteness does not disqualify a sex act from being fully sexual.

Sexual Perversion

The final characteristic of allegedly better sex acts is that they are "natural" rather than "perverted." The ground for classifying sexual acts as either natural or unnatural is that the former type serve or could serve the evolutionary and biological function of sexuality—namely, reproduction. "Natural" sexual desire has as its "object" living persons of the opposite sex, and in particular their postpubertal genitals. The "aim" of natural sexual desire—that is, the act that "naturally" completes it—is genital intercourse. Perverse sex acts are deviations from the natural object (for example, homosexuality, fetishism) or from the standard aim (for example, voyeurism, sadism). Among the variety of objects and aims of sexual desire, I can see no other ground for selecting some as natural, except that they are of the type that can lead to reproduction.[17]

The connection of sexual desire with reproduction gives us the criterion but not the motive of the classification. The concept of perversion depends on a disjointedness between our experience of sexual desire from infancy on and the function of sexual desire—reproduction. In our collective experience of sexuality, perverse desires are as natural as nonperverse ones. The sexual desire of the polymorphously perverse child has many

[14]Jean-Paul Sartre, *Saint Genet* (New York: Braziller, 1963), p. 398; cited and translated by R. D. Laing, *Self and Others* (New York: Pantheon, 1969), pp. 39–40.

[15]Ibid., p. 13.

[16]Sartre, *Being and Nothingness*, p. 386.

[17]See, in support of this point, Sigmund Freud, *Introductory Lectures on Psychoanalysis*, standard ed., vol. 26 (London: Hogarth, 1963), chaps. 20, 21.

objects—for example, breasts, anus, mouth, genitals—and many aims—for example, autoerotic or other-directed looking, smelling, touching, hurting. From the social and developmental point of view, natural sex is an achievement, partly biological, partly conventional, consisting in a dominant organization of sexual desires in which perverted aims or objects are subordinate to natural ones. The concept of perversion reflects the vulnerability as much as the evolutionary warrant of this organization.

The connection of sexual desire with reproduction is not sufficient to yield the concept of perversion, but it is surely necessary. Nagel, however, thinks otherwise. There are, he points out, many sexual acts that do not lead to reproduction but that we are not even inclined to call perverse—for example, sexual acts between partners who are sterile. Perversion, according to him, is a psychological concept while reproduction is (only?) a physiological one. (Incidentally, this view of reproduction seems to me the clearest instance of male bias in Nagel's paper.)

Nagel is right about our judgments of particular acts, but he draws the wrong conclusions from those judgments. The perversity of sex acts does not depend upon whether they are intended to achieve reproduction. "Natural" sexual desire is for heterosexual genital activity, not for reproduction. The ground for classifying that desire as natural is that it is so organized that it *could* lead to reproduction in normal physiological circumstances. The reproductive organization of sexual desires gives us a *criterion* of naturalness, but the *virtue* of which it is a criterion is the "naturalness" itself, not reproduction. Our vacillating attitude toward the apparently perverse acts of animals reflects our shifting from criterion to virtue. If, when confronted with a perverse act of animals, we withdraw the label "perverted" from our own similar acts rather than extend it to theirs, we are relinquishing the reproductive criterion of naturalness, while retaining the virtue. Animals cannot be "unnatural." If, on the other hand, we "discover" that animals can be perverts too, we are maintaining our criterion, but giving a somewhat altered sense to the "naturalness" of which it is a criterion.

Nagel's alternative attempt to classify acts as natural or perverted on the basis of their completeness fails. "Perverted" and "complete" are evaluations of an entirely different order. The completeness of a sex act depends upon qualities of the participants' experience and upon qualities of their relation—qualities of which they are the best judge. To say a sex act is perverted is to pass a conventional judgment about characteristics of the act, which could be evident to any observer. As one can pretend to be angry but not to shout, one can pretend to a complete, but not to a natural, sex act (though one may, of course, conceal desires for perverse sex acts or shout in order to mask one's feelings). As Nagel himself sees, judgments about particular sex acts clearly differentiate between perversion and completeness. Unadorned heterosexual intercourse where each partner has private fantasies is clearly "natural" and clearly "incomplete," but there is nothing prima facie incomplete about exclusive oral-genital intercourse or homosexual acts. If many perverse acts are incomplete, as Nagel claims, this is an important fact *about* perversion, but it is not the basis upon which we judge its occurrence.

Is Better Sex Really Better?

Some sex acts are, allegedly, better than others insofar as they are more pleasurable, complete, and natural. What is the moral significance of this evaluation? In answering this question, official sexual morality sometimes appeals to the social consequences of particular types of better sex acts. For example, since dominantly perverse organizations of sexual impulses limit reproduction, the merits of perversion depend upon the need to limit or increase population. Experience of sexual pleasure may be desirable if it promotes relaxation and communication in an acquisitive society, undesirable if it limits the desire to work or, in armies, to kill. The social consequences of complete sex have not received particular attention, because the quality of sexual experience has been of little interest to moralists. It might be found that those who had complete sexual relations were more cooperative, less amenable to political revolt. If so, complete sexual acts would be desirable in just and peaceable societies, undesirable in unjust societies requiring revolution.

The social desirability of types of sexual acts depends on particular social conditions and independent criteria of social desirability. It may be interesting and important to assess particular claims about the social desirability of sex acts, but this is not my concern. What is my concern is the extent to which we will allow our judgments of sexual worth to be influenced by social considerations. But this issue cannot even be raised until we have a better sense of sexual worth.

The Benefit of Sexual Pleasure

To say that an experience is pleasant is to give a self-evident, terminal reason for seeking it. We can sometimes "see" that an experience is pleasant. When, for example, we observe someone's sensual delight in eating, her/his behavior can expressively characterize pleasure. We can only question the benefit of such an experience by referring to other goods with which it might conflict. Though sensual pleasures may not be sufficient to warrant giving birth or to deter suicide, so long as we live they are self-evidently benefits to us.

The most eloquent detractors of sexual experience have admitted that it provides sensual pleasures so poignant that once experienced they are repeatedly, almost addictively, sought. Yet, unlike other appetites, such as hunger, sexual desire can be permanently resisted, and resistance has been advocated. How can the prima facie benefits of sexual pleasure appear deceptive?

There are several grounds for complaint. Sexual pleasure is ineradicably mixed, frustration being part of every sexual life. The capacity for sexual pleasure is unevenly distributed, cannot be voluntarily acquired, and diminishes through no fault of its subject. If such a pleasure were an intrinsic benefit, benefit would in this case be independent of moral effort. Then again, sexual pleasures are not serious. Enjoyment of them is one of life's greatest recreations, but none of its business. And finally, sexual desire has the defects of its strengths. Before satisfaction, it is, at the least, distracting; in satisfaction, it "makes one little roome, an everywhere." Like psychosis, sexual desire turns us from "reality"—whether the real be God, social justice, children, or intellectual endeavor. This turning away is more than a social consequence of desire, though it is that. Lovers themselves feel that their sexual desires are separate from their "real" political, domestic, ambitious, social selves.

If the plaintiff is taken to argue that sensual pleasures are not peremptory benefits, s/he is probably right. We can still want a good deal and forego sexual pleasures. We often forego pleasure just because we want something incompatible with it, for example, a continuing marriage. We must distinguish between giving up some occasions for sexual pleasure and giving up sexual pleasure itself. If all circumstances of sexual pleasure . . . threaten a peremptory benefit, such as self-respect, then the hope and the possibility of sexual pleasure may be relinquished. Since sexual pleasure is such a great, though optional, benefit, its loss is a sad one.

In emphasizing the unsocial, private nature of sexual experiences, the plaintiff is emphasizing a morally important characteristic of them. But her/his case against desire, as I have sketched it, is surely overstated. The mixed, partly frustrated character of any desire is not particularly pronounced for sexual desire, which is in fact especially plastic, or adaptable to changes (provided perverse sex acts have not been ruled out). Inhibition, social deprivation, or disease make our sexual lives unpleasant, but that is because they interfere with sexual desire, not because the desire is by its nature frustrating. More than other well-known desires (for example, desire for knowledge, success, or power), sexual desire is simply and completely satisfied upon attaining its object. Partly for this reason, even if we are overtaken by desire during sexual experience, our sexual experiences do not overtake us. Lovers turn away from the world while loving, but return—sometimes all too easily—when loving is done. The moralist rightly perceives sexual pleasure as a recreation, and those who upon realizing its benefits make a business of its pursuit appear ludicrous. The capacity for recreation, however, is surely a benefit that any human being rightly hopes for who hopes for anything. Indeed, in present social and economic conditions we are more likely to lay waste our powers in work than in play. Thus, though priest, revolutionary, and parent are alike in fearing sexual pleasure, this fear should inspire us to psychological and sociological investigation of the fearing rather than to moral doubt about the benefit of sexual pleasure.

The Moral Significance of Perversion

What is the moral significance of the perversity of a sexual act? Next to none, so far as I can see. Though perverted sex may be "unnatural" both from an evolutionary and developmental perspective, there is no connection, inverse or correlative, between what is natural and what is good. Perverted sex is sometimes said to be less pleasurable than natural sex. We have little reason to believe that this claim is true and no clear idea of the kind of evidence on which it would be based. In any case, to condemn perverse acts for lack of pleasure is to recognize the worth of pleasure, not of naturalness.

There are many other claims about the nature and consequences of perversion. Some merely restate "scientific" facts in morally tinged terminology. Perverse acts are, by definition and according to psychiatric theory, "immature" and "abnormal," since natural sex acts are selected by criteria of "normal" sexual function and "normal" and "mature" psychological development. But there is no greater connection of virtue with maturity and normality than there is of virtue with nature. The elimination of a village by an invading army would be no less evil if it were the expression of controlled, normal, natural, and mature aggression.

Nagel claims that many perverted sex acts are incomplete, and in making his point, gives the most specific arguments that I have read for the inferiority of perverted sex. But as he points out, there is no reason to think an act consisting solely of oral-genital intercourse is incomplete; it is doubtful whether homosexual acts and acts of buggery are especially liable to be incomplete; and the incompleteness of sexual intercourse with animals is a relative matter depending upon their limited consciousness. And again, the alleged inferiority is not a consequence of perversion but of incompleteness, which can afflict natural sex as well.

Perverted acts might be thought to be inferior because they cannot result in children. Whatever the benefits and moral significance of the procreation and care of children (and I believe they are extensive and complicated), the virtue of proper care for children neither requires nor follows from biological parenthood. Even if it did, only a sexual life consisting solely of perverse acts rules out conception.

If perverted sex acts did rule out normal sex acts, if one were *either* perverted *or* natural, then certain kinds of sexual relations would be denied some perverts—relations that are benefits to those who enjoy them. It seems that sexual relations with the living and the human would be of greater benefit than those with the dead or with animals. But there is no reason to think that heterosexual relations are of greater benefit than homosexual ones. It might be thought that children can only be raised by heterosexual couples who perform an abundance of natural sex acts. If true (though truth seems highly

unlikely), perverts will be denied the happiness of parenthood. This deprivation would be an *indirect* consequence of perverted sex and might yield a moral dilemma: How is one to choose between the benefits of children and the benefits of more pleasurable, more complex sex acts?

Some perversions are immoral on independent grounds. Sadism is the obvious example, though sadism practiced with a consenting masochist is far less evil than other, more familiar forms of aggression. Voyeurism may seem immoral because, since it must be secret to be satisfying, it violates others' rights to privacy.[18] Various kinds of rape can constitute perversion if rape, rather than genital intercourse, is the aim of desire. Rape is always seriously immoral, a vivid violation of respect for persons. Sometimes doubly perverse rape is doubly evil (the rape of a child), but in other cases (the rape of a pig) its evil is halved. In any case, though rape is always *wrong,* it is only perverse when raping becomes the aim and not the means of desire.

Someone can be dissuaded from acting on her/his perverse desires either from moral qualms or from social fears. Although there may be ample basis for the latter, I can find none for the former except the possible indirect loss of the benefits of child care. I am puzzled about this since reflective people who do not usually attempt to legislate the preferences of others think differently. There is no doubt that beliefs in these matters involve deep emotions that should be respected. But for those who do in fact have perverted desires, the first concern will be to satisfy them, not to divert or to understand them. For sexual pleasure is intrinsically a benefit, and complete sex acts, which depend upon expressing the desires one in fact has, are both beneficial and conducive to virtue. Therefore, barring extrinsic moral or social considerations, perverted sex acts are preferable to natural ones if the latter are less pleasurable or less complete.

The Moral Significance of Completeness

Complete sex consists in mutually embodied, mutually active, responsive desire. Embodiment, activity, and mutual responsiveness are instrumentally beneficial because they are conducive to our psychological well-being, which is an intrinsic

[18]I am indebted to Dr. Leo Goldberger for this example.

benefit. The alleged pathological consequences of disembodiment are more specific and better documented than those of perversity.[19] To dissociate oneself from one's actual body, either by creating a delusory body or by rejecting the bodily, is to court a variety of ill effects, ranging from self-disgust to diseases of the will, to faulty mental development, to the destruction of a recognizable "self," and finally to madness. It is difficult to assess psychiatric claims outside their theoretical contexts, but in this case I believe that they are justified. Relative embodiment is a stable, *normal* condition that is not confined to cases of complete embodiment. But psychiatrists tell us that exceptional physical occasions of embodiment seem to be required in order to balance tendencies to reject or to falsify the body. Sexual acts are not the only such occasions, but they do provide an immersion of consciousness in the bodily, which is pleasurable and especially conducive to correcting experiences of shame and disgust that work toward disembodiment.

The mutual responsiveness of complete sex is also instrumentally beneficial. It satisfies a general desire to be recognized as a particular "real" person and to make a difference to other particular "real" people. The satisfaction of this desire in sexual experience is especially rewarding, its thwarting especially cruel. Vulnerability is increased in complete sex by the active desiring of the partners. When betrayal, or for that matter, tenderness or ecstasy, ensues, one cannot dissociate oneself from the desire with which one identified and out of which one acted. The psychic danger is real, as people who attempt to achieve a distance from their desires could tell us. But the cost of distance is as evident as its gains. Passivity in respect to one's own sexual desire not only limits sexual pleasure but, more seriously, limits the extent to which the experience of sexual pleasure can be included as an experience of a coherent person. With passivity comes a kind of irresponsibility in which one can

hide from one's desire, even from one's pleasure, "playing" seducer or victim, tease or savior. Active sexual desiring in complete sex acts affords an especially threatening but also especially happy occasion to relinquish these and similar roles. To the extent that the roles confuse and confound our intimate relations, the benefit from relinquishing them in our sexual acts, or the loss from adhering to them then, is especially poignant.

In addition to being beneficial, complete sex acts are morally superior for three reasons. They tend to resolve tensions fundamental to moral life; they are conducive to emotions that, if they become stable and dominant, are in turn conducive to the virtue of loving; and they involve a preeminently moral virtue—respect for persons.

In one of its aspects, morality is opposed to the private and untamed. Morality is "civilization," social and regulating; desire is "discontent" resisting the regulation. Obligation, rather than benefit, is the notion central to morality so conceived, and the virtues required of a moral person are directed to preserving right relations and social order. Both the insistence on natural sex and the encouragement of complete sex can be looked upon as attempts to make sexual desire more amenable to regulation. But whereas the regulation of perverted desires is extrinsic to them, those of completeness modify the desires themselves. The desiring sensual body that in our social lives we may laugh away or disown becomes our "self" and enters into a social relation. Narcissism and altruism are satisfied in complete sex acts in which one gives what one receives by receiving it. Social and private "selves" are unified in an act in which impersonal, spontaneous impulses govern an action that is responsive to a particular person. For this to be true we must surmount our social "roles" as well as our sexual "techniques," though we incorporate rather than surmount our social selves. We must also surmount regulations imposed in the name of naturalness if our desires are to be spontaneously expressed. Honestly spontaneous first love gives us back our private desiring selves while allowing us to see the desiring self of another. Mutually responding partners confirm each other's desires and declare them good. Such occasions, when we are "moral" without cost, help reconcile us to our moral being and to the usual mutual exclusion between our social and private lives.

The connection between sex and certain emotions—particularly love, jealousy, fear, and anger—is as evident as it is obscure. Complete sex

[19]See, for example, R. D. Laing, *The Divided Self*; D. W. Winnicott, "Transitional Objects and Transitional Phenomena," *International Journal of Psychoanalysis* 34 (1953): 89–97; Paul Federn, *Ego Psychology and the Psychoses* (New York: Basic Books, 1952); Phyllis Greenacre, *Trauma, Growth, and Personality* (New York: International Universities Press, 1969); Paul Schilder, *The Image and Appearance of the Human Body* (New York: International Universities Press, 1950); Moses Laufer, "Body Image and Masturbation in Adolescence," *The Psychoanalytic Study of the Child* 23 (1968): 114–46. Laing's work is most specific about both the nature and consequences of disembodiment, but the works cited, and others similar to them, give the clinical evidence upon which much of Laing's work depends.

acts seem more likely than incomplete pleasurable ones to lead toward affection and away from fear and anger, since any guilt and shame will be extrinsic to the act and meliorated by it. It is clear that we need not feel for someone any affection beyond that required (if any is) simply to participate with him/her in a complete sex act. However, it is equally clear that sexual pleasure, especially as experienced in complete sex acts, is conducive to many feelings —gratitude, tenderness, pride, appreciation, dependency, and others. These feelings magnify their object who occasioned them. When these magnifying feelings become stable and habitual they are conducive to love—not universal love, of course, but love of a particular sexual partner. However, even "selfish" love is a virtue, a disposition to care for someone as her/his interests and demands would dictate. Neither the best sex nor the best love require each other, but they go together more often than reason would expect—often enough to count the virtue of loving as one of the rewards of the capacity for sexual pleasure exercised in complete sex acts.

It might be argued that the coincidence of sex acts and several valued emotions is a cultural matter. It is notoriously difficult to make judgments about the emotional and, particularly, the sexual lives of others, especially culturally alien others. There is, however, some anthropological evidence that at first glance relativizes the connection between good sex and valued emotion. For example, among the Manus of New Guinea, it seems that relations of affection and love are encouraged primarily among brother and sister, while easy familiarity, joking, and superficial sexual play is expected only between cross-cousins. Sexual intercourse is, however, forbidden between siblings and cross-cousins but required of married men and women, who are as apt to hate as to care for each other and often seem to consider each other strangers. It seems, however, that the Manus do not value or experience complete or even pleasurable sex. Both men and women are described as puritanical, and the sexual life of women seems blatantly unrewarding. Moreover, their emotional life is generally impoverished. This impoverishment, in conjunction with an unappreciated and unrewarding sexual life dissociated from love or affection, would argue for a *connection* between better sex and valued emotions. If, as Peter Winch suggests, cultures provide their members with particular possibilities of making sense of their lives, and thereby with

possibilities of good and evil, the Manus might be said to deny themselves one possibility both of sense and of good—namely the coincidence of good sex and of affection and love. Other cultures, including our own, allow this possibility, whose realization is encouraged in varying degrees by particular groups and members of the culture.[20]

Finally, as Sartre has suggested, complete sex acts preserve a respect for persons. Each person remains conscious and responsible, a "subject" rather than a depersonalized, will-less, or manipulated "object." Each actively desires that the other likewise remain a "subject." Respect for persons is a central virtue when matters of justice and obligation are at issue. Insofar as we can speak of respect for persons in complete sex acts, there are different, often contrary requirements of respect. Respect for persons, typically and in sex acts, requires that *actual present* partners participate, partners whose desires are recognized and endorsed. Respect for persons typically requires taking a distance from both one's own demands and those of others. But in sex acts the demands of desire take over, and equal distance is replaced by mutual responsiveness. Respect typically requires refusing to treat another person merely as a means to fulfilling demands. In sex acts, another person is so clearly a means to satisfaction that s/he is always on the verge of becoming merely a means ("intercourse counterfeits masturbation"). In complete sex acts, instrumentality vanishes only because it is mutual and mutually desired. Respect requires encouraging, or at least protecting, the autonomy of another. In complete sex, autonomy of will is recruited by desire, and freedom from others is replaced by frank dependence on another person's desire. Again the respect consists in the reciprocity of desiring dependence, which bypasses rather than violates autonomy.

Despite the radical differences between respect for persons in the usual moral contexts and respect for persons in sex acts, it is not, I think, a mere play on words to talk of respect in the latter case. When, in any sort of intercourse, persons are respected, their desires are not only, in fair measure, *fulfilled*. In addition, their desires are *active* and determine, in fair measure, the form of intercourse

[20]The evidence about the life of the Manus comes from Margaret Mead, *Growing Up in New Guinea* (Harmondsworth, Eng.: Penguin Books, 1942). Peter Winch's discussion can be found in his "Understanding a Primitive Society," *American Philosophical Quarterly* 1 (1964): 307–34.

and the *manner* and *condition* of desire's satisfaction. These conditions are not only met in sexual intercourse when it is characterized by completeness; they come close to defining completeness.

Sartre is not alone in believing that just because the condition of completeness involves respect for persons, complete sex is impossible. Completeness is surely threatened by pervasive tendencies to fantasy, to possessiveness, and to varieties of a sadomasochistic desire. But a complete sex act, as I see it, does not involve an heroic restraint on our sexual interpulses. Rather, a complete sex act is a normal mode of sexual activity expressing the natural structure and impulses of sexual desire.

While complete sex is morally superior because it involves respect for persons, incomplete sex acts do not necessarily involve immoral disrespect for persons. Depending upon the desires and expectations of the partners, incompleteness may involve neither respect nor disrespect. Masturbation, for example, allows only the limited completeness of embodiment and often fails of that. But masturbation only rarely involves disrespect to anyone. Even the respect of Sartre's allegedly desirable sleeping woman may not be violated if she is unknowingly involved in a sex act. Disrespect, though probable, may in some cases be obviated by her sensibilities and expectations that she has previously expressed and her partner has understood. Sex acts provide one context in which respect for persons can be expressed. That context is important both because our sexual lives are of such importance to us and because they are so liable to injury because of the experience and the fear of the experience of disrespect. But many complete sex acts in which respect is maintained make other casual and incomplete sex acts unthreatening. In this case a goodly number of swallows can make a summer.

In sum, then, complete sex acts are superior to incomplete ones. First, they are, whatever their effects, better than various kinds of incomplete sex acts because they involve a kind of "respect for persons" in acts that are otherwise prone to violation of respect for, and often to violence to, persons. Second, complete sex acts are good because they are good for us. They are conducive to some fairly clearly defined kinds of psychological well-being that are beneficial. They are conducive to moral well-being because they relieve tensions that arise in our attempts to be moral and because they encourage the development of particular virtues.

To say that complete sex acts are preferable to incomplete ones is not to court a new puritanism. There are many kinds and degrees of incompleteness. Incomplete sex acts may not involve a disrespect for persons. Complete sex acts only *tend* to be good for us, and the realization of these tendencies depends upon individual lives and circumstances of sexual activity. The proper object of sexual desire is sexual pleasure. It would be a foolish ambition indeed to limit one's sexual acts to those in which completeness was likely. Any sexual act that is pleasurable is prima facie good, though the more incomplete it is—the more private, essentially autoerotic, unresponsive, unembodied, passive, or imposed—the more likely it is to be harmful to someone.

On Sexual Morality: Concluding Remarks

There are many questions we have neglected to consider because we have not been sufficiently attentive to the quality of sexual lives. For example, we know little about the ways of achieving better sex. When we must choose between inferior sex and abstinence, how and when will our choice of inferior sex damage our capacity for better sex? Does, for example, the repeated experience of controlled sexual disembodiment ("desire which takes over will take you too far") that we urge (or used to urge) on adolescents damage their capacity for complete sex? The answers to this and similar questions are not obvious, though unfounded opinions are always ready at hand.

Some of the traditional sexual vices might be condemned on the ground that they are inimical to better sex. Obscenity, or repeated public exposure to sexual acts, might impair our capacity for pleasure or for response to desire. Promiscuity might undercut the tendency of complete sex acts to promote emotions that magnify their object. Other of the traditional sexual vices are neither inimical nor conducive to better sex, but are condemned because of conflicting nonsexual benefits and obligations. For example, infidelity qua infidelity neither secures nor prevents better sex. The obligations of fidelity have many sources, one of which may be a past history of shared complete sex acts, a history that included promises of exclusive intimacy. Such past promises are as apt to conflict with as to accord with a current demand for better sex. I have said nothing about how such a conflict would be settled. I hope I have shown that where the possibility of better sex conflicts with obligations and other benefits, we have a *moral dilemma,* not just an occasion for moral self-discipline.

The pursuit of more pleasurable and more complete sex acts is, among many moral activities, distinguished not for its exigencies but for its rewards. Since our sexual lives are so important to us, and since, whatever our history and our hopes, we are sexual beings, this pursuit rightly engages our moral reflection. It should not be relegated to the immoral, nor to the "merely" prudent.

18/Is Adultery Immoral?

Richard A. Wasserstrom

Many discussions of the enforcement of morality by the law take as illustrative of the problem under consideration the regulation of various types of sexual behavior by the criminal law. It was, for example, the Wolfenden Report's recommendations concerning homosexuality and prostitution that led Lord Devlin to compose his now famous lecture "The Enforcement of Morals." And that lecture in turn provoked important philosophical responses from H. L. A. Hart, Ronald Dworkin, and others.

Much, if not all, of the recent philosophical literature on the enforcement of morals appears to take for granted the immorality of the sexual behavior in question. The focus of discussion, at least, is on whether such things as homosexuality, prostitution, and adultery ought to be made illegal even if they are immoral, and not on whether they are immoral.

I propose in this paper to consider the latter, more neglected topic, that of sexual morality, and to do so in the following fashion. I shall consider just one kind of behavior that is often taken to be a case of sexual immorality—adultery. I am interested in pursuing at least two questions. First, I want to explore the question of in what respects adulterous behavior falls within the domain of morality at all, for this surely is one of the puzzles one encounters when considering the topic of sexual morality. It is often hard to see on what grounds much of the behavior is deemed to be either moral or immoral, for example, private homosexual behavior between consenting adults. I have purposely selected adultery because it seems a more plausible candidate for moral assessment than many other kinds of sexual behavior.

The second question I want to examine is that of what is to be said about adultery if we are not especially concerned to stay within the area of its morality. I shall endeavor, in other words, to identify and to assess a number of the major arguments that might be advanced against adultery. I believe that they are the chief arguments that would be given in support of the view that adultery is immoral, but I think they are worth considering even if some of them turn out to be nonmoral arguments and considerations.

A number of the issues involved seem to me to be complicated and difficult. In a number of places I have at best indicated where further philosophical exploration is required, without having successfully conducted the exploration myself. This essay may very well be more useful as an illustration of how one might begin to think about the subject of sexual morality than as an elucidation of important truths about the topic.

Before I turn to the arguments themselves, there are two preliminary points that require some clarification. Throughout the paper I shall refer to the immorality of such things as breaking a promise, deceiving someone, and so on. In a very rough way I mean by this that there is something morally wrong in doing the action in question. I mean that the action is, in a strong sense of "prima facie," prima facie wrong or unjustified. I do not mean that it may never be right or justifiable to do the action—just that the fact that it is an action of this description always counts against the rightness of the action.

From *Today's Moral Problems* (New York: Macmillan Co., 1975). Reprinted by permission of Richard A. Wasserstrom.

I leave entirely open the question of what it is that makes actions of this kind immoral in this sense of "immoral."

The second preliminary point concerns what is meant or implied by the concept of adultery. I mean by "adultery" any case of extramarital sex, and I want to explore the arguments for and against extramarital sex, undertaken in a variety of morally relevant situations. Someone might claim that the concept of adultery is conceptually connected with the concept of immorality and that to characterize behavior as adulterous is already to characterize it as immoral or unjustified in the sense described above. There may be something to this. Hence the importance of making it clear that I want to discuss extramarital sexual relations. If they are always immoral, this is something that must be shown by argument. If the concept of adultery does in some sense entail or imply immorality, I want to ask whether that connection is a rationally based one. If not all cases of extramarital sex are immoral (again, in the sense described above), then the concept of adultery should either be weakened accordingly or restricted to those classes of extramarital sex for which the predication of immorality is warranted.

One argument for the immorality of adultery might go something like this: What makes adultery immoral is that it involves the breaking of a promise, and what makes adultery seriously wrong is that it involves the breaking of an important promise. For, so the argument might continue, one of the things the two parties promise each other when they get married is that they will abstain from sexual relationships with third parties. Because of this promise both spouses quite reasonably entertain the expectation that the other will behave in conformity with it. Hence, when one of them has sexual intercourse with a third party, he or she breaks that promise about sexual relationships that was made when the marriage was entered into and defeats the reasonable expectations of exclusivity entertained by the spouse.

In many cases the immorality involved in breaching the promise relating to extramarital sex may be a good deal more serious than that involved in the breach of other promises. This is so because adherence to this promise may be of much greater importance to them than is adherence to many of the other promises given or received by them in their lifetime. The breaking of this promise may be much more harmful and painful than is typically the case.

Why is this so? To begin with, it may have been difficult for the nonadulterous spouse to have kept the promise. Hence that spouse may feel the unfairness of having restrained himself or herself in the absence of reciprocal restraint having been exercised by the adulterous spouse. In addition, the spouse may perceive the breaking of the promise as an indication of a kind of indifference on the part of the adulterous spouse. If you really cared about me and my feelings, the spouse might say, you would not have done this to me. And third, and related to the above, the spouse may see the act of sexual intercourse with another as a sign of affection for the other person and as an additional rejection of the nonadulterous spouse as the one who is loved by the adulterous spouse. It is not just that the adulterous spouse does not take the feelings of the nonadulterous spouse sufficiently into account; the adulterous spouse also indicates through the act of adultery affection for someone other than the nonadulterous spouse. I will return to these points later. For the present it is sufficient to note that a set of arguments can be developed in support of the proposition that certain kinds of adultery are wrong just because they involve the breach of a serious promise that, among other things, leads to the intentional infliction of substantial pain on one spouse by the other.

Another argument for the immorality of adultery focuses not on the existence of a promise of sexual exclusivity but on the connection between adultery and deception. According to this argument adultery involves deception. And because deception is wrong, so is adultery.

Although it is certainly not obviously so, I shall simply assume in this essay that deception is always immoral. Thus, the crucial issue for my purposes is the asserted connection between extramarital sex and deception. Is it plausible to maintain, as this argument does, that adultery always involves deception and is, on that basis, to be condemned?

The most obvious person upon whom deceptions might be practiced is the nonparticipating spouse; and the most obvious thing about which the nonparticipating spouse can be deceived is the existence of the adulterous act. One clear case of deception is that of lying. Instead of saying that the afternoon was spent in bed with A, the adulterous spouse asserts that it was spent in the library with B or on the golf course with C.

There can also be deception even when no lies are told. Suppose, for instance, that a person has sexual intercourse with someone other than his or her spouse and just does not tell the spouse about it. Is that deception? It may not be a case of lying if, for example, he or she is never asked by the spouse about the situation. Still, we might say, it is surely deceptive because of the promises that were exchanged at marriage. As we saw earlier, these promises provide a foundation for the reasonable belief that neither spouse will engage in sexual relationships with any other person. Hence the failure to bring the fact of extramarital sex to the attention of the other spouse deceives that spouse about the present state of the marital relationship.

Adultery, in other words, can involve both active and passive deception. An adulterous spouse may just keep silent or, as is often the case, the spouse may engage in an increasingly complex way of life devoted to the concealment of the facts from the nonparticipating spouse. Lies, half-truths, clandestine meetings, and the like may become a central feature of the adulterous spouse's existence. These are things that can and do happen, and when they do they make the case against adultery an easy one. Still, neither active nor passive deception is inevitably a feature of an extramarital relationship.

It is possible, though, that a more subtle but pervasive kind of deceptiveness is a feature of adultery. It comes about because of the connection in our culture between sexual intimacy and certain feelings of love and affection. The point can be made indirectly by seeing that one way in which we can in our culture mark off our close friends from our mere acquaintances is through the kinds of intimacies that we are prepared to share with them. I may, for instance, be willing to reveal my very private thoughts and emotions to my closest friends or to my wife but to no one else. My sharing of these intimate facts about myself is, from one perspective, a way of making a gift to those who mean the most to me. Revealing these things and sharing them with those who mean the most to me is one means by which I create, maintain, and confirm those interpersonal relationships that are of most importance to me.

In our culture, it might be claimed, sexual intimacy is one of the chief currencies through which gifts of this sort are exchanged. One way to tell someone—particularly someone of the opposite sex—that you have feelings of affection and love for them is by allowing them, or sharing with them, sexual behaviors that one does not share with others. This way of measuring affection was certainly very much a part of the culture in which I matured. It worked something like this: If you were a girl, you showed how much you liked a boy by the degree of sexual intimacy you would allow. If you liked him only a little you never did more than kiss—and even the kiss was not very passionate. If you liked him a lot and if your feeling was reciprocated, necking and, possibly, petting were permissible. If the attachment was still stronger and you thought it might even become a permanent relationship, the sexual activity was correspondingly more intense and intimate, although whether it led to sexual intercourse depended on whether the parties (particularly the girl) accepted fully the prohibition on nonmarital sex. The situation for the boys was related but not exactly the same. The assumption was that males did not naturally link sex with affection in the way in which females did. However, since women did link sex with affection, males had to take that fact into account. That is to say, because a woman would permit sexual intimacies only if she had feelings of affection for the male and only if those feelings were reciprocated, the male had to have and express those feelings too, before sexual intimacies of any sort would occur.

The result was that the importance of a correlation between sexual intimacy and feelings of love and affection was taught by the culture and assimilated by those growing up in the culture. The scale of possible positive feelings toward persons of the other sex ran from casual liking, at one end, to the love that was deemed essential to, and characteristic of, marriage, at the other. The scale of possible sexual behavior ran from brief, passionless kissing or hand-holding, at one end, to sexual intercourse, at the other. And the correlation between the two scales was quite precise. As a result, any act of sexual intimacy carried substantial meaning with it, and no act of sexual intimacy was simply a pleasurable set of bodily sensations. Many such acts were, of course, more pleasurable to the participants because they were a way of saying what their feelings were. And sometimes they were less pleasurable for the same reason. The point is, however, that sexual activity was much more than mere bodily enjoyment. It was not like eating a good meal, listening to good music, lying in the sun, or getting a pleasant back rub. It was behavior that meant a great deal concerning one's feelings for persons of the opposite sex in whom one was most interested and with whom one was most involved. It was among the most authoritative ways in which one could communicate to another the nature and degree of one's affection.

If this sketch is even roughly right, then several things become somewhat clearer. To begin with, a possible rationale for many of the rules of conventional sexual morality can be developed. If, for example, sexual intercourse is associated with the kind of affection and commitment to another that is regarded as characteristic of the marriage relationship, then it is natural that sexual intercourse should be thought properly to take place between persons who are married to each other. And if it is thought that this kind of affection and commitment is only to be found within the marriage relationship, then it is not surprising that sexual intercourse should only be thought to be proper within marriage.

Related to what has just been said is the idea that sexual intercourse ought to be restricted to those who are married to each other, as a means by which to confirm the very special feelings that the spouses have for each other. Because our culture teaches that sexual intercourse means that the strongest of all feelings for each other are shared by the lovers, it is natural that persons who are married to each other should be able to say this to each other in this way. Revealing and confirming verbally that these feelings are present is one thing that helps to sustain the relationship; engaging in sexual intercourse is another.

In addition, this account would help to provide a framework within which to make sense of the notion that some sex is better than other sex. As I indicated earlier, the fact that sexual intimacy can be meaningful in the sense described tends to make it also the case that sexual intercourse can sometimes be more enjoyable than at other times. On this view, sexual intercourse will typically be more enjoyable if strong feelings of affection are present than it will be if it is merely "mechanical." This is so in part because people enjoy being loved, especially by those whom they love. Just as we like to hear words of affection, so we like to receive affectionate behavior. And the meaning enhances the independently pleasurable behavior.

More to the point, an additional rationale for the prohibition on extramarital sex can now be developed. For given this way of viewing the sexual world, extramarital sex will almost always involve deception of a deeper sort. If the adulterous spouse does not in fact have the appropriate feelings of affection for the extramarital partner, then the adulterous spouse is deceiving that person about the presence of such feelings. If, on the other hand, the adulterous spouse does have the corresponding feelings for the extramarital partner but not toward the nonparticipating spouse, the adulterous spouse is very probably deceiving the nonparticipating spouse about the presence of such feelings toward that spouse. Indeed, it might be argued, whenever there is no longer love between the two persons who are married to each other, there is deception just because being married implies both to the participants and to the world that such a bond exists. Deception is inevitable, the argument might conclude, because the feelings of affection that ought to accompany any act of sexual intercourse can only be held toward one other person at any given time in one's life. And if this is so, then the adulterous spouse always deceives either the partner in adultery or the nonparticipating spouse about the existence of such feelings. Thus extramarital sex involves deception of this sort and is for that reason immoral even if no deception vis-à-vis the occurrence of the act of adultery takes place.

What might be said in response to the foregoing arguments? The first thing that might be said is that the account of the connection between sexual intimacy and feelings of affection is inaccurate—not in the sense that no one thinks of things that way but in the sense that there is substantially more divergence of opinion than the account suggests. For example, the view I have delineated may describe reasonably accurately the concepts of the sexual world in which I grew up, but it does not capture the sexual *Weltanschauung* of today's youth at all. Thus, whether or not adultery implies deception in respect to feelings depends very much on the persons who are involved and the way they look at the "meaning" of sexual intimacy.

Second, the argument leaves unanswered the question of whether it is desirable for sexual intimacy to carry the sorts of messages described above. For those persons for whom sex does have these implications there are special feelings and sensibilities that must be taken into account. But it is another question entirely whether any valuable end—moral or otherwise—is served by investing sexual behavior with such significance. That is something that must be shown and not just assumed. It might, for instance, be the case that substantially more good than harm would come from a kind of demystification of sexual behavior—one that would encourage the enjoyment of sex more for its own sake and one that would reject the centrality both of the association of sex with love and of love with only one other person.

I regard these as two of the more difficult unresolved issues that our culture faces today in respect of thinking sensibly about the attitudes toward sex and love that we should try to develop in ourselves and in our children.

Much of the contemporary literature that advocates sexual liberation of one sort or another embraces one or the other of two different views about the relationship between sex and love. One view holds that sex should be separated from love and affection. To be sure, sex is probably better when the partners genuinely like and enjoy being with each other. But sex is basically an intensive, exciting sensuous activity that can be enjoyed in a variety of suitable settings with a variety of suitable partners. The situation in respect to sexual pleasure is no different from that of the person who knows and appreciates fine food and who can have a satisfying meal in any number of good restaurants with any number of congenial companions. One question that must be settled here is whether sex can be thus demystified; another, more important, question is whether it would be desirable to do so. What might we gain and what might we lose if we all lived in a world in which an act of sexual intercourse was no more or less significant or enjoyable than having a delicious meal in a nice setting with a good friend? The answer to this question lies beyond the scope of this essay.

The second view of the relationship between sex and love seeks to drive the wedge in a different place. On this view it is not the link between sex and love that needs to be broken, but rather the connection between love and exclusivity. For a number of the reasons already given it is desirable, so this argument goes, that sexual intimacy continue to be reserved to and shared with only those for whom one has very great affection. The mistake lies in thinking that any "normal" adult will have those feelings toward only one other adult during his or her lifetime—or even at any time in his or her life. It is the concept of adult love, not ideas about sex, that needs demystification. What are thought to be both unrealistic and unfortunate are the notions of exclusivity and possessiveness that attach to the dominant conception of love between adults in our culture and others. Parents of four, five, six, or even ten children can certainly claim, and sometimes claim correctly, that they love all of their children, that they love them all equally, and that it is simply untrue to their feelings to insist that the numbers involved diminish either the quantity or the quality of their love. If this is readily understandable in the case of parents and children, there is no necessary reason why it is an impossible or undesirable ideal in the case of adults. To be sure, there is probably a limit to the number of intimate, "primary" relationships that any person can maintain at any given time without affecting the quality of the relationship. But one adult ought surely to be able to love two, three, or even six other adults at any one time without that love being different in kind or degree from that of the traditional, monogamous, lifetime marriage. And between the individuals in these relationships, whether within a marriage or without, sexual intimacy is fitting and good.

The issues raised by a position such as the one described above are also surely worth exploring in detail and with care. Is there something to be called "sexual love" that is different from parental love or the nonsexual love of close friends? Is there something about love in general that links it naturally and appropriately with feelings of exclusivity and possession? Or is there something about sexual love, whatever that may be, that makes these feelings especially fitting? Once again, the issues are conceptual, empirical, and normative all at once: What is love? How could it be different? Would it be a good thing or a bad thing if it were different?

Suppose, though, that having delineated these problems we were now to pass them by. Suppose, moreover, that we were to be persuaded of the possibility and the desirability of weakening substantially either the links between sex and love or the links between sexual love and exclusivity. Would it not then be the case that adultery could be free from all of the morally objectionable features described thus far? To be more specific, let us imagine that a husband and wife have what is today sometimes characterized as an "open marriage." Suppose, that is, that they have agreed in advance that extramarital sex is—under certain circumstances—acceptable behavior for each to engage in. Suppose that as a result there is no impulse to deceive each other about the occurrence or nature of any such relationships and that no deception in fact occurs. Suppose, too, that there is no deception in respect to the feelings involved between the adulterous spouse and the extramarital partner. And suppose, finally, that one or the other or both of the spouses then has sexual intercourse in circumstances consistent with these understandings. Under this description, so the argument might conclude, adultery is simply not immoral. At a minimum adultery cannot very plausibly be condemned either on grounds that it involves deception or on grounds that it requires the breaking of a promise.

At least two responses are worth considering. One calls attention to the connection between marriage and adultery; the other looks to more instrumental arguments for the immorality of adultery. Both deserve further exploration.

One way to deal with the case of the "open marriage" is to question whether the two persons involved are still properly to be described as being married to each other. Part of the meaning of what it is for two persons to be married to each other, so this argument would go, is to have committed oneself to have sexual relationships only with one's spouse. Of course, it would be added, we know that that commitment is not always honored. We know that persons who are married to each other often do commit adultery. But there is a difference between being willing to make a commitment to marital fidelity, even though one may fail to honor that commitment, and not making the commitment at all. Whatever the relationship may be between the two individuals in the case just described, the absence of any commitment to sexual exclusivity requires the conclusion that their relationship is not a marital one. For a commitment to sexual exclusivity is a necessary but not a sufficient condition for the existence of a marriage.

Although there may be something to this suggestion, it is too strong as stated to be acceptable. To begin with it is doubtful that there are many, if any, *necessary* conditions for marriage; but even if there are, a commitment to sexual exclusivity is not such a condition.

To see that this is so, consider what might be taken to be some of the essential characteristics of a marriage. We might be tempted to propose that the concept of marriage requires the following: a formal ceremony of some sort in which mutual obligations are undertaken between two persons of the opposite sex; the capacity on the part of the persons involved to have sexual intercourse with each other; the willingness to have sexual intercourse only with each other; and feelings of love and affection between the two persons. The problem is that we can imagine relationships that are clearly marital and yet lack one or more of these features. For example, in our own society it is possible for two persons to be married without going through a formal ceremony, as in the common-law marriages recognized in some jurisdictions. It is also possible for two persons to get married even though one or both lacks the capacity to engage in sexual intercourse. Thus, two very elderly persons who have neither the desire nor the ability to have intercourse can nonetheless get married, as can persons whose sexual organs have been injured so that intercourse is not possible. And we certainly know of marriages in which love was not present at the time of the marriage, as, for instance, in marriages of state and marriages of convenience.

Counterexamples not satisfying the condition relating to the abstention from extramarital sex are even more easily produced. We certainly know of societies and cultures in which polygamy and polyandry are practiced, and we have no difficulty in recognizing these relationships as cases of marriages. It might be objected, though, that these are not counterexamples because they are plural marriages rather than marriages in which sex is permitted with someone other than one of the persons to whom one is married. But we also know of societies in which it is permissible for married persons to have sexual relationships with persons to whom they are not married, for example, temple prostitutes, concubines, and homosexual lovers. And even if we knew of no such societies, the conceptual claim would still, I submit, not be well taken. For suppose all of the other indicia of marriage were present: suppose the two persons were of the opposite sex; suppose they had the capacity and desire to have intercourse with each other; suppose they participated in a formal ceremony in which they understood themselves voluntarily to be entering into a relationship with each other in which substantial mutual commitments were assumed. If all these conditions were satisfied we would not be in any doubt as to whether or not the two persons were married, even though they had not taken on a commitment of sexual exclusivity and even though they had expressly agreed that extramarital sexual intercourse was a permissible behavior for each to engage in.

A commitment to sexual exclusivity is neither a necessary nor a sufficient condition for the existence of a marriage. It does, nonetheless, have this much to do with the nature of marriage—like the other indicia enumerated above, its presence tends to establish the existence of a marriage. Thus, in the absence of a formal ceremony of any sort an explicit commitment to sexual exclusivity would count in favor of regarding the two persons as married. The conceptual role of the commitment to sexual exclusivity can, perhaps, be brought out through the following example. Suppose we found a tribe that had a practice in which all the other indicia of marriage were present but in which the two parties were *prohibited* even from having sexual intercourse with each other. Moreover, suppose that sexual intercourse with others was clearly permitted. In such a case we would, I think, reject the idea that the two persons were married to each other, and we would describe their relationship in other terms, for example, as some kind of formalized, special friendship relation—a kind of heterosexual "blood-brother" bond.

Compare that case with the following one. Again suppose that the tribe had a practice in which all of the other indicia of marriage were present, but instead of a prohibition on sexual intercourse between the persons in the relationship there was no rule at all. Sexual intercourse was permissible with the person with whom one had this ceremonial relationship, but it was no more or less permissible than with a number of other persons to whom one was not so related (for instance, all consenting adults of the opposite sex). While we might be in doubt as to whether we ought to describe the persons as married to each other, we would probably conclude that they were married and that they simply were members of a tribe whose views about sex were quite different from our own.

What all of this shows is that a *prohibition* on sexual intercourse between the two persons involved in a relationship is conceptually incompatible with the claim that the two of them are married. The *permissibility* of intramarital sex is a necessary part of the idea of marriage. But no such incompatibility follows simply from the added permissibility of extramarital sex.

These arguments do not, of course, exhaust the arguments for the prohibition on extramarital sexual relations. The remaining argument that I wish to consider is—as I indicated earlier—a more instrumental one. It seeks to justify the prohibition by virtue of the role that it plays in the development and maintenance of nuclear families. The argument, or set of arguments, might, I believe, go something like this:

Consider first a far-fetched nonsexual example. Suppose a society were organized so that after some suitable age—say 18, 19, or 20—persons were forbidden to eat anything but bread and water with anyone but their spouse. Persons might still choose in such a society not to get married. Good food just might not be very important to them because they have underdeveloped taste buds. Or good food might be bad for them because there is something wrong with their digestive system. Or good food might be important to them, but they might decide that the enjoyment of good food would get in the way of the attainment of other things that were more important. But most persons would, I think, be led to favor marriage in part because they preferred a richer, more varied diet to one of bread and water. And they might remain married because the family was the only legitimate setting within which good food was obtainable. If it is important to have society organized so that persons will both get married and stay married, such an arrangement would be well suited to the preservation of the family, and the prohibitions relating to food consumption could be understood as fulfilling that function.

It is obvious that one of the more powerful human desires is the desire for sexual gratification. The desire is a natural one, like hunger and thirst, in the sense that it need not be learned in order to be present within us and operative on us. But there is in addition much that we do learn about what the act of sexual intercourse is like. Once we experience sexual intercourse ourselves—and, in particular, once we experience orgasm—we discover that it is among the most intensive, short-term pleasures of the body.

Because this is so it is easy to see how the prohibition on extramarital sex helps to hold marriage together. At least during that period of life when the enjoyment of sexual intercourse is one of the desirable bodily pleasures, persons will wish to enjoy those pleasures. If one consequence of being married is that one is prohibited from having sexual intercourse with anyone but one's spouse, then the spouses in a marriage are in a position to provide an important source of pleasure for each other that is unavailable to them elsewhere in the society.

The point emerges still more clearly if this rule of sexual morality is seen as being of a piece with the other rules of sexual morality. When this prohibition is coupled, for example, with the prohibition on nonmarital sexual intercourse, we are presented with the inducement both to get married and to stay married. For if sexual intercourse is only legitimate within marriage, then persons seeking that gratification that is a feature of sexual intercourse are furnished explicit social directions for its attainment, namely, marriage.

Nor, to continue the argument, is it necessary to focus exclusively on the bodily enjoyment that is involved. Orgasm may be a significant part of what there is to sexual intercourse, but it is not the whole of it. We need only recall the earlier discussion of the meaning that sexual intimacy has in our own culture to begin to see some of the more intricate ways in which sexual exclusivity may be connected with the establishment and maintenance of marriage as the primary heterosexual love relationship. Adultery is wrong, in other words, because a prohibition on extramarital sex is a way to help maintain the institutions of marriage and the nuclear family.

I am frankly not sure what we are to say about an argument such as the preceding one. What I am convinced of is that, like the arguments discussed earlier, this one also reveals something of the difficulty and complexity of the issues that are involved. So what I want now to do in the final portion of this essay is to try to delineate with reasonable precision several of what I take to be the fundamental, unresolved issues.

The first is whether this last argument is an argument for the *immorality* of extramarital sexual intercourse. What does seem clear is that there are differences between this argument and the ones considered earlier. The earlier arguments condemned adulterous behavior because it was behavior that involved breaking a promise, taking unfair advantage of or deceiving another. To the degree to which the prohibition on extramarital sex can be supported by arguments that invoke considerations such as these, there is little question but that violations of the prohibition are properly regarded as immoral. And such a claim could be defended on one or both of two distinct grounds. The first is that action such as promise-breaking and deception are simply wrong. The second is that adultery involving promise-breaking or deception is wrong because it involves the straightforward infliction of harm on another human being—typically the nonadulterous spouse—who has a strong claim not to have that harm so inflicted.

The argument that connects the prohibition on extramarital sex with the maintenance and preservation of the institution of marriage is an argument for the instrumental value of the prohibition. To some degree this counts, I think, against regarding all violations of the prohibition as obvious cases of immorality. This is so partly because hypothetical imperatives are less clearly within the domain of morality than are categorical ones, and even more because instrumental prohibitions are within the domain of morality only if the end that they serve or the way that they serve it is itself within the domain of morality.

What this should help us see, I think, is the fact that the argument that connects the prohibition on adultery with the preservation of marriage is at best seriously incomplete. Before we ought to be convinced by it, we ought to have reasons for believing that marriage is a morally desirable and just social institution. And such reasons are not quite as easy to find or as obvious as it may seem. For the concept of marriage is, as we have seen, both a loosely structured and a complicated one. There may be all sorts of intimate, interpersonal relationships that will resemble but not be identical with the typical marriage relationship presupposed by the traditional sexual morality. There may be a number of distinguishable sexual and loving arrangements that can all legitimately claim to be called *marriages*. The prohibitions of the traditional sexual morality may be effective ways to maintain some marriages and ineffective ways to promote and preserve others. The prohibitions of the traditional sexual morality may make good psychological sense if certain psychological theories are true, and they may be purveyors of immense psychological mischief if other psychological theories are true. The prohibitions of traditional sexual morality may seem obviously correct if sexual intimacy carries the meaning that the dominant culture has often ascribed to it, and they may seem equally bizarre if sex is viewed through the perspective of the counterculture. Irrespective of whether instrumental arguments of this sort are properly deemed moral arguments, they ought not fully convince anyone until questions such as these are answered.

19/Pornography and Respect for Women
Ann Garry

Pornography, like rape, is a male invention, designed to dehumanize women, to reduce the female to an object of sexual access, not to free sensuality from moralistic or parental inhibition. . . . Pornography is the undiluted essence of anti-female propaganda.
    Susan Brownmiller, *Against Our Will: Men, Women and Rape*[1]

It is often asserted that a distinguishing characteristic of sexually explicit material is the degrading and demeaning portrayal of the role and status of the human female. It has been argued that erotic materials describe the female as a mere sexual object to be exploited and manipulated sexually. . . . A recent survey shows that 41 percent of American males and 46 percent of the females believe that "sexual materials lead people to lose respect for women." . . . Recent experiments suggest that such fears are probably unwarranted.
    Presidential Commission on Obscenity and Pornography[2]

The kind of apparent conflict illustrated in these passages is easy to find in one's own thinking as well. For example, I have been inclined to think that pornography is innocuous and to dismiss "moral" arguments for censoring it because many such arguments rest on an assumption I do not share—that sex is an evil to be controlled. At the same time I believe that it is wrong to exploit or degrade human beings, particularly women and others who are especially susceptible. So if pornography degrades human beings, then even if I would oppose its censorship I surely cannot find it morally innocuous.

In an attempt to resolve this apparent conflict I discuss three questions: Does pornography degrade (or exploit or dehumanize) human beings? If so, does it degrade women in ways or to an extent that it does not degrade men? If so, must pornography degrade women, as Brownmiller thinks, or could genuinely innocuous, nonsexist pornography exist? Although much current pornography does degrade women, I will argue that it is possible to have nondegrading, nonsexist pornography. However, this possibility rests on our making certain fundamental changes in our conceptions of sex and sex roles.

I

First, some preliminary remarks: Many people now avoid using 'pornography' as a descriptive term and reserve 'obscenity' for use in legal contexts. Because 'pornography' is thought to be a judgmental word, it is replaced by 'explicit sexual material', 'sexually oriented materials', 'erotica', and so on.[3] I use 'pornography' to label those explicit sexual materials intended to arouse the reader or viewer sexually. I seriously doubt whether there is a clearly defined class of cases that fits my characterization of pornography. This does not bother me, for I am interested here in obvious cases that would be uncontroversially pornographic—the worst, least artistic kind. The pornography I discuss is that which, taken as a whole, lacks "serious literary, artistic, political, or scientific merit."[4] I often use pornographic films as examples because they generate more concern today than do books or magazines.

What interests me is not whether pornography should be censored but whether one can object to it on moral grounds. The only moral ground I consider is whether pornography degrades people;

[1](New York: Simon and Schuster, 1975), p. 394.
[2]*The Report of the Commission on Obscenity and Pornography* (Washington, D.C., 1970), p. 201. Hereinafter, *Report.*

[3]*Report,* p. 3, n. 4; and p. 149.
[4]Roth v. United States, 354 U.S. 476, 489 (1957).

obviously, other possible grounds exist, but I find this one to be the most plausible.[5] Of the many kinds of degradation and exploitation possible in the production of pornography, I focus only on the content of the pornographic work. I exclude from this discussion (i) the ways in which pornographic film makers might exploit people in making a film, distributing it, and charging too much to see it; (ii) the likelihood that actors, actresses, or technicians will be exploited, underpaid, or made to lose self-respect or self-esteem; and (iii) the exploitation and degradation surrounding the prostitution and crime that often accompany urban centers of pornography.[6] I want to determine whether pornography shows (expresses) and commends behavior or attitudes that exploit or degrade people. For example, if a pornographic film conveys that raping a woman is acceptable, then the content is degrading to women and might be called morally objectionable. Morally objectionable content is not peculiar to pornography; it can also be found in nonpornographic books, films, advertisements, and so on. The question is whether morally objectionable content is necessary to pornography.

II

At the beginning of this paper, I quoted part of a passage in which the Presidential Commission on Obscenity and Pornography tried to allay our fears that pornography will lead people to lose respect for women. Here is the full passage:

It is often asserted that a distinguishing characteristic of sexually explicit material is the degrading and demeaning portrayal of the role and status of the human female. It has been argued that erotic materials describe the female as a mere sexual object to be exploited and manipulated sexually.

One presumed consequence of such portrayals is that erotica transmits an inaccurate and uninformed conception of sexuality, and that the viewer or user will (a) develop a calloused and manipulative orientation toward women and (b) engage in behavior in which affection and sexuality are not well integrated. A recent survey shows that 41% of American males and 46% of the females believe that "sexual materials lead people to lose respect for women" (Abelson, et al. 1970). Recent experiments (Mosher 1970a, b; Mosher and Katz 1970) suggest that such fears are probably unwarranted.[7]

The argument to which the Commission addresses itself begins with the assumption that pornography presents a degrading portrayal of women as sex objects. If users of pornography adopt the view that women are sex objects (or already believe it and allow pornography to reinforce their beliefs), they will develop an attitude of callousness and lack of respect for women and will be more likely to treat women as sex objects to be manipulated and exploited. In this argument the moral objection to be brought against pornography lies in the objectionable character of the acquired attitudes and the increased likelihood of objectionable behavior —treating women as mere sex objects to be exploited rather than as persons to be respected.

A second moral argument, which does not interest the Commission, is that pornography is morally objectionable because it exemplifies and recommends behavior that violates the moral principle to respect persons. This argument contains no reference to immoral consequences; there need be no increased likelihood of behavior degrading to women. Pornography itself treats women not as whole persons but as mere sex objects "to be exploited and manipulated sexually." Such treatment is a "degrading and demeaning portrayal of the role and status" (and humanity) of women.

I will explain and discuss the first argument here and the second argument in Part III of this paper. The first argument depends on an empirical premise—that viewing pornography leads to an increase in "sex calloused" attitudes and behavior.[8] My discussion of this premise consists of four parts:

[5]To degrade someone in this situation is to lower her/his rank or status in humanity. This is morally objectionable because it is incompatible with showing respect for a person. Some of the other moral grounds for objecting to pornography have been considered by the Supreme Court: Pornography invades our privacy and hurts the moral tone of the community. See Paris Adult Theatre I v. Slaton, 413 U.S. 49 (1973). Even less plausible than the Court's position is to say that pornography is immoral because it depicts sex, depicts an immoral kind of sex, or caters to voyeuristic tendencies. I believe that even if moral objections to pornography exist, one must preclude any simple inference from "pornography is immoral" to "pornography should be censored" because of other important values and principles such as freedom of expression and self-determination.

[6]See Gail Sheehy, *Hustling* (New York: Dell, 1971) for a good discussion of prostitution, crime, and pornography.

[7]*Report*, p. 201. References cited can be found in notes 12, 13, 14, and 22, below.

[8]'Sex callousness' is a term used by Donald Mosher in the studies to be discussed here. See notes 12 and 13 below. Although the concept of sex callousness will be explained later, the core of the meaning is obvious: To be a sex calloused male is to have attitudes toward women (e.g., lack of respect) conducive to exploiting them sexually.

(1) examples of some who accept the premise (Susan Brownmiller and the Supreme Court); (2) evidence presented for its denial by Donald Mosher for the Presidential Commission; (3) a critical examination of Mosher's studies; and (4) a concluding argument that, regardless of who (Mosher or Brownmiller) is correct, moral grounds exist for objecting to pornography.

1

Although I know of no social scientist whose data support the position that pornography leads to an increase in sex calloused behavior and attitudes, this view has popular support. For example, the Presidential Commission survey cited above finds it supported by 41 percent of American males and 46 percent of the females. In addition, passages from both Susan Brownmiller and the United States Supreme Court illustrate a similar but more inclusive view: that use of pornography leads to sex callousness or lack of respect for women (or something worse) and that we do not need social scientists to confirm or deny it.

The following passage from Brownmiller forms part of her support for the position that liberals should rethink their position on pornography because pornography is anti-female propaganda:

The majority report of the President's Commission on Obscenity and Pornography tried to pooh-pooh the opinion of law enforcement agencies around the country that claimed their own concrete experience with offenders who were caught with the stuff led them to conclude that pornographic material is a causative factor in crimes of sexual violence. The commission maintained that it was not possible at this time to scientifically prove or disprove such a connection.

But does one need scientific methodology in order to conclude that the anti-female propaganda that permeates our nation's cultural output promotes a climate in which acts of sexual hostility directed against women are not only tolerated but ideologically encouraged?[9]

In at least two 1973 opinions, the Supreme Court tried to speak to the relevance of empirical data. They considered antisocial acts in general, without any thought that "sex calloused" behavior

would be particularly antisocial. In *Kaplan* v. *California,* the Court said:

A state could reasonably regard the "hard-core" conduct described by Suite 69 *as capable of encouraging or causing anti-social behavior, especially in its impact on young people. States need not wait until behavioral experts or educators can provide empirical data before enacting controls of commerce in obscene materials unprotected by the First Amendment or by a constitutional right to privacy. We have noted the power of a legislative body to enact such regulatory law on the basis of unprovable assumptions.[10]*

From *Paris Adult Theatre I* v. *Slaton:*

But, it is argued, there is no scientific data which conclusively demonstrates that exposure to obscene materials adversely affects men and women or their society. It is urged on behalf of the petitioner that, absent such a demonstration, any kind of state regulation is "impermissible." We reject this argument. . . . Although there is no conclusive proof of a connection between antisocial behavior and obscene material, the legislature of Georgia could quite reasonably determine that such a connection does or might exist.[11]

The disturbing feature of these passages is not the truth of the view that pornography leads to sex callousness but that the Court and Brownmiller seem to have succumbed to the temptation to disregard empirical data when the data fail to meet the authors' expectations. My intention in citing these passages is not to examine them but to remind the reader of how influential this kind of viewpoint is. For convenience I call it "Brownmiller's view"—the position that pornography provides a model for male sex calloused behavior and has a numbing effect on the rest of us so that we tolerate sex calloused behavior more readily.

2

Donald L. Mosher has put forward evidence to deny that use of pornography leads to sex callous-

---

[9]Brownmiller, *Against Our Will,* p. 395.

[10]413 U.S. 115, 120 (1973).
[11]413 U.S. 49, 60–61.

ness or lack of respect for women.[12] In a study for the Presidential Commission, Mosher found that "sexually arousing pornographic films did not trigger sexual behavior even in the [sex calloused] college males whose attitudes toward women were more conducive to sexual exploitation" (p. 306), and that sex calloused attitudes toward women decreased after the viewers saw pornographic films.

Mosher developed the operative concept of "sex callousness" is one study for the Commission,[13] then used the concept as part of a more comprehensive study of the effects of pornography.[14] In the second study Mosher rated his 194 unmarried undergraduate male subjects for "sex callousness." Men who have sex calloused attitudes approve of and engage in "the use of physical aggression and exploitative tactics such as falsely professing love, getting their dates drunk, or showing pornography to their dates as a means of gaining coitus" (pp. 305–6). Men rated high in sex callousness believe that sex is for fun, believe that love and sex are separate (p. 306), and agree to statements such as "Promise a woman anything, but give her your ———," "When a women gets uppity, it's time to ——— her," and "——— teasers should be raped" (p. 314, expletives deleted in report). Mosher suggests that this attitude is part of the *Macho syndrome*" (p. 323).

The highly sex calloused men rated the two pornographic films they saw as more enjoyable and arousing, and less offensive or disgusting than did other subjects; but, like all of the subjects, these men did not increase their sexual activity. Mosher found no increase in "frequencies of masturbation, heterosexual petting, oral-genital sex, or coitus" in the twenty-four hours after the subjects saw the two films.[15] He did not indicate whether a change occurred in the proportion of exploitative sexual behavior to nonexploitative sexual behavior.

In addition, the data from all the male subjects indicated a *decrease* in their sex calloused attitudes. The sharpest decrease occurred in the twenty-four hours after they saw the films. Two weeks later, their level of sex callousness was still lower than before they viewed the films. Although Mosher used several "equivalent" tests to measure callousness and did not explain the differences among them, the test I saw (*Form B*) was presumably typical: It measured the extent to which the subjects agreed or disagreed with statements such as "——— teasers should be raped."

Mosher's explanation for the decrease in sex calloused attitudes is, in his own words, "speculative." Sex callousness is an expression of "exaggerated masculine style" that occurs during a period of male development ("ideally followed by an integration of love with exploitative sex" [pp. 322–23]). During this period, men, especially young men without occupational success, use the "macho" conquest mentality to reassure themselves of their masculinity. Mosher thinks that seeing a pornographic film in the company of only men satisfies the need for macho behavior—the same need that is satisfied by exploiting women, endorsing calloused attitudes, telling "dirty" jokes, or boasting about one's sexual prowess. Thus the immediate need to affirm the sex calloused statements about women decreases once the men have seen the pornographic films (pp. 322–23, 306–7).

3

For Mosher pornography is an outlet for the expression of calloused attitudes—not, as for Brownmiller, a model for calloused behavior. Some of the limitations of Mosher's study are clear to him; others apparently are not. My comments on his study fall into three categories: the limitations of his design and method, difficulties with his conclusions about sexual behavior, and difficulties with his conclusions about calloused attitudes. I am not raising general methodological issues; for example, I do not ask what measures were used to prevent a subject's (or experimenter's) civil libertarian beliefs

---

[12]"Psychological Reactions to Pornographic Films," *Technical Report of the Commission on Obscenity and Pornography*, vol. 8 (Washington, D.C., 1970), pp. 255–312. Hereinafter, *Tech. Report*, often cited by page number only in body of text.

[13]"Sex Callousness toward Women," *Tech. Report*, vol. 8, pp. 313–25.

[14]"Psychological Reactions to Pornographic Films." See note 12. Both of Mosher's experiments used the same questions to test "sex callousness"; I treat the experiments together, citing only page numbers in the body of the text. As far as I know, no other social scientists are working on the relationship between pornography and sex callousness toward women. Mosher made another study with Harvey Katz that is on even less secure ground. They asked undergraduate males to "aggress verbally" at female student assistants before and after seeing a pornographic film. No increase in verbal aggression occurred after they saw the film. The authors seem to be aware of many limitations of this study; particularly relevant here are the facts that only verbal aggression was tested and that the film did not show violent or aggressive behavior. "Pornographic Films, Male Verbal Aggression Against Women, and Guilt," *Tech. Report*, vol. 8, pp. 357–77.

[15]*Tech. Report*, vol. 8, p. 255. In his "Conclusions" section, Mosher qualifies the claim that no increase occurred in sexual behavior for sex calloused males. He says that they "reported no increased heterosexual behavior" (p. 310).

from influencing a subject's tendency to show less calloused attitudes after seeing the films.

Limitations of Design and Method (i) Mosher's was a very short-term study: His last questions were asked of subjects two weeks after they saw the pornographic films. But since pornography is supposed to provide only a temporary outlet, this limitation may not be crucial. (ii) Mosher believes that, given the standard of commercial pornography, the films he showed displayed more than the usual amount of affection and less than the usual amount of exploitative, "kinky," or exclusively male-oriented appeal. (iii) His test was designed only to measure the most readily testable, gross ways of talking callously about, and acting callously toward, women. Women, especially recently, have become aware of many more and less subtle ways in which men can express hostility and contempt for them. An obvious example is a man who would deny that "most women are cunts at heart" but would gladly talk about women as "chicks" or "foxes" to be captured, conquered, and toyed with. In short, many more men than Mosher thinks might well fall into the "sex calloused" class; and the questions asked of all the men should have included tests for more subtle forms of callousness.

Conclusions About Sexual Behavior One of the most problematic parts of Mosher's study is that he did not test whether exploitative sexual behavior increased after the films were viewed; he tested only whether *any* sexual behavior increased and whether the endorsement of statements expressing calloused attitudes increased. One learns only that no increase occurred in the sexual behavior of the subjects (both calloused and not so calloused). One wants to know how the sex calloused men treated their partners after they saw the films; the frequency of sex, increased or not, implies nothing about the quality of their treatment of their female partners. It is not enough for Mosher to tell us that a decrease occurred in endorsing statements expressing calloused attitudes. Mosher himself points out the gap between verbal behavior in the laboratory and behavior in real-life situations with one's chosen partners.[16]

Conclusions About Calloused Attitudes (i) The most serious difficulty is one that Mosher rec-

ognizes: There was no control for the possibility that the men's level of sex callousness was unusually high in the beginning as a result of their anticipation of seeing pornographic films. (ii) Nor was there a control for the declining "shock value" of the statements expressing calloused attitudes. (iii) No precise indication of the relative decreases in sex calloused attitudes for the high- and low-callousness groups was given. Mosher states the differences for high- and low-guilt groups and has told us that highly calloused men tend to feel less guilt than other men;[17] however, one wants to know more precisely what the different effects were, particularly on the high-callousness group. (iv) Mosher realizes that his explanation for the decrease in calloused attitudes is still speculative. If seeing pornography with a group of men provides an outlet for callousness, there should be a control group of subjects seeing pornography while isolated from others. There should also be a control group experience not involving pornography at all. For example, subjects in such a group could watch a film about a Nazi concentration camp or about the first American presidents.

4

Although I am obviously critical of Mosher's work, let us suspend for a moment our critical judgment about his data and their interpretation. Even if the experience of seeing pornographic movies with other undergraduate men provides an opportunity to let out a small amount of male contempt and hostility toward women, very little follows from this for social policy or moral judgments. No sensible person would maintain that a temporary outlet is an adequate substitute for getting to the root of a problem. Given the existence of a large reservoir of male contempt and hostility toward women, and given that our society is still filled with pressures to "affirm one's manhood" at the expense of women, there is little reason to suppose a "cathartic" effect to be very significant here. Much of the research on the effects of pornography indicates that *any* effect it has—positive or negative—is short lived. At best pornography might divert or delay a man from expressing his callousness in an even more blatantly objectionable manner.

---

[16]"Pornographic Films, Make Verbal Aggression Against Women, and Guilt," *Tech. Report,* vol. 8, pp. 372–73.

[17]*Tech. Report,* vol. 8, p. 274. The low-guilt subjects showed a rebound in sex callousness two weeks after seeing the films; however, the level of callousness still did not reach the prefilm level.

One could make the point in moral terms as follows: Sex calloused attitudes and behavior are morally objectionable; if expressing one's sex calloused attitudes lessens them temporarily, they are still morally objectionable if they persevere at some level. The most that one could say for pornography is that expressing callousness by enjoying pornography in a male group is a lesser evil than, for example, rape or obnoxiously "putting down" a woman in person. This is saying very little on behalf of pornography; it is still morally objectionable.

If pornography is morally objectionable even if Mosher is correct, then given the two alternatives posed, it is surely morally objectionable. For Brownmiller's alternative, remember, was that pornography provides a model for sex calloused behavior and has a numbing effect on many of us so that we more readily tolerate this behavior. This view, much more obviously than Mosher's, implies that pornography is morally objectionable.[18]

Before leaving Mosher and Brownmiller, let me point out that their views are not wholly incompatible. They disagree about pornography's function as an outlet or a model, of course, but Mosher's data (as he interprets their significance) are compatible with the numbing effect of pornography. Pornography may have numbed all of us (previously sex calloused or not) to the objectionable character of exploitative sex; the fact that the sex calloused men were numbed does not imply that they will feel the need to endorse calloused attitudes just after expressing their callousness in other ways. Further, Mosher's data have no bearing at all on the numbing influence on women; certainly Brownmiller means for her claim to apply to women too.

One final point remains to be considered. The Presidential Commission assumes a connection between sex callousness and the lack (or loss) of respect for women; for it appealed to Mosher's data about sex callousness to show that pornography probably will not lead people to lose respect for women.[19] But look at the results of replacing Mosher's talk about sex calloused attitudes with talk about respect for women: One would conclude that seeing pornography (with a group of men) leads to an increase in respect for women. The explanation would be that men who tend toward low respect for women can use pornography as a way of express-

ing their low respect. They then feel no need to endorse statements exemplifying their low respect because they have just expressed it. "Therefore" pornography provides the opportunity for their respect for women to increase. The last idea is bothersome: To think of viewing and enjoying pornography as a way of expressing lack of respect, and at the same time as a way of expressing or increasing respect, seems very strange. This is not to say that such a feat is impossible. Given our complex psychological make-up, we might be able to express both respect and lack of respect at the same time in different ways; it might also be possible to express disrespect that leads to respect (e.g., if shame at feeling disrespect leads to a temporary increase in respect). But one would need far more information about what actually happens before agreeing that any of these possibilities seems very plausible. It is necessary to spell out both the possible connections and suitable explanations for each. Without much more information, one would not want to base either favorable moral judgments about pornography or social policy on the possibility that pornography can lead to more respect for women.

Although much more remains to be said about the connection between pornography and respect for women, I will defer discussion of it to Part III of this paper. For now, let us note that even if the Presidential Commission appropriately allayed our fears about being molested on street corners by users of pornography, it would not have been warranted in placating us with the view that pornography is morally acceptable. It is fortunate that it did not try.

III

The second argument I will consider is that pornography is morally objectionable, not because it leads people to show disrespect for women, but because pornography itself exemplifies and recommends behavior that violates the moral principle to respect persons. The content of pornography is what one objects to. It treats women as mere sex objects "to be exploited and manipulated" and degrades the role and status of women. In order to evaluate this argument, I will first clarify what it would mean for pornography itself to treat someone as a sex object in a degrading manner. I will then deal with three issues central to the discussion of pornography and respect for women: how "losing

---

[18]Of course, pornography might have no effect at all. If this were true, some other basis must be found before calling it morally objectionable.

[19]*Report*, p. 201.

respect" for a woman is connected with treating her as a sex object; what is wrong with treating someone as a sex object; and why it is worse to treat women rather than men as sex objects. I will argue that the current content of pornography sometimes violates the moral principle to respect persons. Then, in Part IV of this paper, I will suggest that pornography need not violate this principle if certain fundamental changes were to occur in attitudes about sex.

To many people, including Brownmiller and some other feminists, it appears to be an obvious truth that pornography treats people, expecially women, as sex objects in a degrading manner. And if we omit 'in a degrading manner,' the statement seems hard to dispute: How could pornography *not* treat people as sex objects?

First, is it permissible to say that either the content of pornography or pornography itself degrades people or treats people as sex objects? It is not difficult to find examples of degrading content in which women are treated as sex objects. Some pornographic films convey the message that all women really want to be raped, that their resisting struggle is not to be believed. By portraying women in this manner, the content of the movie degrades women. Degrading women is morally objectionable. While seeing the movie need not cause anyone to imitate the behavior shown, we can call the content degrading to women because of the character of the behavior and attitudes it recommends. The same kind of point can be made about films (or books or TV commercials) with other kinds of degrading, thus morally objectionable, content—for example, racist messages.[20]

The next step in the argument is to infer that, because the content or message of pornography is morally objectionable, we can call pornography itself morally objectionable. Support for this step can be found in an analogy. If a person takes every opportunity to recommend that men rape women, we would think not only that his recommendation is immoral but that he is immoral too. In the case of pornography, the objection to making an inference

from recommended behavior to the person who recommends is that we ascribe predicates such as 'immoral' differently to people than to films or books. A film vehicle for an objectionable message is still an object independent of its message, its director, its producer, those who act in it, and those who respond to it. Hence one cannot make an unsupported inference from "the content of the film is morally objectionable" to "the film is morally objectionable." Because the central points in this paper do not depend on whether pornography itself (in addition to its content) is morally objectionable, I will not try to support this inference. (The question about the relation of content to the work itself is, of course, extremely interesting; but in part because I cannot decide which side of the argument is more persuasive, I will pass.[21]) Certainly one appropriate way to evaluate pornography is in terms of the moral features of its content. If a pornographic film exemplifies and recommends morally objectionable attitudes or behavior, then its content is morally objectionable.

Let us now turn to the first of our three questions about respect and sex objects: What is the connection between losing respect for a woman and treating her as a sex object? Some people who have lived through the era in which women were taught to worry about men "losing respect" for them if they engaged in sex in inappropriate circumstances find it troublesome (or at least amusing) that feminists—supposedly "liberated" women—are outraged at being treated as sex objects, either by pornography or in any other way. The apparent alignment between feminists and traditionally "proper" women need not surprise us when we look at it more closely.

The "respect" that men have traditionally believed they have for women—hence a respect they can lose—is not a general respect for persons as autonomous beings; nor is it respect that is earned because of one's personal merits or achievements. It is respect that is an outgrowth of the "double standard." Women are to be respected because they are more pure, delicate, and fragile than men, have more refined sensibilities, and so on. Because

[20]Two further points need to be mentioned here. Sharon Bishop pointed out to me one reason why we might object to either a racist or rapist mentality in film: it might be difficult for a Black or a woman not to identify with the degraded person. A second point concerns different uses of the phrase 'treats women as sex objects'. A film treats a subject—the meaninglessness of contemporary life, women as sex objects, and so on—and this use of 'treats' is unproblematic. But one should not suppose that this is the same use of 'treats women as sex objects' that is found in the sentence 'David treats women as sex objects'; David is not treating the *subject* of women as sex objects.

[21]In order to help one determine which position one feels inclined to take, consider the following statement: It is morally objectionable to write, make, sell, act in, use, and enjoy pornography; in addition, the content of pornography is immoral; however, pornography itself is not morally objectionable. If this statement seems extremely problematic, then one might well be satisfied with the claim that pornography is degrading because its content is.

some women clearly do not have these qualities, thus do not deserve respect, women must be divided into two groups—the good ones on the pedestal and the bad ones who have fallen from it. One's mother, grandmother, Sunday School teacher, and usually one's wife are "good" women. The appropriate behavior by which to express respect for good women would be, for example, not swearing or telling dirty jokes in front of them, giving them seats on buses, and other "chivalrous" acts. This kind of "respect" for good women is the same sort that adolescent boys in the back seats of cars used to "promise" not to lose. Note that men define, display, and lose this kind of respect. If women lose respect for women, it is not typically a loss of respect for (other) women as a class but a loss of self-respect.

It has now become commonplace to acknowledge that, although a place on the pedestal might have advantages over a place in the "gutter" beneath it, a place on the pedestal is not at all equal to the place occupied by other people (i.e., men). "Respect" for those on the pedestal was not respect for whole, full-fledged people but for a special class of inferior beings.

If a person makes two traditional assumptions—that (at least some) sex is dirty and that women fall into two classes, good and bad—it is easy to see how that person might think that pornography could lead people to lose respect for women or that pornography is itself disrespectful to women.[22] Pornography describes or shows women engaging in activities inappropriate for good women to engage in—or at least inappropriate for them to be seen by strangers engaging in. If one sees these women as symbolic representatives of all women, then all women fall from grace with these women. This fall is possible, I believe, because the traditional "respect" that men have had for women is not genuine, wholehearted respect for full-fledged human beings but half-hearted respect for lesser beings, some of whom they feel the need to glorify and purify.[23] It is easy to fall from a pedestal. Can we imagine 41

percent of men and 46 percent of women answering "yes" to the question, "Do movies showing men engaging in violent acts lead people to lose respect for men?"?

Two interesting asymmetries appear. The first is that losing respect for men as a class (men with power, typically Anglo men) is more difficult than losing respect for women or ethnic minorities as a class. Anglo men whose behavior warrants disrespect are more likely to be seen as exceptional cases than are women or minorities (whose "transgressions" may be far less serious). Think of the following: women are temptresses; Blacks cheat the welfare system; Italians are gangsters; but the men of the Nixon administration are exceptions—Anglo men as a class did not lose respect because of Watergate and related scandals.

The second asymmetry concerns the active and passive roles of the sexes. Men are seen in the active role. If men lose respect for women because of something "evil" done by women (such as appearing in pornography), the fear is that men will then do harm to women—not that women will do harm to men. Whereas if women lose respect for male politicians because of Watergate, the fear is still that male politicians will do harm, not that women will do harm to male politicians. This asymmetry might be a result of one way in which our society thinks of sex as bad—as harm that men do to women (or to the person playing a female role, as in a homosexual rape). Robert Baker calls attention to this point in "'Pricks' and 'Chicks': A Plea for 'Persons'."[24] Our slang words for sexual intercourse—'fuck', 'screw', or older words such as 'take' or 'have'—not only can mean harm but have traditionally taken a male subject and a female object. The active male screws (harms) the passive female. A "bad" woman only tempts men to hurt her further.

It is easy to understand why one's proper grandmother would not want men to see pornography or lose respect for women. But feminists reject these "proper" assumptions: good and bad classes of women do not exist; and sex is not dirty (though many people believe it is). Why then are feminists angry at the treatment of women as sex objects, and why are some feminists opposed to pornography?

[22]The traditional meaning of "lose respect for women" was evidently the one assumed in the Abelson survey cited by the Presidential Commission. No explanation of its meaning is given in the report of the study. See H. Abelson et al., "National Survey of Public Attitudes Toward and Experience With Erotic Materials," *Tech. Report,* vol. 6, pp. 1–137.

[23]Many feminists point this out. One of the most accessible references is Shulamith Firestone, *The Dialectic of Sex: The Case for the Feminist Revolution* (New York: Bantam, 1970), especially pp. 128–32. [See chapter 4, this volume—eds.]

[24]In Richard Wasserstrom, ed., *Today's Moral Problems* (New York: Macmillan, 1975), pp. 152–71; see pp. 167–71. Also in Robert Baker and Frederick Elliston, eds., *Philosophy and Sex* (Buffalo, N.Y.: Prometheus Books, 1975). [See chapters 1 and 3, this volume, pp. 21–26 and pp. 100–103—eds.]

The answer is that feminists as well as proper grandparents are concerned with respect. However, there are differences. A feminist's distinction between treating a woman as a full-fledged person and treating her as merely a sex object does not correspond to the good-bad woman distinction. In the latter distinction, "good" and "bad" are properties applicable to groups of women. In the feminist view, all women are full-fledged people—some, however, are treated as sex objects and perhaps think of themselves as sex objects. A further difference is that, although "bad" women correspond to those thought to deserve treatment as sex objects, good women have not corresponded to full-fledged people; only men have been full-fledged people. Given the feminist's distinction, she has no difficulty whatever in saying that pornography treats women as sex objects, not as full-fledged people. She can morally object to pornography or anything else that treats women as sex objects.

One might wonder whether any objection to treatment as a sex object implies that the person objecting still believes, deep down, that sex is dirty. I don't think so. Several other possibilities emerge. First, even if I believe intellectually and emotionally that sex is healthy, I might object to being treated *only* as a sex object. In the same spirit, I would object to being treated *only* as a maker of chocolate chip cookies or *only* as a tennis partner, because only one of my talents is being valued. Second, perhaps I feel that sex is healthy, but it is apparent to me that you think sex is dirty; so I don't want you to treat me as a sex object. Third, being treated as any kind of object, not just as a sex object, is unappealing. I would rather be a partner (sexual or otherwise) than an object. Fourth, and more plausible than the first three possibilities, is Robert Baker's view mentioned above. Both (i) our traditional double standard of sexual behavior for men and women and (ii) the linguistic evidence that we connect the concept of sex with the concept of harm point to what is wrong with treating women as sex objects. As I said earlier, 'fuck' and 'screw', in their traditional uses, have taken a male subject, a female object, and have had at least two meanings: harm and have sexual intercourse with. (In addition, a prick is a man who harms people ruthlessly; and a motherfucker is so low that he would do something very harmful to his own dear mother.)[25] Because in our culture we connect sex

with harm that men do to women, and becase we think of the female role in sex as that of harmed object, we can see that to treat a woman as a sex object is automatically to treat her as less than fully human. To say this does not imply that no healthy sexual relationships exist; nor does it say anything about individual men's conscious intentions to degrade women by desiring them sexually (though no doubt some men have these intentions). It is merely to make a point about the concepts embodied in our language.

Psychoanalytic support for the connection between sex and harm comes from Robert J. Stoller. Stoller thinks that sexual excitement is linked with a wish to harm someone (and with at least a whisper of hostility). The key process of sexual excitement can be seen as dehumanization (fetishization) in fantasy of the desired person. He speculates that this is true in some degree of everyone, both men and women, with "normal" or perverted" activities and fantasies.[26]

Thinking of sex objects as harmed objects enables us to explain some of the first three reasons why one wouldn't want to be treated as a sex object: (1) I may object to being treated only as a tennis partner, but being a tennis partner is not connected in our culture with being a harmed object; and (2) I may not think that sex is dirty and that I would be a harmed object; I may not know what your view is; but what bothers me is that this is the view embodied in our language and culture.

Awareness of the connection between sex and harm helps explain other interesting points. Women are angry about being treated as sex objects in situations or roles in which they do not intend to be regarded in that manner—for example, while serving on a committee or attending a discussion. It is not merely that a sexual role is inappropriate for the circumstances; it is thought to be a less fully human role than the one in which they intended to function.

Finally, the sex-harm connection makes clear

---

[25]Baker, in Wasserstrom, *Today's Moral Problems*, pp. 168–169. [Page 102, this volume—eds.]

[26]"Sexual Excitement," *Archives of General Psychiatry* 33 (1976): 899–909, especially p. 903. The extent to which Stoller sees men and women in different positions with respect to harm and hostility is not clear. He often treats men and women alike, but in *Perversion: The Erotic Form of Hatred* (New York: Pantheon, 1975), pp. 89–91, he calls attention to differences between men and women especially regarding their responses to pornography and lack of understanding by men of women's sexuality. Given that Stoller finds hostility to be an essential element in male-oriented pornography, and given that women have not responded readily to such pornography, one can speculate about the possibilities for women's sexuality: their hostility might follow a different scenario; they might not be as hostile, and so on.

why it is worse to treat women as sex objects than to treat men as sex objects, and why some men have had difficulty understanding women's anger about the matter. It is more difficult for heterosexual men than for women to assume the role of "harmed object" in sex; for men have the self-concept of sexual agents, not of passive objects. This is also related to my earlier point concerning the difference in the solidity of respect for men and for women; respect for women is more fragile. Despite exceptions, it is generally harder for people to degrade men, either sexually or nonsexually, than to degrade women. Men and women have grown up with different patterns of self-respect and expectations regarding the extent to which they deserve and will receive respect or degradation. The man who doesn't understand why women do not want to be treated as sex objects (because he'd sure like to be) would not think of himself as being harmed by that treatment; a woman might.[27] Pornography, probably more than any other contemporary institution, succeeds in treating men as sex objects.

Having seen that the connection between sex and harm helps explain both what is wrong with treating someone as a sex object and why it is worse to treat a woman in this way, I want to use the sex-harm connection to try to resolve a dispute about pornography and women. Brownmiller's view, remember, was that pornography is "the undiluted essence of anti-female propaganda" whose purpose is to degrade women.[28] Some people object to Brownmiller's view by saying that, since pornography treats both men and women as sex objects for the purpose of arousing the viewer, it is neither sexist, antifemale, nor designed to degrade women; it just happens that degrading of women arouses some men. How can this dispute be resolved?

Suppose we were to rate the content of all pornography from most morally objectionable to least morally objectionable. Among the most objectionable would be the most degrading—for example, "snuff" films and movies which recommend that men rape women, molest children and puppies, and treat nonmasochists very sadistically.

Next we would find a large amount of material (probably most pornography) not quite so blatantly offensive. With this material it is relevant to use the analysis of sex objects given above. As long as sex is connected with harm done to women, it will be very difficult not to see pornography as degrading to women. We can agree with Brownmiller's opponent that pornography treats men as sex objects, too, but we maintain that this is only pseudoequality: such treatment is still more degrading to women.[29]

In addition, pornography often exemplifies the active/passive, harmer/harmed object roles in a very obvious way. Because pornography today is male-oriented and is supposed to make a profit, the content is designed to appeal to male fantasies. Judging from the content of the most popular legally available pornography, male fantasies still run along the lines of stereotypical sex roles—and, if Stoller is right, include elements of hostility. In much pornography the women's purpose is to cater to male desires, to service the man or men. Her own pleasure is rarely emphasized for its own sake; she is merely allowed a little heavy breathing, perhaps in order to show her dependence on the great male "lover" who produces her pleasure. In addition, women are clearly made into passive objects in still photographs showing only close-ups of their genitals. Even in movies marketed to appeal to heterosexual couples, such as *Behind the Green Door*, the woman is passive and undemanding (and in this case kidnapped and hypnotized as well). Although many kinds of specialty magazines and films are gauged for different sexual tastes, very little contemporary pornography goes against traditional sex roles. There is certainly no significant attempt to replace the harmer/harmed distinction with anything more positive and healthy. In some stag movies, of course, men are treated sadistically by women; but this is an attempt to turn the tables on degradation, not a positive improvement.

What would cases toward the least objectionable end of the spectrum be like? They would be increasingly less degrading and sexist. The genuinely nonobjectionable cases would be non-

---

[27] Men seem to be developing more sensitivity to being treated as sex objects. Many homosexual men have long understood the problem. As women become more sexually aggressive, some heterosexual men I know are beginning to feel treated as sex objects. A man can feel that he is not being taken seriously if a woman looks lustfully at him while he is holding forth about the French judicial system or the failure of liberal politics. Some of his most important talents are not being properly valued.

[28] Brownmiller, *Against Our Will*, p. 394.

[29] I don't agree with Brownmiller that the purpose of pornography is to dehumanize women; rather it is to arouse the audience. The differences between our views can be explained, in part, by the points from which we begin. She is writing about rape; her views about pornography grow out of her views about rape. I begin by thinking of pornography as merely depicted sexual activity, though I am well aware of the male hostility and contempt for women that it often expresses. That pornography degrades women and excites men is an illustration of this contempt.

sexist and nondegrading; but commercial examples do not readily spring to mind.[30] The question is: Does or could any pornography have nonsexist, nondegrading content?

IV

I want to start with the easier question: Is it possible for pornography to have nonsexist, morally acceptable content? Then I will consider whether any pornography of this sort currently exists.

Imagine the following situation, which exists only rarely today: Two fairly conventional people who love each other enjoy playing tennis and bridge together, cooking good food together, and having sex together. In all these activities they are free from hang-ups, guilt, and tendencies to dominate or objectify each other. These two people like to watch tennis matches and old romantic movies on TV, like to watch Julia Child cook, like to read the bridge column in the newspaper, and like to watch pornographic movies. Imagine further that this couple is not at all uncommon in society and that nonsexist pornography is as common as this kind of nonsexist sexual relationship. This situation sounds fine and healthy to me. I see no reason to think that an interest in pornography would disappear in these circumstances.[31] People seem to enjoy watching others experience or do (especially do well) what they enjoy experiencing, doing, or wish they could do themselves. We do not morally object to people watching tennis on TV; why would we object to these hypothetical people watching pornography?

Can we go from the situation today to the situation just imagined? In much current pornography, people are treated in morally objectionable ways. In the scene just imagined, however, pornography would be nonsexist, nondegrading, morally acceptable. The key to making the change is to break the connection between sex and harm. If Stoller is right, this task may be impossible without

changing the scenarios of our sexual lives—scenarios that we have been writing since early childhood. (Stoller does not indicate whether he thinks it possible for adults to rewrite their scenarios or for social change to bring about the possibility of new scenarios in future generations.) But even if we believe that people can change their sexual scenarios, the sex-harm connection is deeply entrenched and has widespread implications. What is needed is a thorough change in people's deep-seated attitudes and feelings about sex roles in general, as well as about sex and roles in sex (sexual roles). Although I cannot even sketch a general outline of such changes here, changes in pornography should be part of a comprehensive program. Television, children's educational material, and nonpornographic movies and novels may be far better avenues for attempting to change attitudes; but one does not want to take the chance that pornography is working against one.

What can be done about pornography in particular? If one wanted to work within the current institutions, one's attempt to use pornography as a tool for the education of male pornography audiences would have to be fairly subtle at first; nonsexist pornography must become familiar enough to sell and be watched. One should realize too that any positive educational value that nonsexist pornography might have may well be as short-lived as most of the effects of pornography. But given these limitations, what could one do?

Two kinds of films must be considered. First is the short film with no plot or character development, just depicted sexual activity in which nonsexist pornography would treat men and women as equal sex partners.[32] The man would not control the circumstances in which the partners had sex or the choice of positions or acts; the woman's preference would be counted equally. There would be no suggestion of a power play or conquest on the man's part, no suggestion that "she likes it when I hurt her." Sexual intercourse would not be portrayed as primarily for

---

[30]Virginia Wright Wexman uses the film *Group Marriage* (Stephanie Rothman, 1973) as an example of "more enlightened erotica." Wexman also asks the following questions in an attempt to point out sexism in pornographic films:

Does it [the film] portray rape as pleasurable to women? Does it consistently show females nude but present men fully clothed? Does it present women as childlike creatures whose sexual interests must be guided by knowing experienced men? Does it show sexually aggressive women as castrating viragos? Does it pretend that sex is exclusively the prerogative of women under twenty-five? Does it focus on the physical aspects of lovemaking rather than the emotional ones? Does it portray women as purely sexual beings? ("Sexism of X-rated Films," Chicago Sun-Times, 28 March 1976.)

[31]One might think, as does Stoller, that since pornography

today depends on hostility, voyeurism, and sado-masochism (*Perversion*, p. 87) that sexually healthy people would not enjoy it. Two points should be noticed here, however: (1) Stoller need not think that pornography will disappear because hostility is an element of sexual excitement generally; and (2) voyeurism, when it invades no one's privacy, need not be seen as immoral; so although enjoyment of pornography might not be an expression of sexual health, it need not be immoral either.

[32]If it is a lesbian or male homosexual film, no one would play a caricatured male or female role. The reader has probably noticed that I have limited my discussion to heterosexual pornography, but there are many interesting analogies to be drawn with male homosexual pornography. Very little lesbian pornography exists, though lesbian scenes are commonly found in male-oriented pornography.

the purpose of male ejaculation—his orgasm is not "the best part" of the movie. In addition, both the man and woman would express their enjoyment; the man need not be cool and detached.

The film with a plot provides even more opportunity for nonsexist education. Today's pornography often portrays the female characters as playthings even when not engaging in sexual activity. Nonsexist pornography could show women and men in roles equally valued by society, and sex equality would amount to more than possession of equally functional genitalia. Characters would customarily treat each other with respect and consideration, with no attempt to treat men or women brutally or thoughtlessly. The local Pussycat Theater showed a film written and directed by a woman *(The Passions of Carol),* which exhibited a few of the features just mentioned. The main female character in it was the editor of a magazine parody of *Viva.* The fact that some of the characters treated each other very nicely, warmly, and tenderly did not detract from the pornographic features of the movie. This should not surprise us, for even in traditional male-oriented films, lesbian scenes usually exhibit tenderness and kindness.

Plots for nonsexist films could include women in traditionally male jobs (e.g., long-distance truckdriver) or in positions usually held in respect by pornography audiences. For example, a high-ranking female Army officer, treated with respect by men and women alike, could be shown not only in various sexual encounters with other people but also carrying out her job in a humane manner.[33] Or perhaps the main character could be a female urologist. She could interact with nurses and other medical personnel, diagnose illnesses brilliantly, and treat patients with great sympathy as well as have sex with

them. When the Army officer or the urologist engage in sexual activities, they will treat their partners and be treated by them in some of the considerate ways described above.

In the circumstances we imagined at the beginning of Part IV of this paper, our nonsexist films could be appreciated in the proper spirit. Under these conditions the content of our new pornography would clearly be nonsexist and morally acceptable. But would the content of such a film be morally acceptable if shown to a typical pornography audience today? It might seem strange for us to change our moral evaluation of the content on the basis of a different audience, but an audience today is likely to see the "respected" urologist and Army officer as playthings or unusual prostitutes —even if our intention in showing the film is to counteract this view. The effect is that, although the content of the film seems morally acceptable and our intention in showing it is morally flawless, women are still degraded.[34] The fact that audience attitude is so important makes one wary of giving wholehearted approval to any pornography seen today.

The fact that good intentions and content are insufficient does not imply that one's efforts toward change would be entirely in vain. Of course, I could not deny that anyone who tries to change an institution from within faces serious difficulties. This is particularly evident when one is trying to change both pornography and a whole set of related attitudes, feelings, and institutions concerning sex and sex roles. But in conjunction with other attempts to change this set of attitudes, it seems preferable to try to change pornography instead of closing one's eyes in the hope that it will go away. For I suspect that pornography is here to stay.[35]

[33]One should note that behavior of this kind is still considered unacceptable by the military. A female officer resigned from the U.S. Navy recently rather than be court-martialed for having sex with several enlisted men whom she met in a class on interpersonal relations.

[34]The content may seem morally acceptable only if one disregards such questions as, "Should a doctor have sex with her patients during office hours?" More important is the propriety of evaluating content wholly apart from the attitudes and reactions of the audience; one might not find it strange to say that one film has morally unacceptable content when shown tonight at the Pussycat Theater but acceptable content when shown tomorrow at a feminist conference.

[35]Three "final" points must be made:
1. I have not seriously considered censorship as an alternative course of action. Both Brownmiller and Sheehy are not averse to it. But as I suggested in note 5, other principles seem too valuable to sacrifice when other options are available. In addition, before justifying censorship on moral grounds one would want to compare pornography to other possibly offensive material: advertising using sex and racial stereotypes, violence in TV and films, and so on.

2. If my nonsexist pornography succeeded in having much "educational value," it might no longer be pornography according to my definition. This possibility seems too remote to worry me, however.
3. In discussing the audience for nonsexist pornography, I have focused on the male audience. But there is no reason why pornography could not educate and appeal to women as well.

Earlier versions of this paper have been discussed at a meeting of the Society for Women in Philosophy at Stanford University, California State University, Los Angeles, Claremont Graduate School, Western Area Meeting of Women in Psychology, UCLA Political Philosophy Discussion Group, and California State University, Fullerton Annual Philosophy Symposium. Among the many people who made helpful comments were Alan Garfinkel, Jackie Thomason, and Fred Berger. This paper grew out of "Pornography, Sex Roles, and Morality," presented as a responding paper to Fred Berger's "Strictly Peeking: Some Views on Pornography, Sex, and Censorship" in a Philosophy and Public Affairs Symposium at the American Philosophical Association, Pacific Division Meeting, March, 1975.

20/What's Wrong with Rape

Pamela Foa

It is clear that rape is wrong. It is equally clear that the wrongness of rape is not completely explained by its status as a criminal assault. Dispute begins, however, when we attempt to account for the special features of rape, the ways in which its wrongness goes beyond its criminal character. I shall argue against those who maintain that the special wrongness of rape arises from and is completely explained by a societal refusal to recognize women as *people*. I shall offer a different explanation: The special wrongness of rape is due to, and is only an exaggeration of, the wrongness of our sexual interactions in general. Thus, a clear analysis of the special wrongness of rape will help indicate some of the essential features of healthy, non-rapine sexual interactions.

I. The Wrongness of Rape Goes Beyond Its Criminality

It is to be expected during this period of resurgent feminism that rape will be seen primarily as a manifestation of how women are mistreated in our society. For example, consider these remarks of Simone de Beauvoir:

All men are drawn to B[rigitte] B[ardot]'s seductiveness, but that does not mean that they are kindly disposed towards her. . . . They are unwilling to give up their role of lord and master. . . . Freedom and full consciousness remain their [the men's] right and privilege. . . . In the game of love BB is as much a hunter as she is a prey. The male is an object to her, just as she is to him. And that is precisely what wounds the masculine pride. In the

Latin countries where men cling to the myth of "the woman as object," BB's naturalness seems to them more perverse than any possible sophistication. It is to assert that one is man's fellow and equal, to recognize that between the woman and him there is a mutual desire and pleasure. . . .

But the male feels uncomfortable if, instead of a doll of flesh and blood, he holds in his arms a conscious being who is sizing him up. "You realize," an average Frenchman once said to me, "that when a man finds a woman attractive, he wants to be able to pinch her behind." A ribald gesture reduces a woman to a thing that a man can do with as he pleases without worrying about what goes on in her mind and heart and body.[1]

And rape is apparently the quintessential instance of women being viewed as objects, of women being treated as entities other than, and morally inferior to, men. It is implicit in this object-view that if men, and therefore society, viewed women as full moral equals, rape would be an assault no different in kind than any other. Thus, it is a consequence of this view that the special wrongness of rape is to be found in the nonsexual aspects of the act.

To this end, Marilyn Frye and Carolyn Shafer suggest in their paper "Rape and Respect" that the wrongness of rape is twofold: first, it is the use of a person without her consent in the performance of an act or event which is against her own best interests; and second, it is a social means of reinforcing the status of women as kinds of entities who lack and ought to lack the full privileges of personhood —importantly, the freedom to move as they will through what is rightfully their domain.[2] What is good

An earlier version of this paper was presented to the Society of Women in Philosophy, Midwestern Division, October 1975, and to the American Philosophical Association, Pacific Division, March 1976. Research for this paper was supported by a generous grant from the University of Pittsburgh. Thanks are due to many colleagues who helped me clarify my views: especially John Cooper, Paul Guyer, Jonathan Himmelhoch, Alexander Nehamas, and, of course, Marilyn Frye and Carolyn Shafer.

[1]Simone de Beauvoir, *Brigitte Bardot and the Lolita Syndrome* (London: New English Library, 1962), pp. 28, 30, 32.

[2]Frye and Shafer characterize a domain as "where . . . a person . . . lives. . . . Since biological life and health are prerequisites for the pursuit of any other interests and goals, . . . everything necessary for their maintenance and sustenance evidently will fall very close to the center of the domain. Anything which exerts an influence on . . . a person's will or dulls its intelligence

From *Feminism and Philosophy* (Totowa, N.J.: Littlefield, Adams & Company, 1977). Reprinted by permission.

about this account is that it provides one way of understanding the sense of essential violation of one's *person* (and not mere sexual abuse), which seems to be the natural concomitant of rape.

This account, further, gives one explanation for the continuous social denial of the common fact of criminal rape. On this view, to recognize rape as a criminal act, one must recognize the domains of women. But if domains are inextricably connected with personhood—if personhood, in fact, is to be analyzed in terms of domains—then it ought to be obvious that where there is no domain there can be no criminal trespass of domain; there can only be misperceptions or misunderstandings. To recognize domains of consent is to recognize the existence of people at their centers. Without such centers, there can be no rape.

Unfortunately, I do not believe that this kind of account can serve as an adequate explanation of what's wrong with rape. I find irrelevant its emphasis on the ontological status of women as persons of the first rank. It is granted that in any act of rape a person is used without proper regard to her personhood, but this is true of every kind of assault. If there is an additional wrongness to rape, it must be that more is wrong than the mere treatment of a person by another person without proper regard for her personhood. Later in this paper, I shall show that there is no need to differentiate ontologically between victim and assailant in order to explain the special wrongness of rape. However, it is important to recognize that rape is profoundly wrong even if it is not an act between ontological equals.

The special wrongness of rape cannot be traced to the fact that in this act men are not recognizing the full array of moral and legal rights and privileges which accrue to someone of equal status. Rape of children is at least as heinous as rape of adults, though few actually believe that children have or ought to have the same large domain of consent adults (male and female) ought to have. In part, this is what is so disturbing about a recent English decision I shall discuss in a moment: it seems to confuse the ontological with the moral. Men's wishes, intentions, and beliefs are given a different (and more important) weight, just because they are (wrongly in this case, perhaps rightly in the case of children) viewed as different kinds of entities than women.

But even if one thinks that women are not people, or that all people (for example, children) do not have the same rights or, prima facie, the same domains of consent, it seems that rape is still especially horrible, awful in a way that other assaults are not. There is, for example, something deeply distressing, though not necessarily criminal, about raping one's pet dog. It is disturbing in ways no ordinary assault, even upon a person, seems to be disturbing. It may here be objected that what accounts for the moral outrage in these two cases is that the first is an instance of pedophilia, and the second of bestiality. That is, the special wrongness of these acts is due to the "unnatural" direction of the sexual impulse, rather than to the abusive circumstances of the fulfillment of a "natural" sexual impulse.

I would argue in response that outrage at "unnatural" acts is misdirected and inappropriate. The notion that acting "against" nature is immoral stems from the false belief that how things are in the majority of cases is, morally speaking, how things always ought to be. Acting unnaturally is not acting immorally unless there is a moral design to the natural order—and there is no such structure to it. This means, then, that if it is reasonable to feel that something very wrong has occurred in the above two cases, then it must be because they are rapes and not because they are "unnatural acts." However, even if this argument is not conclusive, it must be agreed that the random raping of a mentally retarded adult is clearly wrong even though such an individual does not, in our society, have all the legal and moral rights of normal people.[3]

Of course, another very reasonable point to make here may well be that it is not just people who have domains, and that what's wrong with rape is the invasion by one being into another's domain without consent or right. But if something like this is true, then rape would be wrong because it was an "incursion" into a domain. This would make it wrong in the same way that other assaults are wrong. The closer the incursion comes to the center of a person's identity, the worse the act.

The problem here is that such an argument suggests that rape is wrong the same way, and only

---

or affects its own sense of its identity . . . also comes very near the center of the domain. Whatever has a relatively permanent effect on the person, whatever affects its relatively constant surroundings, whatever causes it discomfort or distress—in short, whatever a person has to live with—is likely to fall squarely within its

domain" ("Rape and Respect," [in *Feminism and Philosophy* (Totowa, N.J.: Littlefield, Adams, 1977)] p. 337).

[3]This societal attitude, however, that the mentally retarded are not the equals of normal people is not one with which I associate myself.

the same way, that other assaults are wrong. And yet the evidence contradicts this. There is an emotional concomitant to this assault, one that is lacking in nonsexual criminal assaults. What must be realized is that when it comes to sexual matters, people—in full recognition of the equal ontological status of their partners—treat each other abominably. Contrary to the Frye/Shafer theory, I believe that liberated men and women—people who have no doubts about the moral or ontological equality of the sexes—can and do have essentially rape-like sexual lives.

The following case is sufficient to establish that it is not just the assault upon one's person, or the intrusion into one's domain, that makes for the special features of rape. In New York twenty or so years ago, there was a man who went around Manhattan slashing people with a very sharp knife. He did not do this as part of any robbery or other further bodily assault. His end was simply to stab people. Although he was using people against their own best interests, and without their consent—that is, although he is broadly violating domains—to be the victim of the Mad Slasher was not to have been demeaned or dirtied as a person in the way that the victim of rape is demeaned or dirtied. It was not to be wronged or devalued in the same way that to be raped is to be wronged or devalued. No one ever accused any of the victims of provoking, initiating, or enjoying the attack.

Yet the public morality about rape suggests that unless one is somehow mutilated, broken, or killed in addition to being raped, one is suspected of having provoked, initiated, complied in, consented to, or even enjoyed the act. It is this public response, the fear of such a response and the belief (often) in the rationality of such a response (even from those who do unequivocally view you as a person) that seems to make rape especially horrible.

Thus, what is especially bad about rape is a function of its place in our society's sexual views, not in our ontological views. There is, of course, nothing necessary about these views, but until they change, no matter what progress is made in the fight for equality between the sexes, rape will remain an especially awful act.

II. Sex, Intimacy, and Pleasure

Our response to rape brings into focus our inner feelings about the nature, purpose, and moral-

ity of all sexual encounters and of ourselves as sexual beings. Two areas which seem immediately problematic are the relation between sex and intimacy and the relation between sex and pleasure.

Our Victorian ancestors believed that sex in the absence of (at least marital) intimacy was morally wrong and that the only women who experienced sexual pleasure were nymphomaniacs.[4] Freud's work was revolutionary in part just because he challenged the view of "good" women and children as asexual creatures.[5] Only with Masters and Johnson's work, however, has there been a full scientific recognition of the capacity of ordinary women for sexual pleasure.[6] But though it is now recognized that sexual pleasure exists for all people at all stages of life and is, in its own right, a morally permissible goal, this contemporary attitude is still dominated by a Victorian atmosphere. It remains the common feeling that it is a kind of pleasure which should be experienced only in private and only between people who are and intend to be otherwise intimate. Genital pleasure is private not only in our description of its physical location, but also in our conception of its occurrence or occasion.

For the rape victim, the special problem created by the discovery of pleasure in sex is that now some people believe that *every* sex act must be pleasurable to some extent, including rape.[7] Thus, it is believed by some that the victim in a rape must at some level be enjoying herself—and that this enjoyment in a non-intimate, non-private environment is shameful. What is especially wrong about rape, therefore, is that it makes evident the essentially sexual nature of women, and this has been viewed, from the time of Eve through the time of Victoria, as cause for their humiliation. Note that on this view the special evil of rape is due to the feminine character and not to that of her attacker.[8]

The additional societal attitude that sex is moral only between intimates creates a further dilemma in assessing the situation of the rape victim.

---

[4]Francoise Basch, *Relative Creatures: Victorian Women in Society and the Novel* (New York: Schocken Books, 1974), pp. 8–9, 270–71.

[5]See *The Basic Writings of Sigmund Freud,* ed. A. A. Brill (New York: Random House, 1948), pp. 553–633.

[6]William H. Masters and Virginia E. Johnson, *Human Sexual Response* (Boston: Little, Brown, 1966).

[7]It may well be that Freud's theory of human sexuality is mistakenly taken to support this view. See Sigmund Freud, *A General Introduction to Psychoanalysis* (New York: Washington Square Press, 1962), pp. 329–47.

[8]What is a complete non sequitur, of course, is that the presence of such pleasure is sufficient to establish that no criminal assault has occurred. The two events are completely independent.

On the one hand, if it is believed that the sex act itself creates an intimate relationship between two people, then, by necessity, the rape victim experiences intimacy with her assailant. This may incline one to deny the fact of the rape by pointing to the fact of the intimacy. If one does not believe that sex itself creates intimacy between the actors, but nonetheless believes that sex is immoral in the absence of intimacy, then the event of sex in the absence of an intimate relationship, even though involuntary, is cause for public scorn and humiliation. For the rape victim, to acknowledge the rape is to acknowledge one's immorality. Either way, the victim has violated the social sexual taboos and she must therefore be ostracized.

What is important is no longer that one is the victim of an assault, but rather that one is the survivor of a social transgression. This is the special burden that the victim carries.

There is support for my view in Gary Wills' review of Tom Wicker's book about the Attica prisoners' revolt.[9] What needs to be explained is the apparently peculiar way in which the safety of the prisoners' hostages was ignored in the preparations for the assault on the prison and in the assault itself. What strikes me as especially important in this event is that those outside the prison walls treated the *guards* exactly like the *prisoners.* The critical similarity is the alleged participation in taboo sexual activity, where such activity is seen as a paradigm of humiliating behavior. In his review Wills says,

Sexual fantasy played around Attica's walls like invisible lightning. Guards told their families that all the inmates were animals. . . .

When the assault finally came, and officers mowed down the hostages along with the inmates, an almost religious faith kept faked stories alive against all the evidence—that the hostages were found castrated; that those still living had been raped. . . . None of it was true, but the guards knew what degradation the prisoners had been submitted to, and the kind of response that might call for. . . .

One has to go very far down into the human psyche to understand what went on in that placid town. . . . The bloodthirsty hate of the local community was so obvious by the time of the assault that even Rockefeller . . . ordered that no

correction personnel join the attack. . . . [Nonetheless] eleven men managed to go in. . . . Did they come to save the hostages, showing more care for them than outsiders could? Far from it. They fired as early and indiscriminately as the rest. Why? I am afraid Mr. Wicker is a bit too decent to understand what was happening, though his own cultural background gives us a clue. Whenever a white girl was caught with a black in the old South, myth demanded that a charge of rape be brought and the "boy" be lynched. But a shadowy ostracism was inflicted on the girl. Did she fight back? Might she undermine the myth with a blurted tale or a repeated episode? At any rate, she was tainted. She had, willed she or nilled she, touched the untouchable and acquired her own evil halo of contamination. Taboos take little account of "intention." In the same way, guards caught in that yard were tainted goods. . . . They were an embarrassment. The white girl may sincerely have struggled with her black assailant; but even to imagine that resistance was defiling—and her presence made people imagine it. She was a public pollution—to be purged. Is this [comparison] fanciful? Even Wicker . . . cannot understand the attitude of those in charge who brought no special medical units to Attica before the attack began. . . . The lynch mob may kill the girl in its urgency to get at the boy—and it will regret this less than it admits.[10]

Accounts like the one offered by Frye and Shafer might explain why the *prisoners* were treated so callously by the assaulting troops, but they cannot explain the brutal treatment of the hostages. Surely they cannot say that the guards who were hostages were not and had never been viewed as people, as ontological equals, by the general society. And yet there was the same special horror in being a hostage at Attica as there is for a woman who has been raped. In both cases the *victim* has acquired a "halo of contamination" which permanently taints. And this cannot be explained by claiming that in both cases society is denying personhood or domains of consent to the victim.

The victim in sexual assault cases is as much a victim of our confused beliefs about sex as of the assault itself. The tremendous strains we put on such victims are a cruel result of our deep confusion

[9]Tom Wicker, *A Time to Die* (New York: Quadrangle Books, 1975).

[10]Gary Wills, "The Human Sewer," *New York Review of Books,* 3 April 1975, p. 4.

about the place of, and need for, sexual relationships and the role of pleasure and intimacy in those relationships.

In spite of the fact, I believe, that as a society we share the *belief* that sex is only justified in intimate relationships, we act to avoid real intimacy at almost any cost. We seem to be as baffled as our predecessors were about the place of intimacy in our sexual and social lives. And this is, I think, because we are afraid that real intimacy creates or unleashes sexually wanton relationships, licentious lives—and this we view as morally repugnant. At the same time, we believe that sex in the absence of an intimate relationship is whoring and is therefore also morally repugnant. It is this impossible conflict which I think shows us that we will be able to make sense of our response to rape only if we look at rape as the model of all our sexual interactions, not as its antithesis.

III. The Model of Sex: Rape

Though we may sometimes speak as though sexual activity is most pleasurable between friends, we do not teach each other to treat our sexual partners as friends. Middle-class children, whom I take to be our cultural models, are instructed from the earliest possible time to ignore their sexual feelings. Long before intercourse can be a central issue, when children are prepubescent, boys are instructed to lunge for a kiss and girls are instructed to permit nothing more than a peck on the cheek. This encouragement of miniature adult sexual behavior is instructive on several levels.

It teaches the child that courting behavior is rarely spontaneous and rarely something which gives pleasure to the people involved—that is, it is not like typical playing with friends. It gives the child a glimpse of how adults do behave, or are expected to behave, and therefore of what is expected in future life and social interactions. Importantly, boys are instructed *not* to be attentive to the claims of girls with respect to their desires and needs. And girls are instructed *not* to consult their feelings as a means of or at least a check on what behavior they should engage in.

Every American girl, be she philosopher-to-be or not, is well acquainted with the slippery-slope argument by the time she is ten. She is told that if she permits herself to become involved in anything more than a peck on the cheek, anything but the most innocent type of sexual behavior, she will inevitably become involved in behavior that will result in intercourse and pregnancy. And such behavior is wrong. That is, she is told that if she acquiesces to any degree to her feelings, then she will be doing something immoral.

Meanwhile, every American boy is instructed, whether explicitly or not, that the girls have been given this argument (as a weapon) and that therefore, since everything that a girl says will be a reflection of this argument (and not of her feelings), they are to ignore everything that she says.

Girls are told never to consult their feelings (they can only induce them to the edge of the slippery slope); they are always to say "no." Boys are told that it is a sign of their growing manhood to be able to get a girl way beyond the edge of the slope, and that it is standard procedure for girls to say "no" independently of their feelings. Thus, reasonably enough, boys act as far as one can tell independently of the explicit information they are currently receiving from the girl.

For women, it is very disconcerting to find that from the age of eight or nine or ten, one's reports of one's feelings are no longer viewed as accurate, truthful, important, or interesting. R. D. Laing, the English psychiatrist and theorist, claims that it is this type of adult behavior which creates the environment in which insanity best finds its roots.[11] It is clear, at least, that such behavior is not a model of rationality or health. In any event, rape is a case where only the pretense of listening has been stripped away. It is the essence of what we have all been trained to expect.

In a sexually healthier society, men and women might be told to engage in that behavior which gives them pleasure as long as that pleasure is not (does not involve actions) against anyone's will (including coerced actions) and does not involve them with responsibilities they cannot or will not meet (emotional, physical, or financial).

But as things are now, boys and girls have no way to tell each other what gives them pleasure and what not, what frightens them and what not; there are only violence, threats of violence, and appeals to informing on one or the other to some dreaded peer or parental group. This is a very high-risk, high-stake game, which women and girls, at least, often feel may easily become rape (even though it is usually

[11]See, for example, R. D. Laing and A. Esterson, *Sanity, Madness and the Family* (Baltimore: Penguin, Pelican Books, 1970).

played for little more than a quick feel in the back seat of the car or corner of the family sofa). But the ultimate consequences of this type of instruction are not so petty. Consider, for example, the effects of a recent English high-court decision:

Now, according to the new interpretation, no matter how much a woman screams and fights, the accused rapist can be cleared by claiming he believed the victim consented, even though his belief may be considered unreasonable or irrational.

On a rainy night seven months ago, a London housewife and mother of three claims she was dragged into this dilapidated shed. Annie Baker says she screamed for help and she fought but she was raped. Mrs. Baker lost her case in court because the man claimed he thought when she said no, she meant yes.

One member of Parliament [predicts juries will] "now have the rapist saying that the woman asked for what she got and she wanted what they [sic] gave her."

However, the Head of the British Law Society maintains, "Today juries are prepared to accept that the relationship between the sexes has become much more promiscuous, and they have to look much more carefully to see whether the woman has consented under modern conditions. . . . One mustn't readily assume that a woman did not consent, because all indications are that there is a greater willingness to consent today than there was thirty years ago."[12]

"The question to be answered in this case," said Lord Cross of Chelsea, "as I see it, is whether, according to the ordinary use of the English language, a man can be said to have committed rape if he believed that the woman was consenting to the intercourse. I do not think he can."[13]

This is the most macabre extension imaginable of our early instruction. It is one which makes initially implausible and bizarre any suggestion that the recent philosophical analyses of sexuality as the product of a mutual desire for communication—or even for orgasm or sexual satisfaction—bear any but the most tangential relation to reality.[14]

As we are taught, sexual desires are desires women ought not to have and men must have. This is the model which makes necessary an eternal battle of the sexes. It is the model which explains why rape is the prevalent model of sexuality. It has the further virtue of explaining the otherwise puzzling attitude of many that women will cry "rape" falsely at the slightest provocation. It explains, too, why men believe that no woman can be raped. It is as though what was mildly unsatisfactory at first (a girl's saying "no") becomes, over time, increasingly erotic, until the ultimate turn-on becomes a woman's cry of "rape!"

IV. An Alternative: Sex Between Friends

Understanding what's wrong with rape is difficult just because it is a member of the most common species of social encounter. To establish how rape is wrong is to establish that we have *all* been stepping to the wrong beat. Rape is only different in degree from the quintessential sexual relationship: marriage.

As Janice Moulton has noted, recent philosophical attention to theories of sexuality seem primarily concerned with sex between strangers.[15] On my view, we can explain this primary interest by noticing that our courting procedures are structured so that the couple must remain essentially estranged from each other. They do not ever talk or listen to each other with the respect and charity of friends. Instead, what is taken as the height of the erotic is sex without intimacy.

As long as we remain uncertain of the legitimacy of sexual pleasure, it will be impossible to give up our rape model of sexuality. For it can only be given up when we are willing to talk openly to each other without shame, embarrassment, or coyness about sex. Because only then will we not be too afraid to listen to each other.

Fortunately, to give this up requires us to make friends of our lovers.[16] Once we understand that intimacy enlarges the field of friendship, we can use some of the essential features of friendship as part of the model for sexual interaction, and we can present the pleasures of friendship as a real alternative to predatory pleasures.

[12]CBS Evening News with Walter Cronkite, 22 May 1975.
[13]*New American Movement Newspaper*, May 1975, p. 8.
[14]See R. C. Solomon, "Sex and Perversion," Tom Nagel, "Sexual Perversion," and Janice Moulton, "Sex and Reference," [see chapter 3, this volume, pp. 103–108—eds.] in *Philosophy and Sex*, ed. Robert Baker and Frederick Elliston (Buffalo, N.Y.: Prometheus Books, 1975).

[15]Janice Moulton, "Sex and Sex," unpublished manuscript.
[16]See Lyla O'Driscoll, "On the Nature and Value of Marriage" [in *Feminism and Philosophy*—eds.]. She argues that marriage and the sexual relations it entails should be based on friendship rather than romantic love.

I am not here committing myself to the view that the correct model for lovers is that of friends. Though I believe lovers involved in a healthy relationship have a fairly complex friendship, and though I am at a loss to find any important feature of a relationship between lovers which is not also one between friends, it may well be that the two relationships are merely closely related and not, in the end, explainable with the identical model.

It remains an enormously difficult task to throw over our anachronistic beliefs, and to resolve the conflict we feel about the sexual aspects of ourselves. But once this is done, not only will there be the obvious benefits of being able to exchange ignorance and denial of ourselves and others for knowledge, and fear for friendship, but we will also be able to remove the taboo from sex—even from rape. There will be no revelation, no reminder in the act of rape which we will need so badly to repress or deny that we must transform the victim into a guilt-bearing survivor. An act of rape will no longer remind us of the "true" nature of sex and our sexual desires.

Where there is nothing essentially forbidden about the fact of our sexual desires, the victim of rape will no longer be subject to a taboo or be regarded as dirty and in need of societal estrangement. The victim can then be regarded as having been grievously insulted, without simultaneously and necessarily having been permanently injured.

Further, if the model of sexual encounters is altered, there will no longer be any motivation for blaming the victim of rape. Since sex and rape will no longer be equated, there will be no motive for covering our own guilt or shame about the rapine nature of sex in general by transferring our guilt to the victim and ostracizing her. Rape will become an unfortunate aberration, the act of a criminal individual, rather than a symbol of our systematic ill-treatment and denial of each other.

4
Love

21/Love and Dependency

Sharon Bishop

This is an essay about the sentiment of love in a certain kind of relationship: one between two persons who are at least young adults. Their relationship is sexual, and they may be of the same or different sex. They intend to maintain their relationship for the indefinite future, unless there is some special reason for terminating it that is not associated with their feelings for each other. Their careers might, for example, take them to opposite ends of the country. Their feelings for each other may change over time, but just now they see them as going on indefinitely. If their feelings do change, it will not be simply because their hair has turned color, they lost a few pounds, or their income has fluctuated. It is not that they know what will or will not—or should or should not—lead to changes in their feelings, but that their feelings and attitudes are associated with what are to them important features of their personalities. Of course, what is important to them in this regard can change.

I pick this kind of relationship because it is one that interests very many of us and because there are a number of opinions about the nature of love and dependency that make it difficult, if not impossible, to understand why any moderately healthy and sensible adult would want such a relationship. There is, for example, the theory that the aim of love is to possess another person and to deprive that person of his or her relations with other people.[1] And some have said that the object of love is a set of charac-

teristics that make the loved person appear preeminently beautiful, good, or virtuous. This object may require a certain loss of realism in lovers, and, even in fortuitous circumstances, it puts a high premium on maintaining beauty, goodness, or virtue. There is Freud's view that love is either narcissistic or dependent; that is, either the object of love is some version of yourself that you see in your lover or else it is someone upon whom you can lean. Finally, there are feminists who write that personal relations are political, that men and women cannot have healthy love relations because inevitably, or inevitably in our culture, women are dependent on men psychologically and economically. When filled out, each of these theories can seem quite insightful about the love relations we see in fiction and real life. However, they seem mainly to help us understand relations that are discomforting or have gone awry. Their impact is pessimistic; and, if they are used to project what future relations might be like or as a base for comments about what is possible in adult love relations, it is puzzling why people want such relations. It is also difficult to see how these theories can be used to discuss what it is sensible to want and aim for in adult love relations.

To discuss the attitude of love in these relations, my strategy will be to sketch a set of feelings and attitudes that persons in a relationship of this sort might have, or, more accurately, might have during good days and years. I will take the point of view of someone who is trying to understand what those attitudes are like to those who have them. I want to talk about what they are like from the inside, but I will not restrict the sketch to what anyone

[1] This and the following three views can be found respectively in J. P. Sartre, *Being and Nothingness,* trans. Hazel Barnes (New York: Philosophical Library, 1956), pp. 361–430; Plato, *Symposium,* trans. Walter Hamilton (Baltimore: Penguin Books, 1951); and Rousseau, *Emile,* trans. Barbara Foxley (London: Dent & Sons; New York: Dutton, 1911), pp. 321–444; Sigmund Freud, "On Narcissism," in *General Pscyhological Theory* (New York: Collier, 1963), pp. 68–72; and in Shulamith Firestone, *The Dialectic of Sex* (New York: William Morrow, 1970), this volume, pp. 154–159 and 200–205.

I wish to thank members of the Pacific Division of the Society for Women in Philosophy, especially Ann Garry, for their help and comments.

actually feels or could articulate about what one feels. The result will be idealized in a number of ways. I don't, for example, intend this theory to describe the attitude of love in most persons. Saying anything both plausible and interesting about most people's attitudes seems very hard because there is so much variation even within one culture and time period. Nor do I intend the theory to describe the day to day feelings of the persons I imagine to be in the love relation. Notoriously such feelings vary according to mood, circumstances, problems, and whatnot. And I am not describing the capacity of persons for love relationships. I am trying to describe or characterize the feelings and attitudes of a person who regards a certain relation as important, of someone who wants it, plans for it, and makes room for it, either consciously or behaviorally. There will, I hope, be some connection between the idealized picture and the attitudes and ideals of some, for I want to characterize the features that make these attitudes ones many of us understandably want, and so the sorts of attitudes we want to develop the capacity for.

First, the sentiment of love is a natural one. I do not mean that people are born with it or even that they will inevitably come to have it in the course of their lives, nor do I mean that it would be unnatural never to have the attitude. In saying that it is natural, I contrast it with moral and institutional attitudes like a sense of duty or loyalty to a company or school.[2] It is characteristic of these latter feelings that one cannot have them unless one is committed to principles of duty or a humanly contrived institution. For example, I cannot pay my vet bill from a sense of obligation unless I accept something like the principle that I ought to pay my bills, or anyway my vet bills. I can pay them out of other motives like embarrassment or fear of her collection agency. Likewise, I cannot act out of loyalty to a company unless I have an attachment to it as an institution. Natural attitudes include such things as likings, aversions, attachments, disgust, attraction, admiration, awe, trust, fear, anger, and so on. Characterization of these as natural does not require reference to moral principles or humanly contrived institutions or conventions. The attitudes themselves are outgrowths of naturally occurring human capacities.

The fact that these attitudes are natural means that they need not be expressed through any institution and that the characteristic behavior associated with them is not rule governed and does not require an institutional setting or background. It does not mean that they cannot be expressed institutionally, but where they are, for example, in an exchange of rings, part of the point must always be to express a natural feeling, in this case strong affection and commitment. If a lover finds out later that the exchange meant only that her partner was achieving status in institutionally recognized ways, she would feel betrayed or foolish. Or if she discovers that the exchange meant only that to her, she may feel ashamed. If it is love that she has or receives, then inevitably at least part of what she wants from it or wants to give by it are natural satisfactions, for example, comfort, joy, security, stimulation, sharing, excitement, and the like. A main point is that a lover's interests cannot be solely to conform to a moral principle or an institutional role but to some extent must be in a loved person.

It has been said that personal relations are political. This could be interpreted to mean that the sentiment of love cannot be characterized without referring to some political institutions or power struggle; that is, it could be taken as the claim that personal relations are essentially political. I think it is a necessary and important feature of the sentiment of love that it is not political in this sense. If it were, the behavior characteristic of the attitude could only be understood by seeing it as behavior intended to conform to the appropriate institution. Instead we seem to view evidence that a person's motive is to fulfill some institutional role as evidence that that person does not love. Sometimes people do want to fulfill institutional roles, for example, to be a good wife or father. But the discovery that a person's central motivation in a personal relationship is to fill that role successfully is taken as evidence that the love is less than she thought or that she didn't love at all, as in "I thought I loved him, but I really just wanted to be the wife of a tennis pro."

The claim that love is a natural sentiment is not, however, incompatible with some other ways of taking "the personal is political." It seems correct, for example, that personal relations as they occur in our culture cannot be understood very well unless

[2] A similar distinction is found in Hume's contrast between the natural and artificial virtues, *Treatise on Human Nature,* ed. L. A. Selby-Bigge (Oxford, 1888), Book III, Parts II and III. John Rawls distinguishes between the moral and natural sentiments in characterizing a sense of justice. He also discusses some of the relations between moral and natural sentiments in *A Theory of Justice* (Cambridge, Mass.: Harvard University Press, 1971), pp. 477–484, 574–606, 614–617.

we face the ways in which the people involved engage in role playing and power tactics. An important fact about societies is that people in them are taught, among other things, some way of behaving in their intimate relations. And an important fact about our society is that it teaches women to be passive and obedient while encouraging men to take charge and exercise authority. It also seems correct that people will not fully understand their love lives until they understand what it is they've been taught and what the effects of playing out those roles are. Once they are more articulate about what has been taught and so about what tendencies they are likely to have in intimate relations, they'll understand their actual behavior more thoroughly, and they'll certainly be in a better position to think about the cost of changing the ways they relate. Anyone's behavior in an intimate personal relation may conform quite closely to taught ways, but if a lover's sole object in relating to one she 'loves' is to conform to these ways, then she doesn't have or maintain feelings of love.

While love is a natural sentiment and so can occur and be expressed outside institutional settings, it can also be expressed in institutional settings. For example, marriage is a very complex institution serving numerous purposes. It regulates reproduction and family life and serves as a way of creating economic units and responsibilities. In our culture, it is also designed to provide a setting in which two people publicly express their love and commit themselves to their mutual good. The public commitment places certain constraints on the rest of the community to refrain from interfering with the couple's intimacy. The married partners also place themselves under certain constraints, which presumably provide a good setting for maintaining and deepening their sentiments of love. Their willingness to commit themselves in this way is supposed to be an expression of the strength of their feelings and intentions. The actual effects of an institution of marriage on the sentiment of love may be quite pernicious on the whole. It may, familiarly enough, create inequalities in power and authority between the lovers, or consistently place larger burdens for maintaining the relationship on one of the partners. Whatever the actual effects of an institution on the lives of those who try to make it work for them, there can be an understandable interest in having an institution available that regulates and protects love relations, and through which people can express their commitment to one another. Thus homosexu-

als or couples who emphatically do not wish to found a family may have an interest in it.

A second important feature of the sentiment of love is that it is directed toward an object, and that the object is a particular individual. In general, objects of feelings and attitudes are the things they are directed toward. This makes them the things through which and against which people satisfy the desires that make up their attitudes. For example, if I like trout fishing, it is through trout fishing that I satisfy the desires that make up my liking. If I am angry at a friend, then the desires that make up my anger can only be *satisfied* through her, perhaps by telling her off.

In having an object, love is different from moods that apparently are not directed toward or away from anything. They are just states in which we find ourselves, for example, unaccountably cheerful or grumpy. In having a particular person as an object, love is like hate and revenge and unlike hunger or craving. Simple hunger, for example, can be satisfied by ice cream, snails, cookies, or smoked eel. Hunger for pizza can be satisfied by any number of equally good pizzas. However, a desire for revenge is not satisfied unless the very person who humiliated or harmed you is in turn "done in" by you. The desire may be dissipated or covered over, perhaps by running a marathon or swimming the English Channel, but these activities would not satisfy it. Likewise, the sort of love that can exist between persons has a particular individual as its object. Doubtless there are other sorts of love, too. People who love roses like to look at them, prefer them to other flowers, and appreciate especially beautiful ones. But in choosing among good roses, they are indifferent about which ones they take home. Some people love humankind in this sense, that is, they want to see people prosper, they are dismayed by anyone's pain, and perhaps they even appreciate and like fine examples of human beings. However, anyone's prospering will satisfy the desires associated with this kind of love. Love of pets, a child's attachment to a favorite doll or truck, our interest in souvenirs or meaningful gifts all seem quite different. Having been given a copy of *Anna Karenina* by a special friend on a special occasion, I will not be satisfied with just any copy of equally good quality; it is *that* copy that I want to keep, read, and preserve. If I do not, then my interest in the book is more general. Perhaps it is beautifully bound or well illustrated. If my interest is of the latter sort, then any equally well-bound or illustrated copy will do for me. Similarly if I love somone, it is *that* person whom I care for, wish well for, want to do things with, and so on. If I cannot do something to express my interest in that person, then I cannot express my love or satisfy the desires I have in loving. Again, I may deflect the desires or develop other attachments, but I cannot love if I do not have desires and attitudes that have some particular individual as their object. When someone I love leaves me, I care what happens to that person, not just to people like him. If my feelings toward him are predominantly friendly, then I want him to do well; I may care very little what happens to persons like him. Or if I am predominantly angry, then I may wish that he'll fall in a hole. It would not be sufficient for someone like him to fall in a hole (though it might help).

The object of an attitude or feeling should be distinguished from what causes it. For example, I am frightened at the shadowy dark presence at the far side of the camp site, what causes the fright is a harmless bush. The object of my love is Harry; what causes it is Harry's combination of seriousness and insouciance. With respect to love, this distinction is important because many theories about love seem to be about what causes various people to find others attractive. Such theories are only part of the story. To understand the sentiment one also needs to know what it is directed toward, for the object of love is one of the things that limit what could count as behavior characteristic or expressive of it. Thus if I love someone, then I must have certain attitudes toward that person. In everyday life it is often difficult to know whether we care for each other as persons or solely for what we can do for each other. But if someone I care for seems fickle or inconstant regarding me, that may be evidence that they are not attached to me. Noting the marks of severe neurotic dependency in another may lead one to conclude that one is cared for, not for oneself, but for the needs one satisfies. Or glorifying my friends may be evidence that I am attracted to them for characteristics I see as particularly estimable or admirable, but not to them as individuals. That the object of love is a particular person sets limits on what kinds of things can be expressive of the attitude. Moreover, the fact that the object of love is a particular person picks out some of the legitimate complaints that can be exchanged between lovers. By legitimate complaints I do not mean ones that are morally justifiable, but ones that establish that presumed feelings are not there or are directed toward inappropriate objects;

for example, you don't love me, but my money; you don't care about me, you only wanted a father for your children; or you never loved me, you just thought it was fun to be 'in love' with me; and so on.

The particularity of objects of love is connected with the notion that to be loved is to be singled out in a special way. If I am loved, someone has certain attitudes and feelings toward me. What makes me special is not that I am the exclusive recipient of loving feelings from that person, but that the feelings are directed toward me, and not just toward certain features I have that may be attractive. The behavior expressive of these attitudes will characteristically be encouraging to me and my interests, not just characteristic of promoting the existence and multiplication of the features in virtue of which I am attractive. For example, if I am found attractive because I delight in opera, the behavior characteristic of love will be supportive of *my* interest in opera, not of opera in general. Thus it might take the form of helping me attend special performances, but not necessarily of support for the Metropolitan Opera Company, making good quality performances available to large numbers of people, or encouraging young singers. If this is correct, then being singled out by love is to be found attractive and supported for one's person and not necessarily to be the only recipient of those attitudes from that person. This means that exclusivity is not an essential or defining feature of loving someone, and that the interest in exclusivity has some other explanation. Loving and expressing one's love take time and energy; perhaps there is not enough for more than one love. Or perhaps not being the exclusive object of love raises reasonable doubts about the love or a lover's capacity to love one for oneself. The doubts would be reasonable not because one cannot love nonexclusively, but because exclusivity of affection is particularly good assurance that appropriate sentiments underlie a lover's interests.

So far I have only considered some very general features of the sentiment of love; namely, that it is a natural sentiment with particular persons as its object. Other features of love are more directly experienced by those who have the sentiment. First, loving someone involves liking her, finding her attractive in some way and so enjoying her presence and feeling some affection for her. Secondly and more complexly, it involves caring about her. In this context caring for someone means caring about her good.

There are various theories about what constitutes a person's good. According to one, there are certain kinds of experiences that are good in themselves and not for any further purpose. Whatever list of these experiences is proposed is constitutive of anyone's good. Thus if a list includes sensuous experiences as well as experiences of friendship, beauty, and knowing, then, according to this theory, I can make a contribution to anyone's good simply by increasing her store of these experiences.

For at least two reasons we may reject theories of this kind about an individual's good. First, suppose we grant the rather large assumption that people find friendship, sensuous experience, and so on enjoyable for their own sakes. The difficulty is that there is tremendous variation in the importance of each of these things to different people, not to mention variation in availability of these goods under different conditions. What this theory leaves out is a way of ranking and coordinating these goods in an individual's life. And if one expresses concern for a lover by trying willy nilly to increase his or her store of these experiences, then one is ignoring an important aspect of the lover's good; namely, how important each of these is to her under present conditions.

Secondly, the theory seems to miss altogether a reason for doing things for a lover's good. Experiences that are good for their own sakes provide everyone the same reason for bringing them about. Thus if relief of a certain degree of pain is such an experience, then everyone has exactly the same reason to do what they can to relieve it. One person could have a better reason than another for taking some action to relieve another's pain only if he or she were in a better position to do it. Perhaps one is more skilled than another at relieving that sort of pain, or is closer and so it would be less difficult for them to do it than someone else. Thus, on this theory, to care about another's good is to relieve the pain or produce the satisfying experience as efficiently as possible; it is only rational to care about being the source of those satisfactions oneself if one is the person who can most efficiently produce them. Doubtless total disregard of efficiency in supporting one's lover's interests would indicate something important, ineptitude, perhaps, or anger. However, commitment to nothing but efficiency in supporting a lover's interests may indicate that a person is interested in playing a role and not in expressing love. Contrary to this theory, it seems that one's love and concern itself give one a reason to be the source of satisfaction or relief on certain occasions.

It is also misguided to identify an individual's good with what enables that person to perform her function well. Some people have thought that persons have some special unique human function, and that their own good consists in fulfilling it. Most often this function is thought to be whatever distinguishes people from other creatures and makes them uniquely human. Usually this is said to be their rational nature. Sometimes the theory is taken further and human beings are divided into male and female, each of which is said to have a special function, and an individual's good is identified with that function. Men and women would serve each other's good only by helping them perform their separate but unique functions, which are then associated with their different reproductive roles. However, there just do not seem to be any such functions for human beings. Though it may be true that only human beings are rational, there are other traits that only we seem to have, e.g., the inclination to laugh at others' misfortunes, an interest in sex throughout the reproductive cycle, etc. So far as I know no one has maintained, or would want to maintain, that these features of human nature are identical with human good. This indicates that unique and distinguishing features of human beings cannot be associated with an individual's good in the way these theories require. Moreover, it is easily evident that a wide variety of satisfying lives are compatible with the different part in reproduction that males and females play.

Finally, it is striking how incomplete a person's good seems on such theories. However interested someone may be in her rational and intellectual life or reproductive role, there are many other sorts of things that might bring her harmless satisfactions, for example, sex, music, horseback riding, dining with friends, overcoming fears, developing style, and so on. Sources of satisfaction like these seem especially important when we raise questions about what it is to care for and contribute to a lover's good. When things are going well, we can expect to be interested in her everyday delights as well as in her making constructive life choices expressive of her deepest interests *because* they are the delights and choices of someone we love (and not necessarily because they are intrinsically enjoyable or important to us).

One may want to know why these generalizations about love seem plausible if they do. First, taking an interest in the various things a person finds satisfying is one way of showing and expressing liking and appreciation of him. Secondly, it is a way of evidencing that one cares for him and of expressing that sentiment. This is not enough, however. What is required are reasons for thinking that everyday satisfactions as well as deeper ones are especially appropriate objects of a lover's interests. What people find satisfying and dissatisfying, how they respond to the opportunities and events of daily life are expressive of them as individuals. Their responses may not be the best imaginable but they are what are now chosen, and they are an important source of information about what a person is like. An appreciation and interest in his responses is a reaction to him as he is and to his good as he sees it, rather than as a lover may want him or need him to be. Thus interest in a more or less full range of the things a lover finds satisfying, because he finds them satisfying, is reasonably taken as evidence that the feelings toward him are love rather than admiration, awe, respect, or gratitude. They may also be taken as evidence that the interest is in his person and not in his status, level of achievement, or grace and success in playing some role.

It is difficult to offer a satisfactory characterization of an individual's good. Sometimes it is identified with whatever will give a person the best chance for happiness. This view is often accompanied with a tendency to advise, in a person's best interest, against undertaking difficult or risky projects. Possibly most people will have a better chance for a happy life if they avoid difficulties and risks, but some may want to take them on anyway. In such cases, it seems important to pay attention to what they want.

Occasionally a person's good is said to be what satisfies her needs and/or give her what she wants. But, of course, some of a person's desires can be destructive and some immediate wants incompatible with long term interests. On the face of it it seems mistaken to call a desire to cut oneself or remain in bed through an important appointment a part of one's good. Circumstances can be described where such desires should be seen as a part of an individual's good, but, then, I think they will be linked with what a person wants on reflection or would want for herself if she understood the situation and thought through the alternatives.

Various reasons can be given for identifying a person's good with what he would want on reflection, whether or not that turns out to be what other people would also judge. One such reason is that people have a *right* to make their own choices, including their own mistakes, and in taking their

wants seriously we honor this right. Although this consideration is an interesting one, it does not seem to offer appropriate reasons for taking an interest in the good of a person one loves. To fail to honor a person's rights is to fail to do the minimum required of anyone; whereas it is characteristic of lovers that they have interests in each other that distinguish them from other people. Some of the interests are directly in the good of those they love not because their lovers have a right to such consideration, but because that interest is characteristic and expressive of love. An appreciative response to a person's good as he now sees it is a response to him as he now is or is trying to be.

In general, we show that we care about something by the kind of behavior and attitudes we have surrounding it. Thus a person who cares about someone's good will be inclined to do things to support and encourage it, and to feel bad about undermining it. In some circumstances, one would be willing to give up some of the things one wants. Failure to have any of these tendencies or attitudes would indicate lack of concern for this person or perhaps incapacity to love. A person who cares about a lover's good and has these inclinations could be said to be naturally committed; that is, she supports and encourages the loved person and feels bad when she lets her lover down because she cares. She does not do it simply because she believes she *ought* to behave in this manner toward those she loves. The wish for a commitment of this sort may be behind the suspicion about marriage, that it creates duties and obligations between persons, where caring and inclination are appropriate.

In addition to liking another person and caring about their good, a lover will normally want reciprocation of her feelings and interests. No one wants unrequited love unless there is something she needs to discover with her analyst or unless certain other circumstances obtain.[3] The reciprocity desired in this case is for a return of the same feeling. That is, a lover wants to be liked, and to have her concern returned at a similar level of intensity and complexity. This feature of adult love may be one thing that distinguishes it from parent-child love. Loving parents care about their children's good, but they don't expect that to be returned at the same level.

---

[3] Here I have in mind cases in which reciprocating love involves a conflict with personal integrity in some way. Then there may be some tendency to wish that one's love not be returned. The most familiar examples of this type occur in nineteenth century tales in which someone falls in love with a married person who has a serious, personal commitment to marriage.

Liking another person, being concerned about her good and desiring reciprocity are each constitutive elements of the sentiment of love. If any of these is missing, there is, at least, a presumption that the attitudes toward the other person are not love but something else. That is, unless some acceptable explanation can be given, that the feature is missing is conclusive evidence that the feelings are not love. Limits for acceptable explanations are set by the constitutive features of love. Thus, if someone does not want her love reciprocated, then the explanation must come from a conflict created by another constitutive element of love, for example, desiring a lover's good and believing that his good is incompatible with returning this particular love. I am uncertain whether there really are cases of this sort, but it is important to notice that we could understand this as genuine love; whereas not wanting reciprocation because one is unable to accept love reflects on a person's capacity for love.

Sometimes jealousy is treated as constitutive of love. Lucy complains to Ethyl that Ricky isn't jealous of a high school sweetheart, and zany plans are made to force him to realize that he is and thus to prove his love. Although this requires a more thorough investigation of jealousy, it seems more accurate to say that loving someone creates a liability to jealousy. In love persons are prone to experience anger, frustration, or loss of self-esteem from disappointments and dissatisfactions, but this results from the intensity and importance of the desires that develop as love, not from the character of the desires themselves. Similarly things that are experienced as interfering with, or threatening to, the continued enjoyment of love result in jealousy.

To conclude, I want to discuss some of the connections between the sentiment of love and dependency. "Dependency" is quite often used in a perjorative sense, and talk of one person's dependency on another is taken as an indication that the relation is unhealthy and the dependency morbid. However, another neutral sense is required, if one is to raise questions about whether and/or to what extent lovers may depend on each other and remain moderately healthy adults. Let us say that one person is dependent on another if her desires cannot be satisfied unless the other person is present, has certain attitudes or acts in certain ways.

With respect to the sentiment of love characterized above, it is evident that loving someone is sufficient to create innumerable lover dependent desires. Lovers want to be with one another, and

to express their interest in, and attraction to, each other. This requires the loved person's presence, acceptance, and sensitivity. They may wish to support each other's interests by sharing them in some way. Success in doing this depends on being allowed to share and on having one's sharing seen as supporting and reinforcing. Reciprocation of one's feelings and attitudes of course depends on the other person having them. Loving does, then, involve having interests and desires that can only be satisfied through the person one loves. However, none of these interests, which are essential to love, seem destructive or unhealthy; quite the contrary.

There are other dependent desires often present in intimate relations that may or may not be benign. For example, sometimes people want a lover to be the person who provides relief from various daily pains and discomforts. It may be difficult in real life situations to distinguish between benign desires for relief which one wishes to satisfy through a lover and similar morbid ones. In the first case, what a person wants is relief through some particular person. Here the relief comes not from avoiding the pain, but from having one's lover appreciate the situation one is in and sympathizing. Desires of this type can be satisfied, and normally satisfaction would give rise to feelings of gratitude or increased affection. If the dependency is unhealthy, what is desired is the avoidance of suffering or that the suffering be someone else's. Such desires cannot be satisfied, though notoriously people can project their own sufferings onto others, particularly onto those to whom they are close; that is, they can believe that a particular discomfort is someone else's and not theirs. While this may provide some considerable relief, it is not a desire that could in principle be satisfied; for one wants a particular discomfort that one is now experiencing as one's not to be one's. This situation is bound to create further frustration and probably anger at the intimate who inevitably fails to satisfy one's desire.

In general, a person can be benignly dependent on another for the satisfaction of many of her desires so long as what she wants is return of her feelings, sharing with another person, and the like. The feature of a person's dependent desires that makes them unhealthy is that the object of her desires is to avoid developing her own interests, standards and plans. Thus whether one person is morbidly dependent on another does not depend on whether she has desires that only a particular person can satisfy, but on whether the object of her interest is to engage and share life's problems and joys, or to avoid them and live through another person. Loving may seem dangerous because of uncertainties a person has about the object of her interest, and these uncertainties can be exacerbated or even created by social conditions. For example, many women in our culture have been discouraged in more or less subtle ways from developing interests in creative and constructive work outside a family. And this may contribute to their more frequent (if it is more frequent) inclination to live vicariously. The basis for these problems about dependency, however, seems not to be with what love is, but rather with the capacities people have developed to find and direct their energies to healthy ends. The development of these capacities depends on a variety of factors including personal strength, idiosyncratic experience and social arrangements.

There are other kinds of dependency which come up in discussions of intimate relations to which these distinctions are not obviously related; for example, psychological dependency is created in women who lack economic power and indepen-

dence. There is the fact, too, that when positions of power are closed to women they become dependent on men for the satisfactions of exercising power. Dependencies of these types doubtless affect our intimate relations in interesting and discoverable ways. They don't, however, seem to be aspects of the sentiment of love, but rather ways in which the institutions of our culture affect our intimate personal lives. A full exploration of the theme of dependency would involve ways in which these factors influence our love lives.

In summary and returning to an earlier line of thought to the effect that lovers are appropriately concerned about each other's good: It is evident that this can translate into caring about their independent interests as well as their dependent ones. This means that appreciating the independent interests of someone we love is one way of evidencing love. The sentiment of love, then, creates lover dependent desires, but it also may involve direct concern for the independent interests of those we love. These interests may conflict, and then our love lives will be difficult; but then they are.

22/Love and Women's Oppression
Shulamith Firestone

Love

A book on radical feminism that did not deal with love would be a political failure. For love, perhaps even more than childbearing, is the pivot of women's oppression today. I realize this has frightening implications: Do we want to get rid of love?

The panic felt at any threat to love is a good clue to its political significance. Another sign that love is central to any analysis of women or sex psychology is its omission from culture itself, its relegation to "personal life." (And whoever heard of logic in the bedroom?) Yes, it is portrayed in novels, even metaphysics, but in them it is described, or better, recreated, not analyzed. Love has never

been *understood,* though it may have been fully *experienced,* and that experience communicated.

There is reason for this absence of analysis: *Women and Love are underpinnings. Examine them and you threaten the very structure of culture.*

The tired question "What were women doing while men created masterpieces?" deserves more than the obvious reply: Women were barred from culture, exploited in their role of mother. Or its reverse: Women had no need for paintings since they created children. Love is tied to culture in much deeper ways than that. Men were thinking, writing, and creating, because women were pouring their energy into those men; women are not creating culture because they are preoccupied with love.

That women live for love and men for work is a truism. Freud was the first to attempt to ground this dichotomy in the individual psyche: the male child, sexually rejected by the first person in his attention, his mother, "sublimates" his "libido"—his reservoir of sexual (life) energies—into long term projects, in the hope of gaining love in a more generalized form; thus he displaces his need for love into a need for recognition. This process does not occur as much in the female: most women never stop seeking direct warmth and approval.

There is also much truth in the clichés that "behind every man there is a woman," and that "women are the power behind [read: voltage in] the throne." (Male) culture was built on the love of women, and at their expense. Women provided the substance of those male masterpieces; and for millennia they have done the work, and suffered the costs, of one-way emotional relationships the benefits of which went to men and to the work of men. So if women are a parasitical class living off, and at the margins of, the male economy, the reverse too is true: *(Male) culture was (and is) parasitical, feeding on the emotional strength of women without reciprocity.*

Moreover, we tend to forget that this culture is not universal, but rather sectarian, presenting only half the spectrum. The very structure of culture itself, as we shall see, is saturated with the sexual polarity, as well as being in every degree run by, for, and in the interests of male society. But while the male half is termed all of culture, men have not forgotten there is a female "emotional" half: They live it on the sly. As the result of their battle to reject the female in themselves (the Oedipus Complex as we have explained it) they are unable to take love seriously as a cultural matter; but they can't do without it altogether. Love is the underbelly of (male) culture just as love is the weak spot of every man, bent on proving his virility in that large male world of "travel and adventure." Women have always known how men need love, and how they deny this need. Perhaps this explains the peculiar contempt women so universally feel for men ("men are so dumb"), for they can see their men are posturing in the outside world. . . .

The Culture of Romance

So far we have not distinguished "romance" from love. For there are no two kinds of love, one

healthy (dull) and one not (painful) ("My dear, what you need is a mature love relationship. Get over this romantic nonsense."), but only less-than-love or daily agony. When love takes place in a power context, everyone's "love life" must be affected. Because power and love don't make it together.

So when we talk about romantic love we mean love corrupted by its power context—the sex class system—into a diseased form of love that then in turn reinforces this sex class system. We have seen that the psychological dependence of women upon men is created by continuing real economic and social oppression. However, in the modern world the economic and social bases of the oppression are no longer *alone* enough to maintain it. So the apparatus of romanticism is hauled in. (Looks like we'll have to help her out, Boys!)

Romanticism develops in proportion to the liberation of women from their biology. As civilization advances and the biological bases of sex class crumble, male supremacy must shore itself up with artificial institutions, or exaggerations of previous institutions, e.g., where previously the family had a loose, permeable form, it now tightens and rigidifies into the patriarchal nuclear family. Or, where formerly women had been held openly in contempt, now they are elevated to states of mock worship.[1] Romanticism is a cultural tool of male power to keep women from knowing their condition. It is especially needed—and therefore strongest—in Western countries with the highest rate of industrialization. Today, with technology enabling women to break out of their roles for good—it was a near miss in the early twentieth century—romanticism is at an all-time high.

How does romanticism work as a cultural tool to reinforce sex class? Let us examine its components, refined over centuries, and the modern methods of its diffusion—cultural techniques so sophisticated and penetrating that even men are damaged by them.

1. Eroticism   A prime component of romanticism is eroticism. All animal needs (the affection of a kitten that has never seen heat) for love and warmth are channeled into genital sex: people must never touch others of the same sex, and may touch those of the opposite sex only when preparing for a

---

[1]Gallantry has been commonly defined as "excessive attention to women without serious purpose," but the purpose is very serious: through a false flattery, to keep women from awareness of their lower-class condition.

genital sexual encounter ("a pass"). Isolation from others makes people starved for physical affection; and if the only kind they can get is genital sex, that's soon all they crave. In this state of hypersensitivity the least sensual stimulus produces an exaggerated effect, enough to inspire everything from schools of master painting to rock and roll. Thus *eroticism is the concentration of sexuality—often into highly-charged objects ("Chantilly Lace")—signifying the displacement of other social/affection needs onto sex.* To be plain old needy-for-affection makes one a "drip," to need a kiss is embarrassing, unless it is an erotic kiss; only "sex" is O.K., in fact it proves one's mettle. Virility and sexual performance become confused with social worth.[2]

Constant erotic stimulation of male sexuality coupled with its forbidden release through most normal channels are designed to encourage men to look at women as only things whose resistance to entrance must be overcome. For notice that this eroticism operates in only one direction. Women are the only "love" objects in our society, so much so that women regard *themselves* as erotic.[3] This functions to preserve direct sex pleasure for the male, reinforcing female dependence: women can be fulfilled sexually only by vicarious identification with the man who enjoys them. Thus eroticism preserves the sex class system.

The only exception to this concentration of all emotional needs into erotic relationships is the (sometimes) affection within the family. But here, too, unless they are *his* children, a man can no more express affection for children than he can for women. Thus his affection for the young is also a trap to saddle him into the marriage structure, reinforcing the patriarchal system.

2. The Sex Privatization of Women   Eroticism is only the topmost layer of the romanticism that reinforces female inferiority. As with any lower class, group awareness must be deadened to keep them from rebelling. In this case, because the distinguishing characteristic of women's exploitation as a class is sexual, a special means must be found to make them unaware that they are considered all alike sexually ("cunts"). Perhaps when a man marries he chooses from this undistinguishable lot with care, for as we have seen, he holds a special high place in his mental reserve for "The One," by virtue of her close association with himself; but in general he can't tell the difference between chicks (Blondes, Brunettes, Redheads).[4] And he likes it that way. ("A wiggle in your walk, a giggle in your talk, THAT'S WHAT I LIKE!") When a man believes all women are alike, but wants to keep women from guessing, what does he do? He keeps his beliefs to himself, and pretends, to allay her suspicions, that what she has in common with other women is precisely what makes her different. Thus her sexuality eventually becomes synonymous with her individuality. *The sex privatization of women is the process whereby women are blinded to their generality as a class which renders them invisible as individuals to the male eye.* Is not that strange Mrs. Lady next to the President in his entourage reminiscent of the discreet black servant at White House functions?

The process is insidious: When a man exclaims, "I love Blondes!" all the secretaries in the vicinity sit up; they take it personally because they have been sex-privatized. The blonde one feels personally complimented because she has come to measure her worth through the physical attributes that differentiate her from other women. She no longer recalls that any physical attribute you could name is shared by many others, that these are accidental attributes not of her own creation, that her sexuality is shared by half of humanity. But in an authentic recognition of her individuality, her blondeness would be loved, but in a different way: She would be loved first as an irreplaceable totality, and then her blondness would be loved as one of the characteristics of that totality.

The apparatus of sex privatization is so sophisticated that it may take years to detect—if detectable at all. It explains many puzzling traits of female psychology that take such form as:

Women who are personally complimented by compliments to their sex, i.e., "Hats off to the Little Woman!"

Women who are not insulted when addressed

---

[2]But as every woman has discovered, a man who seems to be pressuring for sex is often greatly relieved to be excused from the literal performance: His ego has been made dependent on his continuously proving himself through sexual conquest; but all he may have really wanted was the excuse to indulge in affection without the loss of manly self-respect. That men are more restrained than are women about exhibiting emotion is because, in addition to the results of the Oedipus Complex, to express tenderness to a woman is to acknowledge her equality. Unless, of course, one tempers one's tenderness—takes it back—with some proof of domination.

[3]Homosexuals are so ridiculed because in seeing men as sex objects they go doubly against the current: Even women don't read Pretty Boy magazines.

[4]"As for his other sports," says a recent blurb about football hero Joe Namath, "he prefers Blondes."

regularly and impersonally as Dear, Honey, Sweetie, Sugar, Kitten, Darling, Angel, Queen, Princess, Doll, Woman.

Women who are secretly flattered to have their asses pinched in Rome. (They'd do better to count the number of times other girls' asses are pinched.)

The joys of "prickteasing" (generalized male horniness taken as a sign of personal value and desirability).

The "clotheshorse" phenomenon. (Women, denied legitimate outlets of expression of their individuality, "express" themselves physically, as in "I want to see something 'different'.")

These are only some of the reactions to the sex privatization process, the confusion of one's sexuality with one's individuality. The process is so effective that most women have come to believe seriously that the world needs their particular sexual contributions to go on. ("She thinks her pussy is made of gold.") But the love songs would still be written without them.

Women may be duped, but men are quite conscious of this as a valuable manipulative technique. That is why they go to great pains to avoid talking about women in front of them ("not in front of a lady")—it would give their game away. To overhear a bull session is traumatic to a woman: So all this time she has been considered only "ass," "meat," "twat," or "stuff," to be gotten a "piece of," "that bitch" or "this broad" to be tricked out of money or sex or love! To understand finally that she is no better than other women but completely indistinguishable comes not just as a blow but as a total annihilation. But perhaps the time that women more often have to confront their own sex privatization is in a lover's quarrel, when the truth spills out: Then a man might get careless and admit that the only thing he ever *really* liked her for was her bust ("Built like a brick shithouse") or legs anyway ("Hey, Legs!"), and he can find that somewhere else if he has to.

Thus sex privatization stereotypes women: it encourages men to see women as "dolls" differentiated only by superficial attributes—not of the same species as themselves—and it blinds women to their sexploitation as a class, keeping them from uniting against it, thus effectively segregating the two classes. A side-effect is the converse: if women

are differentiated only by superficial physical attributes, men appear more individual and irreplaceable than they really are.

Women, because social recognition is granted only for a *false* individuality, are kept from developing the tough individuality that would enable breaking through such a ruse. If one's existence in its generality is the only thing acknowledged, why go to the trouble to develop real character? It is much less hassle to "light up the room with a smile"—until that day when the "chick" graduates to "old bag," to find that her smile is no longer "inimitable."

3. The Beauty Ideal Every society has promoted a certain ideal of beauty over all others. What that ideal is is unimportant, for any ideal leaves the majority out; ideals, by definition, are modeled on *rare* qualities. For example, in America, the present fashion vogue of French models, or the erotic ideal Voluptuous Blonde are modeled on qualities rare indeed: few Americans are of French birth, most don't look French and never will (and besides they eat too much); voluptuous brunettes can bleach their hair (as did Marilyn Monroe, the sex queen herself), but blondes can't develop curves at will —and most of them, being Anglo-Saxon, simply aren't built like that. If and when, by artificial methods, the majority can squeeze into the ideal, the ideal changes. If it were attainable, what good would it be?

For the exclusivity of the beauty ideal serves a clear political function. Someone—most women —will be left out. And left scrambling, because as we have seen, women have been allowed to achieve individuality only through their appearance—looks being defined as "good" not out of love for the bearer, but because of her more or less successful approximation to an external standard. This image, defined by men (and currently by homosexual men, often misogynists of the worst order), becomes the ideal. What happens? Women everywhere rush to squeeze into the glass slipper, forcing and mutilating their bodies with diets and beauty programs, clothes and makeup, anything to become the punk prince's dream girl. But they have no choice. If they don't the penalties are enormous: their social legitimacy is at stake.

Thus women become more and more lookalike. But at the same time they are expected to express their individuality through their physical appearance. Thus they are kept coming and going, at one and the same time trying to express their similarity and their uniqueness. The demands of Sex Privatization contradict the demands of the Beauty Ideal, causing the severe feminine neurosis about personal appearance.

But this conflict itself has an important political function. When women begin to look more and more alike, distinguished only by the degree to which they differ from a paper ideal, they can be more easily stereotyped as a class: They look alike, they think alike, and even worse, they are so stupid they believe they are not alike.

These are some of the major components of the cultural apparatus, romanticism, which, with the weakening of "natural" limitations on women, keep sex oppression going strong. The political uses of romanticism over the centuries became increasingly complex. Operating subtly or blatantly, on every cultural level, romanticism is now—in this time of greatest threat to the male power role— amplified by new techniques of communication so all-pervasive that men get entangled in their own line. How does this amplification work?

With the cultural portrayal of the smallest details of existence (e.g., deodorizing one's underarms), the distance between one's experience and one's perceptions of it becomes enlarged by a vast interpretive network; if our direct experience contradicts its interpretation by this ubiquitous cultural network, the experience must be denied. This process, of course, does not apply only to women. The pervasion of image has so deeply altered our very relationships to ourselves that even men have become objects—if never *erotic* objects. Images become extensions of oneself; it gets hard to distinguish the real person from his latest image, if indeed, the Person Underneath hasn't evaporated altogether. Arnie, the kid who sat in back of you in the sixth grade, picking his nose and cracking jokes, the one who had a crook in his left shoulder, is lost under successive layers of adopted images: the High School Comedian, the Campus Rebel, James Bond, the Salem Springtime Lover, and so on, each image hitting new highs of sophistication until the person himself doesn't know who he is. Moreover, he deals with others through this image-extension (Boy-Image meets Girl-Image and consummates Image-Romance). Even if a woman could get beneath this intricate image facade—and it would take months, even years, of a painful, almost therapeutic relationship—she would be met not with gratitude that she had (painfully) loved the man for his real

self, but with shocked repulsion and terror that she had found him out. What he wants instead is The Pepsi-Cola Girl, to smile pleasantly to his Johnny Walker Red in front of a ski-lodge fire.

But, while this reification affects both men and women alike, in the case of women it is profoundly complicated by the forms of sexploitation I have described. Woman is not only an Image, she is an Image with Sex Appeal. The stereotyping of women expands: Now there is no longer the excuse of ignorance. Every woman is constantly and explicitly informed of how to "improve" what nature gave her, where to buy the products to do it with, and how to count the calories she should never have eaten. The competition becomes frantic, because everyone is now plugged into the same circuit. The current beauty ideal becomes all-pervasive ("Blondes have more fun . . .").

And eroticism becomes erotomania. Stimulated to the limit, it has reached an epidemic level unequalled in history. From every magazine cover, film screen, TV tube, subway sign, jump breasts, legs, shoulders, thighs. Men walk about in a state of constant sexual excitement. Even with the best of intentions, it is difficult to focus on anything else. This bombardment of the senses, in turn, escalates sexual provocation still further: ordinary means of arousal have lost all effect. Clothing becomes more provocative: hemlines climb, bras are shed. Seethrough materials become ordinary. But in all this barrage of erotic stimuli, men themselves are seldom portrayed as erotic objects. Women's eroticism, as well as men's, becomes increasingly directed toward women.

One of the internal contradictions of this highly effective propaganda system is to expose to men as well as women the stereotyping process women undergo. Though the idea was to better acquaint women with their feminine role, men who turn on the TV are also treated to the latest in tummy-control, false eyelashes, and floor waxes (Does she . . . or doesn't she?). Such a crosscurrent of sexual tease and exposé would be enough to make any man hate women, if he didn't already.

Thus the extension of romanticism through modern media enormously magnified its effects. If before culture maintained male supremacy through Eroticism, Sex Privatization, and the Beauty Ideal, these cultural processes are now almost too effectively carried out: the media are guilty of "overkill." The regeneration of the women's movement at this moment in history may be due to a backfiring, an internal contradiction of our modern cultural indoctrination system. For in its amplification of sex indoctrination, the media have unconsciously exposed the degradation of "femininity."

In conclusion, I want to add a note about the special difficulties of attacking the sex class system through its means of cultural indoctrination. Sex objects *are* beautiful. An attack on them can be confused with an attack on beauty itself. Feminists need not get so pious in their efforts that they feel they must flatly deny the beauty of the face on the cover of *Vogue*. For this is not the point. The real question is: is the face beautiful in a *human* way—does it allow for growth and flux and decay, does it express negative as well as positive emotions, does it fall apart without artificial props—or does it falsely imitate the very different beauty of an *inanimate* object, like wood trying to be metal?

To attack eroticism creates similar problems. Eroticism is *exciting*. No one wants to get rid of it. Life would be a drab and routine affair without at least that spark. That's just the point. Why has all joy and excitement been concentrated, driven into one narrow, difficult-to-find alley of human experience, and all the rest laid waste? When we demand the elimination of eroticism, we mean not the elimination of sexual joy and excitement but its rediffusion over—there's plenty to go around, it increases with use—the spectrum of our lives.

23/Marx, Sex, and the Transformation of Society

Virginia Held

I

In that brief passage in the 1844 Manuscripts in which Marx discusses the relation between man and woman, he offers a possible model for a cooperative society in which genuine mutuality of concern and respect for other human beings replaces individual self-interest and the mere plural use by human beings of one another to their own advantage. . . .

But although neither Marx nor the various socialist movements since have yet developed the implications of this fleeting suggestion concerning the relation between man and woman, the time may have come when we can now start seriously so to develop them, in theory and in practice, considering a transformed relation between man and woman as a model for a transformed society. Certainly it is not hard to argue that the relation between man and woman is the key social relation, and that if genuine mutuality of concern and respect did characterize this relation, the effects on the rest of the society would be extraordinary. . . .

II

Let's look more closely at the relation between man and woman as *we* may see it. Can it be a relation of genuine mutuality, of mutual concern and respect, and what is such a relation?

In one sense, the relation between man and woman, as a conscious relation, is abstract and "ideal." At the same time, as Marx says, it is a *natural* relation, it is "sensuously manifested, reduced to an observable fact." We should not, however, be deceived about the sense in which it is observable. It is sensuously observable to ourselves when we privately experience without self-deception what our own deepest feelings in fact are, when we mutually express these feelings, and when we come to experience, directly or indirectly, the conscious feelings of others; it is not observable in the sense of the sex researchers, who can observe secretions, erections, and orgasms, for we know we can induce these in ourselves and others without the accompaniment of the non-inducible feelings of shared concern and respect. When we think we

From *The Philosophical Forum*, 5 (1975). Reprinted by permission. Footnotes have been renumbered.

experience, sensuously, the feelings of love, sometimes we experience only our side of what we mistakenly take to be a relation of mutuality. To "know" that the relation exists may require some education of the sensibilities, but it is still, in Marx's sense, to experience something human and concrete, not a Hegelian abstraction.

A relation of mutuality is quite different from a relation of power, where two persons, as entities possessing power, simply stand in some factual relation to one another, as when we can empirically describe that one person has greater power than another. A relation of mutual concern and respect is also different, although both are conscious, social relations, from a mere mutual recognition by each person of the factual relation of power in which they stand, even when it is one of equal power. Equality is in general a precondition for a relation of mutual concern between man and woman, but we do not necessarily have such a relation with any equal, nor is it in *all* cases absent where power is unequal.

By the relation of mutual concern and respect in its distinctive sense we mean a relation in which neither person uses the other, neither sees the other primarily as a means to the satisfaction of his or her own self-interest. The relation is genuinely mutual; it is only achievable together, and consciously. But the relation of mutuality is different from mere reciprocity, where *both* use the other to increase their own satisfaction, as in a trading relation. If mutual surrender of the primacy of self-interest is absent, or awareness of this surrender not present, there can be no mutual concern and respect, and this relation cannot "exist" as a relation. This does not mean, however, that the relation of mutual concern and respect is *contrary* to self-interest, that it requires altruism or charity towards the other. It is, rather, a relation in which neither the interest of self nor the interest of the other are pitted against one another, because for both persons, cooperation simultaneously replaces competition.[1] We can, perhaps, understand the relation most easily in a sexual context, where genuine mutual consideration between a man and a woman making love is neither the joint pursuit of self-satisfaction nor the joint bestowing of charity, but the mutual pursuit of and awareness of mutual feelings and values.

The value of mutual concern and respect may

be discussed in terms of the conceptual difference between the collective or social value of a relation of mutuality and a sum of the self-interested values of a number of individuals. Applied to the sexual relation between a man and a woman, although the man may gain pleasure from the states of arousal or satisfaction of the woman, if the latter states are considered primarily as factors contributing to his greater pleasure, the resulting value of his initial pleasure, increased by the pleasure which her pleasure gives him, is still an egoistic value. It may often happen that a certain state of consciousness in her may contribute to his pleasure, but if he is a callous man, it may simply not affect his pleasure. Either way, whether her pleasure affects him or not is a contingent matter of fact; concern for her pleasure is not required by the definition of his pleasure as an egoistic value. If a similar interpretation is applied to her, and a summation made of his total pleasure and her total pleasure, the resulting value is a sum of individually self-interested values. Insofar as the values are seen as values *to* individuals, even though their fullest realization may causally depend on other individuals, we have not yet reached the social value of the relation of mutual concern and respect.

The latter would be a mutual relation between two persons in which the man would recognize the woman's pleasure as primarily good-in-itself, not primarily good as a means to his greater pleasure; the woman would do the same with respect to his pleasure, and each would be aware that the other did so. For an extended relation of mutual caring then to exist between them, each would have to value the other for the other's sake as well as for his or her own, and know that the other did the same. Such a relation of mutuality might in fact be less conducive to individual satisfaction, at least at times, than an egoistic relation. Or it might be more so. Either way, the mutuality might itself be judged to have a value, for the society for instance, distinct from the sum of the egoistic values the relation would provide for the individuals involved.

A relation of mutual concern and respect as an immediate and purely sexual relation is not at present altogether rare. But when the same characteristics of genuine mutual concern are sought in other aspects of the relation between sexual partners, the more other aspects are included, the more rare the relation becomes. Men have only for a few decades concerned themselves to a significant ex-

---

[1] I have discussed the conceptual aspects of these distinctions, with further examples, in a paper entitled "Rationality and Social Cooperation," not yet published in final form.

tent with even the sexual satisfactions of women. They are still unaccustomed to regarding the other than sexual needs and satisfactions of the women they make love to in terms of the interests of the woman herself rather than in terms of the threat or source of competition to the man which her achievement of gains in these other areas may produce. Women, trained to expect that the other than sexual satisfactions of their husbands or lovers should satisfy them too, are unaccustomed to expressing, and sometimes even to recognizing, their dissatisfactions in the other than sexual aspects of their lives. In a relation of mutual concern, both would take pleasure in the self-development and wider satisfactions of the other. . . .

A further crucial aspect of the relation between man and woman is that for it to be one of mutual respect, rather than of paternalism or maternalism, each must respect the autonomy of the other, renouncing the right to decide for that other what is best for him or for her. And each must be aware of the other's recognition of such self-denial. Of course, a relation of mutual respect must not involve the imposition of one will upon another, or even the *attempt* to coerce, whether for the benefit of coercer or coerced. In their dealings with one another, man and woman discover not only that man can overpower woman (and I am not talking about physical force or rape, but of the force of sexual attraction) and woman can overpower man—that is, at the level of *sexual* power, as opposed to muscular and other power, they really *are* equal. What human beings also discover is that in this relation, mutual respect is only possible when neither overpowers the other, and coercion of any kind, including the use of sexual power in coercive ways, is transcended.[2] But at present, as with mutual concern, the lesson is too often lost as the relation between man and woman extends into other areas than the purely sexual, and the moment of noncoercive mutuality experienced in bed is crushed under the weight of male dominance beyond. For the relation of mutual respect to develop, coercion must be renounced at all levels, and even more fundamentally than as an aspect of mutual concern where the partners are

inclined to resist being overpowered. To respect another person is to renounce the use of coercion against that person even when he or she is powerless or not inclined to resist.

III

As recent analyses have helped us to realize more acutely than ever before, the relation between man and woman is at present suffused with a monumental disparity of power in all but the capacity to affect purely sexual encounters once man has renounced the power to rape. The wider powerlessness that so often destroys the possibility of mutuality for the woman is often effectively masked by the fact of her capacity and need to hide her feelings while her body and services are being used. Certainly it is more satisfying for the man if he is wanted, and for himself, rather than tolerated in fear, or sought or stayed with for the economic and social favors he can bestow. But the insensitivity which man can so much more easily than woman afford to be wrapped in frequently keeps him ignorant of the woman's dissatisfaction and discontent. And the woman's powerlessness in all the other aspects of their relation frequently assures her need to feign desire, affection, approval, and consent.

Imagine woman now psychologically, economically, socially, politically, as free to ignore man's wishes as he is free to ignore hers. Imagine man having to consider her feelings not only for that brief span of time before her dependence is transferred from her father or former husband to him, but *continually*. The sensitivities of the male rulers of the world and shapers of our future would be bound to be affected, as would the prospects for female participation in the shaping of that future. If, in the relation between man and woman, it would not be possible for one will to impose itself upon another, and not necessary for that other to abdicate its assertion, certainly this would change habits of behavior and thought at wider and higher levels in such a way that present relations between persons would be radically changed for the better. Mutual concern and respect between man and woman would develop not only in their sexual activity but throughout the whole of the association between them. Both men and women would then pursue their economic, political, social, professional and other activities not only as equals but as persons who had become

---

[2]Power is not necessarily coercive, but where its use is unsuccessful, the temptation to resort to coercion is ever present. In "Coercion and Coercive Offers," (*Coercion*, Nomos Vol. XIV, edited by J. Roland Pennock and John W. Chapman, N.Y.: Aldine-Atherton, 1972) I have argued that coercion is the activity of causing someone to do something against his or her will and that it may be brought about through either threats or inducements.

accustomed to mutual concern and respect as a normal condition covering a very extensive part of their lives. Mutuality would no longer be, as it usually now is, a mere isolated and momentary experience.

To argue that mutuality may be possible beyond a few special moments between a very few persons in close contact, as in the case of a man and woman making love, may well be utopian. But just as Marx and his followers dared to reject the Utopianism they inherited, women might consider, now, rejecting the despairing preoccupation with objective reality into which they have been born. One lesson of history is that different times call for different approaches.

To make possible the relation of mutual concern and respect between man and woman, and especially to expand it beyond a fleeting moment in a limited part of their lives to wider and more distantly related aspects of the relations between human beings, most of what militant feminists recommend is indisputably necessary: women must have enough economic, social, political, and psychological independence to be able to subsist satisfactorily without this relation of mutuality. Otherwise the actual relation between man and woman becomes subverted into a relation of dominance and submission. But these economic, social, political, and psychological requirements are *preconditions* of the maintenance of the relation —and in one sense not new, composed as they are of the familiar elements of power. The relation itself, on the other hand, is characterized by a *mutual renunciation of the use of power.* Equality of power may be a precondition for any such satisfactory, voluntary, extended renunciation: otherwise the breakdown of the relation leaves woman, as usual, in a position to be overpowered. But *exploration* of the relation need not await the full achievement of such equality. And if we seek to explore alternative and more satisfactory relations with which to construct society than the relations of power and self-interest which now pertain, women must feel free to build some relations in which they, and men, renounce the use of power, although they must do this in addition to and not instead of building the economic, social, political and psychological foundations with which the power of women can be equal to that of men. . . .

IV

In pursuing the conditions of economic, politi-

cal, social and psychological equality for women, separatism—at least a separatism of feeling—may often seem to recommend itself. Women must support one another and struggle together against the centuries of tradition and experience that leave men so very well trained to be egoists and leaders. Still, if one seeks the transformation of society into a *community* of equals, rather than simply a warring collection of persons or groups with equal power, then separatism is not only not an answer, but it robs us of the most promising source of experience. Certainly women must undertake many activities in concert with other women and against men, but these should not altogether take the place of experimenting with the forms of community and noncoercion possible in the relation between man and woman.

Relations between woman and woman, or man and man, may sometimes also offer experience in mutual concern and respect, but are not a comparable achievement and do not hold out a comparable hope for social transformation. Man and woman each embody within themselves a vast network of group characteristics along with whatever individual characteristics they may have. They bring to their relation their affiliation with two groups possessing an extraordinary disparity of power in the society, and having an armory of conflicting group interests. To transform these antagonisms into a relation of mutual concern and respect is far more significant than is the achievement of such a relation between members of the same sex.

The activities many feminists now recommend are in one sense those of the society we know, since they concern the use of power: how can women marshall their strength to attack, provoke, stir up, win concessions from the structures of entrenched male power and privilege. All women should, I think, take part in and give enthusiastic support to such activities. Where superior power is being used to exploit and oppress women, women must develop power sufficient to attack and overcome such treatment.

They must also, however, I think, develop the possibilities of alternatives to such encounters of power. If men and women are to transform society in ways that will not merely distribute power more equally while remaining based as much as before on its use, then both women and men must learn new habits of dealing with one another in different terms, the terms of cooperation, of trust, of openness, of genuine mutuality—in short, of love. But it is a very real question for women whether the decision—not the mere desire, which can perhaps with effort be overcome, but the decision—to experiment with love can be reconciled with the decision to fight for equal power. It would be helpful for women if they could try to develop relations of love with some men and fight for equality with others, but since the issues often surround the most profound of assumptions and attitudes, it is impossible for women to escape encountering grounds for conflict with the men they could love. Further, even when the groups of men fought and men loved are kept distinct, women sometimes find that as their efforts for equality increase, their opportunities for love decrease, since many men fear independent women even more than totalitarian officials fear independent citizens. If to love is to renounce the fight, it might seem that women who allow themselves to love men betray their sisters. On the other hand, and I think the question may be answered this way, if women refuse to let themselves love men, they betray the goal of a society in which power is not the ultimate arbiter. . . .

In trying to live with a recognition of the importance of both fighting and loving, women will have to accept a kind of schizophrenic existence. But women have the whole of history to call upon for lessons in not flying apart, torn as they have always been by the conflicting wills within them. They have always lived with the will to keep their minds resilient and the conflicting will to not be destroyed for doing so by a society that has expected the minds of all but the most exceptional women slowly to atrophy, at least after young adulthood. They have always known both the will to flee the men who ruled their lives, and the will to avoid the still worse wilderness in which they would find themselves if they yielded to flight. . . .

So women need not fear being both militant and loving alternatively. An integrated stance toward the world is a distant goal to be sought, a luxury they cannot yet afford. But it would be a mistake, I think, to think that love is a luxury they cannot afford, because it is the social experiment, the innovative exploration, the basic research, one might almost say, of this revolution.

24/Separatism and Sexual Relationships

Sara Ann Ketchum and Christine Pierce

The second wave of the feminist movement has always been separatist. From the beginning, there have been political groups organized by and for women, consciousness-raising and support groups by and for women, newspapers and magazines by and for women. Although there are radical feminist separatist positions, some forms of separatism are and have been common to both the conservative and radical wings of the movement. In recent philosophical literature, various kinds of feminist separatism have been lumped together, treated as the radical fringe, and dismissed as sexist and counterrevolutionary without either adequate portrayal of the feminist argument or much effort in the way of counterargument. In particular, Virginia Held and Mihailo Marković, in their respective papers "Marx, Sex, and the Transformation of Society"[1] and "Women's Liberation and Human Emancipation,"[2] construe the separatist position in these purely negative ways. For example, Marković charges that it is "a specific form of sexism, a female chauvinism that consists in expressing resentment, hostility and

An earlier version of this paper was read at the Australian National University, Canberra, August 1975, and at the Society for Women in Philosophy at the State University of New York, New Paltz, October 1975. The research was supported in part by Summer grants from the State University of New York Research Foundation.

[1]Virginia Held, "Marx, Sex, and the Transformation of Society," *Philosophical Forum* 5 (1975): 171–81; reprinted as

Women and Philosophy: Toward a Theory of Liberation (New York: G. P. Putnam, 1976), 171–81. [See immediately preceding article, this volume, pp. 159–163—ed.]

[2]Mihailo Marković, "Women's Liberation and Human Emancipation," *Philosophical Forum* 5 (1975); reprinted in *Women and Philosophy: Toward a Theory of Liberation* (New York: G. P. Putnam, 1976).

even hatred for the opposite sex."[3] He shows no awareness of separatism as an affirmation of sisterhood, only as a rejection of men.

In this paper we will first explain what separatism is and why it is not sexist. Then we will discuss the relationship between feminist separatism and sexual relationships, arguing against Held's claim that "separatism is not an answer."[4]

Separatism

A political theory or movement is separatist to the extent that it claims a special significance and importance for relationships between, and organizations of, members of the relevant oppressed (discriminated against, less powerful) group. The major ideals of separatism are those of solidarity, pride, and the development of an independent or noncontingent culture.[5] Solidarity may mainly pertain to organizing a power base—"United we stand, divided we fall"—or it may shade into concern for a group identity as women, Blacks, workers, gay people, and so on.

The necessity for an independent culture rests in part on the assumption that the recognized culture of a society is that of the dominant group. Thus to the extent that the Black experience is reflected in the dominant culture, it is reflected through the perceptions and needs of whites; the image of women in the dominant culture is that created by men, and so on. The traditional dominant culture is particularly blatant in defining women's interests in terms of relationships with men. A good woman is a woman who serves the interests of the men she is associated with. A woman's needs are identical with those of her man, since she can (by her nature) only be happy when her man is happy. Thus, outside of an independent womanculture, a woman is not offered any noncontingent concept of being a woman—that is, any concept of woman as a being with her own needs, her own interests, her own concerns—rather than a set of interests, needs, and concerns that she might have solely in virtue of her relationship to some other person.

What images the dominant culture might provide of members of the oppressed group tend to be negative and derogatory. Moreover, members of the nondominant group live in the dominant culture; for example, most American Blacks live in, and are part of, a Black culture while living in, but not being part of, the dominant white culture. Since most members of a given society think in terms of the concepts and assumptions of the dominant culture, this situation will foster a sense of inferiority in members of the oppressed group. So a separatist movement which does manage to create an independent culture serves as protection from the contempt, hatred, and prejudices of the dominant group, and it provides a social focus for the attempt to overcome such socially dependent feelings of inferiority.

The emotional and political rejection of such a sense of inferiority is the major element in the notion of pride as used by liberation movements. If racism encourages Blacks to be ashamed of being black, if sexism encourages women to feel inferior as women, and if heterosexism makes gay people hate their capacity to love, then the creation of pride and affirmation of oneself *as* a member of a previously despised group is crucial. A woman who hates women—and consequently hates herself as a woman—will be both her own and other women's oppressor.

At this point, it should be clear why the definition of "separatism" that we cited specified the relationship between members of the oppressed group as crucial to separatism. A call for organizations of dominant groups would presuppose an entirely different kind of political theory with distinct concepts and values. To the extent that any group is dominant, the recognized culture is its own culture, and any attempt at consciously fostering pride is likely to be a process of developing arrogance rather than of overcoming socially entrenched inferiority.

It should also be clear why separatism is not sexism. The union meeting that excludes management would be a more appropriate parallel from mainstream politics than would the exclusion of women and Blacks from the Board of General Motors. The Board of General Motors has a responsibility to be nondiscriminatory because admission to that group is admission to power; its exclusion of Blacks and women is blameworthy because it has important benefits to distribute. There is no particular moral objection to a group of Bowery winos being discriminatory; they have no power to distribute, either fairly or unfairly. There is a moral difference between organizing to keep the presently powerless from power and organizing the powerless as

[3]Marković, "Women's Liberation," p. 165.

[4]Held, "Marx, Sex," p. 179. [Page 162, this volume—eds.]

[5]For a discussion of the noncontingent culture see: Joan Roberts, *Beyond Intellectual Sexism: A New Woman, A New Reality* (New York: David McKay, 1976), pp. 3–60.

such. Thus Marković's accusation that feminist separatism is simply another form of sexism ignores the moral relevance of power and is comparable to the claim that labor unionism is simply a form of classism. This is surprising in the work of a Marxist theorist of the caliber of Marković, who might reasonably be expected to be sympathetic to movements based on principles and assumptions similar to those underlying the Marxist emphasis on class consciousness and solidarity of the working class.

It is important to remember that feminist separatists gather together not simply as women, but *as people who share a particular form of oppression*. Feminist separatists do not exclude men because they hate them any more than unions exclude management *because* they hate management. Certainly individual union members hate either individual managers or management as such; but it would be absurd to claim that the principle of unionism *consists* in expressing hatred and resentment toward management. Black men and gay men, for example, are excluded from some feminist meetings not because they are biologically male nor because they are not oppressed, but because they are oppressed in a different way and by different aspects of the social structure than are women. There may appropriately be coalitions of oppressed groups to fight for common issues or simply for the purpose of solidarity against oppression. However, it is important for members of an oppressed group to understand their particular oppression, to find their own needs, to develop their own culture and their own pride.

Feminist Separatism

Feminist separatism holds that women ought to devote effort and emotional energy to relationships with other women and to organizations and groups of women—this in contrast to the traditional view, which claims that a woman's overriding emotional commitment is, and ought to be, to a man; that men are, and ought to be, the most important people in a woman's life; and that relationships between women are unimportant and trivial. The issue of separatism in the women's movement is particularly sensitive because women are traditionally presumed to have a closer tie to members of the corresponding dominant group—that is, men—than Blacks are assumed to have to whites. The attempts

of women to band together for political advantage—and particularly any claims that women ought to place a special value on relationships with other women—have traditionally been perceived as carrying a threat to the well-entrenched values of heterosexual love and the nuclear family that Black separatism does not pose.

What follows is a schema of the most prominent versions of feminist separatism, ranging from the minimal to the more-or-less radical:

1. *Interest-group Separatism:* According to this version, women ought to organize as an interest group like any other interest group. The point of having an organization composed only of women is to enable women to develop an understanding of their political interests and a base for protecting and furthering those interests through legislation and political reform. In form, this theory is an extension of standard American pluralism. The only radical aspect of this theory is its assumption that women do have political interests *as women* rather than only as wives and daughters of union members or factory workers, as Jews or Catholics, and so on.

2. *The Consciousness-raising (or CR) Model:* One of the major political innovations of the feminist movement is the CR group. The most peculiar feature of such groups is that they aim not so much at public political action as at changing the social structure from the inside, by starting with the way we think about social structures and personal relationships. Such a group has at least two purposes: First, discussion and comparison of basic experiences serve as a grass-roots process for developing a theory and a personal understanding of how problems faced by individual women are part of the social structure of sexism—that is, how the personal is political. This process is also seen as crucial to the development of pride and self-confidence and for developing ways of thinking that are alternatives to the dominant sexist culture. Second, the understanding developed from the first process, as well as the experience of participating in a group of equals with a nonauthoritarian structure, can serve as a model for social change. One of the important points here is that if the personal is political, one of the targets for social change will be relationships otherwise considered personal or apolitical—such as marriage and love relationships.

3. *Lesbianfeminism:* According to this position, a feminist ought to devote her emotional energy primarily (or even exclusively) to other women and to the womanculture, and she ought to define her interests, needs, and womanness through herself and other women. Lesbian relationships have a special importance because the relationship of sexual love is paradigmatically one's major emotional commitment to another person; thus such relationships are thought to have a special potential for the development of equal and loving relationships where the personal and the political merge. On the assumption that love implies some degree of dependence, the lesbian is seen as the model of the woman-identified woman[6]—the woman who feels no need to mold herself into the image of what men want of her.

The interest-group theory would treat changes in sexual relationships or marriages as incidental to the separatist purpose. The other two versions, however, deal directly with such relationships. The CR model implies that women ought to model the structure of their marriages and other relationships with men after the more equal relationships they have found with women. The lesbian-feminist model implies that women ought not to maintain close emotional ties with men or, at least, that such ties ought not to take precedence over feminist commitment and relationships with women.

A pure version of any of these positions, either in an organization or on the part of an individual feminist, is rare; the positions are more or less arbitrary selections from a continuum. They are not mutually exclusive nor are they necessarily correlated with a sexual life style. There are lesbians whose only ties to the feminist movement are through interest-group politics; and, according to one view of lesbianfeminism, one can be a technical heterosexual while maintaining an emotional and political commitment to lesbianfeminism.

Not only are there possible positions that are in between and/or combine these three, but some positions are either more conservative or more radical. On the conservative end would be a feminist who does not favor the creation of even special interest groups for women, either on the grounds that women do not constitute a legitimate interest group—for example, those who take feminism to be an objection to sex roles that oppress men and women equally—or on practical political grounds. Two forms of separatism that might be counted as more extreme than any of the forms mentioned might be called "sexual nationalism" and "asexualism." Sexual nationalism is the position that women ought to form an entirely separate political and geographical entity—the lesbian nation taken literally. Asexualism is the theory that love and sexual relations *as such* are inherently oppressive and ought to be abolished. There is nothing in asexualism per se that makes it a separatist theory; it is perfectly consistent with either separatism or integrationism. However, some feminist separatists—for example, Ti-Grace Atkinson[7]—have argued for asexualism. Other separatists who argue that heterosexual relationships in a sexist society are oppressive recommend that celibacy, combined with strong friendships and/or political ties with women, is preferable—at least for those women who find themselves uncomfortable with explicitly lesbian relationships.

Recent Philosophical Discussion of Feminist Separatism

On the issue of personal relationships, Virginia Held, in "Marx, Sex, and the Transformation of Society," takes a position opposite to that of the separatist. That is, she argues that relationships between women and men, rather than relationships between women, are of primary importance and value. In general, her argument is that the development of relationships of mutuality (i.e., relationships of mutual concern and respect) should be a major social goal and that our present task is to construct models of mutuality to be used in the transformation of society. This argument has two stages: First, she explains how relationships between men and women can be instances or models of mutuality. Second, she argues against separatism, and for the position that women ought to take relationships with men, rather than relationships with women, as models; and that feminists ought to be committed to sexual relationships between men and women.

A main thesis of stage one is that mutuality exists in sexual relations between men and women

[6]See Radicalesbians, "The Woman-Identified Woman," in *Liberation Now: Writings from the Women's Liberation Movement* (New York: Dell, 1971), pp. 287–93.

[7]See Ti-Grace Atkinson, *Amazon Odyssey* (New York: Links, 1974), pp. 13–23, 83–88.

and that such relations should be used as models in extending mutuality to nonsexual relations between men and women:

A relation of mutual concern and respect as an immediate and purely sexual relation is not at present altogether rare. But when the same characteristics of genuine mutual concern are sought in other aspects of the relation between sexual partners, the more other aspects are included, the more rare the relation becomes. . . . [8]

To make possible the relation of mutual concern and respect between man and woman, and especially to expand it beyond a fleeting moment in a limited part of their lives to wider and more distantly related aspects of the relations between human beings, most of what militant feminists recommend is indisputably necessary: women must have enough economic, social, political, and psychological independence to be able to subsist satisfactorily without this relation of mutuality. [9]

Two aspects of this ideal prove problematic for relationships between men and women in a sexist society: respect and equality. We will discuss each in turn, beginning with equality. Strictly speaking, equality is not a part of mutuality but is "in general a precondition for a relation of mutual concern between man and woman." [10] This claim implies at the least that mutuality is more likely in relationships between equals. However, despite her claim that men and women presently have vastly unequal amounts of power, the only relationships she considers as possible models of mutuality are those between men and women.

Held suggests two possible reasons for claiming that social and physical power differentials between men and women may not preclude the possibility of mutuality in individual sexual relationships: (1) men and women have equal power with respect to "the capacity to affect purely sexual encounters once man has renounced rape," [11] and (2) people can and sometimes do renounce the use of power in sexual relationships. [12]

The first claim is unclear. Perhaps all it means

is that men are as sexually attracted to women as women are to men. This may be true, but it does not indicate any equality of power. If Held is claiming that men and women are equally able to seduce those to whom they are sexually attracted, her claim is less likely to be true. Men are still expected to make the first move and are often uneasy if the woman does. Also, wealth and social power serve to a man's advantage in such encounters, since a sexual connection with a man still confers nonsexual economic and social benefits on a woman, while the reverse is seldom true.

Even if men and women are equal in their power to seduce each other, such a limited kind of equality is insufficient for mutuality. The kind of equality needed to *sustain* mutuality would require social, economic, political, and psychological reforms. In the absence of these, Held asks us to accept renunciation of the use of power—presumably the closest we can get.

The relation itself . . . is characterized by a mutual renunciation of the use of power. *Equality of power may be a precondition for any satisfactory, voluntary, extended renunciation; otherwise the breakdown of the relation leaves women, as usual, in a position to be overpowered. But* exploration *of the relation need not await full achievement of such equality.* [13]

Thus Held is asking us to accept, as models for equal relationships, relationships between people who are unequal in power but who have renounced the *use* of power. But renunciation of the *use* of power does not solve the problem of women's vulnerability to the disproportionate social and physical power of men.

Let us assume that a feminist couple, Mary and John, have sincere intentions of building a mutual relationship within a sexist society. Even if John renounces the *use* of his excess power as a male, he has not renounced the *power* and still has more power than Mary. Hence all that stands between Mary and the threat of power is John's good will, while John is not similarly dependent on Mary's good will. As defenders of democracy have often pointed out, a reliance on the good will of the ruler is not a substitute for the power to keep him in check. For the same reasons, the good will of the more

---

[8] Held, "Marx, Sex," p. 174. [Page 160, this volume.]
[9] Held, "Marx, Sex," pp. 176, 177. [Page 162, this volume.]
[10] Held, "Marx, Sex," p. 172. [Page 160, this volume.]
[11] Held, "Marx, Sex," pp. 175, 176. [Page 161, this volume.]
[12] Held, "Marx, Sex," p. 177. [Page 162, this volume.]

[13] Held, "Marx, Sex," p. 177. [Page 162, this volume.]

powerful toward the less powerful should not be accepted as a full substitute for equality of power.[14]

Suppose that John tries to renounce not merely the *use* of his power but the power itself. He may give away the extra money he makes as a man and refuse to take a higher position if a more qualified woman is available. However, this again eliminates only the use of power; he can nonetheless change his mind and the advantages will still be waiting for him—but not for Mary. He can no more effectively relinquish the power due to a man in a sexist society than a white liberal can relinquish his advantage over Blacks. No matter how sincere the white male is, sexism and racism will operate to his advantage with or without his consent, and even the advantages that he is in a position to refuse are waiting for him if he changes his mind. Thus renunciation of the *use* of unequal power on the part of an individual is not sufficient for the creation of equality of power; and, unless we assume that sexual relationships are independent of social and political structures—in a way that, for example, nonsexual friendships between men and women are not—Held has not established her assumption that sexual politics is peculiarly amenable to personal solutions.

The lack of this assumption leaves unsupported her claim that the degree of mutuality possible in male/female sexual relationships is impossible or close to impossible in, for example, male/female friendships, collegial relationships, and nonsexual family relationships: "To argue that mutuality may be possible beyond a few special moments between a very few persons in close contact, as in the case of a man and woman making love, may well be utopian."[15]

Held's assumption that respect is more likely in sexual than in nonsexual relationships between men and women implies that sexism and sexual politics are less evident in the bedroom than outside it. Her extreme pessimism about implementing the ideal of mutual concern and respect to nonsexual relationships between men and women presupposes that there is little respect between men and women. If the nonsexual situation is as dire as she paints it, where does the respect that appears in the bedroom come from? Moreover, the characterization of respect as a feeling that can be momentary and completely unconnected to the rest of a person's life is a somewhat peculiar notion of respect. Thus, although the concept of respect that Held wants us to aim at is perfectly coherent (respect is not using one another, each valuing the other for the other's sake, and so on), the same cannot be said of its starting point, which consists in a man who does not respect women having momentary flashes of respect for a woman as a person during his sexual activities with her.

Given the prevalence of rape, rapelike sexual relations, and wife beating, some feminists are understandably skeptical of the claim that men are more likely to renounce the use of their power and to respect women in sexual and love relationships than in other relationships with women. Moreover, one cannot ignore the fact that in a sexist culture, men gain respect from other men on the basis of the femininity and beauty of the women who are their sexual partners. Hence one might argue that self-interest is actually more likely in sexual relationships between men and women than in friendships between them.

Held's arguments on both issues—respect and power—presuppose that love and sexual relationships take place in a social vacuum, or rather that such relationships can be substantially freer of social context than can other relationships. The CR separatist recommends that women should use relationships with feminist women both as models and as an alternative social context within which to pursue the kind of experiments that Held recommends women take on in isolation from such contacts. Thus the primary disagreements between Held's analysis and the CR theory are: (1) Held recommends that we take sexual relationships between men and women as our models of equal and mutual relationships, while the CR separatist recommends that we take relationships between feminist women as our models; and (2) Held seems to recommend an individual approach to the problem, while the CR separatist recommends the creation of an alternative social context within which women can function as autonomous and equal participants.

Since Held implies that greater inequality between sexual partners usually produces greater difficulty in attaining mutuality, one might expect her to approve of at least those forms of CR separatism that emphasize the necessity of developing personal strength in women. Perhaps her omission of the relevance of relationships between women and of feminist organizations is no more than an omission and should not be interpreted as a denial of

[14]Virginia Held suggested this analogy in correspondence about an earlier draft of this paper.

[15]Held, "Marx, Sex," p. 176. [Page 162, this volume.]

their importance. However, given the widespread acceptance of this model in mainstream feminist practice and theory, this omission is a fairly radical one. Moreover, her discussion of separatism suggests that the omission should indeed be taken as a denial.

If we leave out the covert assumption that sexual relationships have a peculiar relative independence of the social structure and of the character of the individuals involved, Held's assumptions lead us to the conclusion that, in a sexist society, mutuality is as unlikely in heterosexual love and sexual relations as it is in other relations between men and women and must wait on the development of social and economic equality. But, if equality of power and respect is necessary for mutuality, then in a sexist society same-sex relationships are more likely to be mutual than opposite-sex relationships.

The only explanation Held offers of what she thinks separatism is, and consequently which separatist position she is criticizing, is the following:

In pursuing the conditions of economic, political, social, and psychological equality for women, separatism—at least a separatism of feeling—may often seem to recommend itself. Women must support one another and struggle together against the centuries of tradition and experience that leave men so very well trained to be egoists and leaders. [16]

She goes on to say that "separatism is not only not an answer, but it robs us of the most promising source of experience."

Thus Held does seem to be committed to the fundamentally antiseparatist position that relationships between men and women are more valuable than relationships between women: "Relations between woman and woman, or man and man, may sometimes also offer experience in mutual concern and respect, but are not a comparable achievement and do not hold out a comparable hope for social transformation." [17] Her argument for this claim is that:

Man and woman . . . bring to their relation their affiliation with two groups possessing an extraordinary disparity of power in the society, and having an armory of conflicting group interests. To

transform these antagonisms into a relation of mutual concern and respect is far more significant than is the achievement of such a relation between members of the same sex. [18]

It should be noted that there is nothing in this argument to explain the rejection of relationships between women as models. A woman might be committed to the challenge of converting heterosexual relationships to something more nearly resembling mutuality, yet insist on using relationships between women, even lesbian relationships, as the model toward which she is attempting to transform the heterosexual relationship.

Held's argument that heterosexual relationships are more valuable because they are more challenging is a bit puzzling. One might turn it around and ask why we should give priority to such relationships despite the difficulties that Held is so eloquent in describing:

In trying to live with a recognition of the importance of both fighting and loving, women will have to accept a kind of schizophrenic existence. [19]

At this stage in history, women have centuries of experience in relating to men. What we lack, and what the separatist claims we need, is relationships with women in which women are the primary focus of emotional commitment. In contrast, history may already offer us close to the best models of heterosexual relationships obtainable in a sexist society—for example, that of John Stuart Mill and Harriet Taylor Mill. But Held recommends instead a use of that history to enable women to withstand the suffering they accept in choosing a primary emotional commitment to relationships with men:

Women have the whole of history to call upon for lessons in not flying apart, torn as they have always been by the conflicting wills within them. . . . If there is anything they are entitled to use it is the history of their oppression and the skills it has given them. Women know already how to live divided. [20]

Moreover, Held seems to suggest that women should take primary responsibility in the attempt to transform heterosexual relationships into relationships of mutuality:

---

[16]Held, "Marx, Sex," p. 179. [Page 162, this volume.]
[17]Held, "Marx, Sex," p. 179. [Page 162, this volume.]

[18]Held, "Marx, Sex," p. 179. [Page 162, this volume.]
[19]Held, "Marx, Sex," p. 182. [Page 163, this volume.]
[20]Held, "Marx, Sex," p. 182. [Page 163, this volume.]

Women who experience the mutual concern and respect of love even for moments at a time can try to discover ways of extending this alternative to egoism and competition.[21]

Perhaps Held is suggesting that relationships between men and women are preferable to relationships between women in that male-female relationships show a commitment to liberating men as well as women. There is a suggestion here that a feminist woman's commitment to helping other women is selfish in a way that a similar concern for helping men would not be. However, if the separatist is correct in assuming that an essential characteristic of liberation is social self-determination organized around a common oppression, then men must liberate themselves and each other. Thus, such a concern for men on the part of a feminist woman might express, to some degree at least, a self-defeating paternalism, while it is the separatist who respects men's autonomy.

Despite the fact that Held's conclusion presupposes a rejection of lesbianfeminism (even in its least radical form) and of some versions of CR separatism, her criticisms of separatism are mainly aimed at asexual separatism:

An integrated stance toward the world is a distant goal to be sought, a luxury they [women] cannot yet afford. But it would be a mistake, I think, to think that love is a luxury they cannot afford. . . .[22]

This last comment is simply off the point, unless we assume that Held is talking about asexual separatism. Neither lesbianfeminism nor CR separatism recommends that feminists give up love. Since her discussion until this point has only considered whether or not women should love men —rather than whether or not women should love —this remark suggests that her omission of lesbianfeminism is a straightforward expression of heterosexism. Throughout her discussion of sexual relations, Held treats "the sexual relation" and other general characterizations as equivalent to "the relationship between man and woman" and other specifically heterosexual descriptions. This practice is heterosexist in exactly the same way that treating "human being" and "male human being" as interchangeable is sexist; and it is objectionable for similar reasons.

The final part of Held's argument is in terms of goals and means:

If one seeks the transformation of society into a community of equals, rather than simply a warring collection of persons or groups with equal power, then separatism is . . . not an answer. . . .[23]

If our goal is a community of equals, the appropriate model to build would seem to be that which comes closest to being a community of equals. According to the separatist, that model is best pursued in a sexist society through the development of an independent womanculture and in the fostering of pride, mutual respect, and caring between women.

But, says Held,

if women refuse to let themselves love men, they betray the goal of society in which power is not the ultimate arbiter.[24]

The separatist would argue that, in the present society, a woman who is committed to relationships with men in preference to relationships with women is committed to relationships of unequal power. It is the refusal to let unequal power corrupt love that motivates lesbianfeminism. The general separatist commitment to caring about the powerless rather than the powerful would seem to be more reasonably interpreted as a rejection of power than would a commitment to loving the powerful.

Held's discussion of separatism clearly focuses on the fact that feminist separatists may not value love relationships between men and women rather than on the fact that separatism requires a commitment to women. Marković is even more extreme in his portrayal of separatism as primarily an expression of man-hating. To the extent that both writers regard feminist separatism only in terms of its relationship to men, both of them beg the question; since they are assuming that it is the effect on the oppressor or on relationships between the oppressed and the oppressor that should decide the issues. And to the extent that they deal with such aspects of the theory and fail to deal with the central principles of sisterhood, solidarity, the noncontingent womanculture, and pride, they are criticizing side issues and strawwomen. Thus, although there may be serious objections to separatism either from

---

[21] Held, "Marx, Sex," p. 180.
[22] Held, "Marx, Sex," pp. 182, 183. [Page 163, this volume.]

[23] Held, "Marx, Sex," p. 179. [Page 162, this volume.]
[24] Held, "Marx, Sex," p. 180. [Page 163, this volume.]

a moral or a pragmatic point of view, neither Held nor Marković offers any.

However, their seeming preoccupation with a perceived threat to heterosexual love may indicate where some of the political problems lie, and may also indicate some of the ways in which feminist analysis must differ from, for example, an analysis of racism. Racist sexual taboos are those against loving a member of another race. Thus, the Black separatist position on love—that Blacks ought to love and marry only Blacks—is consistent with racist doctrine; and a racist might be perfectly happy with the personal separatism—as opposed to the self-affirmation and power—of Black militancy. The feminist problem is exactly the opposite. Unlike Blacks, women are supposed to be individually dependent on members of the ruling caste, and the primary services required of women are love and sex. Thus feminism calls for a reevaluation of the structure and value of heterosexual relationships, of marriage, and of the family; this may bring into question values and assumptions that are more deeply embedded in the culture than are any of the assumptions of racism.

An analysis of sexual politics is crucial to feminism, since that is one area where it is clear that an analysis of oppression developed to cover racism is not adequately transferable to sexism. Perhaps, now that the issues have been raised, more philosophical work will build on the significant contribution offered by these articles while showing a greater awareness of the feminist separatist literature and a greater willingness to treat feminism as an independent political theory rather than simply as an application of traditional liberalism or Marxism to women's problems.

5
Marriage and Family

25/The Origin of the Family, Private Property, and the State
Friedrich Engels

The overthrow of mother-right was the *world historical defeat of the female sex.* The man took command in the home also; the woman was degraded and reduced to servitude, she became the slave of his lust and a mere instrument for the production of children. This degraded position of the woman, especially conspicuous among the Greeks of the heroic and still more of the classical age, has gradually been palliated and glozed over, and sometimes clothed in a milder form; in no sense has it been abolished.

The establishment of the exclusive supremacy of the man shows its effects first in the patriarchal family, which now emerges as an intermediate form. Its essential characteristic is not polygyny, of which more later, but "the organization of a number of persons, bond and free, into a family, under paternal power, for the purpose of holding lands, and for the care of flocks and herds. . . . (In the Semitic form) the chiefs, at least, lived in polygamy. . . . Those held to servitude, and those employed as servants, lived in the marriage relation."[1]

Its essential features are the incorporation of unfree persons, and paternal power; hence the perfect type of this form of family is the Roman. The original meaning of the word "family" (*familia*) is not that compound of sentimentality and domestic strife which forms the ideal of the present-day philistine; among the Romans it did not at first even refer to the married pair and their children, but only to the slaves. *Famulus* means domestic slave, and *familia* is the total number of slaves belonging to one man. As late as the time of Gaius, the *familia, id est patrimonium* (family, that is, the patrimony, the inheritance) was bequeathed by will. The term was invented by the Romans to denote a new social organism, whose head ruled over wife and children and a number of slaves, and was invested under Roman paternal power with rights of life and death over them all.

This term, therefore, is no older than the iron-clad family system of the Latin tribes, which came in after field agriculture and after legalized servitude, as well as after the separation of the Greeks and Latins.[2]

Marx adds:

*The modern family contains in germ not only slavery (*servitus*), but also serfdom, since from the beginning it is related to agricultural services. It contains* in miniature *all the contradictions which later extend throughout society and its state.*

Such a form of family shows the transition of the pairing family to monogamy. In order to make certain of the wife's fidelity and therefore of the paternity of the children, she is delivered over unconditionally into the power of the husband; if he kills her, he is only exercising his rights. . . . [The monogamous family] develops out of the pairing family, as previously shown, in the transitional period between the upper and middle stages of barbarism; its decisive victory is one of the signs that civilization is beginning. It is based on the supremacy of the man, the express purpose being to produce children of undisputed paternity; such

[1]Morgan, [Lewis H., *Ancient Society, or Researchers in the Lines of Human Progress from Savagery through Barbarism to Civilization* (London: MacMillan, 1877)] p. 474—*Ed.*

[2]*Ibid.*, p. 478.

From *The Origin of the Family, Private Property, and the State* (New York: International Publishers, 1942). Reprinted by permission. The editor referred to in the footnotes is anonymous.

paternity is demanded because these children are later to come into their father's property as his natural heirs. It is distinguished from pairing marriage by the much greater strength of the marriage tie, which can no longer be dissolved at either partner's wish. As a rule, it is now only the man who can dissolve it, and put away his wife. The right of conjugal infidelity also remains secured to him, at any rate by custom (the *Code Napoléon* explicitly accords it to the husband as long as he does not bring his concubine into the house), and as social life develops he exercises his right more and more; should the wife recall the old form of sexual life and attempt to revive it, she is punished more severely than ever.

We meet this new form of the family in all its severity among the Greeks. While the position of the goddesses in their mythology, as Marx points out, brings before us an earlier period when the position of women was freer and more respected, in the heroic age we find the woman already being humiliated by the domination of the man and by competition from girl slaves. Note how Telemachus in the *Odyssey* silences his mother.[3] In Homer young women are booty and are handed over to the pleasure of the conquerors, the handsomest being picked by the commanders in order of rank; the entire *Iliad,* it will be remembered, turns on the quarrel of Achilles and Agamemnon over one of these slaves. If a hero is of any importance, Homer also mentions the captive girl with whom he shares his tent and his bed. These girls were also taken back to Greece and brought under the same roof as the wife, as Cassandra was brought by Agamemnon in Aeschylus; the sons begotten of them received a small share of the paternal inheritance and had the full status of freemen. Teucer, for instance, is a natural son of Telamon by one of these slaves and has the right to use his father's name. The legitimate wife was expected to put up with all this, but herself to remain strictly chaste and faithful. In the heroic age a Greek woman is, indeed, more respected than in the period of civilization, but to her husband she is after all nothing but the mother of his legitimate children and heirs, his chief housekeeper and the supervisor of his female slaves, whom he can and does take as concubines if he so fancies. It is the existence of slavery side by side with monogamy,

the presence of young, beautiful slaves belonging unreservedly to the *man,* that stamps monogamy from the very beginning with its specific character of monogamy *for the woman only,* but not for the man. And that is the character it still has today. . . . [Monogamy] was not in any way the fruit of individual sex-love, with which it had nothing whatever to do; marriages remained as before marriages of convenience. It was the first form of the family to be based, not on natural, but on economic conditions—on the victory of private property over primitive, natural communal property. The Greeks themselves put the matter quite frankly: the sole exclusive aims of monogamous marriage were to make the man supreme in the family, and to propagate, as the future heirs to his wealth, children indisputably his own. Otherwise, marriage was a burden, a duty which had to be performed, whether one liked it or not, to gods, state, and one's ancestors. In Athens the law exacted from the man not only marriage but also the performance of a minimum of so-called conjugal duties.

Thus when monogamous marriage first makes its appearance in history, it is not as the reconciliation of man and woman, still less as the highest form of such a reconciliation. Quite the contrary. Monogamous marriage comes on the scene as the subjugation of the one sex by the other; it announces a struggle between the sexes unknown throughout the whole previous prehistoric period. In an old unpublished manuscript, written by Marx and myself in 1846,[4] I find the words: "The first division of labor is that between man and woman for the propagation of children." And today I can add: The first class opposition that appears in history coincides with the development of the antagonism between man and woman in monogamous marriage, and the first class oppression coincides with that of the female sex by the male. Monogamous marriage was a great historical step forward; nevertheless, together with slavery and private wealth, it opens the period that has lasted until today in which every step forward is also relatively a step backward, in which prosperity and development for some is won through the misery and frustration of others. It is the cellular form of civilized society, in which the nature of the oppositions and contradictions fully active in that society can be already studied.

[3]The reference is to a passage where Telemachus, son of Odysseus and Penelope, tells his mother to get on with her weaving and leave the men to mind their own business (*Odyssey*, Bk. 21, 11. 350 ff.).—*Ed.*

[4]The reference here is to the *Deutsche Ideologie* (*German Ideology*), written by Marx and Engels in Brussels in 1845–46 and first published in 1932 by the Marx-Engels-Lenin Institute in Moscow. See *German Ideology*, New York, 1939.—*Ed.*

The old comparative freedom of sexual intercourse by no means disappeared with the victory of pairing marriage or even of monogamous marriage:

The old conjugal system, now reduced to narrower limits by the gradual disappearance of the punaluan groups, still environed the advancing family, which it was to follow to the verge of civilization. . . . It finally disappeared in the new form of hetaerism, which still follows mankind in civilization as a dark shadow upon the family. [5]

By "hetaerism" Morgan understands the practice, *co-existent with monogamous marriage,* of sexual intercourse between men and unmarried women outside marriage, which, as we know, flourishes in the most varied forms throughout the whole period of civilization and develops more and more into open prostitution. This hetaerism derives quite directly from group marriage, from the ceremonial surrender by which women purchased the right of chastity. Surrender for money was at first a religious act; it took place in the temple of the goddess of love, and the money originally went into the temple treasury. The temple slaves of Anaitis in Armenia and of Aphrodite in Corinth, like the sacred dancing-girls attached to the temples of India, the so-called *bayaderes* (the word is a corruption of the Portuguese word *bailadeira,* meaning female dancer), were the first prostitutes. Originally the duty of every woman, this surrender was later performed by these priestesses alone as representatives of all other women. Among other peoples, hetaerism derives from the sexual freedom allowed to girls before marriage—again, therefore, a relic of group marriage, but handed down in a different way. With the rise of the inequality of property—already at the upper stage of barbarism, therefore—wage-labor appears sporadically side by side with slave labor, and at the same time, as its necessary correlate, the professional prostitution of free women side by side with the forced surrender of the slave. Thus the heritage which group marriage has bequeathed to civilization is double-edged, just as everything civilization brings forth is double-edged, double-tongued, divided against itself, contradictory: here monogamy, there hetaerism, with its most extreme form, prostitution. For hetaerism is as much a social institution as any other; it continues the old sexual

freedom—to the advantage of the men. Actually not merely tolerated, but gaily practiced, by the ruling classes particularly, it is condemned in words. But in reality this condemnation never falls on the men concerned, but only on the women; they are despised and outcast, in order that the unconditional supremacy of men over the female sex may be once more proclaimed as a fundamental law of society.

But a second contradiction thus develops within monogamous marriage itself. At the side of the husband who embellishes his existence with hetaerism stands the neglected wife. And one cannot have one side of this contradiction without the other, any more than a man has a whole apple in his hand after eating half. But that seems to have been the husbands' notion, until their wives taught them better. With monogamous marriage, two constant social types, unknown hitherto, make their appearance on the scene—the wife's attendant lover and the cuckold husband. The husbands had won the victory over the wives, but the vanquished magnanimously provided the crown. Together with monogamous marriage and hetaerism, adultery became an unavoidable social institution—denounced, severely penalized, but impossible to suppress. At best, the certain paternity of the children rested on moral conviction as before, and to solve the insoluble contradiction the *Code Napoléon,* Art. 312, decreed: *"L'enfant conçu pendant le mariage a pour père le mari,"* the father of a child conceived during marriage is—the husband. Such is the final result of three thousand years of monogamous marriage.

Thus, wherever the monogamous family remains true to its historical origin and clearly reveals the antagonism between the man and the woman expressed in the man's exclusive supremacy, it exhibits in miniature the same oppositions and contradictions as those in which society has been moving, without power to resolve or overcome them, ever since it split into classes at the beginning of civilization. I am speaking here, of course, only of those cases of monogamous marriage where matrimonial life actually proceeds according to the original character of the whole institution, but where the wife rebels against the husband's supremacy. Not all marriages turn out thus, as nobody knows better than the German philistine, who can no more assert his rule in the home than he can in the state, and whose wife, with every right, wears the trousers he is unworthy of. But, to make up for it, he considers himself far above his French companion in misfor-

---

[5] Morgan, *op. cit.,* p. 511.—*Ed.*

tune, to whom, oftener than to him, something much worse happens. . . .

But if monogamy was the only one of all the known forms of the family through which modern sex-love could develop, that does not mean that within monogamy modern sexual love developed exclusively or even chiefly as the love of husband and wife for each other. That was precluded by the very nature of strictly monogamous marriage under the rule of the man. Among all historically active classes—that is, among all ruling classes—matrimony remained what it had been since the pairing marriage, a matter of convenience which was arranged by the parents. The first historical form of sexual love as passion, a passion recognized as natural to all human beings (at least if they belonged to the ruling classes), and as the highest form of the sexual impulse—and that is what constitutes its specific character—this first form of individual sexual love, the chivalrous love of the Middle Ages, was by no means conjugal. Quite the contrary. In its classic form among the Provençals, it heads straight for adultery, and the poets of love celebrated adultery. The flower of Provençal love poetry are the Albas (*aubades,* songs of dawn). They describe in glowing colors how the knight lies in bed beside his love—the wife of another man —while outside stands the watchman who calls to him as soon as the first gray of dawn (*alba*) appears, so that he can get away unobserved; the parting scene then forms the climax of the poem. The northern French and also the worthy Germans adopted this kind of poetry together with the corresponding fashion of chivalrous love; old Wolfram of Eschenbach has left us three wonderfully beautiful songs of dawn on this same improper subject, which I like better than his three long heroic poems.

Nowadays there are two ways of concluding a bourgeois marriage. In Catholic countries the parents, as before, procure a suitable wife for their young bourgeois son, and the consequence is, of course, the fullest development of the contradiction inherent in monogamy: the husband abandons himself to hetaerism and the wife to adultery. Probably the only reason why the Catholic Church abolished divorce was because it had convinced itself that there is no more a cure for adultery than there is for death. In Protestant countries, on the other hand, the rule is that the son of a bourgeois family is allowed to choose a wife from his own class with more or less freedom; hence there may be a certain element of love in the marriage, as, indeed, in ac-

cordance with Protestant hypocrisy, is always assumed, for decency's sake. Here the husband's hetaerism is a more sleepy kind of business, and adultery by the wife is less the rule. But since, in every kind of marriage, people remain what they were before, and since the bourgeois of Protestant countries are mostly philistines, all that this Protestant monogamy achieves, taking the average of the best cases, is a conjugal partnership of leaden boredom, known as "domestic bliss." The best mirror of these two methods of marrying is the novel —the French novel for the Catholic manner, the German for the Protestant. In both, the hero "gets" them: in the German, the young man gets the girl; in the French, the husband gets the horns. Which of them is worse off is sometimes questionable. This is why the French bourgeois is as much horrified by the dullness of the German novel as the German philistine is by the "immorality" of the French. However, now that "Berlin is a world capital," the German novel is beginning with a little less timidity to use as part of its regular stock-in-trade the hetaerism and adultery long familiar to that town.

In both cases, however, the marriage is conditioned by the class position of the parties and is to that extent always a marriage of convenience. In both cases this marriage of convenience turns often enough into crassest prostitution—sometimes of both partners, but far more commonly of the woman, who only differs from the ordinary courtesan in that she does not let out her body on piece-work as a wage-worker, but sells it once and for all into slavery. And of all marriages of convenience Fourier's words hold true: "As in grammar two negatives make an affirmative, so in matrimonial morality two prostitutions pass for a virtue."[6] Sex-love in the relationship with a woman becomes, and can only become, the real rule among the oppressed classes, which means today among the proletariat—whether this relation is officially sanctioned or not. But here all the foundations of typical monogamy are cleared away. Here there is no property, for the preservation and inheritance of which monogamy and male supremacy were established; hence there is no incentive to make this male supremacy effective. What is more, there are no means of making it so. Bourgeois law, which protects this supremacy, exists only for the possessing class and their dealings

---

[6]Charles Fourier, *Théorie de l'Unité Universelle.* Paris, 1841–45, Vol. III, p. 120.—*Ed.*

with the proletarians. The law costs money and, on account of the worker's poverty, it has no validity for his relation to his wife. Here quite other personal and social conditions decide. And now that large-scale industry has taken the wife out of the home onto the labor market and into the factory, and made her often the breadwinner of the family, no basis for any kind of male supremacy is left in the proletarian household—except, perhaps, for something of the brutality towards women that has spread since the introduction of monogamy. The proletarian family is therefore no longer monogamous in the strict sense, even where there is passionate love and firmest loyalty on both sides, and maybe all the blessings of religious and civil authority. Here, therefore, the eternal attendants of monogamy, hetaerism and adultery, play only an almost vanishing part. The wife has in fact regained the right to dissolve the marriage, an if two people cannot get on with one another, they prefer to separate. In short, proletarian marriage, and if two people cannot get on with one another, they prefer to separate. In short, proletarian

Our jurists, of course, find that progress in legislation is leaving women with no further ground of complaint. Modern civilized systems of law increasingly acknowledge, first, that for a marriage to be legal, it must be a contract freely entered into by both partners, and, secondly, that also in the married state both partners must stand on a common footing of equal rights and duties. If both these demands are consistently carried out, say the jurists, women have all they can ask.

This typically legalist method of argument is exactly the same as that which the radical republican bourgeois uses to put the proletarian in his place. The labor contract is to be freely entered into by both partners. But it is considered to have been freely entered into as soon as the law makes both parties equal on *paper*. The power conferred on the one party by the difference of class position, the pressure thereby brought to bear on the other party—the real economic position of both—that is not the law's business. Again, for the duration of the labor contract both parties are to have equal rights, in so far as one or the other does not expressly surrender them. That economic relations compel the worker to surrender even the last semblance of equal rights—here again, that is no concern of the law.

In regard to marriage, the law, even the most advanced, is fully satisfied as soon as the partners have formally recorded that they are entering into

the marriage of their own free consent. What goes on in real life behind the juridical scenes, how this free consent comes about—that is not the business of the law and the jurist. And yet the most elementary comparative jurisprudence should show the jurist what this free consent really amounts to. In the countries where an obligatory share of the paternal inheritance is secured to the children by law and they cannot therefore be disinherited—in Germany, in the countries with French law and elsewhere—the children are obliged to obtain their parents' consent to their marriage. In the countries with English law, where parental consent to a marriage is not legally required, the parents on their side have full freedom in the testamentary disposal of their property and can disinherit their children at their pleasure. It is obvious that, in spite and precisely because of this fact, freedom of marriage among the classes with something to inherit is in reality not a whit greater in England and America than it is in France and Germany.

As regards the legal equality of husband and wife in marriage, the position is no better. The legal inequality of the two partners, bequeathed to us from earlier social conditions, is not the cause but the effect of the economic oppression of the woman. In the old communistic household, which comprised many couples and their children, the task entrusted to the women of managing the household was as much a public and socially necessary industry as the procuring of food by the men. With the patriarchal family, and still more with the single monogamous family, a change came. Household management lost its public character. It no longer concerned society. It became a *private service;* the wife became the head servant, excluded from all participation in social production. Not until the coming of modern large-scale industry was the road to social production opened to her again—and then only to the proletarian wife. But it was opened in such a manner that, if she carries out her duties in the private service of her family, she remains excluded from public production and unable to earn; and if she wants to take part in public production and earn independently, she cannot carry out family duties. And the wife's position in the factory is the position of women in all branches of business, right up to medicine and the law. The modern individual family is founded on the open or concealed domestic slavery of the wife, and modern society is a mass composed of these individual families as its molecules.

In the great majority of cases today, at least in

the possessing classes, the husband is obliged to earn a living and support his family, and that in itself gives him a position of supremacy, without any need for special legal titles and privileges. Within the family he is the bourgeois and the wife represents the proletariat. In the industrial world, the specific character of the economic oppression burdening the proletariat is visible in all its sharpness only when all special legal privileges of the capitalist class have been abolished and complete legal equality of both classes established. The democratic republic does not do away with the opposition of the two classes; on the contrary, it provides the clear field on which the fight can be fought out. And in the same way, the peculiar character of the supremacy of the husband over the wife in the modern family, the necessity of creating real social equality between them, and the way to do it, will only be seen in the clear light of day when both possess legally complete equality of rights. Then it will be plain that the first condition for the liberation of the wife is to bring the whole female sex back into public industry, and that this in turn demands the abolition of the monogamous family as the economic unit of society.

We thus have three principal forms of marriage which correspond broadly to the three principal stages of human development. For the period of savagery, group marriage; for barbarism, pairing marriage; for civilization, monogamy, supplemented by adultery and prostitution. Between pairing marriage and monogamy intervenes a period in the upper stage of barbarism when men have female slaves at their command and polygamy is practiced.

As our whole presentation has shown, the progress which manifests itself in these successive forms is connected with the pecularity that women, but not men, are increasingly deprived of the sexual freedom of group marriage. In fact, for men group marriage actually still exists even to this day. What for the woman is a crime, entailing grave legal and social consequences, is considered honorable in a man or, at the worse, a slight moral blemish which he cheerfully bears. But the more the hetaerism of the past is changed in our time by capitalist commodity production and brought into conformity with it, the more, that is to say, it is transformed into undisguised prostitution, the more demoralizing are its effects. And it demoralizes men far more than women. Among women, prostitution degrades only the unfortunate ones who become its victims, and even these by no means to the extent commonly believed. But it degrades the character of the whole

male world. A long engagement, particularly, is in nine cases out of ten a regular preparatory school for conjugal infidelity.

We are now approaching a social revolution in which the economic foundations of monogamy as they have existed hitherto will disappear just as surely as those of its complement—prostitution. Monogamy arose from the concentration of considerable wealth in the hands of a single individual—a man—and from the need to bequeath this wealth to the children of that man and of no other. For this purpose, the monogamy of the woman was required, not that of the man, so this monogamy of the woman did not in any way interfere with open or concealed polygamy on the part of the man. But by transforming by far the greater portion, at any rate, of permanent, heritable wealth—the means of production—into social property, the coming social revolution will reduce to a minimum all this anxiety about bequeathing and inheriting. Having arisen from economic causes, will monogamy then disappear when these causes disappear?

One might answer, not without reason: far from disappearing, it will, on the contrary, be realized completely. For with the transformation of the means of production into social property there will disappear also wage-labor, the proletariat, and therefore the necessity for a certain—statistically calculable—number of women to surrender themselves for money. Prostitution disappears; monogamy, instead of collapsing, at last becomes a reality—also for men.

In any case, therefore, the position of men will be very much altered. But the position of women, of *all* women, also undergoes significant change. With the transfer of the means of production into common ownership, the single family ceases to be the economic unit of society. Private housekeeping is transformed into a social industry. The care and education of the children becomes a public affair: society looks after all children alike, whether they are legitimate or not. This removes all the anxiety about the "consequences," which today is the most essential social—moral as well as economic—factor that prevents a girl from giving herself completely to the man she loves. Will not that suffice to bring about the gradual growth of unconstrained sexual intercourse and with it a more tolerant public opinion in regard to a maiden's honor and a woman's shame? And, finally, have we not seen that in the modern world monogamy and prostitution are indeed contradictions, but inseparable contradictions, poles of the same state of society? Can prostitution disappear without dragging monogamy with it into the abyss?

Here a new element comes into play, an element which, at the time when monogamy was developing, existed at most in germ: individual sex-love.

Before the Middle Ages we cannot speak of individual sex-love. That personal beauty, close intimacy, similarity of tastes and so forth awakened in people of opposite sex the desire for sexual intercourse, that men and women were not totally indifferent regarding the partner with whom they entered into this most intimate relationship—that goes without saying. But it is still a very long way to our sexual love. Throughout the whole of antiquity, marriages were arranged by the parents, and the partners calmly accepted their choice. What little love there was between husband and wife in antiquity is not so much subjective inclination as objective duty, not the cause of the marriage, but its corollary. Love relationships in the modern sense only occur in antiquity outside official society. The shepherds of whose joys and sorrows in love Theocritus and Moschus sing, the Daphnis and Chloe of Longus are all slaves who have no part in the state, the free citizen's sphere of life. Except among slaves, we find love affairs only as products of the disintegration of the old world and carried on with women who also stand outside official society, with *hetairai*—that is, with foreigners or freed slaves: in Athens from the eve of its decline, in Rome under the Caesars. If there were any real love affairs between free men and free women, these occurred only in the course of adultery. And to the classical love poet of antiquity, old Anacreon, sexual love in our sense mattered so little that it did not even matter to him which sex his beloved was.

Our sexual love differs essentially from the simple sexual desire, the Eros, of the ancients. In the first place, it assumes that the person loved returns the love; to this extent the woman is on an equal footing with the man, whereas in the Eros of antiquity she was often not even asked. Secondly, our sexual love has a degree of intensity and duration which makes both lovers feel that non-possession and separation are a great, if not the greatest, calamity; to possess one another, they risk high stakes, even life itself. In the ancient world this happened only, if at all, in adultery. And, finally, there arises a new moral standard in the judgment of a sexual relationship. We do not only ask, was it

within or outside marriage? but also, did it spring from love and reciprocated love or not? Of course, this new standard has fared no better in feudal or bourgeois practice than all the other standards of morality—it is ignored. But neither does it fare any worse. It is recognized just as much as they are—in theory, on paper. And for the present it cannot ask anything more.

At the point where antiquity broke off its advance to sexual love, the Middle Ages took it up again: in adultery. We have already described the knightly love which gave rise to the songs of dawn. From the love which strives to break up marriage to the love which is to be its foundation there is still a long road, which chivalry never fully traversed. Even when we pass from the frivolous Latins to the virtuous Germans, we find in the *Nibelungenlied* that, although in her heart Kriemhild is as much in love with Siegfried as he is with her, yet when Gunther announces that he has promised her to a knight he does not name, she simply replies: "You have no need to ask me; as you bid me, so will I ever be; whom you, lord, give me as husband, him will I gladly take in troth." It never enters her head that her love can be even considered. Gunther asks for Brünhild in marriage, and Etzel for Kriemhild, though they have never seen them. Similarly, in *Gutrun,* Sigebant of Ireland asks for the Norweigan Ute, whom he has never seen, Hetel of Hegelingen for Hilde of Ireland, and, finally, Siegfried of Moorland, Hartmut of Ormany and Herwig of Seeland for Gutrun, and here Gutrun's acceptance of Herwig is for the first time voluntary. As a rule, the young prince's bride is selected by his parents, if they are still living, or, if not, by the prince himself, with the advice of the great feudal lords, who have a weighty word to say in all these cases. Nor can it be otherwise. For the knight or baron, as for the prince of the land himself, marriage is a political act, an opportunity to increase power by new alliances; the interest of the *house* must be decisive, not the wishes of an individual. What chance then is there for love to have the final word in the making of a marriage?

The same thing holds for the guild member in the medieval towns. The very privileges protecting him, the guild charters with all their clauses and rubrics, the intricate distinctions legally separating him from other guilds, from the members of his own guild or from his journeymen and apprentices, already made the circle narrow enough within which he could look for a suitable wife. And who in the circle was the most suitable was decided under this complicated system most certainly not by his individual preference but by the family interests.

In the vast majority of cases, therefore, marriage remained, up to the close of the Middle Ages, what it had been from the start—a matter which was not decided by the partners. In the beginning, people were already born married—married to an entire group of the opposite sex. In the later forms of group marriage similar relations probably existed, but with the group continually contracting. In the pairing marriage it was customary for the mothers to settle the marriages of their children; here, too, the decisive considerations are the new ties of kinship, which are to give the young pair a stronger position in the gens and tribe. And when, with the preponderance of private over communal property and the interest in its bequeathal, father-right and monogamy gained supremacy, the dependence of marriages on economic considerations became complete. The *form* of marriage by purchase disappears, the actual practice is steadily extended until not only the woman but also the man acquires a price—not according to his personal qualities, but according to his property. That the mutual affection of the people concerned should be the one paramount reason for marriage, outweighing everything else, was and always had been absolutely unheard of in the practice of the ruling classes; that sort of thing only happened in romance—or among the oppressed classes, who did not count.

Such was the state of things encountered by capitalist production when it began to prepare itself, after the epoch of geographical discoveries, to win world power by world trade and manufacture. One would suppose that this manner of marriage exactly suited it, and so it did. And yet—there are no limits to the irony of history—capitalist production itself was to make the decisive breach in it. By changing all things into commodities, it dissolved all inherited and traditional relationships, and, in place of time-honored custom and historic right, it set up purchase and sale, "free" contract. And the English jurist, H. S. Maine, thought he had made a tremendous discovery when he said that our whole progress in comparison with former epochs consisted in the fact that we had passed "from status to contract," from inherited to freely contracted conditions—which, in so far as it is correct, was already in *The Communist Manifesto* (Chapter II).

But a contract requires people who can dispose freely of their persons, actions, and possessions, and meet each other on the footing of equal rights. To create these "free" and "equal" people was one of the main tasks of capitalist production. Even though at the start it was carried out only half-consciously, and under a religious disguise at that, from the time of the Lutheran and Calvinist Reformation the principle was established that man is only fully responsible for his actions when he acts with complete freedom of will, and that it is a moral duty to resist all coercion to an immoral act. But how did this fit in with the hitherto existing practice in the arrangement of marriages? Marriage, according to the bourgeois conception, was a contract, a legal transaction, and the most important one of all, because it disposed of two human beings, body and mind, for life. Formally, it is true, the contract at that time was entered into voluntarily: without the assent of the persons concerned, nothing could be done. But everyone knew only too well how this assent was obtained and who were the real contracting parties in the marriage. But if real freedom of decision was required for all other contracts, then why not for this? Had not the two young people to be coupled also the right to dispose freely of themselves, of their bodies and organs? Had not chivalry brought sex-love into fashion, and was not its proper bourgeois form, in contrast to chivalry's adulterous love, the love of husband and wife? And if it was the duty of married people to love each other, was it not equally the duty of lovers to marry each other and nobody else? Did not this right of the lovers stand higher than the right of parents, relations, and other traditional marriage-brokers and matchmakers? If the right of free, personal discrimination broke boldly into the Church and religion, how should it halt before the intolerable claim of the older generation to dispose of the body, soul, property, happiness, and unhappiness of the younger generation?

These questions inevitably arose at a time which was loosening all the old ties of society and undermining all traditional conceptions. The world had suddenly grown almost ten times bigger; instead of one quadrant of a hemisphere, the whole globe lay before the gaze of the West Europeans, who hastened to take the other seven quadrants into their possession. And with the old narrow barriers of their homeland fell also the thousand-year-old barriers of the prescribed medieval way of thought. To the outward and the inward eye of man opened an infinitely wider horizon. What did a young man care about the approval of respectability, or honorable guild privileges handed down for generations, when the wealth of India beckoned to him, the gold and the silver mines of Mexico and Potosi? For the bourgeoisie, it was the time of knight-errantry; they, too, had their romance and their raptures of love, but on a bourgeois footing and, in the last analysis, with bourgeois aims.

So it came about that the rising bourgeoisie, especially in Protestant countries, where existing conditions had been most severely shaken, increasingly recognized freedom of contract also in marriage, and carried it into effect in the manner described. Marriage remained class marriage, but within the class the partners were conceded a certain degree of freedom of choice. And on paper, in ethical theory and in poetic description, nothing was more immutably established than that every marriage is immoral which does not rest on mutual sexual love and really free agreement of husband and wife. In short, the love marriage was proclaimed as a human right, and indeed not only as a *droit de l'homme,* one of the rights of man, but also, for once in a way, as *droit de la femme,* one of the rights of woman.

This human right, however, differed in one respect from all other so-called human rights. While the latter, in practice, remain restricted to the ruling class (the bourgeoisie), and are directly or indirectly curtailed for the oppressed class (the proletariat), in the case of the former the irony of history plays another of its tricks. The ruling class remains dominated by the familiar economic influences and therefore only in exceptional cases does it provide instances of really freely contracted marriages, while among the oppressed class, as we have seen, these marriages are the rule.

Full freedom of marriage can therefore only be generally established when the abolition of capitalist production and of the property relations created by it has removed all the accompanying economic considerations which still exert such a powerful influence on the choice of a marriage partner. For then there is no other motive left except mutual inclination.

And as sexual love is by its nature exclusive—although at present this exclusiveness is fully realized only in the woman—the marriage based on sexual love is by its nature individual marriage. We have seen how right Bachofen was in regarding the advance from group marriage to individual marriage as primarily due to the women. Only the step from pairing marriage to monogamy can be put down to the credit of the men, and historically the essence of this was to make the posi-tion of the women worse and the infidelities of the men easier. If now the economic considerations also disappear which made women put up with the habitual infidelity of their husbands—concern for their own means of existence and still more for their children's future—then, according to all previous experience, the equality of woman thereby achieved will tend infinitely more to make men really monogamous than to make women polyandrous.

But what will quite certainly disappear from monogamy are all the features stamped upon it through its origin in property relations; these are, in the first place, supremacy of the man, and, secondly, indissolubility. The supremacy of the man in marriage is the simple consequence of his economic supremacy, and with the abolition of the latter will disappear of itself. The indissolubility of marriage is partly a consequence of the economic situation in which monogamy arose, partly tradition from the period when the connection between this economic situation and monogamy was not yet fully understood and was carried to extremes under a religious form. Today it is already broken through at a thousand points. If only the marriage based on love is moral, then also only the marriage in which love continues. But the intense emotion of individual sex-love varies very much in duration from one individual to another, especially among men, and if affection definitely comes to an end or is supplanted by a new passionate love, separation is a benefit for both partners as well as for society—only people will then be spared having to wade through the useless mire of a divorce case.

What we can now conjecture about the way in which sexual relations will be ordered after the impending overthrow of capitalist production is mainly of a negative character, limited for the most part to what will disappear. But what will there be new? That will be answered when a new generation has grown up: a generation of men who never in their lives have known what it is to buy a woman's surrender with money or any other social instrument of power; a generation of women who have never known what it is to give themselves to a man from any other considerations than real love, or to refuse to give themselves to their lover from fear of the economic consequences. When these people are in the world, they will care precious little what anybody today thinks they ought to do; they will make their own practice and their corresponding public opinion about the practice of each individual—and that will be the end of it. . . .

26/The Ideology of the Family

Juliet Mitchell

The family as the first form of social organization, has clearly undergone many changes with the advance of the economic methods of production which have always necessitated more and more elaborate social formations to accompany them. In her article "A Woman's Work is Never Done"[1] Peggy Morton points out that under early capitalism the main economic task of the family was to produce large numbers of children for the new industrial jobs which demanded enormous numbers of workers; but under advanced capitalism, labour-intensive industry gives way to capital-intensive and quality rather than quantity of workers is what is required. The family adapts itself accordingly:

Profits depend more and more on the efficient organization of work and on the 'self-discipline' of the workers rather than simply on speed-ups and other direct forms of increasing the exploitation of the workers. The family is therefore important both to shoulder the burden of the cost of higher education, and to carry out the repressive socialization of children. The family must raise children who have internalized hierarchical social relations, who will discipline themselves and work efficiently without constant supervision. . . . Women are responsible for implementing most of this socialization.[2]

I agree with Peggy Morton that the way the family is evolving produces an increased number of contradictions for the woman within it. As there is, likewise, a contradiction within the sector of sexuality alone. However, there is also a further crucial contradiction not just within the family, but between it and the social organization that surrounds it. For though the family *has changed* since its first appearance, it *has also remained*—not just an

idealist concept but as a crucial ideological and economic unit with a certain rigidity and autonomy despite all its adaptations.

Pre-capitalist society flourishes on individual private property—the peasant has his bit of land, the artisan his tools. Capitalist organization of work deprives the individual of his private property and takes all the separate pieces of private property (land, tools, etc.), pools them, and makes the newly accumulated wealth the private property of a few—the capitalists. The appropriation of individual private property necessitates a form of social organization of the property (men have to get together to work it) which is simultaneously denied: the mass of men get together to work it, but what they produce and how they produce it is taken by the 'few' as their own personal private property. However, individual private property for the mass of the people does continue side by side with this new process—it continues in the family. Engels traced the origin of the oppression of women to the demand for individual private property: women had to be 'owned', faithful to marriage to produce an heir for the inheritance of this individual private property. But perhaps more interesting than the 'origin' of the oppression is its maintenance, as Marx and Engels' analyses of other issues demonstrate. In every revolution (whether from tribalism to feudalism, feudalism to capitalism, capitalism to socialism) the new ruling class, in order to overcome the old ruling class, has to *appear* to represent the vast majority of the people in a society (only in the last instance is this *actually* the case): it doesn't, therefore, appear as a particular 'class' but as the whole society:

For each new class which puts itself in the place of the one ruling before it, is compelled, simply in order to achieve its aims, to represent its interests as the common interest of all the members of society, i.e. employing an ideal formula to give its ideas the form of universality and to represent them

[1] Peggy Morton: "A Woman's Work is Never Done," *Leviathan*, vol. II, no. 1.

[2] Ibid., p. 34.

as the only rational and universally valid ones. The class which makes a revolution appears from the beginning not as a class but as the representative of the whole of society, simply because it is opposed to a class. It appears as the whole mass of society confronting a single ruling class. . . . Every new class, therefore, achieves its domination only on a broader basis than that of the previous ruling class. . . . [3]

It is in representing this limited 'class' interest as the general, universal interest, that 'ideas' play such an important part. Emergent capitalist society in confronting and overcoming feudal society has to appear to offer what the majority want—this naturally takes the form of an idealization of what the previous socio-economic system offered as its basis in, inevitably, a totally un-ideal manner. The ideas and desires of all people are conditioned by what they have: they simply want it bigger and better. To put this concretely—the peasant masses of feudal society had individual private property; their ideal was simply more of it. Capitalist society seemed to offer more because it stressed the *idea* of individual private property in a new context (or in a context of new ideas). Thus it offered individualism (an old value) plus the apparently new means for its greater realization—freedom and equality (values that are conspicuously absent from feudalism). However, the only place where this ideal could be given an apparently concrete base was in the maintenance of an old institution: the family. Thus the family changed from being the economic basis of individual private property under feudalism to being the focal point of the *idea* of individual private property under a system that banished such an economic form from its central mode of production —capitalism. In actually owning things, privately and individually, the bourgeois family gives reality to this idea. For the rest, it remains an ideal desire —the possible fulfilment of which is an inducement to work in a manner at loggerheads with it. The working class work socially in production for the private property of a few capitalists *in the hope of* individual private property for themselves and their families.

But, of course, the ruling-class interests that pose, in the first place, as universal interests, increasingly decline into 'mere idealizing phrases,

conscious illusions and deliberate deceits. . . . But the more they are condemned as falsehoods, and the less they satisfy the understanding, the more dogmatically they are asserted and the more deceitful, moralizing and spiritual becomes the language of established society.' [4] Such a state of affairs perfectly describes that of individual private property and its embodiment, the family, towards the end of the nineteenth century in England. During the twentieth century, feudalism having been firmly overcome and capitalism entrenched, the basic ideology remains, but has naturally become more flexible in order to maintain its hold of the reins.

This is not to reiterate the notion that the family had an economic function under feudalism and today under capitalism has only an ideological one. Such a notion misrepresents the specific relationship here between the economic and the ideological and it is further in danger of being interpreted to mean that the family is unnecessary, a part of some con-job. The quotation above which treats ideology from a moral perspective can induce this attitude. There is nothing less 'real' or 'true' or important about the ideological than there is about the economic. Both determine our lives. In any case, the function of the family is not simply one or the other, it is both: it has an economic and ideological role under capitalism. Roughly, the economic role is the provision of a certain type of productive labour-force and of the arena for massive consumption. This is specifically capitalistic. This economic function interacts with the ideology requisite to produce the missing ideals of peasant, feudal society; a place *equally* and *freely* to enjoy individual private property. This ideology which looks backwards for its rationale is, nevertheless, crucial for the present: without it people might hanker back to the past as a 'golden age'; once Utopianism of any sort occurs, after looking backwards, it is liable to look forwards and thus endanger the status quo. The family, thus, embodies the most conservative concepts available: it rigidifies the past ideals and presents them as the present pleasures. By its very nature, it is there to prevent the future. No wonder revolutionaries come up with the vulgar desperation: abolish the family—it does seem *the* block to advance, *the* means of preserving a backwardness that even capitalism makes feel redundant, though, of course, it is essential to it.

---

[3] Karl Marx: *The German Ideology*, 1845–6, *Collected Works*, vol. I, iv, pp. 35–7.

[4] Ibid., p. 27. Actually this language remains on the terrain it is attacking—it is ideological language, moral and descriptive rather than analytical. It is, however, elegantly appropriate here.

This task of ideology to capture and preserve the ideals that arose from a past reality explains, at least in this context, the degree of separation that exists between the ideological superstructure and the economic base. The ideological construct seems to be less variable, to preserve itself across revolutionary changes in the mode of production. It seems that the values of the present-day family are appropriate to peasant production. But it is the function of the ideology precisely to give this sense of continuity in progress. The dominant ideological formation is not separable from the dominant economic one, but, while linked, it does have a certain degree of autonomy and its own laws. Thus the ideology of the family can remain: individualism, freedom and equality; (at home you're 'yourself'), while the social and economic reality can be very much at odds with such a concept. The contradictions between the ideological intentions of the family and its socio-economic base do not mean that we say the former is false. Quite the contrary, as its meshes draw tighter we protest on behalf of the ideology: 'I can't say a thing without you getting at me. . . . I'm not free to think my own thoughts. . . . I've got nothing I can call my own. . . .'

Of course, the ideological concept of the family embodies a paradox which reflects the contradiction between it and the dominant, capitalist method of organizing production. As I have already mentioned, this method of organizing involves social production (a mass or 'team' of workers), and the family provides the relief from the confiscation of this social production by apparently offering individual private property. Now the same contradiction is today contained within the family itself. The family is the most fundamental (the earliest and most primitive) form of social organization. When, under capitalism, it was made to embody as an ideal, what had been its economic function under feudalism, a chronic contradiction took place. What had hitherto been a *united* unit within the overall diversified social structure became, because of changing social conditions, a *divided* one. The peasant family works together for itself—it *is* one. The family and production are homogeneous. But the members of a working-class family work separately, for different bosses in different places and, though the family interest unites them, the separation of their place and conditions of their work fragments, perforce, that unity. Part of the function of the ideology of the family under capitalism is to preserve this unity in the face of its essential break-up. However, in doing this, it ties itself in knots. The social nature of work under capitalism fragments the unitary family; thereby it enforces the social nature of the family itself.

The peasant family owned its individual private property as the family's; but ideological individualism under capitalism cannot relate to a social group (even one as small as the modern family); it must, because it counterposes this to social work, relate to the individual. It is almost as though the family has got smaller and smaller in order to make itself 'one', in a desperate struggle against the disparity of its members in the outside world. Under capitalism, each member of the family is supposed to be 'an individual', it is not the family unit that is individualized. No wonder there are tensions. Each is supposed to be for the other, but every encounter—school, college, work—makes him for himself alone. It is this contradiction between an ideology of the privacy and individuation of the family and its basic social nature, which capitalism by its social organization of work has brought into play, that underlies the psychic problems documented (in England) in the works of the psychiatrists Laing, Esterson, and Cooper. Each member wants to be an individual—but it is the family itself that is supposed to be 'individual' . . . 'Mary's not like my other children, she's always been different . . . she's got a mind of her own and will go places . . . she's so stubborn, that's why things went wrong and I've brought her to you, doctor . . .' The woman's task is to hold on to the unity of the family while its separate atoms explode in different directions.

It seems possible that within this dual contradiction lies the eventual dissolution of the 'family', a future already visible within the conditions of capitalism. The social nature of production restores the family to its social form—a social group of individuals. Restores it, in fact, to something like the days before it was a family in little more than the biological sense. But this is only 'something like'; final forms bear a misleading resemblance to postulated original forms—the difference is the entire intervening social development, and the difference between the social groups prior to the private-interest family, and social groups after it, is the difference between 'golden age' primitive communism and revolutionary communism. It is too late for one and high time for the other. Meanwhile, the self-contradictory ideology of the family, which preserves the individualism of the unit only in the increasingly disruptive individualism of its members, both retards and hastens the day.

27/Liberalism and Marriage Law

Sara Ann Ketchum

Liberals have traditionally excluded the institution of marriage from political criticism, partly on the grounds that the public/private split relegates marriage to the realm of the private and, hence, the apolitical and uncriticizable. In doing so, liberals have left uncriticized laws that enforce with respect to gender the institutionalization of the notion of a natural place assigned by birth which, when applied to class, was the original target of liberal theory. I will deal here with the tradition of granting to marriage law immunity from principles of equality and freedom. I will do this by indicating prima facie violations of basic liberal principles,[1] and then considering some of the arguments for making an exception to these principles in the case of laws regulating marriage.

Historically, standard liberal theories (and, in particular, social-contract theory) tend to leave marriage[2] out of both descriptions and principles which are nonetheless presented as universal in scope. The major starting point of 17th- and 18th-century social-contract theory is the principle (and/or description) that in the state of nature everyone is equal;[3] that there is no natural authority, and there are no natural social bonds. However, many of these philosophers assume that husband and wife form a natural society and that the authority of husbands over wives is a natural authority.[4]

It is still taken by most liberal theory to be inappropriate to apply to marriage those principles of equality and liberty that are presented as universal and hence applied to all political and legal institutions. While classical liberal theory attacked the assumption that the natural authority of lords over serfs and of kings over subjects should be respected because it was natural and not to be interfered with,[5] they left the ideology of marriage more or less intact in that respect.

According to feudal thinking, who rules over whom is given by God and/or nature; authority is assigned by the natural place of classes of people rather than by individual inclination or merit. For this reason, political structures and the organization of society are not legitimately within the realm of human decision. The assumption that males, as such, rather than particular people, are naturally and ought to be the breadwinners and decision-makers within the family is theoretically parallel to the assumption that lords, regardless of their ability, ought to manage estates and rule over peasants.

I. The Inconsistencies

If we treat these liberal assumptions as truly universal and apply them to marriage as a political institution, it would appear that the institution would violate, at least prima facie, some very basic liberal principles.

According to one standard form of liberal

Earlier versions of this paper were read at the Oswego Women's Center, Oswego, New York, in March 1975, and at Alive and Kicking: Women's Studies at SUNY, held on the campus of the State University of New York at Albany in June 1976. I would like to thank Christine Pierce for helpful discussion and comments on this paper.

[1] In particular, I will deal with general principles of equality and justice and with natural-rights liberalism, rather than with utilitarian arguments. For a criticism of the institution of marriage on the grounds of its consequences (particularly for women) see Jessie Bernard, *The Future of Marriage* (New York: Bantam, 1973).

[2] Most of what I will have to say about liberal treatment of marriage is also true of the treatment of other family relationships and of the family itself.

[3] See, for example, Thomas Hobbes, *Leviathan,* pt. 1, chap. 13; John Locke, *The Second Treatise of Government,* chap. 2; Jean-Jacques Rousseau, *The Social Contract,* chap. 4.

[4] See, e.g., Rousseau, bk. 1, chap. 2: "The oldest of all societies and the only natural one, is that of the family." Locke claims that marriage is a contractual relationship (and, thus, not a natural society), but that "the rule . . . naturally falls to the man's share" (chap. 7, par. 82). Also, in at least one place (chap. 5, "Of Property") Locke treats the family, including the wife, as an individual, and that individual is clearly the husband-father (who is the one who gains an individual right to the property which has been created by the whole family—that is, assuming that his wife and children are not simply sitting back amusing themselves).

[5] Hobbes, pt. 1, chap. 14; Locke, chaps. 1, 2; Rousseau, bk. 1, chaps. 4, 5.

From *Feminism and Philosophy* (Totowa, N.J.: Littlefield, Adams & Company, 1977). Reprinted by permission.

theory, there are some basic general rights that everyone has, simply in virtue of being human or in virtue of having some specific characteristic such as rationality or the capacity to make choices. One can give up a basic right or acquire new obligations and rights through a voluntary alienation of that right. The rights and duties of the marriage relationship are special, rather than general rights. That is, they apply to individuals in virtue of a special relationship, rather than to everyone as human beings or citizens. Thus, these obligations and rights arise out of the marriage contract or marriage vows. There are two sets of problems that emerge when we apply this liberal theory of contracts to the legal treatment of marriage: formal problems having to do with the conditions of entering the contract, and problems arising out of the substance or particular provisions of the contract.

Formal Problems

(1) The special rights and obligations of marriage are defined by the laws regarding married persons of the state in which the married couple are living. A man and a woman place themselves under these laws by undergoing a marriage ceremony rather than by signing a contract that specifies these rights and duties in writing. Hence, the contract that would represent the legal relationship into which a couple enters upon getting married is one that is not easily available for perusal before signing. Certainly no one is required to read it or even encouraged to read it before entering into the contract;[6] nor are couples about to be married urged to consult a lawyer as are people about to make a will. The ceremony that commits them to the contractual relationship does not specify the legal duties of marriage. In many cases, the ceremony is identical with the ceremony connected to the religious sacrament of marriage, and, at best, describes the duties of marriage as a sacrament in that particular religion. Special effort may even be taken to obscure the fact that the marriage ceremony legally commits the couple to a contractual relationship; the reason offered may be that such a realization would dampen the religious or romantic fervor of the occasion. This practice is in conflict with the standard liberal and legal principle that a contract may be void if the contractees do not have the opportunity to read it or have it read to them before signing, since the validity of contracts depends on the free, informed consent of the contracting parties.

(2) One of the major aspects of marriage law that makes it feudal rather than liberal in nature is that the roles in the contract are set by birth.[7] It is not the case that, given the two terms of the contract, I could choose to contract to fulfill either the function of husband or that of wife, and the other contractee could also choose. Nor could I choose to enter into this contract with any consenting adult who is not prohibited by other contracts from entering such a contract; women are legally unable to enter into such a contract with other women and men with other men. With respect to a real-estate or employment contract, there is nothing about my birth that would make me legally capable only of being the buyer or employee, or only of being the seller or employer. Similarly, there is no restriction that women can only sell to men, or blacks can only sell to whites. Such restrictions would, in these cases, be seen as clear violations of liberty and equality. However, in marriage law and in marriage contracts the roles are determined by birth because they are defined by sex, rather than by the function that people choose to, or are able to, fulfill. Legally, a wife is female, and no amount of housework and child care will make a man legally capable of falling under the provisions for wives; the husband's housework is legally a gift, while a wife who performs the same work is fulfilling her legal obligations.

(3) Not only is there no choice of roles within the contract, but there is also no choice of contracts.[8] One does not have a choice between *this* contract with unequal apportionment of duties and an alternative contract that spells out an equal division of rights and duties. Presumably, one reason

---

[6]"Although every girl . . . is trained in the School for Wives, such training is no indication that she knows the legal implications of marriage. Before one can get a driver's license one must score 90 percent of the Rules of the Road. To get a marriage license, one must have a blood test and pay a couple of dollars." Karen de Crow, *Sexist Justice* (New York: Random House, 1975), p. 177.

[7]John Stuart Mill, whose rigorous application of liberal principles to marriage stands as a notable exception in the history of liberals' treatment of the family, makes his one major slip on this issue. In *The Subjection of Women* ([1869]; reprinted in *Essays in Sex Equality*, ed. Alice Rossi [Chicago: University of Chicago Press, 1970]), he criticizes the claim that men ought to have legal authority over their wives (pp. 168–69). But, in direct conflict with arguments he advances elsewhere, he assumes that the jobs of housework and child-care are appropriately sex-linked: "when a woman marries, it may in general be understood that she makes choice of the management of the household, and the bringing up of a family, as the first call upon her exertions" (p. 179). Housework and child-rearing are, in his words, "the one vocation in which there is nobody to compete with them" (i.e., women) (p. 183).

[8]The National Organization for Women is proposing legislation to validate marriage contracts other than the present unwritten one. *Do It NOW*, vol. 9, no. 3 (1976), p. 14.

for having a uniform contract is that it is feared that the results of freedom of choice would be chaos. However, the law currently allows for individualized wills and individualized business contracts without undue stress. For those couples who do not devise their own contract, the law could provide a standard contract that would be analogous to laws covering intestacy. There could also be restrictions on the contract similar to laws requiring that a will make adequate provision for surviving spouses and dependent children. In the case of the marriage contract, this might include provision for care and support of children if there are any, guidelines for division of property and child custody in the event of a divorce, etc. One advantage of having such contracts, rather than the usually vaguer legal assumptions that husbands are heads of households and that wives have primary responsibility for housekeeping and child-rearing, would be that it would reduce the problems produced by leaving the details of divorce settlements up to the discretion of the courts. Such a contract might be a better guide to a divorce settlement than the judge's sometimes arbitrary or biased judgement, and would reduce the probability that property settlements and child-custody cases be turned into arenas for character assassination and playing to the prejudices of the court.

All of these aspects of marriage laws constitute prima facie violations of the liberal principle of freedom of choice. The first violates the principle that contracts are only binding if the people who enter into them do so with informed, uncoerced consent. The second violates the principle of equality of opportunity and equal treatment under the law, since it sets the terms of the contract by birth rather than by choice or ability. Such a condition is formally like a law that states that only whites can be bank presidents and only blacks can be ditch-diggers, or that certain political duties and rights apply only to descendants of peasants or only to descendants of aristocrats.

Problems of Content

According to traditional natural-rights theory, there are some contracts that governments ought not to enforce. There are rights that cannot be alienated and, hence, some contracts that are void because of their substance. Two standard cases of such contracts are a contract to give or sell oneself into slavery and a contract under which one gives up

one's civil right to protection by the law against violence and injury.

At the time of the early cooperation between the abolitionist and woman suffrage movements, the legal status of a wife was almost identical with that of a slave, and some of that similarity remains.[9] The following is a description of two legal clauses applying to slaves:

The first clause confirmed his status as property—the right of the owner to his "time, labor and services" and to his obedient compliance with all lawful commands. . . .

The second clause acknowledged the slave's status as a person. The law required that masters be humane to their slaves, furnish them adequate food and clothing and provide care for them during sickness and old age.[10]

Compare that to the following recent description of the rights and duties of wives:

The legal responsibilities of a wife are to live in the home established by her husband; to perform the domestic chores . . . necessary to help maintain that home; to care for her husband and children.

The legal responsibilities of a husband are to provide a home for his wife and children; to support, protect and maintain his wife and children.[11]

Even though the time separating these two legal statements is more than a hundred years, they seem remarkably similar. The legal duties of a wife entail that she has an obligation to work without pay, as does a slave; so a contract between husband and wife which stipulates that the husband will pay the wife for her labor is not legally binding: the courts will not honor a contract to pay someone to do something that she is legally required to do without pay.[12]

If it is morally illegitimate to sell oneself into slavery, and if governments ought not to honor such contracts, then such a contract ought not to be legally enforceable, let alone legally required of married couples. Liberal arguments for the position that voluntarily entered slavery contracts are such that they ought not to be honored by law vary, and some of

[9]Sheila Cronin, "Marriage," in *Radical Feminism,* ed. Anne Koedt, Ellen Levine, and Anita Rapone (New York: Quadrangle Books, 1973), pp. 215–17.

[10]Kenneth M. Stampp, *The Peculiar Institution* (New York: Vintage Books, 1956), p. 192. Quoted in Cronin.

[11]Richard T. Gallen, *Wives' Legal Rights* (New York: Dell, 1967), pp. 4–5. Quoted in Cronin.

[12]Cronin, pp. 216–17; *Miller* v. *Miller,* excerpted in Lon L. Fuller and Melvin Aaron Eisenberg, *Basic Contract Law,* 3d ed.,

them may not apply very clearly to this case. Arguments that base the illegitimacy of slavery contracts on the grounds that the renunciation of freedom is permanent would seem to apply only to the extent to which divorce is unavailable. However, John Stuart Mill, who uses a similar argument against voluntary slavery contracts,[13] claims that the lack of divorce only completes the analogy between slavery and marriage.[14] Arguments that base the illegitimacy of the enforcement of voluntary slavery contracts on the moral objectionability of exploitation or of ownership of people[15] might be more applicable. However, the extension of such arguments to the marriage contract would depend on whether or not such a contract would be exploitation or alienation of one's rights in important ways that go beyond legitimate limits of individual freedom.

The marriage laws also tend to exclude spouses from legal protection against violence or violation of rights by the other spouse. The most obvious and best-known example of this practice is that a wife has no legal protection against rape by her husband, since rape laws explicitly exclude such acts, no matter how forcible and violent, from criminal statutes. There is also a general legal principle of non-interference in marriage, which involves a refusal on the part of the courts to adjudicate many criminal cases and civil suits for injury between spouses.[16] Thus, to borrow the terminology of social-contract theory, spouses are, to some extent, in a state of nature with respect to each other, with no common judge between them unless they choose to file for divorce. The person who is better off in a state of nature is likely to be the one who is stronger. If there is a fight between a two-hundred-pound trained fighter and an untrained ninety-eight-pound weakling, it is fairly clear which one would benefit from outside parties refraining from interference. Since men tend to marry women who are physically weaker than they are, and since men are culturally better trained for violence than women are and usually have greater political and economic power, the principle of non-interference in disputes between spouses will be likely to produce, in effect, a grant of unchecked power to the husband.[17]

Again, it would seem to be consistent with liberal principles as applied elsewhere to argue that no contract should be interpreted as alienating one's right to legal protection against violence and one's right to legal redress of grievance, and to argue further that such a legal principle denies spouses equal protection under the law.

II. Arguments for Immunity

There are three major arguments for excluding marriage law from political criticisms that are otherwise deemed universal: (1) marriage is too important to be meddled with by law; (2) marriage is a religious sacrament and thus does not fall within the realm of political decision; and (3) marriage law is a special case, because marriage is appropriately a relationship of love and mutual trust.

The Importance of Marriage

The first argument is that we ought not to interfere with marriage because marriage is too important:

Our whole society is based on the absolutely fundamental proposition that: "Marriage, as creating the most important relation in life," has "more to do with the morals and civilization of a people than any other institution" (Maynard v. Hill, 125 U.S. 190, 205).[18]

However, a policy allowing people to choose their own contracts would interfere less in the marriage relationship than the laws we already have. Therefore, unless there is something more to the argument, the point that marriage is too important to interfere with would seem to be most appropriate to an argument calling for careful scrutiny and criticism of present marriage law.

The argument might be filled out as follows: It is generally more dangerous to try out new political and social forms than to stick to the ones we have

American Casebook Series (St. Paul: West Publishing Co., 1972), pp. 105–7.

[13]John Stuart Mill, *On Liberty* (1859; New York: Bobbs-Merrill, 1956), p. 125.

[14]*Subjection of Women,* (above, n. 7) p. 161.

[15]Joel Feinberg, "Legal Paternalism," *Canadian Journal of Philosophy* 1 (1971): 118.

[16]Notes: "Litigation between Husband and Wife," *Harvard Law Review* 79 (1966): 1650–65.

[17]For reviews of research on the distribution of power within a marriage, see Bernard (above, n. 1), pp. 6–7, 9–15; and Dair L. Gillespie, "Who Has the Power? The Marital Struggle," in *Women: A Feminist Perspective,* ed. Jo Freeman (Palo Alto, Calif.: Mayfield, 1975), pp. 64–87.

[18]*Bunim* v. *Bunim,* 298 N.Y. 391 (1949). Quoted in de Crow (above, n. 6), p. 198.

already tried. Marriage, in the form we now have institutionalized in the law, is a time-honored and well-tested institution. Any attempt to make the marriage laws egalitarian would constitute a major change in the institution since it would eliminate the special duties and rights of spouses and the corresponding division of labor which have worked so well in the past. Thus, changing the laws would be choosing a risky venture over a well-tested institution. And, since marriage is such an important institution, the risk entails that, if the experiment fails, it will damage not only many individuals, but the very fabric of the society.

This is a fairly standard Burkean conservative argument,[19] and there are two lines of response to it: (1) a standard liberal response to this kind of argument in general, and (2) a criticism of this specific argument about marriage that does not dispute the general conservative thesis.

The liberal response might be as follows: Slavery was a time-hallowed institution, but that does not make it a just institution. The fact that there is uncertainty about the results of just treatment is at the least not a conclusive argument for failing to attempt to make the laws more just.

However, we could also criticize this argument on the grounds that, whether or not the basic conservative theory is correct, it does not apply in this case. This is not a case of a vast political experiment or of trying to change social institutions through government action, but rather an attempt to bring the laws into line with a social institution that has already changed, at least in some segments of the population. Many couples now share responsibilities, and among those who still follow the prescribed pattern to some extent—such that the woman does the housework and the man earns the money—many regard this arrangement as one they have chosen rather than as a necessity that ought to be enforced by law. The experiments have been performed in advance, and there have been a sufficient number of successful ones to make the fears of disaster less plausible. It might also be argued that marriage as we now know it—the patriarchal nuclear family—is a relatively recent historical phenomenon and is an experiment that has not succeeded so very spectacularly.[20] So, there is not much reason to believe that making the marriage

contract less unequal is either particularly experimental or entails more risk than allowing the laws we now have to continue.

The Religious Argument

The second argument, the one from religion, is roughly as follows: marriage is a religious sacrament, the form of which is ordained by particular religions or by God. Therefore, marriage law, which now conforms, more or less, to the religious sacrament, ought not to be changed from that form. However, if we assume that freedom of religion and separation of church and state are good things, then this would more reasonably back up the position that the state ought not to keep this legal institution. If marriage is a religious sacrament, then freedom to choose between marriage contracts would be an element of religious freedom. The exclusive enforcement of a contract that conforms to the religious sacrament of the majority religion would violate the principle of separation of church and state, since it ties the legal institution, which should be open to people of any religion or of no religion at all, to the religious sacrament of a particular religion.

Domestic Harmony

The third argument is based on the claim that marriage laws are a special case, since marriage is appropriately a relationship of love and affection. Thus, we should not apply the same principles to such laws as we would, for example, to a purely economic relationship. This would seem to be a reasonable argument against, for example, an attempt to apply anti-discrimination laws to the choice of marriage partners in the same way that they are applied to the choice of tenants. However, it seems less relevant to an argument for the position that the roles within a marriage ought to be set by law regardless of the choices of the people who have made the contract.

This argument is most often used (1) against allowing contractual relationships other than the existing one between marriage partners, and (2) against court "interference" in the marriage relationship. That is, it is used in defense of the refusal of the courts to enforce civil and, in some cases, criminal laws when the disputants are married to each other.

Lon L. Fuller, an authority on contract law,

---

[19]For a defense of the general principles on which this argument is based, see Michael Oakeshot, *Rationalism in Politics* (London: Methuen, 1967).

[20]See, e.g., Bernard (above, n. 1).

summarizes the arguments for refusing to grant legal status to contracts that regulate the internal affairs of a marriage:

The first of these is that the success of a marriage depends on a shared sense of trust and mutual respect that would be destroyed by any attempt to spell out its implications in numbered paragraphs; unmeasured love and contractually imposed boundary markers hardly go together. A second consideration is that the management of the household is vulnerable to so many shifting contingencies that any attempt to subject it to a regime of rules would inevitably fail.[21]

But if marriages would be destroyed by any legal attempt to spell out marital duties, Fuller does not offer any explanation of how it has survived such specification by past and current common-law regulations of marriage duties. Perhaps it is only when the contract is voluntarily chosen and knowingly entered into that it has such consequences.

Fuller does not seem to notice that his criticism of interspousal contracts on the grounds that marriage duties should not be specified at all is inconsistent with an objection to such contracts on the grounds that they conflict with common-law specification of marriage duties. Thus, the argument he gives is in conflict with the argument used by the court in *Miller* v. *Miller,* the case he cites to support his claim.

In *Miller* v. *Miller,* Mrs. Miller had agreed to stay with her husband, despite serious misconduct on his part, on the basis of a written agreement. This contract specified, among other things, that the wife would care for their children and keep the home in good order, and that the husband would pay the household expenses and, in addition, pay her sixteen and two-thirds dollars a month. He defaulted on the payments and his wife brought suit. The objection made by the court to enforcing the contract entered into by Mr. and Mrs. Miller was that it required him to pay her for the performance of duties which, as his wife, she was already legally required to perform.[22] Fuller seems to see no inconsistency between the bond of love and the legal speci-

fication of the duty of a wife to perform housework without pay.

Nor does Fuller see such a legal specification of duties as one that would run into problems with "shifting contingencies." Surely, a marriage in which the husband loses his outside job and the wife has to work outside the home to support the family would be a shift in the situation which would make that provision of the marriage law inappropriate. As long as the courts decline to honor contracts chosen by a husband and wife, a couple will lack not only the legal option of alternative contracts designed to meet shifting contingencies but, in many cases, will not have the option of choosing a contract that fits their present situation.

The argument of dangers to "domestic harmony" is also used by the courts in refusing to adjudicate civil, and in some cases criminal, cases between spouses. "The flames which litigation would kindle on the domestic hearth would consume in an instant the conjugal bond."[23] Hence, there is a general judicial assumption that the availability of legal redress for personal injury would endanger the stability of marriages. This seems to be an empirical assumption for which no evidence is offered. One might more reasonably assume that fear of unprotected violence would damage the mutual love and trust that the courts hold to be so necessary to the stability of a marriage. The availability of legal redress might serve as a deterrent (at least to cases of intentional injury and refusal to honor either contracts or common-law marriage duties), whereas the refusal of courts to judge disputes between spouses who are living together leaves divorce and separation as the *only* legal recourse.[24] Requiring spouses to separate in order to be eligible for legal protection would appear likely to encourage the dissolution rather than the stability of marriage.

I have argued that the reasons typically advanced for granting to marriage immunity from basic principles of justice are untenable. As sufficient grounds for denying such basic rights as access to legal redress of civil and criminal grievances, religious and contractual freedom, and equality under the law, they are flimsy indeed.

[21]Lon L. Fuller, "The Justification of Legal Decisions," *Archives for Philosophy of Law and Social Philosophy* (Weisbaden, Germany: Franz Steiner Verlag, 1971), no. 7; 82.
[22]Fuller and Eisenberg (above, n. 12), p. 106.

[23]*Ritter* v. *Ritter,* 31 Pa. 396, 398 (1858).
[24]de Crow (above, n. 6), pp. 184–87.

28/Altruism and Women's Oppression

Larry Blum, Marcia Homiak, Judy Housman, Naomi Scheman

I. Introduction

There are two lines of thinking in tension within the contemporary feminist movement in America. According to one (the "positive" view), there are some qualities more likely to be found in women than in men which are humanly good qualities and which should be preserved and fostered in the struggle for the liberation of women. Some of these qualities are grouped around the notion of "altruism" and include supportiveness, compassion, concern for others, ability to help others grow and develop, concern with human relationships. In the process of their struggle to understand and to liberate themselves, the Boston Women's Health Collective "began to really appreciate our capacity to empathize, to nurture."[1] These altruistic qualities can be seen as universal values which are good for men as well as women to possess.

On the other hand there is a line of thinking (the "negative" view) within the women's movement that, for women, being altruistic generally goes along with being self-sacrificing, denying oneself for the sake of others, usually men. Thus the altruistic qualities are intimately tied to the oppressed condition of women. "Studies and common sense suggest that personal 'altruism' in our culture often stems from guilt, fear, and low self-esteem, rather than from freedom or self-love."[2] Margaret Adams says,

The main target of my concern is the pervasive belief . . . that women's primary and most valuable social function is to provide the tender and compassionate components of life and that through the exercise of these particular traits women have set themselves up as the exclusive model for protecting, nurturing, and fostering the growth of others . . . this arbitrary social definition of women's prime function (in value terms) has encouraged the hypertrophied growth of a single circumscribed area of the feminine psyche, while other qualities have been subjected to gradual but persistent attrition.[3]

Women are expected to be supportive and giving to their men and children, or to society (in service and volunteer work), and to neglect their own selves or to deny their self-development in the process. They are to live for others.

The tension between the two strains of thought is a real one; it is not merely illusory or a product of misunderstanding. The strains of thought involve not only differing conceptions of women, but also elements of differing strategies for women's liberation. The positive view will encourage women to preserve and value their qualities of supportiveness and compassion; the negative view, seeing the destructive aspects of these qualities, will not.

The tension is rooted in the actual situation of women; the two discrepant views must be seen as expressions of different aspects of that situation. It is true that for women the "altruistic" qualities are generally connected with self-denial and self-sacrifice, weakness and dependency. They are connected through the ways that women are socialized and through the actual conditions, institutions, and roles in which they typically function. On the other hand there is an important truth in the positive view as well. Compassion, supportiveness, a sense of the importance of human relationships are humanly good qualities. They are qualities which a good person would want to have.

The notion of "humanly good qualities" can present a problem, since we will want to say that

[1] Boston Women's Health Collective, *Our Bodies, Ourselves,* New York, Simon & Schuster, 1971, p. 7.
[2] Phyllis Chesler, *Women and Madness,* New York, Avon, 1971, p. 266.

[3] Margaret Adams, "The Compassion Trap," in Gornick and Moran (eds.), *Women in Sexist Society,* New York, New American Library, p. 556.

From *The Philosophical Forum* 5 (1975). Reprinted by permission. Footnotes have been renumbered.

there are distorted (i.e., in some way bad) forms which such qualities can take. It is the undistorted forms of these qualities which are humanly good. These undistorted forms cannot, however, be identified with an abstract essence which can be detached from concrete persons and situations: that is, taken in abstraction from their actual forms in a particular society, and specifically, in sexist society.

This weakness of the positive view is connected to a failure to see the "altruistic" qualities as part of the person as a whole. The positive view sees that concern and compassion are generally good but does not see that although these qualities can be associated with other positive qualities such as autonomy and independence, they may also be associated with negative qualities such as dependence, sense of inferiority, and self-denial. Conversely, the negative view does not admit the real possibility of the compatibility of altruism with autonomy.[4]

The alleged opposition between concern for self and concern for others is exhibited in the very use of the term "altruism" as referring generally to doing good for others, motivated by concern for them, while disregarding or neglecting one's own interests. "Altruism" thus implies self-neglect, if not actually self-sacrifice. To use the word as a term covering all forms of doing good for others is thus ordinarily to imply that doing good for others generally involves or must involve disregard of oneself.[5]

A failure to recognize that autonomy (and self-concern) and concern for others are not mutually exclusive has deep roots within the individualism of our culture generally. The picture of economic self-sufficiency fostered by capitalist ideology—being owner of one's own enterprise, being one's own "boss"—becomes a model for personal autonomy. Autonomy is equated with (emotional) self-sufficiency and independence of others.[6]

What is lacking is a positive conception of "caring-with-autonomy," i.e., being concerned for oneself as well as being concerned for others. In the rest of this paper we will try to make this conception concrete and to show its importance in understanding the valid insights in both the negative and the positive view of women's "altruism." . . . In section (III) we will give some examples to show that concern, care, and support may be defective unless they are founded on a strong sense of autonomy or independence and a healthy concern for oneself, so that in some sense a genuine and non-defective altruism actually requires autonomy. In our final section (IV) we will propose a positive conception of autonomy with altruism drawn from concrete experiences of women, and specifically consciousness-raising groups, as a context in which the qualities of autonomy yet supportiveness and giving to others are realized, and valued. . . .

III. Examples of the Distortion of "Altruistic" Qualities by the Oppressive Structures in which Women Live

In this section we shall discuss some of the ways in which women's ability to care for others and for relationships with others becomes distorted by structural features of their lives.

The examples we have chosen cluster around marriage and the family, an emphasis which reflects our sense of that institution's centrality to the economic and social conditions which lead to the distortion of altruistic qualities.[7] When we speak of a quality's being "distorted," we do not mean that it must first be exhibited or felt or intended in an undistorted form which subsequently becomes distorted. Rather, the form which the qualities take is determined in part by the context in which they occur.[8]

If our analysis is correct, and "altruistic" qualities do become distorted in relationships based on lack of autonomy, there will be some reason to

---

[4]These incomplete views of the nature of altruistic qualities bear on philosophical conceptions of the nature of altruism. This tendency to abstract a single characteristic from other aspects of a person's life and to take it out of its social context is typical of moral philosophy in general. Yet another strain of thought within philosophy, especially philosophy which is heavily influenced by Christian thought, posits an actual opposition, explicit or implicit, between a concern for self and a concern for others. This opposition can be seen in Kant in the idea of the struggle between morality on the one hand and personal happiness or inclination on the other. (Other strains of thought within Kant, such as the idea that autonomy involves acting out of a law acceptable to all, do not contain this opposition.)

[5]This is not to deny that actual altruism—self-disregard for the sake of others—can be morally admirable and good, but only

that it should not be seen as the paradigm case of doing good for others.

[6]This theme is explored in Philip Slater, *The Pursuit of Loneliness*, Boston, Beacon Press, 1971, ch. 1.

[7]"The family is the primary institution through which women participate in this society . . . Even working women give the family their primary allegiance. Wherever a woman is in this society, it is the family, and the ideology of the family, that contributes most to shaping her beliefs and maintaining her oppression." Eli Zaretsky, "Capitalism and Personal Life," *Socialist Revolution*, #13–14, p. 73.

[8]Distortion also occurs in relationships outside the family. Some is either caused by or mirrors familial relationships, and some is relatively independent and caused by oppressive economic and social features of, e.g., the work situation.

believe that it is within relationships of caring-with-autonomy that such qualities flourish. There are relationships in which one's caring and concern for the other is both reciprocated and enhancing of a sense of self. Ingrid Bengis[9] talks of relationships like this with girl friends when she was young and of the inconceivability then of having such relationships with boys, and the difficulty of the quest later to have them with men. However, the ideology of marriage and the family tells us that here we can find such relationships and such feelings, that here of all places people genuinely care about each other's uniqueness and autonomy. Thus, we often learn as paradigm cases of care and concern what are actually distortions of what those qualities can and should be.

The examples which we discuss fall under two main headings: (A) caring for another person with whom the woman has a particular relationship, and (B) caring for the form and the content of the relationship itself. Under the first heading (A) we consider three factors which lead to the distortion of such caring: (1) the economic dependence of a wife on her husband; (2) the fact that it is typically seen as a wife's role to provide emotional support nonreciprocally for her husband; (3) the lack of avenues for most women to develop a sense of themselves other than derivatively from their roles as (a) wives and (b) mothers.

Under the second heading (B), we consider two distorting factors: (1) the onesidedness of such concern typical of marriage as of many non-marital male-female relationships; (2) the economic and social dependence which women traditionally have on being married.

We will be concerned in each of the examples to indicate defectiveness of the caring as it affects both the woman and the other toward whose supposed good it is directed. In the latter case, the distortion makes the caring either less helpful than it could be or even positively detrimental,[10] or in the case of a woman's concern for a relationship, that concern may help to maintain only a maimed version of the relationship.

[9]Ingrid Bengis, *Combat in the Erogenous Zone*, Knopf, 1972, pp. 106 ff.

[10]The criticism made of [Milton] Mayeroff is particularly relevant here. He would have us not call such distortions cases of caring at all, a rather laudable caveat which unfortunately ignores the fact that it is precisely what we learn as paradigm cases of caring (that shown by mothers and wives) which are most prone to this sort of distortion. We have to deal not so much with individual aberration as with systematic, institutionalized distortion. And that leaves us considerably less able to say "We know just what caring is, and this simply isn't it."

The other side of the defectiveness is in the effects of such distorted caring on the woman herself. Her lack of autonomy, her dependence, the nonreciprocity of her concern are all reinforced by the forms which her "altruism" takes.

A. Effect of Dependence on a Woman's Caring for her Husband

As feminist writers[11] have explained, the root of female dependence is in the wife's economic dependence on the husband. Discouraged or denied economic independence through paid work, the woman is dependent on another for her basic necessities. Even if the wife does work, the husband is still considered the family breadwinner, the real source of family income; the wife's income is often set aside for special, less important purposes. Even when her income is actually essential for the family, this fact is frequently not acknowledged, precisely because her contribution is seen as subsidiary.[12]

The economic security which the woman receives from the husband is at the base of her more general sense of security, of feeling secure as a person in the face of the world. Furthermore, as she becomes accustomed to being dependent on the husband her sense that she is even capable of independence may well begin to disappear. The dependence may stultify her ability to recognize or take advantage of even the limited opportunities open to her to achieve some kind of economic as well as emotional independence (even if she could struggle against her husband's likely opposition). Thus, the structure of marriage is a relationship in which women are objectively dependent and which also causes the individual woman's emotional make-up to be characterized by dependence.

In a marriage in which the wife loves the husband she will care for and care about him. She will want good things for him; she will be concerned at his distress, she will want him to be happy. But this very concern will be expressed in ways which are similar to, and hence likely to be confused with, the expression of her need to continue to be acceptable to him. Because of this she will tend to go along with him, to please him. She will not challenge him or express opinions which diverge from his, even when it regards his welfare.

[11]E.g., by, among others, Simone de Beauvoir, *Second Sex* (trans. Parshley), New York. Knopf, 1952.

[12]Juliet Mitchell, *Women's Estate*, Baltimore, Penguin, 1971, p. 129.

Let us imagine the following example: A scientist working on a research team does not like his job because he is not permitted by his co-workers to exercise complete control of the project. They block his need to dominate. However, he rationalizes this dissatisfaction by complaining, instead, that all of his co-workers are incompetent. His wife accepts this rationalization out of a desire to please her husband and to be supportive in his distress. She has never challenged his desire always to be "top dog," nor even recognized it as an aspect of his character which might work to his detriment in his job situation, and which certainly works to her detriment in her acceptance of her own subordination. Thus she will support and foster the destructive sense of self-importance which the husband gains from having someone subordinate to him, from having someone act indiscriminately to please him. Oriented towards not displeasing her husband, the wife in turn will not assert her own needs, opinions, or wishes if she thinks her husband would disapprove. The caring thus reinforces the suppression of self attendant upon the dependence. Furthermore, the personal ties of caring mask the unequal power relation between the wife and husband.

Thus, the form which caring will typically take in the context of a dependent relationship will be a distortion of a true caring for the other. The focus on the other's needs is clouded by the need to please and by the lack of the development of capacity for independent judgment and perception regarding the other. Thus not only is this a case in which the caring is in some way at the expense of the person who is caring, but the caring is defective on its own terms—the other also is not really aided. For her caring to be helpful to her husband and to herself, it would have to be grounded in an autonomy and independence scarcely possible within the structure of traditional domination and subordination.

B. Effects of the Wife's Role as Emotional Maintainer on her Caring for her Husband

We will now examine a more specific way in which a wife cares for her husband—namely, through her role as the provider and sustainer of emotional support within the family. Before examining the nature of this role, however, one must show how that role emerges as the wife's and why it is important that it is the wife's.[13]

In an advanced capitalist society, where many workers have jobs which the division of labor makes fragmented and unsatisfying, and where contact with other workers is both circumscribed and often competitive, the home and family is an institution which functions to satisfy the emotional needs for warmth and human sociability which are incompatible with the work situation. It is supposed to be an enclave of intimacy and security. In this sense, the family is thought of as an ideal, "a human alternative to the inhumanity of social relations at work."[14] The worker moves from a fragmenting situation to one which is meant to be emotionally compensating; in the family situation he is supposed to be able to be himself and to relax in an atmosphere conducive to the expression of his individuality and to aspects of his personality which were deliberately discouraged in his work situation.[15]

Although it is primarily the emotional needs of the alienated male worker that are satisfied by the family structure (for it is *his* fragmented life that is supposedly compensated for by the family), the family is nevertheless thought to serve the needs of all human beings, since it is within the family that people are thought to find whatever comfort, love, and compassion they know. It is the role of the wife within the family to produce and sustain these values. That she has this function is an effect of her economic dependence on her husband. It is important to see why this is so.

In a society where commodity relations are dominant, where people are valued by how much capital their labor can accumulate, women are devalued because their primary work, which is considered to be that in the home, is not considered to be productive labor at all.[16] It is the husband who, as family breadwinner, provides for the basic necessities of life. In exchange for economic care, protection, and security, the wife is meant to assume the role of promoting and sustaining the emotional needs frustrated by the work situation of the husband. She returns to the husband a different kind of care from that which she receives from him, and it is

---

[13]In this section and elsewhere we appear to ignore the support which, even in traditional contexts, a man often gives to a woman. His care, however, is primarily in providing a calm, level-headed rationality when she is unable to cope.

[14]Sheila Rowbotham, *Woman's Consciousness, Man's World,* Pelican Books, 1973, p. 59.

[15]See Eli Zaretsky, *op. cit.,* pp. 115–116 and elsewhere. Zaretsky traces the development of this conception of the family and shows how the development of capitalism created the conditions for its applying to working class as well as bourgeois families.

[16]This phenomenon has been discussed extensively in feminist literature. See, for example, Juliet Mitchell, *op. cit.,* and Sheila Rowbotham, *op. cit.,* especially chapters 4 and 5.

considered by both to be a fair exchange. Thus, the emotional maintenance which a wife provides within a family is seen as an obligation which she owes to her husband and as a central part of her role.[17] In compensation, the woman's domestic position appears to have certain advantages: the wife is working in the interests of those she cares about and of those who care about her. Although this role involves a great deal of drudgery and is clearly held to be a subordinate one, it is thought that she is at least not subject to the fragmentation experienced by the alienated male worker.

It remains to be explained how this kind of caring within the family structure is limited by its being made the job of the wife. We will consider [two] ways in which this support is shown—in the first, although limited, it is clearly of genuine value to the husband; in the . . . third it is . . . distorted. We will then consider the negative effects on the wife of her role as emotional maintainer.

(i) Given the impersonal and competitive nature of most work in this society, emotional support is hard to come by, and may be most conspicuously absent when it is most needed. For example, a man who is learning a new skill as part of a training program and having difficulty acquiring the necessary expertise may not get encouragement from his co-workers (who may be competing with him for the same position) or from his boss (who does not care who gets promoted). The worker's wife, through her support and encouragement, may be able to promote his self-confidence and thereby help him to feel able to carry the program through and master it. She not only makes him feel that he is cared about, but also that he is worth something, and this feeling may be important for his emotional growth and happiness. The supportiveness is thus genuinely helpful and constructive in overcoming his insecurities and self-doubts and enabling him to return to the work situation with a renewed sense of his own worth. . . .

(iii) Sometimes women realize that, although they feel that they cannot be openly critical of their husbands, there are nonetheless ways that they can influence their behavior. It is often the case that when someone in a subordinate and objectively dependent position develops independent ideas and

[17]Of course, her caring may not be *merely* out of obligation, but we are concerned to examine what happens when caring is, *inter alia,* an obligation which someone in a subordinate position is expected to show to a person on whom she is dependent. No matter what feeling prompts her caring, our argument is that the caring occurs in an objective situation which distorts it.

values which she cannot afford to express, manipulative and devious means are rather naturally turned to as among the few ways of changing the superior's behavior. Women often know (but can't let on that they know) that they are merely boosting their husbands' egos by expressing a faith beyond what they feel; they talk of how fragile men's egos are and of how good they are at "managing" their husbands. One school of anti-feminists extols this ability which some women have as a form of genuine power which women would be foolish to give up. Certainly, such manipulation can sometimes change a husband's behavior, perhaps even in beneficial ways.

For example, if the husband in A(1) is short-tempered as a result of not being in total control, his wife could recast the situation in a way which might lead him to behave differently. She might say, "Well, so-and-so is, as you know, overly sensitive about this and that and likely to get touchy when he thinks someone is criticizing him. So perhaps you should take this into account when dealing with him in the future." In this way the wife gets the husband to think that what might be something to overcome in himself or to struggle against collectively (the aspects of the work situation which make true collective work difficult) is actually something which someone else has to overcome.

This kind of dynamic may actually change the husband's behavior for the better, but it also has the effect of making him feel superior. The wife, in giving the husband a distorted view of himself and others, makes self-knowledge and meaningful change more difficult for him. Hence, her supportiveness may actually be harmful to him.

Thus, the support which the wife gives the husband is a defective form of caring, limited by her role as "emotional supporter."

It is important to note what effect this form of caring may have on her. Her role as the creator of a supportive environment, her sense that the home fills a real need of her husband's and that she is performing a service in exchange for other services rendered her, may prevent her from seeking from him the same kind of support he gains from her. As long as her caring for her husband is entangled with her feeling that it is a *responsibility* which she has toward him, she may be unwilling to trouble him with her own complaints.

On the one hand, since "emotional maintenance" is her job she will be inclined to feel ungrateful and unwomanly if she asks for the kind of support she feels she should be providing. On the other hand, as outlined above, such support isn't seen as "real" work, neither as hard, as draining, as productive, nor as important, and so she may feel that she has much less "right" than her husband to complain about her life. These feelings may be intensified by the fact that she is dependent on him for her livelihood. Thus her supportiveness may actually be harmful to her: it serves to reinforce the limiting role it stems from. In resting content with her half of the marriage bargain, she is denying herself any measure of autonomy and authority.

Thus, what is true of the more general preceding example, A(1), is true as well of these more specific examples: the wife's role as emotional maintainer creates defects in her caring for her husband, from which both she and he suffer. Unless she is more autonomous with regard to her husband and is not forced into the primary and nonreciprocated role of emotional maintainer, it will be difficult to overcome these defects.

C. Effect of the Lack of Adequate Contexts for Self-Development on the Support and Help Given to Others

(a) Wives: The Substitute Success Syndrome   The altruism which we will discuss here is support given to the husband in the context of his career. Phenomena such as that of the ambitious wife who pushes her husband into a success he may not want, or works invisibly for a success in which she does not really participate, have frequently been noted. Here we will explore the connection of the distortions in the wife's help to her lack of opportunity to develop and express interests in life projects of her own.

Wendy Martyna[18] identifies and analyzes the "substitute success syndrome" in upper middle class marriages in which wives who have given up their own career aspirations latch onto their husbands' success as a kind of substitute for what is denied to them. They support their husbands in their work, often in crucial ways, perhaps helping them (e.g., with books they write), taking care of household affairs so that the husband will be free to devote his time to his work. They do this not merely with the sense that this is their proper role but with a direct sense of personal connection to and involvement

in the husband's work. The real credit, however, goes to him.

This situation is reminiscent of Scheler's description of the person who lives through others,[19] and who does not really feel herself distinct from others. We see here how it is the institution of marriage and the socialization of women which brings about such a situation, and not a defect in the individual person.

Furthermore, the support can take distorted forms, because of the frustrated aspirations from which it comes. The wife's ambitions for her husband may really be out of line with his desires for himself. She, however, may continue to push him in such a way that neither he nor they together recognize or take seriously the doubts which he might have, or the possibilities of doing something different.

The form of support and help which this wife gives her husband is also quite damaging to herself, as well as being an obvious product of frustrated aspirations. The illusory satisfactions of vicarious living and substitute success may well prevent the wife from being in touch with her own dissatisfactions and lack of self-expression and development. It will help her to reconcile herself to this form of marital life which is oppressive to her.

(b) Mothers: Living Through One's Children   Another frequently described syndrome is that of mothers' "living through their children." Again, we want to argue that not individual neurosis but institutional structures determine the consequent distortions of caring. The structure of child-care in most American families today is frequently such that it precludes the mother's developing serious interests in activities other than caring for her child. For most people, the kind of employment available outside the home is structured as a full time activity with inflexible hours. Thus it is extremely difficult for parents to arrange schedules that allow for shared responsibility for their children. Adequate day-care is usually unavailable. Furthermore, caring for a home and children "stretches over the whole time of existence broken only by illness and holidays. Its space is the whole space of a woman's life. . . . The routine, in fact, can rarely be overtaken by the woman's efforts, partly because housework is not just effort but continuity as well and also because the

[18]Wendy Martyna, "The Substitute Success Syndrome," in *The Second Wave*, Vol. 1, No. 4, 1972, pp. 28–31.

[19]Max Scheler, *The Nature of Sympathy* (trans. Heath), London, Routledge & Kegan Paul, 1954, p. 42.

infinitely variable needs of children and husband determine the structure of the job."[20] The objective conditions available for child-caring thus force a choice between care for a young child and self-development of other kinds.

Furthermore, the present ideology regarding what constitutes adequate care even for older children limits the ways of caring which the woman will consider adequate for her child's needs. Mothers out of the job market for the early childhood years, facing a difficult re-entry, are likely to fall prey to society's myth of the "supermother."[21] Even after the child has outgrown the early dependent years the belief persists that "caring for the children," arranging their lives and catering to their wants should be a full time occupation which takes precedence over any needs which the mother has for herself.

Because the mother has been denied other outlets for self-expression and development, her relationship to her children takes on a hypertrophied importance which distorts her care for them. Her need to be needed by her children becomes overwhelming because this is the one sphere in which she feels of value. Thus, it may become very difficult for her to recognize their growing needs for autonomy.

Such a woman's major source of satisfaction is vicarious, obtained by identification with the successes of her children. Thus she will frequently push them to gain the achievements she has always dreamed of their attaining. Because she does not have a strong sense of self, she will be unable to separate her needs from their needs and they too may fail to recognize that they are striving toward goals which reflect her values and choices rather than their own.

B. In this section we will be concerned with the fact that women often devote much energy and skill to the preservation and cultivation of the relationships which they have with others. In particular, we will consider two ways in which this concern for

relationships becomes distorted and in turn distorts the relationships—in B(1) the fact that this concern is usually, in relationships with men, largely the woman's, in B(2) the need which women typically feel (and largely have) to become or remain married, a need which can deflect their concern from the content of the relationship to the bare preservation of its form.

1. Effect of Woman's Having Primary Responsibility for Maintaining Emotional and Personal Relationships on Wife's Relationship to Husband

Women's socialization leads them to be more concerned than men with interpersonal and emotional matters, and leads them to know how to maintain and to value personal relationships more than men do.[22] The nature of the woman's role in the marriage reinforces this process, in including emotional support and nurturance as an important part of the wife role. Furthermore, the working situation of most men further erodes men's capacities to work at and to value personal relationships. Often their work situations are essentially competitive with their co-workers, making close trusting relationships difficult.[23] At work they are expected to be unemotional and self-controlled.

Thus the man comes to the marriage situation deficient in the ability to maintain and to give explicit value to emotional ties and personal relationships. The woman comes to the marriage already willing to shoulder the major burden of the emotional resources needed to hold the relationship together emotionally. This situation sets up a dynamic which is debilitating to the relationship between the two of them. Lack of reciprocity is built into the situation. By not asserting her needs in the relationship she may in fact lose touch with them or indeed never become conscious of the fact that the relationship is deeply unsatisfying to her. So her need for acknowledgement of her feelings and of her importance in the relationship is not met.

[20]Rowbotham, op. cit., p. 72.

[21]Pauline Bart discusses the problem of the supermother syndrome in "Depression in Middle-Aged Women" (*Women in Sexist Society,* ed. Gornick and Moran, op. cit., pp. 163–186). She notes that women who have devoted their lives to their children and have failed to develop interests of their own feel threatened and reluctant to relinquish control when their children begin to set forth on their own lives. Such women frequently suffer loss of self-esteem and depression in middle-age when their efforts are no longer required in the day to day burdens of childrearing. The loss of the role of mother is the loss of the role from which they derive their sense of being valued by others and their own sense of being a person of worth.

[22]This is a standard point made in the literature on sex-role

socialization. See, e.g., Adams, op. cit.; Chodorow, "Family Structure and Feminine Personality," in Rosaldo and Lamphere, *Woman, Culture, and Society,* Stanford, Calif., Stanford Univ. Press, 1974, pp. 43–66.

[23]Even work situations which promote a sense of solidarity (e.g., because of a shared sense of grievance or oppression, or because of the necessity of the collective action) exist in conjunction with the aspects of the work role situation discussed here, and only rarely will these negative features be entirely absent. Furthermore, work situations will often be consciously arranged so that they preclude workers' developing a sense of camaraderie. Cf. Howard M. Wachtel, "Class-Consciousness and Stratification in the Labor Process," *Review of Radical Political Economics,* Vol. VI, No. 1, Spring, 1974, pp. 1–31.

The husband may actually remain somewhat oblivious to the fact that maintaining the relationship requires time and energy, which the wife is giving. Thus the wife will remain unappreciated, the lack of reciprocity will not be noticed, and the need for him to take some responsibility will not be acknowledged.

This situation has some analogies to the "invisibility of housework."[24] Since much of housework involves maintaining a *clean* house a man who sees only a clean house and does not concern himself with the process of cleaning will remain unaware of the work involved. Analogously, a man whose relationships have always been maintained by women will remain unaware of and take for granted the activity and energy which goes into maintaining relationships. A woman's capabilities in this area actually contribute to the invisibility of her work. In the case of housework, the better the woman is at keeping the house free from disorder, the less aware her husband will be that houses will become disordered unless they are regularly cleaned. Similarly the better the woman becomes at maintaining a smooth relationship the less will the man notice her efforts.

Furthermore, the very capacities necessary for maintaining close relationships are also requisite to recognizing the concern extended by another. But these are atrophied when one does not attend to relationships. The woman's concern is, thus, increasingly unnoticed because the man becomes increasingly unable to recognize on any deep level his own needs or feelings, or those of the woman.

Thus as the wife continues to maintain the emotional relationship with the husband, the relationship actually becomes emotionally deficient from her perspective. If the man has difficulties expressing his feelings and indeed in knowing what his feelings are, the woman may come to lack confidence that she is really loved and valued. Her insecurity makes her more reluctant to assert herself and challenge her husband's emotional remoteness and irresponsibility in ways which might help the relationship to become more balanced. Furthermore, her task of maintaining the relationship becomes more difficult as the emotional level becomes increasingly alien to the man.

Ironically, though she suffers from the situation, the wife may in one way prefer the man's emotional incapacity. The man's incapacities and the woman's abilities in this area may make her feel that she provides a needed dimension in his life which he could not produce for himself. She will regard this as securing her importance to him.

The effects on men of the suppression of emotion and the inability to acknowledge the emotional importance of others to themselves is portrayed in a story entitled "Frances," by Sarah Wolf,[25] which describes a situation in which the men of a family are unable to support the narrator's dying sister Frances because the caring in the family has been extended in the past primarily by the mothers, sisters, and wives. The men have become incapable of emotional support and expression of care even to a dying member of the family.

Frances' brother Herman is either incapable of adequately valuing his relationship to his dying sister or cannot recognize the necessity for expressions of love and care which such valuing involves.

She grieved for my brother. "It's hard for Herman," she said one day after he had paid one of his frequent but very brief visits. My brother is a nervous man, prone to but afraid of tears, and with the common male tendency to say "I can't" when he means "I won't," as in "I can't neglect my business at this time."

In a sense Herman is right. His frequently repeated "I can't" has actually become an incapacity to give himself to and to value his personal relationships.

Thus the socialization of women to carry the primary burden of maintaining personal relationships works to the detriment of the man, the woman, and the relationship between them.

2. The Distorting Effects of Women's Economic and Social Dependence on Marriage on her Concern for the Relationship

Unmarried women in our society face not only the social stigma of lacking the maritally derived identity expected of women, but in most cases economic hardship, especially if they are middle-aged and have been until now married and jobless. Even for younger women the message is clear. Being an unmarried woman is made to look, as it was for most women in the past (and will be in the future, unless we change it), a lamentable fate, to be borne if necessary, but never to be chosen. And if

---

[24]This is discussed in de Beauvoir, *op. cit.,* pp. 424 ff.

[25]Sarah Wolf, "Frances," *Women: A Journal of Liberation,* Vol. 3, No. 4, pp. 44–47.

one wants to have children, or already has them, the prospects of single parenthood are generally grim. One effect of all of this is to focus a woman's concern on the simple preservation of her marriage (or of a relationship likely to lead to marriage) often to the detriment of the content of that relationship.

Because of the reasons discussed in the previous example it is often very difficult for a woman to attempt to express her feelings and concerns about the relationship she has with her husband. We want to claim further that her very real dependence on his continuing economic and social support may well make her more reluctant to bring up with him, or even, often, to confront in herself, problems and dissatisfactions.[26]

This reluctance to acknowledge and voice one's feelings is especially evident within the relationship itself. Sheila Rowbotham quotes a young wife.

"If he stops loving me, I'm sunk; I won't have any purpose in life, or be sure I exist any more. I must efface myself in order to avoid that, and not make any demands on him, or do anything that might offend him. I feel dead now, but if he stops loving me I am really dead, because I am nothing by myself. I have to be noticed to know I exist. But if I efface myself, how can I be noticed? It is a basic contradiction."[27]

Thus, the energy which the woman is capable and desirous of putting into the relationship becomes focused on the maintenance of its form rather than on the cultivation of its content. "For the sake of her marriage" she overlooks problems, excuses faults, suppresses anger, feigns sexual pleasure, and ignores or lies about any beginnings of dissatisfaction. Not only does this involve a stifling

of her own feelings, but it works against the development of a relationship capable of being responsive to his or her needs. Trying to make a relationship do that is difficult and unlikely to be attempted when the preservation of the marriage *per se* has assumed disproportionate importance.

Thus again, as in the previous examples, we can see how a form of caring which women typically show occurs often within a context which warps it, to the mutual detriment of the woman and the object of her concern.[28]

IV

In Section II [not included herein] we presented a line of philosophical thought which attempts to articulate a positive connection between autonomy and caring. This connection remains, however, an abstract one. This abstractness accounts for the failure of [previous] philosophers to notice that distortions of caring occur not merely as individual failings. Rather these distortions are embedded in the institution which furnishes us with our central nonabstract paradigms of caring: marriage and the family. In arguing for this point in Section III we supported negatively the claim that caring requires autonomy; we have not yet, however, shown concretely what such caring looks like.

The centrality of marriage and the family to our understanding of how people care for each other, combined with the structures of dependence built into traditional marriage, make it difficult for us to understand the importance of autonomy with caring and difficult also to embody such a conception in our relationships. It is helpful, therefore, in developing alternative conceptions of caring, to consider institutions, such as women's

---

[26]For example, this may be part of the reason why she may feel that her support of her husband must be total and uncritical, why, in fact, she may not even admit to herself any critical feelings—cf. [section] A (2) above.

[27]Rowbotham, *op. cit.,* pp. 74–75. Quoted from Meredith Tax, *Woman and Her Mind, the Story of Daily Life,* a Bread & Roses publication, 1970, p. 7.

[28]Our examples have all concerned ways in which women's care and concern is distorted by the forms in which it is expressed in women's lives. It might be useful to mention an example *not* regarding women in which "altruism" is distorted by the forms in which it is expressed, so that the general point that altruism can be distorted by the social and institutional forms in which it exists in a particular society is brought out more clearly. An example is *charity,* a form of giving to others in which the autonomy of the other is not respected or promoted by the giver; rather, the other is regarded as dependent on the beneficence of others, rather than

being able to take care of himself. This aspect of charity is made explicit by Kant in his discussion of the notion of "beneficence" in the *Doctrine of Virtue* (part II of the *Metaphysics of Morals*); he sees to some extent the limits and defects of this form of giving to others, but rather than criticize it he accepts the charity-model as the typical case of giving to others.

Though charity might be motivated by a genuine concern for the other, this concern takes a distorted form in that charity reinforces and expresses a sense of inferiority and lack of autonomy in the recipient. This criticism of charity is made by W. C. MacLagan, "Respect for Persons as a Moral Principle, II," *Philosophy,* 1960. Related points specifically concerning women's role in charity organizations and other volunteer and service work are made by M. Adams, "The Compassion Trap," *op. cit.,* and Doris Gold, "Women and Voluntarism" in Gornick and Moran, *op. cit.*

consciousness-raising groups, which exist largely as a response to the difficulty people feel in relating autonomously and caringly in the context of traditional social structures.[29]

In contrast with the traditional marriage, several structural features of women's consciousness-raising groups promote the members' caring for each other in ways that reinforce their autonomy. A member is neither economically dependent on the others nor forced to rely on them as her sole source of emotional support. Nor does a member feel that criticizing another is being "ungrateful" or overstepping her role. In fact a major aim of such groups is to encourage criticism and a collective questioning of goals.

An example will make clearer how the group functions to promote autonomy and caring. A member feels inadequate to and harassed by the demands of childcare. In voicing her unhappiness she is encouraged by the others' taking her feelings seriously. They, in turn, recognize the similarity of her feelings to theirs. Thus, listening and giving support is bound up not, as typically in marriage, with a suppression of one's own feelings, but with their shared expression.

Furthermore, the seriousness her words are accorded may enable her to become in touch with buried feelings which her immersion in the situation previously prevented her from recognizing.[30] She, and others in the group, may come to acknowledge feelings of anger under the inadequacy.

The supportive criticism of other members may aid her in coming to this recognition. Whereas someone might point out that her efforts to meet *every* demand are self-defeating, someone else may make the deeper criticism that she ought not to feel that she bears sole responsibility for childcare. This sort of criticism, necessary to support someone's developing autonomy, requires one to take an autonomous stance, independent of what the other wants to hear. Thus, growths in autonomy reinforce and are reinforced by the caring within the group.

The increased confidence in the legitimacy of her feelings may enable a member to make changes in her life in response to them. It is likely, however, that the woman will come to see that certain strains are inevitable, no matter how she reacts, given certain features of her situation (her husband holds an exhausting nine to five job; adequate childcare is largely unavailable, etc.) She comes to see that many of these features of her situation are the product of a particular social structure which only concerted political activity could change. Thus the women's group can aid its members to see that their problem cannot be solved by personal change or in the isolated sphere of the group. The women of a group in California expressed this as follows:

Many of us were becoming more and more demoralized as we saw ourselves unable to fit our new concepts of ourselves as women into our daily lives. . . . We now see the group as a place where we can isolate areas of compromise, look at the situation objectively and analyze the most productive form of attack. . . . The group has had a

---

[29]In connection with the feminist and new left movements of the 1960's and 1970's, such structures have emerged, partly in response to the contradictions which we have been discussing. Women's groups, communes, and egalitarian work collectives (including commercial enterprises, political action groups, etc.) are some examples. These groups perform three major functions which are relevant to our concerns:

1. In such groups autonomy and caring reinforce each other. Conflicts between them are seen as opposed to the purpose of the groups rather than inherent in them, as is the case in the examples of section III. Should conflicts between them arise, the conditions exist for their resolution.

2. Within such groups people frequently achieve new ways of relating to others, a changed sense of themselves, and political and social insights which encourage and enable them to ameliorate the oppressive effects of the institutions which structure their lives outside of the groups.

3. In these groups people come to see that many of the contradictions and problems confronted within the groups can be fully resolved only by the sort of full-scale changes in social institutions which necessitate concerted political action.

That these groups give us models for new ways of relating to others should not obscure their limitations. Any group which plays a particular historical role, such as egalitarian collectives under capitalism and women's groups in a sexist society, is likely to be deficient as a "timeless" goal or ideal. These groups may be superseded by others which go further and do more. Their members must retain the awareness that these structures remain within and are deeply affected by features of the society as a whole. Furthermore, such structures usually last for only a limited portion of the lives of their members and often are options really available only to certain groups within the society.

[30]Related to this point is Kathryn Pyne Parsons' observation in "Nietzsche and Moral Change," [in *Nietzsche*, ed. Robert Solomon, New York, 1973] that the women's revolution never would have come about if its "activists had followed the advice" of Michael Walzer: "I should think the immediate goals of the activists must be set by the general consciousness of the oppressed group rather than by their own ideology. The effects can only be judged by those who will feel them. 'Helping' someone usually means doing something for him that he regards or seems likely to regard (given his present state of mind) as helpful" ("The Obligations of Oppressed Minorities," *Commentary*, May 1970, quoted in Parsons, emphasis hers). Part of what Parsons is concerned to argue here is that "People come to recognize that they are oppressed and that they have certain needs in and through the process of social change, and that to regard as legitimate only felt and articulated dissatisfactions is to ignore the deepest problems, the ones which are felt, if they are felt at all, as natural and inevitable."

radicalizing effect on us. Now we understand in our gut something we used to give only lip service to: that there is no personal solution to being a woman in this society. We have realized that if we do not work to change the society it will in the end destroy us.[31]

Thus, while the groups have enabled individual women to discover caring with autonomy, many have also recognized that they will only develop it fully when the political conditions which support the split between autonomy and caring, as well as the other aspects of women's oppression, are transformed.

[31]Pamela Allen, *Free Space: A Perspective on the Small Group in Women's Liberation,* Washington, New Jersey, Times Change Press, 1970, p. 60.

29/Marriage and Its Alternatives

Shulamith Firestone

The Slow Death of the Family

The increasing erosion of the functions of the family by modern technology should, by now, have caused some signs of its weakening. However, this is not absolutely the case. Though the institution is archaic, artificial cultural reinforcements have been imported to bolster it: Sentimental sermons, manuals of guidance, daily columns in newspapers and magazines, special courses, services, and institutions for (professional) couples, parents, and child educators, nostalgia, warnings to individuals who question or evade it, and finally, if the number of dropouts becomes a serious threat, a real backlash, including outright persecution of nonconformists. The last has not happened only because it is not yet necessary.

Marriage is in the same state as the Church: Both are becoming functionally defunct, as their preachers go about heralding a revival, eagerly chalking up converts in a day of dread. And just as God has been pronounced dead quite often but has this sneaky way of resurrecting himself, so everyone debunks marriage, yet ends up married.[1]

What is keeping marriage so alive? I have pointed out some of the cultural bulwarks of marriage in the twentieth century. We have seen how the romantic tradition of nonmarital love, the hetairism that was the necessary adjunct to monogamic marriage, has been purposely confused with that most pragmatic of institutions, making it more appealing—thus restraining people from experimenting with other social forms that could satisfy their emotional needs as well or better.

Under increasing pressure, with the pragmatic bases of the marriage institution blurred, sex roles relaxed to a degree that would have disgraced a Victorian. *He* had no crippling doubts about his role, nor about the function and value of marriage. To him it was simply an economic arrangement of some selfish benefit, one that would most easily satisfy his physical needs and reproduce his heirs. His wife, too, was clear about her duties and rewards: ownership of herself and of her full sexual, psychological, and housekeeping services for a lifetime, in return for long-term patronage and protection by a member of the ruling class, and—in her turn—limited control over a household and over her children until they reached a certain age. Today this contract based on divided roles has been so disguised by sentiment that it goes completely unrecognized by millions of newlyweds, and even most older married couples.

But this blurring of the economic contract, and

[1]Ninety-five percent of all American women still marry and 90 percent bear children, most often more than two. Families with children in the medium range (two to four) are as predominant as ever, no longer attributable to the postwar baby boom.

the resulting confusion of sex roles, has not significantly eased woman's oppression. In many cases it has put her in only a more vulnerable position. With the clear-cut arrangement of matches by parents all but abolished, a woman, still part of an underclass, must now, in order to gain the indispensable male patronage and protection, play a desperate game, hunting down bored males while yet appearing cool. And even once she is married, any overlap of roles generally takes place on the wife's side, not on the husband's: the "cherish and protect" clause is the first thing forgotten—while the wife has gained the privilege of going to work to "help out," even of putting her husband through school. More than ever she shoulders the brunt of the marriage, not only emotionally, but now also in its more practical aspects. She has simply added his job to hers.

A second cultural prop to the outmoded institution is the privatization of the marriage experience: each partner enters marriage convinced that what happened to his parents, what happened to his friends can never happen to him. Though Wrecked Marriage has become a national hobby, a universal obsession—as witnessed by the booming business of guidebooks to marriage and divorce, the women's magazine industry, an affluent class of marriage couselors and shrinks, whole repertoires of Ball-and-Chain jokes and gimmicks, and cultural products such as soap opera, the marriage-and-family genre on TV, e.g., *I Love Lucy* or *Father Knows Best,* films and plays like Cassavetes' *Faces* and Albee's *Who's Afraid of Virginia Woolf?* —still one encounters everywhere a defiant "We're different" brand of optimism in which the one good (outwardly exemplary, anyway) marriage in the community is habitually cited to prove that *it* is possible.

The privatization process is typified by comments like, "Well, I know I'd make a great mother." It is useless to point out that *everyone* says that, that the very parents or friends now dismissed as "bad" parents and "poor" marital partners all began marriage and parenthood in exactly the same spirit. After all, does anyone *choose* to have a "bad" marriage? Does anyone *choose* to be a "bad" mother? And even if it were a question of "good" vs. "bad" marital partners or parents, there will always be as many of the latter as the former; under the present system of universal marriage and parenthood just as many spouses and children must pull a bad lot as a good one; in fact any classes of "good" and "bad"

are bound to recreate themselves in identical proportion.[2] Thus the privatization process functions to keep people blaming themselves, rather than the institution, for its failure: Though the institution consistently proves itself unsatisfactory, even rotten, it encourages them to believe that somehow their own case will be different.

Warnings can have no effect, because logic has nothing to do with why people get married. Everyone has eyes of his own, parents of his own. If he chooses to block all evidence, it is because he must. In a world out of control, the only institutions that grant him an *illusion* of control, that seem to offer any safety, shelter or warmth, are the "private" institutions: religion, marriage/family, and, most recently, psychoanalytic therapy. But, as we have seen, the family is neither private nor a refuge, but is directly connected to—is even the cause of—the ills of the larger society which the individual is no longer able to confront.

But the cultural bulwarks we have just discussed—the confusion of romance with marriage, the blurring of its economic functions and its rigid sex roles, the privatization process, the illusion of control and refuge, all of which exploit the fears of the modern person living within an increasingly hostile environment—still are not the whole answer to why the institution of marriage continues to thrive. It is unlikely that such negatives alone could support the family unit as a vital institution. It would be too easy to attribute the continuation of the family structure solely to backlash. We will find, I am afraid, in reviewing marriage in terms of our four minimal feminist demands, that it fulfills (in its own miserable way) at least a portion of the requirements at least as well as or better than did most of the social experiments we have discussed.

1. Freedom of women from the tyranny of reproduction and childbearing is hardly fulfilled. However, women are often relieved of its worst strains by a servant class—and in the modern marriage, by modern gynecology, "family planning," and the

---

[2]But what does this dichotomy of good/bad really mean? Perhaps after all, it is only a euphemistic *class* distinction: sensitive and educated, as opposed to uneducated, underprivileged, harassed, and therefore indifferent. But even though a child born to educated or upper-class parents is luckier in every respect, and is apt to receive a fair number of privileges by virtue of his class, name, and the property he is due to inherit, the distribution of children is equal among all classes—if indeed children born to the unfortunate do not outnumber the others—in this way reproducing in identical proportion the original inequality.

increasing takeover, by the school, day-care centers, and the like, of the childrearing function.

2. Though financial *independence* of women and children is not generally granted, there is a substitute: physical *security*.

3. Women and children, segregated from the larger society, are integrated within the family unit, the only place where this occurs. That the little interplay between men, women, and children is concentrated in one social unit makes that unit all the more difficult to renounce.

4. Though the family is the source of sexual repression, is guarantees the conjugal couple a steady, if not satisfactory, sex supply, and provides the others with "aim-inhibited" relationships, which are, in many cases, the only long-term relationships these individuals will ever have.

Thus there are practical assets of marriage to which people cling. It is not all a cultural sales job. On a scale of percentages, marriage—at least in its desperate liberalized version—would fare as well as most of the experimental alternatives thus far tried, which, as we have seen, also fulfilled some of the stipulations and not others, or only partially fulfilled all of them. And marriage has the added advantage of being a known quantity.

And yet marriage in its very definition will never be able to fulfill the needs of its participants, for it was organized around, and reinforces, a fundamentally oppressive biological condition that we only now have the skill to correct. As long as we have the institution we shall have the oppressive conditions at its base. We need to start talking about new alternatives that will satisfy the emotional and psychological needs that marriage, archaic as it is, still satisfies, but that will satisfy them better. But in any proposal we shall have to do at least one better than marriage on our feminist scale, or despite all warnings people will stay hooked—in the hope that just this once, just for them, marriage will come across.

Alternatives

The classic trap for any revolutionary is always, "What's your alternative?" But even if you *could* provide the interrogator with a blueprint, this does not mean he would use it: in most cases he is not sincere in wanting to know. In fact this is a common offensive, a technique to deflect revolutionary anger and turn it against itself. Moreover, the oppressed have no job to convince all people. All *they* need know is that the present system is destroying them.

But though any specific direction must arise organically out of the revolutionary action itself, still I feel tempted here to make some "dangerously utopian" concrete proposals—both in sympathy for my own pre-radical days when the Not-Responsible-For-Blueprint Line perplexed me, and also because I am aware of the political dangers in the peculiar failure of imagination concerning alternatives to the family. There are, as we have seen, several good reasons for this failure. First, there are no precedents in history for feminist revolution—there have been women revolutionaries, certainly, but they have been used by male revolutionaries, who seldom gave even lip service to equality for women, let alone to a radical feminist restructuring of society. Moreover, we haven't even a literary image of this future society; there is not even a *utopian* feminist literature in existence. Thirdly, the nature of the family unit is such that it penetrates the individual more deeply than any other social organization we have: it literally gets him "where he lives." I have shown how the family shapes his psyche to its structure—until ultimately, he imagines it absolute, talk of anything else striking him as perverted. Finally, most alternatives suggest a loss of even the little emotional warmth provided by the family, throwing him into a panic. But the model that I shall now draw up is subject to the limitations of any plan laid out on paper by a solitary individual. Keep in mind that these are not meant as final answers, that in fact the reader could probably draw up another plan that would satisfy as well or better the four structural imperatives laid out above. The following proposals, then, will be sketchy, meant to stimulate thinking into fresh areas rather than to dictate the action.

What is the alternative to 1984 if we could have our demands acted on in time?

The most important characteristic to be maintained in any revolution is *flexibility.* I will propose, then, a program of multiple options to exist simultaneously, interweaving with each other, some transitional, others far in the future. An individual may choose one "life style" for one decade, and prefer another an another period.

1. Single Professions

A single life organized around the demands of a chosen profession, satisfying the individual's social and emotional needs through its own particular occupational structure, might be an appealing solution for many individuals, especially in the transitional period.

Single professions have practically vanished, despite the fact that the encouragement of reproduction is no longer a valid social concern. The old single roles, such as the celibate religious life, court roles—jester, musician, page, knight, and loyal squire—cowboys, sailors, firemen, cross-country truck drivers, detectives, pilots had a prestige all their own: there was no stigma attached to being professionally single. Unfortunately, these roles seldom were open to women. Most single female roles (such as spinster aunt, nun, or courtesan) were still determined by their sexual nature.

Many social scientists are now proposing as a solution to the population problem the encouragement of "deviant life styles" that by definition imply nonfertility. Richard Meier suggests that glamorous single professions previously assigned only to men should now be opened to women as well, for example, "astronaut." He notes that where these occupations exist for women, e.g., stewardess, they are based on the sex appeal of a young woman, and thus can be only limited way stations on the way to a better job or marriage. And, he adds, "so many limitations are imposed [on women's work outside the home] . . . that one suspects the existence of a culture-wide conspiracy which makes the occupational role sufficiently unpleasant that 90 percent or more would choose homemaking as a superior alternative." With the extension of whatever single roles still exist in our culture to include women, the creation of more such roles, and a program of incentives to make these professions rewarding, we could, painlessly, reduce the number of people interested in parenthood at all.

2. "Living Together"

Practiced at first only in Bohemian or intellectual circles and now increasingly in the population at large—especially by metropolitan youth—"living together" is becoming a common social practice. "Living together" is the loose social form in which two or more partners, of whatever sex, enter a nonlegal sex/companionate arrangement the duration of which varies with the internal dynamics of the relationship. Their contract is only with each other; society has no interest, since neither reproduction nor production—dependencies of one party on the other—is involved. This flexible non-form could be expanded to become the standard unit in which most people would live for most of their lives.

At first, in the transitional period, sexual relationships would probably be monogamous (single standard, female-style, this time around), even if the couple chose to live with others. We might even see the continuation of strictly nonsexual group living arrangements ("roommates"). However, after several generations of nonfamily living, our psychosexual structures may become altered so radically that the monogamous couple, or the "aim-inhibited" relationship, would become obsolescent. We can only guess what might replace it—perhaps true "group marriages," transexual group marriages which also involved older children? We don't know.

The two options we have suggested so far —single professions and "living together"—already exist, but only outside the mainstream of our society, or for brief periods in the life of the normal individual. We want to *broaden* these options to include many more people for longer periods of their lives, to transfer here instead all the cultural incentives now supporting marriage—making these alternatives, finally, as common and acceptable as marriage is today.

But what about children? Doesn't everyone want children sometime in their lives? There is no denying that people now feel a genuine desire to have children. But we don't know how much of this is the product of an authentic liking for children, and how much is a displacement of other needs. We have seen that parental satisfaction is obtainable only through crippling the child: The attempted extension of ego through one's children—in the case of the man, the "immortalizing" of name, property, class, and ethnic identification, and in the case of the woman, motherhood as the justification of her existence, the resulting attempt to live through the child, child-as-project—in the end damages or destroys either the child or the parent, or both when neither wins, as the case may be. Perhaps when we strip parenthood of these other functions, we will find a real instinct for parenthood even on the part of men, a simple physical desire to associate with the young. But then we have lost nothing, for a basic demand of our alternative system is some form of intimate interaction with children. If a parenthood instinct does in fact exist, it will be allowed to operate even more freely, having shed the practical burdens of parenthood that now make it such an anguished hell.

But what, on the other hand, if we find that there is no parenthood instinct after all? Perhaps all this time society has persuaded the individual to have children only by imposing on parenthood ego concerns that had no proper outlet. This may have been unavoidable in the past—but perhaps it's now time to start more directly satisfying those ego needs. As long as natural reproduction is still necessary, we can devise less destructive cultural inducements. But it is likely that, once the ego investments in parenthood are removed, artificial reproduction will be developed and widely accepted.

3. Households

I shall now outline a system that I believe will satisfy any remaining needs for children after ego concerns are no longer part of our motivations. Suppose a person or a couple at some point in their lives desires to live around children in a family-size unit. While we will no longer have reproduction as the life goal of the normal individual—we have seen how single and group nonreproductive life styles could be enlarged to become satisfactory for many people for their whole lifetimes and for others, for good portions of their lifetime—certain people may still prefer community-style group living permanently, and other people may want to experience it at some time in their lives, especially during early childhood.

Thus at any given time a proportion of the population will want to live in reproductive social structures. Correspondingly, the society in general will still need reproduction, though reduced, if only to create a new generation.

The proportion of the population will be automatically a select group with a predictably higher rate of stability, because they will have had a freedom of choice now generally unavailable. Today those who do not marry and have children by a certain age are penalized: they find themselves alone, excluded, and miserable, on the margins of a society in which everyone else is compartmentalized into lifetime generational families, chauvinism and exclusiveness their chief characteristic. (Only in Manhattan is single living even tolerable, and that can be debated.) Most people are still forced into marriage by family pressure, the "shotgun," economic considerations, and other reasons that have nothing to do with choice of life

style. In our new reproductive unit, however, with the limited contract (see below), childrearing so diffused as to be practically eliminated, economic considerations nonexistent, and all participating members having entered only on the basis of personal preference, "unstable" reproductive social structures will have disappeared.

This unit I shall call a *household* rather than an extended family. The distinction is important: The word *family* implies biological reproduction and some degree of division of labor by sex, and thus the traditional dependencies and resulting power relations, extended over generations; though the size of the family—in this case, the larger numbers of the "extended" family—may affect the strength of this hierarchy, it does not change its structural definition. "Household," however, connotes only a large grouping of people living together for an unspecified time, and with no specified set of interpersonal relations. How would a "household" operate?

Limited Contract   If the household replaced marriage perhaps we would at first legalize it in the same way—if this is necessary at all. A group of ten or so consenting adults of varying ages[3] could apply for a license as a group in much the same way as a young couple today applies for a marriage license, perhaps even undergoing some form of ritual ceremony, and then might proceed in the same way to set up house. The household license would, however, apply only for a given period, perhaps seven to ten years, or whatever was decided on as the minimal time in which children needed a stable structure in which to grow up—but probably a much shorter perioid than we now imagine. If at the end of this period the group decided to stay together, it could always get a renewal. However, no single individual would be contracted to stay after this period, and perhaps some members of the unit might transfer out, or new members come in. Or, the unit could disband altogether.

There are many advantages to short-term households, stable compositional units lasting for only ten-year periods: the end of family chauvinism, built up over generations, of prejudices passed down from one generation to the next, the inclusion of people of all ages in the childrearing process, the integration of many age groups into one social unit,

---

[3]An added advantage of the household is that it allows older people past their fertile years to share fully in parenthood when they so desire.

the breadth of personality that comes from exposure to many rather than to (the idiosyncrasies of) a few, and so on.

Children   A regulated percentage of each household—say one-third—would be children. But whether, at first, genetic children created by couples within the household, or at some future time—after a few generations of household living had served the special connection of adults with "their" children—children were produced artificially, or adopted, would not matter: (minimal) responsibility for the early physical dependence of children would be evenly diffused among all members of the household.

But though it would still be structurally sound, we must be aware that as long as we use natural childbirth methods, the "household" could never be a totally liberating social form. A mother who undergoes a nine-month pregnancy is likely to feel that the product of all that pain and discomfort "belongs" to her ("To think of what I went through to have you!"). But we want to destroy this possessiveness along with its cultural reinforcements so that no one child will be *a priori* favored over another, so that children will be loved for their own sake.

But what if there is an instinct for pregnancy? I doubt it. Once we have sloughed off cultural superstructures, we may uncover a sex instinct, the normal consequences of which *lead* to pregnancy. And perhaps there is also an instinct to care for the young once they arrive. But an instinct for pregnancy itself would be superfluous—could nature anticipate man's mastery of reproduction? And what if, once the false motivations for pregnancy had been shed, women no longer wanted to "have" children at all? Might this not be a disaster, given that artificial reproduction is not yet perfected? But women have no special reproductive *obligation* to the species. If they are no longer willing, then artificial methods will have to be developed hurriedly, or, at the very least, satisfactory compensations—other than destructive ego investments—would have to be supplied to make it worth their while.

Adults and older children would take care of babies for as long as they needed it, but since there would be many adults and older children sharing the responsibility—as in the extended family—no one person would ever be involuntarily stuck with it.

Adult/child relationships would develop just as do the best relationships today: some adults might prefer certain children over others, just as

some children might prefer certain adults over others—these might become lifelong attachments in which the individuals concerned mutually agreed to stay together, perhaps to form some kind of nonreproductive unit. Thus all relationships would be based on love alone, uncorrupted by objective dependencies and the resulting class inequalities. Enduring relationships between people of widely divergent ages would become common.

Legal Rights and Transfers   With the weakening and severance of the blood ties, the power hierarchy of the family would break down. The legal structure—as long as it is still necessary—would reflect this democracy at the roots of our society. Women would be identical under the law with men. Children would no longer be "minors," under the patronage of "parents"—they would have full rights. Remaining physical inequalities could be legally compensated for: for example, if a child were beaten, perhaps he could report it to a special simplified "household" court where he would be granted instant legal redress.

Another special right of children would be the right of immediate transfer: if the child for any reason did not like the household into which he had been born so arbitrarily, he would be helped to transfer out. An adult on the other hand—one who had lived one span in a household (seven to ten years)—might have to present his case to the court, which would then decide, as do divorce courts today, whether he had adequate grounds for breaking his contract. A certain number of transfers within the seven-year period might be necessary for the smooth functioning of the household, and would not be injurious to its stability as a unit so long as a core remained. (In fact, new people now and then might be a refreshing change.) However, the unit, for its own best economy, might have to place a ceiling on the number of transfers in or out, to avoid depletion, excessive growth, and/or friction.

Chores   As for housework: The larger family-sized group (probably about fifteen people) would be more practical—the waste and repetition of the duplicate nuclear family unit would be avoided, e.g., as in shopping or cooking for a small family, without the loss of intimacy of the larger communal experiment. In the interim, any housework would have to be rotated equitably; but eventually cybernation could automate out almost all domestic chores. . . .

Part Three
Some Special Moral Issues in Women's Liberation

6
Abortion

30/A Defense of Abortion

Judith Jarvis Thomson

Most opposition to abortion relies on the premise that the fetus is a human being, a person, from the moment of conception. The premise is argued for, but, as I think, not well. Take, for example, the most common argument. We are asked to notice that the development of a human being from conception through birth into childhood is continuous; then it is said that to draw a line, to choose a point in this development and say "before this point the thing is not a person, after this point it is a person" is to make an arbitrary choice, a choice for which in the nature of things no good reason can be given. It is concluded that the fetus is, or that we had better say it is, a person from the moment of conception. But this conclusion does not follow. Similar things might be said about the development of an acorn into an oak tree, and it does not follow that acorns are oak trees, or that we had better say they are. Arguments of this form are sometimes called "slippery-slope arguments"—the phrase is perhaps self-explanatory—and it is dismaying that opponents of abortion rely on them so heavily and uncritically.

I am inclined to agree, however, that the prospects for "drawing a line" in the development of the fetus look dim. I am inclined to think also that we shall probably have to agree that the fetus has already become a human person well before birth. Indeed, it comes as a surprise when one first learns how early in its life the fetus begins to acquire human characteristics. By the tenth week, for example, it already has a face, arms and legs, fingers and toes; it has internal organs, and brain activity is detectable.[1] On the other hand, I think that the premise is false, that the fetus is not a person from the moment of conception. A newly fertilized ovum, a newly implanted clump of cells, is no more a person than an acorn is an oak tree. But I shall not discuss any of this. For it seems to me to be of greater interest to ask what happens if, for the sake of argument, we allow the premise. How, precisely, are we supposed to get from there to the conclusion that abortion is morally impermissible? Opponents of abortion commonly spend most of their time establishing that the fetus is a person, and hardly any time explaining the step from there to the impermissibility of abortion. Perhaps they think the step too simple and obvious to require much comment. Or perhaps they are simply being economical in argument. Many of those who defend abortion rely on the premise that the fetus is not a person, but only a bit of tissue that will become a person at birth; and why pay out more arguments than you have to? Whatever the explanation, I suggest that the step they take is neither easy nor obvious, that it calls for closer examination than it is commonly given, and that when we do give it this closer examination we shall feel inclined to reject it.

I propose, then, that we grant that the fetus is a person from the moment of conception. How does the argument go from here? Something like this, I take it. Every person has a right to life. So the fetus has a right to life. No doubt the mother has a right to decide what shall happen in and to her body; everyone would grant that. But surely a person's right to life is stronger and more stringent than the mother's right to decide what happens in and to her

I am very indebted to James Thomson for discussion, criticism, and many helpful suggestions.

[1] Daniel Callahan, *Abortion: Law, Choice, and Morality* (New York: Macmillan, 1970), p. 373. This book gives a fascinating survey of the available information on abortion. The Jewish tradition is surveyed in David M. Feldman, *Birth Control in Jewish Law* (New York: New York University Press, 1968), part 5; the Catholic tradition, in John T. Noonan, Jr., "An Almost Absolute Value in History," in *The Morality of Abortion,* ed. John T. Noonan, Jr. (Cambridge, Mass.: Harvard University Press, 1970).

From *Philosophy & Public Affairs* 1 (Fall 1971). Copyright © 1971 by Princeton University Press. Reprinted by permission. Footnotes have been renumbered.

body, and so outweighs it. So the fetus may not be killed; an abortion may not be performed.

It sounds plausible. But now let me ask you to imagine this. You wake up in the morning and find yourself back to back in bed with an unconscious famous violinist. He has been found to have a fatal kidney ailment, and the Society of Music Lovers has canvassed all the available medical records and found that you alone have the right blood type to help. They have therefore kidnapped you, and last night the violinist's circulatory system was plugged into yours so that your kidneys could be used to extract poisons from his blood as well as your own. The director of the hospital now tells you: "Look, we're sorry the Society of Music Lovers did this to you—we would never have permitted it if we had known. But still, they did it and the violinist now is plugged into you. To unplug you would be to kill him. But never mind, it's only for nine months. By then he will have recovered from his ailment and can safely be unplugged from you." Is it morally incumbent on you to accede to this situation? No doubt it would be very nice of you if you did, a great kindness. But do you *have* to accede to it? What if it were not nine months but nine years? Or longer still? What if the director of the hospital said: "Tough luck, I agree, but you've now got to stay in bed, with the violinist plugged into you, for the rest of your life. Because remember this: All persons have a right to life, and violinists are persons. Granted you have a right to decide what happens in and to your body, but a person's right to life outweighs your right to decide what happens in and to your body. So you cannot ever be unplugged from him." I imagine you would regard this as outrageous, which suggests that something really is wrong with that plausible-sounding argument that was mentioned previously.

In this case, of course, you were kidnapped; you did not volunteer for the operation that plugged the violinist into your kidneys. Can those who oppose abortion on the grounds I mentioned make an exception for a pregnancy due to rape? Certainly. They can say that persons have a right to life only if they did not come into existence because of rape; or they can say that all persons have a right to life, but that some have less of a right to life than others, in particular, that those who came into existence because of rape have less. But these statements have a rather unpleasant sound. Surely the question of whether one has a right to life at all, or how much of a right one has, should not turn on the question of whether or not one is the product of a rape. And in

fact the people who oppose abortion on the ground I mentioned do not make this distinction, and hence do not make an exception in case of rape.

Nor do they make an exception for a case in which the mother has to spend the nine months of her pregnancy in bed. They would agree that that would be a great pity and hard on the mother, but would insist all the same that all persons have a right to life, and that the fetus is a person. I suspect, in fact, that they would not make an exception for a case in which, miraculously enough, the pregnancy went on for nine years, or even for the rest of the mother's life.

Some would not even make an exception for a case in which continuation of the pregnancy is likely to shorten the mother's life; they regard abortion as impermissible even to save the mother's life. Such cases are nowadays very rare, and many opponents of abortion do not accept this extreme view. All the same, it is a good place to begin: a number of points of interest come out in respect to it.

1. Let us call the view that abortion is impermissible even to save the mother's life "the extreme view." I want to suggest, first, that it does not issue from the argument I mentioned earlier without the addition of some fairly powerful premises. Suppose a woman has become pregnant, and now learns that she has a cardiac condition such that she will die if she carries the baby to term. What may be done for her? The fetus, being a person, has a right to life; but as the mother is a person too, so has she a right to life. Presumably they have an equal right to life. How is it supposed to come out that an abortion may not be performed? If mother and child have an equal right to life, should not we perhaps flip a coin? Or should we add to the mother's right to life her right to decide what happens in and to her body, which everybody seems to be ready to grant—the sum of her rights now outweighing the fetus' right to life?

The most familiar argument here is the following. We are told that performing the abortion would be directly killing[2] the child, whereas doing nothing would not be killing the mother, but only letting her die. Moreover, in killing the child, one would be killing an innocent person, for the child has committed no crime and is not aiming at his mother's death. And then there are a variety of ways in which

[2]The term "direct" in the arguments I refer to is a technical one. Roughly, what is meant by "direct killing" is either killing as an end in itself or killing as a means to some end, for example, the end of saving someone else's life. See note [5] for an example of its use.

this argument might be continued. (1) As directly killing an innocent person is always and absolutely impermissible, an abortion may not be performed. Or, (2) as directly killing an innocent person is murder, and murder is always and absolutely impermissible, an abortion may not be performed.[3] Or, (3) as one's duty to refrain from directly killing an innocent person is more stringent than one's duty to keep a person from dying, an abortion may not be performed. Or, (4) if one's only options are directly killing an innocent person or letting a person die, one must prefer letting the person die, and thus an abortion may not be performed.[4]

Some people seem to have thought that these are not further premises that must be added if the conclusion is to be reached, but that they follow from the very fact that an innocent person has a right to life.[5] But this seems to me a mistake, and perhaps the simplest way to show this is to point out that while we must certainly grant that innocent persons have a right to life, the theses in arguments 1 through 4 are all false. Take argument 2 for example. If directly killing an innocent person is murder, and thus is impermissible, then the mother's directly killing the innocent person inside her is murder, and thus is impermissible. But it cannot seriously be thought to be murder if the mother performs an abortion on herself to save her life. It cannot seriously be said that she *must* refrain, that she *must* sit passively by and wait for her death. Let us look again at the case of you and the violinist. There you are, in bed with the violinist, and the director of the hospital says to you: "It's all most distressing, and I deeply sympathize, but you see this is putting an additional

strain on your kidneys, and you'll be dead within the month. But you *have* to stay where you are all the same, because unplugging you would be directly killing an innocent violinist, and that's murder, and that's impermissible." If anything in the world is true, it is that you do not commit murder, you do not do what is impermissible, if you reach around to your back and unplug yourself from that violinist to save your life.

The main focus of attention in writings on abortion has been on what a third party may or may not do in answer to a request from a woman for an abortion. This is in a way understandable. Things being as they are, there is not much a woman can safely do to abort herself. So the question asked is, What may a third party do? And what the mother may do, if it is mentioned at all, is deduced, almost as an afterthought, from what it is concluded that a third party may do. But it seems to me that to treat the matter in this way is to refuse to grant to the mother that very status of person that is so firmly insisted on for the fetus. For we cannot simply read off what a person may do from what a third party may do. Suppose you find yourself trapped in a tiny house with a growing child—I mean a very tiny house, and a rapidly growing child; you are already up against the wall of the house and in a few minutes you'll be crushed to death. The child, on the other hand, will not be crushed to death; if nothing is done to stop him from growing he will be hurt, but in the end he will simply burst open the house and walk out a free man. Now I could well understand it if a bystander were to say: "There's nothing we can do for you. We cannot choose between your life and his, we cannot be the ones to decide who is to live, we cannot intervene." But it cannot be concluded that you too can do nothing, that you cannot attack the child to save your life. However innocent the child may be, you do not have to wait passively while it crushes you to death. Perhaps a pregnant woman is vaguely felt to have the status of a house, which we do not allow the right of self-defense. But if the woman houses the child, it should be remembered that she is a person who houses it.

I should perhaps pause to say explicitly that I am not claiming that people have a right to do anything whatever to save their lives. I think, rather, that there are drastic limits to the right of self-defense. If someone threatens you with death unless you torture someone else to death, I think you have not the right, even to save your life, to do so. But the case under consideration here is very different. In our

[3] Cf. *Encyclical Letter of Pope Pius XI on Christian Marriage,* St. Paul Editions (Boston, n.d.), p. 32: "However much we may pity the mother whose health and even life is gravely imperiled in the performance of the duty allotted to her by nature, nevertheless what could ever be a sufficient reason for excusing in any way the direct murder of the innocent? This is precisely what we are dealing with here." Noonan (*The Morality of Abortion,* p. 43) reads this as follows: "What cause can ever avail to excuse in any way the direct killing of the innocent? For it is a question of that."

[4] The thesis in argument 4 is in an interesting way weaker than those in 1, 2, and 3: they rule out abortion even in cases in which both mother and child will die if the abortion is not performed. By contrast, one who held the view expressed in 4 could consistently say that one need not prefer letting two persons die to killing one.

[5] Cf. the following passage from Pius XII, *Address to the Italian Catholic Society of Midwives:* "The baby in the maternal breast has the right to life immediately from God.—Hence there is no man, no human authority, no science, no medical, eugenic, social, economic or moral 'indication' which can establish or grant a valid juridical ground for a direct deliberate disposition of an innocent human life, that is a disposition which looks to its destruction either as an end or as a means to another end perhaps in itself not illicit.—The baby, still not born, is a man in the same degree and for the same reason as the mother" (quoted in Noonan, *The Morality of Abortion,* p. 45).

case there are only two people involved, one whose life is threatened, and one who threatens it. Both are innocent: the one who is threatened is not threatened because of any fault; the one who threatens does not threaten because of any fault. For this reason we may feel that we bystanders cannot intervene. But the person threatened can.

In sum, a woman surely can defend her life against the threat to it posed by the unborn child, even if doing so involves its death. And this shows not merely that the theses in arguments 1 through 4 are false; it shows also that the extreme view of abortion is false, and so we need not canvass any other possible ways of arriving at it from the argument I mentioned at the outset.

2. The extreme view could of course be weakened to say that while abortion is permissible to save the mother's life, it may not be performed by a third party, but only by the mother herself. But this cannot be right either. For what we have to keep in mind is that the mother and the unborn child are not like two tenants in a small house that has, by an unfortunate mistake, been rented to both: the mother *owns* the house. The fact that she does adds to the offensiveness of deducing that the mother can do nothing from the supposition that third parties can do nothing. But it does more than this; it also casts a bright light on the supposition that third parties can do nothing. Certainly it lets us see that a third party who says "I cannnot choose between you" is fooling himself if he thinks this is impartiality. If Jones has found and fastened on a certain coat that he needs to keep himself from freezing but that Smith also needs to keep from freezing, then it is not impartiality that says "I cannot choose between you" when Smith owns the coat. Women have said again and again, "This body is my body!" and they have reason to feel angry, reason to feel that it has been like shouting into the wind. Smith, after all, is hardly likely to bless us if we say to him: "Of course it's your coat; anybody would grant that it is. But no one may choose between you and Jones who is to have it."

We should really ask what it is that says "no one may choose" in the face of the fact that the body that houses the child is the mother's body. It may be simply a failure to appreciate this fact. But it may be something more interesting, namely the sense that one has a right to refuse to lay hands on people, even where it would be just and fair to do so, even where justice seems to require that somebody do so. Thus justice might call for somebody to get Smith's coat back from Jones, and yet you have a

right to refuse to be the one to lay hands on Jones, a right to refuse to do physical violence to him. This, I think, must be granted. But then what should be said is not "no one may choose," but only "*I* cannot choose"—indeed not even this, but rather "*I* will not act," leaving it open that somebody else can or should, in particular that anyone in a position of authority, with the job of securing people's rights, both can and should. So this is no difficulty. I have not been arguing that any given third party must accede to the mother's request that he perform an abortion to save her life, but only that he may.

I suppose that in some views of human life the mother's body is only on loan to her, the loan not being one that gives her any prior claim to it. One who held this view might well think it impartiality to say, "I cannot choose." But I shall simply ignore this possibility. My own view is that if a human being has any just, prior claim to anything at all, he has a just, prior claim to his own body. And perhaps this need not be argued for here anyway, since, as I mentioned, the arguments against abortion we are looking at do grant that the woman has a right to decide what happens in and to her body.

But although they do grant it, I have tried to show that they do not take seriously what is done in granting it. I suggest the same thing will reappear even more clearly when we turn away from cases in which the mother's life is at stake and attend, as I propose we now do, to the vastly more common cases in which a woman wants an abortion for some less weighty reason than preserving her own life.

3. Where the mother's life is not at stake the argument I mentioned at the outset seems to have a much stronger pull. "Everyone has a right to life, so the unborn person has a right to life." And isn't the child's right to life weightier than anything other than the mother's own right to life, which she might put forward as ground for an abortion?

This argument treats the right to life as if it were unproblematic. It is not, and this seems to me to be precisely the source of the mistake.

For we should now, at long last, ask what it comes to, to have a right to life. In some views having a right to life includes having a right to be given at least the bare minimum one needs for continued life. But suppose that what in fact *is* the bare minimum a man needs for continued life is something he has no right at all to be given? If I am sick unto death, and the only thing that will save my life is the touch of Henry Fonda's cool hand on my fevered brow, then all the same, I have no right to be given the touch of Henry Fonda's cool hand on my fevered brow. It would be frightfully nice of him to fly in from the West Coast to provide it. It would be less nice, though no doubt well meant, if my friends flew to the West Coast and carried Henry Fonda back with them. But I have no right at all against anybody that he should do this for me. Or again, to return to the story I told earlier, the fact that for continued life the violinist needs the continued use of your kidneys does not establish that he has a right to be given the continued use of your kidneys. He certainly has no right against you that *you* should give him continued use of your kidneys. For nobody has any right to use your kidneys unless you give him such a right; and nobody has the right against you that you shall give him this right. If you do allow him to go on using your kidneys, this is a kindness on your part, and not something he can claim from you as his due. Nor has he any right against anybody else that they should give him continued use of your kidneys. Certainly he had no right against the Society of Music Lovers that they should plug him into you in the first place. And if you now start to unplug yourself, having learned that you will otherwise have to spend nine years in bed with him, there is nobody in the world who must try to prevent you, in order to see to it that he is given something he has a right to be given.

Some people are rather stricter about the right to life. In their view it does not include the right to be given anything, but amounts to, and only to, the right not to be killed by anybody. But here a related difficulty arises. If everybody is to refrain from killing the violinist, then everybody must refrain from doing a great many different sorts of things. Everybody must refrain from slitting his throat, everybody must refrain from shooting him—and everybody must refrain from unplugging you from him. But does he have a right against everybody that they shall refrain from unplugging you from him? To refrain from doing this is to allow him to continue to use your kidneys. It could be argued that he has a right against us that *we* should allow him to continue to use your kidneys. That is, while he had no right against us that we should give him the use of your kidneys, it might be argued that he anyway has a right against us that we shall not now intervene and deprive him of the use of you kidneys. I shall come back to third-party interventions later. But certainly the violinist has no right against you that *you* shall allow him to continue to use your kidneys. As I said, if you do allow him to use them, it is a kindness on your part, and not something you owe him.

The difficulty I point to here is not peculiar to the right to life. It reappears in connection with all the other natural rights; and it is something that an adequate account of rights must deal with. For present purposes it is enough just to draw attention to it. But I would stress that I am not arguing that people do not have a right to life—quite the contrary, it seems to me that the primary control we must place on the acceptability of an account of rights is that it should turn out in that account to be a truth that all persons have a right to life. I am arguing only that having a right to life does not guarantee having either a right to be given the use of or a right to be allowed continued use of another person's body—even if one needs it for life itself. So the right to life will not serve the opponents of abortion in the very simple and clear way in which they seem to have thought it would.

4. There is another way to bring out the difficulty. In the most ordinary sort of case, to deprive someone of what he has a right to is to treat him unjustly. Suppose a boy and his small brother are jointly given a box of chocolates for Christmas. If the older boy takes the box and refuses to give his brother any of the chocolates, he is unjust to him, for the brother has been given a right to half of them. But suppose that having learned that otherwise it means nine years in bed with that violinist, you unplug yourself from him. You surely are not being unjust to him, for you gave him no right to use your kidneys, and no one else can have given him any such right. But we have to notice that in unplugging yourself you are killing him; and violinists, like everybody else, have a right to life, and thus in the view we are considering, the right not to be killed. So here you do what he supposedly has a right that you shall not do, but you do not act unjustly to him in doing it.

The emendation that may be made at this point is this: the right to life consists not in the right not to be killed but rather in the right not to be killed unjustly. This runs a risk of circularity, but never mind: it would enable us to square the fact that the violinist has a right to life with the fact that you do not act unjustly toward him in unplugging yourself, thereby killing him. For if you do not kill him unjustly, you do not violate his right to life, and so it is no wonder you do him no injustice.

But if this emendation is accepted, the gap in the argument against abortion stares us plainly in the face: it is by no means enough to show that the fetus is a person, and to remind us that all persons have a right to life; we need to be shown also that killing the fetus violates its right to life, that is, that abortion is unjust killing. And is it?

I suppose we may take it as a datum that in a case of pregnancy due to rape the mother has not given the unborn person a right to the use of her body for food and shelter. Indeed, in what pregnancy could it be supposed that the mother has given the unborn person such a right? It is not as if there were unborn persons drifting about the world, to whom a woman who wants a child says "I invite you in."

But it might be argued that there are other ways one can have acquired a right to the use of another person's body than by having been invited to use it by that person. Suppose a woman voluntarily indulges in intercourse, knowing of the chance that it will issue in pregnancy, and then she does become pregnant. Is she not in part responsible for the presence, in fact the very existence, of the unborn person inside her? No doubt she did not invite it in. But doesn't her partial responsibility for its being there itself give it a right to the use of her body?[6] If so, then her aborting it would be more like the boy's taking away the chocolates and less like your unplugging yourself from the violinist—doing so would be depriving it of what it does have a right to, and thus would be doing it an injustice.

And then, too, it might be asked whether or not she can kill it even to save her own life: If she voluntarily called it into existence, how can she now kill it, even in self-defense?

The first thing to be said about this is that it is something new. Opponents of abortion have been so concerned to make out the independence of the fetus, in order to establish that it has a right to life, just as its mother does, that they have tended to overlook the possible support they might gain from making out that the fetus is dependent on the mother, in order to establish that she has a special kind of responsibility for it, a responsibility that gives it rights against her that are not possessed by any independent person—such as an ailing violinist who is a stranger to her.

On the other hand, this argument would give the unborn person a right to its mother's body only if her pregnancy resulted from a voluntary act, undertaken in full knowledge of the chance that a pregnancy might result from it. It would leave out entirely the unborn person whose existence is due

to rape. Pending the availability of some further argument, then, we would be left with the conclusion that unborn persons whose existence is due to rape have no right to the use of their mothers' bodies, and thus that aborting them is not depriving them of anything they have a right to and hence is not unjust killing.

And we should also notice that it is not at all plain that this argument really does go even as far as it purports to. For there are different kinds of cases, and the details make a difference. If the room is stuffy and I therefore open a window to air it and a burglar climbs in, it would be absurd to say, "Ah, now he can stay; she's given him a right to the use of her house—for she is partially responsible for his presence there, having voluntarily done what enabled him to get in, in full knowledge that there are such things as burglars, and that burglars burgle." It would be still more absurd to say this if I had had bars installed outside my windows precisely to prevent burglars from getting in, and a burglar got in only because of a defect in the bars. It remains equally absurd if we imagine it is not a burglar who climbs in but an innocent person who blunders or falls in. Again, suppose it were like this: people-seeds drift about in the air like pollen, and if you open your windows one may drift in and take root in your carpet or upholstery. You do not want children, so you fix up your windows with fine mesh screens, the very best you can buy. As can happen, however, and on very rare occasions does happen, one of the screens is defective; and a seed drifts in and takes root. Does the person-plant who now develops have a right to the use of your house? Surely not, despite the fact that you voluntarily opened your windows, that you knowingly kept carpets and upholstered furniture, and that you knew that screens were sometimes defective. Someone may argue that you are responsible for its rooting, that it does have a right to your house because, after all, you *could* have lived out your life with bare floors and furniture, or with sealed windows and doors. But this will not do, for by the same token anyone can avoid a pregnancy due to rape by having a hysterectomy, or by never leaving home without a (reliable!) army.

It seems to me that the argument we are looking at can establish at most that there are some cases in which the unborn person has a right to the use of its mother's body, and therefore some cases in which abortion is unjust killing. There is room for much discussion and argument as to precisely which cases, if any, are unjust. But I think we should

---

[6]The need for a discussion of this argument was brought home to me by members of the Society for Ethical and Legal Philosophy, to whom this paper was originally presented.

sidestep this issue and leave it open, for the argument certainly does not establish that all abortion is unjust killing.

5. There is, however, room for yet another argument here. We all surely must grant that there may be cases in which it would be morally indecent to detach a person from your body at the cost of his life. Suppose you learn that what the violinist needs is not nine years of your life but only one hour: all you need do to save his life is to spend one hour in that bed with him. Suppose also that letting him use your kidneys for that one hour would not affect your health in the slightest. Admittedly you were kidnapped. Admittedly you did not give anyone permission to plug him into you. Nevertheless it seems to me plain you *ought* to allow him to use your kidneys for that hour—it would be indecent to refuse.

Again, suppose pregnancy lasted only an hour and constituted no threat to life or health. And suppose that a woman becomes pregnant as a result of rape. Admittedly she did not voluntarily do anything to bring about the existence of a child. Admittedly she did nothing at all that would give the unborn person a right to the use of her body. All the same it might well be said, as in the newly emended violinist story, that she *ought* to allow it to remain for that hour—that it would be indecent in her to refuse.

Now some people are inclined to use the term "right" in such a way that it follows from the fact that you ought to allow a person to use your body for the hour he needs, that he has a right to use your body for the hour he needs, even though he has not been given that right by any person or act. They may say that it follows also that if you refuse you act unjustly toward him. This use of the term is perhaps so common that it cannot be called wrong; nevertheless it seems to me to be an unfortunate loosening of what we would do better to keep a tight rein on. Suppose that the box of chocolates I mentioned earlier had not been given to both boys jointly, but was given only to the older boy. There he sits, stolidly eating his way through the box, his small brother watching enviously. Here we are likely to say: "You ought not to be so mean. You ought to give your brother some of those chocolates." My own view is that it just does not follow from the truth of this that the brother has any right to any of the chocolates. If the boy refuses to give his brother any, he is greedy, stingy, callous—but not unjust. I suppose that the people I have in mind will say it does follow that the brother has a right to some of the

chocolates, and thus that the boy does act unjustly if he refuses to give his brother any. But the effect of saying this is to obscure what we should keep distinct, namely the difference between the boy's refusal in this case and the boy's refusal in the earlier case, in which the box was given to both boys jointly, and in which the small brother thus had what was from any point of view clear title to half.

A further objection to so using the term "right," that from the fact that A ought to do a thing for B it follows that B has a right against A that A do it for him, is that it is going to make the question of whether or not a man has a right to a thing turn on how easy it is to provide him with it; and this seems not merely unfortunate but morally unacceptable. Take the case of Henry Fonda again. I said earlier that I had no right to the touch of his cool hand on my fevered brow, even though I needed it to save my life. I said it would be frightfully nice of him to fly in from the West Coast to provide me with it, but that I had no right against him that he should do so. But suppose he isn't on the West Coast. Suppose he has only to walk across the room and place a hand briefly on my brow—and lo, my life is saved. Then surely he ought to do it; it would be indecent to refuse. Is it to be said, "Ah, well, it follows that in this case she has a right to the touch of his hand on her brow, and so it would be an injustice for him to refuse"? So that I have a right to it when it is easy for him to provide it, though no right when it is hard? It's rather a shocking idea that anyone's rights should fade away and disappear as it gets harder and harder to accord them to him.

So my own view is that even though you ought to let the violinist use your kidneys for the one hour he needs, we should not conclude that he has a right to do so; we should say that if you refuse you are, like the boy who owns all the chocolates and will give none away, self-centered and callous—indecent, in fact—but not unjust. And similarly, that even supposing a case in which a woman pregnant due to rape ought to allow the unborn person to use her body for the hour he needs, we should not conclude that he has a right to do so; we should conclude that she is self-centered, callous, indecent, but not unjust, if she refuses. The complaints are no less grave; they are just different. However, there is no need to insist on this point. If anyone does wish to deduce "he has a right" from "you ought," then all the same he must surely grant that there are cases in which it is not morally required of you that you allow that violinist to use your kidneys, and in which he does not have a right to use them, and in which you do not do him an unjustice if you refuse. And so also for mother and unborn child. Except in such cases as the unborn person has a right to demand it—and we were leaving open the possibility that there may be such cases—nobody is morally *required* to make large sacrifices, of health, of all other interests and concerns, of all other duties and commitments, for nine years, or even for nine months, in order to keep another person alive.

6. We have in fact to distinguish between two kinds of Samaritans: the Good Samaritan and what we might call the Minimally Decent Samaritan. The story of the Good Samaritan, you will remember, goes like this:

> *A certain man went down from Jerusalem to Jericho, and fell among thieves, which stripped him of his raiment, and wounded him, and departed, leaving him half dead.*
>
> *And by chance there came down a certain priest that way; and when he saw him, he passed by on the other side.*
>
> *And likewise a Levite, when he was at the place, came and looked on him, and passed by on the other side.*
>
> *But a certain Samaritan, as he journeyed, came where he was; and when he saw him he had compassion on him.*
>
> *And went to him, and bound up his wounds, pouring in oil and wine, and set him on his own beast, and brought him to an inn, and took care of him.*
>
> *And on the morrow, when he departed, he took out two pence, and gave them to the host, and said unto him, "Take care of him; and whatsoever thou spendest more, when I come again, I will repay thee." (Luke 10:30–35)*

The Good Samaritan went out of his way, at some cost to himself, to help one in need of it. We are not told what the options were, that is, whether or not the priest and the Levite could have helped by doing less than the Good Samaritan did; but assuming they could have, then the fact they did nothing at all shows they were not even Minimally Decent Samaritans, not because they were not Samaritans, but because they were not even minimally decent.

These things are a matter of degree, of course, but there is a difference; it comes out perhaps most clearly in the story of Kitty Genovese, who was murdered while thirty-eight peo-

ple watched or listened and did nothing at all to help her. A Good Samaritan would have rushed out to give direct assistance against the murderer. Or perhaps we had better allow that it would have been a Splendid Samaritan who did this, on the ground that it would have involved a risk of death for himself. But the thirty-eight people not only did not do this; they did not even trouble to pick up a phone to call the police. Minimally Decent Samaritanism would call for doing at least that, and their not having done so was monstrous.

After telling the story of the Good Samaritan Jesus said, "Go, and do thou likewise." Perhaps he meant that we are morally required to act as the Good Samaritan did. Perhaps he was urging people to do more than is morally required of them. At all events it seems plain that it was not morally required of any of the thirty-eight that he rush out to give direct assistance at the risk of his own life and that it is not morally required of anyone that he give long stretches of his life—nine years or nine months—to sustaining the life of a person who has no special right (we were leaving open the possibility of this) to demand it.

Indeed, with one rather striking class of exceptions, no one in any country in the world is *legally* required to do anywhere near as much as this for anyone else. The class of exceptions is obvious. My main concern here is not the state of the law in respect to abortion, but it is worth drawing attention to the fact that in no state in this country is any man compelled by law to be even a Minimally Decent Samaritan to any person; there is no law under which charges could be brought against the thirty-eight people who stood by while Kitty Genovese died. By contrast, in most states in this country women are compelled by law to be not merely Minimally Decent Samaritans, but Good Samaritans, to unborn persons inside them. This does not by itself settle anything, because it may well be argued that there should be laws in this country—as there are in many European countries—compelling at least Minimally Decent Samaritanism.[7] But it does show that there is a gross injustice in the existing state of the law. And it shows also that the groups currently working against liberalization of abortion laws, in fact working toward having it declared unconstitutional for a state to permit abortion, had better start

[7] For a discussion of the difficulties involved, and a survey of the European experience with such laws, see *The Good Samaritan and the Law,* ed. James M. Ratcliffe (New York: Peter Smith, 1966).

working for the adoption of Good Samaritan laws generally, or earn the charge that they are acting in bad faith.

I myself think that Minimally Decent Samaritan laws would be one thing, Good Samaritan laws quite another—and in fact highly improper. But we are not here concerned with the law. What we should ask is not whether anybody should be compelled by law to be a Good Samaritan but whether we must accede to a situation in which somebody is being compelled—by nature, perhaps—to be a Good Samaritan. We have, in other words, to look now at third-party interventions. I have been arguing that no person is morally required to make large sacrifices to sustain the life of another who has no right to demand them, and this even where the sacrifices do not include life itself; we are not morally required to be Good Samaritans, or anyway, Very Good Samaritans, to one another. But what if a man cannot extricate himself from such a situation? What if he appeals to us to extricate him? It seems to me plain that there are cases in which we can, cases in which a Good Samaritan would extricate him. There you are: you were kidnapped, and nine years in bed with the violinist lie ahead of you. You have your own life to lead. You are sorry, but you simply cannot see giving up so much of your life to the sustaining of his. You cannot extricate yourself, and ask us to do so. I should have thought that—in light of his having no right to the use of your body—it was obvious that we do not have to accede to your being forced to give up so much. We can do what you ask. There is no injustice to the violinist in our doing so.

7. Following the lead of the opponents of abortion, I have throughout been speaking of the fetus merely as a person; and what I have been asking is whether or not the argument we began with, which proceeds only from the fetus' being a person, really does establish its conclusion. I have argued that it does not.

But of course there are arguments and arguments, and it may be said that I have simply fastened on the wrong one. It may be said that what is important is not merely the fact that the fetus is a person but that it is a person for whom the woman has a special kind of responsibility issuing from the fact that she is its mother. It might be argued that all my analogies are therefore irrelevant—for you do not have that special kind of responsibility for that violinist and Henry Fonda does not have that special kind of responsibility for me. And our attention might be drawn to the fact that men and women

both are compelled by law to provide support for their children.

I have in effect dealt (briefly) with this argument in section 4 above; but a (still briefer) recapitulation now may be in order. Surely we do not have any such "special responsibility" for a person unless we have assumed it, explicitly or implicitly. If a set of parents do not try to prevent pregnancy, do not obtain an abortion, and then at the time of birth of the child do not put it up for adoption but rather take it home with them, then they have assumed responsibility for it, they have given it rights, and they cannot *now* withdraw support from it at the cost of its life because they now find it difficult to go on providing for it. But if they have taken all reasonable precautions against having a child, they do not simply by virtue of their biological relationship to the child who comes into existence have a special responsibility for it. They may wish to assume responsibility for it, or they may not wish to. And I am suggesting that if assuming responsibility for it would require large sacrifices, then they may refuse. A Good Samaritan would not refuse, or, anyway, a Splendid Samaritan would not, if the sacrifices that had to be made were enormous. But then so would a Good Samaritan assume responsibility for that violinist; so would Henry Fonda, if he is a Good Samaritan, fly in from the West Coast and assume responsibility for me.

8. My argument will be found unsatisfactory on two counts by many of those who want to regard abortion as morally permissible. First, while I do argue that abortion is not impermissible, I do not argue that it is always permissible. There may well be cases in which carrying the child to term requires only Minimally Decent Samaritanism of the mother, and this is a standard we must not fall below. I am inclined to think it a merit of my account precisely that it does *not* give a general yes or a general no. It allows for and supports our sense that, for example, a sick and desperately frightened fourteen-year-old schoolgirl, pregnant due to rape, may *of course* choose abortion, and that any law that rules this out is an insane law. And it also allows for and supports our sense that in other cases resort to abortion is even positively indecent. It would be indecent in the woman to request an abortion, and indecent in a doctor to perform it, if she is in her seventh month and wants the abortion just to avoid the nuisance of postponing a trip abroad. The very fact that the arguments I have been drawing attention to treat all cases of abortion, or even all cases of abortion in which the mother's life is not at stake, as morally

on a par ought to have made them suspect at the outset.

Second, while I am arguing for the permissibility of abortion in some cases, I am not arguing for the right to secure the death of the unborn child. It is easy to confuse these two things in that up to a certain point in the life of the fetus it is not able to survive outside the mother's body; hence removing it from her body guarantees its death. But they are different in important ways. I have argued that you are not morally required to spend nine months in bed, sustaining the life of the violinist; but to say this is by no means to say that if when you unplug yourself there is a miracle and he survives, you have a right to turn round and slit his throat. You may detach yourself even if this costs him his life; you have no right to be guaranteed his death by some other means if unplugging yourself does not kill him.

There are some people who will feel dissatisfied by this feature of my argument. A woman may be utterly devastated by the thought of a child, a bit of herself, put up for adoption and never seen or heard of again. She may therefore want not merely that the child be detached from her but, more, that it die. Some opponents of abortion are inclined to regard this as beneath contempt, thereby showing insensitivity to what is surely a powerful source of despair. All the same, I agree that the desire for the child's death is not one that anybody may gratify, should it turn out to be possible to detach the child alive.

At this place, however, it should be remembered that we have only been pretending throughout that the fetus is a human being from the moment of conception. A very early abortion is surely not the killing of a person and so is not dealt with by anything I have said here.

31/On the Moral and Legal Status of Abortion

Mary Anne Warren

We will be concerned with both the moral status of abortion, which for our purposes we may define as the act which a woman performs in voluntarily terminating, or allowing another person to terminate, her pregnancy, and the legal status which is appropriate for this act. I will argue that, while it is not possible to produce a satisfactory defense of a woman's right to obtain an abortion without showing that a fetus is not a human being, in the morally relevant sense of that term, we ought not to conclude that the difficulties involved in determining whether or not a fetus is human make it impossible to produce any satisfactory solution to the problem of the moral status of abortion. For it is possible to show that, on the basis of intuitions which we may expect even the opponents of abortion to share, a fetus is not a person, and hence not the sort of entity to which it is proper to ascribe full moral rights.

Of course, while some philosophers would deny the possibility of any such proof,[1] others will deny that there is any need for it, since the moral permissibility of abortion appears to them to be too

obvious to require proof. But the inadequacy of this attitude should be evident from the fact that both the friends and the foes of abortion consider their position to be morally self-evident. Because proabortionists have never adequately come to grips with the conceptual issues surrounding abortion, most if not all, of the arguments which they advance in opposition to laws restricting access to abortion fail to refute or even weaken the traditional antiabortion argument, i.e., that a fetus is a human being, and therefore abortion is murder.

These arguments are typically of one of two sorts. Either they point to the terrible side effects of the restrictive laws, e.g., the deaths due to illegal abortions, and the fact that it is poor women who suffer the most as a result of these laws, or else they state that to deny a woman access to abortion is to

[1]For example, Roger Wertheimer, who in "Understanding the Abortion Argument" (*Philosophy and Public Affairs,* 1, No. 1 [Fall, 1971], 67–95), argues that the problem of the moral status of abortion is insoluble, in that the dispute over the status of the fetus is not a question of fact at all, but only a question of how one responds to the facts.

From *The Monist,* 57 (January 1973). Reprinted by permission of the author and the publisher.

deprive her of her right to control her own body. Unfortunately, however, the fact that restricting access to abortion has tragic side effects does not, in itself, show that the restrictions are unjustified, since murder is wrong regardless of the consequences of prohibiting it; and the appeal to the right to control one's body, which is generally construed as a property right, is at best a rather feeble argument for the permissibility of abortion. Mere ownership does not give me the right to kill innocent people whom I find on my property, and indeed I am apt to be held responsible if such people injure themselves while on my property. It is equally unclear that I have any moral right to expel an innocent person from my property when I know that doing so will result in his death.

Furthermore, it is probably inappropriate to describe a woman's body as her property, since it seems natural to hold that a person is something distinct from her property, but not from her body. Even those who would object to the identification of a person with his body, or with the conjunction of his body and his mind, must admit that it would be very odd to describe, say, breaking a leg, as damaging one's property, and much more appropriate to describe it as injuring one*self*. Thus it is probably a mistake to argue that the right to obtain an abortion is in any way derived from the right to own and regulate property.

But however we wish to construe the right to abortion, we cannot hope to convince those who consider abortion a form of murder of the existence of any such right unless we are able to produce a clear and convincing refutation of the traditional antiabortion argument, and this has not, to my knowledge, been done. With respect to the two most vital issues which that argument involves, i.e., the humanity of the fetus and its implication for the moral status of abortion, confusion has prevailed on both sides of the dispute.

Thus, both proabortionists and antiabortionists have tended to abstract the question of whether abortion is wrong to that of whether it is wrong to destroy a fetus, just as though the rights of another person were not necessarily involved. This mistaken abstraction has led to the almost universal assumption that if a fetus is a human being, with a right to life, then it follows immediately that abortion is wrong (except perhaps when necessary to save the woman's life), and that it ought to be prohibited. It has also been generally assumed that unless the question about the status of the fetus is answered,

the moral status of abortion cannot possibly be determined.

Two recent papers, one by B. A. Brody,[2] and one by Judith Thomson,[3] have attempted to settle the question of whether abortion ought to be prohibited apart from the question of whether or not the fetus is human. Brody examines the possibility that the following two statements are compatible: (1) that abortion is the taking of innocent human life, and therefore wrong; and (2) that nevertheless it ought not to be prohibited by law, at least under the present circumstances.[4] Not surprisingly, Brody finds it impossible to reconcile these two statements, since, as he rightly argues, none of the unfortunate side effects of the prohibition of abortion is bad enough to justify legalizing the *wrongful* taking of human life. He is mistaken, however, in concluding that the incompatibility of (1) and (2), in itself, shows that "the legal problem about abortion cannot be resolved independently of the status of the fetus problem" (p. 369).

What Brody fails to realize is that (1) embodies the questionable assumption that if a fetus is a human being, then of course abortion is morally wrong, and that an attack on *this* assumption is more promising, as a way of reconciling the humanity of the fetus with the claim that laws prohibiting abortion are unjustified, than is an attack on the assumption that if abortion is the wrongful killing of innocent human beings then it ought to be prohibited. He thus overlooks the possibility that a fetus may have a right to life and abortion still be morally permissible, in that the right of a woman to terminate an unwanted pregnancy might override the right of the fetus to be kept alive. The immorality of abortion is no more demonstrated by the humanity of the fetus, in itself, than the immorality of killing in self-defense is demonstrated by the fact that the assailant is a human being. Neither is it demonstrated by the *innocence* of the fetus, since there may be situations in which the killing of innocent human beings is justified.

It is perhaps not surprising that Brody fails to spot this assumption, since it has been accepted with little or no argument by nearly everyone who has written on the morality of abortion. John Noonan

---

[2]B. A. Brody, "Abortion and the Law," *The Journal of Philosophy*, 68, No. 12 (June 17, 1971), 357–69.

[3]Judith Thomson, "A Defense of Abortion," *Philosophy and Public Affairs*, 1, No. 1 (Fall, 1971), 47–66. [See immediately preceding article, this volume, pp. 207–216—eds.]

[4]I have abbreviated these statements somewhat, but not in a way which affects the argument.

is correct in saying that "the fundamental question in the long history of abortion is, How do you determine the humanity of a being?"[5] He summarizes his own antiabortion argument, which is a version of the official position of the Catholic Church, as follows:

. . . it is wrong to kill humans, however poor, weak, defenseless, and lacking in opportunity to develop their potential they may be. It is therefore morally wrong to kill Biafrans. Similarly, it is morally wrong to kill embryos.[6]

Noonan bases his claim that fetuses are human upon what he calls the theologians' criterion of humanity: that whoever is conceived of human beings is human. But although he argues at length for the appropriateness of this criterion, he never questions the assumption that if a fetus is human then abortion is wrong for exactly the same reason that murder is wrong.

Judith Thomson is, in fact, the only writer I am aware of who has seriously questioned this assumption; she has argued that, even if we grant the antiabortionist his claim that a fetus is a human being, with the same right to life as any other human being, we can still demonstrate that, in at least some and perhaps most cases, a woman is under no moral obligation to complete an unwanted pregnancy.[7] Her argument is worth examining, since if it holds up it may enable us to establish the moral permissibility of abortion without becoming involved in problems about what entitles an entity to be considered human, and accorded full moral rights. To be able to do this would be a great gain in the power and simplicity of the proabortion position, since, although I will argue that these problems can be solved at least as decisively as can any other moral problem, we should certainly be pleased to be able to avoid having to solve them as part of the justification of abortion.

On the other hand, even if Thomson's argument does not hold up, her insight, i.e., that it requires *argument* to show that if fetuses are human then abortion is properly classified as murder, is an extremely valuable one. The assumption she attacks is particularly invidious, for it amounts to the decision that it is appropriate, in deciding the moral

status of abortion, to leave the rights of the pregnant woman out of consideration entirely, except possibly when her life is threatened. Obviously, this will not do; determining what moral rights, if any, a fetus possesses is only the first step in determining the moral status of abortion. Step two, which is at least equally essential, is finding a just solution to the conflict between whatever rights the fetus may have, and the rights of the woman who is unwillingly pregnant. While the historical error has been to pay far too little attention to the second step, Ms. Thomson's suggestion is that if we look at the second step first we may find that a woman has a right to obtain an abortion *regardless* of what rights the fetus has.

Our own inquiry will also have two stages. In Section I, we will consider whether or not it is possible to establish that abortion is morally permissible even on the assumption that a fetus is an entity with a full-fledged right to life. I will argue that in fact this cannot be established, at least not with the conclusiveness which is essential to our hopes of convincing those who are skeptical about the morality of abortion, and that we therefore cannot avoid dealing with the question of whether or not a fetus really does have the same right to life as a (more fully developed) human being.

In Section II, I will propose an answer to this question, namely, that a fetus cannot be considered a member of the moral community, the set of beings with full and equal moral rights, for the simple reason that it is not a person, and that it is personhood, and not genetic humanity, i.e., humanity as defined by Noonan, which is the basis for membership in this community. I will argue that a fetus, whatever its stage of development, satisfies none of the basic criteria of personhood, and is not even enough *like* a person to be accorded even some of the same rights on the basis of this resemblance. Nor, as we will see, is a fetus's *potential* personhood a threat to the morality of abortion, since, whatever the rights of potential people may be, they are invariably overriden in any conflict with the moral rights of actual people.

I

We turn now to Professor Thomson's case for the claim that even if a fetus has full moral rights, abortion is still morally permissible, at least sometimes, and for some reasons other than to save the

[5]John Noonan, "Abortion and the Catholic Church: A Summary History," *Natural Law Forum,* 12 (1967), 125.

[6]John Noonan, "Deciding Who is Human," *Natural Law Forum,* 13 (1968), 134.

[7]"A Defense of Abortion."

woman's life. Her argument is based upon a clever, but I think faulty, analogy. She asks us to picture ourselves waking up one day, in bed with a famous violinist. Imagine that you have been kidnapped, and your bloodstream hooked up to that of the violinist, who happens to have an ailment which will certainly kill him unless he is permitted to share your kidneys for a period of nine months. No one else can save him, since you alone have the right type of blood. He will be unconscious all that time, and you will have to stay in bed with him, but after the nine months are over he may be unplugged, completely cured, that is provided that you have cooperated.

Now then, she continues, what are your obligations in this situation? The antiabortionist, if he is consistent, will have to say that you are obligated to stay in bed with the violinist: for all people have a right to life, and violinists are people, and therefore it would be murder for you to disconnect yourself from him and let him die (p. 49 [208, this volume—eds.]). But this is outrageous, and so there must be something wrong with the same argument when it is applied to abortion. It would certainly be commendable of you to agree to save the violinist, but it is absurd to suggest that your refusal to do so would be murder. His right to life does not obligate you to do whatever is required to keep him alive; nor does it justify anyone else in forcing you to do so. A law which required you to stay in bed with the violinist would clearly be an unjust law, since it is no proper function of the law to force unwilling people to make huge sacrifices for the sake of other people toward whom they have no such prior obligation.

Thomson concludes that, if this analogy is an apt one, then we can grant the antiabortionist his claim that a fetus is a human being, and still hold that it is at least sometimes the case that a pregnant woman has the right to refuse to be a Good Samaritan towards the fetus, i.e., to obtain an abortion. For there is a great gap between the claim that x has a right to life, and the claim that y is obligated to do whatever is necessary to keep x alive, let alone that he ought to be forced to do so. It is y's duty to keep x alive only if he has somehow contracted a *special* obligation to do so; and a woman who is unwillingly pregnant, e.g., who was raped, has done nothing which obligates her to make the enormous sacrifice which is necessary to preserve the conceptus.

This argument is initially quite plausible, and in the extreme case of pregnancy due to rape it is probably conclusive. Difficulties arise, however,

when we try to specify more exactly the range of cases in which abortion is clearly justifiable even on the assumption that the fetus is human. Professor Thomson considers it a virtue of her argument that it does not enable us to conclude that abortion is *always* permissible. It would, she says, be "indecent" for a woman in her seventh month to obtain an abortion just to avoid having to postpone a trip to Europe. On the other hand, her argument enables us to see that "a sick and desperately frightened schoolgirl pregnant due to rape may *of course* choose abortion, and that any law which rules this out is an insane law" (p. 65 [215, this volume—eds.]). So far, so good; but what are we to say about the woman who becomes pregnant not through rape but as a result of her own carelessness, or because of contraceptive failure, or who gets pregnant intentionally and then changes her mind about wanting a child? With respect to such cases, the violinist analogy is of much less use to the defender of the woman's right to obtain an abortion.

Indeed, the choice of a pregnancy due to rape, as an example of a case in which abortion is permissible even if a fetus is considered a human being, is extremely significant; for it is only in the case of pregnancy due to rape that the woman's situation is adequately analogous to the violinist case for our intuitions about the latter to transfer convincingly. The crucial difference between a pregnancy due to rape and the *normal* case of an unwanted pregnancy is that in the normal case we cannot claim that the woman is in no way responsible for her predicament; she could have remained chaste, or taken her pills more faithfully, or abstained on dangerous days, and so on. If, on the other hand, you are kidnapped by strangers, and hooked up to a strange violinist, then you are free of any shred of responsibility for the situation, on the basis of which it could be argued that you are obligated to keep the violinist alive. Only when her pregnancy is due to rape is a woman clearly just as nonresponsible.[8]

Consequently, there is room for the antiabortionist to argue that in the normal case of unwanted pregnancy a woman has, by her own actions, assumed responsibility for the fetus. For if x behaves in

---

[8]We may safely ignore the fact that she might have avoided getting raped, e.g., by carrying a gun, since by similar means you might likewise have avoided getting kidnapped, and in neither case does the victim's failure to take all possible precautions against a highly unlikely event (as opposed to reasonable precautions against a rather likely event) mean that he is morally responsible for what happens.

a way which he could have avoided, and which he knows involves, let us say, a 1 percent chance of bringing into existence a human being, with a right to life, and does so knowing that if this should happen then that human being will perish unless x does certain things to keep him alive, then it is by no means clear that when it does happen x is free of any obligation to what he knew in advance would be required to keep that human being alive.

The plausibility of such an argument is enough to show that the Thomson analogy can provide a clear and persuasive defense of a woman's right to obtain an abortion only with respect to those cases in which the woman is in no way responsible for her pregnancy, e.g., where it is due to rape. In all other cases, we would almost certainly conclude that it was necessary to look carefully at the particular circumstances in order to determine the extent of the woman's responsibility, and hence the extent of her obligation. This is an extremely unsatisfactory outcome, from the viewpoint of the opponents of restrictive abortion laws, most of whom are convinced that a woman has a right to obtain an abortion regardless of how and why she got pregnant.

Of course a supporter of the violinist analogy might point out that it is absurd to suggest that forgetting her pill one day might be sufficient to obligate a woman to complete an unwanted pregnancy. And indeed it *is* absurd to suggest this. As we will see, the moral right to obtain an abortion is not in the least dependent upon the extent to which the woman is responsible for her pregnancy. But unfortunately, once we allow the assumption that a fetus has full moral rights, we cannot avoid taking this absurd suggestion seriously. Perhaps we can make this point more clear by altering the violinist story just enough to make it more analogous to a normal unwanted pregnancy and less to a pregnancy due to rape, and then seeing whether it is still obvious that you are not obligated to stay in bed with the fellow.

Suppose, then, that violinists are peculiarly prone to the sort of illness the only cure for which is the use of someone else's bloodstream for nine months, and that because of this there has been formed a society of music lovers who agree that whenever a violinist is stricken they will draw lots and the loser will, by some means, be made the one and only person capable of saving him. Now then, would you be obligated to cooperate in curing the violinist if you had voluntarily joined this society, knowing the possible consequences, and then your name had been drawn and you had been kidnapped? Admittedly, you did not promise ahead of time that you would, but you did deliberately place yourself in a position in which it might happen that a human life would be lost if you did not. Surely this is at least a prima facie reason for supposing that you have an obligation to stay in bed with the violinist. Suppose that you had gotten your name drawn deliberately; surely *that* would be quite a strong reason for thinking that you had such an obligation.

It might be suggested that there is one important disanalogy between the modified violinist case and the case of an unwanted pregnancy, which makes the woman's responsibility significantly less, namely, the fact that the fetus *comes into existence* as the result of the woman's actions. This fact might give her a right to refuse to keep it alive, whereas she would not have had this right had it existed previously, independently, and then as a result of her actions become dependent upon her for its survival.

My own intuition, however, is that x has no more right to bring into existence, either deliberately or as a foreseeable result of actions he could have avoided, a being with full moral rights *(y),* and then refuse to do what he knew beforehand would be required to keep that being alive, than he has to enter into an agreement with an existing person, whereby he may be called upon to save that person's life, and then refuse to do so when so called upon. Thus, x's responsibility for y's existence does not seem to lessen his obligation to keep y alive, if he is also responsible for y's being in a situation in which only he can save him.

Whether or not this intuition is entirely correct, it brings us back once again to the conclusion that once we allow the assumption that a fetus has full moral rights it becomes an extremely complex and difficult question whether and when abortion is justifiable. Thus the Thomson analogy cannot help us produce a clear and persuasive proof of the moral permissibility of abortion. Nor will the opponents of the restrictive laws thank us for anything less; for their conviction (for the most part) is that abortion is obviously *not* a morally serious and extremely unfortunate, even though sometimes justified act, comparable to killing in self-defense or to letting the violinist die, but rather is closer to being a morally neutral act, like cutting one's hair.

The basis of this conviction, I believe, is the realization that a fetus is not a person, and thus does not have a full-fledged right to life. Perhaps the reason why this claim has been so inadequately defended is that it seems self-evident to those who accept it. And so it is, insofar as it follows from what I take to be perfectly obvious claims about the nature of personhood, and about the proper grounds for ascribing moral rights, claims which ought, indeed, to be obvious to both the friends and foes of abortion. Nevertheless, it is worth examining these claims, and showing how they demonstrate the moral innocuousness of abortion, since this apparently has not been adequately done before.

II

The question which we must answer in order to produce a satisfactory solution to the problem of the moral status of abortion is this: How are we to define the moral community, the set of beings with full and equal moral rights, such that we can decide whether a human fetus is a member of this community or not? What sort of entity, exactly, has the inalienable rights to life, liberty, and the pursuit of happiness? Jefferson attributed these rights to all *men,* and it may or may not be fair to suggest that he intended to attribute them *only* to men. Perhaps he ought to have attributed them to all human beings. If so, then we arrive, first, at Noonan's problem of defining what makes a being human, and, second, at the equally vital question which Noonan does not consider, namely, What reason is there for identifying the moral community with the set of all human beings, in whatever way we have chosen to define that term?

1. On the Definition of 'Human'

One reason why this vital second question is so frequently overlooked in the debate over the moral status of abortion is that the term 'human' has two distinct, but not often distinguished, senses. This fact results in a slide of meaning, which serves to conceal the fallaciousness of the traditional argument that since (1) it is wrong to kill innocent human beings, and (2) fetuses are innocent human beings, then (3) it is wrong to kill fetuses. For if 'human' is used in the same sense in both (1) and (2) then, whichever of the two senses is meant, one of these premises is question-begging. And if it is used in two different senses then of course the conclusion doesn't follow.

Thus, (1) is a self-evident moral truth,[9] and avoids begging the question about abortion, only if 'human being' is used to mean something like "a full-fledged member of the moral community." (It may or may not also be meant to refer exclusively to members of the species *Homo sapiens.*) We may call this the *moral* sense of 'human'. It is not to be confused with what we will call the *genetic* sense, i.e., the sense in which *any* member of the species is a human being, and no member of any other species could be. If (1) is acceptable only if the moral sense is intended, (2) is non-question-begging only if what is intended is the genetic sense.

In "Deciding Who is Human," Noonan argues for the classification of fetuses with human beings by pointing to the presence of the full genetic code, and the potential capacity for rational thought (p. 135). It is clear that what he needs to show, for his version of the traditional argument to be valid, is that fetuses are human in the moral sense, the sense in which it is analytically true that all human beings have full moral rights. But, in the absence of any argument showing that whatever is genetically human is also morally human, and he gives none, nothing more than genetic humanity can be demonstrated by the presence of the human genetic code. And, as we will see, the *potential* capacity for rational thought can at most show that an entity has the potential for *becoming* human in the moral sense.

2. Defining the Moral Community

Can it be established that genetic humanity is sufficient for moral humanity? I think that there are very good reasons for not defining the moral community in this way. I would like to suggest an alternative way of defining the moral community, which I will argue for only to the extent of explaining why it is, or should be, self-evident. The suggestion is simply that the moral community consists of all and only *people,* rather than all and only human beings;[10] and probably the best way of demonstrating its self-evidence is by considering the concept of personhood, to see what sorts of entity are and are not

[9]Of course, the principle that it is (always) wrong to kill innocent human beings is in need of many other modifications, e.g., that it may be permissible to do so to save a greater number of other innocent human beings, but we may safely ignore these complications here.

[10]From here on, we will use 'human' to mean genetically human, since the moral sense seems closely connected to, and perhaps derived from, the assumption that genetic humanity is sufficient for membership in the moral community.

persons, and what the decision that a being is or is not a person implies about its moral rights.

What characteristics entitle an entity to be considered a person? This is obviously not the place to attempt a complete analysis of the concept of personhood, but we do not need such a fully adequate analysis just to determine whether and why a fetus is or isn't a person. All we need is a rough and approximate list of the most basic criteria of personhood, and some idea of which, or how many, of these an entity must satisfy in order to properly be considered a person.

In searching for such criteria, it is useful to look beyond the set of people with whom we are acquainted, and ask how we would decide whether a totally alien being was a person or not. (For we have no right to assume that genetic humanity is necessary for personhood.) Imagine a space traveler who lands on an unknown planet and encounters a race of beings utterly unlike any he has ever seen or heard of. If he wants to be sure of behaving morally toward these beings, he has to somehow decide whether they are people, and hence have full moral rights, or whether they are the sort of thing which he need not feel guilty about treating as, for example, a source of food.

How should he go about making this decision? If he has some anthropological background, he might look for such things as religion, art, and the manufacturing of tools, weapons, or shelters, since these factors have been used to distinguish our human from our prehuman ancestors, in what seems to be closer to the moral than the genetic sense of 'human'. And no doubt he would be right to consider the presence of such factors as good evidence that the alien beings were people, and morally human. It would, however, be overly anthropocentric of him to take the absence of these things as adequate evidence that they were not, since we can imagine people who have progressed beyond, or evolved without ever developing, these cultural characteristics.

I suggest that the traits which are most central to the concept of personhood, or humanity in the moral sense, are, very roughly, the following:

1. consciousness (of objects and events external and/or internal to the being), and in particular the capacity to feel pain;

2. reasoning (the *developed* capacity to solve new and relatively complex problems);

3. self-motivated activity (activity which is relatively independent of either genetic or direct external control);

4. the capacity to communicate, by whatever means, messages of an indefinite variety of types, that is, not just with an indefinite number of possible contents, but on indefinitely many possible topics;

5. the presence of self-concepts, and self-awareness, either individual or racial, or both.

Admittedly, there are apt to be a great many problems involved in formulating precise definitions of these criteria, let alone in developing universally valid behavioral criteria for deciding when they apply. But I will assume that both we and our explorer know approximately what 1–5 mean, and that he is also able to determine whether or not they apply. How, then, should he use his findings to decide whether or not the alien beings are people? We needn't suppose that an entity must have *all* of these attributes to be properly considered a person; 1 and 2 alone may well be sufficient for personhood, and quite probably 1–3 are sufficient. Neither do we need to insist that any one of these criteria is *necessary* for personhood, although once again 1 and 2 look like fairly good candidates for necessary conditions, as does 3, if 'activity' is construed so as to include the activity of reasoning.

All we need to claim, to demonstrate that a fetus is not a person, is that any being which satisfies *none* of 1–5 is certainly not a person. I consider this claim to be so obvious that I think anyone who denied it, and claimed that a being which satisfied none of 1–5 was a person all the same, would thereby demonstrate that he had no notion at all of what a person is—perhaps because he had confused the concept of a person with that of genetic humanity. If the opponents of abortion were to deny the appropriateness of these five criteria, I do not know what further arguments would convince them. We would probably have to admit that our conceptual schemes were indeed irreconcilably different, and that our dispute could not be settled objectively.

I do not expect this to happen, however, since I think that the concept of a person is one which is very nearly universal (to people), and that it is common to both proabortionists and antiabortionists, even though neither group has fully realized the relevance of this concept to the resolution of their dispute. Furthermore, I think that on reflection even the antiabortionists ought to agree not only that 1–5 are central to the concept of personhood, but also that it is a part of this concept that all and only people have full moral rights. The concept of a person is in part a moral concept; once we have admitted that *x* is a person we have recognized, even if we have not agreed to respect, *x*'s right to be treated as a member of the moral community. It is true that the claim that *x* is a *human being* is more commonly voiced as part of an appeal to treat *x* decently than is the claim that *x* is a person, but this is either because 'human being' is here used in the sense which implies personhood, or because the genetic and moral senses of 'human' have been confused.

Now if 1–5 are indeed the primary criteria of personhood, then it is clear that genetic humanity is neither necessary nor sufficient for establishing that an entity is a person. Some human beings are not people, and there may well be people who are not human beings. A man or woman whose consciousness has been permanently obliterated but who remains alive is a human being which is no longer a person; defective human beings, with no appreciable mental capacity, are not and presumably never will be people; and a fetus is a human being which is not yet a person, and which therefore cannot coherently be said to have full moral rights. Citizens of the next century should be prepared to recognize highly advanced, self-aware robots or computers, should such be developed, and intelligent inhabitants of other worlds, should such be found, as people in the fullest sense, and to respect their moral rights. But to ascribe full moral rights to an entity which is not a person is as absurd as to ascribe moral obligations and responsibilities to such an entity.

3. Fetal Development and the Right to Life

Two problems arise in the application of these suggestions for the definition of the moral community to the determination of the precise moral status of a human fetus. Given that the paradigm example of a person is a normal adult human being, then (1) How like this paradigm, in particular how far advanced since conception, does a human being need to be before it begins to have a right to life by virtue, not of being fully a person as of yet, but of being *like* a person? and (2) To what extent, if any, does the fact that a fetus has the *potential* for becoming a person endow it with some of the same rights? Each of these questions requires some comment.

In answering the first question, we need not attempt a detailed consideration of the moral rights of organisms which are not developed enough, aware enough, intelligent enough, etc., to be considered people, but which resemble people in some respects. It does seem reasonable to suggest that the more like a person, in the relevant respects, a being is, the stronger is the case for regarding it as having a right to life, and indeed the stronger its right to life is. Thus we ought to take seriously the suggestion that, insofar as "the human individual develops biologically in a continuous fashion . . . the rights of a human person might develop in the same way."[11] But we must keep in mind that the attributes which are relevant in determining whether or not an entity is enough like a person to be regarded as having some of the same moral rights are no different from those which are relevant to determining whether or not it is fully a person—i.e., are no different from 1–5—and that being genetically human, or having recognizably human facial and other physical features, or detectable brain activity, or the capacity to survive outside the uterus, are simply not among these relevant attributes.

Thus it is clear that even though a seven- or eight-month fetus has features which make it apt to arouse in us almost the same powerful protective instinct as is commonly aroused by a small infant, nevertheless it is not significantly more personlike than is a very small embryo. It is *somewhat* more personlike; it can apparently feel and respond to pain, and it may even have a rudimentary form of consciousness, insofar as its brain is quite active. Nevertheless, it seems safe to say that it is not fully conscious, in the way that an infant of a few months is, and that it cannot reason, or communicate messages of indefinitely many sorts, does not engage in self-motivated activity, and has no self-awareness. Thus, in the *relevant* respects, a fetus, even a fully developed one, is considerably less personlike than is the average mature mammal, indeed the average fish. And I think that a rational person must conclude that if the right to life of a fetus is to be based upon its resemblance to a person, then it cannot be said to have any more right to life than, let us say, a newborn guppy (which also seems to be capable of feeling pain), and that a right of that magnitude could never override a woman's right to obtain an abortion, at any stage of her pregnancy.

[11]Thomas L. Hayes, "A Biological View," *Commonweal*, 85 (March 17, 1967), 677–78; quoted by Daniel Callahan, in *Abortion, Law, Choice, and Morality* (London: Macmillan & Co., 1970).

There may, of course, be other arguments in favor of placing legal limits upon the stage of pregnancy in which an abortion may be performed. Given the relative safety of the new techniques of artifically inducing labor during the third trimester, the danger to the woman's life or health is no longer such an argument. Neither is the fact that people tend to respond to the thought of abortion in the later stages of pregnancy with emotional repulsion, since mere emotional responses cannot take the place of moral reasoning in determining what ought to be permitted. Nor, finally, is the frequently heard argument that legalizing abortion, especially late in the pregnancy, may erode the level of respect for human life, leading, perhaps, to an increase in unjustified euthanasia and other crimes. For this threat, if it is a threat, can be better met by educating people to the kinds of moral distinctions which we are making here than by limiting access to abortion (which limitation may, in its disregard for the rights of women, be just as damaging to the level of respect for human rights).

Thus, since the fact that even a fully developed fetus is not personlike enough to have any significant right to life on the basis of its personlikeness shows that no legal restrictions upon the stage of pregnancy in which an abortion may be performed can be justified on the grounds that we should protect the rights of the older fetus; and since there is no other apparent justification for such restrictions, we may conclude that they are entirely unjustified. Whether or not it would be *indecent* (whatever that means) for a woman in her seventh month to obtain an abortion just to avoid having to postpone a trip to Europe, it would not, in itself, be *immoral,* and therefore it ought to be permitted.

4. Potential Personhood and the Right to Life

We have seen that a fetus does not resemble a person in any way which can support the claim that it has even some of the same rights. But what about its *potential,* the fact that if nurtured and allowed to develop naturally it will very probably become a person? Doesn't that alone give it at least some right to life? It is hard to deny that the fact that an entity is a potential person is a strong prima facie reason for not destroying it; but we need not conclude from this that a potential person has a right to life, by virtue of that potential. It may be that our feeling that it is better, other things being equal, not to destroy a

potential person is better explained by the fact that potential people are still (felt to be) an invaluable resource, not to be lightly squandered. Surely, if every speck of dust were a potential person, we would be much less apt to conclude that every potential person has a right to become actual.

Still, we do not need to insist that a potential person has no right to life whatever. There may well be something immoral, and not just imprudent, about wantonly destroying potential people, when doing so isn't necessary to protect anyone's rights. But even if a potential person does have some prima facie right to life, such a right could not possibly outweigh the right of a woman to obtain an abortion, since the rights of any actual person invariably outweigh those of any potential person, whenever the two conflict. Since this may not be immediately obvious in the case of a human fetus, let us look at another case.

Suppose that our space explorer falls into the hands of an alien culture, whose scientists decide to create a few hundred thousand or more human beings, by breaking his body into its component cells, and using these to create fully developed human beings, with, of course, his genetic code. We may imagine that each of these newly created men will have all of the original man's abilities, skills, knowledge, and so on, and also have an individual self-concept, in short that each of them will be a bona fide (though hardly unique) person. Imagine that the whole project will take only seconds, and that its chances of success are extremely high, and that our explorer knows all of this, and also knows that these people will be treated fairly. I maintain that in such a situation he would have every right to escape if he could, and thus to deprive all of these potential people of their potential lives; for his right to life outweighs all of theirs together, in spite of the fact that they are all genetically human, all innocent, and all have a very high probability of becoming people very soon, if only he refrains from acting.

Indeed, I think he would have a right to escape even if it were not his life which the alien scientists planned to take, but only a year of his freedom, or, indeed, only a day. Nor would he be obligated to stay if he had gotten captured (thus bringing all these people-potentials into existence) because of his own carelessness, or even if he had done so deliberately, knowing the consequences. Regardless of how he got captured, he is not morally obligated to remain in captivity for *any* period of time for the sake of permitting any number of potential people to come into actuality, so great is the margin by which one actual person's right to liberty outweighs whatever right to life even a hundred thousand potential people have. And it seems reasonable to conclude that the rights of a woman will outweigh by a similar margin whatever right to life a fetus may have by virtue of its potential personhood.

Thus, neither a fetus's resemblance to a person, nor its potential for becoming a person provides any basis whatever for the claim that it has any significant right to life. Consequently, a woman's right to protect her health, happiness, freedom, and even her life,[12] by terminating an unwanted pregnancy, will always override whatever right to life it may be appropriate to ascribe to a fetus, even a fully developed one. And thus, in the absence of any overwhelming social need for every possible child, the laws which restrict the right to obtain an abortion, or limit the period of pregnancy during which an abortion may be performed, are a wholly unjustified violation of a woman's most basic moral and constitutional rights.[13]

Postscript on Infanticide

Since the publication of this article, many people have written to point out that my argument appears to justify not only abortion, but infanticide as well. For a new-born infant is not significantly more person-like than an advanced fetus, and consequently it would seem that if the destruction of the latter is permissible so too must be that of the former. Inasmuch as most people, regardless of how they feel about the morality of abortion, consider infanticide a form of murder, this might appear to represent a serious flaw in my argument.

Now, if I am right in holding that it is only people who have a fullfledged right to life, and who can be murdered, and if the criteria of personhood are as I have described them, then it obviously follows that killing a new-born infant isn't murder. It does *not* follow, however, that infanticide is permissible, for two reasons. In the first place, it would be

wrong, at least in this country and in this period of history, and other things being equal, to kill a new-born infant, because even if its parents do not want it and would not suffer from its destruction, there are other people who would like to have it, and would, in all probability, be deprived of a great deal of pleasure by its destruction. Thus, infanticide is wrong for reasons analogous to those which make it wrong to wantonly destroy natural resources, or great works of art.

Secondly, most people, at least in this country, value infants and would much prefer that they be preserved, even if foster parents are not immediately available. Most of us would rather be taxed to support orphanages than allow unwanted infants to be destroyed. So long as there are people who want an infant preserved, and who are willing and able to provide the means of caring for it, under reasonably humane conditions, it is, *ceteris parabis,* wrong to destroy it.

But, it might be replied, if this argument shows that infanticide is wrong, at least at this time and in this country, doesn't it also show that abortion is wrong? After all, many people value fetuses, are disturbed by their destruction, and would much prefer that they be preserved, even at some cost to themselves. Furthermore, as a potential source of pleasure to some foster family, a fetus is just as valuable as an infant. There is, however, a crucial difference between the two cases: so long as the fetus is unborn, its preservation, contrary to the wishes of the pregnant woman, violates her rights to freedom, happiness, and self-determination. Her rights override the rights of those who would like the fetus preserved, just as if someone's life or limb is threatened by a wild animal, his right to protect himself by destroying the animal overrides the rights of those who would prefer that the animal not be harmed.

The minute the infant is born, however, its preservation no longer violates any of its mother's rights, even if she wants it destroyed, because she is free to put it up for adoption. Consequently, while the moment of birth does not mark any sharp discontinuity in the degree to which an infant possesses the right to life, it does mark the end of its mother's right to determine its fate. Indeed, if abortion could be performed without killing the fetus, she would never possess the right to have the fetus destroyed, for the same reasons that she has no right to have an infant destroyed.

---

[12]That is, insofar as the death rate, for the woman, is higher for childbirth than for early abortion.

[13]My thanks to the following people, who were kind enough to read and criticize an earlier version of this paper: Herbert Gold, Gene Glass, Anne Lauterbach, Judith Thomson, Mary Mothersill, and Timothy Binkley.

On the other hand, it follows from my argument that when an unwanted or defective infant is born into a society which cannot afford and/or is not willing to care for it, then its destruction is permissible. This conclusion will, no doubt, strike many people as heartless and immoral; but remember that the very existence of people who feel this way, and who are willing and able to provide care for unwanted infants, is reason enough to conclude that they should be preserved.

7
Preferential Treatment

32/Preferential Hiring

Judith Jarvis Thomson

Many people are inclined to think preferential hiring an obvious injustice. I should have said "feel" rather than "think": it seems to me the matter has not been carefully thought out, and that what is in question, really, is a gut reaction.

I am going to deal with only a very limited range of preferential hirings: that is, I am concerned with cases in which several candidates present themselves for a job, in which the hiring officer finds, on examination, that all are equally qualified to hold that job, and he then straightway declares for the black, or for the woman, because he or she *is* a black or a woman. And I shall talk only of hiring decisions in the universities, partly because I am most familiar with them, partly because it is in the universities that the most vocal and articulate opposition to preferential hiring is now heard—not surprisingly, perhaps, since no one is more vocal and articulate than a university professor who feels deprived of his rights.

I suspect that some people may say, Oh well, in *that* kind of case it's all right, what we object to is preferring the less qualified to the better qualified. Or again, What we object to is refusing even to consider the qualifications of white males. I shall say nothing at all about these things. I think that the argument I shall give for saying that preferential hiring is not unjust in the cases I do concentrate on can also be appealed to to justify it outside that range of cases. But I won't draw any conclusions about cases outside it. Many people do have that gut reaction I mentioned against preferential hiring in *any* degree or form; and it seems to me worthwhile bringing out that there is good reason to think they are wrong to have it. Nothing I say will be in the slightest degree novel or original. It will, I hope, be enough to set the relevant issues out clearly.

I

But first, something should be said about qualifications.

I said I would consider only cases in which the several candidates who present themselves for the job are equally qualified to hold it; and there plainly are difficulties in the way of saying precisely how this is to be established, and even what is to be established. Strictly academic qualifications seem at a first glance to be relatively straightforward: the hiring officer must see if the candidates have done equally well in courses (both courses they took, and any they taught), and if they are recommended equally strongly by their teachers, and if the work they submit for consideration is equally good. There is no denying that even these things are less easy to establish than first appears: for example, you may have a suspicion that Professor Smith is given to exaggeration, and that his "great student" is in fact less strong than Professor Jones's "good student"—but do you *know* that this is so? But there is a more serious difficulty still: as blacks and women have been saying, strictly academic indicators may themselves be skewed by prejudice. My impression is that women, white and black, may possibly suffer more from this than black males. A black male who is discouraged or down-graded for being black is discouraged or down-graded out of dislike, repulsion, a desire to avoid contact; and I suspect that there are very few teachers nowadays who allow

This essay is an expanded version of a talk given at the Conference on the Liberation of Female Persons, held at North Carolina State University at Raleigh, on March 26–28, 1973, under a grant from the S & H Foundation. I am indebted to James Thomson and the members of the Society for Ethical and Legal Philosophy for criticism of an earlier draft.

From *Philosophy & Public Affairs* 2 (Summer 1973). Copyright © 1973 by Princeton University Press. Reprinted by permission. Footnotes have been renumbered.

themselves to feel such things, or, if they do feel them, to act on them. A woman who is discouraged or down-graded for being a woman is not discouraged or down-graded out of dislike, but out of a conviction she is not serious, and I suspect that while there are very few teachers nowadays who allow themselves to feel that women generally are not serious, there are many who allow themselves to feel of the particular individual women students they confront that Ah, this one isn't serious, and in fact that one isn't either, nor is that other one—women generally are, of course, one thing, but these particular women, really they're just girls in search of husbands, are quite another. And I suspect that this will be far harder to root out. A teacher could not face himself in the mirror of a morning if he had down-graded anyone out of dislike; but a teacher can well face himself in the mirror if he down-grades someone out of a conviction that that person is not serious: after all, life is serious, and jobs and work, and who can take the unserious seriously? who pays attention to the dilettante? So the hiring officer must read very very carefully between the lines in the candidates' dossiers even to assess their strictly academic qualifications.

And then of course there are other qualifications besides the strictly academic ones. Is one of the candidates exceedingly disagreeable? A department is not merely a collection of individuals, but a working unit; and if anyone is going to disrupt that unit, and to make its work more difficult, then this counts against him—he may be as well qualified in strictly academic terms, but he is not as well qualified. Again, is one of the candidates incurably sloppy? Is he going to mess up his records, is he going to have to be nagged to get his grades in, and worse, is he going to lose students' papers? This too would count against him: keeping track of students' work, records, and grades, after all, is part of the job.

What seems to me to be questionable, however, is that a candidate's race or sex is itself a qualification. Many people who favor preferential hiring in the universities seem to think it is; in their view, if a group of candidates is equally well qualified in respect of those measures I have already indicated, then if one is of the right race (black) or of the right sex (female), then that being itself a qualification, it tips the balance, and that one is the best qualified. If so, then of course no issue of injustice, or indeed of any other impropriety, is raised if the hiring officer declares for that one of the candidates straightway.

Why does race or sex seem to many to be, itself, a qualification? There seem to be two claims in back of the view that it is. First, there is the claim that blacks learn better from a black, women from a woman. One hears this less often in respect of women; blacks, however, are often said to mistrust the whites who teach them, with the result that they simply do not learn as well, or progress as far, as they would if taught by blacks. Secondly, and this one hears in respect of women as well as blacks, what is wanted is *role models.* The proportion of black and women faculty members in the larger universities (particularly as one moves up the ladder of rank) is very much smaller than the proportion of blacks and women in the society at large—even, in the case of women, than the proportion of them amongst recipients of Ph.D. degrees from those very same universities. Black and women students suffer a constricting of ambition because of this. They need to see members of their race or sex who are accepted, successful, professionals. They need concrete evidence that those of their race or sex *can* become accepted, successful professionals.

And perhaps it is thought that it is precisely by virtue of having a role model right in the classroom that blacks do learn better from a black, women from a woman.

Now it is obviously essential for a university to staff its classrooms with people who can teach, and so from whom its students can learn, and indeed learn as much and as well as possible—teaching, after all, is, if not the whole of the game, then anyway a very large part of it. So if the first claim is true, then race and sex *do* seem to be qualifications. It obviously would not follow that a university should continue to regard them as qualifications indefinitely; I suppose, however, that it would follow that it should regard them as qualifications at least until the proportion of blacks and women on the faculty matches the proportion of blacks and women among the students.

But in the first place, allowing this kind of consideration to have a bearing on a hiring decision might make for trouble of a kind that blacks and women would not be at all happy with. For suppose it could be made out that white males learn better from white males? (I once, years ago, had a student who said he really felt uncomfortable in a class taught by a woman, it was interfering with his work, and did I mind if he switched to another section?) I suppose we would feel that this was due to prejudice, and that it was precisely to be discouraged, certainly not encouraged by establishing hiring ratios. I don't suppose it is true of white males generally that they learn better from white males; I am concerned only with the way in which we should take the fact, if it were a fact, that they did—and if it would be improper to take it to be reason to think being a white male is a qualification in a teacher, then how shall we take its analogue to be reason to think being black, or being a woman, is a qualification in a teacher?

And in the second place, I must confess that, speaking personally, I do not find the claim we are looking at borne out in experience; I do not think that as a student I learned any better, or any more, from the women who taught me than from the men, and I do not think that my own women students now learn any better or any more from me than they do from my male colleagues. Blacks, of course, may have, and may have had, very different experiences, and I don't presume to speak for them—or even for women generally. But my own experience being what it is, it seems to *me* that any defense of preferential hiring in the universities which takes this first claim as premise is so far not an entirely convincing one.

The second claim, however, does seem to me to be plainly true: black and women students do need role models, they do need concrete evidence that those of their race or sex can become accepted, successful, professionals—plainly, you won't try to become what you don't believe you can become.

But do they need these role models right there in the classroom? Of course it might be argued that they do: that a black learns better from a black teacher, a woman from a woman teacher. But we have already looked at this. And if they are, though needed, not needed in the classroom, then is it the university's job to provide them?

For it must surely be granted that a college, or university, has not the responsibility—or perhaps, if it is supported out of public funds, even the right—to provide just *any* service to its students which it might be good for them, or even which they may need, to be provided with. Sports seem to me plainly a case in point. No doubt it is very good for students to be offered, and perhaps even required to become involved in, a certain amount of physical exercise; but I can see no reason whatever to think that universities should be expected to provide facilities for it, or taxpayers to pay for those facilities. I suspect others may disagree, but my own feeling is that it is the same with medical and psychiatric

services: I am sure that at least some students need medical and psychiatric help, but I cannot see why it should be provided for them in the universities, at public expense.

So the further question which would have to be answered is this: granting that black and female students need black and female role models, why should the universities be expected to provide them within their faculties? In the case of publicly supported universities, why should taxpayers be expected to provide them?

I don't say these questions can't be answered. But I do think we need to come at them from a quite different direction. So I shall simply sidestep this ground for preferential hiring in the universities. The defense I give will not turn on anyone's supposing that of two otherwise equally well qualified candidates, one may be better qualified for the job by virtue, simply, of being of the right race or sex.

II

I mentioned several times in the preceding section the obvious fact that it is the taxpayers who support public universities. Not that private universities are wholly private: the public contributes to the support of most of them, for example by allowing them tax-free use of land, and of the dividends and capital gains on investments. But it will be the public universities in which the problem appears most starkly: as I shall suggest, it is the fact of public support that makes preferential hiring in the universities problematic.

For it seems to me that—other things being equal—there is no problem about preferential hiring in the case of a wholly private college or university, that is, one which receives no measure of public support at all, and which lives simply on tuition and (non–tax-deductible) contributions.

The principle here seems to me to be this: no perfect stranger has a right to be given a benefit which is yours to dispose of; no perfect stranger even has a right to be given an equal chance at getting a benefit which is yours to dispose of. You not only needn't give the benefit to the first perfect stranger who walks in and asks for it; you needn't even give him a chance at it, as, e.g., by tossing a coin.

I should stress that I am here talking about *benefits,* that is, things which people would like to have, which would perhaps not merely please them, but improve their lives, but which they don't actually *need.* (I suspect the same holds true of things people do actually need, but many would disagree, and as it is unnecessary to speak here of needs, I shall not discuss them.) If I have extra apples (they're mine: I grew them, on my own land, from my own trees), or extra money, or extra tickets to a series of lectures I am giving on How to Improve Your Life Through Philosophy, and am prepared to give them away, word of this may get around, and people may present themselves as candidate recipients. I do not have to give to the first, or to proceed by letting them all draw straws; if I really do own the things, I can give to whom I like, on any ground I please, and in so doing, I violate no one's *rights,* I treat no one *unjustly.* None of the candidate recipients has a right to the benefit, or even to a chance at it.

There are four caveats. (1) Some grounds for giving or refraining from giving are less respectable than others. Thus, I might give the apples to the first who asks for them simply because he is the first who asks for them. Or again, I might give the apples to the first who asks for them because he is black, and because I am black and feel an interest in and concern for blacks which I do not feel in and for whites. In either case, not merely do I do what it is within my rights to do, but more, my ground for giving them to that person is a not immoral ground for giving them to him. But I might instead give the apples to the sixth who asks, and this because the first five were black and I hate blacks—or because the first five were white and I hate whites. Here I do what I have a right to do (for the apples are *mine*), and I violate no one's rights in doing it, but my ground for disposing of the apples as I did was a bad one; and it might even, more strongly, be said that I ought not have disposed of the apples in the way I did. But it is important to note that it is perfectly consistent, on the one hand, that a man's ground for acting as he did was a bad one, and even that he ought not have done what he did, and, on the other hand, that he had a right to do what he did, that he violated no one's rights in doing it, and that no one can complain he was unjustly treated.

The second caveat (2) is that although I have a right to dispose of my apples as I wish, I have no right to harm, or gratuitously hurt or offend. Thus I am within my rights to refuse to give the apples to the first five because they are black (or because they are white); but I am not within my rights to say to them "I refuse to give you apples because you are black (or white) and because those who are black (or white) are inferior."

And (3) if word of my extra apples, and of my willingness to give them away, got around because I advertised, saying or implying First Come First Served Till Supply Runs Out, then I cannot refuse the first five because they are black, or white. By so advertising I have *given* them a right to a chance at the apples. If they come in one at a time, I must give out apples in order, till the supply runs out; if they come in together, and I have only four apples, then I must either cut up the apples, or give them each an equal chance, as, e.g., by having them draw straws.

And lastly (4), there may be people who would say that I don't really, or don't fully own those apples, even though I grew them on my own land, from my own trees, and therefore that I don't have a right to give them away as I see fit. For after all, I don't own the police who protected my land while those apples were growing, or the sunlight because of which they grew. Or again, wasn't it just a matter of luck for me that I was born with a green thumb?—and why should I profit from a competence that I didn't deserve to have, that I didn't earn? Or perhaps some other reason might be put forward for saying that I don't own those apples. I don't want to take this up here. It seems to be wrong, but I want to let it pass. If anyone thinks that I don't own the apples, or, more generally, that no one really or fully owns anything, he will regard what I shall say in the remainder of this section, in which I talk about what may be done with what is privately owned, as an idle academic exercise. I'll simply ask that anyone who does think this be patient: we will come to what is publicly owned later.

Now what was in question was a job, not apples; and it may be insisted that to give a man a job is not to give him a benefit, but rather something he needs. Well, I am sure that people do need jobs, that it does not fully satisfy people's needs to supply them only with food, shelter, and medical care. Indeed, I am sure that people need, not merely jobs, but jobs that interest them, and that they can therefore get satisfaction from the doing of. But on the other hand, I am not at all sure that any candidate for a job in a university needs a job in a university. One would very much like it if all graduate students who wish it could find jobs teaching in universities; it is in some measure a tragedy that a person should spend three or four years preparing for a career, and then find there is no job available, and that he has in consequence to take work which is less interesting than he had hoped and prepared for. But one thing seems plain: no one *needs* that work which would interest him most in all the whole world of work. Plenty of people have to make do with work they like less than other work—no economy is rich enough to provide everyone with the work he likes best of all—and I should think that this does not mean they lack something they *need*. We are all of us prepared to tax ourselves so that no one shall be in need; but I should imagine that we are not prepared to tax ourselves (to tax barbers, truck drivers, sales-clerks, waitresses, and factory workers) in order that everyone who wants a university job, and is competent to fill it, shall have one made available to him.

All the same, if a university job is a benefit rather than something needed, it is anyway not a "pure" benefit (like an apple), but an "impure" one. To give a man a university job is to give him an opportunity to do work which is interesting and satisfying; but he will only *be* interested and satisfied if he actually does the work he is given an opportunity to do, and does it well.

What this should remind us of is that certain cases of preferential hiring might well be utterly irrational. Suppose we have an eating club, and need a new chef; we have two applicants, a qualified French chef, and a Greek who happens to like to cook, though he doesn't do it very well. We are fools if we say to ourselves "We like the Greeks, and dislike the French, so let's hire the Greek." We simply won't eat as well as we could have, and eating, after all, was the point of the club. On the other hand, it's *our* club, and so *our* job. And who shall say it is not within a man's rights to dispose of what really is his in as foolish a way as he likes?

And there is no irrationality, of course, if one imagines that the two applicants are equally qualified French chefs, and one is a cousin of one of our members, the other a perfect stranger. Here if we declare directly for the cousin, we do not act irrationally, we violate no one's rights, and indeed do not have a morally bad ground for making the choice we make. It's not a morally splendid ground, but it isn't a morally bad one either.

Universities differ from eating clubs in one way which is important for present purposes: in an eating club, those who consume what the club serves are the members, and thus the owners of the club themselves—by contrast, if the university is wholly private, those who consume what it serves are not among the owners. This makes a difference: the owners of the university have a responsibility not merely to themselves (as the owners of an eating

club do), but also to those who come to buy what it offers. It could, I suppose, make plain in its advertising that it is prepared to allow the owners' racial or religious or other preferences to outweigh academic qualifications in its teachers. But in the absence of that, it must, in light of what a university is normally expected to be and to aim at, provide the best teachers it can afford. It does not merely act irrationally, but indeed violates the rights of its student-customers if it does not.

On the other hand, this leaves it open to the university that in case of a choice between equally qualified candidates, it violates no one's rights if it declares for the black because he is black, or for the white because he is white. To the wholly *private* university, that is, for that is all I have so far been talking of. Other things being equal—that is, given it has not advertised the job in a manner which would entitle applicants to believe that all who are equally qualified will be given an equal chance at it, and given it does not gratuitously give offense to those whom it rejects—the university may choose as it pleases, and violates no one's rights in doing so. Though no doubt its grounds for choosing may be morally bad ones, and we may even wish to say, more strongly, that it ought not choose as it does.

What will have come out in the preceding is that the issue I am concerned with is a moral, and not a legal one. My understanding is that the law does prevent an employer wholly in the private sector from choosing a white rather than a black on ground of that difference alone—though not from choosing a black rather than a white on ground of that difference alone. Now if, as many people say, legal rights (or perhaps, legal rights in a relatively just society) create moral rights, then even a moral investigation should take the law into account; and indeed, if I am not mistaken as to the law, it would have to be concluded that blacks (but not whites) do have rights of the kind I have been denying. I want to sidestep all this. My question can be re-put: would a private employer's choosing a white (or black) rather than a black (or white) on ground of that difference alone be a violation of anyone's rights if there were no law making it illegal. And the answer seems to be: it would not.

III

But hardly any college or university in America is purely private. As I said, most enjoy some public support, and the moral issues may be affected by the extent of the burden carried by the public. I shall concentrate on universities which are entirely publicly funded, such as state or city universities, and ignore the complications which might arise in case of partial private funding.

The special problem which arises here, as I see it, is this: where a community pays the bills, the community owns the university.

I said earlier that the members, who are therefore the owners, of a private eating club may declare for whichever chef they wish, even if the man they declare for is not as well qualified for the job as some other; in choosing amongst applicants, they are *not* choosing amongst fellow members of the club who is to get some benefit from the club. But now suppose, by contrast, that two of us who are members arrive at the same time, and there is only one available table. And suppose also that this has never happened before, and that the club has not voted on any policy for handling it when it does happen. What seems to me to be plain is this: the headwaiter cannot indulge in preferential seating, he cannot simply declare for one or the other of us on just any ground he pleases. He must randomize: as it might be, by tossing a coin.

Or again, suppose someone arrives at the dining room with a gift for the club: a large and very splendid apple tart. And suppose that this, too, has never happened before, and that the club has not voted on any policy for handling it when it does happen. What seems to me plain is this: the headwaiter cannot distribute that tart in just any manner, and on any ground he pleases. If the tart won't keep till the next meeting, and it's impossible to convene one now, he must divide the tart amongst us equally.

Consideration of these cases might suggest the following principle: every owner of a jointly owned property has a right to either an equal chance at, or an equal share in, any benefit which that property generates, and which is available for distribution amongst the owners—equal chance rather than equal share if the benefit is indivisible, or for some reason is better left undivided.

Now I have all along been taking it that the members of a club jointly own the club, and therefore jointly own whatever the club owns. It seems to me possible to view a community in the same way: to suppose that its members jointly own it, and therefore jointly own whatever it owns. If a community is properly viewed in this way, and if the principle I set out above is true, then every member of the community is a joint owner of whatever the community owns, and so in particular, a joint owner of its university; and therefore every member of the community has a right to an equal chance at, or equal share in, any benefit which the university generates, which is available for distribution amongst the owners. And that includes university jobs, if, as I argued, a university job is a benefit.

Alternatively, one might view a community as an imaginary Person: one might say that the members of that community are in some sense participants in that Person, but that they do not jointly own what the Person owns. One might in fact say the same of a club: that its members do not jointly own the club or anything which the club owns, but only in some sense participate in the Person which owns the things. And then the cases I mentioned might suggest an analogous principle: every "participant" in a Person (Community-Person, Club-Person) has a right to either an equal chance at, or an equal share in, any benefit which is generated by a property which that Person owns, which is available for distribution amongst the "participants."

On the other hand, if we accept any of this, we have to remember that there are cases in which a member may, without the slightest impropriety, be deprived of this equal chance or equal share. For it is plainly not required that the university's hiring officer decide who gets the available job by randomizing amongst *all* the community members, however well- or ill-qualified, who want it. The university's student-customers, after all, have rights too; and their rights to good teaching are surely more stringent than each member's right (if each has such a right) to an equal chance at the job. I think we do best to reserve the term "violation of a right" for cases in which a man is unjustly deprived of something he has a right to, and speak rather of "overriding a right" in cases in which, though a man is deprived of something he has a right to, it is not unjust to deprive him of it. So here the members' rights to an equal chance (if they have them) would be, not violated, but merely overridden.

It could of course be said that these principles hold only of benefits of a kind I pointed to earlier, and called "pure" benefits (such as apples and apple tarts), and that we should find some other, weaker, principle to cover "impure" benefits (such as jobs).

Or it could be said that a university job is not a benefit which is available for distribution amongst the community members—that although a university job is a benefit, it is, in light of the rights of the students, available for distribution only amongst those members of the community who are best qualified to hold it. And therefore that they alone have a right to an equal chance at it.

It is important to notice, however, that unless *some* such principle as I have set out is true of the publicly owned university, there is no real problem about preferential hiring in it. Unless the white male applicant who is turned away had a right that this should not be done, doing so is quite certainly not violating any of his rights. Perhaps being joint owner of the university (on the first model) or being joint participant in the Person which owns the university (on the second model), do not give him a right to an equal chance at the job; perhaps he is neither joint owner nor joint participant (some third model is preferable), and it is something else which gives him his right to an equal chance at the job. Or perhaps he hasn't a right to an equal chance at the job, but has instead some other right which is violated by declaring for the equally qualified black or woman straightway. It is here that it seems to me it emerges most clearly that opponents of preferential hiring are merely expressing a gut reaction against it: for they have not asked themselves precisely what right is in question, and what it issues from.

Perhaps there is lurking in the background some sense that everyone has a right to "equal treatment," and that it is this which is violated by preferential hiring. But what on earth right is this? Mary surely does not have to decide between Tom and Dick by toss of a coin, if what is in question is marrying. Nor even, as I said earlier, if what is in question is giving out apples, which she grew on her own land, on her own trees.

It could, of course, be argued that declaring for the black or woman straightway isn't a violation of the white male applicant's rights, but is all the same wrong, bad, something which ought not be done. As I said, it is perfectly consistent that one ought not do something which it is, nevertheless, no violation of anyone's rights to do. So perhaps opponents of preferential hiring might say that rights are not in question, and still argue against it on other grounds. I say they *might,* but I think they plainly do better not to. If the white male applicant has no rights which would be violated, and appointing the black or woman indirectly benefits other blacks or women (remember that need for role models), and thereby still more indirectly benefits us all (by widening the available pool of

talent), then it is very hard to see how it could come out to be morally objectionable to declare for the black or woman straightway.

I think we should do the best we can for those who oppose preferential hiring: I think we should grant that the white male applicant has a right to an equal chance at the job, and see what happens for preferential hiring if we do. I shall simply leave open whether this right issues from considerations of the kind I drew attention to, and so also whether or not every member of the community, however well- or ill-qualified for the job, has the same right to an equal chance at it.

Now it is, I think, widely believed that we may, without injustice, refuse to grant a man what he has a right to only if *either* someone else has a conflicting and more stringent right, *or* there is some very great benefit to be obtained by doing so—perhaps that a disaster of some kind is thereby averted. If so, then there really is trouble for preferential hiring. For what more stringent right could be thought to override the right of the white male applicant for an equal chance? What great benefit obtained, what disaster averted, by declaring for the black or the woman straightway? I suggested that benefits are obtained, and they are not small ones. But are they large enough to override a right? If these questions cannot be satisfactorily answered, then it looks as if the hiring officer does act unjustly, and does violate the rights of the white males, if he declares for the black or woman straightway.

But in fact there are other ways in which a right may be overridden. Let's go back to that eating club again. Suppose that now it has happened that two of us arrive at the same time when there is only one available table, we think we had better decide on some policy for handling it when it happens. And suppose that we have of late had reason to be especially grateful to one of the members, whom I'll call Smith: Smith has done a series of very great favors for the club. It seems to me we might, out of gratitude to Smith, adopt the following policy: for the next six months, if two members arrive at the same time, and there is only one available table, then Smith gets in first, if he's one of the two; whereas if he's not, then the headwaiter shall toss a coin.

We might even vote that for the next year, if he wants apple tart, he gets more of it than the rest of us.

It seems to me that there would be no impropriety in our taking these actions—by which I mean to include that there would be no injustice in our taking them. Suppose another member, Jones, votes No. Suppose he says "Look, I admit we all benefited from what Smith did for us. But still, I'm a member, and a member in as good standing as Smith is. So I have a right to an equal chance (and equal share), and I demand what I have a right to." I think we may rightly feel that Jones merely shows insensitivity: he does not adequately appreciate what Smith did for us. Jones, like all of us, has a right to an equal chance at such benefits as the club has available for distribution to the members; but there is no injustice in a majority's refusing to grant the members this equal chance, in the name of a debt of gratitude to Smith.

It is worth noticing an important difference between a debt of gratitude and debts owed to a creditor. Suppose the club had borrowed $1000 from Dickenson, and then was left as a legacy, a painting appraised at $1000. If the club has no other saleable assets, and if no member is willing to buy the painting, then I take it that justice would precisely require *not* randomizing amongst the members who is to get that painting, but would instead require our offering it to Dickenson. Jones could not complain that to offer it to Dickenson is to treat him, Jones, unjustly: Dickenson has a right to be paid back, and that right is more stringent than any member's right to an equal chance at the painting. Now Smith, by contrast, did not have a right to be given anything, he did not have a right to our adopting a policy of preferential seating in his favor. If we fail to do anything for Dickenson, we do him an injustice; if we fail to do anything for Smith, we do *him* no injustice—our failing is, not injustice, but ingratitude. There is no harm in speaking of debts of gratitude and in saying that they are owed to a benefactor, by analogy with debts owed to a creditor; but it is important to remember that a creditor has, and a benefactor does not have, a right to repayment.

To move now from clubs to more serious matters, suppose two candidates for a civil service job have equally good test scores, but that there is only one job available. We could decide between them by coin-tossing. But in fact we do allow for declaring for A straightway, where A is a veteran, and B is not.[1] It may be that B is a nonveteran through no fault of his own: perhaps he was refused induction for flat feet, or a heart murmur. That is, those things in virtue of which B is a nonveteran may be things which it was no more in his power to control or change than it is in anyone's power to control or change the color of his skin. Yet the fact is that B is not a veteran and A is. On the assumption that the veteran has served his country,[2] the country owes him something. And it seems plain that giving him preference is a not unjust way in which part of that debt of gratitude can be paid.

And now, finally, we should turn to those debts which are incurred by one who wrongs another. It is here we find what seems to me the most powerful argument for the conclusion that the preferential hiring of blacks and women is not unjust.

I obviously cannot claim any novelty for this argument: it's a very familiar one. Indeed, not merely is it familiar, but so are a battery of objections to it. It may be granted that if we have wronged A, we owe him something: we should make amends, we should compensate him for the wrong done him. It may even be granted that if we have wronged A, we must make amends, that justice requires it, and that a failure to make amends is not merely callousness, but injustice. But (a) are the young blacks and women who are amongst the current applicants for university jobs amongst the blacks and women who were wronged? To turn to particular cases, it might happen that the black applicant is middle class, son of professionals, and has had the very best in private schooling; or that the woman applicant is plainly the product of feminist upbringing and encouragement. Is it proper, much less required, that the black or woman be given preference over a white male who grew up in poverty, and has to make his own way and earn his encouragements? Again, (b), did we, the current members of the community, wrong any blacks or women? Lots of people once did; but then isn't it for them to do the compensating? That is, if they're still alive. For presumably nobody now alive owned any slaves, and perhaps nobody now alive voted against women's suffrage. And (c) what if the white male applicant for the job has never in any degree wronged any blacks or women? If so, *he* doesn't owe any debts to them, so why should *he* make amends to them?

These objections seem to me quite wrong-headed.

Obviously the situation for blacks and women

[1]To the best of my knowledge, the analogy between veterans' preference and the preferential hiring of blacks has been mentioned in print only by Edward T. Chase, in a Letter to the Editor, *Commentary,* February 1973.

[2]Many people would reject this assumption, or perhaps accept it only selectively, for veterans of this or that particular war. I ignore this. What interests me is what follows if we make the assumption—as, of course, many other people do, more, it seems, than do not.

is better than it was a hundred and fifty, fifty, twenty-five years ago. But it is absurd to suppose that the young blacks and women now of an age to apply for jobs have not been wronged. Large-scale, blatant, overt wrongs have presumably disappeared; but it is only within the last twenty-five years (perhaps the last ten years in the case of women) that it has become at all widely agreed in this country that blacks and women must be recognized as having, not merely this or that particular right normally recognized as belonging to white males, but all of the rights and respect which go with full membership in the community. Even young blacks and women have lived through down-grading for being black or female: they have not merely not been given that very equal chance at the benefits generated by what the community owns which is so firmly insisted on for white males, they have not until lately even been felt to have a right to it.

And even those who were not themselves down-graded for being black or female have suffered the consequences of the down-grading of other blacks and women: lack of self-confidence, and lack of self-respect. For where a community accepts that a person's being black, or being a woman, are right and proper grounds for denying that person full membership in the community, it can hardly be supposed that any but the most extraordinarily independent black or woman will escape self-doubt. All but the most extraordinarily independent of them have had to work harder—if only against self-doubt—than all but the most deprived white males, in the competition for a place amongst the best qualified.

If any black or woman has been unjustly deprived of what he or she has a right to, then of course justice does call for making amends. But what of the blacks and women who haven't actually been deprived of what they have a right to, but only made to suffer the consequences of injustice to other blacks and women? *Perhaps* justice doesn't require making amends to them as well; but common decency certainly does. To fail, at the very least, to make what counts as public apology to all, and to take positive steps to show that it is sincerely meant, is, if not injustice, then anyway a fault at least as serious as ingratitude.

Opting for a policy of preferential hiring may of course mean that some black or woman is preferred to some white male who as a matter of fact has had a harder life than the black or woman. But so may opting for a policy of veterans' preference mean that

a healthy, unscarred, middle class veteran is preferred to a poor, struggling, scarred, nonveteran. Indeed, opting for a policy of settling who gets the job by having all equally qualified candidates draw straws may also mean that in a given case the candidate with the hardest life loses out. Opting for any policy other than hard-life preference may have this result.

I have no objection to anyone's arguing that it is precisely hard-life preference that we ought to opt for. If all, or anyway all of the equally qualified, have a right to an equal chance, then the argument would have to draw attention to something sufficiently powerful to override that right. But perhaps this could be done along the lines I followed in the case of blacks and women: perhaps it could be successfully argued that we have wronged those who have had hard lives, and therefore owe it to them to make amends. And then we should have in more extreme form a difficulty already present: how are these preferences to be ranked? shall we place the hard-lifers ahead of blacks? both ahead of women? and what about veterans? I leave these questions aside. My concern has been only to show that the white male applicant's right to an equal chance does not make it unjust to opt for a policy under which blacks and women are given preference. That a white male with a specially hard history may lose out under this policy cannot possibly be any objection to it, in the absence of a showing that hard-life preference is not unjust, and, more important, takes priority over preference for blacks and women.

Lastly, it should be stressed that to opt for such a policy is not to make the young white male applicants themselves make amends for any wrongs done to blacks and women. Under such a policy, no one is asked to give up a job which is already his; the job for which the white male competes isn't his, but is the community's, and it is the hiring officer who gives it to the black or woman in the community's name. Of course the white male is asked to give up his equal chance at the job. But that is not something he pays to the black or woman by way of making amends; it is something the community takes away from him in order that *it* may make amends.

Still, the community does impose a burden on him: it is able to make amends for its wrongs only by taking something away from him, something which, after all, we are supposing he has a right to. And why should *he* pay the cost of the community's amends-making?

If there were some appropriate way in which the community could make amends to its blacks and women, some way which did not require depriving anyone of anything he has a right to, then that would be the best course of action for it to take. Or if there were anyway some way in which the costs could be shared by everyone, and not imposed entirely on the young white male job applicants, then that would be, if not best, then anyway better than opting for a policy of preferential hiring. But in fact the nature of the wrongs done is such as to make jobs the best and most suitable form of compensation. What blacks and women were denied was full membership in the community; and nothing can more appropriately make amends for that wrong than precisely what will make them feel they now finally have it. And that means jobs. Financial compensation (the cost of which could be shared equally) slips through the fingers; having a job, and discovering you do it well, yield —perhaps better than anything else—that very self-respect which blacks and women have had to do without.

But of course choosing this way of making amends means that the costs are imposed on the young white male applicants who are turned away. And so it should be noticed that it is not entirely inappropriate that those applicants should pay the costs. No doubt few, if any, have themselves, individually, done any wrongs to blacks and women. But they have profited from the wrongs the community did. Many may actually have been direct beneficiaries of policies which excluded or downgraded blacks and women—perhaps in school admissions, perhaps in access to financial aid, perhaps elsewhere; and even those who did not directly benefit in this way had, at any rate, the advantage in the competition which comes of confidence in one's full membership, and of one's rights being recognized as a matter of course.

Of course it isn't only the young white male applicant for a university job who has benefited from the exclusion of blacks and women: the older white male, now comfortably tenured, also benefited, and many defenders of preferential hiring feel that he should be asked to share the costs. Well, presumably we can't demand that he give up his job, or share it. But it seems to me in place to expect the occupants of comfortable professorial chairs to contribute in some way, to make some form of return to the young white male who bears the cost, and is turned away. It will have been plain that I find the outcry now heard against preferential hiring in the universities objectionable; it would also be objectionable that those of us who are now securely situated should placidly defend it, with no more than a sigh of regret for the young white male who pays for it.

IV

One final word: "discrimination." I am inclined to think we so use it that if anyone is convicted of discriminating against blacks, women, white males, or what have you, then he is thereby convicted of acting unjustly. If so, and if I am right in thinking that preferential hiring in the restricted range of cases we have been looking at is *not* unjust, then we have two options: (a) we can simply reply that to opt for a policy of preferential hiring in those cases is not to opt for a policy of discriminating against white males, or (b) we can hope to get usage changed —e.g., by trying to get people to allow that there is discriminating against and discriminating against, and that some is unjust, but some is not.

Best of all, however, would be for that phrase to be avoided altogether. It's at best a blunt tool: there are all sorts of nice moral discriminations (*sic*) which one is unable to make while occupied with it. And that bluntness itself fits it to do harm: blacks and women are hardly likely to see through to what precisely is owed them while they are being accused of welcoming what is unjust.

33/Secondary Sexism and Quota Hiring

Mary Anne Warren

I want to call attention to a pervasive form of discrimination against women, one which helps to explain the continuing male monopoly of desirable jobs in the universities, as elsewhere. Discrimination of this sort is difficult to eliminate or even, in some cases, to recognize, because (1) it is not explicitly based on sex, and (2) it typically *appears* to be justified on the basis of plausible moral or practical considerations. The recognition of this form of discrimination gives rise to a new argument for the use of numerical goals or quotas in the hiring of women for college and university teaching and administrative positions.

I shall argue that because of these de facto discriminatory hiring practices, minimum numerical quotas for the hiring and promotion of women are necessary, not (just) to compensate women for past discrimination or its results, or to provide women with role models, but to counteract this *ongoing* discrimination and thus make the competition for such jobs more nearly fair. Indeed, given the problems inherent in the compensatory justice and role-model arguments for reverse discrimination, this may well be the soundest argument for the use of such quotas.

I. Primary and Secondary Sexism

Most of us try not to be sexists; that is, we try not to discriminate unfairly in our actions or attitudes toward either women or men. But it is not a simple matter to determine just which actions or attitudes discriminate unfairly, and a sincere effort to avoid unfair discrimination is often not enough. This is true of both of the forms of sexism that I wish to distinguish.

In its primary sense, "sexism" means *unfair discrimination on the basis of sex*. The unfairness may be unintentional; but the cause or reason for the discrimination must be the sex of the victim, not merely some factor such as size or strength that happens to be correlated with sex. Primary sexism may be due to dislike, distrust, or contempt for women, or, in less typical cases, for men or hermaphrodites. Or it may be due to sincerely held but objectively unjustified beliefs about women's properties or capacities. It may also be due to beliefs about the properties women *tend* to have, which are objectively justified but inappropriately applied to a particular case, in which the woman discriminated against does not have those properties.

For instance, if members of a philosophy department vote against hiring or promoting a woman logician because they dislike women (logicians), or because they think that women cannot excel in logic, or because they know that most women do not so excel and wrongly conclude that this one does not, then they are guilty of primary sexism. This much, I think, is noncontroversial.

But what should we say if they vote to hire or promote a man rather than a woman because he has a wife and children to support, while she has a husband who is (capable of) supporting her? Or because they believe that the woman has childcare responsibilities which will limit the time she can spend on the job? What if they hire a woman at a lower rank and salary than is standard for a man with comparable qualifications, for one of the above reasons? These actions are not sexist in the primary sense because there is no discrimination on the basis of sex itself. The criteria used *can* at least be applied in a sex-neutral manner. For instance, it might be asserted that if the woman candidate had had a spouse and children who depended upon her for support, this would have counted in her favor just as much as it would in the case of a man.

Of course, appeals to such intrinsically sex-neutral criteria may, in some cases, be mere rationalizations of what is actually done from primary sexist motives. In reality, the criteria cited may not be applied in a sex-neutral manner. But let us assume for the sake of argument that the application of these criteria *is* sex-neutral, not merely a smoke screen for primary sexism. On this assumption, the use of such criteria discriminates against women only because of certain contingent features of this society, such as the persistence of the traditional division of labor in marriage and childrearing.[1]

Many people see nothing morally objectionable in the use of such intrinsically sex-neutral yet de facto discriminatory criteria. For not only may employers who use such criteria be free of primary sexism, but their actions may appear to be justified on both moral and pragmatic grounds. It might, for instance, be quite clear that a department will really do more to alleviate economic hardship by hiring or promoting a man with dependents rather than a woman with none, or that a particular woman's domestic responsibilities will indeed limit the time she can spend on the job. And it might seem perfectly appropriate for employers to take account of such factors.

Nevertheless, I shall argue that the use of such considerations is unfair. It is an example of secondary sexism, which I define as comprising all those actions, attitudes and policies which, while not using sex itself as a reason for discrimination, do involve sex-correlated factors or criteria and do result in an unfair impact upon (certain) women. In the case of university hiring policies, secondary sexism consists in the use of sex-correlated selection criteria which are not valid measures of academic merit, with the result that women tend to be passed over in favor of men who are not, in fact, better qualified. I call sexism of this sort *secondary,* not because it is any less widespread or harmful than primary sexism, but because (1) it is, in this way, indirect or covert, and (2) it is typically parasitic upon primary sexism, in that the injustices it perpetuates—for example, those apparent from the male monopoly of desirable jobs in the universities—are usually due in the first instance to primary sexism.

Two points need to be made with respect to this definition. First, it is worth noting that, although in the cases we will be considering the correlations between sex and the apparently independent but de facto discriminatory criteria are largely due to past

and present injustices against women, this need not always be the case. The discriminatory impact of excluding pregnancy-related disabilities from coverage by employee health insurance policies, for example, probably makes this an instance of secondary sexism. Yet it is certainly not (human) injustice which is responsible for the fact that it is only women who become pregnant. The fact that the correlation is due to biology rather than prior injustice does not show that the exclusion is not sexist. Neither does the fact that pregnancy is often undertaken voluntarily. If such insurance programs fail to serve the needs of women employees as well as they serve those of men, then they can escape the charge of sexism only if—as seems unlikely—it can be shown that they cannot possibly be altered to include disabilities related to pregnancy without ceasing to serve their mutually agreed upon purposes, and/or producing an even greater injustice.

This brings us to the second point. It must be stressed that on the above definition the use of valid criteria of merit in hiring to university positions is not an instance of secondary sexism. Some might argue that merit criteria discriminate unfairly against women, because it is harder for women to earn the advanced degrees, to write the publications, and to obtain the professional experience that are the major traditional measures of academic merit. But it would be a mistake to suppose that merit criteria as such are therefore sexist. They are sexist only to the extent that they understate women's actual capacity to perform well in university positions; and to that extent, they are invalid as criteria of merit. To the extent that they are valid, that is, the most reliable available measurements of capacities which are indeed crucial for the performance of the job, they are not unjust, even though they may result in more men than women being hired.

If this seems less than obvious, the following analogy may help. It is surely not unjust to award first prize in a discus throwing contest to the contestant who actually makes the best throw (provided, of course, that none of the contestants have been unfairly prevented from performing up to their capacity on this particular occasion), even if some of the contestants have in the past been wrongly prevented from developing their skill to the fullest, say by sexist discrimination in school athletic programs. Such contestants may be entitled to other relevant forms of compensation, for example, special free training programs to help them make up for lost time, but they are not entitled to win this particular contest.

---

[1] I mean, of course, the tradition that the proper husband earns (most of) the family's income, while the proper wife does (most of) the housekeeping and childrearing.

For the very *raison d'etre* of an athletic contest dictates that prizes go to the best performers, not those who perhaps *could* have been the best, had past conditions been ideally fair.

So too, a university's central reasons for being dictate that positions within it be filled by candidates who are as well qualified as can be found. Choosing less qualified candidates deprives students of the best available instruction, colleagues of a more intellectually productive environment, and—in the case of state-funded universities—the public of the most efficient use of its resources.[2] To appoint inferior candidates defeats the primary purposes of the university, and is therefore wrongheaded, however laudable its motivations. It is also, as we shall see, a weapon of social change which is apt to backfire against those in whose interest it is advocated.

II. Secondary Racism

Secondary sexism has parallels in secondary racism, as well as secondary antihomosexual bias, and the like.[3] Irving Thalberg has explored some of the arguments used by white liberals to rationalize their refusal to change practices which oppress blacks, without appealing to old-fashioned doctrines of white superiority.[4] Some of the strategies of resistance which he analyzes—for example, the charge of reverse discrimination and the appeal to standards—are frequently used in opposition to special hiring programs not only for blacks but also for women, and will be dealt with in that context later. Conversely, some of the secondary sexist policies which we shall consider may function at times to exclude racial minorities.

Thalberg, however, denies the legitimacy of the analogy between racism and sexism. He finds it ludicrous for a middle-class white woman to compare her oppression with that of blacks:

She *is annoyed because she can't get a baby-sitter when she likes.* They *can barely feed their children . . . She is indignant because a male co-worker gets promoted before she does, or receives more salary for less work.* They *will never get into the same league with their oppressors.*[5]

Such invidious comparisons are not uncommon. George Sher has recently argued that reverse discrimination is justified in the hiring of blacks but not in the hiring of women, since women have not, to the same degree as blacks, been denied the opportunity to obtain the qualifications necessary to compete on an equal basis with white men.[6] I shall have more to say about this argument later. Although I concentrate here on secondary sexism in academic hiring, it is not because I consider secondary racism any less important but because it comprises a somewhat separate set of phenomena.

III. Secondary Sexism in University Hiring

Consider the following policies, which not infrequently influence hiring, retention, and promotion decisions in American colleges and universities:

1. Antinepotism rules, proscribing the employment of spouses of current employees.

2. Giving preference to candidates who (are thought to) have the greater financial need, where the latter is estimated by whether someone has, on the one hand, financial dependents, or, on the other hand, a spouse capable of providing financial support.

3. The "last hired–first fired" principle, used in determining who shall be fired or not rehired as a result of staffing cutbacks.

4. Refusing promotions, tenure, retention seniority, or pro-rata pay to persons employed less than full time, where some are so employed on a relatively long-term basis and where there is no evidence that such persons are (all) less well qualified than full time employees.

---

[2] It might be argued that the hiring process ought not to be based on merit alone, because there are cases in which being a woman, or being black, might itself be a crucial job qualification. As Michael Martin points out, this might well be the case in hiring for, say, a job teaching history in a previously all white-male department which badly needs to provide its students with a more balanced perspective. See "Pedagogical Arguments for Preferential Hiring and Tenuring of Women Teachers in the University," *The Philosophical Forum* 5, no. 2: 325–333. I think it is preferable, however, to describe such cases, not as instances requiring a departure from the merit principle, but as instances in which sex or race itself, or rather certain interests and abilities that are correlated with sex or race, constitutes a legitimate qualification for a certain job, and hence a measure of merit, vis-à-vis that job.

[3] My thanks to Michael Scriven, who discussed this and related points with me, and whose comments have been most helpful.

[4] Irving Thalberg, "Justifications of Institutional Racism," *The Philosophical Forum* 3, no. 2 (Winter 1971–1972): 243–263.

[5] Thalberg, p. 247, emphasis mine.

[6] George Sher, "Justifying Reverse Discrimination in Employment," *Philosophy & Public Affairs* 4, no. 2 (Winter 1975): 168–169.

5. Hiring at a rank and salary determined primarily by previous rank and salary rather than by more direct evidence of a candidate's competence, for example, degrees, publications, and student and peer evaluations.

6. Counting as a negative factor the fact that a candidate has or is thought to have, or to be more likely to have, childcare or other domestic responsibilities which may limit the time s/he can spend on the job.

7. Giving preference to candidates with more or less uninterrupted work records over those whose working careers have been interrupted (for example, by raising children) in the absence of more direct evidence of a present difference in competence.

8. Not hiring, especially to administrative or supervisory positions, persons thought apt to encounter disrespect or lack of cooperation from peers or subordinates, without regard for whether this presumed lack of respect may be itself unjustified, for example, as the result of primary sexism.

9. Discriminating against candidates on the grounds of probable mobility due to the mobility of a spouse, present or possible.

Each of these practices is an example of secondary sexism, in that while the criterion applied does not mention sex, its use nevertheless tends to result in the hiring and promotion of men in preference to women who are not otherwise demonstrably less well qualified. I suggest that in seeking to explain the continuing underrepresentation of women in desirable jobs in the universities, we need to look not only toward primary sexist attitudes within those institutions, and certainly not toward any intrinsic lack of merit on the part of women candidates,[7] but toward covertly, and often unintentionally, discriminatory practices such as these.

Of course, none of these practices operates to the detriment of women in every case; but each operates against women much more often than against men, and the cumulative effect is enormous. No doubt some of them are more widespread than others and some (for example, the use of anti-

nepotism rules) are already declining in response to pressures to remove barriers to the employment of women. Others, such as policies 3 and 4, are still fairly standard and have barely begun to be seriously challenged in most places. Some are publicly acknowledged and may have been written into law or administrative policy, for example, policies 1, 3, 4, and 5. Others are more apt to be private policies on the part of individual employers, to which they may not readily admit or of which they may not even be fully aware, for example, policies 2, 6, 7, and 8. It is obviously much more difficult to demonstrate the prevalence of practices of the latter sort. Nevertheless, I am certain that all of these practices occur, and I strongly suspect that none is uncommon, even now.

This list almost certainly does not include all of the secondary sexist practices which influence university hiring. But these examples are typical, and an examination of certain of their features will shed light on the way in which secondary sexism operates in the academic world and on the reasons why it is morally objectionable.

In each of these examples, a principle is used in choosing between candidates that in practice acts to discriminate against women who may even be better qualified intrinsically than their successful rivals, on any reliable and acceptable measure of merit.[8] Nevertheless, the practice may *seem* to be justified. Nepotism rules, for instance, act to exclude women far more often than men, since women are more apt to seek employment in academic and/or geographical areas in which their husbands are already employed than vice versa. Yet nepotism rules may appear to be necessary to ensure fairness to those candidates and appointees, both male and female, who are *not* spouses of current employees

---

[7]With respect to one such measure, books and articles published, married women Ph.D.'s publish as much or slightly more than men, and unmarried women only slightly less. See "The Woman Ph.D.: A Recent Profile," by R. J. Simon, S. M. Clark, and K. Galway, in *Social Problems* 15, no. 2 (Fall 1967): 231.

[8]I am assuming that whether a candidate is married to a current employee, or has dependents, or a spouse capable of supporting her, whether she is employed on a part-time or a full-time basis, her previous rank and salary, the continuity of her work record, and so on, are not in themselves reliable and acceptable measures of merit. As noted in example 5, more direct and pertinent measure of merit can be obtained. Such measures as degrees, publications, and peer and student evaluations have the moral as well as pragmatic advantage of being based on the candidate's actual past performance, rather than on unreliable and often biased conjectures of various sorts. Furthermore, even if there is or were *some* correlation (it would surely not be a *reliable* one) between certain secondary sexist criteria and job performance, it could still be argued that employers are not morally entitled to use such criteria, because of the unfair consequences of doing so. As Mary Vetterling has observed, there might well be some correlation between having "a healthy and active sex life" and "the patience and good humor required of a good teacher"; yet employers are surely not entitled to take into account the quality of a person's sex life in making hiring and promotion decisions. "Some Common Sense Notes on Preferential Hiring," *The Philosophical Forum* 5, no. 2: 321.

and who, it could be argued, would otherwise be unfairly disadvantaged. Similarly, giving jobs or promotions to those judged to have the greatest financial need may seem to be simple humanitarianism, and the seniority system may seem to be the only practical way of providing job security to *any* portion of the faculty. For policies 5 through 9, it could be argued that, although the criteria used are not entirely reliable, they may still have *some* use in predicting job performance.

Thus each practice, though discriminatory in its results, may be defended by reference to principles which are not intrinsically sex-biased. In the context of an otherwise sexually egalitarian society, these practices would probably not result in de facto discrimination against either sex. In such a society, for instance, men would not hold a huge majority of desirable jobs, and women would be under no more social or financial pressure than men to live where their spouses work rather than where they themselves work; thus they would not be hurt by nepotism rules any more often, on the average, than men.[9] The average earning power of men and women would be roughly equal, and no one could assume that women, any more than men, ought to be supported by their spouses, if possible. Thus the fact that a woman has an employed spouse would not be thought to reduce her need for a job any more—or any less—than in the case of a man. We could proceed down the list; in a genuinely nonsexist society, few or none of the conditions would exist which cause these practices to have a discriminatory impact upon women.

Of course, there may be other reasons for rejecting these practices, besides their discriminatory impact upon women. Nepotism rules might be unfair to married persons of both sexes, even in a context in which they were not *especially* unfair to women. My point is simply that these practices would not be instances of sexism in a society which was otherwise free of sexism and its results. Hence, those who believe that the test of the justice of a practice is whether or not it would unfairly disadvantage any group or individual *in the context of an otherwise just society* will see no sexual injustice whatever in these practices.

But surely the moral status of a practice, as it operates in a certain context, must be determined at least in part by its actual consequences, in that

context. The fact is that each of these practices acts to help preserve the male monopoly of desirable jobs, in spite of the availability of women who are just as well qualified on any defensible measure of merit. This may or may not suffice to show that these practices are morally objectionable. It certainly shows that they are inconsistent with the "straight merit" principle, that is, that jobs should go to those best qualified for them on the more reliable measures of merit. Hence, it is ironic that attempts to counteract such de facto discriminatory practices are often interpreted as attacks on the "straight merit" principle.

IV. Why Secondary Sexism Is Unfair

Two additional points need to be stressed in order to show just why these practices are unfair. In the first place, the contingent social circumstances which explain the discriminatory impact of these practices are themselves morally objectionable, and/or due to morally objectionable practices. It is largely because men *are* more able to make good salaries, and because married women are still expected to remain financially dependent upon their husbands, if possible, that the fact that a woman has an employed husband can be seen as evidence that she doesn't "need" a job. It is because a disproportionate number of women must, because of family obligations and the geographical limitations these impose, accept part-time employment even when they would prefer full time, that the denial of tenure, promotion and pro-rata pay to part-time faculty has a discriminatory impact upon women. That women accept such obligations and limitations may seem to be their own free choice; but, of course, that choice is heavily conditioned by financial pressures—for example, the fact that the husband can usually make more money—and by sexually stereotyped social expectations.

Thus, the effect of these policies is to compound and magnify prior social injustices against women. When a woman is passed over on such grounds, it is rather as if an athlete who had without her knowledge been administered a drug to hamper her performance were to be disqualified from the competition for failing the blood-sample test. In such circumstances, the very least that justice demands is that the unfairly imposed handicap not be used as a rationale for the imposition of further handicaps. If the unfair handicaps that society imposes upon

---

[9]Unless, perhaps, a significant average age difference between wives and husbands continued to exist.

women cause them to be passed over by employers because of a lack of straight merit, that is one thing, and it is unfortunate, but it is not obvious that it involves unfairness on the part of the employers. But if those handicaps are used as an excuse for excluding them from the competition regardless of their merit, as all too often happens, this is quite another thing, and it is patently unfair.

In the second place, practices such as these often tend to perpetuate the very (unjust) circumstances which underlie their discriminatory impact, thus creating a vicious circle. Consider the case of a woman who is passed over for a job or promotion because of her childcare responsibilities. Given a (better) job, she might be able to afford day care, or to hire someone to help her at home, or even to persuade her husband to assume more of the responsibilities. Denying her a job because of her domestic responsibilities may make it almost impossible for her to do anything to lessen those responsibilities. Similarly, denying her a job because she has a husband who supports her may force him to continue supporting her and her to continue to accept that support.

Both of these points may be illustrated by turning to a somewhat different sort of example. J. R. Lucas has argued that there are cases in which women may justifiably be discriminated against on grounds irrelevant to their merit. He claims, for example, that it is "not so evidently wrong to frustrate Miss Amazon's hopes of a military career in the Grenadier Guards on the grounds not that she would make a bad soldier, but that she would be a disturbing influence in the mess room."[10]

But this is a paradigm case of secondary, and perhaps also primary, sexism; it is also quite analogous to practice 8. To exclude women from certain jobs or certain branches of the military on the grounds that certain third parties are not apt to accept them, when that nonacceptance is itself unreasonable and perhaps based on sexual bigotry, is to compound the injustice of that bigotry. If it is inappropriate for soldiers to be disturbed or to make a disturbance because there are women in the mess room, then it is wrong to appeal to those soldiers' attitudes as grounds for denying women the opportunities available to comparably qualified men. It is also to help ensure the perpetuation of those attitudes, by preventing male soldiers from having an opportunity to make the sorts of observations which

might lead to their eventually accepting women as comrades.

Thus, these practices are morally objectionable because they compound and perpetuate prior injustices against women, penalizing them for socially imposed disadvantages which cannot be reliably shown to detract from their actual present capacities. We may conclude that the hiring process will never be fair to women, nor will it be based on merit alone, so long as such practices persist on a wide scale. But it remains to be seen whether numerical hiring quotas for women are a morally acceptable means of counteracting the effects of sexist hiring practices.

V. Weak Quotas

I shall discuss the case for mandatory hiring quotas of a certain very minimal sort: those based on the proportion of women, not in the population as a whole, but among qualified and available candidates in each academic field. Such a "weak" quota system would require that in each institution, and ideally within each department and each faculty and administrative rank and salary, women be hired and promoted at least in accordance with this proportion. If, for instance, a tenured or tenure-track position became available in a given department on an average of every other year, and if women were twenty percent of the qualified and available candidates in that field, then such a quota system would require that the department hire a woman to such a position at least once in ten years.[11]

Needless to say, this is not a formula for rapid change in the sexual composition of the universities. Suppose that the above department has twenty members, all male and all or almost all tenured, that it does not grow, and that it perhaps shrinks somewhat. Under these not atypical circumstances, it could easily take over forty years for the number of women in the department to become proportional to the number of qualified women available, even if the quota is strictly adhered to, and the proportion of

[10]J. R. Lucas, "Because You are a Woman," *Moral Problems,* ed. James Rachels (New York: Harper & Row, 1975), p. 139.

[11]In practice, problems of statistical significance will probably require that quotas be enforced on an institution-wide basis rather than an inflexible department-by-department basis. Individual departments, especially if they are small and if the proportion of qualified women in the field is low, may fail to meet hiring quotas, not because of primary or secondary sexism, but because the best qualified candidates happen in fact to be men. But if no real discrimination against women is occurring, then such statistical deviations should be canceled out on the institutional level, by deviations in the opposite direction.

qualified women does not increase in the meantime. Consequently, some would argue that such a quota system would be inadequate.[12]

Furthermore, it *could* be argued that if the job competition were actually based on merit, women would be hired and promoted at a *higher* rate than such a weak quota system would require, since the greater obstacles still encountered by women on the way to obtaining qualifications ensure that only very able women make it.[13] Or, it might be argued that women should be hired and promoted in more than such proportional numbers, in order to compensate for past discrimination or to provide other women with role models. Indeed, some existing affirmative action plans, so I am told, already require that women be hired in more than proportional numbers. Nevertheless, I will not defend quotas higher than these minimal ones. For, as will be argued in Section IX, higher quotas at least give the appearance of being unfair to male candidates, and it is not clear that either the compensatory justice or the role-model argument is sufficient to dispel that appearance.

VI. Quotas Or Goals?

Before turning to the case for such minimal hiring quotas, we need to comment on the "quotas vs. goals" controversy. Those who oppose the use of numerical guidelines in the hiring of women or racial minorities usually refer to such guidelines as *quotas,* while their defenders usually insist that they are not quotas but *goals.* What is at issue here? Those who use the term "quotas" pejoratively tend to assume that the numerical standards will be set so high or enforced so rigidly that strong reverse discrimination—that is, the deliberate hiring of demonstrably less well qualified candidates—will be

necessary to implement them.[14] The term "goal," on the other hand, suggests that this will not be the case, and that good faith efforts to comply with the standards by means short of strong reverse discrimination will be acceptable.[15]

But whatever one calls such minimum numerical standards, and whether or not one suspects that strong reverse discrimination has in fact occurred in the name of affirmative action, it should be clear that it is not *necessary* for the implementation of a quota system such as I have described. Neither, for that matter, is weak reverse discrimination—that is, the deliberate hiring of women in preference to equally but not better qualified men.[16] For if hiring decisions were solely based on reliable measures of merit and wholly uncorrupted by primary or secondary sexist policies, then qualified women would *automatically* be hired and promoted at least in proportion to their numbers, except, of course, in statistically abnormal cases.[17] Consequently, reverse discrimination will *appear* to be necessary to meet proportional quotas only where the hiring process continues to be influenced by sexist practices—primary or secondary, public or private.

In effect, the implementation of a minimum quota system would place a price upon the continued use of sexist practices. Employers would be forced to choose between eliminating sexist practices, thus making it possible for quotas to be met without discriminating for or against anyone on the basis of sex, and practicing reverse discrimination on an ad hoc basis in order to meet quotas without eliminating sexist practices. Ideally, perhaps, they would all choose the first course, in which case the quota system would serve only to promote an ongoing check upon, and demonstration of, the nonsexist nature of the hiring process.

In reality, however, not all secondary sexist practices can be immediately eliminated. Some

[12]See Virginia Held, "Reasonable Progress and Self-Respect," *The Monist* 57, no. 1: 19.

[13]Gertrude Ezorsky cites in support of this point a study by L. R. Harmon of over 20,000 Ph.D.'s, which showed that "Women . . . Ph.D.'s are superior to their male counterparts on all measures derived from high school records, in all . . . specializations." *High School Ability Patterns: A Backward Look from the Doctorate,* Scientific Manpower [*sic*] Report No. 6, 1965, pp. 27–28; cited by Ezorsky in "The Fight Over University Women," *The New York Review of Books* 21, no. 8 (16 May 1974): 32.

[14]See, for instance, Paul Seaburg, "HEW and the Universities," *Commentary* 53, no. 2 (February 1972): 38–44.

[15]In practice, strong reverse discrimination is specifically prohibited by HEW affirmative action guidelines, and good faith efforts to implement affirmative action programs without resorting to strong reverse discrimination have been accepted as adequate. Nevertheless, though I would not wish to see *these* features of affirmative action policies changed, I prefer the term "quota" for

what I am proposing, because this term suggests a standard which will be enforced, in one way or another, while the term "goal" suggests—and affirmative action is in great danger of becoming —a mere expression of good intentions, compliance with which is virtually unenforceable.

[16]The distinction between strong and weak reverse discrimination is explored by Michael Bayles in "Compensatory Reverse Discrimination in Hiring," *Social Theory and Practice* 2, no. 3: 303–304, and by Vetterling, "Common Sense Notes," pp. 320–323.

[17]This conclusion can be avoided only by assuming either that qualified women would not want better jobs if these were available, or that they are somehow less meritorious than comparably qualified men. The first assumption is absurd, since women who do not want desirable jobs are not apt to take the trouble to become qualified for them; and the second assumption is amply refuted by empirical data. See, for instance, the studies cited in fnn. 6 and 13.

forms of secondary sexism have probably not yet been recognized, and given the nature of the interests involved it is likely that new forms will tend to spring up to replace those which have been discredited. More seriously, perhaps, some secondary sexist policies, such as the seniority system, cannot be eliminated without an apparent breach of contract (or of faith) with present employees. Others —for example, hiring on the basis of need—may survive because they are judged, rightly or wrongly, to be on the whole the lesser evil. A quota system, however, would require that the impact of such secondary sexist practices be counterbalanced by preferential treatment of women in other instances. Furthermore, it would hasten the elimination of all sexist policies by making it in the interest of all employees, men as well as women, that this be done, since until it is done both will run the risk of suffering from (sexist or reverse) discrimination. Certainly their elimination would be more probable than it is at present, when it is primarily women who have a reason based on self-interest for opposing them, yet primarily men who hold the power to eliminate or preserve them.

The most crucial point, however, is that under such a quota system, even if (some) employers do use weak discrimination in favor of women to meet their quota, this will not render the job competition especially unfair to men. For, as I will argue, unfairness would result only if the average male candidate's chances of success were reduced to below what they would be in an ongoing, just society, one in which men and women had complete equality of opportunity and the competition was based on merit alone; and I will argue that the use of weak reverse discrimination to meet proportional hiring quotas will not have this effect.

VII. Quotas and Fairness

Now one way to support this claim would be to argue that in an ongoing, just society women would constitute a far higher proportion of the qualified candidates in most academic fields and that therefore the average male candidate's chances would, other things being equal, automatically be reduced considerably from what they are now. Unfortunately, however, the premise of this argument is overly speculative. It is possible that in a fully egalitarian society women would still tend to avoid certain academic fields and to prefer others, much as they

do now, or even that they would fail to (attempt to) enter the academic profession as a whole in much greater numbers than at present.

But whatever the proportion of male and female candidates may be, it must at least be the case that in a just society the chances of success enjoyed by male candidates must be no greater, on the average, and no less than those enjoyed by comparably qualified women. Individual differences in achievement, due to luck or to differences in ability, are probably inevitable; but overall differences in the opportunities accorded to comparably qualified men and women, due to discrimination, would not be tolerated.

The question, then, is: Would the use of weak discrimination in favor of women, to a degree just sufficient to offset continuing sexist discrimination against women and thus to meet minimum quotas, result in lowering the average chances of male candidates to below those of comparably qualified women? The answer, surely, is that it would not, since by hypothesis men would be passed over, in order to fill a quota, in favor of women no better qualified only as often as women continue to be passed over, because of primary or secondary sexism, in favor of men no better qualified.

In this situation, individual departures from the "straight merit" principle might be no less frequent than at present; indeed, their frequency might even be doubled. But since it would no longer be predominantly women who were repeatedly disadvantaged by those departures, the overall fairness of the competition would be improved. The average long-term chances of success of *both* men and women candidates would more closely approximate those they would enjoy in an ongoing just society. If individual men's careers are temporarily set back because of weak reverse discrimination, the odds are good that these same men will have benefited in the past and/or will benefit in the future—not necessarily in the job competition, but in *some* ways—from sexist discrimination against women. Conversely, if individual women receive apparently unearned bonuses, it is highly likely that these same women will have suffered in the past and/or will suffer in the future from primary or secondary sexist attitudes. Yet, the primary purpose of a minimum quota system would not be to compensate the victims of discrimination or to penalize its beneficiaries, but rather to increase the overall fairness of the situation—to make it possible for the first time for women to enjoy the same opportunity to obtain desirable jobs in the universities as enjoyed by men with comparable qualifications.

It is obvious that a quota system implemented by weak reverse discrimination is not the ideal long-term solution to the problem of sexist discrimination in academic hiring. But it would be a great improvement over the present situation, in which the rate of unemployment among women Ph.D.'s who are actively seeking employment is still far higher than among men with Ph.D.'s, and in which women's starting salaries and chances of promotion are still considerably lower than those of men.[18] Strong reverse discrimination is clearly the least desirable method of implementing quotas. Not only is it unfair to the men who are passed over, and to their potential students and colleagues, to hire demonstrably less well qualified women, but it is very apt to reinforce primary sexist attitudes on the part of all concerned, since it appears to presuppose that women cannot measure up on their merits. But to presume that proportional hiring quotas could not be met without strong reverse discrimination is also to make that discredited assumption. If, as all available evidence indicates, women in the academic world are on the average just as hard-working, productive, and meritorious as their male colleagues, then there can be no objection to hiring and promoting them at least in accordance with their numbers, and doing so will increase rather than decrease the extent to which success is based upon merit.

VIII. Are Quotas Necessary?

I have argued that minimum proportional quotas such as I have described would not make the job competition (especially) unfair to men. But it might still be doubted that quotas are necessary to make the competition fair to women. Why not simply attack sexist practices wherever they exist and then let the chips fall as they may? Alan Goldman argues that quotas are not necessary, since, he says, other measures—for example, "active recruitment of minority candidates, the advertisement and application of nondiscriminatory hiring criteria . . . and the enforcement of these provisions by a neutral gov-

ernment agency"[19] would suffice to guarantee equal treatment for women. Goldman claims that if women candidates are as well qualified as men then, given these other measures, they will automatically be hired at least in proportion to their numbers. Indeed, he suggests that the only basis for doubting this claim is "an invidious suspicion of the real inferiority of women . . . even those with Ph.D.'s."[20] That discrimination against women might continue to occur in spite of such affirmative action measures short of quotas, he regards as "an untested empirical hypothesis without much prima facie plausibility."[21]

In a similar vein, George Sher has argued that blacks, but not women, are entitled to reverse discrimination in hiring, since the former but not the latter have suffered from a poverty syndrome which has denied them the opportunity to obtain the qualifications necessary to compete on an equal basis with white men.[22] He views reverse discrimination—and presumably hiring quotas—as primarily a way of compensating those who suffer from present competitive disadvantanges due to past discrimination, and claims that since women are not disadvantaged with respect to (the opportunity to obtain) qualifications, they are not entitled to reverse discrimination.

What both Goldman and Sher overlook, of course, is that women suffer from competitive disadvantages quite apart from any lack of qualifications. Even if primary sexism were to vanish utterly from the minds of all employers, secondary sexist practices such as those we have considered would in all likelihood suffice to perpetuate the male monopoly of desirable jobs well beyond our lifetimes. Such practices cannot be expected to vanish quickly or spontaneously; to insist that affirmative action measures stop short of the use of quotas is to invite their continuation and proliferation.

IX. The Compensatory Justice and Role-model Arguments

Most of the philosophers who have recently defended the use of goals or quotas in the hiring of women and/or minority group members have as-

---

[18]Elizabeth Scott tells me that her survey of 1974–1976 figures reveals that, in spite of affirmative action policies, unemployment among women Ph.D.'s who are actively seeking work is about twice as high as among men Ph.D.'s and that the starting salaries of women Ph.D.'s average $1,200 to $1,500 lower than those of men.

[19]Alan H. Goldman, "Affirmative Action," *Philosophy & Public Affairs* 5, no. 2 (Winter 1976): 185.

[20]Goldman, p. 186.

[21]Goldman, p. 185.

[22]Sher, p. 168.

sumed that this will necessarily involve at least weak and perhaps strong reverse discrimination, but have argued that it is nevertheless justified as a way of compensating individuals or groups for past injustices or for present disadvantages stemming from past injustices.[23] Others have argued that reverse discrimination is justified not (just) as a form of compensatory justice, but as a means of bringing about certain future goods—for example, raising the status of downtrodden groups,[24] or providing young women and blacks with role models and thus breaking the grip of self-fulfilling expectations which cause them to fail.[25]

If one is intent upon arguing for a policy which would give blacks or women "advantages in employment . . . greater than these same blacks or women would receive in an ongoing just society,"[26] then perhaps it is necessary to appeal to compensatory justice or to the role model or to other utilitarian arguments to justify the prima facie unfairness to white males which such a policy involves. But there is no need to use these arguments in justifying a weak quota system such as the one described here, and indeed, it is somewhat misleading to do so. For, as we have seen, such a system would not lower the average male candidate's overall chances of success to below what they would be if the selection were based on merit alone. It would simply raise women's chances, and lower men's, to a closer approximation of what they would be in an ongoing just society, in which the "straight merit" principle prevailed. This being the case, the fact that quotas may serve to compensate some women for past or present wrongs, or to provide others with role models, must be seen as a fortuitous side effect of their use and not their primary reason for being. The primary reason for weak quotas is simply to increase the present fairness of the competition.

Furthermore, there are problems with the compensatory justice and role-model arguments which make their use hazardous. It is not clear that either suffices to justify any use of reverse discrimination beyond what may in practice (appear to) be necessary to implement weak quotas. For, granted that society as a whole has some obligation to provide compensation to the victims of past

discrimination, and assuming that at least some women candidates for university positions are suitable beneficiaries of such compensation, it is by no means clear that male candidates should be forced to bear most of the burden for providing that compensation. It would be plausible to argue on the basis of compensatory justice for, say, tax-supported *extra* positions for women, since then the burden would be distributed relatively equitably. But compensatory justice provides no case for placing an extra, and seemingly punitive, burden on male candidates, who are no more responsible for past and present discrimination against women than the rest of us.

Similarly, however badly women may need role models, it is not clear that male candidates should be disproportionately penalized in order to provide them. It can be argued on the basis of simple fairness that male candidates' chances should not be allowed to remain *above* what they would be in a just society; but to justify reducing them to *below* that point requires a stronger argument than simply appealing to compensatory justice or the need for role models.

Nor does it help to argue that the real source of the injustice to male candidates, if and when preferential hiring of women results in lowering the former's chances to below what they would be in a just society, is not the preferential hiring policy itself, but something else. Thomas Nagel, for instance, argues that reverse discrimination is not seriously unjust, even if it means that it is harder for white men to get certain sorts of jobs than it is for women and blacks who are no better qualified, since, he suggests, the real source of the injustice is the entire system of providing differential rewards on the basis of differential abilities.[27] And Marlene Fried argues that the root of the injustice is not preferential hiring, but the failure of those with the power to do so to expand job opportunities so that blacks and women could be hired in increasing numbers without hiring fewer men.[28]

Unfortunately, we cannot, on the one hand, reject secondary sexist practices because of their contingent and perhaps unintended discriminatory effects, and, on the other hand, accept extenuations such as these for a policy which would, in practice, discriminate unfairly against (white) men. These

---

[23]See Bayles and Sher, respectively.

[24]Irvine Thalberg, "Reverse Discrimination and the Future," *The Philosophical Forum* 5, no. 2: 307.

[25]See Marlene Gerber Fried, "In Defense of Preferential Hiring," *The Philosophical Forum* 5, no. 2: 316.

[26]Charles King, "A Problem Concerning Discrimination," *Reason Papers*, no. 2 (Fall 1975), p. 92.

[27]Thomas Nagel, "Equal Treatment and Compensatory Justice," *Philosophy & Public Affairs* 2, no. 4 (Summer 1973): 348–363, especially p. 353.

[28]Fried, p. 318.

other sources of injustice are real enough; but this does not alter the fact that if reverse discrimination were practiced to the extent that certain men's chances of success were reduced to below those enjoyed, on the average, by comparably qualified women, then it would at least give every appearance of being unfair to those men. After all, the primary insight necessary for recognizing the injustice of secondary sexist policies is that a policy must be judged, at least in part, by its consequences in practice, regardless of whether or not these consequences are a stated or intended part of the policy. If a given policy results in serious and extensive injustice, then it is no excuse that this injustice has its roots in deeper social injustices which are not themselves easily amenable to change, at least not if there is any feasible way of altering the policy so as to lessen the resulting injustice.

I think we may conclude that while proportional quotas for the hiring of women are justified both on the basis of the merit principle and as a way of improving the overall fairness of the competition, it is considerably more difficult to justify the use of higher quotas. The distinction between such weak quotas and higher quotas is crucial, since although higher quotas have in practice rarely been implemented, the apparent injustice implied by what are typically *assumed* to be higher quotas has generated a backlash which threatens to undermine affirmative action entirely. If quotas are abandoned, or if they are nominally adopted but never enforced, then employers will be free to continue using secondary and even primary sexist hiring criteria, and it is probable that none of us will see the day when women enjoy job opportunities commensurate with their abilities and qualifications.

34/Preferential Treatment

Richard A. Wasserstrom

The instrumental perspective does not require much theoretical attention beyond what has already been said.[1] It is concerned with the question of what would be the best way to move from the social realities to the ideal. The most salient considerations are, therefore, empirical ones—although of a complex sort.

Affirmative action programs, even those which require explicit racial and sexual minimum quotas, are most plausibly assessed from within this perspective.[2] If the social reality is one of racial and sexual oppression—as I think it is—and if, for example, the most defensible picture of a nonracist, nonsexist society is the one captured by the assimilationist ideal, then the chief and perhaps only question to be asked of such programs is whether they are well suited to bring about movement from the existing state of affairs to a closer approximation of the assimilationist ideal. If it turns out, for example, that explicit racial quotas will in fact exacerbate racial prejudice and hostility, thereby making it harder rather than easier to achieve an assimilationist society, that is a reason which counts against the instrumental desirability of racial quotas. This would not settle the matter, of course, for there might also be respects in which racial quotas would advance the coming of the assimilationist society, e.g., by redistributing wealth and positions of power and authority to blacks, thereby creating previously unavailable role models, and by putting persons with different perspectives and interests in a position more directly to influence the course of social change.

[1][The perspective from which one tries to decide the best or most appropriate way to move to an ideal society. See pp. 14–20, this volume—ed.]

[2]Although ostensibly empirical, the question of whether and to what extent affirmative action programs "work" has a substantial nonempirical component. There are many variables that can plausibly be taken into account, and many differing weights to be assigned to these variables. Consequently, how one marshalls and assesses the "evidence" concerning which programs "work" and which do not, has at least as much to do with whether one believes that the programs are or are not justifiable on other grounds as it does with a disinterested marshalling of the "facts." *See, e.g.,* T. SOWELL, AFFIRMATIVE ACTION RECONSIDERED 34–40 (1975); N. GLAZER, AFFIRMATIVE DISCRIMINATION: ETHNIC INEQUALITY AND PUBLIC POLICY (1975).

From "Racism, Sexism, and Preferential Treatment: An Approach to the Topics," *UCLA Law Review* (February 1977), pp. 615–622. Copyright © 1977 by Richard A. Wasserstrom. Reprinted by permission. Footnotes have been renumbered. Earlier sections of this article are reprinted on pages 5–20, this volume—ed.

But persons might be unhappy with this way of thinking about affirmative action—and especially about quotas. They might have three different but related objections. The first objection would be that there are more questions to be asked about means or instruments than whether they will work to bring about a certain end. In particular, there is also the question of the *way* they will work as means to bring about the end. Some means may be morally objectionable as means, no matter how noble or desirable the end. That is the good sense in the slogan: The ends do not justify the means.

I certainly agree with this general point. It is the application to particular cases, for example this one, that vitiates the force of the objection. Indeed, given the way I have formulated the instrumental perspective, I have left a good deal of room for the moral assessment of means to be built in. That is to say, I have described the question as one of the instrumental "desirability," not just the "efficaciousness" in any narrow sense, of the means that are selected.

The second objection is rather more sophisticated. Someone might say something like this: it is just wrong in principle ever to take an individual's race or sex into account. Persons just have a right never to have race or sex considered. No reasons need be given; we just know they have that right. This is a common way of talking today in moral philosophy, but I find nothing persuasive or attractive about it. I do not know that persons have such a right. I do not "see" it. Instead, I think I can give and have given reasons in my discussion of the social realities as well as my discussion of ideals for why they might be said to have rights not to be treated in certain ways. That is to say, I have tried to show something of what was wrong about the way blacks and women were and are treated in our culture. I have not simply proclaimed the existence of a right.

Another form of this objection is more convincing. The opponent of quotas and affirmative action programs might argue that any proponent of them is guilty of intellectual inconsistency, if not racism or sexism. At times past, employers, universities, and many social institutions did have racial or sexual quotas, when they did not practice overt racial or sexual exclusion, and it was clear that these quotas were pernicious. What is more, many of those who were most concerned to bring about the eradication of those racial quotas are now untroubled by the new programs which reinstitute them. And this is just a terrible sort of intellectual inconsistency which at worst panders to the fashion of the present moment and at best replaces intellectual honesty and integrity with understandable but misguided sympathy. The assimilationist ideal requires ignoring race and sex as distinguishing features of people.

Such an argument is a useful means by which to bring out the way in which the analysis I am proposing can respond. The racial quotas and practices of racial exclusion that were an integral part of the fabric of our culture, and which are still to some degree a part of it, were pernicious. They were a grievous wrong and it was and is important that all morally concerned individuals work for their eradication from our social universe. The racial quotas that are a part of contemporary affirmative action programs are, I think, commendable and right. But even if I am mistaken about the latter, the point is that there is no inconsistency involved in holding both views. For even if contemporary schemes of racial quotas are wrong, they are wrong for reasons very different from those that made quotas against blacks wrong.

As I have argued, the fundamental evil of programs that discriminated against blacks or women was that these programs were a part of a larger social universe which systematically maintained an unwarranted and unjust scheme which concentrated power, authority, and goods in the hands of white males. Programs which excluded or limited the access of blacks and women into these institutions were wrong both because of the direct consequences of these programs on the individuals most affected and because the system of racial and sexual superiority of which they were constituents was an immoral one in that it severely and without any adequate justification restricted the capacities, autonomy, and happiness of those who were members of the less favored categories.

Whatever may be wrong with today's affirmative action programs and quota systems, it should be clear that the evil, if any, is not the same. Racial and sexual minorities do not constitute the dominant social group. Nor is the conception of who is a fully developed member of the moral and social community one of an individual who is either female or black. Quotas which prefer women or blacks do not add to the already relatively overabundant supply of resources and opportunities at the disposal of white males. If racial quotas are to be condemned or if affirmative action programs are to be abandoned, it should be because they will not work well to achieve the desired result. It is not because they seek either to perpetuate an unjust society or to realize a corrupt ideal.

Still a third version of this objection might be that when used in affirmative action programs, race and sex are categories that are too broad in scope. They include some persons who do not have the appropriate characteristics and exclude some persons who do. If affirmative action programs made race and sex the sole criteria of selection, this would certainly be a plausible objection, although even here it is very important to see that the objection is no different in kind from that which applies to all legislation and rules. For example, in restricting the franchise to those who are eighteen and older, we exclude some who have all the relevant qualifications for voting and we include some who lack them. The fit can never be precise. Affirmative action programs almost always make race or sex a *relevant* condition, not a conclusive one. As such, they function the way all other classificatory schemes do. The defect, if there is one, is generic, and not peculiar to programs such as these.

There is finally the third objection: that affirmative action programs are wrong because they take race and sex into account rather than the only thing that matters—an individual's qualifications. Someone might argue that what is wrong with these programs is that they deprive persons who are more qualified by bestowing benefits on those who are less qualified in virtue of their being either black or female.

There are many things wrong with the objection based on qualifications. Not the least of them is that we do not live in a society in which there is even the serious pretense of a qualification requirement for many jobs of substantial power and authority. Would anyone claim that the persons who comprise the judiciary are there because they are the most qualified lawyers or the most qualified persons to be judges? Would anyone claim that Henry Ford II is the head of the Ford Motor Company because he is the most qualified person for the job? Or that the one hundred men who are Senators are the most qualified persons to be Senators? Part of what is wrong with even talking about qualifications and merit is that the argument derives some of its force from the erroneous notion that we would have a meritocracy were it not for affirmative action.[3]

[3]The point is a more general one than the few random examples suggest. The more prestige, power, wealth or influence is attached to the job, the less likely it is that there are specifiable qualifications that make it easy to determine who in fact is the most qualified. There are, to be sure, minimum qualifications. But these are satisfied by a large number of individuals. Moreover, for most of these positions the notion simply does not exist that the most qualified individuals from among this large class are the ones who deserve to be selected, *e.g.*, the dean of a college or the head of a federal agency.

But there is a theoretical difficulty as well, which cuts much more deeply into the argument about qualifications. The argument cannot be that the most qualified ought to be selected because the most qualified will perform most efficiently, for this instrumental approach was what the opponent of affirmative action thought was wrong with taking the instrumental perspective in the first place. To be at all persuasive, the argument must be that those who are the most qualified *deserve* to receive the benefits (the job, the place in law school, etc.) because they are the most qualified. And there is just no reason to think that this is a correct premise. There is a logical gap in the inference that the person who is most qualified to perform a task, *e.g.*, be a good student, deserves to be admitted as a student. Of course, those who deserve to be admitted should be admitted. But why do the most qualified deserve anything? There is just no necessary connection between academic merit (in the sense of qualification) and deserving to be a member of a student body. Suppose, for instance, that there is only one tennis court in the community. Is it clear that the two best tennis players ought to be the ones permitted to use it? Why not those who were there first? Or those who will enjoy playing the most? Or those who are the worst and therefore need the greatest opportunity to practice? Or those who have the chance to play least frequently?

We might, of course, have a rule that says that the best tennis players get to use the court before the others. Under such a rule, the best players would deserve the court more than the poorer ones. But that is just to push the inquiry back one stage. Is there any reason to think that good tennis players are entitled to such a rule? Indeed, the arguments that might be given for or against such a rule are many and varied. And few if any of the arguments that might support the rule would depend upon a connection between ability and desert.

Someone might reply that the most able students deserve to be admitted to the university because all of their earlier schooling was a kind of competition, with university admission being the prize awarded to the winners. They deserve to be admitted because that is what the rule of the competition provides. In addition, it would be unfair now to exclude them in favor of others, given the reasonable expectations they developed about the way in which their industry and performance would be rewarded. Minority admission programs, which inevitably prefer some who are less qualified over some who are more qualified, all possess this flaw.

There are several problems with this argument. The most substantial of them is that it is an empirically implausible picture of our social world. Most of what are regarded as the decisive characteristics for higher education have a great deal to do with things over which the individual has neither control nor responsibility: such things as home environment, socioeconomic class of parents, and, of course, the quality of the primary and secondary schools attended. Since individuals do not deserve having had any of these things vis-à-vis other individuals, they do not, for the most part, deserve their qualifications. And since they do not deserve their abilities they do not in any strong sense deserve to be admitted because of their abilities.

To be sure, if there is a rule which connects, say, performance at high school with admission to college, then there is a weak sense in which those who do well at high school deserve, for that reason alone, to be admitted to college. But then, as I have said, the merits of this rule need to be explored and defended. In addition, if persons have built up or relied upon their reasonable expectations concerning performance and admission, they have a claim to be admitted on this ground as well. But it is certainly not obvious that these claims of desert are any stronger or more compelling than competing claims based upon the needs of or advantages to women or blacks.[4]

Qualifications are also potentially relevant in at least three other respects. In the first place, there is some minimal set of qualifications without which the benefits of participation in higher education cannot be obtained by the individuals involved. In the second place, the qualifications of the students within the university will affect to some degree or other the benefits obtainable to anyone within it. And finally, the qualifications of students within the university may also affect the way the university functions vis-à-vis the rest of the world. The university will do some things better and some things worse, depending upon the qualifications of those who make it up. If the students are "less qualified," teachers may have to spend more time with them and less time on research. Some teachers may find

teaching now more interesting. Others may find it less so. But all these considerations only establish that qualifications, in this sense, are relevant, not that they are decisive. This is wholly consistent with the claim that minority group membership is also a relevant but not a decisive consideration when it comes to matters of admission.[5] And that is all that virtually any preferential treatment program—even one with quotas—has ever tried to claim.

I do not think I have shown programs of preferential treatment to be right and desirable, because I have not sought to answer all of the empirical questions that may be relevant. But I have, I hope, shown that it is wrong to think that contemporary affirmative action programs are racist or sexist in the centrally important sense in which many past and present features of our society have been and are racist and sexist. The social realities do make a fundamental difference. It is also wrong to think that these programs are in any strong sense either unjust or unprincipled. The case for programs of preferential treatment can plausibly rest on the view that the programs are not unfair (except in the weak sense described above) to white males, and on the view that it is unfair to continue the present set of unjust—often racist and sexist—institutions that comprise the social reality. The case for these programs also rests on the thesis that it is fair, given the distribution of power and influence in the United States, to redistribute in this way, and that such programs may reasonably be viewed as useful means by which to achieve very significant social ideals.

Conclusion

I do not think that the topics of racism, sexism, and preferential treatment are easily penetrable. Indeed, I have tried to show that they contain complicated issues which must be carefully distinguished and discussed. But I also believe, and have tried to show, that the topics are susceptible to rational analysis. There is a difference between problems that are difficult because confusion is present, and problems that are difficult because a number of distinct ideas and arguments must be considered. It is my ambition to have moved thinking about the topics and issues in question some distance from the first to the second of these categories.

[4] I prefer to focus on these aspects of desert and considerations of fairness rather than principles of compensation and reparation because I can thereby bypass the claim that compensation or reparation is being exacted from the wrong individuals, because they are innocent of any wrongdoing, and causally unconnected with the injuries suffered. I do think the causal link is often present and the claim of innocence often suspect. But my analysis puts these issues to one side. For a discussion of some of the literature that discusses the issues of compensation and reparation, see, e.g., Boxill, The Morality of Reparation, 2 Soc. THEORY & PRAC. 113 (1972).

[5] The preceding six paragraphs appear in substantially the same form in Wasserstrom, ["The University and the Case for Preferential Treatment," 13 Am. Phil. J. 165 (1976),] at 166–67.

Part Four
Theoretical Frameworks
for Women's Liberation

35/Toward a Phenomenology of Feminist Consciousness
Sandra Lee Bartky

I

Contemporary feminism has many faces. The best attempts so far to deal with the scope and complexity of the movement have divided feminists along ideological lines.[1] Thus, liberal, Marxist, neo-Marxist and "radical" feminists have differing sets of beliefs about the origin and nature of sexism and thus quite different prescriptions for the proper way of eliminating it. But this way of understanding the nature of the women's movement, however indispensable, is not the only way. While I would not hesitate to call someone a feminist who supported a program for the liberation of women and who held beliefs about the nature of contemporary society appropriate to such a political program, something crucial to an understanding of feminism is overlooked if its definition is so restricted.

To be a feminist, one has first to become one. For many feminists, this takes the form of a profound personal transformation, an experience which goes far beyond that sphere of human activity ordinarily regarded as "political." This transforming experience, which cuts across the ideological divisions within the women's movement, is complex and multi-faceted. In the course of undergoing the transformation to which I refer, the feminist changes her *behavior*: she makes new friends; she responds differently to people and events; her habits of consumption change; sometimes she alters her living arrangements or, more dramatically, her whole style

of life. These changes in behavior go hand in hand with changes in *consciousness*:[2] to become a feminist is to develop a radically altered consciousness of oneself, of others, and of what for lack of a better term I shall call "social reality."[3] Feminists themselves have a name for the struggle to clarify and to hold fast to this way of apprehending things: they call it "consciousness-raising." A "raised" consciousness on the part of women is not only a causal factor in the emergence of the feminist movement itself but also an important part of its political program: many small discussion groups exist solely for the purpose of consciousness-raising. But what happens when one's consciousness is raised? What is a developed feminist consciousness *like*? In this paper, I would like to examine not the full global experience of liberation, involving as it does new ways of being as well as new ways of perceiving, but, more narrowly, those distinctive ways of perceiving which characterize feminist consciousness. What follows will be a highly tentative attempt at a morphology of feminist consciousness: without claiming to have discovered them all, I shall try to identify some structural features of that altered way of apprehending oneself and the world which is both product and content of a raised consciousness. But first, I would like to make some very general remarks about the nature of this consciousness and about the conditions under which it emerges.

Although the oppression of women is uni-

I would like to thank members of the Society for Women in Philosophy, to whom I read an earlier version of this paper, not only for many helpful critical comments but for their willingness to share experiences both of discrimination and of personal transformation.

[1]"Four Views of Women's Liberation," read by Alison Jaggar at the American Philosophical Association meeting, Western Division, 4–6 May 1972. [See immediately following article, this volume, pp. 258–265—eds.]

[2]In what follows, the consciousness I discuss is the consciousness of a feminist who is female. I do not discuss the modes of awareness, whatever they may be, of men who are feminists.

[3]By "social reality" I mean the ensemble of formal and informal relationships with other people in which we are now enmeshed or in which we are likely to become enmeshed, together with the attitudes, values, types of communication, and conventions which accompany such relationships. "Social reality" is the social life world, the social environment as it is present to my consciousness.

From *Social Theory and Practice* 3 (Fall 1975). Reprinted by permission.

versal, feminist consciousness is not. While I am not sure that I could demonstrate the necessity of its appearance in this time and place and not in another, it is possible to identify two features of current social reality which, if not necessary and sufficient, are at least necessary conditions for its emergence. These features constitute, in addition, much of the *content* of this consciousness. I refer first to the existence of what Marxists call "contradictions" in our society and second, to the presence, due to these contradictions, of specific conditions which permit a significant alteration in the status of women.

In Marxist theory, the stage is set for social change when existing forms of social interaction —property relations as well as values, attitudes, and beliefs—come into conflict with new social relations which are generated by changes in the mode of production.

At a certain stage of their development, the material forces of production in society come in conflict with the existing relations of production or—what is but a legal expression for the same thing—with the property relations within which they had been at work before. From forms of development of the forces of production these relations turn into their fetters. Then comes the period of social revolution. [4]

To date, no one has offered a comprehensive analysis of those alterations in the socioeconomic structure of contemporary American society which have made possible the emergence of feminist consciousness. [5] This task is made doubly difficult by the fact that these changes are no convenient object for dispassionate historical investigation but part of the fluid set of circumstances in which each of us find our way from one day to another and whose ultimate direction is as yet unclear.

Nevertheless, certain changes in contemporary social life are too significant to escape notice: the development of cheap and efficient types of contraception; the reentry, beginning in the early

fifties, of millions of women into the market economy; the growing and unprecedented participation of women in higher education during the same period; innovations in production (such as prepared foods) to ease the burden of housekeeping; a general undermining of traditional family life; and the social upheavals and mass movements of the 1960s. When the position of women within the social whole is altered, new conceptions of self and society come directly into conflict with older ideas about a woman's role, her destiny, and even her "nature."

Clearly, any adequate account of the "contradictions" of late capitalism—i.e., of the conflicts, the instabilities, the ways in which some parts of the social whole are out of phase with others—would be a complex and elaborate task. But even in the absence of a comprehensive analysis, it is essential to understand as concretely as possible how the contradictory factors we are able to identify are lived and suffered by particular people. The facts of economic development are crucial to an understanding of any phenomenon of social change, but they are not the phenomenon in its entirety. While only dogmatic Marxists have regarded consciousness as a mere reflection of material conditions and therefore uninteresting as an object for study in and of itself, even Marxist scholars of a more humane cast of mind have not paid sufficient attention to the ways in which the social and economic tensions they study are played out in the lives of concrete individuals. There is an anguished consciousness—an inner uncertainty and confusion which characterizes human subjectivity in periods of social change (and I shall contend that feminist consciousness, to some degree, is "anguished")—of whose existence Marxist scholars seem largely unaware. Indeed, the only sort of consciousness that is discussed with any frequency in the literature is "class consciousness," a somewhat unclear idea whose meaning Marxists themselves dispute. The incorporation of a phenomenological perspective into Marxist analysis is necessary if the proper dialectical relations between human consciousness and the material modes of production are ever to be grasped in their full concreteness.

Women have long lamented their condition, but a lament, pure and simple, need not be an expression of feminist consciousness. As long as their situation is apprehended as natural, inevitable, and inescapable, women's consciousness of themselves, no matter how alive to insult and inferiority, is not yet feminist consciousness. This conscious-

[4]Karl Marx, *A Contribution to the Critique of Political Economy* (Chicago: Charles H. Kerr & Co., 1904), pp. 11–12.

[5]See, however, Margaret Benston, "The Political Economy of Women's Liberation," *Monthly Review*, vol. 21, no. 4; also Valerie K. Oppenheimer, *The Female Labor Force in the United States: Demographic and Economic Factors Governing Its Growth and Changing Composition* (Berkeley: University of California Press, 1970). Highly recommended, too, is the special issue, "The Political Economy of Women," *Review of Radical Political Economics*, vol. 4, no. 3 (July 1972), as well as Juliet Mitchell, *Woman's Estate* (New York: Vintage Books, 1973), pp. 19–39.

ness, as I contended earlier, emerges only when the partial or total liberation of women is possible. This possibility is more than a mere accidental accompaniment of feminist consciousness: feminist consciousness *is* the apprehension of possibility. The very *meaning* of what the feminist apprehends is illuminated by the light of what ought to be: the given situation is first understood in terms of a state of affairs not yet actual and in this sense a possibility, a state of affairs in which what is given would be negated and radically transformed. To say that feminist consciousness is the experience in a certain way of certain specific contradictions in the social order is to say that the feminist apprehends certain features of social reality *as* intolerable, as to be rejected in behalf of a transforming project for the future. "It is on the day that we can conceive of a different state of affairs that a new light falls on our troubles and we *decide* that these are unbearable."[6] What Sartre would call her "transcendence," her project of negation and transformation, makes possible what are specifically feminist ways of apprehending contradictions in the social order. Women workers who are not feminists know that they receive unequal pay for equal work, but they may think that the arrangement is just; the feminist sees this situation as an instance of exploitation and an occasion for struggle. Feminists are not aware of different things than other people; they are aware of the same things differently. Feminist consciousness, it might be ventured, turns a "fact" into a "contradiction"; often, features of social reality are only apprehended *as* contradictory from the vantage point of a radical project of transformation.

Thus, we understand what we are and where we are in the light of what we are not yet. But the perspective from which I understand the world must be rooted in the world, too. That is, my comprehension of what I and my world can become must take account of what they *are*. The possibility of a transformed society that allows the feminist to grasp the significance of her current situation must somehow be contained in the way she apprehends her current situation: the contradictory situation in which she finds herself is perceived *as* unstable, as carrying within itself the seeds of its own dissolution. There is of course no way of telling, by a mere examination of some form of consciousness, whether the possibilities it incorporates are realizable or not; this

depends on whether the situation is such as to contain within itself the sorts of material conditions that will bring to fruition a human expectation. To sum up, the relationship between consciousness and concrete circumstances can best be described as "dialectical." Feminist consciousness is more than a mere reflection of external material conditions, for the transforming and negating perspective which it incorporates first allows these conditions to be revealed as the conditions they *are*—that is, as contradictions. The mere apprehension of some state of affairs as intolerable does not, of course, transform it. This only power can do.

II

Feminist consciousness is consciousness of *victimization*. To apprehend oneself as victim is to be aware of an alien and hostile force which is responsible for the blatantly unjust treatment of women and for a stifling and oppressive system of sex-roles; it is to be aware, too, that this victimization, in no way earned or deserved, is an *offense*. For some feminists, this hostile power is "society" or "the system"; for others, it is, simply, men. Victimization is impartial, even though its damage is done to each of us personally. One is victimized as a woman, as one among many, and in the realization that others are made to suffer in the same way that I am made to suffer lies the beginning of a sense of solidarity with other victims. To come to see oneself as victim is not to see things in the same old way while merely judging them differently or to superimpose new attitudes on things like frosting on a cake: the consciousness of victimization is immediate and revelatory; it allows us to discover what social reality really *is*.

The consciousness of victimization is a divided consciousness. To see myself as victim is to know that I have already sustained injury, that I live exposed to injury, that I have been at worst mutilated, at best diminished, in my being. But at the same time, feminist consciousness is a joyous consciousness of one's own power, of the possibility of unprecedented personal growth and of the release of energy long suppressed. Thus, feminist consciousness is consciousness both of weakness and of strength. But this division in the way we apprehend ourselves has a positive effect, for it leads to the search both for ways of overcoming those weaknesses in ourselves which support the sys-

[6]Jean-Paul Sartre, *Being and Nothingness* (New York: Philosophical Library, 1956), p. 531.

tem and for direct forms of struggle against the system itself.

But consciousness of victimization is a consciousness divided in still another way. This second division does not have the positive effect of the first, for its tendency is to produce confusion, guilt, and paralysis in the political sphere. The awareness I have of myself as victim rests uneasily alongside the awareness that I am at the same time more privileged than the overwhelming majority of the world's population. I enjoy both white-skin privilege and the advantage of comparative wealth.[7] I have some measure of control, however small, over my own productive and reproductive life. The implications of this split in consciousness for feminist political theory and the obstacles it presents to the formulation of a coherent feminist strategy are frequently mentioned in the literature of the women's movement. It is not my task in this paper to develop a conception of political praxis appropriate to a consciousness of oppression so divided; I only intend to identify this division. But two things follow upon consideration of the phenomenon of the "guilty victim": first, that an analysis of "psychological" oppression is essential to feminist political theory; second, that any feminist analysis that ignores the guilty-victim phenomenon or else sees in it the expression of a low level of political awareness will fail to do justice to the disturbing complexity of feminist experience.

To apprehend myself as victim in a sexist society is to know that there are few places where I can hide, that I can be attacked anywhere, at any time, by virtually anyone. Innocent chatter—the currency of ordinary social life—or a compliment ("You don't think like a woman"), the well-intentioned advice of psychologists, the news item, the joke, the cosmetics advertisement—none of these is what it is or what it was. Each is revealed (depending on the circumstances in which it appears) as a threat, an insult, an affront—as a reminder, however subtle, that I belong to an inferior caste—in short, as an instrument of oppression or as the articulation of a sexist institution. Since many things are not what they seem to be, and since many apparently harmless sorts of things can suddenly exhibit a sinister dimension, social reality is revealed as *deceptive*.

Contemporary thinkers as diverse as Heidegger and Marcuse have written about the ambiguity and mystification which are so prominent a feature of contemporary social life. Feminists are alive to one certain dimension of a society which seems to specialize in duplicity—the sexist dimension. But the deceptive nature of this aspect of social reality itself makes the feminist's experience of life, her anger and sense of outrage, difficult to communicate to the insensitive or uninitiated: it increases her frustration and reinforces her isolation. There is nothing ambiguous about racial segregation or economic discrimination: it is far less difficult to point to these abuses than it is to show how, for example, the "tone" of a news story can transform it from a piece of reportage into a refusal to take women's political struggles seriously or even into a species of punishment. The male reporter for a large local daily paper who described the encounter of Betty Friedan and the Republican Women's Caucus at Miami never actually used the word "fishwife" nor did he say outright that the political struggles of women are worthy of ridicule; he merely chose to describe the actions of the individuals involved in such a way as to make them appear ridiculous. (Nor, it should be added, did he fail to describe Ms. Friedan as "petite.") It is difficult to characterize the tone of an article, the patronizing implications of a remark, the ramifications of some accepted practice, and it is even more difficult to describe what it is like to be bombarded ten or a hundred times daily with these only half-submerged weapons of a sexist system. This, no doubt, is one reason why, when trying to make a case for feminism, we find ourselves referring almost exclusively to the "hard data" of discrimination, like unequal pay, rather than to those pervasive intimations of inferiority which rankle at least as much.

Many people know that things are not what they seem to be. The feminist knows that the thing revealed in its truth at last will, likely as not, turn out to be a thing that threatens or demeans. But however unsettling it is to have to find one's way about in a world that dissimulates, it is worse to be unable to determine the nature of what is happening at all. Feminist consciousness is often afflicted with category confusion—an inability to know how to classify things. The timidity I display at departmental meetings, for instance—is it nothing more than a personal shortcoming, or is it a typically female trait, a shared inability to display aggression, even verbal aggression? And why is the suggestion I make ignored? Is it intrinsically unintelligent or is it because I am a woman and therefore not to be taken seri-

---

[7]Clearly, this is not a description of any feminist consciousness whatsoever. Some feminists must contend with poverty, racism and imperialism as part of their oppression as women.

ously? The persistent need I have to make myself "attractive," to fix my hair and put on lipstick—is it the false need of a chauvinized woman, encouraged since infancy to identify her value as a person with her attractiveness in the eyes of men? Or does it express a wholesome need to express love for one's own body by adorning it, a behavior common in primitive societies, allowed us but denied to men in our own still-puritan culture? Uncertainties such as these make it difficult to decide how to struggle and whom to struggle against, but the very possibility of understanding one's own motivations, character traits and impulses is also at stake. In sum, feminists suffer what might be called a "double ontological shock": first, the realization that what is really happening is quite different from what appears to be happening; and second, the frequent inability to tell what is really happening at all.

Since discriminatory sex-role differentiation is a major organizing principle of our society, the list of its carriers and modes of communication would be unending: the sorts of things already mentioned were chosen at random. Little political, professional, educational, or leisure-time activity is free of the blight of sexism. Few personal relationships are free of it. Feminist consciousness is something like paranoia, especially when the feminist first begins to apprehend the full extent of sex discrimination and the subtle and various ways in which it is enforced. The System and its agents are everywhere, even inside her own mind, since she can fall prey to self-doubt or to a temptation to compliance. In response to this, the feminist becomes vigilant and suspicious: her apprehension of things, especially of direct or indirect communication with other people, is characterized by what I shall call "wariness." Wariness is anticipation of the possibility of attack, of affront or insult, of disparagement, ridicule, or the hurting blindness of others; it is a mode of experience which anticipates experience in a certain way. While it is primarily the established order of things of which the feminist is wary, she is wary of herself, too. She must be always on the alert lest her pervasive sense of injury provoke in her without warning some public display of emotion, such as violent weeping. Many feminists are perpetually wary lest their own anger be transformed explosively into behavior too hostile to be prudently or safely displayed.

Some measure of wariness is a constant in feminist experience, but the degree to which it is present will be a function of other factors in a feminist's life—her level of political involvement,

perhaps, the extent of her sensitivity to the social milieu, or the degree to which she allows resignation or humor to take away the sting. Characteristic of this kind of consciousness, too, is the alternation of a heightened awareness of the limitations placed on one's free development with a duller self-protecting sensibility without which it would be difficult to function in a society like ours.

The revelation of the deceptive character of social reality brings with it another transformation in the way the social milieu is present in feminist experience. Just as so many apparently innocent things are really devices to enforce compliance, so are many "ordinary" sorts of situations transformed into opportunities or *occasions* for struggle against the system. In a light-hearted mood, I embark upon a Christmas-shopping expedition, only to have it turn, as if independent of my will, into an occasion for striking a blow against sexism. On holiday from political struggle, I have abandoned myself to the richly sensuous atmosphere of Marshall Field's. I have been wandering about the toy department, looking at chemistry sets and miniature ironing boards. Then, unbidden, the following thought flashes into my head: what if, just this once, I send a doll to my nephew and an erector set to my niece? Will this confirm the growing suspicion in my family that I am a crank? What if the children themselves misunderstand my gesture and covet one another's gifts? Worse, what if the boy believes that I have somehow insulted him? The shopping trip turned occasion for resistance now becomes a *test*. I will have to answer for this, once it becomes clear that Marshall Field's has not unwittingly switched the labels. My husband will be embarrassed. A didactic role will be thrust upon me, even though I have determined earlier that the situation was not ripe for consciousness-raising. The special ridicule reserved for movement women will be heaped upon me at the next family party—all in good fun, of course.

Ordinary social life presents to the feminist an unending sequence of such occasions, and each occasion is a test. It is not easy to live under the strain of constant testing. Some tests we pass with honor, but often as not we fail, and the price of failure is self-reproach and the shame of having copped out. To complicate things further, much of the time it is not clear what criteria would allow us to distinguish the honorable outcome of an occasion from a dishonorable one. Must I seize every opportunity? May I never take the easy way out? Is what I call prudence and good sense merely cowardice? On the occasion in question, I compromised and sent both children musical instruments.

The transformation of day-to-day living into a series of invitations to struggle has the important consequence for the feminist that she finds herself, for a while at least, in an ethical and existential impasse. She no longer knows what sort of person she ought to be, and therefore she does not know what she ought to do. One moral paradigm is called into question by the laborious and often obscure emergence of another. The ethical issues involved in my shopping trip were relatively trivial, but this is not true of all occasions. One thinks of Nora's decision in *A Doll's House* to leave her husband and children and seek independence and self-fulfillment on her own. Ibsen, her creator, betrays a certain lack of sensitivity to feminist experience: Nora makes the decision too easily; a real-life Nora would have suffered more.

To whom will a woman in such a predicament turn for guidance? To choose a moral authority, as Sartre tells us, is already to anticipate what kind of advice we are prepared to take seriously. Having become aware of the self-serving way in which a male-dominated culture has defined goodness for the female, a woman may decide on principle that the person she wants to be will have little patience, meekness, complaisance, self-sacrifice, or any of the other "feminine" virtues. But will such a solution satisfy a reflective person? Must the duty I have to myself (if we have duties to ourselves) always win out over the duty I have to others? To develop feminist consciousness is to live a part of one's life in the sort of *ambiguous ethical situation* which existentialist writers have been most adept at describing. Here it might be objected that this feature of feminist experience is characteristic not of a fully emergent feminist consciousness but of periods of transition to such consciousness, that the feminist is a person who has chosen her moral paradigm and who no longer suffers the inner conflicts of those in ambiguous moral predicaments. I would deny this. Even the woman who has decided to be this new person and not that old one can be tormented by recurring doubts. Moreover, the pain inflicted on other persons in the course of finding one's way out of an existential impasse, one continues to inflict. The feminist is a person who, at the very least, has been marked by the experience of ethical ambiguity: she is a moral agent with a distinctive history.

Feminist consciousness, it was suggested earlier, can be understood as the negating and transcending awareness of one's own relationship to a society heavy with the weight of its own contradictions. The inner conflicts and divisions which make up so much of this experience are just the ways in which each of us, in the uniqueness of her own situation and personality, *lives* these contradictions. In sum, feminist consciousness is the consciousness of a being radically alienated from her world and often divided against herself, a being who sees herself as victim and whose victimization determines her being-in-the-world as resistance, wariness, and suspicion. Raw and exposed much of the time, she suffers from both ethical and ontological shock. Lacking a moral paradigm, sometimes unable to make sense of her own reactions and emotions, she is immersed in a social reality that exhibits to her an aspect of malevolent ambiguity. Many "ordinary" social situations and many human encounters organized for quite a different end she apprehends as occasions for struggle, as frequently exhausting tests of her will and resolve. She is an outsider to her society, to many of the people she loves, and to the still-unemancipated elements in her own personality.

But this picture is not as bleak as it appears; indeed, its "bleakness" would be seen in proper perspective had I described what things were like *before.* Coming to have a feminist consciousness is the experience of coming to know the truth about oneself and one's society. This experience, the acquiring of a "raised" consciousness, is an immeasurable advance over that false consciousness which it replaces. The scales fall from our eyes. We are no longer required to struggle against unreal enemies, to put others' interests ahead of our own, or to hate ourselves. We begin to see why it is that our images of ourselves are so depreciated and why so many of us are lacking any genuine conviction of personal worth. Understanding things makes it possible to change them. Coming to see things differently, we are able to make out possibilities for liberating collective action as well as unprecedented personal growth—possibilities that a deceptive sexist social reality has heretofore concealed. No longer do we have to practice upon ourselves that mutilation of intellect and personality required of individuals, caught up in an irrational and destructive system, who are nevertheless not permitted to regard it as anything but sane, progressive, and normal. Moreover, that feeling of alienation from established society which is so prominent a feature of feminist experience is counterbalanced by a new identification with women of all conditions and a growing sense of solidarity with other feminists. It is a fitting commentary on our society that the growth of feminist consciousness, in spite of its ambiguities, confusion, and trials, is apprehended by those in whom it develops as an experience of liberation.

36/Political Philosophies of Women's Liberation

Alison Jaggar

Feminists are united by a belief that the unequal and inferior social status of women is unjust and needs to be changed. But they are deeply divided about what changes are required. The deepest divisions are not differences about strategy or the kinds of tactics that will best serve women's interests; instead, they are differences about what *are* women's interests, what constitutes women's liberation.

Within the women's liberation movement, several distinct ideologies can be discerned. All[1] believe that justice requires freedom and equality for women, but they differ on such basic philosophical questions as the proper account of freedom and equality, the functions of the state, and the notion of what constitutes human, and especially female, nature. In what follows, I shall outline the feminist ideologies which are currently most influential and show how these give rise to differences on some particular issues. Doing this will indicate why specific debates over feminist questions cannot be settled in isolation but can only be resolved in the context of a theoretical framework derived from reflection on the fundamental issues of social and political philosophy.

The Conservative View

This is the position against which all feminists are in reaction. In brief, it is the view that the differential treatment of women, as a group, is not unjust. Conservatives admit, of course, that some individual women do suffer hardships, but they do not see this suffering as part of the systematic social oppression of women. Instead, the clear differences between women's and men's social roles are rationalized in one of two ways. Conservatives either claim that the female role is not inferior to that of the male, or they argue that women are inherently better adapted than men to the traditional female sex role. The former claim advocates a kind of sexual apartheid, typically described by such phrases as "complementary but equal"; the latter postulates an inherent inequality between the sexes.[2]

All feminists reject the first claim, and most feminists, historically, have rejected the second. However, it is interesting to note that, as we shall see later, some modern feminists have revived the latter claim.

Conservative views come in different varieties, but they all have certain fundamentals in common. All claim that men and women should fulfill different social functions, that these differences should be enforced by law where opinion and custom are insufficient, and that such action may be justified by reference to innate differences between men and women. Thus all sexual conservatives presuppose that men and women are inherently unequal in abilities, that the alleged difference in ability implies a difference in social function and that one of the main tasks of the state is to ensure that

---

This paper is a revised version of my "Four Views of Women's Liberation," read at the American Philosophical Association meeting, Western Division, 4–6 May, 1972.

[1] All except one: as we shall see later, Lesbian separatism is evasive on the question whether men should, even ultimately, be equal with women.

[2] The inequalities between the sexes are said to be both physical and psychological. Alleged psychological differences between the sexes include women's emotional instability, greater tolerance for boring detail, incapacity for abstract thought, and less aggression. Writers who have made such claims range from Rousseau (*Émile, or Education* [1762; translation, London: J. M. Dent, 1911]; see especially Book 5 concerning the education of "Sophie, or Woman"), through Schopenhauer (*The World As Will and Idea* and his essay "On Women"), Fichte (*The Science of Rights*), Nietzsche (*Thus Spake Zarathustra*), and Freud down to, in our own times, Steven Goldberg with *The Inevitability of Patriarchy* (New York: William Morrow, 1973–74).

---

the individual perform his or her proper social function. Thus, they argue, social differentiation between the sexes is not unjust, since justice not only allows but requires us to treat unequals unequally.

Liberal Feminism

In speaking of liberal feminism, I am referring to that tradition which received its classic expression in J. S. Mill's *The Subjection of Women* and which is alive today in various "moderate" groups, such as the National Organization for Women, which agitate for legal reform to improve the status of women.

The main thrust of the liberal feminist's argument is that an individual woman should be able to determine her social role with as great freedom as does a man. Though women now have the vote, the liberal sees that we are still subject to many constraints, legal as well as customary, which hinder us from success in the public worlds of politics, business and the professions. Consequently the liberal views women's liberation as the elimination of those constraints and the achievement of equal civil rights.

Underlying the liberal argument is the belief that justice requires that the criteria for allocating individuals to perform a particular social function should be grounded in the individual's ability to perform the tasks in question. The use of criteria such as "race, sex, religion, national origin or ancestry"[3] will normally not be directly relevant to most tasks. Moreover, in conformity with the traditional liberal stress on individual rights, the liberal feminist insists that each person should be considered separately in order that an outstanding individual should not be penalized for deficiencies that her sex as a whole might possess.[4]

This argument is buttressed by the classic liberal belief that there should be a minimum of state intervention in the affairs of the individual. Such a belief entails rejection of the paternalistic view that women's weakness requires that we be specially protected.[5] Even if relevant differences between women and men in general could be demonstrated, the existence of those differences still would not constitute a sufficient reason for allowing legal restrictions on women as a group. Even apart from the

possibility of penalizing an outstanding individual, the liberal holds that women's own good sense or, in the last resort, our incapacity to do the job will render legal prohibitions unnecessary.[6]

From this sketch it is clear that the liberal feminist interprets equality to mean that each individual, regardless of sex, should have an equal opportunity to seek whatever social position she or he wishes. Freedom is primarily the absence of legal constraints to hinder women in this enterprise. However, the modern liberal feminist recognizes that equality and freedom, construed in the liberal way, may not always be compatible. Hence, the modern liberal feminist differs from the traditional one in believing not only that laws should not discriminate against women, but that they should be used to make discrimination illegal. Thus she would outlaw unequal pay scales, prejudice in the admission of women to job-training programs and professional schools, and discrimination by employers in hiring practices. She would also outlaw such things as discrimination by finance companies in the granting of loans, mortgages, and insurance to women.

In certain areas, the modern liberal even appears to advocate laws which discriminate in favor of women. For instance, she may support the preferential hiring of women over men, or alimony for women unqualified to work outside the home. She is likely to justify her apparent inconsistency by claiming that such differential treatment is necessary to remedy past inequalities—but that it is only a temporary measure. With regard to (possibly paid) maternity leaves and the employer's obligation to reemploy a woman after such a leave, the liberal argues that the bearing of children has at least as good a claim to be regarded as a social service as does a man's military or jury obligation, and that childbearing should therefore carry corresponding rights to protection. The liberal also usually advocates the repeal of laws restricting contraception and abortion, and may demand measures to encourage the establishment of private day-care centers. However, she points out that none of these demands, nor the father's payment of child support, should really be regarded as discrimination in favor of women. It is only the customary assignment of responsibility for children to their mothers which makes it possible to overlook the fact that fathers have an equal obligation to provide and care for their children. Women's traditional responsibility for

---

[3] This is the language used by Title VII of the Civil Rights Act with Executive Order 11246, 1965, and Title IX.

[4] J. S. Mill, *The Subjection of Women* (1869; reprint ed., London: J. M. Dent, 1965), p. 236[See chapters 1 and 2, this volume, pp. 2–5, 52–59—eds.]

[5] Ibid., p. 243.

[6] Ibid., p. 235.

child care is culturally determined, not biologically inevitable—except for breast-feeding, which is now optional. Thus the liberal argues that if women are to participate in the world outside the home on equal terms with men, not only must our reproductive capacity come under our own control but, if we have children, we must be able to share the responsibility for raising them. In return, as an extension of the same principle of equal responsibility, the modern liberal supports compulsory military service for women so long as it is obligatory for men.

Rather than assuming that every apparent difference in interests and abilities between the sexes is innate, the liberal recognizes that such differences, if they do not result entirely from our education, are at least greatly exaggerated by it. By giving both sexes the same education, whether it be cooking or carpentry, the liberal claims that she is providing the only environment in which individual potentialities (and, indeed, genuine sexual differences) can emerge. She gives little weight to the possible charge that in doing this she is not liberating women but only imposing a different kind of conditioning. At the root of the liberal tradition is a deep faith in the autonomy of the individual which is incapable of being challenged within that framework.

In summary, then, the liberal views liberation for women as the freedom to determine our own social role and to compete with men on terms that are as equal as possible. She sees every individual as being engaged in constant competition with every other in order to maximize her or his own self-interest, and she claims that the function of the state is to see that such competition is fair by enforcing "equality of opportunity." The liberal does not believe that it is necessary to change the whole existing social structure in order to achieve women's liberation. Nor does she see it as being achieved simultaneously for all women; she believes that individual women may liberate themselves long before their condition is attained by all. Finally, the liberal claims that her concept of women's liberation also involves liberation for men, since men are not only removed from a privileged position but they are also freed from having to accept the entire responsibility for such things as the support of their families and the defense of their country.

Classical Marxist Feminism

On the classical Marxist view, the oppression of women is, historically and currently, a direct result of the institution of private property; therefore, it can only be ended by the abolition of that institution. Consequently, feminism must be seen as part of a broader struggle to achieve a communist society. Feminism is one reason for communism. The long-term interests of women are those of the working class.

For Marxists, everyone is oppressed by living in a society where a small class of individuals owns the means of production and hence is enabled to dominate the lives of the majority who are forced to sell their labor power in order to survive. Women have an equal interest with men in eliminating such a class society. However, Marxists also recognize that women suffer special forms of oppression to which men are *not* subject, and hence, insofar as this oppression is rooted in capitalism, women have additional reasons for the overthrow of that economic system.

Classical Marxists believe that the special oppression of women results primarily from our traditional position in the family. This excludes women from participation in "public" production and relegates us to domestic work in the "private" world of the home. From its inception right up to the present day, monogamous marriage was designed to perpetuate the consolidation of wealth in the hands of a few. Those few are men. Thus, for Marxists, an analysis of the family brings out the inseparability of class society from male supremacy. From the very beginning of surplus production, "the sole exclusive aims of monogamous marriage were to make the man supreme in the family, and to propagate, as the future heirs to his wealth, children indisputably his own."[7] Such marriage is "founded on the open or concealed domestic slavery of the wife,"[8] and is characterized by the familiar double standard which requires sexual fidelity from the woman but not from the man.

Marxists do not claim, of course, that women's oppression is a creation of capitalism. But they do argue that the advent of capitalism intensified the degradation of women and that the continuation of capitalism requires the perpetuation of this degradation. Capitalism and male supremacy each reinforce the other. Among the ways in which sexism benefits the capitalist system are: by providing a supply of cheap labor for industry and hence exerting

---

[7]Friedrich Engels, *The Origin of the Family, Private Property and the State* (1884; reprint ed., New York: International Publishers, 1942), pp. 57–58. [See chapter 5, this volume, pp. 172–180—ed.]

[8]Ibid., p. 65.

a downward pressure on all wages; by increasing the demand for the consumption goods on which women are conditioned to depend; and by allocating to women, for no direct pay, the performance of such socially necessary but unprofitable tasks as food preparation, domestic maintenance and the care of the children, the sick and the old.[9]

This analysis indicates the directions in which classical Marxists believe that women must move. "The first condition for the liberation of the wife is to bring the whole female sex back into public industry."[10] Only then will a wife cease to be economically dependent on her husband. But for woman's entry into public industry to be possible, fundamental social changes are necessary: all the work which women presently do—food preparation, child care, nursing, etc.—must come within the sphere of public production. Thus, whereas the liberal feminist advocates an egalitarian marriage, with each spouse shouldering equal responsibility for domestic work and economic support, the classical Marxist feminist believes that the liberation of women requires a more radical change in the family. Primarily, women's liberation requires that the economic functions performed by the family should be undertaken by the state. Thus the state should provide child care centers, public eating places, hospital facilities, etc. But all this, of course, could happen only under socialism. Hence it is only under socialism that married women will be able to participate fully in public life and end the situation where "within the family [the husband] is the bourgeois and the wife represents the proletariat."[11]

It should be noted that "the abolition of the monogamous family as the economic unit of society"[12] does not necessitate its disappearance as a social unit. Since "sexual love is by its nature exclusive,"[13] marriage will continue, but now it will no longer resemble an economic contract, as it has done hitherto in the property-owning classes. Instead, it will be based solely on "mutual inclination"[14] between a woman and a man who are now in reality, and not just formally, free and equal.

It is clear that classical Marxist feminism is based on very different philosophical presupposi-

tions from those of liberal feminism. Freedom is viewed not just as the absence of discrimination against women but rather as freedom from the coercion of economic necessity. Similarly, equality demands not mere equality of opportunity to compete against other individuals but rather approximate equality in the satisfaction of material needs. Hence, the classical Marxist feminist's view of the function of the state is very different from the view of the liberal feminist. Ultimately, the Marxist pays at least lip service to the belief that the state is an instrument of class oppression which eventually will wither away. In the meantime, she believes that it should undertake far more than the minimal liberal function of setting up fair rules for the economic race. Instead, it should take over the means of production and also assume those economic responsibilities that capitalism assigned to the individual family and that placed that woman in a position of dependence on the man. This view of the state presupposes a very different account of human nature from that held by the liberal. Instead of seeing the individual as fundamentally concerned with the maximization of her or his own self-interest, the classical Marxist feminist believes that the selfish and competitive aspects of our natures are the result of their systematic perversion in an acquisitive society. Viewing human nature as flexible and as reflecting the economic organization of society, she argues that it is necessary for women (indeed for everybody) to be comprehensively reeducated, and to learn that ultimately individuals have common rather than competing goals and interests.

Since she sees women's oppression as a function of the larger socioeconomic system, the classical Marxist feminist denies the possibility, envisaged by the liberal, of liberation for a few women on an individual level. However, she does agree with the liberal that women's liberation would bring liberation for men, too. Men's liberation would now be enlarged to include freedom from class oppression and from the man's traditional responsibility to "provide" for his family, a burden that under liberalism the man merely lightens by sharing it with his wife.

Radical Feminism

Radical feminism is a recent attempt to create a new conceptual model for understanding the many different forms of the social phenomenon of oppression in terms of the basic concept of sexual

---

[9]This is, of course, very far from being a complete account of the ways in which Marxists believe that capitalism benefits from sexism.

[10]Engels, op. cit., p. 66.

[11]Ibid., pp. 65–66.

[12]Ibid., p. 66.

[13]Ibid., p. 72.

[14]Ibid.

oppression. It is formulated by such writers as Ti-Grace Atkinson and Shulamith Firestone.[15]

Radical feminism denies the liberal claim that the basis of women's oppression consists in our lack of political or civil rights; similarly, it rejects the classical Marxist belief that basically women are oppressed because they live in a class society. Instead, in what seems to be a startling regression to conservatism, the radical feminist claims that the roots of women's oppression are biological. She believes that the origin of women's subjection lies in the fact that, as a result of the weakness caused by childbearing, we became dependent on men for physical survival. Thus she speaks of the origin of the family in apparently conservative terms as being primarily a biological rather than a social or economic organization.[16] The radical feminist believes that the physical subjection of women by men was historically the most basic form of oppression, prior rather than secondary to the institution of private property and its corollary, class oppression.[17] Moreover, she believes that the power relationships which develop within the biological family provide a model for understanding all other types of oppression such as racism and class society. Thus she reverses the emphasis of the classical Marxist feminist by explaining the development of class society in terms of the biological family rather than explaining the development of the family in terms of class society. She believes that the battles against capitalism and against racism are both subsidiary to the more fundamental struggle against sexism.

Since she believes that the oppression of women is basically biological, the radical feminist concludes that our liberation requires a biological revolution. She believes that only now, for the first time in history, is technology making it possible for women to be liberated from the "fundamental inequality of the bearing and raising of children." It is achieving this through the development of techniques of artificial reproduction and the consequent

possibility of diffusing the childbearing and child-raising role throughout society as a whole. Such a biological revolution is basic to the achievement of those important but secondary changes in our political, social and economic systems which will make possible the other prerequisites for women's liberation. As the radical feminist sees them, those other prerequisites are: the full self-determination, including economic independence, of women (and children); the total integration of women (and children) into all aspects of the larger society; and the freedom of all women (and children) to do whatever they wish to do sexually.[18]

Not only will technology snap the link between sex and reproduction and thus liberate women from our childbearing and child-raising function; the radical feminist believes that ultimately technology will liberate both sexes from the necessity to work. Individual economic burdens and dependencies will thereby be eliminated, along with the justification for compelling children to attend school. So both the biological and economic bases of the family will be removed by technology. The family's consequent disappearance will abolish the prototype of the social "role system,"[19] the most basic form, both historically and conceptually, of oppressive and authoritarian relationships. Thus, the radical feminist does not claim that women should be free to determine their own social roles: she believes instead that the whole "role system" must be abolished, even in its biological aspects.

The end of the biological family will also eliminate the need for sexual repression. Male homosexuality, lesbianism, and extramarital sexual intercourse will no longer be viewed in the liberal way as alternative options, outside the range of state regulation, in which the individual may or may not choose to participate. Nor will they be viewed, in the classical Marxist way, as unnatural vices, perversions resulting from the degrading influence of capitalist society.[20] Instead, even the categories of

---

[15]Ti-Grace Atkinson, "Radical Feminism" and "The Institution of Sexual Intercourse" in *Notes from the Second Year: Major Writings of the Radical Feminists,* ed. S. Firestone (N.Y., 1970); and Shulamith Firestone, *The Dialectic of Sex: The Case for Feminist Revolution* (N.Y.: Bantam Books; 1970). [See chapters 4 and 5, this volume, pp. 154–159, 200–205—eds.]

[16]Engels recognizes that early forms of the family were based on what he calls "natural" conditions, which presumably included the biological, but he claims that monogamy "was the first form of the family to be based, not on natural, but on economic conditions—on the victory of private property over primitive, natural communal property." Engels, op. cit., p. 57.

[17]Atkinson and Firestone do talk of women as a "political class," but not in Marx's classic sense where the criterion of an

individual's class membership is her/his relationship to the means of production. Atkinson defines a class more broadly as a group treated in some special manner by other groups: in the case of women, the radical feminists believe that women are defined as a "class" in virtue of our childbearing capacity. "Radical Feminism," op. cit., p. 24.

[18]These conditions are listed and explained in *The Dialectic of Sex,* pp. 206–9.

[19]"Radical Feminism," op. cit., p. 36.

[20]Engels often expresses an extreme sexual puritanism in *The Origin of the Family, Private Property and the State.* We have already seen his claim that "sexual love is by its nature exclusive." Elsewhere (p. 57) he talks about "the abominable practice of sodomy." Lenin is well known for the expression of similar views.

homosexuality and heterosexuality will be abandoned; the very "institution of sexual intercourse," where male and female each play a well-defined role, will disappear.[21] "Humanity could finally revert to its natural 'polymorphously perverse' sexuality."[22]

For the radical feminist, as for other feminists, justice requires freedom and equality for women. But for the radical feminist "equality" means not just equality under the law nor even equality in satisfaction of basic needs: rather, it means that women, like men, should not have to bear children. Correspondingly, the radical feminist conception of freedom requires not just that women should be free to compete, nor even that we should be free from material want and economic dependence on men; rather, freedom for women means that any woman is free to have close relationships with children without having to give birth to them. Politically, the radical feminist envisions an eventual "communistic anarchy,"[23] an ultimate abolition of the state. This will be achieved gradually, through an intermediate state of "cybernetic socialism" with household licenses to raise children and a guaranteed income for all. Perhaps surprisingly, in view of Freud's reputation among many feminists, the radical feminist conception of human nature is neo-Freudian. Firestone believes, with Freud, that "the crucial problem of modern life [is] sexuality."[24] Individuals are psychologically formed through their experience in the family, a family whose power relationships reflect the underlying biological realities of female (and childhood) dependence. But technology will smash the universality of Freudian psychology. The destruction of the biological family, never envisioned by Freud, will allow the emergence of new women and men, different from any people who have previously existed.

The radical feminist theory contains many interesting claims. Some of these look almost factual in character: they include the belief that pregnancy and childbirth are painful and unpleasant experiences, that sexuality is not naturally genital and heterosexual, and that technology may be controlled by men and women without leading to totalitarianism. Other presuppositions are more clearly normative: among them are the beliefs that technology should be used to eliminate all kinds of pain, that hard work is not in itself a virtue, that

sexuality ought not to be institutionalized and, perhaps most controversial of all, that children have the same rights to self-determination as adults.

Like the other theories we have considered, radical feminism believes that women's liberation will bring benefits for men. According to this concept of women's liberation, not only will men be freed from the role of provider, but they will also participate on a completely equal basis in childbearing as well as child-rearing. Radical feminism, however, is the only theory which argues explicitly that women's liberation also necessitates children's liberation. Firestone explains that this is because "The heart of woman's oppression is her childbearing and child-rearing roles. And in turn children are defined in relation to this role and are psychologically formed by it; what they become as adults and the sorts of relationships they are able to form determine the society they will ultimately build."[25]

New Directions

Although the wave of excitement about women's liberation which arose in the late '60's has now subsided, the theoretical activity of feminists has continued. Since about 1970, it has advanced in two main directions: lesbian separatism and socialist feminism.

Lesbian separatism is less a coherent and developed ideology than an emerging movement, like the broader feminist movement, within which different ideological strains can be detected. All lesbian separatists believe that the present situation of male supremacy requires that women should refrain from heterosexual relationships. But for some lesbian separatists, this is just a temporary necessity, whereas for others, lesbianism will always be required.

Needless to say, all lesbian separatists reject the liberal and the classical Marxist beliefs about sexual preferences; but some accept the radical feminist contention that ultimately it is unimportant whether one's sexual partner be male or female.[26]

---

[21]"The Institution of Sexual Intercourse," op. cit.

[22]*The Dialectic of Sex,* p. 209.

[23]Ibid., final chart, pp. 244–45.

[24]Ibid., p. 43.

[25]Ibid., p. 72.

[26]"In a world devoid of male power and, therefore, sex roles, who you lived with, loved, slept with and were committed to would be irrelevant. All of us would be equal and have equal determination over the society and how it met our needs. Until this happens, how we use our sexuality and our bodies is just as relevant to our liberation as how we use our minds and time." Coletta Reid, "Coming Out in the Women's Movement," in *Lesbianism and the Women's Movement,* ed. Nancy Myron and Charlotte Bunch (Baltimore: Diana Press, 1975), p. 103.

However, in the immediate context of a male-supremacist society, the lesbian separatist believes that one's sexual choice attains tremendous political significance. Lesbianism becomes a way of combating the overwhelming heterosexual ideology that perpetuates male supremacy.

Women . . . become defined as appendages to men so that there is a coherent ideological framework which says it is natural for women to create the surplus to take care of men and that men will do other things. Reproduction itself did not have to determine that. The fact that male supremacy developed the way it has and was institutionalized is an ideological creation. The ideology of heterosexuality, not the simple act of intercourse, is the whole set of assumptions which maintains the ideological power of men over women.[27]

Although this writer favors an ultimate de-institutionalization of sexual activity, her rejection of the claim that reproduction as such determines the inferior status of women clearly places her outside the radical feminist framework; indeed, she would identify her methodological approach as broadly Marxist. Some lesbian separatists are more radical, however. They argue explicitly for a matriarchal society which is "an affirmation of the power of female consciousness of the Mother."[28] Such matriarchists talk longingly about ancient matriarchal societies where women were supposed to have been physically strong, adept at self-defense, and the originators of such cultural advances as: the wheel, pottery, industry, leather working, metal working, fire, agriculture, animal husbandry, architecture, cities, decorative art, music, weaving, medicine, communal child care, dance, poetry, song, etc.[29] They claim that men were virtually excluded from these societies. Women's culture is compared favorably with later patriarchal cultures as being peaceful, egalitarian, vegetarian, and intellectually advanced. Matriarchal lesbian separatists would like to re-create a similar culture which would probably imitate the earlier ones in its exclusion of men as full members. Matriarchal lesbian separatists do not claim unequivocally that "men are

genetically predisposed towards destruction and dominance,"[30] but, especially given the present research on the behavioral effects of the male hormone testosterone,[31] they think it is a possibility that lesbians must keep in mind.

Socialist feminists believe that classical Marxism and radical feminism each have both insights and deficiencies. The task of socialist feminism is to construct a theory that avoids the weaknesses of each but incorporates its (and other) insights. There is space here for only a brief account of some of the main points of this developing theory.

Socialist feminists reject the basic radical feminist contention that liberation for women requires the abolition of childbirth. Firestone's view is criticized as ahistorical, anti-dialectical, and utopian. Instead, socialist feminists accept the classical Marxist contention that socialism is the main precondition for women's liberation. But though socialism is necessary, socialist feminists do not believe that it is sufficient. Sexism can continue to exist despite public ownership of the means of production. The conclusion that socialist feminists draw is that it is necessary to resort to direct cultural action in order to develop a specifically feminist consciousness in addition to transforming the economic base. Thus their vision is totalistic, requiring "transformation of the entire fabric of social relationships."[32]

In rejecting the radical feminist view that the family is based on biological conditions, socialist feminists turn toward the classical Marxist account of monogamy as being based "not on natural but on economic conditions."[33] But they view the classical Marxist account as inadequate, overly simple. Juliet Mitchell[34] argues that the family should be analyzed in a more detailed, sophisticated, and historically specific way in terms of the separate, though interrelated, functions that women perform within it: production, reproduction, sexuality, and the socialization of the young.

Socialist feminists agree with classical Marx-

---

[27]Margaret Small, "Lesbians and the Class Position of Women," in *Lesbianism and the Women's Movement*, p. 58.

[28]Jane Alpert, "Mother Right: A New Feminist Theory," *Ms.*, August 1973, p. 94.

[29]Alice, Gordon, Debbie, and Mary, *Lesbian Separatism: An Amazon Analysis*, typescript, 1973, p. 5. (To be published by Diana Press, Baltimore.)

[30]Ibid., p. 23.

[31]It is interesting that this is the same research on which Steven Goldberg grounds his thesis of "the inevitability of patriarchy"; see note 2 above.

[32]Barbara Ehrenreich, "Socialist/Feminism and Revolution" (unpublished paper presented to the National Socialist-Feminist Conference, Antioch College, Ohio, July 1975), p. 1.

[33]Engels, op. cit., p. 57.

[34]Juliet Mitchell, *Woman's Estate* (New York: Random House, 1971). Lively discussion of Mitchell's work continues among socialist feminists. [See chapter 5, this volume, pp. 181–183—ed.]

ists that women's liberation requires the entry of women into public production. But this in itself is not sufficient. It is also necessary that women have access to the more prestigious and less deadening jobs and to supervisory and administrative positions. There should be no "women's work" within public industry.[35]

In classical Marxist theory, "productive labor" is viewed as the production of goods and services within the market economy. Some socialist feminists believe that this account of productiveness obscures the socially vital character of the labor that women perform in the home. They argue that, since it is clearly impossible under capitalism to bring all women into public production, individuals (at least as an interim measure) should be paid a wage for domestic work. This reform would dignify the position of housewives, reduce their dependence on their husbands and make plain their objective position, minimized by classical Marxists, as an integral part of the working class.[36] Not all socialist feminists accept this position, however, and the issue is extremely controversial at the time of this writing.

One of the main insights of the feminist movement has been that "the personal is political." Socialist feminists are sensitive to the power relations involved in male/female interaction and believe that it is both possible and necessary to begin changing these, even before the occurrence of a revolution in the ownership of the means of production. Thus, socialist feminists recognize the importance of a "subjective factor" in revolutionary change and reject the rigid economic determinism that has characterized many classical Marxists. They are sympathetic to attempts by individuals to change their life styles and to share responsibility for each other's lives, even though they recognize that such attempts can never be entirely successful within a capitalist context. They also reject the sexual puritanism inherent in classical Marxism, moving closer to the radical feminist position in this regard.

Clearly there are sharp differences between socialist feminism and most forms of lesbian separatism. The two have been dealt with together in this section only because each is still a developing theory and because it is not yet clear how far either represents the creation of a new ideology and how far it is simply an extension of an existing ideology. One suspects that at least the matriarchal version of lesbian separatism may be viewed as a new ideology: after all, the interpretation of "freedom" to mean "freedom from men" is certainly new, as is the suggestion that women are innately superior to men. Socialist feminism, however, should probably be seen as an extension of classical Marxism, using essentially similar notions of human nature, of freedom and equality, and of the role of the state, but attempting to show that women's situation and the sphere of personal relations in general need more careful analysis by Marxists.[37]

This sketch of some new directions in feminism completes my outline of the main contemporary positions on women's liberation. I hope that I have made clearer the ideological presuppositions at the root of many feminist claims and also shed some light on the philosophical problems that one needs to resolve in order to formulate one's own position and decide on a basis for action. Many of these philosophical questions, such as the nature of the just society, the proper account of freedom and equality, the functions of the state and the relation between the individual and society, are traditional problems which now arise in a new context; others, such as the role of technology in human liberation, are of more recent origin. In either case, feminism adds a fresh dimension to our discussion of the issues and points to the need for the so-called philosophy of man to be transformed into a comprehensive philosophy of women and men and their social relations.

[35]For one socialist feminist account of women's work in public industry see Sheila Rowbotham, *Woman's Consciousness, Man's World* (Baltimore: Penguin Books, 1973), chap. 6, "Sitting Next to Nellie."

[36]One influential exponent of wages for housework is Mariarosa Dalla Costa, *The Power of Women and the Subversion of Community* (Bristol, England: Falling Wall Press, 1973).

[37]Since I wrote this section, I have learned of some recent work by socialist feminists which seems to provide an excitingly new theoretical underpinning for much socialist feminist practice. An excellent account of these ideas is given by Gayle Rubin in "The Traffic in Women: Notes on the 'Political Economy' of Sex." This paper appears in *Toward an Anthropology of Women,* ed. Rayna R. Reiter (New York: Monthly Review Press, 1975). If something like Rubin's account is accepted by socialist feminists, it will be a difficult and important question to work out just how far they have moved from traditional Marxism and how much they still share with it.

Selected Bibliography

Part I: Sexism and Sex Roles

Historical Philosophical Works

Hume, David. "Of Chastity and Modesty." In *A Treatise Concerning Human Nature,* book 3, part 2. Garden City, N.Y.: Dolphin, 1961.

Korsmeyer, Carolyn W. "Reason and Morals in the Early Feminist Movement: Mary Wollstonecraft." *Philosophical Forum* 5 (1973–74): 97–111.

Nietzsche, Friedrich. "Beyond Good and Evil." In *The Philosophy of Nietzsche,* sections 144, 145. New York: Random House, 1970.

Nietzsche, Friedrich. "On Little Old and Young Women" and "On Child and Marriage." In *Thus Spake Zarathustra.* Translated by Walter Kaufmann, part 1, sections 18 and 20. New York: Viking, 1966.

Rossi, Alice S., ed. *The Feminist Papers.* New York: Columbia University Press, 1973.

Rousseau, Jean Jacques. *Emile.* Translated by Barbara Foxley, chapter 5. London: J. M. Dent & Sons, 1911.

Schopenhauer, Arthur. "On Women." In *Essays.* New York: Simon & Schuster, 1928.

Wollstonecraft, Mary. *A Vindication of the Rights of Women.* Edited by Charles W. Hagelman, Jr. New York: Norton, 1967.

Contemporary Philosophical Works

Braggin, Mary V.; Elliston, Frederick; and English, Jane, eds. *Feminism and Philosophy.* Sections 2 and 3. Totowa, N.J.: Littlefield, Adams, 1977.

Garside, Christine. "Can a Woman be Good in the Same Way as a Man?" *Dialogue* 10 (1971): 534–44.

Govier, Trudy R. "Woman's Place." *Philosophy* 49 (1974): 305–9.

Hill, Thomas E., Jr. "Servility and Self-Respect." *The Monist* 57 (1973): 87–104.

Lucas, J. R. "Because You are a Woman." *Philosophy* 48 (1973): 161–71.

Marković, Mihailo. "Women's Liberation and Human Emancipation." *Philosophical Forum* 5: 242–58.

Pierce, Christine. "Natural Law Language and Women." In *Woman in Sexist Society.* Edited by Vivian Gornick and Barbara K. Moran. New York: Mentor, 1971.

Tormey, Judith Farr. "Exploitation, Oppression and Self-Sacrifice." *Philosophical Forum* 5 (1973–74): 206–21.

Trebilcot, Joyce. "Sex Roles: The Argument from Nature." *Ethics* 85 (1975): 249–55.

Trebilcot, Joyce. "Two Forms of Androgynism." *Journal of Social Philosophy* 8 (1977): 4–8.

Whitbeck, Caroline. "Theories of Sex Differences." *Philosophical Forum* 5 (1973–74): 54–80.

Social Scientific Works

Baker, Jean, ed. *Psychoanalysis and Women.* Baltimore: Penguin, 1973.

Bardwick, Judith M. *Psychology of Women.* New York: Harper & Row, 1971.

Bardwick, Judith M., ed. *Readings on the Psychology of Women.* New York: Harper & Row, 1972.

Bardwick, J. M.; Douvan, E.; Horner, M. S.; and Gutman, D. *Feminine Personality and Conflict.* Belmont, Calif.: Brooks/Cole, 1970.

Bernard, Jessie. *Academic Women.* New York: Meridian, 1964.

Freeman, Jo. *Women: A Feminist Perspective.* Palo Alto, Calif.: Mayfield, 1975.

Freud, Sigmund. "Female Sexuality." In *Standard Edition.* Vol. 21. London: Hogarth Press, 1961.

Freud, Sigmund. *New Introductory Lectures in Psychoanalysis.* New York: Norton, 1933.

Freud, Sigmund. "Three Essays on the Theory of Sexuality." In *Standard Edition.* Vol. 7. London: Hogarth Press, 1953.

Garskof, Michele H., ed. *Roles Women Play: Readings Toward Women's Liberation.* Belmont, Calif.: Brooks/Cole, 1971.

Gornick, Vivian, and Moran, Barbara K., eds. *Woman in Sexist Society.* New York: Mentor, 1971.

Horney, Karen. *Feminine Psychology.* New York: Norton, 1967.

Jaquette, Jane S., ed. *Women in Politics.* New York: Wiley, 1974.

Maccoby, Eleanor, and Jacklin, Carol, eds. *The Psychology of Sex Differences.* Stanford, Calif.: Stanford University Press, 1974.

Money, John, and Ehrhardt, Anke A. *Man & Woman, Boy & Girl.* New York: Mentor, 1972.

Oakley, Ann. *The Sociology of Housework.* New York: Pantheon, 1974.

Political and Social Viewpoints

Daly, Mary. *The Church and the Second Sex.* New York: Harper Colophon, 1975.

de Crow, Karen. *Sexist Justice.* New York: Vintage, 1975.

Densmore, Dana. "On the Temptation to Be a Beautiful Object." In *Female Liberation.* Edited by Roberta Salper. New York: Knopf, 1972.

Gilder, George. *Sexual Suicide.* New York: Quadrangle, 1973.

Goldberg, Herb. *The Hazards of Being Male: Surviving the Myth of Masculine Privilege.* New York: New American Library, 1976.

Goldberg, Steven. *The Inevitability of Patriarchy.* New York: William Morrow, 1973.

Greer, Germaine. *The Female Eunuch.* New York: McGraw-Hill, 1970.

Hardwick, Elizabeth. *Seduction & Betrayal: Women and Literature.* New York: Vintage, 1975.

Koedt, Anne: Levine, Ellen; and Rapone, Anita, eds. *Radical Feminism.* New York: Quadrangle, 1973.

Millett, Kate. *Sexual Politics.* New York: Avon, 1969.

Mitchell, Juliet. *Psychoanalysis and Feminism.* New York: Pantheon, 1974.

New York Radical Women. *Notes from the Second Year: Women's Liberation.* Boston: 1969. (P.O. Box 621, Old Chelsea Station, New York, N.Y. 10011.)

Nichols, Jack. *Men's Liberation: A New Definition of Masculinity.* New York: Penguin, 1975.

Roszak, Betty, and Roszak, Theodore, eds. *Masculine/Feminine.* New York: Harper Colophon, 1969.

Summers, Anne. *Damned Whores and God's Police: The Colonization of Women in Australia.* Harmondsworth, Middlesex, England: Penguin, 1975.

Tiger, Lionel. *Men in Groups.* New York: Random House, 1969.

Part II: Sex, Love, and Marriage

Historical Philosophical Works

Fichte, Johann G. *The Science of Rights.* Pp. 394–401, 406–7, 440–42. Philadelphia: Lippincott, 1869.

Kant, Immanuel. *Lectures on Ethics.* Translated by Louis Infield, pp. 162–71. London: Methuen, 1930.

Kierkegaard, Sören. *Fear and Trembling.* Translated by Walter Lowrie, pp. 52–61. New York: Doubleday, 1954.

Mill, John Stuart. "The Subjection of Women." In *Essays on Sex Equality.* Edited by Alice S. Rossi, chapter 2. Chicago: University of Chicago Press, 1970.

Morgan, Douglas N. *Love: Plato, the Bible and Freud.* Englewood Cliffs, N.J.: Prentice-Hall, 1964.

Norton, David L., and Kille, Mary F., eds. *Philosophies of Love.* San Francisco: Chandler, 1971.

Ortega y Gassett, Jose. *On Love.* Translated by Toby Talbot. Cleveland: Meridian, 1957.

Plato. *Republic.* Translated by Francis Cornford, pp. 457–64. Oxford: Oxford University Press, 1945.

Russell, Bertrand. *Marriage and Morals.* New York: Bantam, 1929.

Sartre, Jean-Paul. *Being and Nothingness.* Translated by Hazel Barnes, pp. 471–84, 487–91. New York: Washington Square Press, 1966.

Schopenhauer, Arthur. "The Metaphysics of the Love of the Sexes." In *The Philosophy of Schopenhauer.* Edited by Irwin Edman. New York: Modern Library, 1928.

Singer, Irving. *The Nature of Love: Plato to Luther.* New York: Random House, 1966.

Stendhal. *On Love.* Garden City, N.Y.: Doubleday, 1957.

Verene, D. P., ed. *Sexual Love and Western Morality: A Philosophical Anthology.* New York: Harper Torch, 1972.

Contemporary Philosophical Works

Bayles, Michael D. "Marriage, Love and Procreation." In *Philosophy and Sex.* Edited by Robert Baker and Frederick Elliston. Buffalo: Prometheus, 1975.

Braggin, Mary V.; Elliston, Frederick; and English, Jane, eds. *Feminism and Philosophy.* Sections 5 and 6. Totowa, N.J.: Littlefield, Adams, 1977.

Clark, Lorenne M. G., and Lewis, Debra J. *Rape: The Price of Coercive Sexuality.* Toronto: Canadian Women's Educational Press, 1976.

Curley, E. M. "Excusing Rape." *Philosophy and Public Affairs* 5(1976): 325–60.

Elliston, Frederick. "In Defense of Promiscuity." In *Philosophy and Sex.* Edited by Robert Baker and Frederick Elliston. Buffalo: Prometheus, 1975.

Margolis, Joseph "The Question of Homosexuality." *Philosophy and Sex.* Edited by Robert Baker and Frederick Elliston. Buffalo: Prometheus, 1975.

McMurtry, John. "Monogamy: A Critique." In *Philosophy and Sex.* Edited by Robert Baker and Frederick Elliston. Buffalo: Prometheus, 1975.

Moulton, Janice. "Sexual Behavior: Another Position." *Journal of Philosophy* 74(1977): 537–46.

Nagel, Thomas. "Sexual Perversion." *Journal of Philosophy* 66(1969): 1–15.

Newton-Smith, W. "A Conceptual Investigation of Love." In *Philosophy and Personal Relations.* Edited by A. Montefiore. London: Routledge & Kegan Paul, 1973.

Rapaport, Elizabeth. "On the Future of Love: Rousseau and the Radical Feminists." *Philosophical Forum* 5(1973–74): 185–205.

Solomon, Robert. "Sexual Paradigms." *Journal of Philosophy* 71(1974): 336–45.

Solomon, Robert. "Sex and Perversion." In *Philosophy and Sex.* Edited by Robert Baker and Frederick Elliston. Buffalo: Prometheus, 1975.

Social Scientific Works

Bernard, Jessie. *The Future of Marriage.* New York: Macmillan, 1971.

Curtin, Mary Ellen, ed. *Symposium on Love.* New York: Behavioral Publications, 1973.

Freud, Sigmund. "On Narcissism." In *General Psychological Theory.* Edited by Philip Rieff. New York: Collier, 1963.

Hite, Shere. *The Hite Report.* New York: Dell, 1977.

Masters, William H., and Johnson, Virginia. *Human Sexual Response.* Boston: Little, Brown, 1966.

Political and Social Viewpoints

Abbott, Sidney, and Love, Barbara. *Sappho was a Right-On Woman: A Liberated View of Lesbianism.* New York: Stein & Day, 1972.

Atkinson, Ti-Grace. "The Institution of Sexual Intercourse." In *Notes from the Second Year: Women's Liberation.* Boston: 1969.

Brownmiller, Susan. "Speaking Out on Prostitution." In *Radical Feminism.* Edited by Anne Koedt, Ellen Levine, and Anita Rapone. New York: Quadrangle, 1973.

Brownmiller, Susan. *Against Our Will: Men, Women and Rape.* New York: Simon & Schuster, 1975.

Cronan, Sheila. "Marriage." In *Radical Feminism.* Edited by Anne Koedt, Ellen Levine, and Anita Rapone. New York: Quadrangle, 1973.

Densmore, Dana. "On Celibacy." In *Voices from Women's Liberation.* Edited by Leslie B. Tanner. New York: Signet, 1970.

Johnston, Jill. *Lesbian Nation: The Feminist Solution.* New York: Touchstone, 1973.

Jones, Beverly. "The Dynamics of Marriage and Motherhood." In *Sisterhood is Powerful.* Edited by Robin Morgan. New York: Vintage, 1970.

Koedt, Anne. "The Myth of the Vaginal Orgasm." In *Radical Feminism.* Edited by Anne Koedt, Ellen Levine, and Anita Rapone. New York: Quadrangle, 1973.

Lessing, Doris. "To Room Nineteen." In *A Man and Two Women.* New York: Simon & Schuster, 1958.

Masters, William H., and Johnson, Virginia E. *The Pleasure Bond.* New York: Bantam, 1976.

Millett, Kate. *Flying.* New York: Ballantine, 1975.

Millett, Kate. *The Prostitution Papers: "A Quartet for Female Voices."* New York: Ballantine, 1976.

O'Neill, George, and O'Neill, Nena. *Open Marriage.* New York: M. Evans, 1972.

Rowbotham, Sheila. *Woman's Consciousness, Man's World.* Chapters 4 and 5. Baltimore: Penguin, 1973.

Shulman, Alix Kates. *Memoirs of an Ex-Prom Queen.* New York: Bantam, 1972.

Taylor, Gabrielle. "Love." *Proceedings of the Aristotelian Society.* Supplementary volume (1976–77): 147–64.

Part III: Some Special Moral Issues in Women's Liberation

Abortion

Baker, Robert, and Elliston, Frederick, eds. *Philosophy and Sex.* Section titled "Feminism and Abortion." Buffalo: Prometheus, 1975.

Braggin, Mary V.; Elliston, Frederick; and English, Jane, eds. *Feminism and Philosophy.* Section 7. Totowa, N.J.: Littlefield, Adams, 1977.

Callahan, Daniel. *Abortion: Law, Choice and Morality.* New York: Macmillan, 1970.

Cohen, Marshall; Nagel, Thomas; and Scanlon, Thomas, eds. *The Rights and Wrongs of Abortion.* Princeton, N.J.: Princeton University Press, 1974.

Feinberg, Joel, ed. *The Problem of Abortion.* Belmont, Calif.: Wadsworth, 1973.

Grisez, Germain. *Abortion: The Myths, the Realities and the Arguments. New York: Corpus, 1970.*

Noonan, John T., ed. *The Morality of Abortion: Legal and Historical Perspectives.* Cambridge: Harvard University Press, 1970.

Roe v. *Wade,* 410 U.S. 113, 93 S.Ct. 705 (1973).

Werner, Richard. "Abortion: The Moral Status of the Unborn." *Social Theory and Practice* 3(1974): 201–222.

Preferential Treatment

Bakke v. *Regents of the University of California,* 18 Cal. 3d 34, 553 P. 2d 1152, 132 Cal. Rptr. 680 (1976).

Bayles, Michael. "Compensatory Reverse Discrimination in Hiring." *Social Theory and Practice* 2(1973): 301–12.

Braggin, Mary V.; Elliston, Frederick; and English, Jane, eds. *Feminism and Philosophy.* Section 4. Totowa, N.J.: Littlefield, Adams, 1977.

Cohen, Carl. "Race and the Constitution." *The Nation,* 8 February 1975.

Cohen, Marshall; Nagel, Thomas; and Scanlon, Thomas, eds. *Equality and Preferential Treatment.* Princeton, N.J.: Princeton University Press, 1976.

Ezorsky, Gertrude. "Hiring Women Faculty." *Philosophy and Public Affairs* 7(1977): 82–91.

Fried, Marlene Gerber. "In Defense of Preferential Hiring." *Philosophical Forum* 5(1973–74): 309–19.

Gross, Barry R., ed. *Reverse Discrimination.* Buffalo: Prometheus, 1977.

Ketchum, Sara Ann, and Pierce, Christine. "Implicit Racism." *Analysis* 36(1976): 91–95.

Martin, Michael. "Pedagogical Arguments for Preferential Hiring and Tenuring of Women Teachers in the University." *Philosophical Forum* 5(1973–74): 325–33.

Nagel, Thomas. "Equal Treatment and Compensatory Justice." *Philosophy and Public Affairs* 2(1973): 348–63.

Nell, Onora. "How Do We Know When Opportunities Are Equal?" *Philosophical Forum* 5(1973–74): 334–46.

Office of Federal Contract Compliance. *Revised Order No. 4, Affirmative Action Guidelines*. Subpart B—Required Contents of Affirmative Action Programs. Washington, D.C.

Thalberg, Irving. "Reverse Discrimination and the Future." *Philosophical Forum* 5(1973–74): 294–308.

U.S. Department of Health, Education and Welfare, Office of Civil Rights. *Higher Education Guidelines Executive Order 11246.* Washington, D.C.: U.S. Government Printing Office, 1972.

Vetterling, Mary. "Some Common Sense Notes on Preferential Hiring." *Philosophical Forum* 5(1973–74): 320–24.

Wasserstrom, Richard A. "The University and the Case for Preferential Treatment." *American Philosophical Quarterly* 13(1976): 165–70.

Part IV: Theoretical Frameworks for Women's Liberation

General Works

Parsons, Kathryn Pyne. "Nietzsche and Moral Change." In *Nietzsche: A Collection of Critical Essays.* Edited by Robert Solomon. Garden City, N.Y.: Doubleday, 1973.

Rubin, Gayle. "The Traffic in Women." In *Towards an Anthropology of Women.* Edited by Rayna Reifer. New York: Monthly Review Press, 1976.

Liberal Feminism

Friedan, Betty. *The Feminine Mystique.* New York: Dell, 1963.

Mill, John Stuart. "The Subjection of Women." In *Essays on Sex Equality.* Edited by Alice S. Rossi, chapters 1 and 4. Chicago: University of Chicago Press, 1970.

Existentialism

Daly, Mary. Beyond God the Father: Toward a Philosophy of Women's Liberation. Chapter 1. Boston: Beacon Press, 1973.

de Beauvoir, Simone. *The Second Sex.* Translated by H. M. Parshley, conclusion. New York: Bantam, 1961.

Classical Socialism

Bebel, August. *Woman Under Socialism.* Translated by Daniel de Leon. New York: Schocken Books, 1971.

Engels, Friedrich. *The Origin of the Family, Private Property, and the State.* New York: International Publishers, 1974.

Lenin, V. I. *The Emancipation of Women.* New York: International Publishers, 1934.

Trotsky, Leon. *Women and the Family.* New York: Pathfinder, 1970.

Contemporary Socialist Feminism

Mitchell, Juliet. *Woman's Estate.* Chapters 3–5. New York: Vintage, 1973.

Rowbotham, Sheila. *Woman's Consciousness, Man's World.* Baltimore: Penguin, 1973.

Rowbotham, Sheila. *Women, Resistance and Revolution: A History of Women and Revolution in the Modern World.* New York: Vintage, 1974.

Radical Feminism

Burris, Barbara. "The Fourth World Manifesto." In *Radical Feminism.* Edited by Anne Koedt, Ellen Levine, and Anita Rapone. New York: Quadrangle, 1973.

Firestone, Shulamith. *The Dialectic of Sex: The Case for Feminist Revolution.* New York: William Morrow, 1970.

Johnston, Jill. *Lesbian Nation: The Feminist Solution.* New York: Touchstone, 1973.

Koedt, Anne. "Lesbianism and Feminism." In *Radical Feminism.* Edited by Anne Koedt, Ellen Levine, and Anita Rapone. New York: Quadrangle, 1973.